AMONG WOMEN

AMONG WOMEN

From the Homosocial
to the Homoerotic
in the Ancient World

Edited by
Nancy Sorkin Rabinowitz
and Lisa Auanger

University of Texas Press, Austin

Library of Congress Cataloging-in-Publication Data

Among women : from the homosocial to the homoerotic
in the ancient world / edited by Nancy Sorkin Rabinowitz
and Lisa Auanger.
        p.   cm.
  Includes bibliographical references and index.
  ISBN 0-292-77113-4 (alk. paper)
    1. Lesbians—History—To 500.   2. Lesbians in art.
  3. Art, Classical.   4. Lesbians in literature.   5. Literature,
  Classical.   6. Civilization, Classical.   I. Rabinowitz,
  Nancy Sorkin.   II. Auanger, Lisa, 1965–

HQ75.5 .A485   2002
305.48'9664'09—dc21   2001034790

For Peter, Michael, and Rachel, always patient, always loving

For Victor Estevez

Contents

Abbreviations   xiii

Acknowledgments   xv

1. Introduction   1
   Nancy Sorkin Rabinowitz

2. Imag(in)ing a Women's World in Bronze Age Greece: 34
   The Frescoes from Xeste 3 at Akrotiri, Thera
   Paul Rehak

3. Aphrodite Garlanded: *Erôs* and Poetic Creativity in Sappho   60
   and Nossis
   Marilyn B. Skinner

4. Subjects, Objects, and Erotic Symmetry in Sappho's Fragments   82
   Ellen Greene

5. Excavating Women's Homoeroticism in Ancient Greece: 106
   The Evidence from Attic Vase Painting
   Nancy Sorkin Rabinowitz

6. Women in Relief: "Double Consciousness" in Classical Attic   167
   Tombstones
   John G. Younger

7. Glimpses through a Window: An Approach to Roman Female   211
   Homoeroticism through Art Historical and Literary Evidence
   Lisa Auanger

8. Ovid's Iphis and Ianthe: When Girls Won't Be Girls   256
   Diane T. Pintabone

9. Lucian's "Leaena and Clonarium": Voyeurism or a Challenge   286
   to Assumptions?
   Shelley P. Haley

10. "Friendship and Physical Desire": The Discourse of Female   304
Homoeroticism in Fifth-Century CE Egypt
    Terry G. Wilfong

Works Cited   331
Notes on Contributors   373
Index   375

Illustrations

2.1. Plan of Xeste 3 at Akrotiri, Thera.   35

2.2. Lustral-basin fresco, Xeste 3, ground floor.   38

2.3. Stone relief rhyton, Zakros palace, Crete.   39

2.4. Detail of lustral-basin women, Xeste 3, ground floor.   40

2.5. Male figures, Xeste 3, ground floor.   43

2.6. Goddess and girls, Xeste 3, upper floor.   44

2.7. Detail of goddess, Xeste 3, upper floor.   45

2.8. Mature woman, Xeste 3, upper floor.   47

5.1. Red-figure cup. Woman carding wool.   111

5.2a, b. Red-figure cup, fragments. Women exchanging gifts.   114

5.3. Red-figure krater. Women musicians.   118

5.4. Red-figure calyx krater. Women musicians.   118

5.5 I, a, b. Red-figure kylix. Interior (I), woman leading another; (a) and (b) exterior, pairs of women.   120–121

5.6. Red-figure pyxis. Bride and groom, with another woman.   122

5.7. Red-figure lebes gamikos. Woman placing necklace on the bride.   123

5.8. Red-figure lebes gamikos. Bride examining flute, while companion plays harp.   123

5.9. Red-figure lebes gamikos. Crowning of a bride.   124

5.10. Red-figure squat lekythos. Aphrodite and her companions.   127

5.11. Red-figure cup. Maenads.   128

5.12. Black-figure neck amphora. Dionysos and Maenads.   129

5.13. Black-figure lekythos. Two women sharing mantle.   131

5.14 a, b, c. Black-figure pyxis. Male-male, male-female, female-female couples.   132

5.15. Red-figure cup. Women's symposion.   136

5.16. Red-figure hydria. Women's symposion.   136

5.17. Red-figure amphora. Women bathing.   137

5.18 I, a, b. Red-figure cup. (I) Interior. Women dressing; (a) pairs of youths and women, two women together; (b) women and youth, women and boy.   139

5.19. Red-figure pelikê. Woman watering penis plants.   141

5.20. Red-figure cup. Women dancing at an erect phallus.   141

5.21 a, b. Red-figure cup. Women at bath with dildos.   143

5.22. Red-figure cup. Women with dildos.   144

5.23. Red-figure kantharos. Sexual scene with double-headed dildo.   144

5.24. Plate. Women with wreaths.   147

5.25. Red-figure cup. Sexual stimulation.   149

6.1. View of Plot 34 in Kerameikos cemetery.   168

6.2. Plan of Kerameikos cemetery.   169

6.3. Stele for seated woman, in front of whom second woman stands and holds box.   175

6.4. Stele for woman who died in childbirth; woman stands and looks at seated woman; between, woman (servant?) holds infant; in back of chair, another woman.   175

6.5. Stele for seated woman who clasps hands with second woman who stands and looks at her; in back of chair, girl.   177

6.6. Red-figure epinetron by the Eretria Painter.   180

6.7. Red-figure epinetron by the Eretria Painter.   180

6.8. Red-figure epinetron by the Eretria Painter.   180

6.9. Stele for Pausimakhe.   184

6.10. Cast of the stele for Demetria and Pamphile, from Kerameikos plot 20.   187

6.11. Relief from Pharsalus, Thessaly.   189

7.1. Sarcophagus showing Graces and Erotes.   224

7.2. Sarcophagus showing Muses.   227

7.3. Sarcophagus showing musical activity.   229

7.4. End of a sarcophagus showing two musicians dancing around an altar.   229

7.5. Helen and Aphrodite relief.   231

7.6. Archaistic women from Neo-Attic krater.   233

7.7. Eros, from Neo-Attic krater.   233

7.8. Engraving of Venus and Adonis.   234

7.9. Aldobrandini Wedding.   235

7.10. Male-female chamber scene.   235

7.11. Situla from Herculaneum.   238

7.12. Women at an Amor market.   241

7.13. Eros between Two Women.   241

7.14. Nereid Thiasos with Erotes.   244

10.1. Map of Egypt showing the location of Shenutean and Pachomian monastic communities.   306

10.2. Record of punishment of women for homoerotic activity.   309

Abbreviations

ABV	Beazley, John. D. *Attic Black-Figure Vase-Painters.* Oxford: Oxford UP, 1956.
ARV	Beazley, John D. *Attic Red-Figure Vase-Painters.* 3 vols. 2nd. ed. Oxford: Oxford UP, 1956; New York: Hacker, 1984.
Add.	Carpenter, Thomas H., ed. *Beazley Addenda: Additional References to* Attic Black-Figure Vase-Painters, Attic Red-Figure Vase-Painters² *and* Paralipomena. Oxford: Oxford UP, 1989. (Also Beazley *Addenda*)
Clairmont, Christoph W.	*Classical Attic Tombstones.* 9 vols. Kilchberg, Switzerland: Akanthus, 1993.
Gow-Page	Gow, A. S. F., and D. L. Page, eds. *The Greek Anthology: Hellenistic Epigrams.* 2 vols. Cambridge: Cambridge UP, 1965.
L-P	Lobel, E., and D. Page, eds. *Poetarum Lesbiorum Fragmenta.* Oxford: Clarendon P, 1963 [1955].
LIMC	*Lexicon Iconographicum Mythologiae Classicae.* Zurich and Munich, 1981–1997.
NMA	National Archaeological Museum, Athens.
Paralipomena (also *Para.*)	Beazley, John D. *Paralipomena: Additions to* Attic Black-Figure Vase-Painters *and to* Attic Red-Figure Vase-Painters. 2nd ed. Oxford: Clarendon P, 1971.

ACKNOWLEDGMENTS

The editors would like to take this opportunity to thank the editorial staff at University of Texas Press: Ali Hossaini Jr. for approaching us at the APA and Jim Burr for taking over the project, patiently answering questions and waiting for the manuscript; Leslie Tingle, Allison Faust, and Nancy Moore have been unfailingly courteous and wise. We would also like to thank the anonymous reviewers for their words of praise and for their suggestions about ways to improve the manuscript; we hope we have answered all their questions.

Each of the editors has incurred many debts to others for their careful reading of our work. Lisa Auanger thanks in particular Patricia Crown, Dan Hooley, and Kathleen Slane of the University of Missouri, and Laurel Boeckman of the State Historical Society of Missouri, for their comments on her chapter. We would like to thank each other for energy, commitment, and countless emails even when it seemed the process would never be over. Most of all, we thank the contributors who were adventurous enough to write for this volume and who were willing to revise and revise again.

For gracious permission to publish a revised version of Marilyn Skinner's essay, "Aphrodite Garlanded: *Erôs* and Poetic Creativity in Sappho and Nossis," which originally appeared in *Rose di Piereia*, ed. Francesco De Martino, we thank Levante Editori, Bari, Italy.

AMONG WOMEN

CHAPTER ONE

INTRODUCTION[1]

Nancy Sorkin Rabinowitz

 This volume is unusual in the field of classics in that it bridges literary and archaeological evidence and defines antiquity expansively (preclassical Greece to fifth-century CE Egypt), whereas most similar anthologies or books have been either literary/historical or art historical/archaeological and have tended to define the field more narrowly. But most importantly, it focuses exclusively on women's relationships with other women. The essays published here present new interpretations and new evidence about the homosocial and homoerotic relationships between women in the ancient world.

Over the last twenty-five years there has been an enormous amount of research undertaken and published on women in antiquity, but aside from recent work on Sappho and Bernadette Brooten's groundbreaking book, relatively little has addressed women as sexual subjects or addressed their possible homoeroticism.[2] On the other hand, while there has been an explosion of interest in sexuality in antiquity over the last ten to fifteen years, following Michel Foucault, that attention has mostly been devoted to men.[3] In this volume, we bring together both the study of women and the study of sexuality, broadly construed.[4]

Developments in feminist theory, gay and lesbian studies, and queer theory have made this book possible by shaping questions and suggesting directions in which one can look for answers; with this collection, we hope to make a contribution to those discourses by studying the ancient world. More pragmatically, such studies have created a climate of interest and expanded the possibilities for publication and readership. Although the expansion in sexuality studies is sometimes called "fashionable" or a "growth industry" even by its friends, implying it is merely a fad (a terrible insult in classics), it is also still treated to extremely homophobic responses[5] that expose the politicized nature of the current academy and the importance of continuing to work on same-sex desire.

Given the stature of Sappho (a seventh-century BCE Greek poet from the island of Lesbos), whose name has become synonymous with women's love for women, classical studies would seem to be a privileged site for the study of female homoeroticism; yet examining female relationships and homoeroticism in antiquity is a daunting task. In general, classicists seeking information about social life have much less data at their disposal and much less unambiguous data than scholars studying later periods; the ravages of time and the cultural practices of antiquity conspire against the project. For instance, there are no diaries, few textual records documenting private life, and no first-person accounts of the everyday life of ordinary people.[6] What we have are images and texts, crafted and written by artists and authors for their own purposes. In brief, we have no direct access to "women's relations to women"—no actual voices, no recordings—only representations. Moreover, ancient culture was male dominated, and except for the fragments of Sappho and some few later women poets,[7] the material remaining to us was produced by men. Thus they are more remote still from women's actual experience. Our literary sources are further distorted because they are often embedded in discourses of invective, satire, and insult. Thus, there are many layers between us in the present and women in the past.

Female relations not centered on men are even harder to document, since in ancient Greece and Rome, the culture of male sexuality was placed in high relief, while female sexuality was repressed or pressed into the service of masculinity. Moreover, until quite recently, discussions about women in antiquity focused on their social status, which was determined by their ties to men (father, husband); that focus led scholars to overlook women's relationships to other women.[8] It becomes still more difficult to discuss sexuality since the dominant ideology, from antiquity to the recent past, required married or marriageable ruling-class women to be chaste, and as a result, their erotic lives were hidden. Even Sappho's writing was not sufficiently "explicit" to escape generations of misreading.

WHAT'S IN A NAME?

But what do we mean by explicit? Some definitions are in order. Writing this introduction has been like walking through a minefield because every word that comes to mind (e.g., sexual) has been the subject of academic scrutiny and, in some cases, is even at the heart of critical debates; thus, any word can detonate in your face. In our title, we use the term "homosocial" to refer to the various social relationships between women and to underline the idea that ancient societies were to a great extent sex-segregated and that women were therefore brought together with other women on many occasions and in many settings.

"Homosocial" was a relatively easy choice. Less simple was the choice of "homoerotic" over, say, "homosexual" or "lesbian."[9] Why? First, the word homosexual (as a noun) continues to connote gay men and also seems to accept in advance a concept of transhistorical homosexuality that is highly contested today. At least for the time being, "homoerotic" does not have an association with a congealed identity, although it may be colonized for that purpose in the future. Second, while "lesbian" obviously avoids the problem of masculinity, it seems to us to apply more appropriately to a modern sexual identity; thus, for instance, Brooten generally adopts the term homoerotic, even though she argues strongly for the possibility of a lesbian history, perhaps because of these distinctions. Third, there are advantages to pairing "homo" (from the Greek for the "same") with "erotic" rather than "sexual." Scholars following Foucault and other constructionists in the study of the history of sexuality have destabilized the notion of an unchanging biological determination of the sexual, pointing out that we do not even know for sure what would have counted as sex in the Mediterranean region in antiquity and that we most assuredly cannot assume it is the same as what counts as sexual in western Europe or the United States today.[10] There is debate about whether the realm of things "sexual" constituted a meaningful category in antiquity, and as to whether sexual object choice (as in homo-/hetero-) was a significant axis of experience within that problematicized "realm."[11] Despite the debate, however, the words sex and sexuality still carry the baggage of phallocentric definitions, in which "having sex" often means (vaginal) penetration; at the least, the term seems to refer to physical expressions of desire and is not consistent with much of the evidence from antiquity about women's relations to women.

"Erotic" has a broader ambit because it derives from Eros, cosmogonic force and child of Aphrodite; in Greek, *eros* connotes sexual love as distinct from *philia*, or family love, but its focus is on the desire.[12] Thus, in discussions of representations of sexual material, erotica have tended to be distinguished from pornography, which is taken to seek to arouse sexual feelings and to lead to sexual acts. Homoerotic, by this genealogy, suggests the possibility of desire without consummation, turns our gaze away from genital sexuality, and inscribes a more expansive field of relationships than does "homosexual."[13] As a result of this etymology, "homoerotic" better tallies with the nature of our evidence about women's lives in antiquity.

The material presented in this volume falls along a spectrum from the implicit (Rehak, Rabinowitz, Younger, Auanger) to the more explicit (Greene, Skinner, Pintabone, Haley, Wilfong). To interpret this evidence through an exclusive emphasis on the overtly sexual would be a mistake, for it would ignore many other dimensions especially important in the lives of ancient women. Moreover, such an emphasis depends on a paradigm of modern practices that would not necessarily have been available to women in antiquity; by looking for evidence of physical genital consummation, we would moreover be maintaining a very high standard for what counts as "lesbian"[14] and almost guaranteeing the erasure of women's desire from all but a very few places. The question of "how can you be sure" about lesbians seems simultaneously homophobic (in its requirement of proof) and masculinist (what constitutes proof is a sexual act modeled on penetrative intercourse), when in heterosexual contexts, the assumption of sexual significance often requires little more than a glance.

The word "women" is hardly unproblematic either, though it may seem to be less politically charged. Given differences among women of sexual orientation, race, and class, the word does not always have the same referent in the present, and ancient peoples not only had different words but used the words they did have for female human beings in different ways. Indeed, the ancient conception of "women" can be viewed as being constituted in part by the very artifacts and texts that we are studying. As the texts by Ovid and Lucian confirm, the category was not stable and fixed (see Pintabone's and Haley's essays in this volume). To what extent were females who were attracted to other women imagined as men in antiquity? If they were, were female homoerotic relationships analogous to heterosexual relationships? Or to male homoerotic ties? To neither? Or to both?

Finally, we do not mean the small words, the prepositions, to delineate a straight line, a progression, much less a teleology, "from" one "to" the other, but rather we use them to delineate a range of women's relationships. They define a plane, not a ray. By asserting the linkage of social and erotic, we announce our intention to look at the spectrum of the relationships between women, asking if they were erotic as well as social. Our title underlines that link, which not only makes the most of the evidence we have but also enriches our analyses by putting a variety of women's relationships in context with one another instead of extracting one aspect (the physically sexual) for consideration. Indeed, the sexual desire implied by the erotic may be more productively associated with other forms of pleasure or with other forms of relationship, as it is in this volume, rather than set apart.[15]

IDEOLOGICAL SCHOLARSHIP: FLASHBACK

These problems of the paucity of evidence and the attendant ambiguities can profitably encourage us to reflect on how we construct a "world" in the past. All scholarship and interpretation may be said to be ideological in that they derive, consciously or unconsciously, from the scholar's positions and preoccupations, but the significance of ideology becomes more apparent when the evidence is fragmentary, for in such cases we must "read in" to create a whole from the remains.[16] This ideological dimension of (classical) scholarship is not new; what is new is that some of us now acknowledge it. Since earlier generations of scholars were not self-conscious about their ideological investment in their research, their biases went undetected. They were there nonetheless. However, as Marilyn Katz writes in the conclusion to her essay on "the history of the history of women," we will move ahead not by "dismissing as outdated what has gone before, but by exposing the ideological foundations of a hegemonic discourse that has dominated the discussion of ancient women, and that continues to make its powerful influence felt in the discussion of women generally as part of civil society at the present moment in history."[17] To some extent, the earlier generations still set the terms of current discussions. This next section of the introduction will show that ideology in the past worked in ways relevant to the study we are embarked on in the present.

In the late eighteenth and nineteenth centuries, western Europeans studied antiquity, first Rome and then increasingly Greece,[18] to affirm their own notions of racialized nation, class, and gender and indeed as a way of writing about themselves. In Britain, the study of the classics served to define the colonial ruling class; as a result, colonial rule and classical education went hand in hand.[19] Some of the same men were key figures in both arenas. To take one example, William Gladstone, British prime minister and an expert on colonial policy, devoted himself to promoting the study of Homer late in his career because of the importance of "the Greek mind . . . in which was shaped and tempered the original mould of the modern European civilization."[20]

These men did not simply discover a pre-existing Greece, however: they invented it to meet their needs. The European idea of "Greece" was mapped along the intersecting lines of color/whiteness, east/west and femininity/masculinity, as well as ancient/modern.[21] When ancient Greece supplanted Rome as the model for the west, standing as the idealized origin of western culture and manliness, it was largely on the basis of its supposed rationality and the much-vaunted simplicity of the sculpture being rediscovered at the time. That simplicity was associated with the statues' putative whiteness; although they were originally painted, they had lost their color through the action of time. Eighteenth-century writers denied that the statues had been painted in classical antiquity: "We cannot believe that the architects of the best days of Greece would so carefully select the purest materials in the prospect of their concealment by a mask of tawdry colour." Explorers and members of the Dilletanti Society, James Stuart and Nicholas Revett decided that they must have been painted after the Classical period.[22] The statues had to be white: this idea was one way in which scholars constructed the Greeks as white and is evidence of the investment that they had in the view of Greece as white.

Greece was not simply "western" either. At the time that ancient Greece was being rediscovered, modern Greece had been conquered by the Ottoman empire, and the Turks were not considered white or western. In part, Europeans adopted the view of ancient Greek men, who contrasted themselves to women and to the "barbarians" of the east (viewed as slavish and effeminate), but in modern times, "the barbarian" had won. The Romantics were simultaneously Hellenes (defined as lovers of ancient Greece) and Philhellenes (literally, lovers of Greece but taken to mean defenders of modern Greece); they involved themselves not only in the reclamation of Greek art but also in the struggle for Greek independence in 1821. Contradictions ensued: contemporary Greece was viewed as wild terrain, though ancient Greece was taken to be civilization itself.[23] Among themselves, Greek freedom fighters acknowledged that Greece had submitted to multiple influences, including that of Turkish culture, but when appealing to the west, they represented Greek culture as untouched and the direct heir to antiquity, utilizing what Michael Herzfeld terms the "Hellenic" discourse.[24]

The social position of actual Greek women (both modern and ancient) carried meaning in this matrix of barbarian/civilized, east/west.[25] Nationalists using the Hellenic mode clothed the emerging nation state in the glamour of ancient Greece on the basis of the similarity of women's roles in the past and present. That very persistence of the past, however, risked making Greece seem less modern, and so the nationalists still had to be careful to distinguish modern Greek women from their Turkish sisters, who were even more anchored in tradition. Herzfeld points out the dilemma: if for the Greek folklorist the treatment of women provided a continuity with the ancient world, "in a world in which Greece claims 'European' status, the nation's women must be correspondingly well educated."[26]

A palpable discourse of masculinity underlay the idealization of ancient Greece: the men of the past were a model for modern men. As a result, ancient women—who were a link to modern Greek women and thus possibly to the east—were a troubling node in British men's identification with Greece as western. In the early part of the nineteenth century, critical orthodoxy held that Athenian women were kept as a lower order of beings than men; they were little better than slaves, ill-educated and confined to the women's quarters; marriage was a matter of procreation, and their husbands had their meaningful friendships with other men and sex with *hetairai* (high-class prostitutes, typically assumed to be foreign born).[27] Since Greece was taken as the point of origin for western culture, this view of women's lives presented a problem for male scholars. Some felt they had to face "the woman question," as we can see in this passage from Gladstone: "No view of a peculiar civilization can on its ethical side be satisfactory, unless it includes a distinct consideration of the place held in it by women."[28] I would argue that Gladstone and others strategically deployed the term "oriental" to displace the objectionable behavior from the west and minimize the possibility that it would appear familiar to bourgeois classicists.[29] In this discourse, the women's quarters were identified with "the Oriental harem" and women's condition with "Oriental seclusion." The phrase "the oriental seclusion of women" was so common in classics that A. E. Haigh could use it offhandedly in his discussion of theatrical conventions ("Undoubtedly Athenian women were kept in a state of almost Oriental seclusion.").[30]

Victorians also responded to the orthodox view (indeed, to some extent we are still trying to deal with it) by emphasizing other aspects of Greek culture. In *Studies on Homer*, written in part to encourage more instruction on Homer at Oxford, Gladstone goes on to argue that the place of women in Homeric times was elevated "both absolutely and in comparison with what it became in the historic ages of Greece and Rome."[31] Gilbert Murray cites those who called the Greeks "trampler[s] on women" but adds this disclaimer: "But it is not those people that constitute Greece. . . . It is not anything fixed and stationary that constitutes Greece: what constitutes Greece is the movement which leads from all these to the Stoic or fifth-century 'sophist' who condemns and denies slavery, who has abolished all cruel superstitions and preaches some religion based on philosophy and humanity, who claims for women the same spiritual rights as for men."[32]

Yet another strategy was to adopt a strong defense of the Greeks, discrediting the severity of the orthodox view. As the discussion of women expanded in the twentieth century, some scholars defended the ancient Greek treatment of women by comparing it to the treatment of women in modern Europe. A. W. Gomme wrote in 1925 that "I consider it very doubtful if Greek theory and practice differed fundamentally from the average, say, prevailing in mediaeval and modern Europe." [33] H. D. F. Kitto shared this opinion, comparing Greek men to modern western men; he goes even further than Gomme and refers specifically to his home city of Manchester. [34] By saying that the Greeks were like "us," these scholars were saying that nothing was wrong with the Greeks. By defending the Greeks, male classicists of course also defended bourgeois British treatment of women and the status quo (as I will show below, this is a strand in discussions of women in antiquity practically up to the present day). [35]

Discourses of sex and sexuality were part and parcel of these constructions of antiquity and were similarly laced with ideology. [36] Just as the newly discovered statues were considered to be white, they were also supposedly sexless. Catherine Johns observes an "unfortunate coincidence" between early collecting and the "rapid development of a refinement in speech and manners which eventually became sheer prudery, and even led on occasion to the most regrettable and unscholarly hypocrisy." [37] Jean Marcadé points out that the prudery was located in assumptions about Hellenism ("the 'noble simplicity' and 'calm grandeur' spoken of by Winckelmann"). [38] The explicitly sexual wall paintings at Pompeii and Herculaneum were published separately from the rest of the discovery, while sexual vases were hidden away in private collections. [39]

The new nineteenth-century discourse of homosexuality was enhanced by a review of the curriculum being undertaken at Oxford in this period. By instituting the study of Plato, the so-called Greats course in classics became a legitimate avenue for the development of intense ties between men and for the strengthening of the nation. [40] Oxford's curriculum explored and redefined Socrates' relationship to men; in the ascetic readings (e.g., Benjamin Jowett's) and the erotic ones (e.g., John Symonds' and Walter Pater's), the past was seen as analogous to the present, whether the relationships were those between students and teachers or between friends. In other words, nineteenth-century scholars such as Symonds and Pater looked to Plato for justification of their own lives and loves. [41]

The overlap between classical studies and sexuality studies was still closer, however, since some of those same men trained in classics were also involved in the movement to legitimate male-male sexual relationships, and they used Greek *paederastia* and the high status of Greece as the origin of culture to counter the assertion that male homosexuality, as it was coming to be called, was somehow "primitive."[42] Edward Carpenter applauds the Greek ideal of "the trained male, the athlete, the man temperate and restrained, even chaste, for the sake of bettering his powers. It was round this conception that the Greeks kindled their finer emotions." He goes on to say: "And so of their love: a base and licentious indulgence was not in line with it." He distinguishes between procreative, physical love and the philosophical creations of "homogenic love."[43] The title and introduction to John Symonds' *A Problem in Greek Ethics, Being an Inquiry into the Phenomenon of Sexual Inversion Addressed Especially to Medical Psychologists and Jurists* are quite explicit. He addresses himself to the medical psychologists who would pathologize homosexuality and to the jurists who would criminalize it, and he uses ancient Greece for support:

> Here alone in history have we the example of a great and highly-developed race not only tolerating homosexual passions, but deeming them of spiritual value, and attempting to utilise them for the benefit of society. . . . What the Greeks called paiderastia, or boy-love, was a phenomenon of one of the most brilliant periods of human culture, in one of the most highly organized and nobly active nations.[44]

The reference to the Greeks granted legitimacy where it was needed. Symonds refers to homoerotic Greek legends and sums up their meaning by saying that "the chivalry of Hellas found its motive force in friendship rather than in the love of women. . . . The fruit which friendship bore among the Greeks was courage in the face of danger, indifference to life when honor was at stake, patriotic ardor, the love of liberty, and lion-hearted rivalry in battle."[45] For both Carpenter and Symonds, the ancient Greek love of men for men was the basis of desire for liberty and was not effeminate but was consonant with military vigor.

Several elements are intertwined in this complicated matrix of British classical studies. Just as the emerging category of homosexuality was related to the place of classics in the curriculum and to the idealization of the manly nation, so the hierarchies of feminine/masculine and east/west found their way into the discourse of homosexuality. According to Carpenter and Symonds, not all male-male desire was vigorous, and they distinguished between masculine and feminine forms, associating the former with Greece and the latter with the "Orient." Symonds identified two strands in "Greek love," Dorian and Phoenician ("military freedom" and "Oriental luxury"), which were brought together with the Hellenic "organising, moulding and assimilating spirit."[46] He was at pains to distinguish this Greek love from other "unisexual practices," "from the effeminacies, brutalities and gross sensualities which can be noticed alike in imperfectly civilised and in luxuriously corrupt communities."[47] In fact, Symonds claims Greek love as distinctive in a way reminiscent of current debates about the contributions of Egypt to Greek thought. The origins of pederasty could be seen as oriental, but "whatever the Greeks received from adjacent nations, they distinguished with the qualities of their own personality. Paiderastia in Hellas assumed Hellenic characteristics, and cannot be confounded with any merely Asiatic form of luxury." He further asserts that the "nobler type of masculine developed by the Greeks" is "almost unique in the history of the human race. It is that which more than anything else distinguishes the Greeks from the barbarians of their own time, from the Romans, and from modern men in all that appertains to the emotions."[48]

This discourse of male homosexuality not only defines Greek love as manly, it barely touches on women. Women's lives are mentioned three times (taking up several paragraphs) in Symonds' *Problem.* Carpenter claims to speak of men and women but for the most part fails to do so, as he acknowledges, saying, "The remarks in this essay have chiefly had reference to boys' schools."[49] Symonds connects Athenian women's social situation to the institution of pederasty and asserts that male love was preferred over female love because of problems in the types of women available to Greek men: "Athenian women were comparatively uneducated and uninteresting, and . . . the hetairai had proverbially bad manners."[50] The "social disadvantages of women" explain the "idealisation of boy-love among the Athenians."[51] "Sexual inversion" among women, on the other hand, is merely a "parenthetical investigation" in the discussion of Greek love, because it did not attain the status of men's love in antiquity.[52] Symonds' project of justifying male same-sex desire requires a Greek love that was masculine and not Oriental, but he orientalizes women's sexuality by naming the women's quarters (*gynaikonitis*) "the harem or the zenana" and then accounting for "Lesbian" love by women's seclusion in the harem.[53]

Sappho's erotic relationships to women were obscured by scholars who tried to salvage her good name, which was thought to have been besmirched by the ancient comic poets.[54] For instance, Henry Wharton introduced Sappho to England ("Sappho, the Greek poetess whom more than eighty generations have been obliged to hold without a peer, has never, in the entirety of her works, been brought within the reach of English readers") and tried to correct "current calumnies" that Friedrich Welcker had "seriously inquired into and found to be based on insufficient evidence."[55] In publishing his work on Sappho, David Robinson similarly felt obliged to defend the poet's "moral purity":

> She expresses herself, no doubt, in very passionate language, but passionate purity is a finer article than the purity of prudery, and Sappho's passionate expressions are always under the control of her art. A woman of bad character and certainly a woman of such a variety of bad character as scandal . . . has attributed to Sappho might express herself passionately and might run on indefinitely with erotic imagery. But Sappho is never erotic.[56]

J. M. Mackail makes this admonition: "Round the life of Sappho, and the nine books of her lyrics . . . a whole mythology, not of the most attractive nature, grew up in later Greece. It is not necessary to go into this; it would be hardly necessary to mention it, except that a word of warning is not even now superfluous against treating it seriously." Embarrassed though he is, he feels compelled to defend Sappho from the bias against women that led to the calumny.[57] The German philological tradition of Friedrich Welcker and Ulrich von Wilamowitz introduced the notion of Sappho the schoolmistress, which similarly eliminated the possibility that there were sexual relations between women.[58] For countercultural figures like Baudelaire, Swinburne, and Symonds, she was erotic though not necessarily lesbian; it was only in Renée Vivien's group that she was taken up as lesbian and made the center of the coterie.[59]

Victorian classical studies were thus political in several ways. First, studying the classics was the basis of education for the ruling class of the British empire, and Greece furnished the ideal for educational philosophy. Second, once democratic Greece succeeded republican Rome as origin and mirror, it was further constructed as western, white, and masculine. Third, studies of women and sexuality were implicated in the privileging of Greek civilization, but not in any univocal way, for though shaped by the dominant discourse, these areas to some extent also contradicted it. Thus, there is not a single politics that one can point to: rather, there were crosscurrents. If the status of women debate drew upon a conservative strand in classics, the liberatory discourse on male sexuality contributed to and benefited from the valorization of the Greeks. At the same time, that discourse orientalized passive male homoerotic behaviors and explicitly eliminated women from view.

There are important continuities between the past and present in classics. Scholars working on women in antiquity are heirs to the ways in which these scholars set out the field; that is, the issue of seclusion and the question of women's status dominated what little discussion there was. While the argument of some male classicists that women's seclusion did not entail dis-respect may seem naive, there are ongoing debates within feminism about whether separate always means unequal. Indeed, this volume's emphasis on the homosocial is grounded in the prominence of the private sphere in the lives of women in antiquity and in the possibility that women's space might provide a productive as well as a restrictive site.[60] The discourse on sexuality provides a similar point of continuity as well as discontinuity; for instance, the Victorian construction of homosexuality, with its exclusion of women, seems to haunt some aspects of contemporary discussions. Modern scholars continue to find hope in the paradigm offered by the ancient world as well as power in the canonical status of ancient texts. Perhaps, as Foucault's treat-ment of the "repressive hypothesis" would suggest, the compulsion to dis-cuss sexuality is only another facet of the Victorian silencing of Sappho's sexuality.[61]

IDEOLOGICAL SCHOLARSHIP: CUT TO THE PRESENT

In labeling the Victorian studies ideologically motivated, I am not claiming superiority for contemporary classicists over these scholars. I am, however, trying to counter those who would say that progressive classicists are the only ideologues. Most assuredly, we do have motives for pursuing this work; any superiority to which we can lay claim comes from admitting that fact. In this volume, we do not pretend to have gotten at the undisputable truth, nor do we expect to eliminate all our own preconceptions. In fact, it would be dangerous to do so, for if you go digging without knowing what you are looking for, you run the risk of missing it or even burying it in the haste to move on; on the other hand, if you have too sharply defined a model in mind, you will overlook what does not fit (and what might conceivably chal-lenge your notion of what "it" is). In either case, the very knowing and look-ing will shape what you can see.[62] The key is to be open to the ancient ma-terial, even though modern interests may motivate the research.

In the beginning of the twenty-first century, we, like the earlier generation, put the past to current uses, but, as was the case for them, these uses differ. As there were currents and crosscurrents in the tradition I have delineated, so modern scholars of antiquity are not a monolithic "we." Some look at the recent past as the "bad old days" from which they are liberated or which they are correcting; others defend the past and by so doing defend a present that is seen as not so different from the past.[63] Some go back to the Greeks for reasons very similar to those of the Victorian writers; their goal is to re-store the ideal held by men like Gladstone and Jowett. For instance, in *The*

Closing of the American Mind, Allan Bloom seems to be calling for a return to the days of Oxford and Cambridge, where a group of good men studied Plato.[64]

But there have been important changes in the academy since the Victorian era: classics on the whole is in a much more defensive posture today than it was in the nineteenth century. Studying Greek and Latin will no longer assure students a position in government, and in fact, the contrary seems more likely to undergraduate students who increasingly turn toward pre-professional education. To the extent that classics retains its canonical status, those arguing for a multicultural and inclusive curriculum often attack the field as a haven for "dead white European male" authors. These attacks have led to a defense of the ancient authors, which casts feminists and others in favor of opening up the academy as the enemy.[65]

But those of us who simultaneously find classics "guilty as charged," and yet remain in the field, clearly do not intend to throw it all out. Rather, we find our own reasons to continue the study of antiquity. If, as I have argued, the eighteenth- and nineteenth-century scholars looked first to Rome and then to Greece for similarities with themselves (though what they sought changed as their self-conception changed), today's scholars who are interested in women in antiquity, or sexuality, or both are divided between schools stressing similarity and those stressing difference. One strand of feminist scholars, whom we might call optimists, have seen differences between the past and the present, even locating a matriarchy in pre-Hellenic society; the pessimists on the whole have seen similarities or even causal connections.[66] Those engaged in studying "sexuality" are also invested in a division over similarities and differences, in particular the question of whether it makes sense to speak of homosexuality, taken to be an exclusive sexual orientation to partners of the same gender, in the premodern period.[67] This is the philosophical crux of a larger debate in classics about whether the past is "familiar" or "strange," which seems like the field's variant of the struggle over postmodernism, between essentialism and constructionism, in the academy.

Although there are divisions within feminism and within sexuality studies, for the sake of clarity, I will take as exempla the positions staked out by Amy Richlin and David Halperin. Richlin is a feminist committed to the possibility of improving women's lives. She maintains that in significant ways the Greeks and Romans were like us and

that it is important to find out as much as possible about women's lives in the past, for two reasons: both because memory and remembering are a major part of what history writing is, and because by putting women into our histories we move toward some balance in our lives. . . . I believe that we cannot know the measure of our own problems unless we know how long they have been going on.[68]

Positions like Richlin's energized the early feminist project of uncovering bias in antiquity; by understanding the power that humanist versions of canonical works had in shaping contemporary patriarchal ideology, feminist criticism attacked the alleged universality of these male authors. By focusing on the continuity between then and now, feminist critics also sought to transform the present.

For the most part, those involved in the study of the history of sexuality are no less committed to political change, to the possibility of escaping the constraints of current sexual categories, but they tend to take hope from the distance between the past and the present. The discussion of male sexuality in classics has been grounded in the essentialist/constructionist debate and has addressed itself to the question of whether it is appropriate to call male-male sexual relations homosexual, as Kenneth Dover did in his groundbreaking study of 1978, or whether pederasty is not really a more accurate term. In antiquity, it is argued, the significant variables were not sex/gender but age and the hierarchy active/passive (or dominant/submissive). Adult males were supposed to be sexual initiators and penetrators but could penetrate either women or boys without incurring opprobrium because they would retain dominance.[69]

That ancient Greeks and Romans had different sexual practices from our own can be crucial to realizing that change is possible. Halperin takes an extreme position here: "Homosexuality and heterosexuality, as we currently understand them, are modern, Western, bourgeois productions. Nothing resembling them can be found in classical antiquity."[70] This statement from Halperin makes overt the agenda of much of his work: "I believe that if classical scholarship is ever to challenge heterosexuality's claims to normality and universality—its claims to be the sexuality of the majority of the population in all times and all places—it will have to do what it can to hang on to Foucault's fundamental insight."[71] Paul Veyne and John Clarke are also explicit about the hopefulness they find in difference.[72]

This view of ancient male sexuality has become a new form of doctrine, as if pederasty were the only form of male-male desire, but it should not be taken as the total picture when it is not even the whole of what was represented.[73] Amy Richlin has argued strongly against the dematerialism behind the constructionist position, pointing out that in Rome at least, mature men who chose the pathic role did constitute a stigmatized group.[74] Thus, while it is strictly accurate to say that there was no such thing as homosexuality (a sexuality organized completely around object choice) in antiquity, it does not follow that there was nothing that we would recognize as similar to what we call homosexuality, and it does not follow that all forms of male same-sex desire met with equal approval.

These positions within classics have arisen from various theoretical developments in the current academy. Let me begin with a brief (and admittedly superficial) outline of what is often called the second wave of feminism in the academy. Feminism in the early 1970s used gender as the primary category of analysis and focused on women's oppression under patriarchy, itself taken to be universal. Theories abounded as to whether the oppression was based on the traffic in women or the sexual division of labor or the division into public and private.[75] Feminist historians were engaged in a similar investigation, although they used the terminology of separate spheres, based on the language of the nineteenth-century ideologues.[76] Studies of women in the modern Mediterranean world, as well as in the European west, analyzed the segregation of men and women in everyday life, looking on "separate spheres" as a possible source of power for women as well as their oppression.[77] As Carroll Smith-Rosenberg argued for the United States in the nineteenth century, the maintenance of separate spheres facilitated a peaceful coexistence between heterosexual marriage and intimate relationships between women.[78] In her now classic paper, Adrienne Rich called attention to what she called the "lesbian continuum," in addition to lesbian existence, to account for women's relations to women; she posited that many women who might otherwise simply have been defined as married actually led a double life. Lillian Faderman's work on romantic friendship offered another way to conceptualize women's intimate relationships.[79] The work of feminists such as Smith-Rosenberg and Rich stressed the similarities between women and identification along the lines of gender; Rich in particular opposed working with gay men, whom she saw as benefiting from male privilege in a patriarchal society. This strand of feminist theory, especially Rich's work, was associated with the definition of a lesbian as a woman-identified woman who exemplified an androgynous ideal of nonpatriarchal sexual activity.

While such historical work and feminist theory opened up the study of women, it has been criticized for blind spots, for underestimating differences between women (on the basis of race, class, nation, ability, and sexual orientation), and for downplaying the significance of sexual desire in its view of lesbianism. Some critics claimed that the early feminist theory was heterosexist in its attention to women in the world of men and to the binary of male/female.[80] The attacks on the dominant discourse of feminism for ignoring the erotic component in lesbian relationships stimulated feminist attention to sexuality in the early 1980s. Feminists such as Gayle Rubin defined themselves as "pro-sex" and against anti-pornography feminists (e.g., Andrea Dworkin, Catharine MacKinnon) who arose out of the context of radical feminism; they challenged feminism's view of women as sexual victims (and a focus on the danger of sex) and provided another perspective on women's sexuality (one that emphasized the pleasure of sex).[81] These self-proclaimed sex radicals rebelled against a supposedly orthodox sexual ideology of lesbian feminism and emphasized sexual diversity; opposing the repression of sexual practices taken to deviate from a feminist ideal, they also shifted the focus from romantic friendship and egalitarian sexual practices to a valorization of sadomasochism and butch/femme roles.[82] But if the sexual and particularly the butch woman was overlooked in women's studies, lesbians were overlooked in gay studies, which tended to be male dominated. Changing the name to gay and lesbian studies was an attempt to change the discourse, but it was not entirely successful. In a recognition of the difficulties, de Lauretis adopted the term *queer* to emphasize the shared outsider status of gay men and lesbians as outsider.[83] Gayle Rubin, who had launched feminist theory with the phrase the "sex/gender system" in her essay "The Traffic in Women" (1975), distinguished between feminist studies and sexuality studies in "Thinking Sex" (1984), saying, "Feminism is the theory of gender oppression. To automatically assume that this makes it the theory of sexual oppression is to fail to distinguish between gender, on the one hand, and erotic desire, on the other."[84] Though Rubin did not mean this as a call for a radical break with feminism, it has been taken as such.[85]

The fissures have widened since Rubin made her statement, however, and there now seems to be a polarity between women's studies and gay/lesbian studies on the one hand, and queer theory on the other. Gay and lesbian studies as a field tends to look for the antecedents of modern movements or identities in the past, whereas queer theory focuses on the dissimilarities between present and past and tries to problematize heterosexual orthodoxy by recognizing many sexualities, without tracing out an alternative history for a gay sexuality.[86] Much of queer theory seeks to displace and decenter heteronormativity. Towards this end, it takes up the history of sexuality, following Foucault's distinction between acts and identities: "The sodomite had been a temporary aberration; the homosexual was now a species."[87] Thus, despite obvious affinities (these bodies of theory are related to liberation struggles; sex, sexuality, and gender are interrelated categories, etc.), there is not a direct lineage from feminist theory to queer theory, via gay and lesbian studies. Rather, the terrain is contested.

This history yields different definitions of female homoeroticism and suggests different lines of inquiry when we turn back to the ancient material. I started this section with the debate between Richlin and Halperin, and the question of similarity or difference: were women in antiquity like modern women or were they radically different? Whatever the empirical reality, we run the risk of making them seem similar by reading ancient women in the light of modern conceptions unless we are aware of our biases. These different perspectives show up clearly in readings of Sappho. For instance, contemporary feminists looking for a woman-centered culture have worshiped at Lesbos and used Sappho as a name to conjure with since the publication of *Sappho Was a Right-On Woman* in 1972, a book that mentions Sappho only once, aside from the title, and then only as a forerunner of feminism.[88] Those arguing for the continuity of sexualities across time and a lesbian tradition point to Sappho: of course the Greeks practiced lesbianism; they invented it.[89] A woman from Lesbos—a Lesbian—and a woman who sexually desires other women—a lesbian—were not interchangeable in early antiquity or even in the early modern period.[90] In the early ancient texts, *Lesbiazein* connoted female lasciviousness and especially fellatio and was not dissimilar from *laikazein,* to indulge in any kind of promiscuity; by Hellenistic and Roman times the homoerotic connotation was added to the term. But in the Latin poetic tradition, Sappho was repeatedly interpreted through the lens of masculine sexuality.[91]

Feminist theories of separate spheres and lesbian-feminist emphasis on romantic friendship, emotion, and gender are fruitful approaches for many of the ancient materials, because they broaden the range of women's activities that might be considered erotic in the homosocial world of women. The academic field of "women in antiquity" drew extensively on this phase of feminism and women's studies scholarship.[92] This early construction of women does fit some of the evidence that we have, which points to non-hierarchical erotic relations in women's communities.

Much has changed in the interim, however; notions of seclusion are contested, and the lesbian continuum was challenged even in its original publication in *Signs.* The critique of the sex radicals adjusts the lens by heightening our awareness of specifically sexual desire between women, leading us to ask whether the sexual roles of butch or dyke have anything to do with gender presentation and sexual behavior in ancient societies or in ancient representations. If a man had to be sexually active to be acceptably masculine in ancient societies, what did that mean about women who desired other women? Would such a woman necessarily have been considered masculine? Was there a place for active feminine sexual desire for other women?

The growth of queer theory provides a constructionist model that can be helpful for the study of ancient women's sexuality. Aside from Brooten's work, which is devoted to women, there are only brief references to women and female homoeroticism, and these have not been nuanced.[93] The assumption of "difference" in studies of masculine sexuality could also be useful if carefully applied to the study of female relationships.[94] What does it mean to call Sappho or any ancient Greek woman a lesbian, beyond the geographic denotation? If we take the specifics of the male pederastic model and look for examples of women's sexuality resembling ancient male hierarchical relations of older/younger and dominant/submissive, what will we uncover? Given the differences in male and female socialization, we should not expect to find a replica, but looking at men's homoerotic relationships could be valuable (as a hermeneutic device). Finally, attention to work in queer theory can enable a queer reading practice that challenges the assumption of heterosexuality not by a claim to have found something new in the past, but by a claim to read the past differently.

As a result of the complex history I have just sketched in, we seem to have several partially overlapping and partially successful interpretive grids, each with advantages and disadvantages. As scholars writing in the midst of these theoretical developments, we have the opportunity to pick our way eclectically, taking what is useful and making an amalgam of our own. If we can manage to keep feminism's attention to women and its notion of a continuity between homosocial/heterosexual/homoerotic, while recognizing differences within female eroticism, and adding queer theory's attention to the mobility of desire and its careful analysis of discursive practices, we may gain a more complete understanding of women in antiquity. The focus on women will be enriched by consideration of the material on sexuality and the queer focus, which puts into question stable identities; the focus on sexuality will be enriched by turning the lens on women.

THE CURRENT VOLUME: SITUATED SCHOLARSHIP

The essays in this volume are similar in that each argues from a specific body of evidence, not trying to fit it into a preconceived idea of women's relations to women, but they differ in that they adopt a variety of strategies, examine a wide range of periods and forms, and come from a broad spectrum of disciplinary perspectives, including art history, archaeology, classical philology, and comparative literature. There are disagreements among us, indeed the editors have not always agreed, but we have deliberately not tried to impose a single point of view on the authors of the individual essays.

Paul Rehak's essay, "Imag(in)ing a Women's World in Bronze Age Greece: The Frescoes from Xeste 3 at Akrotiri, Thera," is located in the field of archaeology. Rehak examines the homosocial environment represented in Cretan frescoes that were preserved at Akrotiri on the island of Thera, destroyed by volcanic activity in 1625 BCE. Because "Aegean art contains virtually no explicit depictions of sexual activity or even personal affection," Rehak's work is concerned with the implicit and raises the question of what we are seeing when there is no "sex." Given the differences represented between men and women, as well as between different ages of men and women, he argues for the existence of ritual stages. In women's lives these stages are based on their knowledge and control of plant life, in particular the saffron crocus plant. This evidence supports the notions that there were coming-of-age rituals for girls in the Aegean and that female power and female knowledges were developed in women's communities. While age differentiation between the figures seems clear, Rehak does not make assumptions about power differentials between them but instead emphasizes the possibility that women gained power over their own bodies and lives from control over saffron, a plant useful as medicine. On the basis of the implication of initiation, Rehak hypothesizes a homoerotic connection between the participants.

With the essay of Marilyn B. Skinner, "Aphrodite Garlanded: *Erôs* and Poetic Creativity in Sappho and Nossis," the collection turns simultaneously to textual evidence and to female authors. Skinner opens with a famous citation from Adrienne Rich (about "the lesbian within us") and develops the idea that Greek women writers could take strength as poets not only from the Muses as images of poetry but also from Aphrodite. Her view hypothesizes a reciprocal, nonhierarchal, homoerotic relationship between goddess, poet, and women of the community. Skinner attends not so much to the explicit expressions of erotic desire in Sappho and Nossis as to the significance of the poetic expression of that desire. She emphasizes the homosocial end of the continuum, placing Sappho and Nossis in tightly knit female worlds where creativity and desire are realized in art. This essay asks the probing question of whether "self-sufficient female imagination unshackled from conventional perceptions of the creative process" can fittingly be troped as "lesbian." In Skinner's interpretation of these Greek women poets, we have not sexual lesbianism but literary lesbianism.

Ellen Greene, in contrast, considers the erotic elements in Sappho's poetry. "Subjects, Objects, and Erotic Symmetry in Sappho's Fragments" thus complements Skinner's view. Greene argues that Sappho's poetry rejects the conventional Greek pattern of dominant lover and passive object of desire; she analyzes the way desire is configured in Sappho, disentangling the poetic dramatization of desire both from ancient male models and from modern conceptions of female sexuality. Greene's essay reveals that through manipulation of voice and gaze, Sappho's poetry dissolves rigid categories of lover and beloved so prevalent in ancient Greek male homoerotic culture. This reading of Sappho is consistent with modern lesbian feminist notions of nonhierarchical sexuality. Greene argues that Sappho's erotic discourse and practice may constitute an alternative to the competitive and hierarchical models of eroticism common in male patterns of erotic discourse. Greene also relates the nonobjectifying quality of the Sapphic gaze to the flexibility of subject positions in the poems, a view of Sappho that is also consistent with queer theory's emphasis on the shifting nature of sexual subjectivity.

Nancy Sorkin Rabinowitz's essay, "Excavating Women's Homoeroticism in Ancient Greece: The Evidence from Attic Vase Painting," raises questions about the ways in which what viewers think they know determines what they see. Placing women's relations to women on a continuum from the homosocial to the homoerotic, the essay's underlying question might be, "When is a dildo not a dildo?" As Rabinowitz points out, most claims about women on Greek vases are the result of assumptions and can be contested. Her essay analyzes the evidence for erotic ties between women in several homosocial settings, for instance, home, dance, wedding, and bath. The relations that can be glimpsed, Rabinowitz argues, cannot be securely interpreted either through the lens of male pederastic forms of sexuality or through the lens of heterosexuality, but a bifocal combination of the two can provide some guidance in how to read the images of women with women. Rabinowitz confronts the male domination of the form and culture but holds out hope for excavating some of what women saw when they looked at these paintings.

John G. Younger's essay, "Women in Relief: 'Double Consciousness' in Classical Attic Tombstones," focuses on Attic sculpture and its construction of a homosocial women's space in the cemetery of Kerameikos. Because of the nature of the evidence, Younger's essay, like the other pieces on art and archaeology, emphasizes the implied intimacy and affection in the representations of pairs of women, particularly on gravestones. Ancient Greek women had important roles in mourning; the grave markers are often ambiguous in their referents, but women indisputably feature prominently in the inscriptions and scenes. In performing the tasks involved with mourning, women were constructed as subjects, active viewers, and participants. The homosocial environment (a woman looking at the scene would be looking at a woman looking at another [the deceased] with a gaze full of yearning) makes plausible the insertion of homoerotic feelings in the circle of the gaze. Younger's essay reveals a shifting of subject positions made possible by the instability of reference for the stelai, positing not a specific lesbian sensibility but rather a mobile desire circulating among the figures and the audience. As Younger points out, in some cases a homoerotic reading of the women on the stelai is called for.

In "Glimpses through a Window: An Approach to Roman Female Homoeroticism through Art Historical and Literary Evidence," Lisa Auanger provides an overview of literary and art historical materials that serves in part as an introduction to the essays on later antiquity. Roman views of Sappho reveal a negative stereotype of the *tribas* or *frictrix* (literally, one who rubs), which, like the Greek *lesbiazein*, connoted sexual promiscuity, not simply homoeroticism. Another form of homoeroticism, however, more consistent with normative feminine behavior, was not so harshly judged. Her claim that certain versions of female homoeroticism were acceptable and indeed normative is supported by her analysis of representations of women's groups in myth and the arts. As Auanger speculates, the hostility to female homoeroticism may be hostility to only one form: an explicitly sexual "lesbianism" discursively constructed by comedy and satire.

Returning to literary evidence, in "Ovid's Iphis and Ianthe: When Girls Won't Be Girls," Diane T. Pintabone deals with explicitly physical sexual desire in Ovid's *Metamorphoses* (a Roman author writing from first century BCE to first century CE), showing that many different readings of the story of Iphis and Ianthe are possible depending on how one understands sex and gender in the work. Iphis has been treated as an example of the masculine lesbian, the *tribas* who is considered the active partner. By placing the narrative within the modern discourse on women's sexuality in Rome as well as in the context of the overall structure of the *Metamorphoses*, with its focus on power, Pintabone counters that interpretation of Iphis; she is brought up as a boy but thinks and acts like a Roman female. Her desire is expressed in a way consistent with Roman norms of femininity; she is passive and judges her passion negatively. In Pintabone's view female-female passion emerges in the story as egalitarian but impossible to maintain. Though Ovid as narrator never denounces the love of woman for woman, in the end, Pintabone finds that the narrative reinforces stereotypes of sex/gender and the structure of patriarchy.

Shelley P. Haley's essay, "Lucian's 'Leaena and Clonarium': Voyeurism or a Challenge to Assumptions?," takes up Lucian's (a second-century CE Roman author from Syria, writing in Greek) *Dialogue of the Courtesans* 5. Haley's essay crosses geographical, gender, and theoretical boundaries. She raises explicitly the question of what it means for a man to write an essay or dialogue treating female homoerotic motifs. Haley discusses the position of the male author, but she complicates that category by considering Lucian as a member of a multiculture and speculating on his own sexual practices, asking whether his ethnicity or sexuality would perhaps have encouraged him to take a sympathetic view of his characters. On the other hand, as Haley points out, voyeurism or the desire to hear details is the driving force behind the narration, and it may have been the force behind its writing as well. Haley is self-conscious about the problem: is the utilization of contemporary categories of analysis anachronistic? Can those categories nonetheless reveal the depths of interest in the dialogue?

Finally, Terry G. Wilfong takes us to fifth-century CE Egypt and the discourse of the law with his essay "'Friendship and Physical Desire': The Discourse of Female Homoeroticism in Fifth-Century CE Egypt." Wilfong studies a document from the White Monastery, which imposed punishment on two nuns for "running after" other women in "friendship and physical desire." The homosocial setting of the monastery and convent made women's desire troublesome; as is often the case, the laws that were inscribed to control their actions also conjure up the reality they were designed to repress. They leave us evidence of active erotic groups within the monastery community as well as what their actions were (for instance, shaving one another's heads). The problem of studying female homoeroticism is made clear by the striking asymmetry between male and female: while some of the language correlates male and female friendship groups, there was a specific term for men sleeping together, which did not apply to women. Sexuality and discourse are explicitly related: in the monastery, controlling women's sexuality gives the monks power. Thus, the sinfulness of female homoeroticism is correlated with the sin of challenging the authority of the monks to teach. This text makes glaringly clear the ways in which sexual practices and discourses of women were controlled by men.

Feminism, gay/lesbian studies, queer theory, and classics form the immediate intellectual background to this current volume; they evoke different approaches to women's lives and female homoeroticism in antiquity. The prominence of these grounding discourses undoubtedly has shaped what we have seen and what has still remained invisible to us. There are of course dangers in using modern theories for understanding representation in antiquity, particularly in the light of current emphasis on the differences between cultures; if the premodern and postmodern do not have much in common, how useful can our theories be? The new theories cannot be applied wholesale to antiquity, but they can be productive when used to raise possibilities; ways of thinking developed in the present can help us look at the past with fresh eyes. We hope that others will be able to take our work and build on it.

NOTES

1. This volume had its origin in an email correspondence between the editors, which resulted in a session at the meetings of the American Philological Association in 1997 entitled "Homosocial to Homoerotic: Problems and Methods in the Study of Women's Relations to Women in Antiquity." Commentators on the original panel, Mireille Lee and Louise Hitchcock, made invaluable suggestions. Portions of the introduction were also read at Loyola University of Chicago in 1995. Thanks to my coeditor Lisa Auanger, Patricia Cholakian, Katheryn Doran, Françoise Frontisi-Ducroux, Barbara Gold, Martine Guyot-Bender, Lydia Hamessley, François Lissarrague, Dana Luciano, Maureen Miller, Peter J. Rabinowitz, and the anonymous reviewers of University of Texas Press for their advice on this introduction. They are not responsible, of course, for advice not taken.

2. On Sappho's eroticism, see Jane Snyder, *Lesbian Desire in the Lyrics of Sappho* (New York: Columbia UP, 1997); cf. Margaret Williamson, *Sappho's Immortal Daughters* (Cambridge, MA: Harvard UP, 1995); in *Sappho Is Burning* (Chicago: U of Chicago P, 1995), Page duBois criticizes Foucault for ignoring Sappho, but she emphasizes the cultural significance of the poems, not their sexual significance.

Bernadette Brooten's *Love between Women: Early Christian Responses to Female Homoeroticism* (Chicago: U of Chicago P, 1996) is perhaps the most important predecessor for this volume, but her focus is on late antiquity.

For bibliography (before 1993) on women and gender, see Nancy Sorkin Rabinowitz and Amy Richlin, eds., *Feminist Theory and the Classics* (New York: Routledge, 1993). Since its publication, several new collections have appeared, especially for the literary and historical evidence: Mary DeForest, ed., *Woman's Power, Man's Game: Essays on Classical Antiquity in Honor of Joy K. King* (Wauconda, IL: Bolchazy-Carducci, 1993); Léonie J. Archer, Susan Fischler, and Maria Wyke, eds., *Women in Ancient Societies: An Illusion of the Night* (New York: Routledge, 1994); Richard Hawley and Barbara Levick, eds., *Women in Antiquity: New Assessments* (London: Routledge, 1995). On text and image, see Elaine Fantham, Helene Peet Foley, Natalie Boymel Kampen, Sarah B. Pomeroy, and H. Alan Shapiro, eds., *Women in the Classical World:*

Image and Text (Oxford: Oxford UP, 1994); James Davidson, *Courtesans and Fishcakes: The Consuming Passions of Classical Athens* (New York: HarperCollins, 1997). On art, see Ellen D. Reeder, ed., *Pandora: Women in Classical Greece* (Baltimore: Walters Art Gallery, in association with Princeton UP, 1995).

Several volumes on sexuality and visual representation in antiquity have come out recently, but these pay little or no attention to women's relations to women: Ann Koloski-Ostrow and Claire L. Lyons, eds., *Naked Truths: Women, Sexuality and Gender in Classical Art and Archaeology* (New York: Routledge, 1997); Natalie Kampen, ed., *Sexuality in Ancient Art* (Cambridge: Cambridge UP, 1996); Andrew Stewart, *Art, Desire, and the Body in Ancient Greece* (Cambridge: Cambridge UP, 1997); John Clarke, *Looking at Lovemaking: Constructions of Sexuality in Roman Art 100 B.C.–A.D. 250* (Berkeley: U of California P, 1998). Martin Kilmer, *Greek Erotica on Attic Red-Figure Vases* (London: Duckworth, 1993), is an exception in that he presents an extensive discussion of imagery, including female homoeroticism, but he focuses exclusively on the physical aspects of the erotic.

3. *The Use of Pleasure*, Vol. 2, *History of Sexuality*, trans. Robert Hurley (New York: Vintage, 1985) 22, is explicit: "It was an ethics for men." On masculine bias in Foucault, see Brooten, *Love between Women*; on Foucault and classics, see David H. J. Larmour, Paul Allen Miller, and Charles Platter, eds., *Rethinking Sexuality: Foucault and Classical Antiquity* (Princeton: Princeton UP, 1998), and on the masculine bias of Foucault, see especially the essays in that volume by Page duBois, "The Subject in Antiquity after Foucault," 87, and Amy Richlin, "Foucault's *History of Sexuality:* A Useful Theory for Women?" in David H. J. Larmour, Paul Allen Miller, and Charles Platter, eds., *Rethinking Sexuality* (Princeton: Princeton UP 1998). On the centrality of Foucault for sexuality theory in classics, see also Judith Hallett and Marilyn Skinner, eds., *Roman Sexualities* (Princeton: Princeton UP, 1997) 6; cf. David M. Halperin, John J. Winkler, and Froma I. Zeitlin, eds., *Before Sexuality: The Construction of Erotic Experience in the Ancient Greek World* (Princeton: Princeton UP, 1990) 5–7. David Halperin, *One Hundred Years of Homosexuality and Other Essays on Greek Love* (New York: Routledge, 1990), and Craig Williams, *Roman Homosexuality: Ideologies of Masculinity in Classical Antiquity* (Oxford: Oxford UP, 1999), follow Foucault and emphasize masculinity. John J. Winkler, *The Constraints of Desire: The Anthropology of Sex and Gender in Ancient Greece* (New York: Routledge, 1990), touches on both male and female experiences. *Naked Truths*, ed. Koloski-Ostrow and Lyons, is an exception in its emphasis on women.

Earlier scholarly work on sex in antiquity, mostly about men, includes Hans Licht (P. Brandt), *Sexual Life in Ancient Greece*, trans. J. H. Freese (London: Abbey Library, 1932); Robert Flacelière, *Love in Ancient Greece*, trans. James Cleugh (New York: Crown, 1962); Pierre Grimal, *L'Amour à Rome* (Paris: Hachette, 1963); Gaston Vorberg, *Glossarium Eroticum* (Hanau: Verlag Müller and Kleipenheuer, 1965). Kenneth Dover, *Greek Homosexuality* (New York: Vintage, 1978), did groundbreaking work on male homosexuality and included a chapter on women; see also Félix Buffière, *Eros adolescent: la pédérastie dans la Grèce antique* (Paris: Belles Lettres, 1980).

Cf. Amy Richlin's *The Garden of Priapus: Sexuality and Aggression in Roman Humor* (New Haven: Yale UP, 1983) for an early feminist analysis of the priapic paradigm in Rome; on text and image in Greece, see Eva Keuls, *The Reign of the Phallus: Sexual Politics in Ancient Athens* (New York: Harper and Row, 1985).

4. The two rarely overlap in classics, and in the academy, feminism and queer theory

have recently been locked in acrimonious dispute. For a statement of the problem, see Elizabeth Weed and Naomi Schor, eds., *Feminism Meets Queer Theory*, books from *differences* (Bloomington: Indiana UP, 1997).

5. The review by Danielle Gourevitch ("La sexualité de l'Antiquité: essai à propos de publications récentes," *Antiquité Classique* 68 [1999]: 334) is clear: "Therefore, it is not possible in my eyes to be at the same time a militant homosexual and a historian. The program of these 'colleagues' is not historical. . . . " But what makes a militant homosexual? She continues in an even more vitriolic vein: "For this American position contributes to destroying the very conditions of life, and hedonism is not, will never be, the foundation of life or truth." Thanks to François Lissarrague for bringing this review to my attention; the translation is mine. For "fashion," see Mark Golden, "Thirteen Years of Homosexuality (and Other Recent Work on Sex, Gender and the Body in Ancient Greece)," *Échos du Monde Classique/Classical Views* 35 n.s. 10 (1991): 327.

6. For recent summaries of the problem, see Lisa Nevett, *House and Society in the Ancient Greek World* (Cambridge: Cambridge UP, 1999); Sarah Pomeroy, *Families in Classical and Hellenistic Greece: Representations and Realities* (Oxford: Clarendon P, 1997) 12–16.

7. Jane Snyder, *The Woman and the Lyre: Women Writers in Classical Greece and Rome* (Carbondale: Southern Illinois UP, 1989); Marilyn Skinner, "Nossis *Thēlyglōssos:* The Private Text and the Public Book," in Sarah B. Pomeroy, ed., *Women's History and Ancient History* (Chapel Hill: U of North Carolina P, 1991) 20–47; "Sapphic Nossis," *Arethusa* 22 (1989): 5–18; "Woman and Language in Archaic Greece, or, Why Is Sappho a Woman?," in Nancy Sorkin Rabinowitz and Amy Richlin, eds., *Feminist Theory and the Classics* (New York: Routledge, 1993) 125–144; Diane Rayor, ed. and trans., *Sappho's Lyre: Archaic Lyric and Women Poets of Ancient Greece* (Berkeley: U of California P, 1991). Recent attention to Hrosvitha, a medieval woman writing in Latin, attempts to compensate for this lack (Barbara Gold, "Hroswitha Writes Herself: *Clamor Validus Gandeshemensis,*" in *Sex and Gender in Medieval and Renaissance Texts: The Latin Tradition,* ed. Barbara K. Gold, Paul Allen Miller, and Charles Platter [Albany: State University of New York P, 1997] 41–70); scholars also try to disentangle a women's perspective from medical writers, e.g., Aline Rousselle, *Porneia: On Desire and the Body in Antiquity,* trans. Felicia Pheasant (Oxford: Basil Blackwell, 1988).

8. See Marilyn Arthur Katz, "Ideology and the 'Status of Women' in Ancient Greece," *History and Theory* 31 (1992): 70–97; H. S. Versnel, "Wife and Helpmate: Women of Ancient Athens in Anthropological Perspective," in *Sexual Asymmetry: Studies in Ancient Society,* ed. Josine Blok and Peter Mason (Amsterdam: J. C. Gieben, 1987) 59–85, for considerations of the ideological roots of the status discourse.

9. On other terminology, see Williams, *Roman Homosexuality* 6, and Clarke, *Looking at Lovemaking* 12–16.

10. See Winkler, *Constraints* of Desire 17 with note, for a cogent statement of the cultural nature of sex; Jeffrey Henderson, "Greek Attitudes toward Sex," in *Civilization of the Ancient Mediterranean: Greece and Rome,* Vol. 2, ed. Michael Grant (New York: Charles Scribner's and Sons, 1988) 1251; Clarke, *Looking at Lovemaking* 15–16.

11. For opposition to the post-Foucauldian position, see Amy Richlin, "Not before Homosexuality: The Materiality of the *Cinaedus* and the Roman Law against Love between Men," *Journal of the History of Sexuality* 3 (1993): 523–573, and "Zeus and Metis: Foucault, Feminism, Classics," *Helios* 18 (1991): 160–180.

12. In Hesiod's *Theogony* 115–123, Eros is a creative force, emerging in the beginning before the other gods and making possible heterosexual reproduction, but he is also anthropomorphized as Aphrodite's attendant; for a recent study, see Claude Calame, *The Poetics of Eros in Ancient Greece*, trans. Janet Lloyd (1992; Princeton: Princeton UP, 1999). It is possible to see Eros as asexual; for instance, in contrast to the satyrs he is never ithyphallic (François Lissarrague, Seminar on Eros, Centre Louis Gernet, March 22, 2000).

13. The asymmetry between usage of homoerotic and heterosexual is interesting and casually inscribed in otherwise self-conscious texts. Thus, the heterosexual norm is still not scrutinized but remains the unmarked category. In fact, sexuality studies can in general be taken as gay sexuality studies.

14. For an overview of the problem facing lesbian studies, see Martha Vicinus, *Lesbian Subjects: A Feminist Studies Reader* (Bloomington: Indiana UP, 1996), and "Lesbian History: All Theory and No Facts or All Facts and No Theory," *Radical History Review* 60 (1994): 57–75.

15. For a study making a connection between sex and food, see Davidson, *Courtesans*; see also Foucault, *Use of Pleasure*.

16. On ancient historiography, see Neville Morley, *Writing Ancient History* (Ithaca: Cornell UP, 1999) esp. ch. 2.

17. "Ideology" 97.

18. On the problem of the "privileging of Greece at the expense of Rome," see Thomas N. Habinek, *The Politics of Latin Literature: Writing, Identity, and Empire in Ancient Rome* (Princeton: Princeton UP, 1998) 3–33. As a consequence of this historical phenomenon (as well as the prominence of Sappho in studies of female eroticism), this introduction also emphasizes Greece, though the volume as a whole does not.

19. On colonialism in classics, see Martin Bernal, *Black Athena: The Afroasiatic Roots of Classical Civilization*, Vol. 1, *The Fabrication of Ancient Greece 1785–1985* (New Brunswick: Rutgers UP, 1987), particularly chs. 7 and 8. On Victorian ideas of Greece, especially the formation of the ruling class, see Frank M. Turner, *The Greek Heritage in Victorian Britain* (New Haven: Yale UP, 1981) 5, 8; and Richard Jenkyns, *The Victorians and Ancient Greece* (Cambridge, MA: Harvard UP, 1980) esp. 63, 65; cf. Bernal, *Black Athena*, 282, 288, on Germany.

20. *Studies on Homer and the Homeric Age*, Vol. 1 (Oxford: Oxford UP, 1858) 5; cf. vol. 3, 3: "Nothing in those poems offers itself, to me at least, as more remarkable, than the deep carving of the political characters; and what is still more, the intense political spirit which pervades them. I will venture one step farther, and say that, of all the countries of the civilized world, there is no one of which the inhabitants ought to find that spirit so intelligible and accessible as the English: because it is a spirit, that still largely lives and breathes in our own institutions." Lest we think this way of thinking is over, see Gourevitch, "Sexualité" 333: "La grandeur de la Grèce puis de Rome est d'avoir fondé la société occidentale." ("The glory of Greece and then of Rome is to have founded western society.") Even a recent film like *The Browning Version* can mourn the passing of a time in education when the teaching of Latin and Greek inculcated the values of civilization.

21. For the classic statement of the ideology of Oriental Studies behind this east/west binary, see Edward Saïd, *Orientalism* (New York: Vintage, 1979) esp. 1–14. Janet R. Jakobsen, "Queer Is? Queer Does? Normativity and the Problem of Resistance," *GLQ* 4 (1998): 523, has an elegant discussion of how shifting binaries work to manage inconsistencies:

"When one binary is challenged, threatened, insufficient, problematic, or itself incoherent, it is possible to slip discursively to another, thus protecting the network as a whole."

22. James Stuart and Nicholas Revett, *Antiquities of Athens and Other Monuments of Greece*, 2nd ed. (London: Henry G. Bohn, 1858) 11; Jenkyns, *Victorians* esp. 145–150.

On the racist element of such descriptions, see Katz, "Ideology"; Bernal (*Black Athena* 201–215, 244, 292–294) relates appreciation for the Greeks to racism; despite her disagreement with Bernal, Emily Vermeule, "The World Turned Upside Down," in Mary Lefkowitz and Guy McLean Rogers, eds., *Black Athena Revisited* (Chapel Hill: U of North Carolina P, 1996) 272, connects the German belief that they were spiritually close to the Greeks to a systematic "historical revision . . . in the treatment of historic sites."

23. "Constantly they risked death from disease or the knife." Jenkyns, *Victorians* 3.

24. Michael Herzfeld, "Within and Without: The Category of 'Female' in the Ethnography of Modern Greece," in *Gender and Power in Rural Greece*, ed. Jill Dubisch (Princeton: Princeton UP, 1986) 215–233.

25. On the relation of gender to colonialism, see Leila Ahmed, *Women and Gender in Islam* (New Haven: Yale UP, 1992) esp. 151.

26. "Within and Without" 225, see also 218, 223. "In other words, at the same time as the Greek woman is upheld as a model of intelligence by comparison with her Turkish counterpart, she is to be kept in a relatively submissive role, far more so than her counterpart in the countries of Western Europe" (225). See also his "Silence, Submission, Subversion: Toward a Poetics of Womanhood," in *Contested Identities: Gender and Kinship in Modern Greece*, ed. Peter Loizos and Evthymios Papataxiarchis (Princeton: Princeton UP, 1991) 79–87.

27. Katz, "Ideology" 76–77 (quoting from philologist Wilhelm Becker, *Charicles*, with an excursus on "The Women"). The debate about that orthodoxy, as Katz points out, is the status of women debate; see also Versnel, "Wife and Helpmate."

On the origins of *hetairai*, see Leslie Kurke, *Coins, Bodies, Games, and Gold: The Politics of Meaning in Archaic Greece* (Princeton: Princeton UP, 1999) ch. 5; on distinctions within categories of prostitution, see Davidson, *Courtesans* esp. 73–97; see Haley's essay in this volume.

28. *Studies on Homer*, vol. 2, 479.

29. Gladstone, *Studies on Homer*, vol. 2, 519, differentiates Greek and "barbarian," saying that "the woman was not with them equivalent to the slave. Throughout their history they continued to be a nation of monogamists, except where they became locally tainted with oriental manners." Cf. John Addington Symonds, *Studies of the Greek Poets*, Vol. 1 (New York: Harper & Brothers, 1880) 385–386, on the "Asiatic extravagance of pleasure." These scholars deployed the word "oriental" in a manner consistent with Saïd's second definition of orientalism, *Orientalism* 2: "Orientalism is a style of thought based upon an ontological and epistemological distinction made between 'the Orient' and (most of the time) 'the Occident.'"

30. *The Attic Theatre*, 3rd ed. (Oxford: Clarendon P, 1907) 324. Blinders are selective, and our sensitivity to some issues may not extend to others; this comment follows hard upon his caveat about gender bias.

Even though the terminology is currently in disrepute, it is invoked: for instance, Raphael Sealey, *Women and the Law in Ancient Greece* (Chapel Hill: U of North Carolina P, 1990) 153–154, ends his book by contrasting "oriental seclusion" with "genteel withdrawal."

31. 2, 479.

32. "The Value of Greece to the Future of the World," in *The Legacy of Greece*, ed. Richard W. Livingstone (Oxford: Clarendon P, 1928) 15.

33. "The Position of Women in Athens in the Fifth and Fourth Centuries," *Classical Philology* 20 (1925): 25.

34. *The Greeks* (Harmondsworth: Penguin, 1951) 219–231; see also Versnel, "Wife and Helpmate."

35. Barbara McManus, *Classics and Feminism: Gendering the Classics* (New York: Twayne, 1997) 8–9, 12–14.

36. Jenkyns, *Victorians* 149, 152, not only points out the homosexuality of Walter Pater and John Symonds in a disdainful way ("And yet we keep hearing those quietly troubling overtones; as he slides around within his cluster of metaphors, a soft insinuating voice seems to whisper some message that it dares not speak aloud." "Symonds, another homosexual") but also argues that literary texts could cite Pater's language as a code indicating homosexuality (152). On Winckelmann's homosexuality and the statuary, see Bernal, *Black Athena* 213.

37. *Sex or Symbol: Erotic Images of Greece and Rome* (Austin: U of Texas P, 1982) 15. She believes that there has been a change in norms, ways of collection, for the better (9).

38. *Eros Kalos: Essay on Erotic Elements in Greek Art* (Geneva: Nagel, 1962) 5. On Winckelmann's ascetic homoeroticism, see Whitney Davis, "Winckelmann's 'Homosexual' Teleologies" in Kampen, ed., *Sexuality in Ancient Art* 262–276. The repudiation of the earlier (prudish) version of Greek culture becomes a refrain in modern writing on the subject. Robert Sutton states it explicitly in "Pornography and Persuasion on Attic Pottery," in *Pornography and Representation in Greece and Rome*, ed. Amy Richlin (New York: Oxford UP, 1992) 7, "Though earlier avoided by scholars or published with censored illustration, since the 1920s this material has been collected in a number of specialized picture books and is now one of the most completely illustrated and conveniently studied categories of the genre scenes on Greek vases."

39. Clarke, *Looking at Lovemaking* 148; Catherine Johns, *Sex or Symbol: Erotic Images of Greece and Rome* (Austin: U of Texas P, 1982) 19–32.

40. Linda Dowling, *Hellenism and Homosexuality in Victorian Oxford* (Ithaca: Cornell UP, 1994) 31.

41. Dowling, *Hellenism* 64–66 on Jowett's role in Plato studies; cf. ch. 3 on the "Socratic Eros."

42. George Chauncey, "From Sexual Inversion to Homosexuality: Medicine and the Changing Conceptualization of Female Deviance," *Salmagundi* 58–59 (1982–1983): 134. See also Jenkyns, *Victorians* 153, about Symonds. Symonds, *Studies*, vol. 2, 372, implicitly argues for a male homoerotic "sense of beauty which was inherent in the Greeks." Cf. Walter Pater, *Plato and Platonism* (London: Macmillan, 1899), on Sparta and Greek aesthetics.

43. *The Intermediate Sex: A Study of Some Transitional Types of Men and Women* (London: George Allen, 1912) 68, 70. On the basis of his analysis of Spartan society, Carpenter argues, "It is easy to see that while on the one hand marriage is of indispensable importance to the State as providing the workshop as it were for the breeding and rearing of children, another form of union is almost equally indispensable to supply the basis for social activities of other kinds" (73).

44. *A Problem in Greek Ethics* (New York: Haskell Hall House, 1971) 1. Plato's *Symposium* was viewed as relevant to the decision of the Georgia court in the case of Bowers v. Hardwick and in the Colorado law making it illegal to give civil rights to lesbians and gays (Martha Nussbaum, "Platonic Love and Colorado Law: The Relevance of Ancient Greek Norms to Modern Sexual Controversies," *Virginia Law Review* 80 [1994]: 1515–1651).

45. Symonds, *Studies*, vol. 1, 113; cf. Carpenter, *Intermediate* 73–74; Pater, *Plato and Platonism* 200–210, makes the connection between Plato's idealization of Lacedaimon and Spartan idealization of male beauty and emphasis on honor. He explicitly relates the Spartan system to the British public schools (201, 209–210; cf. Carpenter, *Intermediate* 105, below, n49).

46. *Problem* 18. Cf. Walter Pater, *Walter Pater: Three Major Texts (The Renaissance, Appreciations, and Imaginary Portraits)*, ed. William E. Buckler (New York: New York UP, 1986) 191, 200, who links Greek art and homoeroticism via Winckelmann, while distinguishing it from the east.

47. *Problem* 19.

48. *Problem* 5, 7.

49. He maintains that "they apply in the main to girls' schools—with this difference, that in girls' schools friendships instead of being repressed are rather encouraged by public opinion." *Intermediate* 105; on male bonding in the discourse, see Joan DeJean, *Fictions of Sappho, 1546–1937* (Chicago: U of Chicago P, 1989) 229: "The chastity [of Sappho] theory's success story corresponds perfectly to the paradigm for sexual politics articulated so famously by Luce Irigaray in *Speculum de l'autre femme:* men found a cultural order through the creation of a shared discourse of female sexuality."

50. *Problem* 33.

51. *Problem* 64.

52. *Problem* 70–72.

53. *Problem* 71.

54. See DeJean, *Fictions* 229.

55. *Sappho: Memoir, Text, Selected Renderings, and a Literal Translation*, 2nd ed. (London: Simpkin, Marshall, Hamilton, Kent, 1898) xv, 23; on Welcker, see n58.

56. *Sappho and Her Influence* (Boston: Marshall Jones, 1924) 43. Cf. R. C. Jebb, *The Growth and Influence of Classical Greek Poetry* (Boston and New York: Houghton, Mifflin, 1893) 111, on calumny; he asserts that "Sappho was married and had a daughter to whom she was devoted" (112). Similarly, Mary Mills Patrick, author of *Sappho and the Island of Lesbos* (London: Methuen, 1912) 110, argues away the eroticism in Sappho's famous Fragment 31 (*phainetai moi*): "The words do not describe love at all, but the unhappiness occasioned by the loss of the affection of her friend was of so deep a nature that its full expression required a stronger use of language than is at present the custom."

57. *Lectures on Greek Poetry* (London: Longmans, Green, 1911) 93, 94. He also agrees that Sappho was married and had children.

58. Friedrich Gottlieb Welcker, *Sappho von einem herrschenden Vorurtheil befreyt* (Göttingen: Vandenhoek und Ruprecht, 1816); Ulrich von Wilamowitz-Moellendorff, *Sappho und Simonides* (Berlin: Weidmannsche Buchhandlung, 1913). On the tradition of Sappho scholarship in England, see Yopie Prins, *Victorian Sappho* (Princeton: Princeton UP, 1999); for the history in France and its German influences, see DeJean, *Fictions*, in particular 207–230.

59. Renée Vivien (1877–1909) is the pen name of Pauline Mary Tarn, who translated

Sappho and gathered a group of artists and writers around her in Paris in the early twentieth century. Susan Gubar, "Sapphistries," in *The Lesbian Issue from Signs*, ed. E. Freedman et al. (Chicago: U of Chicago P, 1984) 91–110; DeJean, *Fictions* 266–299.

60. Ahmed (*Women* 27) points out that strict segregation also creates opportunities for women's work.

61. *The History of Sexuality: An Introduction*, Vol. 1, trans. Robert Hurley (New York: Vintage, 1978) 17–35; on Victorian and modern, 3–13.

62. It is frightening to recognize our own vulnerability to error, but one must do so nonetheless. Feminist postmodernism, with its emphasis on partial point of view, is not a cure, only a recognition of the disease. Bruce Thornton, "Constructionism and Ancient Greek Sex," *Helios* 18 (1991): 181–193, argues that there has to be some way of adjudicating between conflicting interpretations, but there may not be *one* way, only a variety of ways.

63. The debate between Bernal and his critics is symptomatic of these divisions. Bernal argues that classics as a discipline developed during an intensely racist period of European history (1815–1830); he hopes to change fundamental assumptions about ancient Greece and its relationship to Egypt and Phoenicia. He explicitly aims "to open up new areas of research to women and men with far better qualifications that I have. The political purpose of *Black Athena* is, of course, to lessen European cultural arrogance" (73). Mary Lefkowitz ("Ancient History, Modern Myths," in Mary Lefkowitz and Guy MacLean Rogers, eds., *Black Athena Revisited* [Chapel Hill: U of North Carolina P, 1996] 22) objects strenuously to the bias she sees in Afrocentrism, but she unwittingly reveals her own emotional sympathy for the Greeks ("The Greeks, *least of all peoples*, deserve the fate to which the Afrocentrists have subjected them" [emphasis added]). Other opponents of Bernal point out that if two centuries of classicists have been wrongly following ideologically motivated models, so might he be. See particularly the essays by Robert Norton, "The Tyranny of Germany over Greece?" in Mary Lefkowitz and Guy MacLean Rogers, eds., *Black Athena Revisited* (Chapel Hill: U of North Carolina P, 1996) 410, and Richard Jenkyns, "Bernal and the Nineteenth Century," in Mary Lefkowitz and Guy MacLean Rogers, eds., *Black Athena Revisited* (Chapel Hill: U of North Carolina P, 1996) 413. Many of Bernal's detractors concede his main point, which is that the construction of classics, with its privileging of Greece, was politically motivated.

64. *The Closing of the American Mind* (New York: Simon and Schuster, 1987) 332–333, 381.

65. In addition to Bloom, see Bruce Thornton, *Eros: The Myth of Ancient Greek Sexuality* (Boulder: Westview P, 1997) 76; for an extended attack, see Victor Hanson, *Who Killed Homer?: The Demise of Classical Education and the Recovery of Greek Wisdom* (Berkeley, U of California P, 2000).

66. For optimism and pessimism, see Amy Richlin, "The Ethnographer's Dilemma and the Dream of a Lost Golden Age," in Nancy Sorkin Rabinowitz and Amy Richlin, eds., *Feminist Theory and the Classics* (New York: Routledge, 1993) 272–303. On the problem of the myth of matriarchy for archaeology, see Shelby Brown, "Feminist Research in Archaeology: What Does It Mean? Why Is It Taking So Long?" in Nancy Sorkin Rabinowitz and Amy Richlin, eds., *Feminist Theory and the Classics* (New York: Routledge, 1993) 254–257; "'Ways of Seeing'" Women in Antiquity: An Introduction to Feminism in Classical Archaeology and Ancient Art History," in Ann Koloski-Ostrow and Claire Lyons, eds., *Naked Truths* (New York: Routledge, 1997) 20, 33n44, 34n51.

67. To name just the most vocal one, Halperin, *One Hundred Years*, who argues strongly for difference; on the other side, John Boswell (*Christianity, Social Tolerance, and Homosexuality: Gay People in Western Europe from the Beginning of the Christian Era to the Fourteenth Century* [Chicago: U of Chicago P, 1980]), who argues as strenuously for continuity, and now Brooten, *Love between Women*.

68. "Foucault's *History*" 168.

69. E.g., Dover, *Greek Homosexuality*; Halperin, *One Hundred Years*, *Before Sexuality*; Winkler, *Constraints of Desire*. Halperin analyzes the *kinaidos* (passive, effeminate partner in same-sex relationships) figure, pointing out that he was not the stigmatized modern-day homosexual and that pederasty is not homosexuality. Clarke, *Looking at Lovemaking* 86–87, challenges the view that there were always status differences between male lovers; cf. Charles Hupperts, "Greek Love: Homosexuality or Paederasty? Greek Love in Black Figure Vase-painting," in Jette Christiansen and Torben Melander, eds., *Proceedings of the 3rd Symposium on Ancient Greek and Related Pottery*, Copenhagen August 31–Sept. 4 1987 (Copenhagen: Nationalmuseet Ny, Carlsberg Glyptotek and Thorvaldsens Museum, 1988) 255–268, who argues that this has become the new orthodoxy but that vase painting does not bear out the ubiquity of age distinctions between lover and beloved. Davidson, *Courtesans* 174–180, 313, questions Foucault's emphasis on active/passive. The Greek picture was more complicated than the dominant/subordinate pederastic scenario allows for, and the modern situation is more complicated than a monolithic homosexuality/heterosexuality binary implies, as well. On this last point, see Eve Kosofsky Sedgwick, *Epistemology of the Closet* (Berkeley: U of California P, 1990) 1–66, esp. 25–26, 44–48.

70. *One Hundred Years* 8. Halperin restates his commitment to the "strangeness" of antiquity in his review of Brooten, Elizabeth Castelli, "Lesbian Historiography before the Name?" *GLQ* 4 (1998): 560; see also Ann Pellegrini's section of that review (587).

71. "Questions of Evidence: Commentary on Koehl, DeVries, and Williams," in *Queer Representations: Reading Lives, Reading Cultures*, ed. Martin Duberman (New York: New York UP, 1997) 53, citing Foucault's review of Dover: "De Caresses d'hommes considérées comme un art," *Libération* (1 June 1982) 27.

72. Paul Veyne, "Homosexuality in Ancient Rome," in *Western Sexuality: Practice and Precept in Past and Present Times*, ed. Philippe Ariès and André Béjin, trans. Anthony Forster (Oxford: Blackwell, 1985) 34; Clarke, *Looking at Lovemaking* 3–4.

73. See above, n69. The Greek vases sometimes represent men of the same age engaging in sexual activities together; these are often ignored. Hupperts ("Greek Love" 257) holds that "in the sixth century the paederastic relation was not the only form of homosexuality. In my view the scholars haven't paid enough attention up till now to vases that make clear that other forms of homosexual practice must have existed. Mostly the scholars have interpreted the data from the vases with a homoerotic and homosexual iconography from a too strict, presupposed idea of what Greek homosexuality implies." Cf. Clarke, *Looking at Lovemaking* 20 (on Dover), 35–42.

74. "Not before Homosexuality."

75. Gayle Rubin, "The Traffic in Women: Notes on the 'Political Economy' of Sex," in *Toward an Anthropology of Women*, ed. Rayna R. Reiter (New York: Monthly Review P, 1975) 175–210; on division of labor, see Heidi Hartmann, "The Unhappy Marriage of Marxism and Feminism: Towards a More Progressive Union," in *Women and Revolution: A Discussion*

of the Unhappy Marriage of Marxism and Feminism, ed. Lydia Sargent (Boston: West End P, 1981) 1–42; Michelle Rosaldo, "Woman, Culture, and Society: A Theoretical Overview," in *Woman, Culture, and Society,* ed. Michelle Zimbalist Rosaldo and Louise Lamphere (Stanford: Stanford UP, 1974) 17–42. Rosaldo rethought her position on the public/private a few years later, in "The Uses and Abuses of Anthropology: Reflections on Feminism and Cross-cultural Understanding," *Signs* 5 (1980): 389–417.

76. See the epigraphs to Linda K. Kerber, "Separate Spheres, Female Worlds, Woman's Place: The Rhetoric of Women's History," *Journal of American History* 75 (1988): 9–39.

77. Christiane Sourvinou-Inwood, "Male and Female, Public and Private, Ancient and Modern," in Ellen D. Reeder, ed., *Pandora* (Baltimore, MD: Trustees of the Walters Art Gallery in association with Princeton UP, 1995) 111, is dismissive of the tendency to group together ancient and modern Greek women under that rubric; she also argues against the idea that public and private were complementary spheres in antiquity, arguing that women were also subordinated in the household.

78. "Female World of Love and Ritual: Relations between Women in Nineteenth-Century America," *Signs* 1 (1975): 1–29.

79. "Compulsory Heterosexuality and Lesbian Existence," *Signs* 5 (1980): 631–660, rev. in *Signs Reader: Women, Gender, and Scholarship,* ed. Elizabeth Abel and Emily Abel (Chicago: U of Chicago P, 1983): 139–168. Lillian Faderman, *Surpassing the Love of Women: Romantic Friendships and Love between Women from the Renaissance to the Present* (New York: William Morrow, 1981).

80. Judith Butler, "Against Proper Objects," in Elizabeth Weed and Naomi Schor, eds., *Feminism Meets Queer Theory,* books from *differences* (Bloomington: Indiana UP, 1997) 2, recounts the history of this critique of feminist theory as heterosexist. See also her interview with Gayle Rubin in that volume.

81. Carole S. Vance, ed., *Pleasure and Danger: Exploring Female Sexuality* (New York: Routledge, 1984); see also Ann Snitow, Christine Stansell, and Sharon Thompson, eds., *Powers of Desire: the Politics of Sexuality* (New York: Monthly Review P, 1983). For a good overview that makes its own contribution, see Lisa Duggan and Nan. D. Hunter, *Sex Wars: Sexual Dissent and Political Culture* (New York: Routledge, 1995).

82. While butch-femme are studied as modern (post-WWII) styles, they do have forebears in the nineteenth-century construct of the invert and in the early twentieth-century emphasis on the manly lesbian. On the paradigm, see Esther Newton, "The Mythic Mannish Lesbian: Radclyffe Hall and the New Woman," *Signs* 9 (1984): 557–575.

83. "Queer Theory: Lesbian and Gay Sexualities," *differences* 3 (1991): iii–xxviii.

84. "Thinking Sex: Notes for a Radical Theory of the Politics of Sexuality," in Carole S. Vance, ed., *Pleasure and Danger: Exploring Female Sexuality* (Boston: Routledge and Kegan Paul, 1984) 307. For her intentions, and her view of the history, see also her interview with Judith Butler, "Sexual Traffic. *Interview,*" in Elizabeth Weed and Naomi Schor, eds., *Feminism Meets Queer Theory,* books from *differences.* Bloomington: Indiana UP, 1997) 68–108.

85. "Sexual Traffic," 73.

86. For a strong working out of the differences between gay/lesbian and queer studies, see Eric Savoy, "You Can't Go Homo Again: Queer Theory and the Foreclosure of Gay Studies," *English Studies in Canada* 20 (1994): 129–152.

87. *History of Sexuality,* vol. 1, 43. Of course, these notions were not invented by Foucault,

though his fame has obscured his social science predecessors (for a reminder, see Butler's interview of Gayle Rubin, "Sexual Traffic").

88. Sydney Abbott and Barbara Love, *Sappho Was a Right-On Woman* (Briarcliff Manor, NY: Stein and Day, 1972) 178; see also Judy Grahn, *Another Mother Tongue: Gay Words, Gay Worlds* (Boston: Beacon, 1984) 5; Dolores Klaich (*Woman + Woman: Attitudes toward Lesbianism* [New York: Simon and Schuster, 1974; New York: Morrow, 1975]) puts the poet in the lineage of writing as well as sexuality: "Sappho was a poet who loved women. She was not a lesbian who wrote poetry" (160). The importance of Sappho as a writer for women who were struggling to write is clear in Judy Grahn's book-length study of Sappho and women's literary tradition (*The Highest Apple: Sappho and the Lesbian Poetic Tradition* [San Francisco: Spinsters, Ink, 1985]).

89. Brooten (*Love between Women* 23) argues that there is a long history for the term and that there is no radical break between late antiquity and the Byzantine period. Her introduction gives an excellent summary (20–26).

90. In addition to Brooten, *Love between Women*, see summaries in Dover, *Greek Homosexuality* 182; H. D. Jocelyn, "A Greek Indecency and Its Students: LAIKAZEIN," *Proceedings of the Cambridge Philological Society* 206 n.s. 26 (1980) 12–66, esp. 30–34, 48n66; Alan Cameron, "Love (and Marriage) between Women," *Greek, Roman, and Byzantine Studies* 39 (1998): 137–156. The reputation of Lesbos for women who loved women may be taken from a poem by Anakreon, 358 Page; Peter Bing and Rip Cohen, trans., *Games of Venus: An Anthology of Greek and Roman Erotic Verse from Sappho to Ovid* (New York: Routledge, 1991) 90: "Once more Eros of the golden hair / hits me with his purple ball, / calls me out to play with the girl / with the flashy slippers. / But she, since she comes from noble / Lesbos, scoffs at my hair, / since it's white, and gapes for another girl."

91. See Auanger's essay in this volume; Greene explicitly challenges that tradition. Cf. Pam Gordon, "The Lover's Voice in *Heroides* 15: Or, Why Is Sappho a Man?" in Judith Hallett and Marilyn B. Skinner, eds., *Roman Sexualities* (Princeton: Princeton UP, 1997) 274–291; Holt Parker, "Sappho Schoolmistress," *Transactions of the American Philological Association* 123 (1993): 309–351.

92. For a summary, see McManus, *Classics* 15–19.

93. Above, n3. Grimal, *L'Amour à Rome*, does not mention women at all; Craig A. Williams' volume, *Roman Homosexuality*, is subtitled *Ideologies of Masculinity in Classical Antiquity*. Eva Cantarella (*Bisexuality in the Ancient World*, trans. Cormac Ó Cuilleanáin [New Haven: Yale UP, 1992] 78) claims that she started out looking for women's homoeroticism and gave up because of the lack of evidence.

94. Judith Hallett, "Female Homoeroticism and the Denial of Roman Reality in Latin Literature," *Yale Journal of Criticism* 3 (1989) 209–227, points out the casualness about terminology in ancient Rome: "Clearly these Latin literary sources, and the culture they come from, did not sort out, systematize, and rank their thoughts and feelings about the phenomenon of tribadism in the way that they did their reactions to male same-sex love, much less integrate tribadism into their cultural milieu. To them, female homoeroticism was an undifferentiated, unassimilated conglomeration of alien and unnatural Greek behaviors . . . " (223).

CHAPTER TWO

Imag(in)ing a Women's World in Bronze Age Greece

The Frescoes from Xeste 3 at Akrotiri, Thera*

Paul Rehak

 Although many images of women have survived from the Late Bronze Age Aegean world (ca. 1700–1100 BCE), it has proved extremely difficult for us to recover information about how they constructed their own sexuality at the time.[1] For in contrast to the other cultures of the eastern Mediterranean at the time, or the later cultures of Greece,[2] Aegean art contains virtually no explicit depictions of sexual activity or even personal affection: there are no scenes of women or men engaged in sexual intercourse (or other natural bodily functions, for that matter), no individuals who embrace, kiss, hold hands, or show other signs of intimacy.[3] In addition, we have no literary texts from the Aegean that might describe or discuss sexuality, in contrast to civilizations such as Egypt, which preserve large bodies of literature on the subject. This does not mean, however, that we have no hope of recovering women's sexuality in prehistoric Greece but simply that the search is more difficult than for other periods and cultures.

One potentially useful source of information in our search for female sexuality consists of the images preserved in Aegean fresco paintings, especially those from the earlier phase of the Late Bronze Age, when the Minoan culture on Crete exerted a powerful influence in the Aegean world. This era, the Neopalatial period (ca. 1700–1490 BCE),[4] saw the decoration of palaces and houses on Crete and important buildings at other Aegean sites with paintings executed in true fresco technique, painted on damp lime plaster, with occasional additions made after the wall surface had dried. The Cretan paintings have generally survived only in small pieces, but almost complete wall paintings have survived from Akrotiri on Thera, which was engulfed in a volcanic eruption ca. 1625 BCE.

I focus attention here on a series of paintings from room 3 in Xeste 3 at Akrotiri, a large freestanding structure of approximately thirty rooms, constructed on three levels and generally regarded as a public building (fig. 2.1).[5]

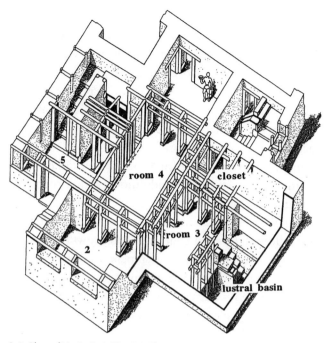

2.1. Plan of Xeste 3 at Akrotiri, Thera. Drawing: Author.

Though several attempts have been made to interpret these important frescoes,[6] most discussions have minimized the sexual implications of the scenes that depict women in homosocial environments.

In this essay, I shall attempt a more detailed reading of the compositions, concentrating on the activities, gestures, and costumes of the women and the landscape they inhabit, and I shall suggest that the main theme is female rites of passage at all stages of a woman's life, centering around the medicinal use of saffron. If this is so, then it is possible, using Eva Cantarella's hypothesis that rites of passage fostered same-sex relationships in early societies, to imagine a homoerotic element among women in prehistoric Greece.[7]

CONVENTIONS OF AEGEAN WALL PAINTING

Aegean art used a color convention to differentiate between women (who are shown with white flesh) and men (who are painted red).[8] We must look to physiognomy, pose, scale, costume, hairstyles, jewelry, and the interactions among figures for additional visual clues. The Aegean frescoes pay particular attention to different age grades and body types as figures mature from childhood into adulthood.

Several analyses of hairstyles in the paintings, in conjunction with observations about body morphology and facial physiognomy, suggest that both
sexes selectively cut and grew their hair in standard styles that mark specific
age grades as they matured, a practice important in later Greece and one that
has been documented in many other societies.[9] Prepubescent girls wore a
forelock and backlock but shaved the rest of their skulls; at the beginning
of the pubescence, the cranial hair was allowed to grow in curls, and the
fore- and backlocks grew even longer. By the end of puberty, girls had a full
head of hair and may have cut their forelocks, as they did in Classical times,
to mark the important transition to adulthood. Adult women wore their
hair long or tied it in a kerchief like the Classical *sakkos*. A few female hairstyles depicted in the frescoes do not fit into this progression, and thus some
girls may have followed different courses of hair growth and cutting, and—
we may therefore assume—social development, as they matured.

Less work has been done on male coiffures, but it is clear that the hairstyle for prepubescent boys was very similar to that of girls. Perhaps young-
sters were considered a single (asexual) gender, despite the difference in skin
colors, as the later Greek word παιδιά and our own neutral term "children"
suggest.[10]

The cut, color, and decoration of clothing can also be important sources
of social information, particularly among the women who actually produced
the textiles.[11] At all periods, Aegean women tend to wear more elaborate
and voluminous costumes than men. Both girls and women wear a short-
sleeved robe, which is open above the waist to expose the chest area even in
the case of children; this garment is calf-length for girls and ankle-length for
adult women. Although the female breast is often depicted exposed, there is
no evidence that it had a sexual connotation, as it did in historical Greece or
does in modern western cultures.[12] In fact, since Aegean artists show a great
awareness of several stages of breast development, it is possible that women
used the exposure of the chest to monitor and communicate the stages of
their own physical development to one another.

Women of all ages may wear a heavy apron that is wrapped around the
hips and secured at the waist with ties, or a type of girdle (apparently a single
or double roll of fabric) encircling the waist just above the hips. The combination of robe, apron, and girdle may represent special costumes rather
than everyday wear. Men, by contrast, often wear kilts or a breechcloth and
codpiece, while boys and even youths may be nude or wear only a belt.

Jewelry also communicates important social information about age, rank, status, and occupation.[13] Excavated finds also attest many types of Aegean jewelry that are represented in the Xeste 3 frescoes: hairpins, earrings, necklaces, bracelets, and anklets. Jewelry tassels could also be attached to clothing.

Finally, Aegean art tends to show both women and men in outdoor settings, where architecture serves as a backdrop or a frame of reference for human activities. Within these settings, women and men usually form sexually segregated groups, even when they appear together in towns or palaces, and women are usually shown on a larger scale, in more central positions, and they perform more important acts.

The crocus that is being gathered and that is depicted throughout the frescoes of Xeste 3 is probably saffron crocus, the *crocus sativus*, a cultivated plant whose bulbs need to be replanted on a 6–7-year cycle, rather than *crocus cartwrightianus*, which grows wild.[14] *Crocus sativus* blossoms in late October for just a few days, and it is then that its yellow-orange stigmas must be harvested quickly and dried for use as saffron, the many uses of which will be considered in more depth later. In the frescoes, the plants have yellow, not green, leaves, and the living stigmas are painted red, the color they actually take only when dried. The blossoms originally had brilliant purple petals, which have now faded or turned gray.

THE PAINTINGS OF XESTE 3

In Xeste 3, it is very likely that most public rooms (as opposed to service areas) had painted wall decorations, although not all these have yet been restored and reconstructed. Aside from those with women, which we shall examine in detail, the first large room that one encountered upon entering the building, room 4, contained a fresco depicting blue monkeys wielding swords and playing lyres.[15] Since blue monkeys (*cercopithecus aethiops aethiops*) were imported from Egypt to Crete and thence to other islands such as Thera, their presence immediately signals that the visitor has entered an exotic, liminal zone.[16] In Egypt, monkeys are usually associated with women and female sexuality;[17] since they sometimes appear with women in the Aegean, but never with men, they probably also imply that women were the main users of Xeste 3.[18]

The adjacent ground-floor room 3 has been subdivided into compartments by pier and door partitions (*polythyra*), a feature that allowed parts of ceremonial rooms to be opened up or closed off from view. One compartment, a sunken pit or "lustral basin," is set into the northeast corner of the ground-floor room 3, approached by a short flight of steps. The two walls above it are painted with a Minoan-style shrine facade and a composition of three women in a rocky landscape that includes crocuses (fig. 2.2). The function of "lustral basins" has received much attention, but no consensus has been reached; they are evidently not bathrooms, since they lack drains, and because they have flights of steps, they were obviously meant to be entered.[19] Some have a low balustrade along one side, evidently so observers could watch from above: thus, the basins were settings for spectacle.

The shrine facade painted on one wall is surmounted by the so-called horns of consecration, which probably represent a stylized mountain peak rather than animal horns.[20] Extraordinarily, the horns are streaked red. These streaks were first interpreted as drops of blood, but a recent examination suggests instead that they are coated with saffron stigmas.[21] The red horns may be an apotropaic sign, meant to turn aside evil. Set in the painted facade below is a pair of door panels, likewise streaked with red and carrying a design of red lily flowers.

This facade is reminiscent of the peak sanctuary carved in low relief on the impressive stone "Sanctuary Rhyton" from Zakros in east Crete (fig. 2.3).[22] That shrine is set in a mountainous landscape that also includes rockwork with crocus, wild goats (*agrimia*), and birds but no human figures. The shrine painting on the lustral basin wall, however, suggests that the observer is located out of doors in a mountain setting, not in a sunken pit. Perhaps the floor of the lustral basin can be equated with the courtyard in front of the shrine, as represented on the stone vase.

On the adjacent wall of the Xeste 3 lustral basin, we see three female figures: these include, from left to right, a woman swinging a necklace, a seated

2.2. Lustral-basin fresco, Xeste 3, ground floor. Drawing after N. Marinatos.

2.3. Stone relief rhyton, Zakros palace, Crete. Drawing: Author.

woman with a bleeding foot, and a girl on tiptoe enveloped in a yellow veil (fig. 2.4). The Necklace Swinger and seated Wounded Woman have similar long coiffures, firm chins, shallow breasts, and ankle-length skirts that indicate that they are fully pubescent and sexually mature, about 14–16 years of age. By contrast, the shorter, slighter Veiled Girl to the right is still in early pubescence, age 12–14: since she extends both arms in front of her, we cannot see her chest, but her short, calf-length skirt and partially shaved head with a few long locks indicate that she is not yet an adult.

A shared ground line and close physical proximity link the Wounded Woman and Veiled Girl and locate them in the open area before the shrine facade; the Necklace Swinger stands apart at a lower level, as if approaching the sanctuary with an offering of jewelry. The similarity in physiognomy and hairstyle link the Necklace Swinger and Wounded Woman, but their differences in costume and jewelry clearly distinguish the one from the other.

Several features call attention to the Wounded Woman in this composition: she is located near the center of the scene, she is much larger in scale

2.4. Detail of lustral-basin women, Xeste 3, ground floor. Drawing: Author.

than the others, and she is framed by the rockwork on which she sits and by pendant rockwork that hangs from the top of the scene like a canopy. Since she is the only one so framed, she seems isolated from the other two figures.

Seated figures in Aegean art are often goddesses or important individuals,[23] but the posture of the Wounded Woman is unique: she appears to have her right leg crossed over the left knee, and she leans forward slightly. She rests her head against the palm of her left hand and extends the right arm toward her foot, the sole of which is elevated slightly above the ground line. Red streaks of blood stream from the underside of the foot toward a single large crocus blossom underneath it. It is not clear whether the young woman is reaching to touch her bleeding foot or to pick up the blossom, but since this flower is not attached to a plant and simply hangs in space, it must serve as a sign or symbol standing for or referring to something else and perhaps carries a multiplicity of associations.[24]

In addition to the unique pose, the Wounded Woman has an unusual costume and jewelry. Along with her blouse, which is open to reveal the chest, she wears a draped but untied apron with lappets that somewhat recall the dangling strands of a hula skirt. In historical times, the loosened belt can be a reference to impending childbirth, but the Wounded Woman's abdomen is slim and flat, indicating that she is not pregnant.[25] The form of the apron also recalls that of the prehistoric "string skirt," which Elizabeth Barber has noted was used in many early European societies to advertise sexual maturity, readiness for marriage, and sexual activity.[26]

In *Iliad* Book 14, Homer describes how Hera borrows such a tasseled garment from Aphrodite when she sets out to seduce Zeus on Mt. Ida, to distract him from directing the fortunes of the Trojan War. A garment that simultaneously conceals and reveals the body underneath it has usually been considered an erotic device to make a woman more attractive to a man. An important aspect of the myth, however, is that the goddesses share an intimate article of apparel with one another. Because the garment of the Wounded Woman is simply draped but not tied, it hints at the presence of the naked body underneath, since it would fall off if she were to stand up. Her only observer in the painting, however, is another woman—the Necklace Swinger.

As if to emphasize that the link between the image of the blood/crocus blossom and the Wounded Woman is not coincidental, the belt of her garment is decorated with a chain of crocus buds.[27] This design has not been noticed in previous discussions, but it is clearly important, because it also echoes the clumps of crocus growing from the rocks on which the Wounded Woman sits. These visual repetitions reinforce the notion that crocus is central to the meaning of this figure.

The floral hairpins worn by the Wounded Woman, one over the forehead in the shape of a myrtle twig and the other with an iris finial in a knot of hair at the nape, are also unusual. Related hairpins of gold and silver have been excavated on Crete, where they sometimes carry Linear A inscriptions.[28] The surface of one surviving example is even incised with a row of crocus blossoms.[29] The plants that the pins imitate carry a special meaning. Myrtle, for example, was specifically associated in historical times with Aphrodite and thus with marriage, but the plant can also be used medicinally to induce abortion or cause the onset of labor in pregnant women.[30]

The identity of this figure is clearly crucial to our understanding of the lustral-basin scene. Her gesture of hand to forehead has usually been interpreted as one of pain or grief,[31] but it could be shock at the sight of the blood or even a gesture of introspection and self-awareness. The severely contracted, seated pose might also be intended to relieve abdominal cramps.

The features enumerated above suggest that the Wounded Woman has been dressed and bejeweled deliberately, probably by other women, for a particular ritual occasion. She is not an individual who has had an accident, as some scholars have maintained, nor is she completely recognizable as a mythological figure such as Persephone, Demeter, or Eurydice.[32]

The repeated references to crocus in the lustral-basin scene suggest that the juxtaposition of blood and blossom could be a metaphor or substitute for several types of female bleeding, including menstruation, the rupture of the hymen, or childbirth. All these occasions were often marked and celebrated by female rites of passage in ancient and early modern societies,[33] reinforcing the sense that the shedding of female blood is significant. Because no man is present, there is no obvious reference to defloration, and since there is also no infant, childbirth seems excluded. Menstruation therefore seems the likeliest possibility. If this is so, it is important to note that the event is being celebrated with rich garments and adornment with special jewelry, not marginalized or stigmatized. The ritualization of the event is suggested as well by the shrine facade on the adjacent wall and by the location of the paintings in a lustral basin, a special architectural area.

The Veiled Girl averts her eyes from the bloodshed of the Wounded Woman and looks back toward the shrine with its red-streaked horns. She may be too young to participate or even understand whatever activity or experience is taking place in front of her, but her diaphanous yellow veil covered with red spots that envelops her body suggests that she too is undergoing a transition. In historical Greece, garments dyed yellow with saffron crocus stigmas include the wedding veil[34] and the *krokotos*, which was put on briefly by the prepubescent girls who served Artemis at Brauron in preparation for their assumption of adult roles and duties.[35] Both are costumes that were worn only to mark a rite of passage and are restricted to females. In historical times, saffron-dyed garments were generally considered inappropriate for men, and Aristophanes mocks as effeminate the men who wore this color.[36] The red spots on the Thera veil, however, make the garment unlike those attested in Classical times and suggest that the veil has been sprinkled with blood.

Since the Veiled Girl turns toward the shrine and away from the onset of the Wounded Woman's first menses, and since she has continued to shave her hair long after the others have begun to grow theirs, it may be that she has already chosen a different role in life, signaled by her hairstyle.

It is surely significant that all three figures in the Thera lustral-basin painting are associated with crocus flowers or the saffron-yellow dye derived from its stigmas. The Necklace Swinger and Veiled Girl have blouses adorned with blossoms and stigmas (the purple petals are much faded but can still be made out) and by yellow garments. The Necklace-Swinger also has a garland of crocus stigmas draped across her chest and over her shoulders.[37] As noted above, the Wounded Woman's unusual belt carries a repeating pattern of crocus buds, her foot bleeds over a crocus blossom, and she sits on rocks from which clumps of crocus grow. There is thus a complex interweaving of color and floral imagery that unites all the women despite their individual differences.

A separate ground-floor compartment located near the lustral basin in Xeste 3 depicts four male figures whose body types and facial features indi-

2.5. Male figures, Xeste 3, ground floor. Drawing: Author.

cate that they are shown at four distinct age grades: a prepubescent child (8–10), a boy in early pubescence (10–12), a young man in full pubescence (16–18), and a seated mature man with a slight paunch, clad in a white kilt (fig. 2.5).[38] The last is the only one of these individuals who is clothed, and none wears jewelry, indicating that all are of relatively low status or a different class, particularly noteworthy when we compare them with the richly adorned women from the building. At the same time, it would be a mistake to think of these as inconsequential figures: seated male figures are very rare in Aegean art,[39] and the eldest youth turns his head back in the same manner as the Veiled Girl, a highly unusual pose.

Each male figure holds a metal vessel or piece of fabric; the gold-colored cup once held by the youngest boy has unfortunately been erased in cleaning. Comparisons for these metal vessels can be found among the containers excavated on Crete, Thera, and the mainland, most of which were probably manufactured at a few Minoan palace centers, such as Knossos.[40] The fabric that one individual holds does not resemble any of the costumes worn by women in the building, but its red, white, blue, and black colors, along with the presence of undulating bands, somewhat recalls the decoration of the abstract relief fresco, modeled in plaster and then painted, from a third-floor room in Xeste 3.[41] The procession fresco from the west Entrance Corridor of the Knossos palace shows other men carrying metal containers and a man offering another piece of fabric to an important woman.[42]

The youngest boy in Xeste 3 differs from the rest because his skin is painted an orange-yellow color, in contrast to the older males who have darker red skins; we shall return to this anomaly later.

Directly above the lustral basin, in room 3 on the upper floor, a composition over two walls depicts four young girls who gather crocus blossoms

2.6. Goddess and girls, Xeste 3, upper floor. Drawing after N. Marinatos.

in a mountainous landscape and offer them in baskets to a goddess enthroned on a high platform set atop Minoan incurved bases (fig. 2.6). One
girl stands on the foot of the platform and empties a basket of crocus blossoms into a large pannier, while another girl approaches from the far right,
with her basket balanced on her shoulder, its handle steadied by a string.[43]
On the adjacent wall are two more girls, both of whom are picking the blossoms.[44] The first holds her basket in one hand and turns her head back toward her companion; the other has set her basket on the ground and climbs
a small hillock to reach for a new blossom to add to those cupped in the
palm of her other hand.

Because all the girls wear short skirts, have snub noses, receding chins,
partially shaved heads with short curls, and flat chests with barely budding
nipples, they must be prepubescent, about 8–10 years of age. The girl with
the basket on her shoulder has red hair and blue eyes, as if she represents a
different, non-Greek ethnic type. If so, she is almost the only "other" person shown in Aegean art.[45]

Despite minor differences among the girls in terms of hairstyle and physiognomy, the two conjoined compositions on the adjacent walls of this upper-
floor room both have clumps of crocus depicted as a repeating background
pattern. Thus, the scenes appear to form a unified narrative, an interpreta-

2.7. Detail of goddess, Xeste 3, upper floor.
Drawing: Author.

tion that is supported by the gathering of crocus blossoms and stigmas for saffron and their presentation to the divinity.

The central goddess on one wall is the most important figure, and every visual element in her representation draws our eye (fig. 2.7). She is enthroned on the highest stage of a tripartite platform and is flanked by unusual animals in a heraldic composition—a blue monkey to the left who offers her saffron stigmas with a courtly gesture[46] and a rampant griffin to the right, illusionistically tethered by a red collar and leash to the edge of an actual window set in the wall of the room. She is thus a Mistress of Animals or *Potnia Theron*, a well-known aspect in historical times of Artemis.[47]

The goddess is the largest as well as the most richly dressed, coiffed, and bejeweled figure painted in Xeste 3. She wears a diaphanous blue robe decorated and bordered with crocus blossoms and over it, a blue and white apron. Her elaborate jewelry includes a string of beads in her hair, necklaces of duck- and dragonfly-shaped beads, earrings, and several bracelets. A pair of crocus stigmas hangs against one cheek; as elsewhere, the purple petals have faded, but this is probably a blossom hanging over one ear, rather than a tattoo.[48] She also wears a distinctive forehead band like all the young girls, but her shallow breast and facial features are so similar to those of the Necklace Swinger and the Wounded Woman from the floor below that we must imagine her as being about the same age, 14–16 years old. The relative youth of this divinity and her association with young girls strongly imply that she incorporates some of the functions of the later historical Artemis, who was attended by young girls in sanctuaries at Brauron and elsewhere.

Three other compositions from the upper floor, possibly belonging to other walls of this room, are still undergoing conservation and restoration. A separate marsh scene with two types of reeds, half a dozen male and female ducks, a nest with ducklings waiting to be fed, and red dragonflies against a white background suggest a different type of landscape setting from the mountaintop where the crocus gathering takes place.[49] The ducks and dragonflies, however, recur as beads in the goddess' necklaces, while the birds' nests find parallels in a frieze from ground-floor room 4. In Bronze Age Egypt, ducks were associated with women and with female sexuality, while in later Archaic Greek art, the birds are a frequent attribute of Artemis as "mistress of animals."[50]

Another scene from the upper floor shows a file of mature women with full breasts and hair tied in snoods (fig. 2.8).[51] Unlike the younger female figures from Xeste 3, these adults lack earrings and elaborate jewelry, but their costumes are rich in floral iconography. One wears a saffron-yellow blouse decorated with red lilies and over it, a yellow garment with undulating borders (perhaps a dyed fleece rather than cloth) draped across one shoulder and covered with red roses.[52] Another has a yellow blouse with red crocus stigmas and wears a crocus over one ear, like the seated goddess. Her fleecy overgarment is blood red, and she holds a basket like those of the crocus-gathering girls; perhaps she performed this activity as a girl.[53] A third woman carries a sheaf of white lilies and wears a single lily blossom at the back of the head.[54] Possibly related to this scene is a large panel that depicts white lilies against a red background.[55] These matrons could be the mothers of the crocus-gathering girls described earlier.

INTERPRETATION

I have already suggested some possible interpretations of individual scenes within Xeste 3. It is now time to consider the pictorial program of the building as a whole. While the extraordinary iconographic content of the frescoes was recognized from the moment the paintings were unearthed, scholars have long debated whether Aegean frescoes generally are mainly decorative (like wallpaper) or are primarily religious, with a wide range of opinion between these two extremes.[56]

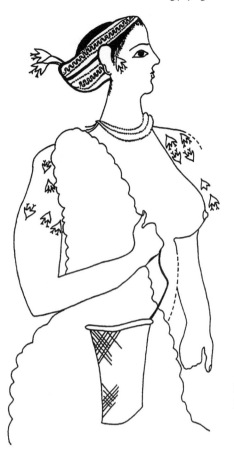

2.8. Mature woman, Xeste 3, upper floor. Drawing: Author.

For example, Nanno Marinatos has proposed and argued a primarily religious interpretation of the Xeste 3 frescoes in several studies. She identifies the program of Xeste 3 as a general representation of women's puberty rites and the seasonal renewal of nature.[57] Suzanne Amigues, by contrast, has focused on the economic importance of the saffron gathering in the frescoes for a source of food and dyestuff and takes the position that the scenes from Xeste 3 simply depict the centrality of saffron culture as an economic commodity in the lives of ancient Theran women.[58] Both views may be partially correct, since it is likely that early societies made less of a distinction between secular and religious spheres than we do today.[59]

Saffron is obviously important in these frescoes, and obviously important to women. It is probably significant too that while males are also depicted, they appear in a separate room and are apparently of lesser status. At the same time, similar physiognomies for both sexes indicate the existence of four parallel age grades. The earliest stage of prepubescence includes the boy with the yellowish skin and the flower-gathering girls; for the latter, this stage coincides with a period of service to a goddess in whose presence they are shown. A more advanced state is represented by the Veiled Girl and the boy with the metal basin: they are taller than the children and have similar facial features; the penis of the boy is relatively small but clearly indicated. Full puberty, the third stage, is illustrated by the Necklace Swinger, Wounded Woman, and the youth holding the cloth. A fourth stage, of full adulthood, includes the matronly processional women (who are the least elaborately adorned of the female figures) and the seated man with the hydria.

The different type of pubescence marked by the Veiled Girl's unusual hairstyle and different costume may indicate the existence of a separate, different course open to some girls as they matured; and since she veils herself and averts her eyes toward the shrine from the bloodshed associated with full pubescence, she may be destined ultimately for the status of virgin priestess.

If my hypotheses are correct, they seem to indicate that the identification of the scenes as general puberty rites for women is far too simplistic, and the frescoes instead are outlining the importance in Aegean society of successive rituals of maturation for women at all ages with reference to a specific goddess, localizing each stage within a more inclusive society of women. Moreover, references to saffron abound for all these women, whatever their age and status within this homosocial sisterhood.

An understanding of the properties of saffron crocus may provide clues for a more detailed interpretation of the various scenes with women. A wide range of uses for saffron is known or suggested in the medical pharmacopoeia, past and present, from around the world: it can reportedly be used as a digestive, stimulant, aromatic, aphrodisiac, narcotic, and emmenagogue; it can ease menstruation and in higher doses can induce abortion.[60] In very high doses, it is said to cause insanity and death. In addition to its well-attested use as a food and dyestuff, saffron has also been documented to provide an important source of vitamins. Saffron is extremely rich in vitamins A and B (riboflavin) and carotenids, especially carotenes[61]—all of which are lacking from most of the foods we know were consumed in the Bronze Age Aegean, where the diet consisted largely of grains, legumes, oil, figs, grapes, and wine.[62] Saffron thus has a variety of applications pertaining to general good health.

In an article some years ago, Ellen Davis called attention to an unusual detail in the way the eyes of some figures in these frescoes were depicted.[63]

Several individuals have light blue streaks in the corners of the corneas, which Davis interpreted as a sign of relative youth, while the red streaks in the corneas of other figures were identified as a sign of age. Now that more figures have been published in detail, it is clear that this hypothesis does not adequately explain the evidence. The goddess and young girls, along with all the lustral-basin women and the youngest boy, have blue-streaked corneas. The matrons all have plain white corneas. The two youthful males and the one adult man have red-streaked eyes (the eyes of another youth are not preserved). What the red and blue streaks indicate is not age and youth but rather a condition that links the young women and the youngest boy.

The medicinal properties of saffron are responsible for the different condition of the eyes.[64] A marked symptom of vitamin A or riboflavin deficiency is a clinically distinct red streaking of the corneas, which, if untreated, can lead to significant ocular problems. These include corneal lesions, conjunctivitis, sensitivity to light, eye irritation and increased tearing, and a decrease in the sharpness of vision. An accompanying factor is an inflammation of mucous membranes of the face, especially around the lips (cheilosis) and tongue (glossitis). The modern remedy for these conditions is simple: dietary supplementation with the normal required doses of vitamins A and B. Individuals with diets high in these two vitamins tend to have better visual acuity and healthier eyes.

Saffron, however, is also very high in carotenes. An occasional temporary side effect of high carotene levels (sometimes now caused by eating too many carrots) is a condition resembling jaundice, in which the color of the skin turns yellow (caretenemia). The youngest boy, the only male figure in Xeste 3 with blue-streaked corneas, in fact exhibits just this trait: his skin is painted a unique pale yellow-orange, instead of the brick-red color used for the other male figures. Because carotene is turned into vitamin A in the body, a high carotene diet translates to a diet high in vitamin A, which results in good ocular health.[65] But unlike jaundice, in which the eyes also turn yellow, this condition results in bright, healthy eyes, and the yellow skin typically disappears when the dietary level of carotenes is reduced.

Even though the women in the building are represented with white, rather than yellowish, skins, the frescoes seem to be telling us that the culture and ingestion of saffron was principally a female activity, and one that was relevant at all stages of a woman's life, not just at puberty. Young boys may have had similar access to saffron because they were dependent on their mothers before they entered pubescence, when they presumably started taking part in male activities. Even the mature women, who have plain white corneas, must have received adequate amounts, since their eyes show no signs of the reddening associated with vitamin A or riboflavin deficiency.

It is probable therefore that the Theran women not only cultivated and harvested the crocus and supplied themselves and their dependent children with the saffron, but since the red eyes of males apparently indicate that they had low levels of vitamin A, they also denied men access to saffron.

Since an adequate supply of vitamins A and B is essential to good health, we can assume that women carefully controlled their saffron-rich diet; we also know that this kind of diet contributes directly to high birth weights in babies and thus promotes reproductive success.[66] Its use as an emmenagogue, to induce and ease menstruation, would have allowed women to regulate their own menses, to afford some control over conception, and even to induce abortions if they wished.[67] High levels of these vitamins promote good eyesight and general health and may reduce the risk of some cancers, lower the incidence of coronary disease, and retard aging. The women of Thera must have had a detailed experiential knowledge of the medicinal properties of saffron, a knowledge that should also have been an important source of women's power and ability to experience a personal control of their bodies and thus their lives.

The frescoes from Xeste 3 thus document Aegean women's extraordinary awareness of, and attention to, their body, its development, and its maintenance. In this female homosocial world depicted in a public building at Akrotiri, where men are obviously of lesser status and deprived of access to a source of nutrition that gave power instead to women, it would be surprising indeed if these healthy women did not express their care and attention for each other erotically.

Because there is a gap in our literary sources between the Bronze Age and the historical period, we cannot be sure that such social traditions survived unchanged. Nevertheless, the evidence of later authors suggests that even after the prehistoric period, floral landscapes were understood as a setting where women could express and explore their sexuality with one another. In Fragment 2, Sappho invokes Aphrodite to visit a paradise landscape with flowers that excludes men and permits homosocial, even erotic, relationships among women, very much like the construction I have tried to suggest here for the Bronze Age.[68] She is the exception, however. The landscape that Sappho envisions as a protected realm in which women could express their sexuality with other women has been transformed into a landscape that reflects a patriarchal need for ownership and control.

In the Archaic and Classical periods, descriptions of the sexualized female body, and even that of the adolescent male, are often couched in terms of the natural landscape or compared to flowers, with a complex interweaving of images.[69] Thus, when Zeus in the form of a bull rapes Europa as she gathers flowers, he "breathes out a crocus flower from his mouth" to entice the unwary girl.[70] In *Homeric Hymn to Demeter*, the four (unmarried) daughters of King Keleus and Queen Metaneira are "like goddesses in the flower of their youth" and have hair that "streams about their shoulders like a crocus flower," presumably because it has not been cut yet in anticipation of marriage.[71] Landscapes with flowers that include crocus are the setting for the rape of Persephone by her uncle, Hades, and the lovemaking of Hera and Zeus in the *Iliad*.[72]

Though more examples could be added, these few examples illustrate the ways in which the prehistoric homosocial landscape of women had changed by the historical period. Women with detailed knowledge of plants and their properties were often considered potential poisoners or witches such as Medea. The sharing of knowledge among women at festivals that excluded men had become a locus for male insecurity, as Aristophanes' play, *Thesmophoriazousai*, indicates. Certainly by the Classical period in Athens, the homosocial landscape of women had become the erotic domain of men.

The frescoes from Xeste 3 seem to document that a different situation obtained during the Late Bronze Age, at least for one Aegean society. Women are the protagonists throughout the painted program of an important building of the town, and they are shown in different roles than those revealed in other frescoes from Minoan and Mycenaean sites. Rather than marginalizing women, these paintings from Thera illustrate the centrality of women's personal relationships with one another, and present occasions when women could explore their own sexuality with one another.

NOTES

*I am grateful to the following individuals for their help: Mireille Lee, Barbette Spaeth, Ann Suter, and John G. Younger. Much of the medical material documented here was compiled by Roman R. Snihurowych in the course of an independent study with me at Duke University in 1997. Some of our joint conclusions were presented in P. Rehak and Roman R. Snihurowych, "Is Female to Male as Nature Is to Culture? Medicine, Myth and Matriarchy in the Thera Frescoes," *American Philological Association Abstracts of Papers Presented at the One Hundred Twenty-Ninth Annual Meeting* (New York: American Philological Association, 1997): 180. Nancy S. Rabinowitz and Lisa Auanger provided a number of helpful suggestions on this text.

1. Paul Rehak, "The Construction of Gender in Late Bronze Age Aegean Art—A Prolegomenon," *Redefining Archaeology: Feminist Perspectives. Proceedings of the 3rd Australian Women in Archaeology Conference*, edited by Mary Casey, Denise Donlon, Jeannette Hope, and Sharon Wellfare (Canberra: Australian National University Publications, 1998): 191–98.

2. E.g., A. Mulas, *Eros in Antiquity* (New York: Erotic Book Society 1978); M. Kilmer, *Greek Erotica* (London: Duckworth, 1993); Andrew Stewart, *Art, Desire, and the Body in Ancient Greece* (Cambridge: Cambridge UP, 1997); Lisa Manniche, *Sexual Life in Ancient Egypt* (London/New York: Kegan Paul, 1987).

3. The few sexual images from the Aegean include copulating goats: Nicholas Platon, I. Pini, and G. Salies. 1977. *Corpus der Minoischen und Mykenischen Siegel, II, Iraklion Archäologisches Museum, 2, Die Siegel der Altpalastzeit* (Berlin: Gebrüder Mann Verlag 1977), no. 306a; V. E. G. Kenna, *Corpus der Minoischen und Mykenischen Siegel, VII, Die Englischen Museen, II* (Berlin: Gebrüder Mann Verlag, 1967), no. 78; nude man and dressed woman: Ingo Pini, *Corpus der Minoischen und Mykenischen Siegel, II, Iraklion Archäologisches Museum, 5, Die Siegelabdrücke von Phästos* (Berlin: Gebrüder Mann Verlag, 1970), no. 324.

4. For a recent critical survey of this period, see Paul Rehak and John G. Younger, "Review of Aegean Prehistory VII: Neopalatial, Final Palatial, and Postpalatial Crete," *American Journal of Archaeology* 102 (1998): 91–173. For paintings, see Sara A. Immerwahr, *Aegean Painting in the Bronze Age* (University Park: Pennsylvania State UP, 1990).

5. Spyridon Marinatos, *Excavations at Thera*, III (Athens: Athens Archaeological Society, 1970) 38–39; Spyridon Marinatos, *Excavations at Thera*, V (Athens: Athens Archaeological Society, 1972) 26–27, pls. 50b–53; Spyridon Marinatos, *Excavations at Thera*, VII (Athens: Athens Archaeological Society, 1976) 22–28, col. pls. A–L, pls. 32–42, 58–66; Clairy Palyvou, "Architectural Design at Late Cycladic Akrotiri," in *Thera and the Aegean World III: Proceedings of the Third International Congress, Santorini, Greece, 3–9 September 1989*, ed. David A. Hardy, Christos G. Doumas, John A. Sakellarakis, and Peter M. Warren (London: Thera Foundation, 1990), vol. 1, 44–56. Xeste 3 lacks the deposits of domestic pottery characteristic of private houses.

6. E.g., Nanno Marinatos, *Art and Religion in Thera: Reconstructing a Bronze Age Society* (Athens: D. and I. Mathioulakis, 1984) 61–84; Nanno Marinatos, *Minoan Religion: Ritual, Image, and Symbol* (Columbia: U. of South Carolina Press, 1993); Nanno Marinatos, "Role and Sex Division in Ritual Scenes of Aegean Art," *Journal of Prehistoric Religion* 1 (1987): 23–34; Gösta Säflund, "The Agoge of the Minoan Youth as Reflected by Palatial Iconography," in *The Function of the Minoan Palaces: Proceedings of the Fourth International Symposium at the Swedish Institute in Athens, 10–16 June, 1984*, ed. Robin Hägg and Nanno Marinatos (Stockholm: Swedish Institute in Athens, 1987) 227–233; Suzanne Amigues, "Le crocus et le safran sur une fresque de Théra," *Revue Archéologique* 1988: 227–242; Paul Rehak, "The Aegean Landscape and the Body: A New Interpretation of the Thera Frescoes," in *From the Ground up: Beyond Gender Theory in Archaeology. Proceedings of the Fifth Gender & Archaeology Conference, University of Wisconsin-Milwaukee, October 1998*, ed. N. L. Wicker and B. Arnold (London: BAR-IS 812, 1999) 11–21.

7. Eva Cantarella, *Bisexuality in the Ancient World* (New Haven: Yale UP, 1992) 3–8; see Younger's essay in this volume, for Classical Greece.

8. Sinclair Hood, "The Primitive Aspects of Minoan Artistic Convention," in Pascal Darcque and Jean-Claude Poursat, eds., *L'Iconographie Minoenne: Actes de la table ronde d'Athènes (21–22 avril 1983)* (Paris, *Bulletin de Correspondence Héllenique* Suppl. 11, Paris 1985) 21–26.

9. A. Van Gennep, *Les rites de passage* (Paris: E. Nourry, 1909; Paris: Éditions A. and J. Pi-

card, 1994); Ellen Davis, "Youth and Age in the Thera Frescoes," *American Journal of Archaeology* 90 (1986): 399–406; Diana Withee, "Physical Growth and Aging Characteristics Depicted in the Theran Frescoes," *American Journal of Archaeology* 96 (1992): 336 (abstract); Christina Televantou, "Η απόδοση της ανθρώπινης μορφής στις θηραϊκές τοιχογραφίες," *Αρχαιολογική Εφημερίς* 1988: 135–166; Vassos Karageorghis, "Rites de Passage at Thera: Some Oriental Comparanda," in D. A. Hardy, C. G. Doumas, J. A. Sakellarakis, and P. M. Warren, eds., *Thera and the Aegean World III: Proceedings of the Third International Congress, Santorini, Greece, 3–9 September 1989* (London: Thera Foundation, 1990), vol. 1, 67–71; Susan G. Cole, "The Social Function of Rituals of Maturation: The Koureion and the Arkteia," *Zeitschrift für Papyrologie und Epigraphik* 55 (1984): 233–244; Evelyn B. Harrison, "Greek Sculptural Coiffures and Ritual Haircuts," *Early Greek Cult Practice: Proceedings of the Fifth International Symposium at the Swedish Institute at Athens, 26–29 June 1986*, ed. Robin Hägg, Nanno Marinatos, and Gullog C. Nordquist (Stockholm: Swedish Institute in Athens, 1988) 247–254; E. David, "Hair as Language," *Eranos* 90 (1992): 11–21.

10. Anita E. Klein, *Child Life in Greek Art* (New York: Columbia UP, 1932); Mark Golden, *Children and Childhood in Classical Athens* (Baltimore: Johns Hopkins UP, 1990).

11. Christine Televantou, "Η γυναικεία ενδυμασία στην προϊστορική Θήρα," *Αρχαιολογική Εφημερίς* 1982: 113–135; I. Tzachili-Douskou, "All Important Yet Elusive: Looking for Evidence of Cloth-Making at Akrotiri," in D. A. Hardy, C. G. Doumas, J. A. Sakellarakis, and P. M. Warren, eds. *Thera and the Aegean World III: Proceedings of the Third International Congress, Santorini, Greece, 3–9 September 1989* (London: Thera Foundation, 1990), vol. A1, 380–389; Elizabeth J. W. Barber, *Prehistoric Textiles: The Development of Cloth in the Neolithic and Bronze Ages with Special Reference to the Aegean* (Princeton: Princeton UP, 1991); Elizabeth J. W. Barber, *Women's Work: The First 20,000 Years* (London: W. W. Norton, 1994); Mireille Lee, "Deciphering Gender in Minoan Dress," in *Reading the Body: Representations and Remains in the Archaeological Record*, ed. Alison E. Rautman (Philadelphia: U of Pennsylvania P 2000) 111–123; Bernice R. Jones, "Revealing Minoan Fashion," *Archaeology* 53.3 (2000): 36–41; Paul Rehak, "Crocus Costumes in Aegean Art," (forthcoming). For men's clothing, see Paul Rehak, "Aegean Breechcloths, Kilts, and the Keftiu Paintings," *American Journal of Archaeology* 100 (1996): 35–51. For comparative work, see Ruth Barnes and Joanne B. Eichler, eds., *Dress and Gender: Making and Meaning in Cultural Context* (Providence: Berg, 1997).

12. In Archaic Greece, by contrast, men are sometimes shown touching or grasping an exposed female breast as an allusion to intercourse or marriage or, in the case of divinities, the hieros gamos or sacred marriage. See Beth Cohen, "Divesting the Breast of Clothes in Classical Sculpture," in A. Koloski-Ostrow and C. Lyons, eds., *Naked Truths* (London: Routledge, 1997) 66–92.

13. Christina Televantou, "Κοσμήματα από την προϊστορική Θήρα," *Αρχαιολογική Εφημερίς* 1984: 14–54; John G. Younger, "Representations of Minoan-Mycenaean Jewelry," in Robert Laffineur and J. Crowley, eds., *EIKΩN. Aegean Bronze Age Iconography. Shaping a Methodology* (Liège: *Aegaeum* 8, 1992) 257–293; John G. Younger, "Non-sphragistic Uses of Minoan-Mycenaean Sealstones and Rings," *Kadmos* 16 (1977): 141–159. Cf. M. Effinger, *Minoischer Schmuck* (Oxford: Tempus Reparatum, *BAR-IS* 646, 1996).

14. I. Douskos, "The Crocuses of Santorini," in *Thera and the Aegean World*, ed. C. Doumas (London: Thera Foundation, 1980), vol. II.1, 141–145; O. Höckmann, "Theran Floral Style in Relation to That of Crete," in *Thera and the Aegean World*, ed. C. Doumas, vol. II.1, 755–

764; Amigues, "Le crocus et le safran." R. Porter instead suggests *crocus cartwrightianus:* "The Theran Wall Paintings' Flora: Living Plants and Motifs—Sea Lily, Crocus, Iris, Ivy," in *The Wall Paintings of Thera: Proceedings of the First International Symposium: Petros M. Nomikos Conference Centre, Thera, Hellas: 30 August–4 September 1997,* ed. S. Sherratt (Piraeus, Greece: Petros M. Nomikos and the Thera Foundation, 2000) vol. 2, 603–629.

15. Christos Doumas, *The Wall-Paintings of Thera* (Athens: Thera Foundation, 1992) pls. 95–99. For recent discussion of these fragments and an attempted reconstruction, see Paul Rehak, "The Monkey Frieze from Xeste 3, Room 4: Reconstruction and Interpretation," in *MELETEMATA: Studies in Aegean Archaeology Presented to Malcolm H. Wiener as He Enters His 65th Year,* ed. P. P. Betancourt, V. Karageorghis, R. Laffineur, and W.-D. Niemeier (Liège: *Aegaeum* 20, 1999) 705–709.

16. Christos Doumas, "Conventions artistiques à Théra et dans la Méditerranée orientale à l'époque préhistorique," in Pascal Darcque and Jean-Claude Poursat, eds., *L'Iconographie Minoenne: Actes de la table ronde d'Athènes (21–22 avril 1983)* (Paris, *Bulletin de Correspondance Héllenique* Suppl. 11, Paris 1985) 31; Eric Cline, "Monkey Business in the Bronze Age Aegean: The Amenhotep II Faience Figurines at Mycenae and Tiryns," *Annual of the British School at Athens* 86 (1991): 29–42; Thomas Strasser, "The Blue Monkeys of the Aegean and Their Implications for Bronze Age Trade," *American Journal of Archaeology* 101 (1997): 348 (abstract); Patricia Parker, "African Vervets on Crete and Thera during MM IIIB–LM IA," *American Journal of Archaeology* 101 (1997): 348 (abstract). For a fragmentary monkey from Melos, see Lyvia Morgan, "Island Iconography: Thera, Kea, Milos," in *Thera and the Aegean World III: Proceedings of the Third International Congress, Santorini, Greece, 3–9 September 1989,* ed. David A. Hardy, Christos G. Doumas, John A. Sakellarakis, and Peter M. Warren (London: Thera Foundation, 1990), vol. A1, 252–266, esp. 256, fig. 7. Colin Renfrew et al., *The Archaeology of Cult: The Sanctuary at Phylakopi* (London: British School of Archaeology at Athens, Supplementary vol. 18, 1985) 14–21.

17. Manniche, *Sexual Life in Ancient Egypt* 43–44. For representations of monkeys on women's cosmetic vessels, see Jean A. Bourriau, *Pharaohs and Mortals: Egyptian Art in the Middle Kingdom* (Cambridge: Cambridge UP, 1988) 142, no. 144 and fig. 144 a–b; E. Terrace, "'Blue Marble' Plastic Vessels and Other Figures," *Journal of the American Research Center in Egypt* 5 (1966): 59–60; H. G. Fischer, "Another Pithemorphic Vessel of the Sixth Dynasty," *Journal of the American Research Center in Egypt* 30 (1993): 1–9.

18. E.g., on a seal in Heraklion: Nicholas Platon and Ingo Pini, *Corpus der Minoischen und Mykenischen Siegel,* 11, *Iraklion Archäologisches Museum,* 3, A. *Die Siegel der Neupalastzeit* (Berlin: Gebrüder Mann Verlag, 1984) no. 103.

19. Walter Graham, *The Palaces of Crete,* rev. ed. (Princeton: Princeton UP, 1987) 99–100; Nicholas Platon, "Bathrooms and Lustral Basins in Minoan Dwellings," in *Europa: Studien zur Geschichte und Epigraphik frühen Ägäis, Festschrift für Ernst Grumach,* ed. William C. Brice et al. (Berlin: Walter de Gruyter, 1967) 236–245; Stelios Alexiou, "Περί μινωϊκῶν δεξαμενῶν καθαρμοῦ," *Kretika Chronika* 14 (1972): 414–434; Geraldine Gesell, *Town, Palace, and House Cult in Minoan Crete* (Göteborg: *Studies in Mediterranean Archaeology* 67, 1985) 22–26 (discussion and catalogue of lustral basins); Nanno Marinatos and Robin Hägg, "On the Ceremonial Function of the Minoan Polythyron," *Opuscula Atheniensia* 16 (1986): 57–73; AnnCharlotte Nordfeldt, "Residential Quarters and Lustral Basins," in R. Hägg and N. Marinatos, eds., *The*

Function of the Minoan Palaces: Proceedings of the Fourth International Symposium at the Swedish Institute in Athens, 10–16 June 1984. Acta Instituti Atheniensis Regni Suciae 4, 35 (Stockholm: Swedish Institute in Athens, 1987) 187–193.

20. This portion of the painting remains unpublished, but see N. Marinatos, *Art and Religion in Thera* 75 fig. 53 for a color reconstruction. Anna Lucia D'Agata, "Late Minoan Crete and Horns of Consecration: A Symbol in Action," in R. Laffineur and J. L. Crowley, eds., *EIKΩN: Aegean Bronze Age Iconography: Shaping a Methodology: Proceedings of the 4th International Aegean Conference, University of Tasmania, Hobart, 6–9 April 1992.* Aegaeum 8 (Liège: Université de Liège, Histoire de l'art et archéologie de la Grèce antique, 1992) 247–256. Parts of two stone horns have been found at Akrotiri: one in Well 66 (S. Marinatos, *Thera* VII 21) and the other near the entrance into block Delta (S. Marinatos, *Excavations at Thera* VI [Athens: Archaeological Society, 1974] 34, pl. 83a). Horns that surmount a building where women are present occur on the Miniature Fresco from the West House: Doumas, *Wall-Paintings of Thera* pl. 38.

21. Geraldine Gesell, "Blood on the Horns of Consecration?" in *The Wall Paintings of Thera: Proceedings of the First International Symposium: Petros M. Nomikos Conference Centre, Thera, Hellas: 30 August–4 September 1997,* ed. S. Sherratt (Piraeus, Greece: Petros M. Nomikos and the Thera Foundation, 2000) vol. 2, 947–956.

22. A rhyton (pl. rhyta) is a vessel designed with a hole in its bottom so that liquids poured in at the top will drain out. We assume that these are ritual vessels, though some rhyta may have served a domestic function as fillers or funnels. Nicholas Platon, *Zakros: The Discovery of a Lost Palace of Ancient Crete* (New York: Scribner, 1971) 161–169; Joseph Shaw, "Evidence for the Minoan Tripartite Shrine," *American Journal of Archaeology* 82 (1978): 429–448; Anne P. Chapin, "The Sanctuary Rhyton from Kato Zakros and the Representation of Space in Aegean Art of the Bronze Age," *American Journal of Archaeology* 96 (1992): 334 (abstract). On stone vases, see Peter Warren, *Minoan Stone Vases* (Cambridge: Cambridge UP, 1969) 174–181; Bernd Kaiser, *Untersuchung zum minoischen Relief* (Bonn: Habelts Dissertationsdrücke, 1976).

23. Paul Rehak, "Seated Figures in Aegean Art and the Function of the Mycenaean Megaron," in *The Role of the Ruler in the Prehistoric Aegean: Proceedings of a Panel Discussion Presented at the Annual Meeting of the Archaeological Institute of America, New Orleans, Louisiana, 28 December 1992,* ed. Paul Rehak (Liège: Aegaeum 11, 1995) 95–117.

24. A. Potts, "Sign," in *Critical Terms for Art History,* ed. R. S. Nelson and R. Schiff (Chicago: U of Chicago P 1996): 17–29.

25. Pausanias 1.31.1 on the cult of Leto at Zoster.

26. Barber, *Women's Work* 42–70, ch. 2: "The String Revolution." Cf. Christopher Faraone, "Aphrodite's ΚΕΣΤΟΣ and Apples for Atalanta: Aphrodisiacs in Early Greek Myth and Ritual," *Phoenix* 44 (1990): 219–243.

27. This detail was misinterpreted by Barber, *Prehistoric Textiles* 317 and fig. 15.3, as a "yo-yo pattern with oval fillers." A similar pattern of crocus buds enclosed by wavy lines occurs on a jug of late Neopalatial date found at Ayia Triada: Federico Halbherr, Enrico Stefani, and Luisa Banti, "Haghia Triada nel periodo tardo palaziale," *Annuario della Scuola Italiana di Atene* 31 (1977 [1980]): 68, 67 fig. 37. See Rehak, forthcoming.

28. Stelios Alexiou, "Καθαρισμός αργυρών αντικειμένων στο εργαστήριο του Μουσείου

Ἡρακλείου, ἐνεπίγραφες περόνες καὶ ἐγχειρίδια," *Athens Annals of Archaeology* 8 (1975): 133–139; William C. Brice, "A Silver Pin from Mavro Spelio with an Inscription in Linear A: Heraklion Museum 540," *Kadmos* 11 (1972): 113–124.

29. Sinclair Hood, *The Arts in Prehistoric Greece* (Harmondsworth: Penguin, 1978) 200 fig. 198 A.

30. John M. Riddle, *Eve's Herbs: A History of Contraception and Abortion in the West* (Cambridge, MA: Harvard UP, 1997) 185.

31. E.g., N. Marinatos, *Art and Religion in Thera* 79; and N. Marinatos, *Minoan Religion* 207, 208.

32. N. Marinatos, *Art and Religion in Thera* 78–80, interprets her both as Eurydice and as a crocus picker who has dropped a blossom, ignoring the fact that she lacks the basket of the flower-picking girls in the fresco from the upper floor and is much older than they are. Barber, *Women's Work* 115, argues that she is a crocus-gathering girl who has stubbed her foot on the rocks.

33. Helen King, "Bound to Bleed: Artemis and Greek Women," in *Images of Women in Antiquity*, ed. A. Cameron and A. Kuhrt (Detroit: Wayne State UP, 1983) 109–27; G. Sissa, *Greek Virginity* (Cambridge MA: Harvard UP, 1990); A. E. Hanson, "Conception, Gestation, and the Origin of Female Nature in the Corpus Hippocraticum," *Helios* 19 (1992): 31–71; Nancy Demand, *Birth, Death and Motherhood in Classical Greece* (Baltimore: Johns Hopkins UP, 1994); K. Dowden, *Death and the Maiden: Girls' Initiation Rites in Greek Mythology* (New York: Routledge, 1989). On the importance of blood in sacrificial ritual, see Walter Burkert, *Homo Necans: The Anthropology of Ancient Greek Sacrificial Ritual and Myth* (Berkeley: U. of California P, 1983) 20–21; R. Snowden and B. Christian, eds., *Patterns and Perceptions of Menstruation: A World Health Organization International Collaborative Study in Egypt, India, Indonesia, Jamaica, Mexico, Pakistan, Philippines, Republic of Korea, United Kingdom, and Yugoslavia* (New York: Croom Helm in cooperation with the World Health Organization, and St. Martin's P, 1983); T. Buckley and A. Gottlieb, *Blood Magic: The Anthropology of Menstruation* (Berkeley: U. of California P, 1988); K. Christopher, *Blood Relations: Menstruation and the Origins of Culture* (New Haven: Yale UP, 1991); D. Taylor, *Red Flower: Rethinking Menstruation* (Freedom, CA: Crossing Press, 1988).

34. Aeschylus, *Agamemnon* 239–241: κρόκου βαφάς δ' ἐς πέδον χέουσα ἔβαλλ' ἔκαστον θυτήρων ἀπ' ὄμ-/ματος βέλει φιλοίκτῳ. ("Then, as her yellow robe slipped to the ground, she struck each of her sacrificers with a glance entreating pity.") For discussion of this problematic passage, see D. Armstrong and A. Ratchford, "Iphigenia's Veil: Aeschylus, *Agamemnon* 228–248," *Bulletin of the Institute of Classical Studies, London* 32 (1985): 1–12, and more recently by R. Edgeworth, "Saffron-Coloured Terms in Aeschylus," *Glotta* 66 (1988): 179–182; Ruth Scodel, "Δόμων ἄγαλμα: Virgin Sacrifice and Aesthetic Object," *Transactions of the American Philological Association* 126 (1996): 111–128. In Classical Greece, the veil is also associated with the wedding and the gesture of unveiling (*anakalypsis*): John Oakley, "The Anakalypteria," *Archäologischer Anzeiger* (1982): 113–118; John Oakley and Rebecca H. Sinos, *The Wedding in Ancient Athens* (Madison: U of Wisconsin P 1993); D. L. Cairns, "Veiling, Αἰδώς, and a Red Figure Amphora by Phintias," *Journal of Hellenic Studies* 116 (1996): 152–158.

35. C. Sourvinou-Inwood, *Studies in Girls' Transitions. Aspects of the Arkteia and Age Representation in Attic Iconography* (Athens: Kardamitsa, 1988); C. Sourvinou-Inwood, "Ancient Rites and Modern Constructions: On the Brauronian Bears Again," *Bulletin of the Institute of Clas-*

sical Studies, London 37 (1990): 1–14; Gloria F. Pinney, "Fugitive Nudes: The Woman Athlete," *American Journal of Archaeology* 99 (1995): 303–304 (abstract); Catalog, in Ellen Reeder, ed., *Pandora: Women in Classical Greece* (Princeton: Princeton UP, 1995) esp. 321–328.

36. Aristophanes, *Ekkleziazousai* 331–332; cf. *Lysistrata* 49–51 on yellow as a women's color. Unusually, Jason has a yellow mantle (κροκόεν εἷμα) in Pindar's *Fourth Olympian Ode* 232. I thank M. Kwintner for this reference. A colossal statue of Dionysos, carried in the great procession of Ptolemy II Philadelphus in Alexandria, was draped with a diaphanous kroko-tos (κροκωτὸν διαφανῆ), perhaps because of the god's androgenous qualities or his appeal to women: Athenaios, *Deipnosophistae* 5.198.c. The ghost of the barbarian king Darius in the Persians of Aeschylus wears yellow sandals: κροκόβαπτον ποδὸς εὔμαριν, 660.

37. Noted by Porter, "Theran Wall Paintings' Flora."

38. Doumas, *Wall-Paintings of Thera* pls. 109–115. Cf. Christos Doumas, "Η Ξεστὴ 3 καὶ οἱ κυανοκέφαλοι στὴν τέχνη τῆς Θήρας," *ΕΙΛΑΠΙΝΗ. Τόμος τιμητικός για τον Καθηγητή Νικολάο Πλάτωνα* (Athens: Athens Archaeological Society, 1987) 151–159.

39. Rehak, "Seated Figures in Aegean Art."

40. Ellen Davis, *The Vapheio Cups and Aegean Gold and Silver Ware* (New York: Garland, 1977); Hartmut Matthäus, *Die Bronzegefässe der kretisch-mykenischen Kultur* (Munich: Prähistorische Bronzefunde II.1, 1980).

41. Doumas, *Wall-Paintings of Thera* pls. 113, 136–137.

42. Christos Boulotis, "Nochmals zum Prozessionsfresko von Knossos: Palast und Darbringung von Prestige-Objekten," in R. Hägg and N. Marinatos, eds., *The Function of the Minoan Palaces: Proceedings of the Fourth International Symposium at the Swedish Institute in Athens, 10–16 June 1984.* Acta Instituti Atheniensis Regni Suciae 4, 35 (Stockholm: Swedish Institute in Athens, 1987) 145–156.

43. Doumas, *Wall-Paintings of Thera* pls. 122–124, 129–130.

44. Doumas, *Wall-Paintings of Thera* pls. 116–121.

45. Black figures, perhaps sub-Saharan African natives, appear in frescoes at Knossos, Mycenae, and Pylos: Immerwahr, *Aegean Painting* 176 Kn no. 27, 191 My no. 6, 197 Py no. 7.

46. Nanno Marinatos, "An Offering of Saffron to the Minoan Goddess of Nature: The Role of the Monkey and the Importance of Saffron," in *Gifts to the Gods,* ed. T. Linders and G. C. Nordquist (Uppsala: Academia Ubsaliensis, 1987) 123–132.

47. *Lexicon Iconographicum Mythologiae Classicae* (Zurich and Munich: Artemis Verlag, 1981–1997) vol. 1.2 (1981), 618–624 *s.v.* Artemis. Homer, *Iliad* 21.470 calls her πότνια θηρῶν. For a concise summary of Artemis and her cults, see Walter Burkert, *Greek Religion* (Cambridge, MA: Harvard UP, 1985): 149–152.

48. Some terracotta figurines appear to have facial tattoos. Cf. the large plaster head from Mycenae: Spyridon Marinatos and Max Hirmer, *Crete and Mycenae* (New York: Harry N. Abrams, 1960) col. pls. XLI, XLII.

49. Doumas, *Wall-Paintings of Thera* pl. 135. Several new additions were presented at the 1997 Thera conference (publication forthcoming). I thank Karen P. Foster for discussing these with me.

50. For Egyptian cosmetic vessels in the form of ducks or with duck iconography, see Arele P. Kozloff and Betsy M. Bryan, *Egypt's Dazzling Sun: Amenhotep III and His World* (Cleveland: Cleveland Museum of Art/Indiana UP, 1992) 347–348, no. 75.

51. Doumas, *Wall-Paintings of Thera* pls. 131–134.

52. On fleecy garments, see I. Tzachili-Douskou, "Τα ποίκιλα θηραϊκά ιμάτια και η τοιχογραφία του στόλου. Μία ιδιόμορφη τεχνική στα ύφαντα της Θήρας," *Athens Annals of Archaeology* 14 (1981): 251–265.

53. Cf. Aristophanes' chorus of women, describing its service to Artemis in *Lysistrata* 641–647: "At seven I carried the sacred container; at ten I ground the sacred grain; next I played the bear at Brauron wearing the yellow garment (*krokotos*), and finally—as a beautiful maiden—I wore a string of figs and served as a basket-carrier (*kanephoros*)."

54. *Αρχαιολογικόν Δελτίον* 29B (1973–1974): pl. 31; *Archaeological Reports* 26 (1980): 5, fig. 2; Immerwahr, *Aegean Painting* 188, uncatalogued no. 15.

55. S. Marinatos, *Thera* VI 17, pl. 24c. S. Marinatos noted that the figure of a woman found nearby may belong to the same composition—a continuation of the procession of women, perhaps?

56. Robin Hägg, "Pictorial Programmes in Minoan Palaces and Villas?" in Pascal Darcque and Jean-Claude Poursat, eds., *L'Iconographie minoenne: Actes de la table ronde d'Athènes (21–22 avril 1983). Bulletin de Correspondance Héllenique* Suppl. 11, Paris, 1985) 209–217; Nanno Marinatos, "The Function and Interpretation of the Theran Frescoes," in Darcque and Poursat, *L'Iconographie minoenne* 219–230; Wolf-Dietrich Niemeier, "Iconography and Context: The Thera Frescoes," in Laffineur and Crowley, *ΕΙΚΩΝ: Aegean Bronze Age Iconography: Shaping a Methodology: Proceedings of the 4th International Aegean Conference, University of Tasmania, Hobart, 6–9 April 1992.* Aegaeum 8. (Liège: Université de Liège, Histoire de l'art et archéologie de la Grèce antique, 1992) 97–104. Litsa Kontorli-Papadopoulou assumes a religious function for most wall paintings: *Aegean Frescoes of Religious Character: Studies in Mediterranean Archaeology* 117 (Göteborg: P. Åströms Förlag, 1996).

57. N. Marinatos, *Art and Religion in Thera* and *Minoan Religion.*

58. Amigues, "Le crocus et le safran."

59. Rehak and Younger, "Review of Aegean Prehistory VII" 141–148.

60. B. T. Burton, *Human Nutrition* (New York: McGraw-Hill 1988) 289; John M. Riddle, *Contraception and Abortion from the Ancient World to the Renaissance* (Cambridge, MA: Harvard UP, 1992) 85; John M. Riddle, *Eve's Herbs* 55, 151, 190, 230; cf. J. Scarborough, "The Pharmacology of Sacred Plants, Herbs, and Roots," in *Magika Hiera: Ancient Greek Magic and Religion,* ed. C. Faraone and D. Obbink (Oxford: Oxford UP, 1991) 138–174.

61. C. L. Madan, B. M. Kapur, and U. S. Gupta, "Saffron," *Economic Botany* 20 (1966): 377–385; R. H. Garrison, *The Nutrition Desk Reference* (New Canaan, CT: Keats Publishing, 1985) 45.

62. P. J. P. McGeorge, "Νέα στοιχεία για το μέσο όρο ζωής στη μινωϊκή Κρήτη," *Κρητική Εστία* 4th ser. 1 (1987): 9–15; P. J. P. McGeorge, "Biosocial Evolution in Bronze Age Crete," in *ΕΙΛΑΠΙΝΗ* (Athens: Athens Archaeological Society, 1987) 407–416; P. J. P. McGeorge, "A Comparative Study of the Mean Life Expectation of the Minoans," *Τα Πεπραγμένα του 6° Διεθνούς Κρητολογικού Συνεδρίου,* vol. A1 (Herakleion, 1990) 419–428; Robert Arnott, *Disease, Healing and Medicine in the Aegean Bronze Age* (Leiden: E. J. Brill, forthcoming).

63. Davis, "Youth and Age."

64. D. Basker and M. Negbi, "Uses of Saffron," *Economic Botany* 37 (1983): 228–236.

65. R. S. Harris and W. H. Sebrell, *The Vitamins* (New York: Academic Press, 1967) 292; Garrison, *Nutrition Desk Reference* 36–37.

66. Harris and Sebrell, *The Vitamins*, vol. 1, 28; A. T. Diplock, *Fat Soluble Vitamins* (Lancaster, PA: Technomic Publishing, 1985): 44.

67. *The Lawrence Review of Natural Products* (St. Louis: Facts and Comparisons, June 1996): s.v. saffron; V. P. Kamboj, "A Review of Indian Medicinal Plants with Interceptive Activity," *Indian Journal of Medical Research* 87 (1988): 336–355; Madan et al., "Saffron"; K. M. Nadkarni, *Indian Materia Medica*, vol. 1 (Bombay: Popular Prakashan, 1927) 388–391; W. H. Lewis and M. P. F. Elvin-Lewis, *Medical Botany* (New York: John Wiley and Sons, 1977) 325–329.

68. This view was persuasively argued by J. M. Snyder in a lecture, "Love in the Apple Orchard: Sacred Space in the Lyrics of Sappho," presented by the Department of Classics at the University of North Carolina at Chapel Hill, February 6, 1998.

69. Bernard Sergent, *Homosexuality in Greek Myth* (Boston: Beacon Press, 1986) 81–101.

70. Scholiast on *Iliad* 12.92: ἤλλαξεν ἑαυτὸν εἰς ταῦρον καὶ ἀπὸ τοῦ στόματος κρόκον ἔπνει· οὕτως τε τὴν Εὐρώπην ἀπατήσας. ("So he transformed himself into a bull and breathed out a crocus flower from his mouth. Thus he tricked Europa.")

71. *Homeric Hymn to Demeter* 108: ὥστε θεαί, κουρήιον ἄνθος ἔχουσαις ("They were like goddesses being in the first flower of their youth."); 177–178: ἀμφὶ δὲ χαῖται ὤμοις ἀίσσοντο κροκηίῳ ὁμοῖαι. ("And around their shoulders their long locks streamed like a crocus flower.")

72. *Iliad* 14.347–350: τοῖσι δ' ὑπὸ χθὼν δῖα φύεν νεοθηλέα ποίην, / λωτόν θ' ἑρσήεντα ἰδὲ κρόκον ἠδ' ὑάκινθον / πυκνὸν καὶ μαλακόν, ὃς ἀπὸ χθονὸς ὑψόσ' ἔεργε. ("And beneath them the divine earth made new grass grow up, along with dew-sprinkled lotus and crocus and hyacinth thick and soft, which cushioned them high above the ground.")

CHAPTER THREE

APHRODITE GARLANDED

Erôs and Poetic Creativity in Sappho and Nossis*

Marilyn B. Skinner

> When I finished speaking, there was immediate reaction to my statement that "it is the lesbian in us who is creative, for the dutiful daughter of the fathers in us is only a hack." It became clear during the ensuing discussion that different women had heard this sentence in different ways. Some women asserted that they created out of their bisexuality, not their "female side"; others, that their creativity came from their commitment to black struggle; others, that they created out of love for their (male) children as much as out of love for women. One lesbian asserted that if "the lesbian in us" was to become a figurative term, she, as a woman who had been oppressed for physically expressing her love for women, wanted another name for who she was. Some women heard me as saying that all creation has simply a sexual basis (vide Freud) and that women can create only out of erotic experience with other women. My intention was, of course, to say something more complex.
>
> Adrienne Rich, footnote to "'It Is the Lesbian in Us' ..." (1979)

 Can a woman poet have a muse? Feminists have debated this question urgently ever since they realized the pitfalls of subscribing to the androcentric and heterosexist paradigm of creativity that describes poetry as the product of intercourse between the artist and his own powers of inspiration personified as his mistress.[1] As numerous critics have observed, this model symbolically appropriates female reproductive ability, subordinating it to a genius regarded as intrinsically masculine.[2] Implicitly, then, it denies flesh-and-blood women the capacity to make anything other than babies, even as it devalues biological, in contrast to intellectual, paternity.[3] When the heterosexual framework is inverted, and the woman writer is visited by a hypothetical male muse, she risks the same fate as the prophetess Cassandra, doomed to unintelligibility for resisting the god Apollo's advances.[4] Feminist literary criticism has responded to this dilemma by envisioning a self-sufficient female imagination unshackled from conventional perceptions of the creative process. Much of that criticism, however, has been involved in a "war of images" dealing with whether the dynamics of pure, autonomous female creativity can fittingly be troped as "lesbian."[5]

By declaring, in a paper given at the Modern Language Association meeting in December 1976 and published in 1979, that "it is the lesbian *in us* who is creative, for the dutiful daughter of the fathers *in us* is only a hack" (my italics), Adrienne Rich pioneered the theoretical application of the term "lesbian" as a metaphor for each and every woman's inherent capacity to record her personal experience.[6] When I attended my first National Women's Studies Association (NWSA) meeting in June 1984, controversy over Rich's dictum was still heated. I vividly remember an agitated debate that sprang up at a publisher's reception—of all places!—where one woman-identified woman expressed rage at the perceived insinuation that "being straight only a little bit and only to communicate" might doom her to "hackhood." For even when acknowledged as figurative, the language is open to a reductionist rendering. Rich, of course, was careful to distinguish her use of "lesbian" from the strictly carnal, "the fact that two women might go to bed together," and to define it as "a sense of desiring oneself; above all, of choosing oneself" and as "a primary intensity between women." One could argue, though, that by requiring the woman poet to repudiate her duty to the fathers, Rich was fabricating an artists' ghetto where the lesbian imagination, secluded from both the patriarchal literary tradition and the general community of readers, can speak intelligibly only to itself.[7] My acquaintance at NWSA was expressing precisely this concern: although herself lesbian, she feared being marginalized as a "lesbian writer."

That incident provided an initial stimulus for the following essay. Its point of departure was the recognition of a marked difference between classical and modern women writers in respect to one's sense of authority to speak as an artist. In her definitive account of women's contributions to Greek and Roman literature, Jane Snyder contends that ancient female poets did not experience a personal "anxiety of authorship" comparable to that of present-day women. She attributes ancient women's artistic confidence in themselves to a cultural presumption of the "inherently female nature of literary creativity," as incorporated in the mythic figures of the nine Muses.[8] The Homeric and classical Greek Muse is a goddess who acts as intermediary between the divine and mortal spheres, bestowing both the ability to sing and the knowledge of past events that forms the content of the poet's song.[9] Far from being the artist's mere helper, much less his mistress, she, like all divinities, commands awed respect, and her blessings can be dangerous: Homer's archetypal bard Demodokos, whom the Muse "favored above all" (τὸν πέρι Μοῦσ' ἐφίλησε) received sweet song as a gift but at the price of his eyesight (*Odyssey* 8.63–64).[10] For the ancient woman singer or composer, then, comparison with the Muse as she is represented in Greek epic and lyric would have been an affirmation of the paradoxical and awesome quality of the artist's poetic faculty, not a reminder of the female biological imperative.[11]

Reading the sixth-century BCE lyricist Sappho and her Hellenistic imitator, the epigrammatist Nossis, with Snyder's suggestion in mind, I gradually became aware that these poets, even while professing themselves servants and worshipers of the Muses, depict the process of creative inspiration within their respective circles of women as somehow "other" than being prompted by an agent from outside and above. The psychological dynamic taken for granted by modern performers—in which the cognitive skills of the artist and, in particular, her ability to invent "on the spot" are heightened in response to an audience's emotional engagement with her charismatic personality—is depicted as a manifestation of sexual desire (*erôs*) in Sappho's and Nossis' compositions and externalized as the goddess of love, Aphrodite. For them, her felt presence serves as the embodiment of the creative tension experienced in a performance setting and also as a conceptual foil to the Muse or external preceptor. Aphrodite is thus both matrix and vector of inspiration within the women-oriented song circle.[12] While the poets I discuss do not depict the goddess as garlanded, it was easy to imagine her wearing a festive wreath in token of her sympotic and poetic office—and thus I portray her in my title.

In the final paragraph of the original essay, I associated that alternative model of creativity, in which the artist's inspiration proceeds from intimate bonding with her companions, with what appeared to be a similar phenomenon expressed in the writings of modern women poets, particularly those who, like Rich, affirm a "lesbian" literary identity. While I do not believe I was mistaken in forging that tentative link between ancient and present-day conditions of composition—indeed, discussions of Sappho's impact upon other contemporary women authors appear to confirm my hypothesis[13]— I would not go so far as to map twentieth-century constructions of lesbianism upon the affective experience of Sappho and Nossis.[14] Moreover, the homoeroticism, however conceptualized, that informs the creative activity of these two poets does not sequester them or ghettoize them as artists: they also speak to a larger community. Finally, although they venerate Aphrodite as their chief patron, they also render homage to the Muses as secondary benefactors, thus providing an example of an inclusive poetics, one that militates against overly reductionist interpretations of Rich's trope. I will discuss that final point in a brief afterword to my essay. Meanwhile, readers are invited to consider the critical remarks that follow as provisional extensions of a profoundly Delphic pronouncement upon the craft of poetry advanced by a major contemporary poet and theorist.

For every ancient Greek author, poetic inspiration is a mysterious and numinous phenomenon, but poets employ various symbolic devices to encode their empirical awareness of creative insight.[15] Paradigmatic accounts in Homer and Hesiod characterize inspiration as arising from an external divine source, the Muses. The aid furnished by the daughters of Zeus and Memory is twofold: they first endow the singer with permanent poetic ability (*Odyssey* 8.44–45, 63–64; *Theogony* 22–34), then provide him with temporary help in composition as a supplement to his own skills (*Iliad* 2.484–92; *Odyssey* 8.73, 488–491, 22.347–348). Plato transmits a contrary concept of inspiration as a form of possession or *mania*, visited upon the poet who serves as a wholly passive mouthpiece for the divine voice (*Apology* 22a–c, *Ion* 533d–534e, *Phaedrus* 245a, *Laws* 719c, etc.).[16] Penelope Murray observes, however, that these two conflicting views of imagination stand at opposite ends of a spectrum and are not contradictory.[17] Between the two extremès, she thinks, other and different notions of the creative process can probably be identified.

One example of such an alternative view of creativity, reflecting the particular circumstances of Greek women's lived experience, is its figuration as a process in poetry composed by women themselves. From surviving verses addressed to members of their own sex, it would appear that Sappho and her later imitator Nossis depict not the male bard's Muse but Aphrodite as their divine source of artistic inspiration. In Greek poetry generally, to be sure, the goddess of love is regularly mentioned along with the Muses in festive contexts; furthermore, both Sappho and Nossis formally acknowledge the Muses, too, as patrons of their craft. Yet the woman poet's relationship to those orthodox divinities of inspiration appears relatively distant or austere in comparison to her consciousness of Aphrodite's sensual aura and almost tangible presence. During her epiphanies to Sappho and in her temple visited by Nossis, the Cyprian goddess becomes a member of the poet's circle of companions. The graces she confers upon her worshipers embrace the sphere of poetry. Through corrective allusions to Hesiod, Sappho and

Nossis invest Aphrodite with the functions of a Muse, endowing her with a simultaneous command of both desire and discourse. As a fountainhead of homoerotic energy, the goddess in fact transmutes one into the other: through Aphrodite's agency, the kinetic urgency of sexual tension, as it oscillates between singer and audience and among audience members, is channeled into a creative impetus heightening the intensity of the performance.

To understand this departure from ordinary literary conventions, we should reflect upon the social setting in which an Archaic Greek woman poet like Sappho would have produced songs or texts for and about her immediate companions.[18] Those circumstances of literary production seem to have differed radically from the contexts of elite male poetic activity, such as the symposium: more competitive as a rule, male performance was likewise, in emotional terms, more guarded. In celebrating the life of her community, a milieu in which close homoerotic friendships were presumably encouraged (insofar as romantic desire between community members was artistically memorialized), Sappho's songs appeal directly to the aesthetic, religious, and emotive sensibilities of her listeners.[19] Nossis follows Sappho in artistically recreating her own tightly knit female world through the subgenre of the dedicatory epigram and in expressing an ardent homoerotic attachment to the donors whose gifts she commemorates.[20]

In the intimate surroundings of a communal environment, recitations of Sappho's songs or Nossis' epigrams must have been deeply moving occasions for composer and listeners alike. Audience response would have taken on a sexually charged intensity: that circumstance seems likely, for example, in L-P 22, where desire is said to "hover around" the singer as she performs.[21] As she felt her creative powers stimulated and heightened by reciprocal *erôs*, the performer saw herself as receiving an inrush of divine illumination from her patroness Aphrodite. This process of creativity is formally distinct from both the Homeric and the Platonic paradigms of inspiration, because each of those concentrates upon the exclusive hierarchical dyad of Muse and individual poet, without reference to the surrounding audience of listeners. Let us now examine the texts of Sappho and Nossis to learn more precisely how this fusion of erotic and creative energy is realized in art.

As she reminds her daughter Cleis in a well-known fragment, Sappho considers it unsuitable to lament within her household, designating it as a place where the Muses are reverenced (L-P 150). She appeals to them when beginning a song ("Here again, Muses . . . ," L-P 127), twice more in company with the Graces ("holy Graces and Muses of Pieria," L-P 103.8; "come here now, delicate Graces and beautiful-haired Muses," L-P 128), and acknowledges that she has been honored by their gifts (L-P 32). With the possible exception of one broken line (L-P 124) in which she addresses Calliope individually, however, her dealings with the nine goddesses seem somewhat formal. Her fullest surviving testimony to their importance for her is couched in negative terms. In Fragment 55, she prophesies oblivion after death for an uneducated woman:[22]

> Once dead you will lie there, nor will there ever be memory of you
> nor yearning for you in future; for you have no share
> in the roses of Pieria. . . .

The recipient of the abuse is implicitly contrasted with the speaker herself, who, endowed with a share of song by the Pierian Muses, can look forward confidently to artistic immortality.[23] Yet, precisely because it testifies indirectly to the benefits she has received from the nine goddesses, Sappho's language sets both gifts and givers apart from contact with ordinary mortals. Only the select few enjoy the Muses' poetic favors, given concrete form as the archetypally perfect rose of their birthplace.

In contrast, the thrill of Aphrodite's proximity is felt at once by all the women in attendance at a Sapphic gathering. L-P 2, for example, is a delicate description of a temple within a sacred grove of apple trees that seems to capture, in its muted sensuality, one aspect of female erotic experience. Evoking an atmosphere of ritual enchantment, sensory images of smoking incense, cool babbling water, shivering leaves, and softly blowing winds excite the visual, aural, olfactory, and tactile imagination; meanwhile, references to a *kôma* or deep lethargy and to flowers blooming in a horse-pasturing meadow, in Greek poetry a frequent allusion to sexual initiation, hint at yet more intimate physical enjoyments.[24] Here the goddess is invited to materialize within the circle of human celebrants to perform the office of cupbearer:

> There, Cypris, taking [garlands?], pour out
> nectar richly mixed for our festivities
> in golden cups. . . .

Song would be an indispensable part of such a celebration. Since it figuratively resembles nectar, both in its sweetness and in its power to confer eternal life, poetry, in later Greek literature at least, is often metaphorically equated with the beverage of the gods.[25] The drink Cypris serves may therefore be a veiled reference to Sappho's own music. A similar epiphany seems to occur at the fragmentary conclusion of L-P 96, which consoles Atthis for the loss of her beloved. There again Aphrodite's sweet potion may symbolize the transformative and healing effects of poetic art.[26] Described figuratively as nectar, poetry becomes the goddess' hospitable gift to Sappho's companions, linking them as communicants in convivial ecstasy. That is, the sexually vibrant aura of the meeting graced by Aphrodite's presence intensifies the worshipers' shared appreciation of the song that commemorates it.

Moved by longing (*pothos*) for departed companions, members of the group comfort themselves by singing about their absent loves. In Fragment 22, another sadly tattered scrap, a girl whose name may be Abanthis is urged to express her yearning, aroused by seeing a dress that had formerly belonged to her beloved Gongyla.[27] With the restorations proposed by West,[28] the text now reads:

> I charge you, Abanthis, to take up [your] harp
> and sing of Gongyla, as desire again hovers around you . . .
> the beautiful one; for the fall of her garment aroused you
> as you looked upon it. And I rejoice,
> for at one time the holy Cyprus born herself blamed me
> for praying . . . this word (?) . . .

The word "again" (*dêute*) tells us that Abanthis' longing is a recurrent one. Her songs about Gongyla have been heard, we infer, on many previous occasions. In addition, the adverb has important programmatic resonances, as I will demonstrate below.[29] Meanwhile, Sappho's own position as onlooker is hardly detached. She is joyful, because, as she explains, Aphrodite herself had once "blamed me for praying." Whatever the content of that earlier, now mutilated, prayer might have been, the speaker at this present moment apparently invokes the goddess while identifying vicariously with the lovesick Abanthis. In giving voice to her own sorrow, Abanthis meanwhile enthralls her companions, thereby becoming a surrogate for her mentor Sappho. Fused into a single resonant harmonic field, desire and poetry, under kindly divine protection, once more serve to bond the participants together.

Sappho's most compelling realization of Aphrodite's power over the creative process is contained in her only complete ode, L-P 1, in which the goddess is called upon to assist the speaker in a love affair. Beginning as a hymn in which a divinity is summoned from afar, the song quickly modulates into a recollection of a prior face-to-face encounter with Aphrodite. Contemporary scholars interpret this text not as a candid report of mystical experience but rather as a dense reflex of epic type-scenes, whose adaptation betrays a keen artistic self-consciousness.[30] Finding a Homeric model for Aphrodite's epiphany in Hera and Athena's descent to the battlefield and Athena's subsequent confrontation with Diomedes (*Iliad* 5.720–777 and 793–834), they consider it to be a transposition of the epic ideal of "manly excellence" (*aretê*) into the feminine domain of *erôs*. Winkler has now proposed, however, that Sappho's ode is in fact an intertextual critique of Diomedes' martial exploits, including his battlefield triumph over Aphrodite, in *Iliad* 5 and thus an instance of a woman composer's aesthetic response to the male heroic tradition.[31] The intriguing hypothesis that L-P 1 serves, in part, as a critique of earlier literature may be taken one step further.

The opening word of the text, Aphrodite's descriptive epithet *poikilothronos*, may prepare us to interpret the ode programmatically by associating the goddess with the craft of weaving, the metaphor *par excellence* for the poet's art.[32] Coupled with *poikilo-* ("manifold, intricate"), the element *-thron* is usually traced back etymologically to *thronos* ("chair or seat") and the compound taken to mean "of the elaborately carved throne." As numerous scholars have suggested, however, it could also be derived from the rare noun *throna* ("embroidered flowers").[33] The single Homeric instance of that word is found together with *poikilos* at *Iliad* 22.441, in the well-known passage in which Andromache, about to learn of Hector's death, is described as working *throna poikila* ("variegated flowers") into a purple cloth: the repetition of the noun-adjective combination lends weight to the claim that Sappho might be explicitly alluding to this particular epic moment.[34] Keeping that possibility in mind, let us now see how Aphrodite's statements, as narrated to us, reflect on the singer's own activity and so on the production of the present song.

Upon her entry, Aphrodite inquires the reason for the summons in a series of sharp questions (13–18), first reported indirectly—"You, blessed lady . . . asked what I suffered *again* (ὄττι δηὖτε πέπονθα) and why I was calling on you *again* (κὤττι δηὖτε κάλημμι)"—then in direct discourse, "Whom am I to persuade *again* (τίνα δηὖτε πείθω) . . . ?" As a strategy of characterization, the triple anaphora or repetition *dêute . . . dêute . . . dêute* sounds a facetious note, implying that Aphrodite has grown slightly exasperated at being invoked once too often. But the figure of speech also conveys a witty metatextual observation. As Snell commented long ago, *dêute* is a formulaic opening element in Archaic Greek love poetry, found as early as Alcman:[35]

Eros again, at the behest of the Cyprian,
pouring down sweetly melts my heart.

Through this conventional expression, singers present themselves as *perpetual* victims of sexual passion. Unsatisfied longing is not an occasional but a habitual condition; as such, it supplies the motive for the artist's entire repertoire of love poetry.[36] In L-P 130, Sappho uses the exordium straightforwardly ("limb-loosening Eros again shakes me"); the adverb recurs, as we have seen, in L-P 22, where Abanthis is invited to take Sappho's place as musician. As she confronts the speaker with "who wrongs you, Sappho?" (τίς σ', ὦ | Ψάπφ', ἀδικήει), Aphrodite recognizes her as not only a repeatedly frustrated lover—Sappho's dramatic role in the fictive scenario—but also, through that reiterated formula, as an established love poet extratextually. "Once Aphrodite's speculations about the source of the speaker's distress are understood as designed particularly for a poetess' ears," Mace remarks, "the thrice-repeated δηὖτε takes on a whole new—and primarily 'literary'— dimension. The goddess' words begin to sound, above all, like an ironic parody of what we are to understand is this poetess-speaker's most characteristic way of expressing her distress."[37] Perhaps Aphrodite's incisive questions might even paraphrase, or otherwise echo, the opening words of certain other Sapphic monodies.

Finally, Aphrodite's epiphany to Sappho has a Hesiodic as well as a Homeric predecessor. At the opening of the *Theogony*, the bardic narrator provides a quasi-autobiographical tale of his initiation by the Muses as he was pasturing his lambs below Mount Helicon. The words he puts into their mouths in lines 26–28 are widely recognized as a cryptic pronouncement upon the character and operations of poetic discourse:[38]

> Back-country shepherds, loutish disgraces, mere bellies,
> we know how to tell many fictions that seem like truths,
> and we know how to utter the truth when we want to.

In its first-hand report of a divine manifestation and its quotation of the deity's actual words, in which a reference to the poet's literary *persona* (and, in Sappho's case, the use of her own name) functions as a kind of authorial seal, the manifestation of Aphrodite in L-P 1 so closely resembles Hesiod's allegory of his investiture that Sappho might well be emulating that passage. Indeed, it is also conceivable that Sappho's original Alexandrian editors, having arrived at the same conclusion, placed this ode at the head of her collection precisely because of its similarity to a poetic *prooimion* or introductory section.[39] Yet we should still observe the dramatic contrast in tone between the Muses' manner of addressing Hesiod and Aphrodite's corresponding greeting to Sappho: while the goddesses of Helicon haughtily assert their superiority to mortals, Aphrodite's amused smile and teasing words bridge the gap separating herself from her worshiper and establish a bond of intimacy between them. Accordingly, as Ellen Greene points out elsewhere in this volume, the dissolution of boundaries between divinity and human being in L-P 1 is an idealized reflex of the nonhierarchical female homoerotic relationships celebrated in other Sapphic monodies.[40]

As the source of a heightened inspiration on the part of the artist—as well as its immediate cause, the responsive desire of her audience—the goddess of love can perform for Sappho those functions conventionally assigned to the Muse within the epic and lyric tradition. Hesiod asserts the comprehensiveness of epic knowledge by investing his Muses with authority over the opposing polarities of truth and falsehood. In the realm of erotic discourse, Aphrodite's power is just as sweeping: as she reminds Sappho in lines 21–24, she can effect a reversal of the singer's habitual misfortune by compelling the disdainful beloved to desire in turn "even unwillingly" (κωὐκ ἐθέλοισα). The composer of erotic songs, for her part, has another theme in store besides suffering, for she can also celebrate the happiness of love reciprocated. We find the poet dealing with this opposite theme in L-P 48, which apparently recalls a joyful tryst ("you cooled my heart burning with longing" ὂν δ' ἔψυξας ἔμαν φρένα καιομέναν πόθῳ), and more poignantly in L-P 94, where the memory of mutually enjoyed pleasures is to serve as balm for present grief.[41] Given the troping of homoerotic desire as a stimulus to song throughout the ode, we may conclude that when Sappho resumes her petition for help in the last stanza, she is not simply asking to be delivered from the pains of desire. The battle of love in which Aphrodite is to be her ally, her *summachos*, is likewise the creative struggle of the artist.[42]

Over the course of centuries, Sappho's lyrics inspired a host of ancient imitations. For the history of women's literature, none are as important as those of Nossis, an epigrammatist active in south Italian Locri in the third century BCE. There we meet Sappho refracted through eleven, or perhaps twelve, unusually subjective epigrams composed by a learned Hellenistic woman.[43] In poem 11, the epilogue to what was originally a published collection of her quatrains, Nossis acknowledges Sappho as her primary literary exemplar and, if the text as it is now emended is correct, proclaims herself at the same time "dear to the Muses," Μούσαισι φίλαν.[44] Yet this is the only explicit mention of the Muses in her surviving verses. Aphrodite, however, is invoked four times: most conspicuously in Nossis' prologue poem, then in three subsequent dedicatory epigrams. In all four passages, the goddess' cultic and literary functions are decidedly reminiscent of those assigned to her in Sappho's lyrics.[45]

Nossis 1 is an introductory *sphragis* or signature poem in which the author, in the process of identifying herself, simultaneously articulates her artistic principles and defines her poetic concerns:[46]

> Nothing is sweeter than desire. All other delights
> (ὄλβια) are second.
> From my mouth I spit even honey.
> Nossis says this. Whom Aphrodite does not love,
> knows not her flowers, what roses they are.

Here again a likely reminiscence of Hesiod has been noted. In its structure, imagery, and actual phrasing, the epigram patently imitates his familiar glorification of the *aoidos* or epic minstrel at *Theogony* 96−97:[47]

> Happy (ὄλβιος) the man whom the Muses love.
> Sweet flows the speech from his mouth.

Nevertheless, we must note two striking alterations, each a telling example of Hellenistic *arte allusiva*, the practice of calling the reader's attention to earlier textual models.[48] First, Hesiod makes the daughters of Zeus confer the power of sweetly flowing speech upon their favorites. His language draws a tacit equation between poetry and honey, the epitome of sweetness itself.[49] In her initial distich, Nossis pointedly recasts Hesiod's declaration by asserting that nothing, not even honey, is sweeter than *erôs*. Echoes of L-P 16.1−4 and 130 imbue her remark with delicate Sapphic undertones.[50] Second, the place of Hesiod's Muses is once again usurped in the last couplet by Aphrodite, albeit in a privative way: whom the goddess does *not* love is unaware of "what roses her flowers are." As Degani has convincingly demonstrated,[51] the primary antecedent of the feminine pronoun "her" must be Nossis' own name, proclaimed in line 3: these "flowers" (*anthea*) are therefore the speaker's collection of epigrams, further characterized as "roses," in evident homage to Sappho.[52] In L-P 55, as we have seen, Nossis' predecessor had described poems as "roses of Pieria"; the association of Sappho's own verse with that particular flower is encapsulated in Meleager's characterization of her anthologized pieces as "few but roses" (Meleager 1.6 Gow-Page = *Anthologia Palatina* 4.1). Explicit reference to Aphrodite, however, must naturally bring the heavy sexual nuances of the two nouns into play.[53] Because of the intentional ambiguities of the third-person pronoun[54] and the dense symbolic overtones of "flowers" and "roses," poetry becomes indistinguishable from sexuality.[55] Appreciation of either, or both, is a blessing Aphrodite reserves for her favorites. They alone will be able to savor—and, for that matter, to write—poems conceived under the impulse of *erôs*, as the author has programmatically declared her verse to be. Thus Nossis' complex intertextual corrections of Hesiod signify that for her, as for her predecessor Sappho, the goddess of love, source of homoerotic desire, is the true and proper Muse.

Of the extant pieces by this epigrammatist, none is overtly erotic. One might conclude, as I did in an earlier study, that all her frank professions of desire have simply been lost.[56] It is equally plausible, however, that the poet's commemorations of temple donations served as her true medium for expressing a love of her own sex kindled by an extraordinary sensitivity to female beauty.[57] The *erôs* Nossis identified as the dominant theme of her book, prompting later connoisseurs such as Meleager to classify her as an amatory poet (Meleager 1.9–10 Gow-Page = *Anthologia Palatina* 4.1), reveals itself in those poems as a visual excitement aroused by the donor herself as much as by her gift, for in every instance the speaker ultimately transfers her rapturous attention from the dedicated object to the allure of its dedicant. Support for this contention may be found in the part Aphrodite plays as recipient of the offerings provided in poems 4, 5, and 6 by the respective givers Polyarchis, Samytha, and Callo: the goddess makes her pleasure and delight known by imparting to each woman a corresponding share in her own supernatural powers. Thus Aphrodite's gilded cult statue, commissioned for her temple by the wealthy courtesan Polyarchis, is an object of admiration worthy of a special visit by Nossis and her friends, who discover, reflected in it, the splendor (*aglaïa*) of Polyarchis' own body, for the courtesan, we must infer, had also served as the sculptor's model. A headdress dedicated by Samytha is still redolent of her hair oil—not pomade, however, but Aphrodite's nectar, a comparison that fleetingly glances back toward the literary symbolism of nectar in Sappho. Lastly, Callo offers a painted portrait of herself termed "wholly like" (*pant' . . . isan*), but with no object specified: is it like the sitter, then, or like the divinity who receives it? As each donor is identified with the goddess herself, her fragile mortal bloom is invested with a luminous transcendence. In the atmosphere of Aphrodite's temple, filled with the goddess' tangible presence, that preternatural beauty evokes a swift creative response from the artist. Along with her offering, the donor's charm will be remembered in a commemorative quatrain—a poem affecting to be a spontaneous exclamation of awed appreciation. Thus endowed with Aphrodite's divine favor, gifts and givers alike are at length intertwined into the garland of roses that is this epigram collection.[58]

In the respective compositions of Sappho and Nossis, the occurrence of various passages in which Aphrodite discharges the office of a Muse suggests that each poet nurtured a notion of artistic creativity proper to a communal, woman-identified, setting. Inspiration is breathed into male bards such as Hesiod by an external agent, who, in her divine detachment, personifies the arbitrary nature of the poetic gift and the extraordinary status of those chosen to receive it. In Sappho's and Nossis' verse, the currents of creativity originate in physical and emotional yearning for another woman and find their true fulfillment in song, as it is performed before a group of intimate friends within the familiar surroundings of the community. Raised to a pitch of intensity, bittersweet *erôs* suffuses the very lyrics it calls forth. For the duration of the performance, the composer and her receptive audience are bound together emotionally, immersed in thrilling desire—the same desire that, though muted, still radiates today from the written text to the empathetic reader. Palpably present amidst this gathering of companions, receiving homage and dispensing grace in turn, Aphrodite, precisely because she is the divine wellspring of reciprocal *erôs*, can also replace the traditional epic Muse as fountainhead of literary inspiration.

Encased in other metaphors, this alternative model of creativity is a phenomenon that contemporary female poets are beginning to explore anew. In the last twenty-five years, a large company of writers—both those of an older generation, working within a more traditional vein, like May Sarton and Denise Levertov, as well as such committed lesbian poets as Rich herself, Olga Bromas, Judy Grahn, and Audre Lorde, have undertaken the project of "re-visioning" or "re-imagining" the muse. For these authors, the muse is inevitably female, although not necessarily divine. She assumes many mortal guises, among them biological mother, sister, older relative, mentor (as in Elizabeth Bishop's "Invitation to Miss Marianne Moore"), lover, or *doppelgänger* ("ghostly double"); her mythic incarnation may be that of Medusa, Kali, or Demeter.[59] Encounters between muse and poet often occur in the presence, or through the mediation, of other women, or serve as the catalyst that empowers the poet to speak on behalf of other women: they therefore encapsulate many other modes of homosocial or homoerotic affiliation between women. In any given text, the muse's figuration is determined by the particular dynamics of her rendezvous with the poet, who asks of her not inspiration per se, but the psychic integration, the self-completion, that permits full and authoritative speech, as in the closing lines of Rich's "Transcendental Etude":

> Such a composition has nothing to do with eternity,
> the striving for greatness, brilliance—
> only with the musing of a mind
> one with her body, experienced fingers quietly pushing
> dark against bright, silk against roughness,
> pulling the tenets of a life together
> with no mere will to mastery,
> only care for the many-lived, unending
> forms in which she finds herself,
> becoming now the sherd of broken glass
> slicing light in a corner, dangerous
> to flesh, now the plentiful, soft leaf
> that wrapped round the throbbing finger, soothes the wound;
> and now the stone foundation, rockshelf further
> forming underneath everything that grows.[60]

The relationship, as Carruthers notes, is "not one of possession but of communal bonding,"[61] with other women, of course, and finally, also, with nature as a whole. The genesis and maturation of this woman-oriented muse is arguably a response to the speaker's anticipation, earlier in "Transcendental Etude," of "a whole new poetry beginning here." In this respect, as in so much else, the works of Sappho and her ancient female successors, fragmentary though they are, can still point the way.

AFTERWORD

In my own professional writing, I have profited from maintaining a constant sensitivity to the distinction between the lesbian and the dutiful daughter, but I confess that, being a scholar and critic rather than an imaginative artist, I have allowed myself an intentional misprision. On my reading, the "dutiful daughter" is the academic who blindly subscribes to the entrenched *communis opinio* of classical studies, with all its attendant gender, race, and class biases. The "lesbian in us" is one who, by questioning its ingrained patriarchal assumptions, risks being branded a "dubious" authority, the mark of Cain in our profession. As my personal contribution to correcting error, I have repeatedly targeted the fossilized assumption that texts of the female poets of Greece and Rome may safely be left unread, since women's writing in antiquity (Sappho naturally excepted) was at best a curious anomaly—sentimental effusions by girlish amateurs, devoid of art and decidedly free of homoerotic resonances. On the contrary, the female poetic tradition was of crucial importance to Greek literature as a whole and the artistic accomplishments of its many participants and contributors were often affirmed in antiquity by learned male readers.

Still, a solemn duty to the past is built into our discipline: I would not be a classicist if I did not believe that prior entrenched opinion, however flawed, should not be discarded entirely but rather integrated into a coherent and comprehensive program of scholarly reception. Here, again, Sappho and Nossis may be taken as models, for they do not reject the traditional Muses but instead metonymize them. In their poems, I would speculate (even if I cannot prove it), the Hesiodic goddesses of inspiration function as symbols of a dominant, mainstream, male-oriented poetics, which, though duly appreciated, still plays a subordinate part in the operations of the female creative process. Insofar as inspiration originates communally, the Muses cannot behave in their normal authoritarian way. Instead, the "household of the Muses," to use Sappho's phrase, becomes the enveloping background, the *mise-en-scène*, for Aphrodite's informing presence. Resistance to tradition, to a patriarchal notion of the artist, to "dutiful daughterhood," takes the form of employing that tradition as a setting for creative events happening apart from it. Thus one final lesson the ancient female poets can teach us is that by venerating the Muses, the creative or scholarly writer allows the fathers the opportunity to hear what they want to hear, even as, loving Aphrodite, she speaks the unspeakable to women.

It is not, I think, a poor trade-off.

NOTES

*This is a revised and augmented version of M. B. Skinner, *"Aphrodite Garlanded: Erôs and Poetic Creativity in Sappho and Nossis,"* in F. De Martino, ed., *Rose di Pieria,* "Le Rane" Collana di Studi e Testi 9 (Bari: Levante Editori, 1991) reprinted here by permission of Levante Editori. I have appended an explanatory preface and afterword, expanded references to primary sources, made numerous alterations in wording, added my own translations, and incorporated subsequent scholarship. Considerations of space unfortunately did not permit me to take into account all the important research published since the earlier appearance of this essay. For helping me unpack many of its underlying assumptions, I am grateful to Ellen Greene and Nancy Sorkin Rabinowitz. Citations of Sappho follow the text of Lobel and Page (L-P), except where indicated. For Nossis' epigrams, I have used Page's Oxford University Press edition.

1. Harold Bloom's Oedipal scheme of creativity, in which the poet is said to battle with his precursor to possess the muse sexually, makes the dilemma excruciatingly apparent: see the extensive critique of Bloom's *The Anxiety of Influence: A Theory of Poetry* (New York: Oxford UP, 1973) in S. M. Gilbert and S. Gubar, *The Madwoman in the Attic: The Woman Writer and the Nineteenth-Century Literary Imagination* (New Haven and London: Yale UP, 1979) 46 – 53. In this essay I capitalize the noun "muse" when speaking of the ancient Greek goddess; references to the modern construct are in lower case.

2. E.g., M. R. Farwell, "Toward a Definition of the Lesbian Literary Imagination," *Signs* 14 (1988): 107: the poet "not only expends his seed on an object, but he also bears the fruit: in˚other words he has a self-sufficient power to create."

3. T. Olsen, "One out of Twelve: Writers Who Are Women in Our Century," *Silences* (New York: Dell, 1978 [1971]) 28 – 32; cf. S. S. Friedman, "Creativity and the Childbirth Metaphor: Gender Difference in Literary Discourse," in *Speaking of Gender*, ed. Elaine Showalter (New York and London: Routledge, 1989 [1987]) 84: "The male comparison of creativity with woman's procreativity equates the two as if both were valued equally, whereas they are not. This elevation of procreativity seemingly idealizes woman and thereby obscures woman's real lack of authority to create art as well as babies. As an appropriation of women's (pro)creativity, the male metaphor subtly helps to perpetuate the confinement of women to procreation."

4. J. F. Diehl, "'Come Slowly — Eden': An Exploration of Women Poets and Their Muse," Signs 3 (1978); M. J. Carruthers, "The Re-Vision of the Muse: Adrienne Rich, Audre Lorde, Judy Grahn, Olga Broumas," *Hudson Review* 36 (1983): 295; M. K. DeShazer, *Inspiring Women: Reimagining the Muse* (New York and Oxford: Pergamon P, 1986) 1 – 7.

5. Farwell, "Lesbian Literary Imagination" 100.

6. C. Stimpson, "Adrienne Rich and Lesbian/Feminist Poetry," *Parnassus* 12.2 – 13.1 (1985): 256, preserves the memory of Rich making her presentation in a hotel ballroom, speaking the famous sentence "quietly, tautly," as she leaned forward from the dais.

7. For "lesbian" as a theoretical formulation, see A. Rich, "'It Is the Lesbian in Us' . . . ," in *On Lies, Secrets, and Silence: Selected Prose 1966 – 1978* (New York and London: Norton, 1979) 200, expanded in her concept of a "lesbian continuum" (A. Rich, "Compulsory Heterosexuality and Lesbian Existence," *Signs* 5 [Summer 1980]). Cf. Stimpson's sensitive explication of Rich's "lesbian/feminism" in "Adrienne Rich." On the possibility of reductionism: Farwell, "Lesbian Literary Imagination" 101 – 102.

8. Jane McIntosh Snyder, *The Woman and the Lyre: Women Writers in Classical Greece and Rome* (Carbondale: Southern Illinois UP, 1989) 154 – 155.

9. W. G. Thalmann, *Conventions of Form and Thought in Early Greek Epic Poetry* (Baltimore and London: Johns Hopkins UP, 1984) 126 – 133; on the truth value of the information they provide, see further ch. 5.

10. The muse is not eroticized or identified with the poet's mistress until Roman times (Catullus 35.16 – 17, Propertius 2.1.3 – 4); DeShazer, *Inspiring Women* 9 – 10, is incorrect in maintaining that possession by the muse at Plato, *Phaedrus* 245a has sexual implications.

11. Comparison of Sappho to a Muse was a standard motif: see *Anthologia Palatina* 7.14 and 9.66 (Antipater of Sidon); 7.407.1 – 4 (Dioscorides); 9.571.7 – 8 (anonymous); Plutarch, *Amatorius* 18. Antipater of Thessalonica draws an analogy between the nine Muses and the Alexandrian canon of nine female poets: *Anthologia Palatina* 9.26.

12. E. Robbins,"Sappho, Aphrodite, and the Muses," *Ancient World* 26.2 (1995), discusses appearances of Aphrodite and the Muses in Sappho but does not observe a distinction in how they are presented to the reader.

13. See especially S. Gubar, "Sapphistries," in Ellen Greene, ed., *Re-reading Sappho: Reception and Transmission* (Berkeley: U of California P, 1996); E. Rohrbach, "H.D. and Sappho: A 'Precious Inch of Palimpsest',," in Greene, ed., *Re-reading Sappho;* and Jane McIntosh Snyder, *Lesbian Desire in the Lyrics of Sappho* (New York: Columbia UP, 1997) 123–159.

14. The most recent account of female homoeroticism in the Greco-Roman world is Bernadette J. Brooten, *Love between Women: Early Christian Responses to Female Homoeroticism* (Chicago: U of Chicago P, 1996). Since her primary area of investigation is late Roman antiquity, however, she limits her discussion of Sappho to a consideration of the poet's reception in subsequent eras, noting in passing that Sappho's increasing disrepute in the Roman world may have affected Nossis' reputation as well (Brooten, *Love between Women* 29–41). For express identification of desire in Sappho's poems as "lesbian" in the contemporary sense, see John J. Winkler, *The Constraints of Desire: The Anthropology of Sex and Gender in Ancient Greece* (New York: Routledge, 1990) 162–187, and Snyder, *Lesbian Desire,* esp. ch. 2. Page du Bois, *Sappho Is Burning* (Chicago: U of Chicago P, 1995) 13–15, insists that the adjective is inappropriate and suggests that Sapphic eroticism is instead aristocratic in outlook and "polymorphous, constructed with an [*sic*] view toward domination rather than exclusively toward women." See further André Lardinois, "Lesbian Sappho and Sappho of Lesbos," in *From Sappho to de Sade: Moments in the History of Sexuality,* ed. Jan Bremmer (London: Routledge, 1989), and Margaret Williamson, *Sappho's Immortal Daughters* (Cambridge, MA: Harvard UP, 1995) ch. 4.

15. For Archaic Greek concepts of poetic inspiration, consult R. Harriott, *Poetry and Criticism before Plato* (London: Methuen, 1969) 34–51; P. Murray, "Poetic Inspiration in Early Greece," *Journal of Hellenic Studies* 101 (1981); and Thalmann, *Conventions of Form and Thought* 126–130. J. S. Clay, *The Wrath of Athena: Gods and Men in the* Odyssey (Princeton: Princeton UP, 1983) 9–25, examines the thematic significance of the Muse in the *Odyssey.*

16. See E. R. Dodds, *The Greeks and the Irrational* (Boston: Beacon Press, 1957 [1951]; Berkeley: U of California Press, 1968) 80–82; Harriott, *Poetry and Criticism* 78–91; and E. N. Tigerstedt, "Furor Poeticus: Poetic Inspiration in Greek Literature before Democritus and Plato," *Journal of the History of Ideas* 31 (1970): 163–178.

17. Murray, "Poetic Inspiration" 88.

18. I operate on the assumption that Sappho's poetry was composed and delivered orally (for further discussion, see M. B. Skinner, "Woman and Language in Archaic Greece, or, Why Is Sappho a Woman?" in *Feminist Theory and the Classics,* ed. N. Rabinowitz and Amy Richlin [New York: Routledge, 1993]). Eva Stehle, *Performance and Gender in Ancient Greece* (Princeton: Princeton UP, 1997) ch. 6, takes the contrary position that Sappho employed writing as a primary medium of composition.

19. Sappho's social environment and the circumstances in which her poetry was performed are intensely contested matters. Representative earlier inquiries into the religious and paideutic activities of her putative *thiasos* or sodality include R. Merkelbach, "Sappho und ihr Kreis," *Philologus* 101 (1957); C. Calame, *Les choeurs de jeunes filles en Grèce archaïque I: Morphologie, fonction religieuse et sociale* (Rome: Edizioni dell'Ateno & Bizzarri, 1977) 367–372; Bruno Gentili, *Poetry and Its Public in Ancient Greece: From Homer to the Fifth Century,* trans. A. Thomas Cole (Baltimore: Johns Hopkins UP, 1988) 77–89; on the socializing function of poetry in

such surroundings, see also Judith Hallett's classic article, "Sappho and Her Social Context: Sense and Sensuality," *Signs* 4 (1979). The tradition that Sappho was a teacher of young girls has now been vigorously attacked by Holt N. Parker, "Sappho Schoolmistress," *Transactions of the American Philological Association* 123 (1993): 309–352, who contends that her songs were composed for an audience of adult women and performed at banquets. André Lardinois, "Subject and Circumstance in Sappho's Poetry," *Transactions of the American Philological Association* 124 (1994) accepts Parker's position that the "schoolmistress" notion of Sappho is anachronistic but insists that she was an instructor of young women's choruses. Following Lardinois, I avoid the word *thiasos* in this essay and speak instead of Sappho's "circle" or "group." Claude Calame, "Sappho's Group: An Initiation into Womanhood," in Ellen Greene, ed., *Reading Sappho: Contemporary Approaches* (Berkeley: U of California P, 1996) offers a convenient overview of recent studies; see also L. H. Wilson, *Sappho's Sweetbitter Songs: Configurations of Female and Male in Ancient Greek Lyric* (London and New York: Routledge, 1996) 117–121.

20. M. B. Skinner, "Sapphic Nossis," *Arethusa* 22 (1989) and "Nossis *Thēlyglōssos:* The Private Text and the Public Book," in *Women's History and Ancient History*, ed. Sarah B. Pomeroy (Chapel Hill and London: Johns Hopkins UP, 1991). On the intimate relationships between Nossis and the other members of her circle, see P. L. Furiani, "Intimità e socialità in Nosside di Locri," in *Rose di Pieria*, "Le Rane" Collana di Studi e Testi 9, ed. F. De Martino (Bari: Levante Editori, 1991); cf. the discussion of her homoeroticism by K. J. Gutzwiller, *Poetic Garlands: Hellenistic Epigrams in Context* (Berkeley, Los Angeles, and London: California UP, 1998) 80–84. L. Bowman, "Nossis, Sappho and Hellenistic Poetry," *Ramus* 27 (1998), rejects my claim that the epigrams assume a primary female audience by distinguishing between the implied internal addressees, who may well have been fictive, and the external readership for which they were actually destined. I regret that constraints of publication make it impossible to give proper consideration to Bowman's critique.

21. A fuller text and explication of L-P 22 is provided below. Cf. Margaret Williamson, "Sappho and the Other Woman," in Ellen Greene, ed., *Reading Sappho: Contemporary Approaches* (Berkeley: U of California P, 1996) 256–257, making a related point about the "circulation of desire" between Sapphic singer and audience.

22. For useful discussion of this fragment, see Denys Page, *Sappho and Alcaeus: An Introduction to the Study of Ancient Lesbian Poetry* (Oxford: Oxford UP, 1955) 137; R. Jenkyns, *Three Classical Poets: Sappho, Catullus and Juvenal* (Cambridge, MA: Harvard UP, 1982) 76–77; T. Compton, "The Barbed Rose: Sappho as Satirist" *Favonius* 1 (1987); and Calame, "Sappho's Group" 117.

23. Aelius Aristides (*Orationes* 28.51 = Fr. 193) may be alluding to this passage when he represents Sappho boasting to other women that "the Muses had made her truly fortunate and enviable and even in death she would not be forgotten."

24. For the erotic ambience in Sappho L-P 2, see especially G. Lanata, "Sappho's Amatory Language," trans. W. Robins, in Ellen Greene, ed., *Reading Sappho: Contemporary Approaches* (Berkeley: U of California P, 1996) 15–17 and Wilson, *Sweetbitter Songs* 34–41, 76–77. Both A. Burnett, *Three Archaic Poets: Archilochus, Alcaeus, Sappho* (Cambridge, MA; Harvard UP, 1983) 259–276, and Winkler, *Constraints of Desire* 186, interpret it as a symbolic evocation of female sexual pleasure; Winkler comments that virtually every word "suggests a sensuous ecstasy in the service of Kyprian Aphrodite." On the sexual connotations of the flowering

meadow, see C. Segal, "The Tragedy of the *Hippolytus:* The Waters of Ocean and the Untouched Meadow," *Harvard Studies in Classical Philology* 70 (1965).

25. See especially Pindar, *Olympian Odes* 7.7; later examples include Theocritus 7.82, Meleager 1.35–36 Gow-Page = *Anthologia Palatina* 4.1 and *Antipater of Sidou* 16.4 Gow-Page = *Anthologia Palatina* 7.29. On the common referent of "immortality," see D. Steiner, *The Crown of Song: Metaphor in Pindar* (New York: Oxford UP, 1986) 129–130. Robbins, "Sappho, Aphrodite, and the Muses" 236, observes the associative link between Aphrodite's nectar, poetry, and immortality in Fragment 2.

26. Burnett, *Three Archaic Poets* 312: "Atthis has been led out of desire, taken briefly to a cool realm of memory, and then brought finally to a place that is sacred. . . . She brings a kind of knowledge with her into the final (imaginary) festivity. This *gnôsis* is one with Sappho's song."

27. On the "configuration of desire" in 22, see the definitive discussion of Snyder, *Lesbian Desire* 38–42, with whom I am largely in agreement: "Desire, then, as it is articulated in the Gongula fragment . . . is not a frustrated attempt to grasp an object, as later Platonic dialogues sometimes suggest as a definition, but rather a heightened experience of what is beautiful, a fluttering excitement aroused by motion and by visual stimulus, an active sense of repeated engagement in which the desirer is moved to express desire through song." I differ only with her assumption that Abanthis' beloved is present to her gaze.

28. Here I follow M. L. West, "Burning Sappho," *Maia* 22 (1970): 319, rather than L-P.

29. My own observations about the programmatic character of *dêute* here and in L-P 1 have now been independently confirmed by Mace's thorough examination of its general function in erotic Greek lyric. In this context the adverb serves to identify the kind of composition Abanthis is being asked to produce (Sarah Mace, "Amour, Encore! The Development of δηὖτε in Archaic Lyric," *Greek, Roman, and Byzantine Studies* 34 [1993]: 354).

30. For a lengthy survey of earlier critical opinion about L-P 1, consult H. Saake, *Zur Kunst Sapphos: Motiv-analytische und kompositionstechnische Interpretationen* (Munich: F. Schöningh, 1971) 39–78. As an example of those who interpreted it as an account of actual religious experience, see C. M. Bowra, *Greek Lyric Poetry*, 2nd rev. ed. (Oxford: Clarendon, 1961) 193–195. Objections to that reading were advanced by A. Cameron, "Sappho's Prayer to Aphrodite," *Harvard Theological Review* 32 (1939); touches of dispassionate wit were famously noted by Page, *Sappho and Alcaeus* 12–18. Studies that read the ode as an attempt to impart a Homeric or epic coloring to erotic events include K. Stanley, "The Rôle of Aphrodite in Sappho Fr. 1," *Greek, Roman, and Byzantine Studies* 17 (1976); J. D. Marry, "Sappho and the Heroic Ideal: *erôtos aretê*," *Arethusa* 12 (1979); and Leah Rissman, *Love as War: Homeric Allusion in the Poetry of Sappho* (Beitrage zur klassischen Wissenschaft 157. Königstein: Anton Hain, 1983) 1–29. According to Snyder, *Lesbian Desire* 17, "Homer is always present as a kind of palimpsest in Sappho's songs."

31. Winkler, *Constraints of Desire* 167–170.

32. On the common analogy between weaving and poetry, see Janet McIntosh Snyder, "The Web of Song: Weaving Imagery in Homer and the Lyric Poets," *Classical Journal* 76 (1981) and the comprehensive study of weaving tropes by J. Scheid and J. Svenbro, *The Craft of Zeus: Myths of Weaving and Fabric* (Cambridge, MA: Harvard UP, 1996) esp. 111–130. For the Indo-European roots of the trope, consult R. Schmitt, *Dichtung und Dichtersprache in indogermanischer Zeit* (Wiesbaden: Otto Harrassowitz, 1967) 299–301 and M. Durante, *Sulla pristo-*

ria della tradizione poetica greca, II: Risultanze della comparazione indoeuropea (Rome: Edizioni dell'Ateneo, 1976) 173–179. While our most immediate source for the poem, *POxy.* 2288, gives *poikilothron'*, an alternative reading *poikilophron* ("many-minded"), is elsewhere attested. The latter, however, is also associated with weaving through its close connection with "deviousness" (*mêtis*), a standard attribute of the weaver; see M. Detienne and J.-P. Vernant, *Cunning Intelligence in Greek Culture and Society*, trans. J. Lloyd (Atlantic Highlands, NJ: Humanities Press, 1978) 299–300 and A. L. T. Bergren, "Language and the Female in Early Greek Thought," *Arethusa* 16 (1983).

33. M. C. J. Putnam, "*Throna* and Sappho 1.1," *Classical Journal* 56 (1960) contains a concise summary of earlier bibliography.

34. See especially G. Bolling, "POIKILOS and THRONA," *American Journal of Philology* 79 (1958); cf. Winkler, *Constraints of Desire* 172–174, who stresses the connections between *throna*, weaving, and erotic magic.

35. *Poetae Melici Graeci*, ed. D. L. Page (Oxford: Clarendon P, 1962) no. 59; B. Snell, *The Discovery of the Mind: The Greek Origins of European Thought*, trans. T. G. Rosenmeyer (New York and Evanston: Harper & Row, 1960) 57–58. See now Mace, "Amour, Encore!" passim.

36. For Eros providing the impulse to poetic creation, see Euripides Fragment 664 N², repeated as a proverbial remark in Aristophanes, *Wasps* 1074 and Plato, *Symposium* 196e.

37. Mace, "Amour, Encore!" 359–360.

38. Consult, for example, M. Detienne, *Les maîtres de vérité dans la Grèce archaïque* (Paris: Maspero, 1967); P. Pucci, *Hesiod and the Language of Poetry* (Baltimore and London: Johns Hopkins UP, 1977) 8–44; Bergren, "Language and the Female"; and M. B. Arthur, "The Dream of a World without Women: Poetics and the Circles of Order in the *Theogony* Proemium," *Arethusa* 16 (1983).

39. F. De Martino, "Saffo ed Esiodo, fr. 1, 21–24, Voight," *Giornale filologico ferrarese* 10 (1987).

40. See Greene's essay in this volume. As Greene observes, the mutuality of the relationship between Sappho and Aphrodite is stressed in the closing line of the poem, where the mortal woman asks the divinity to become her "battle partner" (*summachos*). Euripides, I would add, accentuates that reciprocity in a pointed allusion to L-P 1: "Woman is by nature a kind of battle partner to woman" (γυνὴ γυναικὶ σύμμαχος πέφυκέ πως, Fr. 108 N²), which suggests that ancient audiences perceived an egalitarian overtone in the metaphor. My reading of the entire ode has been greatly improved by Professor Greene's personal comments.

41. A. Burnett, "Desire and Memory (Sappho Frag. 94)," *Classical Philology* 74 (1979), a reading elaborated in *Three Archaic Poets* 290–300.

42. W. Schadewaldt, *Sappho* (Potsdam: Eduard Stichnote, 1950) 93, comes close to expressing this notion when he states that the repeated experience of being helplessly in love constitutes at once both Sappho's "being" (*Dasein*) and the source of her creative energy. One must add, however, that the experience is that of the poet-character "Sappho" depicted in the ode and not necessarily, as Schadewaldt thought, that of the composer.

43. A good bibliographic survey of recent work on Nossis is provided by O. Specchia, "Recenti studi su Nosside," *Cultura e scuòla* 23 (1984). For a defense of the debated authenticity of Nossis 12, see M. Gigante, "Nosside," *Parola del Passato* 29 (1974) 29–30.

44. On the textual problems posed by verses 3–4, see Gow-Page *ad loc.* and I. Caz-

zaniga, "Critica testuale ed esegesi a Nosside *A.P.* VII 718," *Parola del Passato* 25 (1970). While Gow-Page obelize the transmitted *phila* in line 3, Cazzaniga accepts Brunck's emendation *philan,* as does Page himself in his subsequent edition.

45. For treatments of Aphrodite's cult and character at Locri, see Christiane Sourvinou-Inwood, "Persephone and Aphrodite at Locri: A Model for Personality Definitions in Greek Religion," *Journal of Hellenic* Studies 98 (1978) and B. C. MacLachlan, "Love, War, and the Goddess in Fifth-Century Locri," *Ancient World* 26.2 (1995).

46. On poem 1 as prologue to a published collection, see now the contribution of Gutzwiller, *Poetic Garlands* 75–79, who regards it as Nossis' attempt to define her own volume of epigrams as erotic, as distinct from those of the earlier Hellenistic woman poet Erinna. G. Luck, "Die Dichterinnen der griechischen Anthologie," *Museum Helveticum* 11 (1954) 183, was the first to recognize the programmatic character of this quatrain; Gigante, "Nosside" 26–27 and "Il manifesto poetico di Nosside," in *Letterature comparate, problemi e metodo: Studie in onore de Ettore Paratore,* vol. 1 (Bologna: Pàtron Editore, 1981) discusses it as an example of literary polemic. I treat other programmatic aspects of this manifesto in Skinner, "Sapphic Nossis" and "Nossis *Thēlyglōssos*" 32–33. C. Riedweg, "Reflexe hellenistischer Dichtungstheorie im griechischen Epigramm," *Illinois Classical Studies* 19 (1994) skeptically dismisses a "poetologische Deutung," but his efforts to disprove the existence of references to Sappho and Hesiod in Nossis 1 rest on too narrow and mechanical an understanding of the conventions of Hellenistic allusion.

47. See E. Cavallini, "Noss. A.P. V 170," *Sileno* 7 (1981); cf. Gutzwiller, *Poetic Garlands* 76.

48. Vital theoretical contributions to the study of this literary device in Greek and Latin poetry include G. Pasquali, "Arte allusiva," *Italia che scrive* 25 (1942); Giangrande, "Alexandrian Epic Poetry"; C. Segal, "Underreading and Intertextuality: Sappho, Simaetha, and Odysseus in Theocritus' Second Idyll," *Arethusa* 17 (1984); G. B. Conte, *The Rhetoric of Imitation: Genre and Poetic Memory in Virgil and Other Latin Poets,* trans. C. Segal (Ithaca and London: Cornell UP, 1986) 23–95; and R. F. Thomas, "Virgil's *Georgics* and the Art of Reference," *Harvard Studies in Classical Philology* 90 (1986). P. Bing, *The Well-Read Muse: Present and Past in Callimachus and the Hellenistic Poets. Hypomnemata Heft* 90 (Göttingen: Vandenhoeck & Ruprecht, 1988) 72–90, treats Hellenistic allusion in the light of the poet's general relationship to the literary past; S. Hinds, *Allusion and Intertext: Dynamics of Appropriation in Roman Poetry* (Cambridge: Cambridge UP, 1998), is a systematic and authoritative exploration of "reflexive annotation" in Roman poetry.

49. J. H. Waszink, *Biene und Honig als Symbol des Dichters und der Dichtung in der griechisch-römischen Antike. Rheinisch-Westfälische Akademie der Wissenschaften Vorträge* G 196 (Opladen: Westdeutscher Verlag, 1974), provides a comprehensive study of this metaphor; for its implications in the Hesiodic passage under discussion, see Pucci, *Hesiod* 19–21.

50. On the reminiscence of L-P 16.1–4, consult Gigante, "Nosside" 25; for the additional echo of L-P 130, see Skinner, "Nossis *Thēlyglōssos*" 33.

51. E. Degani, "Nosside," *Giornale filologico ferrarese* 4 (1981): 51–52.

52. For a survey of earlier futile attempts to resolve this crux, consult Gow-Page *ad loc.*

53. On the sexual implications of "flowers" and "roses" in Greek, see H. White, "The Rose of Aphrodite," in *Essays in Hellenistic Poetry,* ed. Heather White (Amsterdam: J. C. Gieben, 1980) and Snyder, *Woman and the Lyre* 78–79. The conjunction of honey, Aphrodite and

anthea may be intended to recall Pindar's own warning at *Nemean Odes* 7.52–53, "even honey and the pleasant flowers of Aphrodite have a surfeit" (Skinner, "Sapphic Nossis" 10).

54. Theoretically, the feminine pronoun "of her" (*tênas*), could also refer to a hypothetical feminine object of the verb, i.e., "*she* whom Aphrodite does not love," or conceivably to Cypris herself, although both of those explanations seem somewhat redundant.

55. Degani, "Nosside," concludes that Nossis pronounces herself directly inspired by Aphrodite (52). Additional support for his reading is provided by Cavallini, "Noss. A.P. V 170" 181–182; see further Skinner, "Sapphic Nossis" 8–9.

56. Skinner, "Sapphic Nossis."

57. Gutzwiller, *Poetic Garlands* 80.

58. On Nossis' innovation in referring to a collection of poems as an "anthology," or gathering of blossoms, see Gutzwiller, *Poetic Garlands* 87–88.

59. DeShazer, *Inspiring Women* 1–44, offers a broad survey of the construction of the muse in the work of modern women poets.

60. The lines are from "Transcendental Etude," from *The Dream of a Common Language: Poems 1974–1977* by Adrienne Rich. Copyright © 1978 by W. W. Norton & Company, Inc. Used by permission of the author and W. W. Norton & Company, Inc.

61. Carruthers, "Re-Vision" 321–322.

CHAPTER FOUR

Subjects, Objects, and Erotic Symmetry in Sappho's Fragments

Ellen Greene

Ever since she composed her poems on the island of Lesbos at the end of the seventh century BCE, the life and lyrics of Sappho have haunted the Western imagination. Sappho is not only the earliest surviving woman writer in the West, but she is also one of the few and certainly one of the earliest woman writers before the twentieth century to explicitly express in verse the (erotic) desire of one woman for another.[1] Indeed, Sappho's provocative images of lesbian love have disturbed readers through the ages and have given rise to a multitude of fantasies, fictions, and myths about both her poetics and her persona.[2] From Ovid in ancient Rome who "masculinized" Sappho in his portrayal of her in his *Heroides* to twentieth-century scholars who have often attempted to rationalize away the homoerotic aspects of Sappho's poetry, we can see a distinct pattern of unease at the homoerotic elements in Sappho's fragments. As Pamela Gordon has argued, Ovid's depiction of Sappho in the *Heroides* fits a pattern in the treatment of female homoeroticism in Roman literature; in Roman texts it is often the case that women who desire other women "are explicitly masculinized, sometimes so radically that their very bodies become male."[3] The Sapphic tradition becomes reconfigured, in Latin texts, as a vehicle for expression of heterosexual love. As a number of scholars have shown, this heterosexualization of Sapphic desire, the appropriation of feminine (homoerotic) desire by the male poetic voice, can be traced throughout the tradition of love lyric in the West.[4]

Moreover, in scholarship on Sappho, particularly in the early decades of this century, we see an obsession with Sappho's "abnormal" female psychology and supposed sexual deviance.[5] This obsession, I believe, not only stems from a discomfort with the expression of female homoeroticism in Sappho's poems but also from Sappho's female narrator assuming what Joan DeJean calls "a male prerogative," that is, the expression of *active* erotic desire. The expression of that desire—normally considered "masculine" in the context of male-dominated ancient Greek society—has led some scholars to regard Sappho's poems as perpetuating the hierarchies found in both heterosexual and homoerotic relationships.

What I find most remarkable about Sappho's poems, aside from their powerful lyric evocations of erotic desire, is their dramatization of desire in a way that rejects the conventional roles of a dominant lover and a passive object of desire. For the Greeks, erotic relationships were essentially hierarchical and defined in terms of the opposition between active and passive. One was either in the active position of a lover (*erastes*) or in the passive position of a beloved (*eromenos*).[6] As Eva Stehle contends, "The phallus was the central signifier of sexual relations as constructed in social norms and in language in ancient Greece; . . . one was positioned in relation to the phallus: one was penetrator, penetrated, neither or both. A woman or a boy could only be penetrated or not . . . a hegemonic, adult man was (by definition) a penetrator but not penetrated."[7] By contrast, in the segregated woman-centered world described in Sappho's poems, distinctions between lover and beloved, subject and object, often dissolve through a complex merging of female voices and through the speaker's dynamic, rather than static, visual descriptions of the desired woman and the environment they both inhabit.

Sappho dissolves the rigid categories of lover and beloved so prevalent in ancient Greek homoerotic male culture not only through the coalescence of female voices in her fragments but also through her use of the erotic gaze. Joan DeJean has argued that assuming the male prerogative means that the Sapphic speaker must also be "in control of the gaze that objectifies the beloved woman."[8] While it is true that in Sappho's verse, desire often operates through the eyes and that the female narrator is portrayed as an "active subject controlling the gaze," Sappho's protagonist articulates her desire within the context of a woman-centered society that appears to be detached from male public arenas. What is fascinating about Sappho's use of the erotic gaze is not the way it usurps male prerogatives but the way in which it demonstrates a different, alternative way of looking at what one loves, whether it be a person or a line of infantry. Luce Irigaray's assertion that "woman takes pleasure more from touching than from looking"[9] clearly does not apply to Sappho, as DeJean persuasively argues. Indeed, Sapphic desire is often activated through the gaze. But it is a gaze that although active, is neither controlling nor possessive, nor does it aestheticize the desired woman. Rather, the flexibility of subject positions in Sappho's fragments emphasizes the nonobjectifying quality of the Sapphic gaze and, more importantly, offers an erotic discourse and practice that may constitute an alternative to the competitive and hierarchical models of eroticism common in male patterns of erotic discourse.[10]

FRAGMENT 1

I begin my analysis with a discussion of Sappho's Fragment 1, often called the "Hymn to Aphrodite." This poem uses the relationship between the narrator and the goddess to represent a nonhierarchical ideal for relationships between women, and it is also sometimes employed by scholars to illustrate how Sappho, like her male contemporaries, offers a vision of *eros* as a scene of struggle and conquest.[11] Page duBois has argued, for example, that the "Hymn to Aphrodite" reflects Sappho's participation in "the aristocratic drive for domination."[12] DuBois' argument is based on her view that the last stanza of the poem stresses the element of conquest in the relationship Sappho envisions between the two female lovers. My own reading of this poem will attempt to refute this view. I agree that Sappho's poems may be said to reflect an aristocratic worldview—with their depictions of women at leisure to pursue literary interests and their idealized environments of beauty and abundance.[13] But I think that the chief relevance this has to her erotic poetry is that the aristocratic atmosphere in Sappho's poems provides environments suited to the idealization of female beauty and feminine desire.

The language of the "Hymn to Aphrodite," in particular the merging of the voices of the speaker and the goddess, points to a dissolution of hierarchy between subject and object, lover and beloved, and thus presents a view of *eros* as both symmetrical and intersubjective.

Richly-enthroned, immortal Aphrodite, daughter of
Zeus, weaver of wiles, I beseech you,
do not subdue me with pain and anguish.

But come to me, if ever in the past you heard my
cries from afar, and leaving the house
of your father, you came,

Your golden chariot yoked. Beautiful sparrows
brought you swiftly over the black earth,
their wings fluttering from heaven through
mid-air,

And quickly they came. But you, Blessed One,
with a smile on your immortal face,

asked what did I suffer, this time again,
and why, again, I called,

And what I most want in my frenzied heart,
Whom, again, am I to persuade back to your heart?
Who, O Sappho, does you wrong?

For if she flees, soon she will pursue; and if she
does not receive gifts, soon she will give them.
And if she loves not, soon she will love even against her will.

Come to me even now, and release me from cruel
anxieties; and fulfill all that my heart desires,
you yourself be my ally.

Poikilothron' athanat' Aphrodita
pai Dios doloploke, lissomai se,
me m' asaisi med' oniaisi damna,
4   *potnia, thumon.*

Alla tuid' elth', ai pota katerota
tas emas audas aioisa peloi
eklues, patros de domon lipoisa
8   *chrusion elthes.*

Arm' upasdeuxaisa; kaloi de s' agon
okees strouthoi peri gas melainas
pukna dinnentes pter' ap' oranoaithe-
12   *ros dia messo,*

Aipsa d' exikonto; su d', o makaira,
meidiaisais' athanatoi prosopoi
ere' otti deute pepontha kotti
16   *deute kallemmi,*

kotti moi malista thelo genesthai
mainolai thumoi; tina deute peitho
. . . sagen es san philotata; tis s', o
20   *Psaph', adikesi?*

Kai gar ai pheugei, tacheos dioxei,
ai de dora me deket' alla dosei,
ai de me philei, tacheos philesei,
24   *kouk etheloisa.*

Elthe moi kai nun, chalepan de luson
ek merimnan, ossa de moi telessai
thumos imerrei, teleson, su d' auta
28   *summachos esso.*[14]

Most commentators on the poem agree that Sappho's invocation of Aphrodite does not describe a religious or cultic experience but is used as a "literary fantasy" or fiction to externalize psychological phenomena.[15] However, Sappho's use of traditional prayer formula and ritual elements of song in her apostrophe does have an important function in the way the poet reconciles the speaker with her object of desire. Sappho accomplishes this reconciliation through a merging of the voice of suffering "Sappho" with the divine voice of her impassive goddess.

We can see from the beginning of Fragment 1 that the Aphrodite of Homeric epic is Sappho's point of departure for her depiction of Aphrodite. The first stanza abounds in conventional epithets for Aphrodite that stress Aphrodite's authority and power as well as the distance between the speaker and the goddess. The throne image in particular (*poikilothron'*) expresses a sense of awe at Aphrodite's power—in sharp contrast to the helplessness of the speaker. The tension between Aphrodite's immortality (her status as daughter of Zeus) and the mortal pain of the speaker is suggestive of a division in the speaker between passivity and empowerment.

Although the poem begins with the speaker at a distance from her goddess, the speaker asks Aphrodite *not* to subdue her with cares. Sappho's speaker uses the word *damna* (subdue), a word often associated with conquest and domination, to express what she does *not* want from Aphrodite. We start out here, as we do in several of Sappho's fragments, with two distinct, fully individuated voices that seem to reflect opposing points of view and ways of looking at the world. However, from the start, the speaker in the poem implicitly expresses the wish that she be reconciled with Aphrodite. The memory of a past situation in which, on another occasion, Aphrodite responded to the speaker's distress, begins to take the speaker out of the present moment and signals the beginning of her ability to transcend her anguished state of mind. The image of the speaker's cries being heard from afar reinforces the sense that the speaker is attempting to overcome her feelings of powerlessness. Indeed, the description of Aphrodite's descent in the third stanza of the poem is, in another sense, a description of the speaker's ascent. At the same time as the speaker imagines Aphrodite coming down to her level, she raises herself to a higher level through her close identification with the goddess. The swiftness and rapid movement of Aphrodite's descent and the image of sparrows fluttering their wings over the black earth suggest that through the power of the poetic voice, the speaker herself is taking flight and bringing heaven down to earth.

As some scholars have noted, Sappho models Aphrodite's descent on the descents of Athena and Hera in *Iliad* 5 coming to help the wounded Diomedes.[16] On the surface, Sappho seems to be transferring the language of warfare to the experience of women in love and to be attaching an attitude of militance to the normally unwarlike attributes of Aphrodite. However, sparrows, instead of horses, draw Aphrodite's chariot as it makes its descent. This deviation from the Iliadic model adds an element of delicacy and beauty to the warlike mood and suggests that the speaker is not merely declaring war on her beloved but wants to persuade her with the enchantment of her charms.

The effect of the speaker's transformation begins to become evident in stanza 4, where the speaker suddenly addresses Aphrodite in a more personal way ("But you, Blessed One") than she did earlier in the poem when her address to Aphrodite was mediated by a series of epithets. As many commentators of the poem have observed, the serene detachment of Aphrodite (her smile) in the face of the speaker's tumultuous emotions allows the speaker to see those emotions from a somewhat comic, light-hearted perspective. The repetition of the word "again" (*deute*) in stanzas 4 and 5 reinforces this effect. As Sarah Mace has observed, the repetition of "again" (*deute*) is often used in Archaic Greek poetry in a context in which the erotic subject wants to emphasize a feeling of helplessness in the face of repeated onslaughts of desire.[17] The speaker's ability to observe and comment on how her experience *as a victim of love* is like other situations she has experienced in the past necessarily implies a certain degree of objectivity toward her current predicament. In Sappho's poem, we may also be able to detect a degree of self-mockery in Aphrodite's questions to the speaker. Aphrodite's reminder that the speaker has gone through a similar situation before has the effect of making the speaker's feelings, which seemed insurmountable at the beginning of the poem, seem smaller and less significant within the larger context of love's vicissitudes.

But Sappho's use of "again" (*deute*) here goes beyond "an ironic commentary on the speaker's recurrent susceptibility to desire."[18] Aphrodite's questions in stanza 5 about the cause of the speaker's anguish are not posed directly in the second person, as one might expect, but are put in the first person instead. Aphrodite does not say, "What do you suffer, why do you call, what do you want. . . . " Instead, the speaker reports Aphrodite's questions as though she, the speaker, is speaking them directly, "What again did I suffer, why again have I called, what do I want, whom again do I persuade . . . ?" This has the effect of making it seem as though the speaker is asking the questions to herself and is making the identities of the speaker and Aphrodite no longer distinct, as in the first half of the poem. Moreover, *deute* (again) is mentioned three times, each time immediately preceding a verb in the first person. *Deute* (again) is linked respectively to the verbs, "I suffer," "I call," and "I persuade." The actions of suffering and calling are connected with the speaker, while the action of persuading is normally linked to Aphrodite.

The connection that is drawn between these three actions, in part through the use of *deute* (again), implies a blurring of the boundaries between the speaker and her goddess. Further, the persistence of first-person verbs in Aphrodite's questions to the speaker ("I suffer," "I call," "I want," "I persuade") suggests a unified identity that governs all those actions. The verbs of calling and wishing placed between verbs of suffering and persuading bridge the gap, both syntactically and figuratively, between the powerless victim of love and the all-powerful goddess. Also, at the moment the voices of speaker and goddess seem to merge, Sappho implies that Aphrodite gazes intimately at the desiring speaker. Before Aphrodite speaks, she smiles "with her immortal face." The mention of Aphrodite's look suggests that the goddess is face to face with the speaker. This action of gazing helps to dissolve the boundaries between the speaker and the goddess and to break down the hierarchy that defined their relationship at the beginning of the poem.

The sixth stanza of this poem (in which Sappho does not identify clearly who is speaking) has provoked controversy, chiefly because of its apparent portrayal of *eros* as an endless game of flight and pursuit. It is a game that suggests a model of erotic relations based on conquest and domination.[19] Many have read Aphrodite's reassurance to the speaker in this stanza as confirmation of the view that the roles of lover and beloved will eventually be reversed. In other words, the speaker will some day outgrow her position as lover and will become the object of another's affections, while the speaker's beloved will eventually become the lover of some younger beloved. Anne Carson, for example, holds that Aphrodite offers the speaker in the poem a form of erotic revenge that guarantees a reversal of the roles of lover and beloved. Carson bases her argument on the observation that Aphrodite's statements to Sappho contain no direct object. In other words, Carson contends that Aphrodite does not say that the speaker "*Sappho*" will be the object of the beloved's pursuit or the recipient of her gifts, only that the beloved will someday pursue, give gifts, and love. Thus, from the "observation" that Aphrodite is *not* offering the speaker reconciliation with her beloved, Carson infers that she is *not* asking Aphrodite to turn the affections of the beloved toward her—rather, the speaker is merely asking Aphrodite for justice or revenge.

I agree that the lack of a direct object in Aphrodite's consolation of the speaker is very important. But the real significance of the lack of direct objects (of fleeing, pursuing, and loving) in these lines is that the speaker is suggesting that neither she nor her beloved are objects of each other's love. The speaker does not imagine that the consummation of (her) love involves either domination or submission. The beloved is figured as a subject whether she is fleeing or pursuing, giving or receiving. Indeed, the subject *she* in these lines can be either the speaker or her beloved. The speaker is describing, in general terms, the reciprocal movements of desire in which she and her beloved both participate in the process of giving and receiving, loving and being loved—a process that, according to the grammar of the poem, involves only subjects. Moreover, the incantatory quality of the lines evokes what Charles Segal calls "the hypnotic effect of love's *thelxis*"(enchantment).[20] Segal argues that "the rhythmical echo between the first and third lines . . . almost seems to assure the success of this spell-like promise" (149). If it is true, as Segal argues, that the fulfillment of love depends on *thelxis*, then surely both lover and beloved must fall under the same spell for love to be fully realized. By definition, it seems, the "magic of *eros*" implicates both lovers in a circularity of desire that requires reciprocity.

In the context of the whole poem, it seems much more likely that the speaker seeks reconciliation rather than revenge. The initial and final stanzas frame the poem with the speaker's invocation of Aphrodite in the present, but the body of the poem is in the past tense. We learn through the speaker's narration of her past encounter with Aphrodite that the speaker has called on the goddess before for the same purpose: to ask Aphrodite's help in persuading the speaker's beloved to turn her affections back in the speaker's direction. If it is merely erotic justice the speaker wants, then once she recalls Aphrodite's "words of justice" from that earlier encounter, she would have no reason to call on Aphrodite again to enact the same revenge, the same universal law of justice. The language of the last stanza of the poem reinforces this reading. It returns to the present moment of discourse and reminds us of the speaker's original prayer to Aphrodite in the first and second stanzas. Although the imperative "come" (*elthe*) in line 25 recalls the earlier "come" (*elthe*) in line 5, the absence of the qualifying "but" (*alla*) here and

the repetition of imperatives ("release," "accomplish," "be") suggest a far
more powerful voice than the voice of helpless supplication we hear at the
beginning of the poem. The narrator speaks with a confidence in the fulfillment of her desires. There are no negative verbs here, as in the previous
stanza, to suggest the possibility of defeat.

Sappho's use of military terminology in the speaker's request to Aphrodite to be her ally in the last line of the poem may seem to identify Sappho
with masculine values of conquest and militarism.[21] In asking Aphrodite to
be her co-fighter or fellow soldier in the "battle" of love, the speaker asks
Aphrodite to come into an alliance of mutuality with her. The speaker's use
of the word "ally" (*summaxos*) to describe her relationship with the goddess
suggests that she is imagining a relationship based on equality and reciprocity. Further, this trope may refer to an alliance between states rather than
between warriors, thus heightening the sense in which the speaker envisions
herself in an equal partnership with Aphrodite based not on a model of dominance and aggression but on political affiliations between equals.[22] In light
of Aphrodite's (Homeric) reputation for ineffectual, obstructive conduct in
martial affairs and her clearly inappropriate presence in the exclusively male
world of the battlefield, it would seem that Aphrodite's role as the speaker's
ally would not follow the male model for battle partners.[23] Thus, we cannot assume that an alliance between the speaker and Aphrodite involves the
attempt to conquer an adversary at all. It seems that Sappho negates the values associated with martial conquest and substitutes in its place an alliance
with Aphrodite that turns the domination of one over the other into *persuasion:* the power to seduce another into a relationship of mutual desire.[24]
Moreover, as I have argued above, in lines 21–24, the voices of Aphrodite
and the speaker "Sappho" are no longer clearly differentiated. That Sappho
does not clearly identify the speaker in these lines suggests not only a dissolving of the boundaries between the speaker and the goddess but also an
incorporation within the speaker of Aphrodite's persuasive powers.

The speaker's assertive tone in the last stanza expresses a confidence in her
own ability to conjure longing in the beloved. The ability to imagine herself
in an alliance with Aphrodite elevates the speaker to a position of empowerment. The speaker asks Aphrodite to be her ally not in order to conquer
or dominate the beloved, and certainly not to make the beloved passively
accept her affections. Rather, the speaker calls on Aphrodite to help stir the
beloved from passive indifference into active affection. The speaker imagines a situation in which her beloved actively pursues. In addition, we should
not assume that the speaker has to become passive if her beloved is to become

active. That would be simply to assume the male model of dominance and submission. The poem itself in no way suggests this. On the contrary, the purpose of the speaker's alliance with Aphrodite is to rouse her beloved, so that each is to be both lover and beloved, active participants in a circularity of desire—both of them active, desiring subjects.

FRAGMENT 94

As we have seen in the discussion of the "Hymn to Aphrodite," Sappho presents a model of erotic relations between women in which the positions of lover and beloved are symmetrical. Neither woman (in the sixth stanza) is presented as fixed in the role of either active or passive, dominant or submissive. I now turn to a discussion of Fragments 94 and 16, poems that explicitly show how the sight of the beloved triggers desire in the Sapphic lover but does not entail either possession or objectification of the desired woman. The speaker in these poems never describes the beauty of the beloved as static, nor does she portray the beloved as a passive object of desire. Rather, she describes her exclusively in terms of her *effect* on the speaker herself and on their surroundings.

Fragment 94, the only surviving poem of Sappho's that specifically dramatizes an erotic encounter between two women, exemplifies how the Sapphic gaze gives rise to a blurring of the boundaries between lover and beloved. Indeed, the speaker in the poem never portrays the beloved as separate from herself, as an object either to gaze at or describe.[25]

> Honestly, I wish I were dead.
> Weeping, she left with many tears,
>
> And said: "Oh what terrible things
> we endured. Sappho, truly,
> against my will I leave you."
>
> And I answered: "Go, be
> happy, and remember me;
> For you know how we cared for you.
>
> And if not, then I want
> to remind you . . . of the wonderful
> things we shared.
>
> For many wreaths of violets and
> roses . . .
> you put on by my side,

And many woven garlands
fashioned of flowers,
you tied round your soft neck,

And with rich myrrh,
fit for a queen,
you anointed . . .

And on a soft bed,
tenderly,
you satisfied (your) desire.

And there was
no sacred place
from which we were absent,

no grove,
no dance,
no sound.

tethnaken d'adolos thelo.
2   *a me psisdomena katelimpanen*

polla kai tod' eeipe [moi
oim' os deina pep[onth]amen,
5   *Psaph', e man s' aekois' apulimpano.*

tan d' ego tad' ameiboman.
chairois' ercheo kamethen
8   *memnais', oistha gar os se pedepomen.*

ai de me, alla s' ego thelo
omnaisai . . . eai
11   *os . . . kai kal' epaskomen.*

po[llois gar stephan]ois ion
kai br[odon . . .]kion t' umoi
14   *ka . . . par emoi perethekao*

kai pollais upathumidas
plektais amph' apalai derai
17   *antheon e . . . pepoemenais.*

kai p . . . muroi

brentheoi . . . ru . . . n

20 *exal<e>ipsao ka[i bas]ileioi*

kai stromn[an e]pi molthakan

apalan par[ ]onon

23 *exies potho[n] nidon*

koute tis[ou]te ti

iron oud' u . . .

26 *eplet' opp[othen am]mes apeskomen,*

ouk alsos [ ] ros

] psophos

29 *] . . . oidiai.*

The fragment opens with the expression of a wish to die. Since the beginning of the poem is missing, the text does not tell us who speaks the first extant line: the speaker or the other woman. It makes the most sense to attribute the opening line to the other woman rather than to the speaker, since that would be consistent with the other woman's despondent attitude toward her separation from the speaker.[26] Moreover, attributing the opening line to the other woman heightens the tension in the poem between the two speakers, whose different approaches toward the separation are reflected in their correspondingly different modes of discourse.

The wish to die at the beginning is expressed baldly, without the embellishment of poetic images. The use of the word "honestly" (*adolos*) initiates a conversational diction and tone that accentuate the contingencies of circumstance. The time-bound world of circumstance evoked here is reinforced by the speaker's use of third-person narrative to describe a past event ("Weeping, she left with many tears"). The poem implies that the two lovers are faced with a separation that is not of their own choosing. Some scholars have proposed that the likely reason for the departure of the other woman is her impending marriage. But there is no evidence within the poem to support this interpretation. If marriage was the reason Sappho had in mind, then she chooses to make it peripheral to the intense relationship she depicts between the two women in the poem. That is itself important, since it emphasizes the primacy of female relationships within the context of a society in which heterosexual marriage was expected. In Sappho's famous *phainetai moi* poem, she explicitly portrays the speaker's female beloved sitting with a man whom many scholars suppose to be a husband or fiancé. In that poem, the figure of separation between the speaker and her beloved is the man, but as in Fragment 94, the circumstances of separation fade out as the speaker's powerful emotions at the sight of the beloved come to the fore.[27]

Like the "Hymn to Aphrodite," Fragment 94 is a response to a situation over which the speaker has little control, and it begins also in a mood of helpless despair. Like the speaker in Fragment 1, the speaker here is able to raise herself out of her distressed state of mind by demonstrating the capacity of her poetic voice to conjure past erotic fulfillment. Through a merging of the voices of lover and beloved (much like the merging of the voices of speaker and goddess in Fr. 1), Sappho dramatizes the shift from the time-bound world of circumstance to an idyllic world of memory and imagination.

The drama of separation unfolds as we hear the distinct voices of the speaker and her departing lover shift back and forth in nearly ritualized responsion to one another.[28] The phrase "I leave" (*apulimpano*) in line 5 resonates to the phrase "she left" (*katelimpanen*) in line 2. Both verbs refer to the act of leaving and reflect the point of view of the woman who is constrained to act against her will and for whom there seems to be no way out. In addition, "we cared" (*pedepomen*) and "we shared" (*epaskomen*) in the third and fourth stanzas of "Sappho's" speech answer "I leave" (*apulimpano*), and focus attention away from the pain of separation to the shared experience of the two lovers. The voice of the speaker responding to the voice of the departing woman begins to remove us from the immediate moment of departure to the experience of love in the past. The speaker's request in line 8 that the woman remember draws the poem away from the dramatic portrayal of the woman leaving to the more inward situation of remembering. And although we are still in the narrative frame, the speaker's verbal imperatives to the woman (go and remember) are spoken as direct address. The speaker has moved from reporting a past event in the third person to reporting the reciprocal apostrophes spoken by the two lovers. These two modes of discourse—third-person narrative and the reporting of second-person address—both remain within a temporal frame. It is not until the "we" emerges at line 8 that the speaker begins to turn away from narrative altogether. The "we" of "we shared" (*pedepomen*) initiates a shift from reported speech to a detemporalized mode of discourse in which the individual voices of the two lovers are no longer differentiated.

In stanza 4, the pattern of shifting voices changes as the speaker's own point of view and poetic voice take over. The speaker's assertion at line 9 that she will remind her beloved if she does not remember focuses attention on the poetic voice and its ability to activate the past and make it come alive in the present. The phrase "I wish" (*thelo*) at the end of line 9, expressing the speaker's wish to remind her departing lover about their past happiness, echoes the earlier wish to die in the opening line of the fragment. The repetition of wishing in the parallel contexts of death and memory suggests the active transformative power of the poetic voice as it replaces the will to die with the will to create. The speaker's clearly delineated voice offering her beloved an abstract consolation about how great the past was gives way to the dissolution of both their voices—voices that become subsumed within a detemporalized, intersubjective space inclusive of speaker, addressee, and perhaps an audience of women as well. Stanza 4 brings about a transition to a more remote time and introduces a use of language that abounds in poetic images.

As against the clearly delineated voices and personalities at the beginning, here, the "I," "you," and "we" of the poem are all linked in the aura of sensations and erotic stimulation. Boundaries of person, object, and place seem to break down as everything in the environment dissolves into a totality of sensation. Despite the speaker's rapt absorption in the woman whose presence she invokes, there is no emphasis on describing the woman as *independent* of the effect she has on the narrator herself or as separate from the atmosphere their shared erotic experience generates. Jane Snyder has argued that Sappho often emphasizes the visual impression made by the beloved woman. But Snyder points out that the Sapphic gaze produces an image of the beloved that does not present her as static, as something that can be possessed. Rather, the Sapphic lover focuses on the "total affect" of the beloved that arouses desire: the movement of the beloved's body, the flow of her garments, the smells and textures that surround her.[29] Here, in what is perhaps the best example of Sappho's portrayal of the beloved woman, the speaker does not depict the beloved as a passive object of desire, nor does she present the beauty of the beloved as something satisfying in itself. Rather, the speaker presents the body of the beloved as a site of erotic agency.

The dynamic actions associated with the beloved (putting around, putting on, anointing, satisfying) emphasize the active desire of the beloved woman. She is not merely a static entity to be gazed upon with pleasure; she is presented, instead, through a series of actions that involve both her and the speaker. The speaker celebrates their shared experiences by calling to mind images of the beloved woman as the subject of her own desires, as one who acts rather than as one who is acted upon. This oscillation between subject and object in the poem is reinforced by the way in which the be-loved's actions are all framed by the speaker's statement in line 11 that "we shared wonderful things."

In the last two stanzas, the sense of fullness expressed in the repetition of negatives that negate the lovers' absence at the shrine, the grove, and the dance contrasts with the emptiness implicit in the earlier verbs of abandon-ment and departure. The negation of place to denote presence suggests that it is the mutual experience of the two lovers that gives form to the world; the implication is that place comes alive only in the presence of the other. The space inhabited by the two lovers expands outwards to the seemingly endless spaces of streams, temples, and groves. The effortless motion from interior to exterior space that suggests the dissolving of spatial boundaries corre-lates with the breakdown in clearly distinct positions of self and other, sub-ject and object. The voice of the speaker, which earlier expressed its clearly distinct emotions and demands, becomes incorporated into the description of the lovers' shared experiences. The description of the beloved's actions (putting on, anointing, satisfying) in stanzas 5 through 8 flow into the ac-tions the two lovers undertake together in the ninth stanza of the poem. At line 26, "*apeskomen*" (we are [not] absent) echoes "*epaskomen*" (we shared) at line 11. The two verbs frame the scene of erotic bliss not only through their assonance but also through their use of the third-person plural. In the re-turn to "we" as the subject, the speaker reminds us that the fulfillment of desire depends on a symmetrical arrangement between lover and beloved— an arrangement in which they are both actively engaged in the pursuit of erotic fulfillment.

In the last two stanzas of the fragment, after the climactic moment of fulfilled desire in line 23, the rhythm slows down, and the poem turns to a quieter, more peaceful mood. The piling on of highly descriptive nouns and adjectives that characterizes the more excited tempo of stanzas 5 through 8 narrows down to a sparer use of speech. The repetition of negatives turns the poem from the contemplation of sensual abundance, with its emphasis on intense tactile and visual stimulation, to the awareness of inaction, of *be-ing* instead of doing. The main verb in stanza 9, "there was," (*eplet'*) contrasts sharply with the verbs in the preceding stanzas—verbs that involve intricate, external actions, such as weaving, anointing, making, and of course leaving. That the voice of the speaker asserts that there was *no place* from which the lovers were absent suggests a denial of both time and place altogether. It is presence, mutual presence, rather than possession that characterizes the de-sire of the two lovers at the end.

FRAGMENT 16

In the most programmatic of Sappho's surviving poems, Fragment 16, Sappho not only asserts that the most beautiful thing on earth is what one loves but also demonstrates the way in which individual identity and agency are inextricably entwined with *eros*. In this poem Sappho dramatizes active female desire through a refashioning of the legend of Helen. Sappho portrays Helen as actively pursuing erotic fulfillment by abandoning her husband and sailing to Troy. While Sappho uses the example of Helen to make her point about the general characteristics of desire, in the process she also posits a version of desire that goes against conventional Greek (male) conceptions of the erotic gaze as a vehicle for perpetuating hierarchical erotic relationships. One of the most interesting facets of this poem is the way it emphasizes *the manner in which one gazes* rather than the appearance of the object of the gaze. While Sappho may identify the speaker's perspective as uniquely feminine, she also presents an alternative way of looking at what one loves, a way that may be applicable to *both* men and women. Accordingly, it is more appropriate to speak in terms of the *Sapphic gaze* rather than merely the *female gaze* in Sappho's erotic poems.[30] I will argue that in Fragment 16, Sappho presents a radical way of understanding relations between lover and beloved that runs counter to prevailing conceptions of *eros* as a game based on domination, conquest, and the objectification of the other.

> Some say that a troop of horsemen,
> some of foot soldiers, some a fleet of ships
> is the most beautiful thing on the dark earth;
> but I say that it is whatever anyone loves.
>
> It is completely simple to make this
> intelligible to all, for the woman
> who far surpassed all mortals in beauty,
> Helen, abandoning her most brave husband,
>
> went sailing to Troy and took no thought
> for child or dear parents, but
> the [Cyprian goddess]
> led her away . . .
>
> [All of which] now reminds me
> of Anaktoria absent;
> Her lovely step and the bright sparkle

of her face I would rather see than
all the Lydian chariots
and armed men fighting on foot . . .

[O]i men ippeon stroton, oi de pesdon,
oi de naon phais' ep[i] gan melai[n]an
e]mmenai kalliston, ego de ken' ot-
4   *to tis eratai.*

pa]gchu d' eumares suneton poesai
p]anti t[o]ut', a gar polu perskethoisa
kallos [anth]ropon Elena [to]n andra
8   *ton [ar]iston*

kall[ipoi]s' eba 's Troian pleoi[sa
koud[e pa]idos oude philon to[k]eon
pa[mpan] emnasth[e], alla paragag'
autan
12   *]san*

]ampton gar[
] . . . kouphost [ ]oe.[.]n
..]me nun Anaktori[as o]nemnai-
16   *s' ou] pareoisas.*

ta]s <k>e bolloiman eraton te bama
k' amaruchma lampron iden prosopo
e ta Ludon armata kan oploisi
20   *pesdom]achentas.*

(Fragments of a few more lines follow
that are largely unintelligible.)

In their essays on Fragment 16, both Page duBois and Jack Winkler argue that the poem is not, as many critics have thought, a commentary on the
system of values in heroic poetry.[31] Both argue against the view that the poem
sets up a contrast between the value of military prowess and the value of personal desire. The catalogue of choices that recalls the language of the Homeric poems and the values of the heroic life seems to be in direct conflict
with the speaker's emphatic declaration that the most beautiful is whatever
anyone loves or desires. However, we can see the paradox in the speaker's assertion through the way she contrasts the emphatic *ego* ("I") of line 3 with

the impersonal force in the words "some" and "anyone" in the first stanza of the fragment.[32] The contrast makes it appear that the speaker is elevating the values of personal desire, associated with the feminine and the erotic, over public, masculine, heroic values. To be sure, stating her view as a personal one against an array of impersonal choices reinforces a sharp distinction between competing systems of value. However, both the "some" in the first part of stanza 1 and the specific images of horsemen and foot soldiers become subsumed under the indefinite and all-encompassing "whatever" and "anyone" in line 4, so that public and private, personal and impersonal become inextricably entwined.

On the surface it appears that the speaker is offering her preference as a contrast to the preference of those who find horsemen, infantry, and ships "the most beautiful." But the speaker's expression of what she finds beautiful, although emphatically an articulation of her particular identity, is presented as an instance of a general interconnectedness between beauty and desire. The inclusiveness of the word "whatever" in line 4 is reinforced in the poem through the way Sappho links the images of weaponry and war with the image of Anaktoria. Further, the emphasis Sappho gives to *ego* in the context of the speaker's general assertion about desire strongly suggests that people reveal their individual identities through their erotic pursuits. To say that the most beautiful is whatever one desires (loves) is to say that one is defined by what one loves and that the self is precipitated in desire, in the process of pursuing something that one considers beautiful. Sappho implies that the desiring subject gives testimony to (her) identity through the action of loving. While the *ego* of line 3 is not clearly identified, and is certainly not presented as gendered, it does, nonetheless, affirm its identity through erotic pursuit. The indefinite "whatever" (the thing that one loves) is made beautiful through the action not only of desire itself but of speaking one's desire. The speaker's emphatic expression of personal identity through an association with an unspecified "object" of desire suggests that the lover and the "loved thing" are deeply intertwined.

The contrast between the particularity of *ego* and the indefiniteness of the "loved thing" is reinforced in the second stanza. The speaker juxtaposes the particular example of Helen with a claim that her general point about desire can be entirely (*pagchu*) made intelligible to all. This claim, as Snyder argues,[33] accentuates the authority of the *ego* in the poem, but it also provides a link between the specific examples offered by the speaker to prove her point.[34] The centrality of the figure of Helen in the speaker's argument about desire clearly focuses on female subjectivity and agency. Helen is portrayed neither as the Homeric object of male desire nor as a passive victim but rather as an active seeker of what she considers beautiful, the "hero of her own life," as Page duBois has put it.[35] The speaker offers the image of Helen as both beautiful (*kallos*) and as an actively desiring figure (leaving, sailing, going) and thus implicitly presents her as an object of the speaker's own desiring gaze. The speaker asserts that it is what one loves that is the most beautiful, and then in the next stanza calls forth an image of Helen as "the most beautiful." Helen is the particular example that will help to make the speaker's assertion easily intelligible (*suneton*) to all. The Greek word *suneton* (intelligible) can be associated with seeing or perception in general; the example of Helen is "seen" by both the speaker herself and her audience—those to whom the speaker will show her images of desiring and desired women. The speaker's description of Helen parallels the speaker's portrayal of the beloved in Fragment 94. While it is implied that the woman described by the speaker in Fragment 94 is her "object" of desire, the speaker does not portray the woman as an object at all. Rather, the speaker emphasizes the woman's agency and autonomy and describes her through a series of dynamic actions. Likewise, we can see in the figure of Helen a coalescence of subject and object. She both arouses desire through her surpassing beauty and, like the speaker's beloved in Fragment 94, actively engages in the fulfillment of her own desire as well.

The blurring of the boundaries between subject and object of desire in the figure of Helen links her with Anaktoria, whose image the speaker calls to mind in the fourth stanza. Although Helen does not remember those she once loved and the speaker does recall the absent Anaktoria, the use of verbs of remembering in reference to both Helen and Anaktoria serves to link the two female figures. This link is formed not only through verbal repetition but also through the speaker's forceful expression of desire in the first stanza, which leads her to make "intelligible" those (Helen and Anaktoria) who both arouse desire and also actively pursue. In stanza 4, Sappho's poem moves from the world of legend, from a past where the cycles of desire and fulfillment were played out, to the present moment of desire. The word "now" in line 13, along with the name of Anaktoria, takes us back to the *ego* in line 4 and to the moment of vivid presence. But in line 18, the speaker's expression of desire to gaze upon Anaktoria, "I would rather see," is less emphatic than her earlier assertion in the first stanza. Not only is the *ego* lacking, but, as Snyder points out, the verb that expresses the speaker's desire, *bolloiman* ("I would rather"), is in the optative mood and thus expresses a wish rather than a declaration.[36] While it is true that the speaker's statement that she *would* wish to see Anaktoria gives the statement a generalizing force, it also has the effect of weakening the speaker's subject position in relation to her desired "object." The speaker's emphatic presentation of self recedes as the image of the beloved comes into sharp focus, in much the same way as the speaker's clearly delineated voice in Fragment 94 becomes incorporated into the speaker's description of the beauty of the beloved and the lovers' shared experiences.

In this poem, unlike Fragment 94, the speaker explicitly states that she wishes to gaze upon her beloved. She thus implies in a general sense that looking at what one loves arouses desire for it; the logic of the speaker's argument leads to the conclusion that "if what one desires is considered to be the most beautiful, and desire is awakened by gazing upon what one considers the most beautiful (as the speaker demonstrates through her desire for Anaktoria), then it follows that the gaze is the mechanism that both animates desire and seeks its fulfillment in the beauty of the beloved." As in Fragment 94, Sappho here accords agency to the speaker's "object" of desire by focusing on the dynamic qualities of the beloved's beauty. Helen's movement to Troy, described through a series of dynamic actions, becomes in the present moment of desire the "lovely step" (*eraton . . . bama*) of Anaktoria. Although the speaker wishes to look upon her beloved, she does not present her as the fixed object of her gaze, nor does she depict her in a way that suggests possession. Rather, the images of Anaktoria emphasize the elusive effects of her beauty; both her step and her radiant, sparkling face resist containment and control. Anaktoria not only animates desire in the speaker but is herself animated.

The image of Anaktoria's radiance links her beauty and the act of gazing with the concluding images of Lydian chariots and fighting infantry. The military imagery at the end brings the poem back to its beginning, and appears to negate the values associated with the world of war and weaponry. The speaker seems to reiterate her assertion that she prefers to follow the path of personal desire rather than that of public duty and military glory. Although the speaker mentions the accoutrements of war in the process of demonstrating her opening proposition about *eros*, she recasts the glittering spectacle of military might within the context of Sapphic *eros*. The worlds of love and war do indeed seem far apart at the beginning of the poem. But, as Margaret Williamson has argued, Helen's voyage to Troy combines the two worlds together.[37] In sailing to Troy and leaving her family, Helen emulates the action of Homeric warriors and, at the same time, enacts the value of *eros* in pursuing what she considers the most beautiful. That value is maintained not only in the speaker's evocation of Anaktoria's radiant beauty but also in the way the speaker draws an implicit parallel between the luminescence of the beloved woman and the gleam of chariots and marching soldiers.[38] That parallel is reinforced by the link between Anaktoria's step (*bama*) and the steps of the soldiers who fight on foot (*pesdomachentas*).

In linking the images of Anaktoria and of war in this way, Sappho not only destabilizes the opposition between them but also implies that even a line of infantry may seem beautiful when seen through the lens of desire. I take issue with the view of some scholars who hold that in the end Sappho argues for a new set of values that replaces the value of masculine military heroism with a more personal form of *eros*—the desire of one woman for another.[39] This view does not adequately take into account the continuity of desire that links rather than separates the examples of *eros* the speaker uses to illustrate her point. Helen, Anaktoria, and the foot soldiers are all presented by the speaker as active agents (of their own desires) and as objects of the speaker's gaze (as things that can be viewed as "the most beautiful" and are depicted as such by the speaker). The speaker characterizes an object of desire *as beautiful* not by merely observing it but by noticing that it is beautiful in its action, in its own pursuits. The Sapphic speaker turns her gaze to the mythical figure of Helen, to her own beloved Anaktoria, and to the spectacle of soldiers and armor, to demonstrate a way of looking at what one loves that resists the oppositions between viewer and viewed, subject and object.

While the poem clearly celebrates active female desire through the examples of Helen and of the speaker herself, it also asserts the primary importance of *eros* in determining what has value for an individual, irrespective of gender. Sappho shows us not only that people pursue different things but more importantly that the erotic impulse itself does not have to involve possession of what one desires or power over it. Moreover, Sappho's constant emphasis on the flexibility of subject/object positions in women's erotic relations with one another suggests that these relationships may serve as a paradigm for imagining nonhierarchical, symmetrical erotic relationships in general. Despite the Sapphic lover's own preference for other women, Sappho suggests that what matters most is not what we desire but rather the ability to make "intelligible" to ourselves our own particular conceptions of beauty.

NOTES

1. For discussions of the debate concerning Sappho's sexual proclivities, see Judith Hallett, "Sappho and Her Social Context: Sense and Sensuality," *Signs* 4 (1979): 447–464; Joan

DeJean, *Fictions of Sappho, 1546–1937* (Chicago: University of Chicago Press, 1989); André Lardinois, "Lesbian Sappho and Sappho of Lesbos," in *From Sappho to de Sade: Moments in the History of Sexuality*, ed. Jan Bremmer (London: Routledge, 1989) 15–35; Margaret Williamson, *Sappho's Immortal Daughters* (Cambridge: Harvard UP, 1995) 5–33 and 90–132; Jane McIntosh Snyder, *Lesbian Desire in the Lyrics of Sappho* (New York: Columbia UP, 1997).

2. For recent discussions of Sappho reception and transmission in both the literary and scholarly traditions, see DeJean, *Fictions of Sappho;* Williamson, *Sappho's Immortal Daughters* 5–33; Glenn Most, "Reflecting Sappho," in *Re-Reading Sappho: Reception and Transmission,* ed. Ellen Greene (Berkeley: University of California Press, 1996) 11–35; Holt Parker, "Sappho Schoolmistress," *Transactions of the American Philological Association* 123 (1993): 309–351; Yopie Prins, "Sappho's Afterlife in Translation," in Ellen Greene, ed., *Re-Reading Sappho: Reception and Transmission* (Berkeley: U of California P, 1996) 36–67.

3. Pamela Gordon, "The Lover's Voice in *Heroides* 15: Or, Why is Sappho a Man?" in Judith Hallett and Marilyn Skinner, eds., *Roman Sexualities* (Princeton: Princeton UP, 1997) 275.

4. For a discussion of the ways in which male poets have appropriated the Sapphic voice, see especially, Lawrence Lipking, *Abandoned Women and Poetic Tradition* (Chicago: U of Chicago P, 1988) 57–126; Eva [Stigers] Stehle, "Retreat from the Male: Catullus 62 and Sappho's Erotic Flowers," *Ramus* 6 (1977): 83–102; Elizabeth Harvey, "Ventriloquizing Sappho, or the Lesbian Muse," in Ellen Greene, ed., *Re-Reading Sappho: Reception and Transmission* (Berkeley: U of California P, 1996) 79–104; Gordon, "The Lover's Voice"; Ellen Greene, "Re-Figuring the Feminine Voice: Catullus Translating Sappho," *Arethusa* 32 (1999): 1–18.

5. For notable examples of critical essays that promote the view of Sappho as "deviant," see Miroslav Marcovich, "Sappho Fr. 31: Anxiety Attack or Love Declaration?" *Classical Quarterly* 22 (1972): 19–32; George Devereux, "The Nature of Sappho's Seizure in Fr. 31 L-P as Evidence of Her Inversion," *Classical Quarterly* 20 (1970): 17–31. For critiques of this view, see especially Mary Lefkowitz, "Critical Stereotypes and the Poetry of Sappho," *Greek, Roman, and Byzantine Studies* 14 (1973): 113–123; Joan DeJean, "Sex and Philology: Sappho and the Rise of German Nationalism," *Representations* 27 (1989): 148–171; Parker, "Sappho Schoolmistress"; Snyder, *Lesbian Desire.*

6. For important discussions of ancient Greek sexuality, see Kenneth J. Dover, *Greek Homosexuality* (Cambridge: Harvard UP, 1978); Michel Foucault, *The History of Sexuality: The Use of Pleasure.* Volume 2 (New York: Vintage, 1985); David Halperin, *One Hundred Years of Homosexuality and Other Essays on Greek Love* (New York: Routledge, 1990).

7. Eva Stehle, "Sappho's Gaze: Fantasies of a Goddess and a Young Man," *differences* 2 (1990): 88–125.

8. Joan DeJean, "Female Voyeurism: Sappho and Lafayette," *Rivista di letterature moderne e comparate* 40 (1987): 204.

9. Luce Irigaray, *This Sex Which Is Not One,* trans. Catherine Porter, with Carolyn Burke (Ithaca: Cornell UP, 1985) 25–26.

10. Jane McIntosh Snyder and Eva Stehle have shown how the gaze is crucial in the dynamics of Sapphic desire, particularly in poems that explicitly focus on erotic relations between a female narrator and another woman; see Stehle, "Sappho's Gaze"; Jane Snyder, "The Configuration of Desire in Sappho Fr. 22 L-P," *Helios* 21 (1994): 3–8; and Snyder, *Lesbian Desire.* For discussions of how Sappho's poetry emphasizes mutuality between lover

and beloved rather than possession of the beloved by the lover, see especially Eva Stehle, "Sappho's Private World," in *Reflections of Women in Antiquity*, ed. Helene Foley (New York: Gordon and Breach, 1981) 45–61; Marilyn Skinner, "Woman and Language in Archaic Greece, or Why is Sappho a Woman?" in Nancy Rabinowitz and Amy Richlin, eds., *Feminist Theory and the Classics* (New York: Routledge, 1993) 125–144; Williamson, *Sappho's Immortal Daughters* 133–174; Ellen Greene, "Apostrophe and Women's Erotics in the Poetry of Sappho," *Transactions of the American Philological Association* 124 (1994): 41–56.

11. In *Lesbian Desire* 15, Snyder suggests that we may regard the "Hymn to Aphrodite" as providing a "positive construction of lesbian desire."

12. Page duBois, *Sappho Is Burning* (Chicago: U of Chicago P, 1995) 9.

13. See Williamson's discussion of Sappho's involvement in aristocratic culture, in *Sappho's Immortal Daughters* 84–89.

14. Throughout this essay, I provide a transliterated version of the Greek text for each of the poems I discuss. I include this in order to give the non-Greek reader a sense of what the Greek sounds like and to enable me to refer to specific Greek words in my analyses of particular poems.

15. In *Sappho and Alcaeus: An Introduction to the Study of Ancient Lesbian Poetry* (Oxford: Oxford UP, 1955) 16, Denys Page writes: "This (Frag. 1) is not a cult-song, an appeal for epiphany with ritual accompaniment on a formal occasion in honor of Aphrodite; yet it is constructed in accordance with the principles of cult song." Page goes on to say that the poem imitates a type of ritual prayer used as a demand for a particular service rather than as a general act of worship. Hermann Fränkel, *Early Greek Poetry and Philosophy*, trans. Moses Hadas and James Willis (New York: Harcourt, Brace, Jovanovich, 1973) 178, calls the descent of Aphrodite "an inward event."

16. See Page, *Sappho and Alcaeus*; John J. Winkler, "Double Consciousness in Sappho's Lyrics," *Constraints of Desire: The Anthropology of Sex and Gender in Ancient Greece* (New York: Routledge, 1990) 162–187.

17. See Sarah Mace, "Amour, Encore! The Development of *Deute* in Archaic Lyric," *Greek, Roman, and Byzantine Studies* 34 (1993): 335–364.

18. Mace, "Amour, Encore!" 358.

19. See Anne Carson, "The Justice of Aphrodite in Sappho Fr. 1," *Transactions of the American Philological Association* 110 (1980): 135–142; see also duBois' discussion of how this poem presents love as a battlefield (*Sappho Is Burning* 9). duBois argues that the last stanza of the poem shows that we cannot read a vision of "reciprocal feminine sexuality" into this poem. My interpretation of the last stanza will show that the last stanza does indeed offer a vision of *eros* as one of equality and reciprocity.

20. Charles Segal, "Eros and Incantation: Sappho and Oral Poetry," *Arethusa* 7 (1974): 149.

21. See Leah Rissman, *Love as War: Homeric Allusion in the Poetry of Sappho*. Beitrage zur klassischen Wissenschaft 157 (Konigstein: Hain, 1983), for an analysis of military imagery in Sappho's poetry.

22. I thank Marilyn Skinner for pointing out to me that *summaxos* (ally) may refer to an alliance between states.

23. In "Double Consciousness" (*Constraints*), see Winkler's discussion of Aphrodite's descent in the *Iliad*, where she attempts to come to the rescue of the wounded Diomedes.

24. I wish to thank Paul Allen Miller for suggesting to me the importance of *damna* in the context of reciprocal, nonhierarchical desire.

25. The two poems I discuss next, Fragments 94 and 16, both illustrate the fragmentary quality of many of Sappho's texts. Gaps in the original text are indicated with ellipses (. . .). Square brackets indicate scholars' educated guesses as to missing words or phrases.

26. See Anne Burnett, "Desire and Memory (Sappho Frag. 94)," *Classical Philology* 74 (1979): 23; and Jane Snyder, *Lesbian Desire* 56. Burnett and Snyder agree that the first line of the fragment ought to be attributed to the other woman and not the speaker. Burnett writes: "The disconsolate girl thinks that parting is the end of life and love, but her wiser mistress commands her to go her way rejoicing."

27. See Prins, "Sappho's Afterlife"; and Greene, "Apostrophe and Women's Erotics."

28. See Thomas McEvilley, "Sappho, Fragment 94," *Phoenix* 25 (1971): 1–11, for a useful discussion of the way responsion between the two lovers works in the poem.

29. See Snyder, *Lesbian Desire* ch. 2.

30. Women's position on the margins of ancient Greek society may have offered them a unique perspective, one that allowed them to imagine alternatives to cultural norms. In "Woman and Language," Marilyn Skinner argues that Sappho's poetry was likely to have exerted a powerful influence on Greek culture in general. In particular, Skinner argues that the "diffused eroticism" we can perceive in Sappho's poems allowed male listeners and readers "a socially permissible escape from the strict constraints of masculinity" (137). With respect to erotic relationships, I take "constraints" to imply the fixed categories of lover and beloved that appear to be the hallmark of ancient Greek male homoerotic relationships.

31. See Page duBois, "Sappho and Helen," *Arethusa* 11 (1978): 89–99; and Winkler, "Double Consciousness," *Constraints*.

32. I refer to the use of *ego* as emphatic since Greek is a highly inflected language; that is, the meaning of words depends on case endings, which tell us whether a noun, for example, is the subject, direct object, or indirect object in a sentence. In the case of verbs, the endings tell us what person a particular verb form is in. So there is no need grammatically in Greek to include the personal pronoun. When a personal pronoun is used, it is often for emphasis, as here in Sappho's poem.

33. Snyder, *Lesbian Desire* 68.

34. I refer to the speaker as a she not because the poem provides direct evidence that the speaker is a woman. But I assume that the speaker is a woman because she is identified as such in other poems of Sappho. See Williamson on this point in *Sappho's Immortal Daughters* 167.

35. See duBois, "Sappho and Helen."

36. Snyder, *Lesbian Desire* 69.

37. Williamson, *Sappho's Immortal Daughters* ch. 5.

38. In archaic Greek poetry, weapons and armor are typically described as giving off a nearly blinding radiance. See in particular Homer's description of Achilles' armor in the *Iliad* and the description of the glittering weapons of the Greek soldiers as they march against the Trojans in Book 4 of the *Iliad*.

39. Snyder, *Lesbian Desire* 71, for example, asserts that "by setting the example of Anaktoria in opposition to the Lydian forces in stanza 5, Sappho in effect creates an opposition between war and *eros*."

CHAPTER FIVE

EXCAVATING WOMEN'S HOMOEROTICISM IN ANCIENT GREECE

The Evidence from Attic Vase Painting[1]

Nancy Sorkin Rabinowitz

 This essay focuses on the representation of women's relationships to women on ancient Greek vases. In some ways, it is the obverse of my first book, a study of asymmetrical compulsory heterosexuality in the plays of Euripides (*Anxiety Veiled: Euripides and the Traffic in Women*) in which I argued that the exchange of women takes women out of relation to other women and places them in primary relationships with men, simultaneously strengthening relationships between men. Having finished the book, I started to ask to what extent women were really taken from other women and began to look for those very relationships that I had hypothesized as interrupted. Canonical literature written by men shed very little light on the subject, and given the masculinity of the tragic genre (the authors and the performance practices), I turned from tragedy to vase painting where I hoped to find something less mediated and less ideologically laden.

MEANS OF REPRESENTATION

I soon realized that my hope was vain; there are as many challenges to interpreting these seemingly physical objects as there are to interpreting the fragments of Sappho; most statements about the vases are debatable. The very terms we choose to refer to the objects (vases or pots) carry different connotations. Whereas pot suggests archaeology, the domain of utility and function, "vases" suggests the realm of art and art history, the domain of aesthetics.[2] We can see their current importance and value in the way vases are treated—we revere them and show them in museums as "works of art" —and the prices they command on the market.[3] But does this importance mirror the status of the artifacts in antiquity? In a controversial stance, Michael Vickers argues to the contrary that the high status and value of Attic pottery were created by the Baron d'Hancarville to establish a market for

William Hamilton's recently acquired collection; in antiquity, they were the cheap imitations of valuable silverware.[4]

Emphasis on the value of the objects and the art of the painters was the basis of d'Hancarville's aestheticist view of Greek vases, which has its heirs in the traditional art historical perspective on vase painting. This school, dominated by scholars such as John Boardman, Dietrich von Bothmer, and Martin Robertson, follows J. D. Beazley in focusing on the style of individual vases in an attempt to attribute them to a particular painter or a school. There are other ways of looking at vase painting as well. More recently, and more useful for my purposes here, a social critical or semiotic school has emerged that tends to explore "the exotic and distant world of Greek culture, through the imagery of Attic vases of the sixth and fifth centuries."[5] The point of this work is not to attribute the vase to an artist but to analyze the function of the visual images in ancient society; it revels in the coded nature of representation on vases and tends to emphasize the role of the audience more than the maker. From this perspective, the vases' lack of high cultural value is a plus, and study of them is a form of cultural studies.[6]

The Greek pottery I will discuss was for the most part made in Attica between roughly 600 and 400 BCE; the pots were found in sites around the Mediterranean and are now located in museums around the world. They utilize two techniques, called black figure (black figures on reserved red ground) and red figure (red figures on a black background).[7] Pots are often catalogued by their shape, which were associated with certain uses (for instance, a shallow cup for drinking [*kylix*] or covered containers for jewelry or cosmetics [*pyxides*]) and, often, gendered users. Because the drinking party was generally a male affair, it is hypothesized that the cups were probably generally used by men, while the boxes were used by women in their toilet, as their contents reveal.[8] The long-necked *loutrophoros hydria*, a water-carrying vessel for ritual baths and associated with weddings and funerals; the *alabastron* for perfume; and the *lebes gamikos* (wedding vase) were almost exclusively used by women and are often decorated with images of women.[9]

Very little is certain, however, and what we think we know is determined by the ways in which we see these objects. While almost all the vases were functional as well as decorative (though they sometimes functioned as signs of honor or as gifts), we see them as photographs in books or in museums. In books, they are flat, not in the round, so that relationships between the figures may be obscured. If we are fortunate enough to see the objects in an art museum, they are still outside their original setting, and we often see only one side of a three-dimensional piece. Moreover, ways of displaying construct a context and a perspective. The curator determines the organization of the exhibition, whether it is by period, by type of object, or by material, and thus determines how individual pieces will be perceived. Crucially for interpretation, the images are labeled, and the descriptive tag lines, for example, "woman," "*hetaira*" (translated as concubine or mistress), "maenad" (woman follower of Dionysos), "mistress/maid," shape our ways of viewing and receiving information.

These names may have the ring of objective truth, but they are often conclusions drawn by the editor or curator, even if they are based on good reasoning and sound thinking.[10] The representations on the vases are not transparent; rather, many of the details are like part of a code, a conventional language that we no longer speak. In the absence of explicit depictions of primary sex organs, even the simplest attribution of gender (let alone postmodern deconstructions of gender) is made on the basis of conventions. For instance, there is a series of vases (sometimes called Anakreontic because the poet Anakreon is named in a group of them, or "booners" because they are taken to feature his boon companions) that display figures with headdress, earrings, and parasol (all markers of femininity) but also sporting a beard. Are these women with beards or men in women's garb? Since the dress, earring, and parasol may signify easternness, or effeminacy, or both,[11] the femininity or masculinity must be ascribed by the viewer who knows the conventions.

If marks of gender are external and can be put on, if effeminacy is associated with the east, then it is very difficult to be sure what it is that you are seeing. Reading according to modern codes, gender seems ambiguous even in less striking examples. In early black-figure painting, for instance, the nude female body appears masculine in the hips and shoulders; ironically, color (dark for men, light for women), which was based on the ideological construction of gender (outside space for men, inside space for women), is a more secure signifier than physiognomy on these vases.[12] By the end of the fifth century and in late red-figure style, both male and female are softer and more voluptuous and again often indistinguishable when genitals are hidden from view. For instance, scholars debate whether a late terracotta fragment from Pergamon (second century BCE) represents "tender sexual intercourse between a man and a boy"—because the figure on the bottom "lacks female breasts"—or whether it must be male-female lovemaking—because the front-facing position of the couple is assumed to characterize male-female intercourse.[13] The debate is telling and relevant to earlier Greek material as well; in large measure, what you believe or think you know, in this case about what constitutes male-male intercourse, will determine what you see.

Moreover, vase painting does not escape the male domination of Greek tragedy or Athenian culture in general. As there were only male actors and male playwrights and male judges for tragedy, so the vases might have been made by men and decorated by men. There is, however, at least one vase that shows a woman painter in one of the shops.[14] Were there other examples of women potters or painters? Given the fragmentary state of the evidence, we cannot say for sure that there were not, and there may well have been.[15] The existence of a few female painters and potters would not, however, have changed the structure of the form, and so in any case, interpretation must at least take into account the effect male framing would have had on the images we see.

The question of audience is equally vexed. One school of thought holds that the women on the vases are "always objects on display for the pleasure of the male viewer."[16] Since some of the shapes were designed for women's use, one can easily see women as the intended viewers for at least some vases.[17] Moreover, even the cups, which were mostly used by men at symposia, might have been handled and seen by women: if there were not separate symposion cups, women might also have used them, and at any rate, they presumably served and washed up. The idea that the vases were not seen by women is based in part on a false assumption of complete sequestration, with the resulting idea that men even bought the vases, but only propertied women who had slaves and servants could have been totally secluded.[18] Thus, even if the vases were designed for men, women would have had access to them.[19] As in the case of the production of pottery, however, these possibilities do not mean that the form escaped the overall male domination of the culture; vessels made for women's use might have encoded only what men thought women wanted to see, how they thought women wanted to be represented, or how they thought women should behave or should be represented. On the other hand, even if the notional audience for the vases was male, we need not exclude the possibility that women had different and multiple points of view on what they were seeing.[20] To assume the seamlessness of a single male point of view is to flatten the terrain unnecessarily. We can at least hypothesize differences in spectatorship, though women would not necessarily or even probably have taken a counter-hegemonic view.[21]

THE "THING" REPRESENTED?

Like any art form, the vase paintings present a selective view. They do not reflect a preexisting reality but rather construct versions of a reality—and although these are not entirely parallel universes, we cannot be certain of how much they overlap. While I went into this study out of a desire for "information" about women, I discovered that the vase paintings clearly follow conventions of representation as well as of behavior. Women are represented over and over again handling or surrounded by the same objects, performing the same actions. Toward what end? Let us take the relatively common scenes of women working with wool as an example. Literary and archaeological evidence demonstrate that weaving and textile work were important for women, both economically (inside and outside the household) and ideologically (for instance, it was a great honor to be one of the girls chosen to weave the *peplos* (robe) dedicated to the goddess Athena at the Panathenaic festival in her honor.[22] In Xenophon's *Oeconomicus* the young bride will oversee wool working (7.34–36) to increase the wealth of the household. While the frequency of the representation of wool work on the vases may attest its prominence in women's lives, that does not exhaust the meaning of the vases. There is room for interpretation, and the critic's reading of the way the activities are depicted will come in part from his or her predisposition. Thus, Claude Bérard takes the vases as signs of pride in wool working, whereas Eva Keuls sees them as male fantasy propaganda.[23]

Keuls further argues that the male point of view is revealed in the eroticization of weaving and its correlation to primping. As others have noted, there is frequently ambiguity between the spindle and the mirror, so that we literally do not know what it is that we see, and that interplay itself is the subject of discussion. The similarity brings adornment and wool work closer together.[24] Both Keuls and Françoise Frontisi-Ducroux recognize the significance of the confusion; they see wool working as eroticized for the male gaze.[25] The center of a red-figure cup by Douris (fig. 5.1) shows one woman seated carding wool and exposing her leg in the process, while another woman stands before her, looking down; she raises her dress in what Keuls calls a "flirtatious gesture."[26] How do we know if they are flirting, or who is flirting with whom? I accept the eroticism but suggest that it might be addressed to the other woman in the vase or even to a female audience. The divergence of opinion alone is a sign of the complexity of the images and the process of interpretation and should therefore remind us to exercise care in our assessment of what information the vases convey.

This ambiguity in analyzing the Douris cup brings me to the even more complicated realm of desire. How would an artist depict women's desire in ancient Greece?[27] Do the changes we can perceive over time in vase painting result from changing artistic conventions, changing interests of the painters, or changing social conventions? How should viewers interpret the imagery

5.1. Red-figure cup. Woman carding wool. Douris. Berlin Staatliche Museen 2289. (c) Bildarchiv Preussischer Kulturbesitz. Courtesy Staatliche Museen zu Berlin.

2,500 years later? Given the ideological stance of Greek culture regarding "respectable" women's chastity, it is not surprising to find that the vase paintings are circumspect about women's sexuality outside the confines of heterosexual relations (and critics tend to assume that the women in sexually explicit heterosexual scenes are prostitutes). This reticence presents a special challenge to those of us who are interested in the spectrum of women's relationships to women; like critics and historians of other early periods, "the difficulty we face is not necessarily the lack of erotically desiring women, but our inability to crack the code organizing the conceptual categories of an earlier culture."[28] Few would deny the existence of any erotic behavior between women, but was it represented? What shapes did it take? Is there a code that we must crack in order to begin to read?

Our use in this volume of "homoerotic," like Traub's term "erotically desiring women," attempts to avoid imposing contemporary categories on the past in what might seem an essentialist search for lesbian foremothers (see the Introduction in this volume).[29] I am explicitly not seeking lesbianism because I do not want to presume a continuity between ancient and modern practices and cultures. With this strategy I also hope to sidestep some of the debates over lesbianism, for instance, whether sex with women or love for women is the defining characteristic and whether we have to know whether women "are doing it" to identify them as "lesbian."[30] The erotic must not be reduced to some concept of foreplay, for an image can be erotic without implying the future goal of genital consummation, though in ordinary language labeling something erotic often suggests that it tends in that direction. By emphasizing the erotic or what might be called "romantic,"[31] however, I do not mean to deny women's explicitly sexual relations with other women. I use the term because it provides a better hermeneutic device for understanding the Greek vases where genitally focused sex between women is not often (or ever) represented, though male-female and male-male sexual encounters are.[32]

In what follows I have tried to be as inductive as possible and to work by looking at the representations, without imposing a definition on them, but of course, we do have preconceptions that may lead us to recognize only what fits our own categories. These preconceptions may also cause us to misrecognize a great deal. For instance, in modern society, "masculine" women are often read as lesbians, whereas "feminine" women who desire other women may be visible only when accompanied by another woman who fulfills the stereotype. We must be sensitive to the ways in which desire might be revealed in a womanly woman, since the vases show little evidence of the *tribas*, one who rubs, or the "mannish lesbian" we see in later antiquity, for instance in Lucian's *Dialogue of the Courtesan* 5 (see Auanger's and Haley's essays in this volume).[33]

When we call an image of ancient women homoerotic, we are doubtless "reading in," filling in the gaps between women occupying the same vase or in some cases imagining an absent woman. On what basis or with what methodology do we perform these operations? In what follows, I call homoerotic those looks and touches that seem to point to intimacy; following Adrienne Rich, Carroll Smith-Rosenberg, and Lillian Faderman, I look for them in women's homosocial spaces.[34] What do these looks mean? In early red-figure vase painting, women facing men lower their glance, arguably to express modesty;[35] by the end of the fifth century, however, that convention has changed, and "a woman may gaze directly into a man's face," sometimes suggesting an erotic charge.[36] When women are represented with other women, the gaze is typically not averted so sharply, which gives their interactions an appearance of intimacy. If a gaze is actually exchanged between two women, is that a sign of desire between them? I hypothesize that it can be, though I am aware that that interpretation might be in the eye of the beholder. Particularly late in the fifth century, women are also sometimes represented touching one another on the shoulder or around the waist, and in some cases sitting on another woman's lap; these touches seem to the modern viewer, at least, to connote intimacy and affection, if not explicit erotic interest.[37]

What encourages or justifies the interpretation? There are two overarching strategies of reading one can adopt: first, one can attempt to find the ancient meaning, what the representation would have meant or what the painter might have intended; second, one can attend to the meaning to a modern audience. There are several ways to try to get at the ancient meaning. In some cases, ancient texts can supply support of the homoerotic interpretation. In other cases, one can look to the context of the rest of the vase for such support. For instance, if there are multiple pairs of women or more obviously sexual imagery in other areas of a vase, then we can justify taking the ambiguous image as sexual. Critics also sometimes look for scenes that are analogous to male pederastic scenes, which have been more thoroughly analyzed and which are more explicitly sexual.[38] For example, if women give flowers to each other, are they potentially love tokens, as the male gift of cock or hare is?[39] In the fragments of a cup from Douris, women seem to take on the role of gift giver; we can see two pairs of women, one pair exchanging flowers, one exchanging a flower and an egg (fig. 5.2a, b). Garlands form the decorative frieze surrounding the women, making their flowers part of the vase itself. From the association of the flower with gift giving in heterosexual settings, we can infer that these are love gifts.[40]

Though these readings attempt to limit themselves to the ancient meaning of the imagery, the critic nonetheless makes a choice of how to interpret or even read; without a grammar and a lexicon at hand, it is not clear that we are right, or that we are even justified in making the leap between the images on different faces of the vase or between male and female practices. Indeed, the tendency to read from male to female is sometimes problematic because of the differences in the construction of masculinity and femininity and thus can be indulged in only with caution.[41] If we nonetheless make these comparisons, it is best that they be explicit so that we can understand what trajectory we are pursuing.

5.2a, b. Red-figure cup, fragments. Women exchanging gifts. Douris. Leipzig T 550. Courtesy Institut für Klassische Archäologie und Antikenmuseum.

The second strategy of reading avowedly goes beyond trying to recover the ancient meaning and takes the image as a free-floating signifier.[42] If we exceed the likely past meaning, we may nonetheless make these vases useful to us in the present,[43] a not insignificant consideration, since we are the audience, and our concerns are not only legitimate but important. From Winckelmann on, art history has unfolded through erotic engagement with ancient art.[44] We bring our perspectives with us when we view these objects; as we read them for what they can tell us about the past, we also constitute ourselves in the present.[45] The images on the vases are for the most part idealized and made beautiful; they seem to have been meant to arouse desire, but whose desire is elicited and what is it a desire for? Not all desire is sexual; for instance, my desire, which to some extent is at stake here, is to find gaps in the total masculinity of ancient culture, to find women escaping male domination.

Because of the difficulties I have sketched out here, this essay is more metacritical than interpretive. I will look first at the homosocial dimension of women's lives, and then I will turn to those vases and settings that seem to yield a more erotic reading. Placing different interpretations side by side will reveal some of the assumptions underneath them as well as the problems we face in decoding Greek vases. I do not hope to come up with a single positive argument for the representation of women's homoeroticism on Greek vases but rather to make a space for a multiplicity of new interpretations by raising questions about the relationship between the homosocial and the homoerotic. Thus, I place scenes of women on a spectrum from the homosocial to the homoerotic and consciously question readings of ambiguous representations that simplify them by assuming heterosexuality. To say that there are no representations of female homoeroticism because there are no representations of female homoeroticism is circular and means that women's homoeroticism will remain invisible.[46] My goals are sympathetic both with the new lesbian studies, in that I do not focus on the history of a specific identity, as well as with queer theory, with its focus on resistance to norms.[47] While I "queer the vase," to make it possible to see women's homoeroticism, I also intend to point out the shortcomings of using theory based on male sexuality for dealing with women's lives in the past.

"In the Gynaeceum"?

Because of the requirements of exhibition labeling, vases depicting women in an indoor setting are often entitled "the women's quarters," or "the gynaeceum," as if we knew for sure that such "women's quarters" existed and what the term meant. Neither is entirely accurate, and the topic of the so-called gynaeceum (*gynaikonitis*) is a vexed one. Fourth-century evidence from the orators (Lysias 1.9–10, 3.23; Demosthenes 37.45–46) emphasizes physical separation and the restriction of women to the *gynaikonitis* (as does Xenophon, *Oeconomicus* 9.5); in this, however, it differs from the depiction of heroic women in fifth-century tragedy, which shows women in public.

Furthermore, the archaeological legend is inconclusive: the excavations of houses reveal remains of a room that might well have been used as a dining room (there are signs of spaces for the couches typical of the symposion), but the rest of the house is not architecturally distinguished, and there is no sign of a corollary specific women's quarters.[48] "With the exception of a single, clearly specialized room (usually referred to in modern discussions as the *andron*), archaeology provides no criteria for assigning different parts of the house to the two genders, and our texts, in turn, provide no indication of a standard location for the two types of space. It is quite arbitrary to mark one or more rooms on a ground plan as male or female."[49] The iconography of the vases signals inner space with columns or double doors; they may point to the existence of the *gynaikonitis*, but the space indicated was not necessarily structurally marked off from the rest of the house, as the term "women's quarters" suggests.[50] Whether women were sequestered or locked up in these so-called quarters and whether that sequestration connoted low status are yet other questions.

Women of the citizen class did not have political power, but they were not entirely restricted to the household. In a society where there were frequent religious holidays—some of which lasted for two to three days, were celebrated by women, and led by priestesses—women would have had ample occasion to appear in public and to act collectively. Thus, "the convenient opposition between public and private does not always hold true in these images."[51] Nonetheless among representations of women, domestic scenes do preponderate, particularly later in the fifth century, when they replace scenes of men visiting *hetairai*, Amazons, and maenads as favored subjects. As a result, it comes to seem that both before and after marriage, Greek women occupied a largely homosocial world, a world in which they shared rituals and responsibilities. From the number of interior scenes representing women adorning themselves surrounded by their vessels,[52] with jewels, and with mirrors,[53] we would think that was how they spent their days. That is not likely; rather, these aspects of women's lives were often chosen for emphasis on the containers used for cosmetics, so that there is an element of self-referentiality in the motif (perhaps indicating that we should not read them literally). The scenes of women at their toilet are constructions, whether we take them as an indication of how important it was that women be attractive,[54] as propaganda from a male point of view,[55] or as part of an overall idealization of life useful because women were supposed to be decorative.[56]

One crucial element emerges: women were not isolated but were placed in relation to other women.[57] At home there might have been a group of women, sisters, children, and servants—we do not know precisely which women lived together—and there would also have been friends and guests.[58] Whether inside the home or outside it, women are often represented in homosocial groups: groups dancing, bringing gifts to a bride, preparing a body for burial and mourning, working in wool, drawing water at the fountain, or playing music. These occasions and situations set the stage for women's relationships, be they co-workers, friends, or relatives. I will be asking whether the homosocial was not also homoerotic and suggesting that some of these occasions provided the opportunity for the experience of physical attraction for one another.

Interior scenes frequently represent women playing music, and at least one image of women on the bell *krater* in the Metropolitan Museum attributed to the Danae Painter shows signs of a connection between music and female desire (fig. 5.3).[59] There are three women on the obverse and three on the reverse. In the primary image, one woman leans fondly over the shoulder of another with her arms around her, and both look languorously at the third, who is playing the lyre. Richter notes the "affectionate gesture" with which "their hands meet."[60] It is difficult to characterize a gaze, but in this case, at the very least we can say that it is intense and direct. The representation does not come with its own interpretation, and we do not know if the figures listening were involved with one another, whether their gaze indicates desire for the singer, or if I am justified in hypothesizing anything more than a shared touch and excitement generated by the music, which is the traditional interpretation. The description accompanying the piece in the case at the Metropolitan Museum speculates that the musician is Sappho; is that because of the eroticism suffusing the representation? Song and eros for women characterized Sappho's group,[61] but she was not singular; lines from the later poet Nossis (see Skinner's paper this volume) and vase painting suggest that this linkage was not limited to her circle. There is a very similar piece in the British Museum (fig. 5.4) where the hands of the woman behind are in a slightly different position, higher up.[62]

The overlap of women's space with other forms of women's learning, with erotic overtones, can be seen in a red-figured kylix also in the Metropolitan Museum (fig. 5.5). The interior of the cup (fig. 5.5 I) shows two women, one leading the other, with her hand on her left wrist. The woman (girl?) behind has a tablet in her right hand. Uncertainty surrounds the representation; indeed, the Metropolitan Museum catalogue entry on this vase calls it "an uncertain subject," and Richter says that this might be a writing lesson "though she seems rather big for this" and then hypothesizes that the woman has received a letter.[63] But she seems to be hanging back or being dragged along. It is difficult to define the reluctance that we sense, but there are reasons to give an eroticized reading for the interaction. First, the gesture of hand on wrist is reminiscent of the conventions of heterosexual marriage (see fig. 5.6

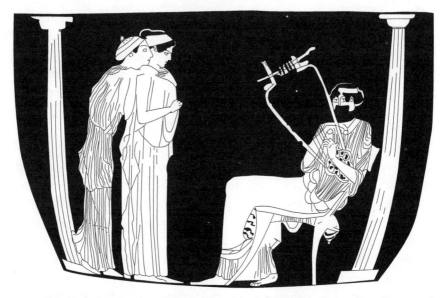

5.3. Red-figure krater. Women musicians. Danae Painter. New York, Metropolitan Museum of Art 23.160.80. Drawing: Christine Ingersoll, after Lindsley Hall, in Gisela Richter and Lindsley Hall, *Red-Figured Athenian Vases in the Metropolitan Museum.*

5.4. Red-figure calyx krater. Women musicians. Niobid Painter, British Museum E 461. Courtesy The Trustees of the British Museum.

and below); second, the outside of the cup (fig. 5.5a, b) shows women in pairs conversing, an echo perhaps of male homoeroticism, given that each of the pairs consists of a woman who is fully draped and one who is more animated and less covered up.[64] In the background on the outside of the vessel are the appurtenances iconographically linked to women's apartments, which thus associate women's reading and writing not with a separate school space but with ordinary women's lives.

MARRIAGE AS WOMEN'S RITUAL

Some speculate that the increase in the representation of domestic scenes toward the end of the fifth century BCE was related to a transformation in the iconography of courtship, which may have reflected "a change in Athenian ideals or a change in the audience for which the scenes were intended, or both. . . . Romance between the sexes was in fact idealized on the vases."[65] As a result, there was an increasing eroticization of the women depicted. While the alabastra, lekythoi, and pyxides with scenes of women's toilet typically display figures of women at rest and apart from one another, there are also an increasing number of scenes of women at home with Erotes.[66] Because of the objects used and the addition of Erotes, these so-called genre scenes are very close to scenes of the preparation of the bride, where the eroticism is more pronounced and more expected. Indeed, it is often unclear whether we are seeing the dressing of the bride or a woman at her toilet.[67] The ideological import of the representation of women at home is made more apparent by this similarity. Not only were women idealized on the vases, but they were idealized as beautiful brides.

Although marriage as an institution was explicitly heterosexual and procreative—the bride was given to the husband for the purpose of raising legitimate offspring (Menander, *Perikeiromenê* [*Cropped*] 1013–1014)—both the betrothal or *eggyê* (which took place between the father of the bride and the groom-to-be) and the ritual were in large part homosocial. Greek marriage rituals were very complex and have been much studied; I will summarize briefly the main stages of this private ritual, which, like other rites of passage (for instance, the funeral), was comprised of several parts and lasted several days.[68] Before the wedding, the bride consecrated her toys and other items of her girlhood to the goddess Artemis; additional sacrifices were also made to Artemis, Aphrodite, or other goddesses; the bride's family gave offerings on the day before the wedding (*proaulia*); and both bride and groom took a nuptial bath. On the wedding day (*gamos*), both houses were deco-

rated with crowns; the bride was dressed by friends or servants—there was a position for the woman who oversaw the wedding (the *nympheutria*) and for the one who prepared the bride (the *nymphokomos*);[69] the father of the bride held a bridal feast, at which time libations were poured, special marriage songs were sung, and crucially, the bride would lift her veil and receive the gifts associated with the moment of uncovering (*anakalypteria*); and the bride and groom departed for the groom's house in a cart, surrounded by friends and the *nympheutria*, who would at this point carry torches. On the next day, the bride received gifts from her relations (*epaulia*).

In black-figure vases, the heterosexual aspects of the ritual predominate because the painters most often represent the wedding procession, but in the later red-figure paintings, the homosocial elements rise in importance. In this later period, we have many more examples of the adornment of the bride and of the *epaulia* (which are often indistinguishable because the evidence is simply the presentation of similar objects), both of which took place among women. The transitional moment between homo- and hetero- is represented visually, for a common motif on vases is that of the groom taking the bride

5.5 I (on page 120), a, b. Red-figure kylix. Interior (I), woman leading another; (a) and (b) exterior, pairs of women. Painter of Bologna 417. New York, Metropolitan Museum of Art 06.1021.167. All rights reserved, The Metropolitan Museum of Art. Drawing: Christine Ingersoll, after Lindsley Hall, in Gisela Richter and Lindsley Hall, *Red-Figured Athenian Vases in the Metropolitan Museum.* Courtesy The Metropolitan Museum of Art, Rogers Fund, 1906.

5.6. Red-figure pyxis, bride and groom, with another woman. Paris, Louvre L 55. Courtesy Musée du Louvre.

by the wrist; the vases also reveal that she is being taken from a woman. A red-figure pyxis in the Louvre shows a woman adjusting the bride's robe from behind and touching her elbow; the groom holds her by the wrist (fig. 5.6). While the two women seem immobilized, the groom is moving forward, suggesting his power and dominance.[70] The implication of dominance and repressed violence in the gesture (*cheir epi karpou*) is corroborated by the tradition of the *thyroros*, in which a friend of the groom stood guard outside the wedding chamber. There were women outside the door as well, and they sang "so that the voice of the virgin might not be heard as she is violated by her husband, but might go unnoticed, covered by the maidens' voices."[71]

What was going on among these women? Red-figure vases, especially those by the Washing Painter (who seems to have specialized in wedding scenes), evoke a strong connection between the women engaged in the preparations for marriage. For instance, on an Attic red-figure wedding vase (lebes gamikos) (fig. 5.7), the bride sits in the center of the vase, while another

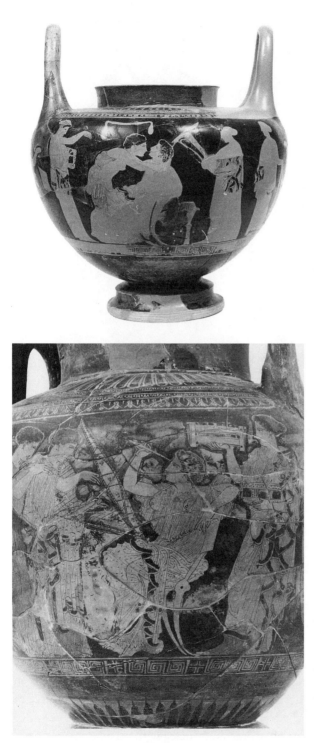

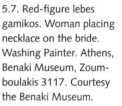

5.7. Red-figure lebes gamikos. Woman placing necklace on the bride. Washing Painter. Athens, Benaki Museum, Zoumboulakis 3117. Courtesy the Benaki Museum.

5.8. Red-figure lebes gamikos. Bride examining flute, while companion plays harp. Washing Painter. Athens, National Archaeological Museum 14791. Courtesy National Archaeological Museum.

5.9. Red-figure *lebes gamikos.* Crowning of a bride. Painter of Athens 1454. Athens, National Archaeological Museum 1454. Courtesy National Archaeological Museum.

woman is reaching around her neck, fastening a necklace. Other women surround them. Oakley and Sinos label the woman with her arms around the bride's neck an attendant;[72] that decision minimizes the implicit affection, but if we think of her as a friend, we might ask if there is anything more than an instrumental relationship between the two. The woman sitting might be thinking any number of thoughts, and the woman fastening the necklace looks at her, not at what she is doing. Moreover, the small distance between them seems highly charged. Another Attic red-figure lebes gamikos by the Washing Painter shows a bride examining a flute, while one of her companions plays the harp (fig. 5.8). One woman (far left) leans over another, with her arm over her shoulder; the softness in their eyes suggests that this is an intimate touch, although we cannot be sure. They occupy the centerpiece of the vase, which implies their importance.[73]

In this homosocial setting, women's intimacy with other women is literally "eroticized," for in the late fifth century, not only the bridal couple but also the bride with her companions are frequently accompanied by *erotes* or cupids. In the red-figure epinetron by the Eretria Painter (Younger fig. 6.6, with discussion),[74] Eros and Aphrodite accompany Harmonia, Peitho (Persuasion), and Kore (the Maiden); Harmonia seems to be the bride. On a second panel we have mortal women from myth bringing marriage gifts to Alcestis, lounging on her marriage bed. Oakley and Sinos describe the action on another Attic red-figure wedding vase (fig. 5.9) thus: "A woman holds the bride on her lap as she puts the bridal crown in place; Eros further links the two with the garlands he extends above them."[75]

How should we interpret these images? The poetry of Alcman and Sappho—though not a direct parallel because they are not Athenian and are not from the same time period as these images—suggests that love between women was part of some young women's experience at least before marriage (the choral performance in the case of Alcman and the lyrics in the case of Sappho indicate an erotic charge between marriageable girls).[76] For Athens, evidence from Artemis' sanctuary at Brauron demonstrates that girls danced nude in all-female groups as part of their transition to womanhood.[77] Interpretation of this material must be tentative, for we cannot say securely that women's initiations existed in Athens or that these rituals were homoerotic; like the creation of Sappho the schoolmistress, that reading may be based on assumptions about male patterns and must be viewed with suspicion. For my purposes here, it is not necessary to make such a claim. Women who had such youthful experience might have desired one another, though publicly and officially eroticized for a man.

The signs of physical affection in the women's tenderly leaning on one another or gazing into one another's eyes are discounted in a perspective focused on the future event (the marriage) but could be emphasized in one that puts homosocial relations at the center of analysis.[78] If we are justified in reading ahead to a heterosexual future not represented literally, then perhaps we can also read back to the homosocial/homoerotic past. These representations of marriage as a rite celebrated by women are not of course realistic and do not attempt to document daily life; on the vases, as in today's magazines, all brides are beautiful, elegant, and happy, whatever the prospects of happiness in their married life. As part of this romanticized view, however, women are imbued with an erotic aura; consequently, the representation seems to accept not only women's sense of community but also their physical and emotional intimacy.

Given the potentially homoerotic experiences of these women as girls, we should at least consider the possibility that the Greek women who received gifts of vases depicting women accompanied by Erotes (e.g., fig. 5.9) could have understood Eros/desire to have been linking the women. Since Eros was active in pederastic and other male homoerotic settings as well as in het-eroerotic scenes, he might have stood for desire between the women rep-resented as well as for the absent male.[79] To be sure, the lack of rigid dis-tinctions between homo- and hetero-relations for men might well not have applied to women. Nonetheless, if, as is claimed, object choice did not de-fine sexuality in Greek culture, then women might have experienced desire for one another at the same time that they married men.

To sum up, especially toward the end of the century, women on vases oc-cupy potentially eroticized spaces; the domestic scenes slide into the roman-tic register, sometimes embellished with Erotes. The pre-wedding rituals are similar to other interior scenes of women, but they center on the bride and her female attendants; affection and touch are shared among women. Al-though I am not saying that these women were "lesbians" or that we *know* that their relationships were erotic, an ancient Greek woman might have seen them as sensual at a minimum and perhaps as sexual. While these mo-tifs might also have simply been part of a male fantasy about women's lives, we can reclaim them now for different purposes. As a hermeneutic device, a homocentric perspective enables us to see new possibilities of women's pleasures.

CHORAL GROUPS

In working on women or, more particularly, female homoeroticism, you quickly find out that you cannot exclude mythological scenes, for no sharp line distinguishes the representation of mortal and immortal female; women (especially brides) are sometimes represented as goddesses or other personi-fications, as is the case in the vases from the Meidias Painter and his circle or in the epinetron of the Eretria Painter (described above).[80] In this late red-figure squat lekythos in the Manner of the Meidias Painter (fig. 5.10), the goddess and her companions are named (Kleopatra, Eunomia, Paidia, Peitho, Eudaimonia); Eros perches on Aphrodite's shoulder. But these could easily be mortal women in another setting; as Lucilla Burn points out, only their names indicate that they are personifications. The pose of the figures on the left—the one behind has her arm around the shoulder of the one in front of her, her hand touches her waist above her hip—suggests to me that they nonetheless found pleasure with one another.[81] Reference to a divinity may shed radiance on the mortal who accompanies her; at the same time, the

2. IM BRITISH MUSEUM

5.10. Red-figure squat lekythos. Manner of the Meidias Painter. London, British Museum E 697. Courtesy The Trustees of the British Museum.

goddess can hypostatize a particular event (marriage in this case). Thus, when we look at mythic marriages, such as that of Peleus and Thetis, or images of Aphrodite and her attendants, we may also be seeing a version of human existence (on Aphrodite, see Skinner's and Auanger's papers in this volume).

"Maenads" or "maenads and satyrs" are a common mythological subject for vase painting, and they are labeled as such in books and museums. What would the ancient viewer actually have seen, however? Would he or she assimilate maenad to woman or distinguish them from one another? The maenads have external signs of bacchic revelry or worship (usually a wand called a thyrsus, ivy branches, wild animals) but are not physiologically marked, as are satyrs, who have tails or horns or large, erect penises. Thus the viewer would have to decide how to categorize this female being. By identifying all females in the company of satyrs as maenads, scholars seem to imply that they are not human, but the lack of physiological marker indicates that the potential for maenadism is latent: any woman could become a maenad.[82]

Legends of Dionysos driving women mad (maenad comes from the word for mania), for instance, the Minyades and the daughters of Cadmus, until they accepted his worship, confirm this interpretation.[83] On a red-figure cup

5.11. Red-figure cup. Maenads. Makron. Berlin, Staatliche Museum 2290. © Bildarchiv Preussischer Kulturbesitz, Berlin. Courtesy Berlin, Staatliche Museen.

by Makron, the wild revelry of women alone is animated and powerful; their dance seems orgiastic, marked by their heads flung back in a manner typical of their dance (fig. 5.11).[84] As Lillian Lawler remarks, "The large groups of women dancers without men tend to be ecstatic." Some of the figures seem to her coquettish. Lawler hypothesizes that in the later period, the Bacchic revelry "acquired a strong measure of immorality and degenerated into a pleasure-spectacle."[85] Perhaps that was an element earlier on as well.

Other iconographic evidence suggests that Dionysiac worship was a time of women's intimacy: take, for instance, this black-figure neck-amphora by Amasis, which depicts women alone with the god (fig. 5.12).[86] They hold out a hare to Dionysos and look at him, but their arms are around one another, and their bodies practically merge. Women engaged in nightlong revels (*pannychides*) not only for Aphrodite but also for Dionysos; they were accused of licentiousness by Pentheus in Euripides' *Bacchae* (225, 236–237, 354). In that play, Agave and the women of Thebes are driven mad as punishment for rejecting the god Dionysos; they wander far from the city, leaving their women's work of weaving behind. Because they are outside his control, Pentheus thinks that the bacchants who follow Dionysos are holding orgies on the mountain. His suspicion that the maenads' all-night revels were sexual has some cultural currency, since it is shared to some extent by the shepherd,

5.12. Black-figure neck amphora. Dionysos and Maenads. Amasis Painters. Paris, Cabinet des Médailles 222. Courtesy Bibliothèque Nationale de France, Paris.

at least until he has first-hand knowledge. But there is no implication that men were present, so it was women's relationships to women that were at stake. It would of course be a dangerous mistake to take Pentheus' point of view, but it raises the possibility that the absence of limits meant that women expressed desire for other women on those occasions.

Maenads represent an extreme of women's behavior; they danced wildly, but many girls and women danced.[87] Both the followers of Dionysos and chorus members constitute a "guild" (*thiasos*) of women; furthermore, nude dancing was associated with female initiation at Brauron (see above, n74) and Sparta, which was also known for its female homoeroticism (Plutarch, *Lykurgus* 14–18). We can see that women's musical performance and dance presented another occasion for female intimacy, and its eroticization is underlined when the musicians are given the names of Muses, or handmaidens of Aphrodite.[88] The dance was primarily a women's institution that brought women together, sometimes overnight for weddings, the harvest, or a name day.[89] While there is nothing explicitly sexual about the stately dances often represented, literary sources indicate the possible erotic significance of dance. In Sappho's circle and Alcman's poems for maidens (*partheneia*), girls are clearly attractive to one another; graceful dancing accompanied song and was a source of erotic pleasure. For instance, Sappho's Fragment 94 portrays a woman telling Sappho how miserable she is at leaving her; Sappho replies with positive memories, one of which is the dance: "And there was / no sacred place / from which we were absent, / no grove, / . . . dance, / . . . sound . . . " (trans. Ellen Greene).[90] Fragment 96 praises the women of Sardis in Lydia for their dance, and another (L-P 16, not securely attributed to Sappho) praises Cretan women for the way they dance. Dance accompanied choral singing, and movement is specifically part of the attraction in the *Partheneia* of Alcman. The choral performance was an occasion for the demonstration of feminine charm and desirability, articulated in poetry, and women were not immune to it.

SHARING THE MANTLE

The Amasis vase discussed above (fig. 5.12) is similar to a series of sixth-century black-figure paintings of women sharing a mantle (fig. 5.13).[91] We do not know if this image referred to anything in reality or if it is an artistic convention. Gundel Koch-Harnack argues that this image and others like it are erotic in meaning; I would agree, but with some caveats.[92] On a black-figure pyxis (fig. 5.14), we see male couples practicing intercrural sex or preparing for it (fig. 5.14a), a male-female couple facing one another (fig. 5.14b), and a female couple facing one another under a mantle (fig. 5.14c).[93] In this case, the surrounding evidence powerfully supports reading the female couple as sexual as well. But pederasty and heterosexuality are not always appropriate models for decoding women's sexuality. The female homoeroticism I have teased out from the other representations was muted and mutual, with no sign of age or power differential between the participants, while there often is in male pederastic scenes. In this example, there is no visible disparity between the women sharing the mantle, whereas one can see elements of hierarchy in the other two sets of images (age or gender).

This distinction supports the notion that female homoeroticism did not share the dominant/submissive organization of heterosexuality and male-male pederasty. Thus, the fact that men represented as sharing a robe are engaging in sexual activity does not mean that women sharing a robe are always similarly occupied.[94] We may be justified in interpreting the joint cloaking as sexual when the members of the couple gaze at one another, gesture toward one another, touch one another, or hold a wreath, which was a

5.13. Black-figure lekythos. Two women sharing mantle. Pharos Painter. New York, Metropolitan Museum of Art 75.2.10. The Metropolitan Museum of Art, Gift of Samuel G. Ward, 1987.

sign of ancient courtship. But in others, where the women's gaze is averted, there is no contact between them, and in fact a great distance separates them (e.g., black-figure kylix, London B 409), we cannot assume there is an erotic connection simply on the basis of the mantle. The position of the figures often seems determined by aesthetic considerations, especially when the space between the women fills the entire panel or vase.

The motif of the mantle once again underlines the interpretive difficulties facing those of us engaged in this form of detective work. First, the difference in representation of men and women may be based on a difference in norms for representation; that is, it may be part of the overall tendency toward greater frankness about representing masculine sexuality. Representation and behavior are not easily separable, however, and the same code may shape both: we do not represent it because it is not done. Alternatively, lack of representation might mean that something is so taken for granted as not to need representing. In much the same way, we can only guess at what an outsider to our culture would assume on the basis of the nonrepresentation of some of our own everyday practices, say, toenail clipping. As viewers, then, it is hard to tell what are the reasons for absences.

5.14a, b, c. Black-figure pyxis. Mississippi University Museum
1972.3.72. Courtesy the University Museums, University of Mississippi Cultural Center.

Second, our own assumptions as viewers undoubtedly shape our interpretation. In contemporary western culture, unless Adrienne Rich's theory of the lesbian continuum is invoked, women's emotional intimacy is generally called friendship and distinguished from physical intimacy, which is called lesbianism.[95] This point of view demands that the sexual be visible for us to take a representation as erotic. Without explicit markers of sexuality (markers observable to the naked modern eye), it is easy to interpret these simply as representations of women's social ties instead of seeing desire as a component of that friendship. It bears repeating that the same level of "proof" is not required for the interpretation, say, of representations of Ganymede and Zeus or for heterosexual couples.[96] Obviously, one needs a lot more evidence to convince people of something they do not already believe exists.

By placing these images in the context of the earlier scenes (the women with Erotes, the wedding vases, the musicians), we can hypothesize a relation between the affection, which is represented, and its more sexual expression, which is not. On the other hand, modern social mores may also be leading me to overemphasize the sexual or the erotic and to assume either that the physical dimension is always present (though literally absent) or that a relationship is insignificant without the sexual dimension. These are obviously very difficult issues; by reiterating the ambiguity, I hope at least to minimize the risk of overinterpreting or underinterpreting.

SOCIAL CLASS AND EROTICISM

The line of mortal/immortal is not the only permeable boundary that makes interpretation difficult; it is similarly unclear whether the women depicted are servants/slaves or free women and whether or not they are professional sex workers. The discursive categories of seclusion and women's sphere, from which I began, operate in conjunction with the division of women into the categories of "respectable" and, by inference, not respectable.[97] The term "respectable" in descriptions of vase painting appears to denote the "married or the unmarried daughters of Athenian citizens," who were allegedly secluded in the private domain and thus not represented in certain ways, for example, at symposia or nude; contrariwise, certain activities, like wool working, are presumed to denote respectability.[98]

The debate about the latter is telling: women's weaving or spinning depicted on vases has been seen by some as a sign that they were housewives, while others argue that gender, not respectability, was at issue in the representation and that there were spinning *hetairai*.[99] Not only is the word "respectable" circular, based on assumptions about what Athenian women of the citizen class did or did not do and then using that attribution to define what they could do, but it also makes the biased assumption that no professional sex workers were respectable in antiquity. The ancients, however, distinguished between the courtesan (*hetaira*) and the common prostitute (*pornê*), disturbing a too-easy binary organization of respectability, though it is difficult to pin down the meaning of *hetaira* and what it includes.[100] Finally, the labeling practice ironically distinguishes *hetairai* from women, but sex work does not make prostitutes any the less women; on the contrary, their gender is a prerequisite of the job.[101]

The secondary literature tends to assume that all overtly eroticized women in the vase paintings were *hetairai* and that they were heterosexual. The term *hetaira* is parallel to the male friend or companion (*hetairos*);[102] and *hetairai* might also have been friends or women who desired other women.[103] In discussions of the age of Sappho's companions, for instance, scholars note that she sometimes calls them *hetairai* (Fr. 96.6; *Suda* 107 = T 2 Loeb) instead of girls.[104] The term *hetaira* is very close to *hetairistria,* a word we hear only in Plato's *Symposion* 191e (though it is later used by Lucian in the *Dialogue of the Courtesans* 5 [see Haley's essay in this volume]). When the symposiasts are speaking of love, Aristophanes recounts a myth to explain why some men desire only men, some women desire only women, while others desire members of the "opposite" sex. *Hetairistriai* are those who seek only women as partners. The postmodern discussion of this passage in Plato has tended to focus on whether or not the gender of the sexual object defined an identity in antiquity. Some, such as Brooten, say that it must have; others, such as Halperin, discount the Aristophanes passage as historical evidence, on the grounds that it is a myth.[105] The myth, however, at least reveals that it was conceivable to the Greeks that sexual object choice would define a kind of person; more interesting to me is the possibility that the word suggests an association between the *hetaira* and such women. The masculine form of the word for companion indicates closeness between men; might the feminine form of the word not similarly suggest closeness between women as well as the sale of sexual services to men?

When looking at cups representing women with men at the symposion, a setting for elite male drinking, entertainment, and sexual activity, we may for the most part correctly assume that they were prostitutes or *hetairai,* because citizen-class Athenian women reputedly did not attend symposia and almost certainly would not have been represented in amorous poses.[106]

However, some vases show women alone at what seems to be a symposion. Scholars differ as to whether these figures are to be viewed as *hetairai*, because they are depicted as nude and drinking at the symposion, or simply as any women at a symposion of their own.[107] The vases of course might not represent anything that actually took place but may have been an ironic inversion of a men's symposion.[108] After all, in Aristophanes' comedy, *Ecclesiazousae*, females are depicted running the city, but that does not mean that they ever did so; rather, the very idea was so ludicrous as to be a joke.

If, however, women (whether *hetairai* or not) did indeed hold their own symposia, they might well have been erotic partners for one another, as men and boys were. In his section entitled "Lesbian Copulation," Kilmer cites some of these vases and says both that they represent women's symposia and that they are not erotic. He hypothesizes that the women are nude because "most males find the naked female body attractive to look at."[109] But the cup by Oltos (fig. 5.15) represents two women, one with a double pipe, one extending a kylix (flat cup) and holding a skyphos (a tall cup), with their legs intertwined, which seems to be a sign of intimacy and evidence of an erotic charge between them.[110] The shoulder of a red-figure hydria by Phintias (fig. 5.16) depicts two young women naked from the waist up; they play *kottabos*, a game that involves flicking drops of wine from the cup. The intrusion of a man's name in the inscription ("this is for you, Euthymides") may suggest that their nudity is for the male gaze, but it is just as possibly a joke at the expense of another vase painter, Euthymides.[111]

The assumption that nudity always signifies "lack of respectability" for women is countered by a series of vases representing the bride bathing.[112] But there are also other kinds of scenes of women bathing or preparing to bathe. Are we to assume that these women were *hetairai* on the basis of their nudity? Or "respectable" given the evidence of nude brides? I incline to the latter view; if they are shown exclusively in the company of other women, there would be no male spectator and therefore no impropriety. Some might object that the male spectator would be supplied by the viewer of the vase, if that were a man. We do not need to hypothesize a male viewer in all cases, however, especially in the case of the vase shapes intended for women's use (for instance, the hydria, fig. 5.16). Thus, some of these images were undoubtedly designed with women in mind as the potential viewer.

The number of representations of women bathing increased in the late fifth century.[113] Are such scenes, like the wedding pictures, sometimes (always) of erotic interest? If so, whose desire is elicited? Kilmer asserts both that female nudity is aimed at male satisfaction (cited above) and that "lesbian

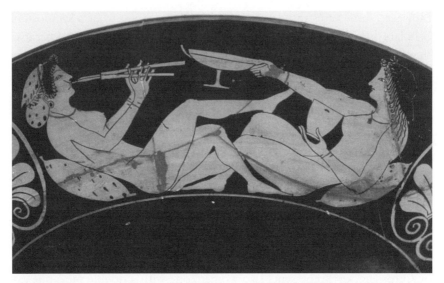

5.15. Red-figure cup. Women's symposion. Oltos. Madrid, Museo Arqueológico Nacional 11.267. Courtesy Archivo Fotográfico. Museo Arqueológico Nacional.

5.16. Red-figure hydria. Women's symposion. Phintias. Munich 2421. Courtesy Staatliche Antikensamlungen und Glyptothek München. Photograph: Keppermann.

5.17. Red-figure amphora. Women bathing. Andokides. Paris, Louvre F 203. Courtesy Musée du Louvre.

implications are common in bathing scenes" (cf. males in *palaistra*).[114] Which is it? Of a red-figure amphora by Andokides (fig. 5.17), he says,

> The nudity of the women is natural for bathers but also has a sexual aspect. The somewhat phallic fish, the unusual shape of the sakkos and the little oil-jar from which one woman pours, all have mild sexual implications; but the overall impression gives no specific indication that the women plan sexual activity among themselves.[115]

Kilmer seems to suggest that the aura of sexuality is aimed at men. But it could emanate from and be directed at the women depicted in the scene; they seem content with themselves. There is no internal male audience, and there is no reason to hypothesize a male viewer, given that the shape of the vase does not designate it as for one gender or the other. We can see tenderness in the way the standing woman on the right leans over and reaches out to the swimmer, and care in the woman who is pouring oil on the swimmer. The reverse side shows Amazons, one on horseback, half smiling at another, armed with a lance, who looks at her and reaches toward her. In this case, as in so many, the visual evidence requires interpretation.

If the objects conjured up a space known to have homoerotic connotations (as the gymnasium did for men), then the viewer might have provided that context, as we could for objects in our own culture.[116] Again, we must ask who was that viewer. The so-called lesbian implications in the scene could have been displayed for the delectation of a male audience, as in the case of modern pornography.[117] But there was not a single audience or even one sort of audience, and male and female audiences might have had different ways of looking at the same object.[118] By hypothesizing a female spectator, we can avoid assuming that women are always represented as fetish objects for men. My point is that it does not have to be either/or but might have been read by men and women for their own pleasure.

While we have only a few scenes of women swimming, there are many scenes of women bathing in a courtyard at home or dressing. These might or might not have had an erotic effect and might or might not be homoerotic. We can sometimes use the context provided by other sections of a pot to help define an ambiguous image. For instance, the interior of this cup by Douris showing two women (or a woman and a girl?) "disrobing" (fig. 5.18 I) seems erotic because they are nude and one woman is looking over her shoulder at the other. That interpretation is supported by the images on the outside of the cup (fig. 18a, b). Side a depicts two pairs of youths and women, and one pair of two females (girl and woman?), one presenting a fillet to the other. The erotic potential seems clear, given the combination of couples, nudity, and gaze. The fillet might be a gift suggesting courtship.[119] Side b shows a woman with a plemochoe, facing a beardless youth, who holds a lyre; another woman faces them; two women surround a boy with a lyre. Three of the women and one man hold flowers. Erotic *and* homoerotic?

The ambiguity in such an exegesis is more problematic in another example that Kilmer includes in this category, a red-figure cup from a painter in the Pezzino group, in which a seated nude woman cleans her boot; a standing nude woman faces her with alabastron and cloak over her arm. Kilmer finds "lesbian implications" in the women's nakedness and their obvious pubic hair and large breasts. The vases more typically represent small breasts, and the large breasts on the standing woman seem awkward (they are represented frontally, while she is turned in profile). Since breasts were eroticized in antiquity, his interpretation seems convincing. Kilmer argues in addition that certain of the vase shapes were associated with sexual activity, notably, the perfume jar or alabastron, which is also a frequent accompaniment of women in the scenes of adornment. His interpretation of the objects that the women carry ("the slender alabastos, with the oil it contains,

5.18 I, a, b. Red-figure cup. (I) Interior. Women dressing; (a) pairs of youths and women, two women together; (b) women and youth, woman and boy. Douris. New York, Metropolitan Museum 23.160.54.

could be used as a penis substitute, supplying its own lubricant") is interesting, though of course not conclusive and may be a mistaken result of assimilating female to male homoeroticism, since it is not clear why women with other women would require a lubricant any more than would women with men.[120] The presence of this scene on a cup most likely to be used by men, as well as the outside of the cup, which contains scenes of a komos and of Dionysos with satyrs and maenads, suggests that the representation of the internal implied homoeroticism was intended for a male audience.

WHEN IS A DILDO NOT A DILDO?

Vases combining bathing women and representations of male genitals would seem to be more explicitly sexual. Given the phallocentric nature of Greek cult, however, images of the genitals were not necessarily intended as exclusively erotic and could symbolize fertility. We are again confronted with the extent to which an editor's or author's labeling practices determine our response. Some phallic objects on these vases are very large, even gargantuan; scholars typically label these "phalluses" and relate them to ritual. Some smaller phallic objects are called *olisboi* (or dildos), and scholars relate them to erotic practices.[121] In short, a decision has to be made as to how to contextualize and interpret these pictures, whether to consider an object a dildo or a phallus. A red-figure *pelikê* shows a woman holding an *olisbos* (?), stepping into a basket full of phalluslike objects with eyes. It is not entirely clear what she is meant to be doing, nor whether the objects are ritual or erotic in import. Keuls labels this "Hetaera leaps into basket full of dildos."[122] Why is this a *hetaira*? Why is she leaping into the basket? Keuls' label implies joy or sexual desire with "leaps"; the assumption that it is a *hetaira* with dildos removes the image from domestic or ritual contexts. Dover notes the ambiguity, labeling it "a woman with a basket full of olisboi or phalloi," but Angelika Dierichs takes the opposite tack to Keuls and simply labels them "künstlichen Phallen."[123] Significant for an erotic reading, the woman holds a dildo or phallus in one hand as she grips the basket with another.

Further, in ancient Greek religion, the erotic and the ritual did not occupy distinct spheres; thus, even if these are phalluses, and this is a representation of ritual, that does not exclude an erotic component. For instance, this red-figure pelikê depicts a woman sprinkling upright phallic objects (phallus plants?) (fig. 5.19) emerging from the ground;[124] it may refer to the Haloa, a ritual celebrated by women to encourage the growth of wheat, which became an all-night banquet with a reputation for indecency. At the feast held in honor of Demeter and Dionysos, women carried models of male and

5.19. Red-figure pelikê. Woman watering penis plants. Hasselman Painter. London, British Museum E 819. Courtesy The Trustees of the British Museum.

5.20. Red-figure cup. Women dancing at an erect phallus. Apollodorus. Rome, Villa Giulia 50404. Courtesy Soprintendenza Archeologica per l'Etruria Meridionale.

female genitalia, indulged in obscene language, and exchanged ritual insults. Cakes in the shape of male and female sex organs were also on the table.[125] Another red-figure cup (fig. 5.20) that shows two women dancing around an erect phallus may also refer either to a religious occasion or to a simple dance with a naked woman and a clothed one.[126] I would suggest that the image can be read as erotic: not only is the phallus inscribed "*kalê*" (feminine for "beautiful") but the foot of the clothed woman points directly at the genitals of the naked woman, drawing attention to them. Almost touching her, she may intend to stimulate her dance partner. Literary evidence seems to suggest that feet arouse desire; in Sappho's Fragment 16, Helen's walk reminds the speaker of Anaktoria. There are references to feet in Fragment 39 as well as Fragment 57 (here we can compare Alkaios Fragment 130B); in what is usually taken as a sexual joke, Fragment 110 draws attention to the size of the bridegroom's feet. Sandals are associated with sexual scenes, where they seem to increase sexual pleasure through an addition of aggression; they are also associated with wedding scenes. It is not clear what they mean in the latter, but the combination with the connotations in the erotic vases leads me to think that they are suggestive of heightened sexual pleasure there as well.[127]

Even if we are sure that we are looking at a dildo and not a phallus, there is considerable debate as to what the object signifies. Although the dildo does not necessarily denote female homoeroticism, these two examples seem pertinent. First, the two sides of a cup by the Pedieus Painter (fig. 5.21) suggest the confluence of bathing and homoerotic use of the dildo.[128] On one side are three naked women bathing at a basin, one with her hands already in it, the other two running toward her; the middle figure is looking back at the woman behind her. On the reverse side, there is a more fanciful scene with perhaps humorous intent: two naked women are shown with dildos on the wall and a phallus bird (a bird with a phallus head) in between them.[129] The women hold out their hands to one another and are playful (given the missing piece, it is difficult to be sure what the figure on the right is doing with her feet). They seem to show keen interest in one another and are engaged in energetic action, which supports the notion that this is a scene of homoerotic sexuality. Second, another vase shows several women using several dildos on one side, and on the other, at least one woman with a strap-on dildo approaching another woman leaning over a pillow from the rear (fig. 5.22). This is the only example where the dildo is undoubtedly employed in a homoerotic, as opposed to heterosexual or autoerotic, setting.[130] We can contrast this with the presence of a double-headed dildo hanging on the wall on a Boston kantharos (fig. 5.23); in the scene depicted, the sexual

5.21a, b. Red-figure cup. Women at bath with dildos. Pedieus Painter. Paris, Louvre G 14. Courtesy Musée du Louvre.

5.22. Red-figure cup. Women with dildos. Near Epiktetos. Once Rome, Castellani. Courtesy Martin Kilmer, Vicky Bennet. Drawing: Christine Ingersoll, after Vicky Bennet, in Martin Kilmer, *Greek Erotica on Attic Red-Figure Vases.*

5.23. Red-figure kantharos. Nikosthenes Painter. Boston, Museum of Fine Arts 95.61. Catharine Page Perkins Fund. Courtesy, Museum of Fine Arts, Boston. All rights reserved. Reproduced with permission. © 2000 Museum of Fine Arts, Boston.

encounters are all heterosexual, but the dildo suggests that other permutations and combinations might follow, whether of men with men, or women with women, who desire mutual penetration.[131]

But what does it mean that we find the dildo represented on vases? First, a caveat: dildos are not numerous, especially in comparison with the number of scenes of women dressing or of the wedding. The question is, "Why are they there at all?" Given the male dominance of ancient Athenian culture, we cannot overlook the probability that it was for male pleasure. Frontisi-Ducroux agrees with those who find the intrusion of the *olisbos* an emblem of the masculine and supportive of male fantasies.[132] Johns reiterates the notion that this play with dildos is for the entertainment of men, since "there is no need for such equipment between female lovers, though most men would like to think there is."[133] Marcadé allows that "the same instrument could be used for relations between women, but female homosexuality does not seem to have been very widespread in Greece."[134] Kilmer includes the dildo images in his section on lesbian copulation but then reiterates the notion that the dildo and any lesbian implications are there for the pleasure of male fantasy. This line of reasoning is based on the assumption that men would find it delightful that women use dildos. In this view, the dildo does not suggest women's ability to find sexual pleasure apart from men but rather women's excessive sexual desire and dependence on some form of phallic implement.[135] The critics focus not on the replaceability of the man but on the presence of the imitation. To these critics, this group of vases, like the image of women symposiasts toasting a man's name, domesticates images of women without men, placing them under the sign of masculinity.

But it arguably works another way as well: perhaps these women do not want a *man* (a male human being socialized into masculinity) at all but do want the pleasure of penetration. The dildo can then suggest women's desire for other women. The vase that shows a woman with a dildo strapped on (extreme right, fig. 5.22) might represent a hermaphrodite with penis and breasts, but the size and form of the "penis" and the presence of other women with dildos make that unlikely. The recurring image of woman/women with dildo(s), the representation of at least one double-headed dildo, and this strap-on dildo taken together make it plausible that the dildo was used to give women pleasure, even if its representation also entertained men.[136] In these vases, we have to admit that the gap is as prominent as either object or body, leaving us still having to fill in the blank from our ideologically laden imaginations.

The question of the masculinity of the dildo reminds me of the sexuality debates in feminism. Nowadays, the association of dildo with lesbian sex seems obvious, but it has been problematic. Like scholars in art history, feminists who criticize the use of the dildo tend to see it as reproducing and reinscribing heterosexual norms. Those who defend the dildo in theoretical terms stress its detachability and separation from economic and social masculinity, as well as its suitability for parodic inversion of gender conformity. The antidildo position is generally associated with the woman-identified woman, radical feminist, separatist branch of lesbianism, while the prodildo position is usually associated with the pro-sex, anti-censorship, butch/femme, s/m supporting wing of "lesbian"ism.[137] The sexuality debates, the pornography debates, and internal fights within feminism might jokingly be said to be based on the lowly dildo. Those who dismiss the dildo in these vases as an invasion of male sexuality, or the effect of male fantasy, ignore the difference between the dildo and penis: there is no man attached to the former. In some sense, the dildo stands for women's sexual agency and therefore for the possibility of the pleasure of penetration without male domination. It also destabilizes a single lesbian identity, thus perhaps causing a new form of "panic" about sex/gender definition.[138]

SEXUALLY EXPLICIT?

All this is still conjectural. The line between homosocial and homoerotic is hard to draw, and whatever we have that is called explicit is still very much in the eye of the beholder (and clearly disproportionate to the number of images of same-sex male activity). This early plate from Thera depicts two women, one with her hand under the chin of the other, and they exchange a wreath (fig. 5.24).[139] This positioning recalls male homoerotic scenes in which the hand under the chin and the exchange of wreaths are common.[140] Wreaths are present in heterosexual wedding scenes as well. The double repertory for the gesture and the object obviates some of the danger in moving from male to female realms. While we cannot always argue from one to the other (given the differences between male and female experience, especially sexual experience), in this case, there are sufficient grounds for doing so: the wreath in particular is shown in male and female spheres. But as in the case of the shared cloaks, there are also significant distinctions between the women in this pose and the male prototypes. In the latter, there is a very clear age distinction (Dover compares it to two images of men and boys), but there is no such clear distinction between the women on the basis of size or clothing.[141]

5.24. Plate. Women with wreaths. Thera, Thera Museum. CE 34.
Courtesy Deutsches Archäologisches Institut, Athen, Neg. 1100.

Keuls, Brooten, and Petersen also cite a late Apulian pelikê, which corre-
lates garlands and affectionate touch and, if interpreted in the light of comparable heterosexual pairs, would seem erotic. One woman is standing holding a wreath, and a seated woman, holding another wreath, reaches up to
touch her breast. They look into one another's eyes. The gesture in the direction of the breast seems erotic, given conventional emphasis on the breast
in heterosexual scenes, and the mutual gaze supports that interpretation.[142]

Two women, one standing, one crouching; one hand of the crouching
woman is on the standing woman's thigh, the other at her crotch. Is it an example of mutual stimulation, "fingering," and titillation, or of delousing or
depilation (fig. 5.25)?[143] The glosses on this red-figure cup reveal the problems we face when we try to decode female sexuality from the past. Dietrich
von Bothmer views this as the only lesbian scene from the entire corpus of
vases to the best of his knowledge.[144] Others dismiss that interpretation on
the grounds of that very uniqueness; for instance, John Boardman adds this
comment to the image: "Two Hetaerae. This curious cup treats a thoroughly
unusual theme. A naked girl stands holding a bowl which probably contains

perfumed water or oil. Another girl, also naked and on her knees, is touching her, probably anointing her with perfume. So this cup is one of those depicting hetaerae preparing for the *komos*, though the chosen theme is unique. In fact, vase painters usually show hetaerae at their bath or at symposia in the company of men. It is not likely that this scene depicts an erotic relationship between the women, since there are no examples of this in Attic vase painting, although such things must have occurred often in a society where the segregation of the sexes was so rigid." [145] Frontisi-Ducroux strongly believes that the scene shows depilation, but if it is depilation (see above, n43), it may also be erotic. As Sutton says, the two are not mutually exclusive:

> Since all of these acts could be performed without assistance, it is not impossible to suggest some erotic overtones, though there is nothing to suggest arousal in the attitude of either woman. The scene is therefore "soft-core" pornography, like the bathing scenes of the period.[146]

Boardman's caption reveals how quickly assumptions change and how those assumptions shape our viewing. What seems "obvious" depends on your view of what is sexual and what is pleasure. Given how socially constructed that is, nothing is obvious any more.

Now is the time to pull the rabbit out of the hat, the one clear example that only I have found. Unfortunately for the magician, I do not have a rabbit. If we define the sexually explicit as entailing genital activity, there is really nothing to see when women are alone with women. This should sound familiar to readers who have been involved in women's studies research, for that is often the view of women's sexuality per se. One question that used to be asked of lesbians was (and is), "But what do you do in bed?" The standard of sexually explicit, genitally focused, behavior is not maintained for heterosexual identity, however, and maintaining it leads to the continued invisibility of women's homoeroticism.

Throughout this essay I have been raising questions about the effect of the lenses we use to view antiquity. As a result, it is difficult to write a traditional conclusion. Let me just state what I have found. First, the vase painters endow women's homosocial world with affection, which is sometimes physically expressed, especially toward the end of the fifth century. Women in their spaces are eroticized, and the homosocial setting (the wedding scene in particular) is suffused with eroticism, which we may take as shared among the women. Second, there are more erotically explicit representations of women in the bath, with dildos, and touching one another.

It is clear from the imagery we have seen that you cannot understand

5.25. Red-figure cup. Apollodorus. Tarquinia. Photograph: Martin Kilmer, *Greek Erotica on Attic Red-Figure Vases.*

women's erotic lives simply on the model of men's lives, for there is no consistent pattern of age or status differences between these representations of women. Similarly, there do not seem to be any consistent role distinctions between the women. Nonetheless, comparisons with male-male relations and heterosexual relations may help us to detect what were signs of courtship and desire in ancient Greece. I have been trying to make women's relations to women in ancient Greece more salient and to interrupt the glib assumptions that "though women's eroticism was not much represented, it can be assumed to be analogous to men's." Women's homoeroticism was sometimes represented, if you have eyes to see, and in ways substantially different from the eroticism characteristic of men's lives.

The invisibility of lesbians and gay men is no longer the issue that it once was, but excluding the possibility that these vases represented same-sex desire among women reinscribes that invisibility. When students refuse even to entertain an erotic interpretation of a relationship between women, it is often a sign of homophobic resistance. That resistance may be a factor in the scholarship as well and certainly may be an (unintended) effect of the scholarly silence. There are consequences to the way we frame our studies, in particular whether we deny or stress the continuity of lesbian experience. To emphasize the continuity of lesbianism risks essentializing and fixing a category by stripping it of differences across time and space; to deny the similarity between present and past may be to deny a bit of history that could empower those struggling for rights and representation in the present. These depictions of women's lives taken together show a wide range of modes and sites for the expression of women's desire, although neither the women represented nor the women viewing them would have thought of themselves as "lesbians." Our viewing them may constitute a kind of lesbian continuum: what we see in them can be constructive in the present as well as instructive about the past.

NOTES

1. This essay has been years in the making. Thanks to Hamilton College, especially President Gene Tobin and Dean Bobby Fong, for their generous research support during my two leave years; to colleagues, especially Paula Schwartz and Tracey Jean Boisseau, at the Five Colleges Women's Studies Research Center, where I began this research; to the Smith College Art Library; to Lydia Hamessley, Catie Mihalopoulos, Maureen Miller, and Peter Rabinowitz for careful readings of many drafts; to Françoise Frontisi-Ducroux for her honest disagreement with an earlier version; and to François Lissarrague for his encouragement and support. Donna Kurtz, Thomas Mannack, and Florence Maskell at the Beazley Archive; Lucilla Burn, Keith Lowe, and Roger Flint at the British Museum; and Martine Denoyelle, Marianne Hamiaux, and Alexandra Kardianou at the Musée du Louvre were all extremely kind, as were Sandra Fritz and Rebecca Akhan at the Metropolitan Museum of Art, Claire Hills-Nova at the Institute of Fine Arts, and Rebecka Lindau at New York University. Librarians Glynis Asu, Lynn Mayo, Kristin Strohmeyer, and Joan Wolek at Hamilton College have been unfailingly helpful. Their support makes research at a small liberal arts college possible. Keith DeVries generously shared relevant pages of his manuscript with me. For answering many questions, I thank Joan Connelly, Larissa Bonfante, Natalie Kampen, H. Alan Shapiro, Rebecca Sinos, Christiane Sourvinou-Inwood, Robert Sutton, and especially Martin Kilmer and Dietrich von Bothmer, who assisted me in tracking down images. Finally, research assistants Sascha Arbouet, Adinah Bradberry, Martin Brooks, and Rebecca Libed have helped in innumerable ways. Versions of this article were presented at the meetings of the American Philological Association, at Loyola University of Chicago, Manchester University, University of Hartford, and Hamilton College.

2. The title of David Gill's article, "Art and vases vs. craft and pots," *Antiquity* 67 (1993): 452–455, indicates the status implied in the words vase and pot.

3. For a strong statement, see Tom Rasmussen and Nigel Spivey, eds., *Looking at Greek Vases* (Cambridge: Cambridge UP, 1991) xi: "Greek vases are important. Even in a culture

such as our own, enslaved to the lords of cash and quick profit, the importance of Greek vases can be measured in terms of the millions of dollars, pounds, and yen annually expended in their trade. . . . Men go to jail for the sake of Greek vases; academic careers are constructed on expertise in Greek vases; and exceptional students of Greek vases may receive knighthoods."

4. *Artful Crafts: Ancient Greek Silverware and Pottery* (Oxford: Oxford UP, 1994) 4n15; Rasmussen and Spivey, *Looking* xiii, agree. Lucilla Burn, *The Meidias Painter* (Oxford: Oxford UP, 1987) 1, notes d'Hancarville's importance in recognizing the "beauty and the technical accomplishment of Greek vase painting."

5. Jean-Pierre Vernant, "Preface," in Claude Bérard et al., eds., Deborah Lyons, trans., *A City of Images: Iconography and Society in Ancient Greece* (Princeton: Princeton UP, 1989) 7.

6. For the difference between the art historical and the semiotic approaches, see the contributions of Martin Robertson and Mary Beard, "Adopting an Approach I and II," in Tom Rasmussen and Nigel Spivey, eds., *Looking at Greek Vases* (Cambridge: Cambridge UP, 1991) 1–35.

7. For a detailed study of technique, see Joseph Veach Noble, *The Techniques of Painted Attic Pottery*, rev. ed. (New York: Thames and Hudson, 1988). At a later date, I hope to study the white *lekythoi*, mostly funerary objects, which constitute an important corpus of their own. Though these have many images of women, they present substantially different formal issues than the red-figure vases.

8. What did women drink from? Was it the deeper *skyphos*, or did they actually use the flat kylix as well? Two women on an Attic red-figure *amphora*, attributed to the Flying-Angel Painter by Robert Guy, are drunk. One holds a pitcher, the other, a skyphos. They embrace or hold one another up. See Bernadette Brooten, *Love between Women: Early Christian Responses to Female Homoeroticism* (Chicago: U of Chicago P, 1996) fig. 4, discussion 58; Michael Padgett, "The Workshop of the Syleus Sequence: A Wider Circle," in John H. Oakley, William D. E. Coulson, and Olga Palagia, eds., *Athenian Potters and Painters,* (Oxford: Oxford UP 1997) 216–218nn52–56, thinks they are *hetairai* in "sisterly comradery."

9. For a good summary, see Christiane Bron and François Lissarrague, "Looking at the Vase," in Claude Bérard et al., Deborah Lyons, trans., *A City of Images: Iconography and Society in Ancient Greece* (Princeton: Princeton UP, 1989) 11–21; Gisela Richter and Marjorie J. Milne, *Shapes and Names of Athenian Vases* (New York: Metropolitan Museum of Art, 1935). Victoria Sabetai, "Aspects of Nuptial and Genre Imagery in Fifth-Century Athens: Issues of Interpretation and Methodology," in John H. Oakley, William D. E. Coulson, and Olga Palagia, eds., *Athenian Potters and Painters* (Oxford: Oxford UP, 1997) 320, takes the presence of the loutrophoros on a vase as an allusion to the wedding preparations. For differences between loutrophoroi used for funerals or weddings, as well as the lebetes gamikoi, see Victoria Sabetai, "The Washing Painter: A Contribution to the Wedding and Genre Iconography in the Second Half of the Fifth-Century B.C." 2 vols. (Dissertation, U of Cincinnati, 1995). On lebetes gamikoi, see also Marina Sgourou, "Attic Lebetes Gamikoi" (Dissertation, U of North Carolina at Chapel Hill, 1995).

10. On the often-used mistress and maid categories as misnomers, see Joan Reilly, "Many Brides: 'Mistress and Maid' on Athenian Lekythoi," *Hesperia* 58 (1989): 411–444.

11. Donna Kurtz and John Boardman, "Booners," in *Greek Vases in the J. Paul Getty Museum*, vol. 3 (Malibu, CA: J. Paul Getty Museum, 1986) 35–70, publish many of the vases in ques-

tion. M. C. Miller, "The Parasol: An Oriental Status-Symbol in Late Archaic and Classical Athens," *Journal of Hellenic Studies* 112 (1992): 91–105, sums up the debate: this is a male revel, a male crossdressing ritual, or a female ritual crossdressing. Because it is Asian in origin, the parasol is also sometimes taken as an emblem not of femininity but of status. Leslie Kurke, "The Politics of ἀβροσύνη" *Classical Antiquity* 11 (1992): 91–170, reads the figures as mature men celebrating "aristocratic luxury" (97). She notes pointedly: "We seem determined to read these costumes as somehow effeminate. What motivates this modern trend?" (98).

12. On conventions for representing gender, see K. J. Dover, *Greek Homosexuality* (New York: Vintage, 1978) 68–73; Martin Kilmer, *Greek Erotica on Attic Red-Figure Vases* (London: Duckworth, 1993) 180–186; and Rehak's essay (this volume).

13. John Clarke, *Looking at Lovemaking: Constructions of Sexuality in Roman Art 100 B.C.–A.D. 250* (Berkeley: U of California P) 36; see his discussion at 35–36, 285nn28, 29, 30.

14. Red-figure hydria, Milan C 278, attributed to the Leningrad Painter; Beazley *ARV* 571.73; Bérard et al., *City of Images* 10, fig. 1.

15. Keith DeVries shared his opinion that there were other women potters and painters in the discussion after this paper was delivered at the American Philological Association meetings in 1997; J. D. Beazley, "Potter and Painter in Ancient Athens," *Proceedings of the British Academy* 30 (1946): 1–43, collects three pots that include female figures; Kilmer, *Greek Erotica* 197n18, points out that the evidence is weak in either direction; Lisa C. Nevett, *House and Society in the Ancient Greek World* (Cambridge: Cambridge UP, 1999) 11, similarly concludes that women painters were rare. Catie Mihalopoulos argues in her dissertation, "Images of Women and Concepts of Popular Culture in Classical Athens: 450–400 B.C.," Dissertation, U of Southern California, 2001, that both the Washing Painter and the Eretria Painter were women (private correspondence, 2/18/01).

16. François Lissarrague, "Figures of Women," in *A History of Women in the West*, Vol. 1. *From Ancient Goddesses to Christian Saints*, ed. Pauline Schmitt Pantel, trans. Arthur Goldhammer. General eds. Georges Duby and Michelle Perrot (Cambridge, MA: Belknap P of Harvard UP, 1992) 229; cf. Eva Keuls, *The Reign of the Phallus: Sexual Politics in Ancient Athens* (New York: Harper and Row, 1985) 117–118, who affirms the "male conceptual framework; the women's pots were made and decorated by men. . . ."

17. Claude Bérard, "The Order of Women," in Claude Bérard et al., eds., Deborah Lyons, trans., *A City of Images: Iconography and Society in Ancient Greece* (Princeton: Princeton UP, 1989) 89; cf. Keuls, *Reign of the Phallus* 118.

18. As Robert Sutton, "Pornography and Persuasion on Attic Pottery," in Amy Richlin, ed., *Pornography and Representation in Greece and Rome* (New York: Oxford UP, 1992) 5, among others, points out.

19. Jeffrey Henderson, *The Maculate Muse: Obscene Language in Attic Comedy*, 2nd ed. (New York: Oxford UP, 1991) 33, 34–35, makes this point in comparing tragedy and pottery.

20. John J. Winkler, "The Ephebes' Song: *Tragôidia* and *Polis*," in *Nothing to Do with Dionysos: Athenian Drama in Its Social Context*, ed. John J. Winkler and Froma I. Zeitlin (Princeton: Princeton UP, 1990) 39n58, makes use of the concept of notional audience for tragedy (male though women might have been present); he introduces the notion of double consciousness in *Constraints of Desire: The Anthropology of Sex and Gender in Ancient Greece* (New York: Routledge, 1990) to explain the poetry of Sappho.

Lauren Petersen, "Divided Consciousness and Female Companionship: Reconstructing

Female Subjectivity on Greek Vases," *Arethusa* 30 (1997): 36, admits the difficulty of seeing a female point of view but argues that "women could have variously experienced their own subjectivity and sexuality within the constructs of patriarchy." Cf. Eva Stehle and Amy Day, "Women Looking at Women: Women's Ritual and Temple Sculpture," in Natalie Kampen, ed., *Sexuality in Ancient Art* (Cambridge: Cambridge UP, 1996) 101–116. In their consideration of monumental art, which is public and therefore different from the pottery, they make the point that it is a "serious distortion" to treat the mythic narratives as if they presented "only this single stable meaning, for this is tantamount to asserting that all viewers always looked only from a universalizing hegemonic male perspective" (101). Françoise Frontisi-Ducroux, "Eros, Desire, and the Gaze," in Natalie Kampen, ed., *Sexuality in Ancient Art* (Cambridge: Cambridge UP, 1996) 94–95, argues, however, that only men had both desire and the gaze.

21. Ellen Reeder, ed. *Pandora: Women in Classical Greece* (Baltimore: Walters Gallery, 1995) 13, is more optimistic than I would be about the extent to which we can "hear the voice of ancient Greek women." But as she points out, we do have "objects that women dedicated in sanctuaries, and we have works of art that were intentionally created to please women."

22. Compare the weaving at Sparta at the Hyakinthia (Pausanias 3.16.2) and in Elis in honor of Hera (Louise Bruit Zaidman, "Pandora's Daughters and Rituals in Grecian Cities," in *A History of Women in the West*, Vol. 1, *From Ancient Goddess to Christian Saints*, ed. Pauline Schmitt Pantel, trans. Arthur Goldhammer, general eds. Georges Duby and Michelle Perror [Cambridge, MA: Belknap P of Harvard UP, 1992] 353–355); the Law Code of Gortyn indicates that women during marriage occupied themselves with weaving (*Inscriptiones Creticae* iv, col. 2.48–52, col. 3.17–24, cited in Sarah B. Pomeroy, *Xenophon* Oeconomicus [Oxford: Clarendon P, 1994] 64n48).

23. Bérard, "Order," 90; Keuls, *Reign of the Phallus* 245.

24. Eva Keuls, "Attic Vase-Painting and the Home Textile Industry," in Warren G. Moon, ed., *Ancient Greek Art and Iconography* (Madison: U of Wisconsin P, 1983) 209–230, esp. 216–219, also *Reign of the Phallus*, takes this as evidence of male production of images of women; Françoise Frontisi-Ducroux, in Françoise Frontisi-Ducroux and Jean-Pierre Vernant, *Dans l'oeil du miroir* (Paris: Odile Jacob, 1997) 96–111, discusses the ambiguity and agrees that the images are erotic and directed to men, but disagrees with Keuls' overall interpretation.

25. Keuls, "Attic Vase-Painting" 214–215, 221; Frontisi-Ducroux, *Dans l'oeil* 111.

26. Berlin 2289 *ARV* 435.95; cf. cup by Stieglitz Painter, Florence 3918, *ARV* 826.7; Keuls, *Reign of the Phallus* 254, fig. 232.

27. For thinking about women's desire, primarily in the matrix of male-female relationships, see Natalie Kampen, "Epilogue: Gender and Desire," in Ann Koloski-Ostrow and Claire Lyons, eds., *Naked Truths: Women, Sexuality and Gender in Classical Art and Archaeology* (New York: Routledge, 1997) 267–277, and the essays in Kampen's edited volume, *Sexuality in Ancient Art*.

28. Valerie Traub, "The (In)significance of 'Lesbian Desire' in Early Modern England," in *Erotic Politics: Desire on the Renaissance Stage*, ed. Susan Zimmerman (New York: Routledge, 1992) 152.

29. Though the vases reproduced in Kilmer's *Greek Erotica* are very helpful, his casual use of the term "lesbian" and the category "lesbian copulation" is problematic.

30. David Halperin, "Lesbian Historiography before the Name?" *GLQ* 4 (1998): 562,

recounts an amusing anecdote from a class of his that differentiates "the history of women who *fucked* other women" from "the history of women who *loved* other women."

31. See Sutton, "Pornography and Persuasion" 31, 33, for a comparison to modern romance. Ann Pellegrini, "Lesbian Historiography before the Name?" *GLQ* 4 (1998): 586, criticizes Brooten, *Love between Women,* for ignoring sex in lesbianism.

32. Pederastic scenes of men or youths reaching for boys' genitals and chucking them under the chin, e.g., Berlin 2279, attributed to Peithinos, *ARV* 115.2, popular in the period 560–475 BCE, are called "courtship scenes," following J. D. Beazley, "Some Attic Vases in the Cyprus Museum," *Proceedings of the British Academy* 33 (1947): 195–244. One aspect of "courtship" shows a mature man with his penis between the youth's thighs (called intercrural sex), e.g., Berlin 1773, *ABV* 198; *Para.* 80, attributed to the Painter of the Boston Polyphemos; Sèvres Musée Céramique 6405; Dover, *Greek Homosexuality* figs. B486, 70, 78, 98. Later representations of heterosexual intercourse are more graphic and are usually assumed to involve women paid for their services; these often represent anal intercourse and fellatio, e.g., Paris G 13, attributed to the Pedieus Painter, *ARV* 86, Kilmer, *Greek Erotica* R 156; Boston 95.61, attributed to the Nikosthenes Painter, *ARV* 132, fig. 5.23 below; Kilmer, *Greek Erotica* R 223; Dover, *Greek Homosexuality* 98–99.

On sexuality in antiquity, especially as represented in art, there are now many popular and scholarly studies; in most of them, female homoeroticism receives only brief mention. Some are glossy picture books: John Boardman and Eugenio La Rocca, *Eros in Greece* (Milan: Arnoldo Mondadori, 1975); Theodore Bowie and Cornelia V. Christenson, eds., *Studies in Erotic Art* (New York: Basic Books, 1970); Catherine Johns, *Sex or Symbol: Erotic Images of Greece and Rome* (Austin: U of Texas P, 1982). Others are academic: Kampen, *Sexuality in Ancient Art;* Keuls, *Reign of the Phallus;* Clarke, *Looking at Lovemaking;* Andrew Stewart, *Art, Desire, and the Body in Ancient Greece* (Cambridge: Cambridge UP, 1997).

Koloski-Ostrow and Lyons, *Naked Truths,* has no article specifically on female homoeroticism, though it is mentioned often. Kilmer, *Greek Erotica,* presents many relevant vases and extensive discussion; Brooten, *Love between Women,* attends to visual imagery from Greece in her introduction; Juan Francisco Martos Montiel, *Desde Lesbos con Amor: Homosexualidad femenina en la antigüedad,* Supplementa Mediterránea, 1 (Madrid: Ediciones Clásicas, 1996), devotes ch. 5 (67–102) to iconography.

33. Esther Newton, "The Mythic Mannish Lesbian: Radclyffe Hall and the New Woman," *Signs* 9 (1984): 557–575 on the problem of that terminology for modern butches; Brooten, *Love between Women* 16; Ann Pellegrini, "Lesbian Historiography" 581–582, for a critique of Brooten.

34. For work on the gaze in Sappho, see Greene's essay this volume. Adrienne Rich, "Compulsory Heterosexuality and Lesbian Existence," in *Signs Reader: Women, Gender, and Scholarship,* ed. Elizabeth Abel and Emily Abel (Chicago: U of Chicago P, 1983) 139–168; Carroll Smith-Rosenberg, "Female World of Love and Ritual: Relations between Women in Nineteenth-Century America," *Signs* 1 (1975): 1–29; Lillian Faderman, *Surpassing the Love of Men: Romantic Friendships and Love between Women from the Renaissance to the Present* (New York: William Morrow, 1981); see the Introduction to this volume for discussion. Martha Vicinus, "Lesbian History: All Theory and No Facts or All Facts and No Theory?" *Radical History Review* 60 (1994): 57, points out the problem of privileging "either the visibly marked mannish woman or the self-identified lesbian" when looking at earlier periods. When that hap-

pens, much of women's experience simply disappears from view. She emphasizes "the 'not said' and the 'not seen' as conceptual tools for the writing of lesbian history" (58). She also notes that romantic friendship has disappeared from current typology, but it might nonetheless be relevant to antiquity. Cf. Judith Butler, "Imitation and Gender Insubordination," *Inside/Out: Lesbian Theories, Gay Theories*, ed. Diana Fuss (New York: Routledge, 1991) 13–17, on the limitations of categorization.

Petersen, "Divided Consciousness" 49, issues some important caveats about using the work of Rich and Smith-Rosenberg because, as she notes, both have been accused of omitting the sex from lesbianism; nonetheless, they remain useful for examining a time period when women's sexual relations with other women appear to have been left inexplicit.

35. Ellen Reeder, "Catalogue," in Ellen Reeder, ed., *Pandora: Women in Classical Greece* (Baltimore, MD: Trustees of the Walters Art Gallery, in association with Princeton UP, 1995) 123–126, e.g., red-figure *stamnos*, Kleophon Painter, St. Petersburg, G (cyrillic) 1145 (St. 1428, B 809), *ARV* 1143.3; *Para.* 455; *Add.* 334; Reeder, "Catalogue," in *Pandora* 155–156, no. 18; red-figure amphora, Painter of the Louvre Centauromachy, Warsaw 147367, *ARV* 1683.90bis; *Para.* 449; Reeder, "Catalogue," in *Pandora* 157, fig. 19.

36. Reeder, "Catalogue," in *Pandora* 125. Greek desire was thought to operate through the eyes; for summaries of this relationship, see Claude Calame, *The Poetics of Eros in Ancient Greece*, trans. Janet Lloyd (Princeton: Princeton UP, 1999) 5, 20–23, 186–191; Frontisi-Ducroux, "Eros"; Stewart, *Art, Desire, and the Body* 13–23, esp. 19.

37. Leaning: Attic red-figure lebes gamikos by the Washing Painter, Athens, National Museum 14791 (fig. 8 below); British Museum E 226, attributed to the Washing Painter, *ARV* 1317.3. Arm around the waist: red-figure hydria by the Meidias Painter (*ARV* 1313.5) British Museum E 224. On lap: Attic red-figure lebes gamikos by the Painter of Athens 1454, Athens, National Museum 1454 (fig. 5.9 below).

38. Keith DeVries, *Homosexuality and the Athenian Democracy* (Oxford: Oxford UP, forthcoming), uses both strategies; on gifts as parallel, see Younger's essay in this volume.

39. On the lotus flower as homoerotic symbol, see Gundel Koch-Harnack, *Erotische Symbole: Lotosblüte und gemeinsamer Mantel auf antiken Vasen* (Berlin: Gebrüder Mann Verlag, 1989) 78–79; Martos Montiel, *Desde Lesbos* 80; Younger's essay in this volume, n94.

40. Leipzig T 550, *ARV* 438.139. Diana Buitron-Oliver, *Douris: A Master-Painter of Athenian Red-Figure Vases*, Kerameus 9 (Mainz: Verlag Philipp von Zabern, 1995) 37, assays this hypothesis and also cites DeVries, *Homosexuality*.

41. Holt Parker, "Sappho Schoolmistress" *Transactions of the American Philological Association* 123 (1993): 309–351, attacks the myth of Sappho schoolmistress, pointing out that it is based on forcing female sexuality into a male mold (328n40). There might nonetheless be reasons for retaining elements of that earlier interpretation, for instance, the notion that there was a group of women connected by music, writing, and desire.

42. For a similar distinction, see Christiane Sourvinou-Inwood, *Reading Greek Culture: Texts and Images, Rituals and Myths* (Oxford: Oxford UP, 1991) 9.

43. One motive for this kind of reading is contemporary interest in the field of sexuality, as well as political movements against the invisibility of marginalized sexualities. Thus, the whole project is fraught with difficulties and political consequences: is it good or bad to look for the sexual when gay men and lesbians are stigmatized as only sexual beings?

44. Whitney Davis, "Winckelmann's 'Homosexual' Teleologies," in Natalie Kampen, ed., *Sexuality in Ancient Art* (Cambridge: Cambridge UP, 1996) 262–276.

45. See Tamsin Wilton, *Lesbian Studies: Setting an Agenda* (London: Routledge, 1995) 26, for a recent attempt to give multiple definitions of lesbianism, one of which is a way of "reading."

46. Boardman and La Rocca, *Eros* 110, about the Apollodorus cup from Tarquinia (fig. 5.25): "It is not likely that this scene depicts an erotic relationship between the women, since there are no examples of this in Attic vase painting." See below for further discussion.

47. See the Introduction. Wilton, *Lesbian Studies* 26, tries to avoid the static view of lesbian studies by calling it "a complex, amorphous and *shifting* entity." She states boldly that "of course it makes no sense to ask was Sappho a lesbian" because that is the wrong question (ix), but she goes on to say that there is a form of myth-making in lesbian studies that is a powerful part of the mix, and Sappho has her place there. There is a whole group of texts reconstituting lesbian studies in the wake of queer theory: Bonnie Zimmerman and Toni A. McNaron, eds., *The New Lesbian Studies: Into the Twenty-first Century* (New York: Feminist P, 1996); Andy Medhurst and Sally R. Munt, eds., *Lesbian and Gay Studies: A Critical Introduction* (London: Cassell, 1997); Mandy Merck, Naomi Segal, and Elizabeth Wright, eds., *Coming Out of Feminism?* (Oxford: Blackwell, 1998).

48. Sarah B. Pomeroy, *Goddesses, Whores, Wives and Slaves* (Boston: Beacon, 1975) 60, held that the divergence of opinion was a matter of the difference in genres; Marilyn Arthur Katz, "Ideology and the 'Status of Women' in Ancient Greece," *History and Theory* 31 (1992): 80, sees it as a shift in ideology; Pomeroy, *Xenophon* 32, later considered the possibility that there was an historical shift between the fifth century and the fourth century that accounts for the perceived difference. For an interesting and balanced view, see Nevett, *House and Society* esp. 4–20; for reviews of the debate, see Ian Morris, "Archaeology and Gender Ideologies in Early Archaic Greece," *Transactions of the American Philological Association* 129 (1999): 305–317, and Sarah B. Pomeroy, *Families in Classical and Hellenistic Greece: Representations and Realities* (Oxford: Clarendon, 1997) 29–31, 32, 58, 72; Pomeroy, *Xenophon* 295–297.

49. Michael Jameson, "Private Space and the Greek City," in *The Greek City from Homer to Alexander*, ed. Oswyn Murray and Simon Price (Oxford: Clarendon, 1990) 172. See also R. E. Wycherley, *How the Greeks Built Cities*, 2nd ed. (Garden City, NY: Doubleday, 1969), who sees a *gynaikonitis* (196) but finds it impossible to distinguish it on the basis of the floor plan (200).

50. Keuls, "Attic Vase-Painting" 216, takes it as axiomatic that women were locked in; cf. Lissarrague, "Figures" 194–197. The doors on the pyxides may stand for the house and do not necessarily imply sequestration. Sally Roberts, *The Attic Pyxis* (Chicago: Ares, 1978) 178–182, suggests that the emphasis on doors emblematizes the view of marriage as a transition rather than an abrupt rupture.

51. Lissarrague, "Figures" 194. For an extensive study of women and ritual, see Barbara Goff, *Citizen Bacchae: Women's Ritual Practice in Ancient Greece* (Berkeley: U of California P, forthcoming). I am delighted to have had the opportunity to read Goff's manuscript just before this manuscript went to press.

52. François Lissarrague, "Women, Boxes, Containers: Some Signs and Metaphors," in Ellen Reeder, ed., *Pandora: Women in Classical Greece* (Baltimore, MD: Trustees of the Walters Art Gallery, in association with Princeton UP, 1995) 91–101, figs. 1–13, argues that women

are represented with these objects "not only because they are connected with female activities but also because symbolic values connected with these activities defined, in the eyes of the painters and their clients, the status of women" (91). On the sexual significance of the box, see Henderson, *Maculate Muse* 130, citing Aristophanes, *Peace* 666, *Lysistrata* 1184.

53. On the mirror, see Frontisi-Ducroux and Vernant, *Dans l'oeil* 53–91. The mirror, sign of beauty, and the distaff, sign of labor, are iconographically similar, perhaps marking the eroticization of women's work (see above, 100, 153n24; Keuls, "Attic Vase Painting" 216–18, 221; *Reign of the Phallus* 245; Frontisi-Ducroux and Vernant, *Dans l'oeil* 92–111; Aleksandra Wasowicz, "Miroir ou quenouille? La représentation des femmes dans la céramique attique," in *Mélanges Pierre Lévêque*, ed. Marie Madeleine and Evelynne Gery, vol. 82 [Paris: Centre de recherches d'Histoire Ancienne, 1989] 413–438; e.g., New York, Metropolitan Museum, red-figure lekythos by the Sabouroff Painter, *ARV* 844.151, Keuls, *Reign of the Phallus* fig. 222; Avignon, Musée Calvet, inv. D 598, black-figure lekythos attributed to the Haimon Painter, in Odile Cavalier, ed. *Silence et fureur: La Femme et le mariage en Grèce: Les antiquités grecques du Musée Calvet* (Fondation du Muséum Calvet, 1996) fig. 72.

54. Robert Sutton, "The Interaction between Men and Women Portrayed on Attic Red-Figure Pottery," Dissertation, U of North Carolina at Chapel Hill, 1981, 351–352, notes that the most common feminine activity is dressing and self-adornment; he hypothesizes that the women so represented were *hetairai*, "for to hetairai, even more than to respectable women, a well-kept appearance must have been an asset." Lissarrague, "Women, Boxes" 91, notes that they "allow a metaphorical expression of views about women." Frontisi-Ducroux and Vernant, *Dans l'oeil* 104, connects the weaving and adornment in that both reveal the attraction women exercised over men and the desire they knew how to inspire.

55. On propaganda function, see Keuls, *Reign of the Phallus* 240–259. Bérard, "Order" 93, is optimistic about the significance of the images and takes them as evidence that women's lives were "less monotonous and boring, more varied and animated, than commonly supposed. While men discussed politics in the agora or banqueted in joyous comaraderie [sic], women assembled in the orchards to gather fruits . . . , or for animated discussions about flowers or perfume." He takes the images literally, as presenting "an extremely positive view of female society and of the dignity of women."

56. Burn, *Meidias Painter* 18–19; she also argues that the personifications so prominent in the vases attributed to the Meidias Painter further glamorize these representations and indicate that they are not merely decorative. The style appears feminine, too, and Beazley's dislike of it and preference for a spare style is expressed in ways that seem to make a distinction between masculine and feminine (Beazley, *Vases in American Museums* 185; letter to Christoph Clairmont, *Yale Classical Studies* 15 [1957]: 171n18, cited in Burn, *Meidias Painter* 2n15, 3n16).

57. Lissarrague, "Figures" 194, notes that "the various images of ritual discussed thus far portray women as a group, acting collectively, whether around the body of a deceased individual or an effigy of a god."

58. See Bruce Thornton, *Eros: The Myth of Ancient Greek Sexuality* (Boulder: Westview P, 1997) 169, who assumes the existence of an extended family. Cf. Jameson, "Private Space," who assumes a nuclear family: "The *oikos*, the household formed around a nuclear family" (195). Since the vases sometimes depict the wedding party arriving at a house and being greeted by a woman, assumed to be the mother of the groom, it seems that this is the house of the groom's family, not a new house for the couple.

59. New York, Metropolitan Museum 23.160.80. Gisela Richter and Lindsley Hall, *Red-Figured Athenian Vases in the Metropolitan Museum of Art*, 2 vols. (New Haven: Yale UP, 1936) 142–143; *ARV* 1075.10. Cf. red-figure hydria British Museum E 191, women with flute and lyre, attributed to the Duomo Painter, *ARV* 1119.29; red-figure *calyx krater*, British Museum E 461, attributed to the Niobid Painter, women or muses, *ARV* 601.20; red-figure hydria, Vatican 16549, attributed to Phiale Painter, *ARV* 1020.92, *Para.* 441; *Add.* 154, shows one woman with one hand around the shoulder of another, and the other at her waist in a solicitous gesture; both watch Thamyris with lyre; cf. Wurzburg 521, which features a cithara player and Eros; red-figure hydria, Brunswick 219, near the Hector Painter, *ARV* 1037.2, has a woman with a lyre, and Eros tying the sandal of a seated woman (like Brunswick 220). Red-figure hydria, British Museum E 189, attributed to the Group of Polygnotos, *ARV* 1060.147, shows three women with instruments (standing woman with double flute, seated woman with lyre, standing woman with lyre) and Eros approaching the seated woman with a wreath. On brides and music in the work of the Washing Painter, see Sabetai, *Washing Painter* 170.

60. Richter and Hall, *Red-Figured Athenian Vases* 142.

61. The phrase is taken from Eva Stehle, *Performance and Gender in Ancient Greece* (Princeton: Princeton UP, 1997) 287. See red-figure hydria from Athens, National Museum 1260, attributed to the group of Polygnotos, *ARV* 1060.145, for a representation of Sappho reading a papyrus, surrounded by women with musical instruments and showing signs of affection. Jane Snyder, "Sappho in Attic Vase Painting," in A. Koloski-Ostrow and C. Lyons, eds., *Naked Truths: Women, Sexuality and Gender in Classical Art and Archaeology* (New York: Routledge, 1997) 115, points out that this could easily be entitled "enjoyment in the women's quarters."

62. Red-figure calyx krater, E 461, attributed to the Niobid Painter, *ARV* 601.20, cf. n59 above.

63. New York, Metropolitan Museum 06.1021.167, attributed to the Painter of Bologna 417, *ARV* 908.13. Richter and Hall, *Red-Figured Athenian Vases* 107–108, pl. 80.

64. Keith DeVries, *Homosexuality* 13 (draft) points out that "there is a tendency for eromenoi to be shown heavily wrapped in himatia and to be standing stock-still in contrast to the more loosely dressed and more freely moving erastai" (his fig. 13).

65. Robert Sutton, "Interaction" 380; Andrew Stewart, "Rape?," in Ellen Reeder, ed. *Pandora: Women in Classical Greece* (Baltimore, MD: Trustees of the Walters Art Gallery, in association with Princeton UP, 1995) 84, outlines three reasons (sexual, literary, sociopolitical) for a sudden rise and fall in the popularity of rape and abduction scenes, both heterosexual and homoerotic, but none is artistic. He concludes, "They mobilize these worlds [heroic and divine] to promote the cause of Athenian masculine self-assertion" (86). The change in imagery does not, however, indicate a change in women's power or status.

66. Women with erotes: red-figure pyxis, Metropolitan Museum 06.1021.120, Richter and Milne, *Shapes* 20–21, fig. 136; red-figure pyxis, Metropolitan Museum 06.1021.123, Richter and Milne, *Shapes* 20–21, fig. 138; red-figure kylix, Museo Archeológico, Florence, Martos Montiel, *Desde Lesbos* fig. 13; red-figure pyxis, British Museum E 775, with Aphrodite among them, *ARV* 1328.92, *Add.* 364; red-figure *lekanis* in the manner of the Meidias Painter, Metropolitan Museum 15.166.

67. The similarity has been noted by others, for instance, Reilly, "Many Brides"; Lissarrague, "Women, Boxes"; Sabetai, "Aspects"; Lissarrague, "Figures"; John Oakley, "Nuptial

Nuances: Wedding Images in Non-Wedding Scenes of Myth," in Ellen Reeder, ed., *Pandora: Women in Classical Greece* (Baltimore, MD: Trustees of the Walters Art Gallery, in association with Princeton UP, 1995) 64, points out that the adornment of the bride is "the most common red-figure motif" of the wedding.

68. For this summary, see François Lissarrague, "Regards sur le mariage grec," in Odile Cavalier, ed., *Silence et fureur: La Femme et le mariage en Grèce: Les Antiquités grecques du Musée Calvet* (Avignon: Fondation du Muséum Calvet, 1996) 417, and John Oakley and Rebecca Sinos, *The Wedding in Ancient Athens* (Madison: U of Wisconsin P, 1993).

69. Oakley and Sinos, *Wedding* 16, 134n41, citing Aristophanes, *Acharnians* 1056; Plutarch, *Lykurgus* 15; Pollux 3.41; Pausanias 9.3.7; Hesychius, *Suda*, Photius, *s.v. nympheutria;* on *nymphokomos*, see Hesychius, *s.v.*

70. Louvre L 55; *ARV* 924.33, *Para.* 431; *Add.* 305. Christiane Sourvinou-Inwood, "Male and Female, Public and Private, Ancient and Modern," in Ellen Reeder, ed., *Pandora: Women in Classical Greece* (Baltimore, MD: Trustees of the Walters Art Gallery, in association with Princeton UP, 1995) 113, makes a similar point, emphasizing the mothers of bride and bridegroom. On the gesture, *cheir epi karpou,* see C. H. E. Haspels, "Deux fragments d'une coupe d'Euphronios," *Bulletin de correspondance hellenique* 54 (1930): 422–451; Sutton, "Interaction" 181–187; I. D. Jenkins, "Is There Life after Marriage? A Study of the Abduction Motif in Vase Paintings of the Athenian Wedding Ceremony," *Bulletin of the Institute of Classical Studies* 30 (1983): 137–145.

71. Scholia to Theocritus 18, cited by Oakley and Sinos, *Wedding* 37, 138nn106, 107.

72. Benaki Museum 3117, attributed to the Washing Painter; Oakley and Sinos, *Wedding* 17, fig. 22; Sabetai, "Washing Painter," vol. 2, 12, calls her simply a woman.

73. Athens, National Museum 14791, attributed to the Washing Painter; *ARV* 1126.5. Oakley and Sinos, *Wedding* 70 (fig. 38); Sabetai, "Washing Painter," vol. 2, 9, with bibliography.

74. Cf. British Museum E 226, attributed to the Painter of the Athens Wedding, *ARV* 1318.3, which shows Helen with Eros and women, one leaning on another, and one leaning on a tymbalon. For discussion, see Sabetai, "Washing Painter," vol. 1, 171–174.

75. *Wedding* 66 (figs. 28 and 29). Athens, National Museum 1454, attributed to the Painter of Athens 1454, *ARV* 1178.1, 1685; *Para.* 480.

76. I do not wish to enter the debate about the age of the women or girls in Sappho's group, what to call the group, whether it was for purposes of initiation, and whether it is reasonable to compare her to Alcman. On Alcman, see Claude Calame, *Choruses of Young Women in Ancient Greece: Their Morphology, Religious Role, and Social Functions,* trans. Derek Collins and Jane Orion (Lanham, MD: Rowman and Littlefield, 1997) 208–209, 244–258 on homoeroticism. Cf. Stehle, *Performance and Gender* 76–79, 87, 87n55, who disagrees with Calame about the homoeroticism, though she acknowledges that these are songs for maidens about to be married in which the singers are made desirable. Eva Cantarella, *Bisexuality in the Ancient World,* trans. Cormac O Cuilleanáin (New Haven: Yale UP, 1992) 81–82, goes further and analyzes the maiden songs of Alcman as evidence of an initiation marriage between the women. She asserts the parallels between male and female initiation rituals, though pointing out this fundamental difference: while men are prepared for further male bonding in war, women are prepared for relations with men.

See the vigorous disagreement between Parker "Sappho Schoolmistress," and André Lardinos, "Subject and Circumstance in Sappho's Poetry," *Transactions of the American Philo-*

logical Association 124 (1994): 57–84, who supports the idea of Sappho as someone who produces choruses of young girls though stops short of asserting initiatory significance for the choruses. Sappho as leader of choruses of young girls is, however, consistent with an initiation interpretation.

77. Lilly Kahil, "Mythological Repertoire of Brauron," in Warren G. Moon, ed., *Ancient Greek Art and Iconography* (Madison: U of Wisconsin P, 1983) 240, says that among the many pots that pertain to women's activity, there is one representation of a kiss, but unfortunately she does not say more or reproduce the image.

78. See Oakley, "Nuptial Nuances" 72, on polysemy in Greek vase painting: "An allusion can be faint, obvious, or somewhere between."

79. On Eros represented between women, see Martos Montiel, *Desde Lesbos* 79–81. For Eros as a lover, see H. Alan Shapiro, "Eros in Love: Pederasty and Pornography in Greece," in Amy Richlin, ed., *Pornography and Representation in Greece and Rome.* (New York: Oxford UP, 1992) 53–72.

80. On the slippage, see the following: David Harvey, "Painted Ladies: Fact, Fiction and Fantasy," in Jette Christiansen and Torben Melander, eds., *Proceedings of the 3rd Symposium on Ancient Greek and Related Pottery,* Copenhagen, Aug. 31–Sept. 4, 1987 (Copenhagen: Nationalmuseet Ny; Carlsberg Glyptotek and Thorvaldsens Museum, 1988) 242–254; Dyfri Williams, "Women on Athenian Vases: Problems of Interpretation," in Averil Cameron and Amélie Kuhrt, eds., *Images of Women in Antiquity* (Detroit: Wayne State UP, 1983) 92–106; Sabetai, "Aspects" 320, on the iconography of the red-figure pyxis in New York, Metropolitan Museum, 1972.118.148; Oakley, "Nuptial Nuances" 63; Burn, *Meidias Painter* 26–44, on the role of personification in the Meidias Painter's work; T. B. L. Webster, *Potter and Patron in Classical Athens* (London: Methuen, 1972).

81. See Colombe Couëlle, "La loi d'Aphrodite: entre la norme et le plaisir," in Odile Cavalier, ed., *Silence et fureur: La Femme et le mariage en Grèce: Les Antiquités grecques du Musée Calvet* (Avignon: Fondation du Muséum Calvet, 1996) 229–249, on this pot (British Museum E 697, in the manner of the Meidias Painter, *ARV* 1324.45, *Para.* 478, *Add.* 181, *LIMC* ii, pl. 127, Aphrodite 1271) and a red-figure pyxis (British Museum E 775, *ARV* 1328.92). Couëlle argues that Athenian women did not have high expectations of marital pleasure but depended on order, which explains the presence of the personifications in wedding iconography. On this vase, Aphrodite and weddings, and personification in general, see Burn, *Meidias Painter* 30–44.

82. E. R. Dodds, *The Greeks and the Irrational* (Berkeley: U of California P, 1968) 278, affirms that the maenad is not a mythological figure but human. On maenads in art, see Mark Edwards, "Representation of Maenads on Archaic Red-Figure Vases," *Journal of Hellenic Studies* 80 (1960): 78–87; Sheila McNally, "The Maenad in Early Greek Art," *Arethusa* 11 (1978): 101–135, makes the point that without a satyr a maenad is not truly Dionysian (117). On satyrs, see François Lissarrague, "The Sexual Life of Satyrs," in David M. Halperin, John J. Winkler, and Froma I. Zeitlin, eds., *Before Sexuality: The Construction of Erotic Experience in the Ancient Greek World* (Princeton: Princeton UP, 1990) 53–81; Robin Osborne, "Desiring Women on Athenian Pottery," in Natalie Kampen, ed., *Sexuality in Ancient Art* (Cambridge: Cambridge UP, 1996) 65–80.

83. Plutarch, *Greek Questions* 38; cf. daughters of Proetus, who convinced the Argive women to kill their children and to take to the mountains (Apollodorus 2.2.2).

84. Berlin, Staatliche Museum 2290, *ARV* 462.48.

85. "The Maenads: A Contribution to the Study of the Dance in Ancient Greece," *Memoirs of the American Academy in Rome* 6 (1927): 78, 84, 99; as examples of coquetry I would cite her pl. 18.1 (Bologna 258); 19.1 (Baltimore kylix, Hartwig 30.3); 21.1 (Berlin 2471). Keuls, *Reign of the Phallus* 357–371, includes the maenads in her section on anti-masculinity.

86. Cabinet des Médailles 222, *ABV* 152.25, 687, *Add.* 43; Oakley, Coulson, and Palagia, eds., *Athenian Potters* 30–31, figs. 33, 34, 36.

87. Women's dance at weddings, see Attic red-figure lebes gamikos by the Syriskos Painter, Mykonos Museum 970, Oakley and Sinos, *Wedding* figs. 54–58.

88. See Auanger's essay in this volume. Calame, *Choruses* 208–209; see 244–258 on homoeroticism; cf. Stehle, *Performance and Gender* 73, 78. For women with names of Muses, see Marie-Christine Villaneuva-Puig, *Images de la vie quotidienne en Grèce dans l'antiquité* (Paris: Hachette, 1992) 102–103. For examples, see red-figure oinochoe, Louvre G 440, attributed to the Methyse Painter, *ARV* 633.11; red-figure amphora, British Museum E 271, attributed to the Peleus Painter, *ARV* 1039.13; red-figure lekanis, Third Ephoria, M 26, attributed to the Meidias Painter by M. Zaphiropoulou, *Archaiologikon Deltion* 31 (1976) part B'1, 30 and pl. 35, cited by Burn, *Meidias Painter* 99, discussed on 59.

89. Lissarrague, "Figures" 184, points out that "most choruses were exclusively female: of some one hundred surviving paintings, nearly eighty depict choruses made up of women or girls"; Bérard, "Order" 91, on women's parallel cultural institutions; Lillian Beatrice Lawler, *The Dance in Ancient Greece* (Middletown, CT: Wesleyan UP, 1964) 116, 117.

90. "Apostrophe and Women's Erotics in the Poetry of Sappho," *Transactions of the American Philological Association* 124 (1994): 47.

91. New York, Metropolitan Museum 75.2.10, attributed to the Pharos Painter; *ABV* 698.

92. *Erotische Symbole* 143, with figs. 13–18. Compare British Museum B 163, a black-figure amphora showing two women with satyrs and bird with hands in a similar position. The series has been defined by H.-G. Buchholz, "Das Symbol des gemeinsamen Mantels," *Jahrbuch des Deutschen Archäologischen Instituts* 102 (1987) 1–55; Martos Montiel, *Desde Lesbos* 74–79, agrees with the homoerotic interpretation; Dover, *Greek Homosexuality* 173, disagrees and places the image of two women facing one another only in the context of lines of women facing in the same direction. Nina Strawczynski's fine unpublished 1993 essay, "Échange sous le manteau: analyse iconographique d'un motif archaïque," places the motif in the context of Charis and the Charites. Neither Dover's reading nor Strawczynski's interpretation necessarily discounts the homoerotic reading, however.

93. Mississippi University Museum 1972.3.72; Koch-Harnack, *Erotische Symbole* 118, fig. 3. Koch-Harnack compares this pyxis to Athens, Kerameikos Museum 1636 (119, fig. 4).

94. See, for instance, the black-figure lekythos, Leningrad, Hermitage 1440 (Koch-Harnack, *Erotische Symbole* 141, fig. 12), a man and boy closely entwined under a mantle like the women's cloaks show the pederastic "up and down" position of the hands. For women with a similar but less pointed gesture, see black-figure lekythos, Berlin F 1738; black-figure lekythos Athens 18674 (Koch-Harnack, *Erotische Symbole* 144, figs. 13, 15). The figures are much farther away from one another on a black-figure lekythos from Syracuse but still display a similar gesture with their hands (Koch-Harnack, *Erotische Symbole* 145, fig. 18).

95. Eve Sedgwick, *Between Men: English Literature and Male Homosocial Desire* (New York: Co-

lumbia UP, 1985) 5, points to "an asymmetry between, on the one hand, the relatively continuous relation of female homosocial and homosexual bonds, and, on the other hand, the
radically discontinuous relation of male homosocial and homosexual bonds." In doing so,
she uses the Greeks as an example of a time when male homosocial and homosexual bonds
were "quite seamless" (4). I disagree about women in the present, but I wonder whether
Greek women might not have enjoyed such a seamless continuum between homosocial and
homosexual bonds.

96. Thanks to Lisa Auanger for the contrast with Zeus and Ganymede.

97. Cf. Harvey, "Painted Ladies" 245. See also Reilly, "Many Brides" 412, about the lack
of definition of generally accepted terms.

98. Alan Shapiro puts the term in quotation marks in "Eros in Love" 54; he doubts that
any "respectable" women were at symposia. Bérard, "Order" 89, objects to the labeling as
bourgeois ideology and asks whether it is likely that vases intended for women's use would
have been decorated with large numbers of *hetairai.*

99. On the respectability of wool work, see James Davidson, *Courtesans and Fishcakes: The
Consuming Passions of Classical Athens* (New York: HarperCollins, 1997) 86–90, who believes
on the basis of archaeological evidence (loomweights in an identifiable brothel) that prostitutes were weavers; Keuls, "Attic-Vase Painting" passim and esp. 229, holds that *hetairai* spin
and weave; for a complete study of the debate, see Carola Reinsberg, *Ehe, Hetärentum und
Knabenliebe im antiken Griechenland* (Munich: C. H. Beck, 1989). For an interpretation of alleged
money bags on the walls in domestic scenes as knucklebones, see Gloria Pinney, "Money
Bags?" *American Journal of Archaeology* 90 (1986) 218.

100. Leslie Kurke, "Inventing the *Hetaira:* Sex, Politics, and Discursive Conflict in Archaic Greece," *Classical Antiquity* 16 (1997): 106–150, takes the distinction between *hetaira* and
pornê, courtesan/mistress and prostitute, as defining a semantic field. On the erasure of
the distinction, see Davidson, *Courtesans* 73–77. From a feminist perspective, the focus on
hetairai's education and witty conversation, the supposedly elite aspects that distinguished
them from ordinary prostitutes, seems romanticization of what was for the most part forced
labor; Davidson, however, finds ample ancient evidence to document those aspects (though
of course that might only put the romanticization back into antiquity; none of the evidence
is from an *hetaira*'s point of view).

101. Although there were male prostitutes in antiquity, we seem to have no representations of them, to the best of my knowledge (see Shapiro, "Eros in Love" for the evidence).

102. Kurke, "Inventing" 136 (see also *Coins, Bodies, Games, and Gold: The Politics of Meaning in
Archaic Greece* [Princeton: Princeton UP, 1999] 185–186) argues that the *hetaira* was invented
as a corollary of the male *hetairos* to reinforce the distinctiveness of the symposium and its
egalitarian atmosphere.

103. For the suggestion that *hetairai* were also lesbians or tribads, see Geneviève Pastre,
Athènes et "le péril saphique": Homosexualité féminine en Grèce Ancienne (Paris: "Les Mots à la bouche,"
1987) 36–37, 63. Cf. Viveca Liventhal, "What Goes on among the Women: The Settings
of Some Attic Vase Paintings of the Fifth Century B.C.," *Analecta Romana Institute Danici* 14
(1985): 37–52, on lesbianism in scenes of dancers dressed in armor (Pyrrhic dances) who
are also often taken to be *hetairai.*

The connection between disparate deviant categories is telling. In the late nineteenth
century, overly large clitorises were attributed to sexually active women, equally often cate-

gorized as masturbators, prostitutes, and lesbians; clitoridectomy was prescribed (Thomas Laqueur, "Amor Veneris, vel Dulcedo Appeletur," in *Fragments for a History of the Human Body*, pt. 3, ed. Michael Feher [New York: Zone, 1989] 91–131, esp. 119), as it was in antiquity (Brooten, *Love between Women* 173). See also Valerie Traub, "The Psychomorphology of the Clitoris," *GLQ* 2 (1995): 81–113.

104. See Parker, "Sappho Schoolmistress," and Lardinois, "Subject," for the argument.

105. Brooten, *Love between Women* 41; David M. Halperin, *One Hundred Years of Homosexuality and Other Essays on Greek Love* (New York: Routledge, 1990) 18–22, and "Lesbian Historiography" 567, for an attack on Brooten.

106. Here as elsewhere, the evidence is ambiguous. Jean-Marie Dentzer, *Le Motif du banquet couché dans le proche-orient et le monde grec du VII au IV siècle avant J.-C.* (Rome: École française de Rome, 1982) 84; cf. the distinctions elaborated on 123–124. Dentzer argues that "three modes of representation of the women correspond to three types of social status." Sutton, "Pornography and Persuasion" 8, believes that women "with a reputation to uphold" would not have attended; but see Kilmer, *Greek Erotica* 161n77, on the lateness of the evidence (Theopompus; Lysias 1; Pseudo-Demosthenes, *Against Neaira*) against women at the symposion.

107. Kilmer, *Greek Erotica* 159–163. Cf. Dyfri Williams, "Women on Athenian Vases" 99; Larissa Bonfante, "Nudity as a Costume in Classical Art," *American Journal of Archaeology* 93 (1989): 543–570, esp. 549, 559, argues that for men, nudity was heroic, for women, a sign of vulnerability; when erotic, it is also a sign of weakness and related to slave or commodity status. Dentzer, *Motif du banquet* 123, argues that when the symposiasts are only women, the nudity might not define them as *hetairai* but simply women banqueting amongst themselves.

108. Gloria Pinney, "Meaningful Figures," paper delivered at Archaeological Institute of America meetings; abstract published in *American Journal of Archaeology* 100 (1996): 361.

109. *Greek Erotica* 26; he cites three unpublished vases by Onesimos, which are erotic (26n39) and show genitals delineated.

110. Red-figure cup attributed to Oltos, Madrid, Museo Arqueológico Nacional 11.267; *ARV* 58.53.

111. Munich 2421, ca. 525–510, *ARV* 23.7. For an extensive interpretation, see Peter Evans and Lyle Eveille, *Symposia and Women on Greek Vases* (London: Old Vicarage Publications, 1992) 18–19. Kilmer, *Greek Erotica* 26, does not discuss this scene, but says that "all-female drinking parties, sometimes with everyone present shown nude, are quite common, but normally have no explicit erotic content."

112. For instance, a red-figure pyxis, New York, Metropolitan Museum of Art 1972.118.148, unattributed, D. von Bothmer, *Ancient Art from New York Private Collections* (New York: Metropolitan Museum of Art, 1961) 61–62, pls. 91–92; Sabetai, "Aspects" fig. 1; Sutton, "Pornography and Persuasion" 24–25, fig. 1.9; Reilly, "Many Brides," 421.

113. For a thorough study, see René Ginouvès, *Balaneutikè: recherches sur le bain dans l'antiquité grecque* (Paris: Boccard, 1962). Ginouvès makes the point that the expansion of scenes of women bathing is comparable to the new focus on scenes of women's lives in general (163–169).

114. *Greek Erotica* 89.

115. *Greek Erotica* 89, 90. Louvre F 203, *ARV* 4.13.

116. On the connection of Spartan women's exercise and homoeroticism, see Plutarch, *Lykurgus* 18.9, 14–15; Euripides, *Andromache* 595–600; Aristophanes, *Lysistrata* 79–84. Plutarch

explicitly mentions sexual relations, while other sources focus on education in physical activity. Poetry from Sparta includes Alcman's maiden songs with their homoerotic overtones.

117. Feminist attempts to develop a theory of spectatorship can perhaps help us here in articulating a non-masochistic feminine position: for instance, Laura Mulvey, *Visual and Other Pleasures* (Bloomington: Indiana UP, 1989); Griselda Pollock, *Vision and Difference: Femininity, Feminism and Histories of Art* (New York: Routledge, 1988); Mary Ann Doane, *The Desire to Desire: The Woman's Film of the 1940's* (Bloomington: Indiana UP, 1987), "Film and the Masquerade: Theorising the Female Spectator," *Screen* 23 (1982): 74–87. For an excellent summary, see Shelby Brown, "'Ways of Seeing' Women in Antiquity," in A. Koloski-Ostrow and C. Lyons, eds., *Naked Truths: Women, Sexuality and Gender in Classical Art and Archaeology* (New York: Routledge, 1997) 12–42.

118. I take this to be the main point of Petersen, "Divided Consciousness."

119. Red-figure cup attributed to Douris, New York, Metropolitan Museum 23.160.54; *ARV* 441.186, 1653. DeVries, *Homosexuality* 21 (draft); Buitron-Oliver, *Douris* 37, speaks of the artist's lesbian scenes, without discussing any specifically. Richter and Hall, *Red-Figured Athenian Vases* 80, states that the women "have taken off their clothes, rolled them up into neat bundles, and are putting" them on the stool. Cf. red-figure neck-amphora by the Phiale Painter (*ARV* 1016.38), Prague Museum Z.260.7, in which a nude woman looks at her clothed companion, who has a boot in her hand.

120. Kilmer, *Greek Erotica* 26, 27, fig. R 73 (*ARV* 32.4). Naples SA 5; cf. red-figure cup, attributed to the Boot Painter (*ARV* 821.5), Boston 10.572; red-figure stamnos, attributed to the Polygnotos group (*ARV* 1051.18, *Add.* 321), Munich Staatliche Antikensammlungen und Glyptothek inv. 2411. Keuls, *Reign of the Phallus* 120, sees sexual significance in the alabastron. On the question of eroticism and genital hair or genital depilation, see Martin Kilmer, "Genital Phobia and Depilation," *Journal of Hellenic Studies* 102 (1982): 104–112; Aaron J. Paul, "A New Vase by the Dinos Painter: Eros and an Erotic Image of Women in Greek Vase Painting," *Harvard University Art Museums* 3.2 (1994–1995): 60–67. If representations of depilation were erotic, there is also a possibility of homoeroticism (see below). Paul correlates depilation scenes with the iconography of a cross-breast strap on women dancers, which Liventhal, "What Goes On," sees as homoerotic.

121. On *olisboi* and women, see Aristophanes, *Lysistrata* 107–109; Herodas, *Mimes* 6 and 7. In antiquity as in the present, dildos are not used by all women and are not used exclusively by lesbians.

122. Keuls, *Reign of the Phallus* 84, fig. 76; Syracuse 20065, pelike, *ARV* 238.5. Padgett, "Workshop" 218, argues that the large phallos on the Flying-Angel amphora must be "a fantasy, an olisbos that waxes with every stroke of the woman's hand."

123. Dover, *Greek Homosexuality* R 1071; Angelika Dierichs, "Erotik in der Kunst Griechenlands," *Antike Welt. Zeitschrift für Archäologie und Kulturgeschichte* 19 (1988): 67, fig. 111. In the 1993 version (Mainz: Verlag Philipp von Zabern, 1993) 100, fig. 179, she calls them *olisboi*. Cf. Dover, *Greek Homosexuality* R 414, Petit Palais 307. These two vases are similar, yet Keuls labels one dildos and the other, phalluses (*Reign of the Phallus* 84).

124. London, British Museum E 819, attributed to the Hasselmann Painter, *ARV* 1137.25; Kilmer, *Greek Erotica* R 940; Johns, *Sex or Symbol* 48.

125. H. W. Parke, *Festivals of the Athenians* (Ithaca: Cornell UP, 1977) 98–99, from the scholiast to Lucian 179.24. According to Demosthenes 59.116, this festival was associated

with *hetairai;* on this vase, see A. B. Cook, *Zeus,* vol. 1 (Cambridge: Cambridge UP, 1914) 685, fig. 510a; Ludwig Deubner, *Attische Feste* (Berlin: H. Keller, 1932) 65 and pl. 3.3.

126. Villa Giulia 50404, attributed to Apollodorus, *ARV* 1565.1; Johns, *Sex or Symbol* 43; Kilmer, *Greek Erotica* R 607; Keuls, *Reign of the Phallus* pl. 78; Deubner, *Attische Feste* pl. 4.1.

127. Sandals are sexual toys, perhaps in the cup from the Pezzino group described above, or in the scenes where it is used for spanking. On heterosexual use, as a weapon, see Kilmer, *Greek Erotica* 36—37 (figs. R 156, 486, 518), 46 (figs. R 464, 490), 52 (fig. R 156), 98 (fig. R 223), 108—121, 145n38. He does not find any lesbian scenes, but we do not know what the frequent representation of shoes, tying sandals, etc., means on the vases.

For shoes on wedding vases, see Keuls, *Reign of the Phallus* 121—122, who takes them as signs of copulation or sexual danger; Oakley and Sinos, *Wedding* 16 (Hesychius, *s.v. nymphides,* the word for wedding shoes), on Eros and the binding of the sandals, 18, 19, on Aphrodite and the removal of sandals, 33; sandals might have been part of the wedding gifts, 38; as part of seductiveness of bride, 46. On feet, see Auanger's essay in this volume.

128. Louvre G 14, *ARV* 85.1; Kilmer, *Greek Erotica* R 152 a, b; 26, 27, 29, 30, 86, 89, 90—92 and nn28—29, 93, 98, 194, 197.

129. On the phallos bird, see Kilmer, *Greek Erotica* 192—197; Frontisi-Ducroux, "Eros."

130. Kilmer, *Greek Erotica* R 141.3. Thanks to Professor Kilmer and Vicky Bennett for gracious permission to reprint this drawing. This vase has been lost, but it is cited as having been at Rome, in the Castellani collection, by Gaston Vorberg, *Glossarium Eroticum* (Hanau: Verlag Müller and Kleipenheuer, 1965) 409.

131. Museum of Fine Arts 95.61; *ARV* 132; Kilmer, *Greek Erotica* R 223. Thanks to our anonymous reviewer who encouraged me to mention this example. Cf. Red-figure kylix, American School of Classical Studies, Corinth, *ARV* 1519.13, Q Painter, showing what seems to be a woman in a satyr's costume, replete with phallus and tail, facing Dionysos; Claude Bérard and Christiane Bron, "Satyric Revels," in Claude Bérard et al., eds., Deborah Lyons, trans., *A City of Images: Iconography and Society in Ancient Greece* (Princeton: Princeton UP, 1989) 144—145, fig. 198; Martos Montiel, *Desde Lesbos* 94, fig. 25.

132. "Eros" 90, 99n77: "The term 'lesbian' hardly seems appropriate for women who, in the absence of men, think only of being penetrated by phalli" (cf. Kilmer, *Greek Erotica* 29—32, 197). Jane Snyder, *Lesbian Desire in the Lyrics of Sappho* (New York: Columbia UP, 1997) 115, points out that the appearance of the dildo in a lyric attributed either to Sappho or to Alkaios "may be a figment of papyrological imagination, and if so, the question then arises as to why scholars have been so eager to find it in an almost illegible fragment of dubious authorship and uncertain context. The elements of scandal and masquerade in the notion of the Sapphic dildo are worth exploring further ('WOMAN POET WEARS FAKE PENIS!')."

133. *Sex or Symbol* 102.

134. *Eros* 142.

135. John Younger is similarly dismissive of the idea that the dildo vases are lesbian. In Greek texts such as Aristophanes' *Lysistrata* 107—109 and Herodas, *Mimes* 6 and 7, the dildo is associated with heterosexual women and is evidence of their desire for intercourse.

136. On seeing both ways, although not about dildos, see Petersen, "Divided Consciousness" 51, 69.

137. For a good summary, see Lynda Hart, *Between the Body and the Flesh: Performing Sado-*

masochism (New York: Columbia UP, 1998) 92–123. On the dildo as evidence of the commodification of lesbianism, see Sue-Ellen Case, "The Student and the Strap: Authority and Seduction in the Class(room)," in *Professions of Desire,* ed. George E. Haggerty and Bonnie Zimmerman (New York: Modern Language Association of America, 1995) 39–46; on fetishism of the dildo, see Heather Findlay, "Freud's 'Fetishism' and the Lesbian Dildo Debates," in *Out in Culture: Gay, Lesbian, and Queer Essays on Popular Culture,* ed. Corey K. Creekmur and Alexander Doty (Durham: Duke UP, 1995) 328–342. Colleen Lamos, "The Postmodern Lesbian Position: *On Our Backs,*" *The Lesbian Postmodern,* ed. Laura Doan (New York: Columbia UP, 1994) 85–103, focuses on the way the lesbian is represented in a pornographic magazine for lesbians and addresses the issue of "undesignated readers" (89). According to Lamos, the power and danger of the dildo is that it is part of "a queer lesbian culture that blurs distinctions between masculine and feminine and between gay and straight sexuality" (94).

138. Hart, *Between* 123; Lamos, "Postmodern" 99. See June L. Reich, "Genderfuck: The Law of the Dildo," *Discourse* 15.1 (Fall 1992) 121, for a radical claim: "The consequences of the dildo-as-phallus are potentially far reaching for emancipating theory from the appeal to Truth. At the very least, the dildo schema announces the arbitrariness of the hegemonic phallus = penis construction, while attending to the rigid logic of the phallic economy. At its most radical, the dildo, as an equal-opportunity accessory, and as a simulacrum (an object circulating without origin), undermines the penis as a meaningfully stable organ, denaturalizing the body without erasing its materiality."

139. Thera CE 34; Dover, *Greek Homosexuality* 173, CE 34; for the wreaths, see his B 271, Munich 1468, *ABV* 315; B 502, Munich 2290a (both black-figure scenes of male courtship). On the gesture of touching the chin, common in courtship, see, e.g., B 271, B 342, B 598 in Dover. On this vase, see Brooten, *Love between Women* 57, fig. 1; Petersen "Double Consciousness" (65–66, fig. 13). Kilmer does not include this example.

140. The hand under the chin resembles vases in Beazley's alpha group, while the wreath is characteristic of the beta group ("Some Attic Vases").

141. The state of preservation is poor, making sure description difficult.

142. Red-figure pelikê. Taranto, Museo Nazionale di Taranto (48033). Keuls, *Reign of the Phallus* 85, 87, fig. 81; Brooten, *Love between Women* 58 (fig. 6); Petersen, "Double Consciousness" 65–66 (fig. 14).

143. Red-figure cup, attributed to Apollodoros, Tarquinia. Kilmer, *Greek Erotica* 26; Dover, *Greek Homosexuality* 173, R 207.

144. Private conversation.

145. Boardman and La Rocca, *Eros* 110.

146. *Interactions* 137n68; Brooten, *Love between Women* 57–58, makes a similar observation while discussing the red-figure kylix, perhaps by the Boot Painter, J. Paul Getty Museum 83.AE.251; on related images of depilation, see Paul, "A New Vase by the Dinos Painter."

CHAPTER SIX

Women in Relief

"Double Consciousness" in Classical Attic Tombstones*

John G. Younger

Introduction

In much recent scholarship on the lives of women in Athens of the Classical period (broadly, fifth and fourth centuries BCE), there is a recurring insistence that women were objects in a patriarchal system, the property of men, and the objects of male sexual desire and an all-encompassing male gaze. Were women ever subjects? Could women feel their own personhood even within the confines of a patriarchal system? And if so, under what circumstances?

Lauren Petersen argues that "it was possible for a woman of ancient Greece to liberate herself from the oppression of patriarchal constructs by actively reading her subjectivity";[1] she cites several vase paintings that could serve to facilitate such feelings.

Circumstances in which women could feel liberated "from the oppression of patriarchal constructs" could logically include occasions when and locations where women were physically beyond the reach of men. The home, once the men went to the *agora* (the marketplace) or the assembly, became a female homosocial environment; so did house rooftops during the Adonia and the Pnyx hill during the Thesmophoria (see Rabinowitz's essay in this volume).[2]

This study looks at another place that, on occasion, became primarily a woman's space, the Kerameikos cemetery located outside the fortification walls in northwest Athens; in that space, I concentrate on its sculpted tombstones (*stêlai:* στῆλαι) of the later Classical period (fourth century BCE).

Like all cemeteries, the Kerameikos was a heterotopia, a space other than that which humans usually inhabit,[3] and its gardenlike appearance and calm contrasted greatly with the traffic that clustered at the entrance to the city at the Dipylon and Sacred Gates. For women, going to the Kerameikos cemetery to perform occasional funerary rites at the tombs of their relatives may have provided some relief from the everyday pressures of a patriarchal world. I suggest that in that space, women visitors could also be subjects, the active viewers of the deceased women depicted on the stelai.

6.1. View of Plot 34 in Kerameikos cemetery. Left to right, cast of stele of Hegeso daughter of Proxenos (Athens, National Archaeological Museum 3624; Clairmont no. 2.150), stele of Koroibos and family, and stele of Kleidimos and family (Kerameikos P 1072; Clairmont no. 2.115a). Photograph: Author.

PAYING HONORS TO THE DEAD

Classical Greek cemeteries usually lay outside the city, with the tombs lining the roads leading into it. Both men and women visited the tombs on formal occasions, but otherwise these areas were more the preserve of women. Women attended those who lay dying, women provided formal mourning for the deceased when they were taken for burial, and women paid continuous honor to the dead on informal occasions thereafter. In Athens the excesses of mourning were limited by successive laws, but women remained central to honoring the dead.[4]

Paying honors to the dead was a prerequisite for men holding office (Aristotle, *Athenaion Politeia* 55.3; Xenophon, *Memorabilia* 2.2.13) and for inheriting

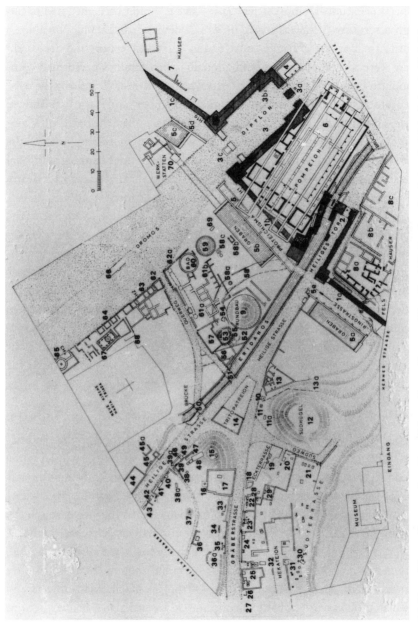

6.2. Plan of Kerameikos cemetery. From Knigge, *Kerameikos von Athen* fig. 165. Courtesy Deutsches Archäologisches Institut, Athen.

property ([Pseudo-Demosthenes] 43.57–58): to hold office, men had to undergo a scrutiny (*dokimasia*), part of which demanded that they be able to identify their ancestral tombs; next-of-kin heirs had to bury the deceased.[5] There were formal occasions held annually when families performed commemorative rites at the tombs; the festival called Genesia (honoring the tribe [*genos*]) took place on 5 Boedromion (mid September) and is the best known, perhaps because it preceded the state commemoration of the battle of Marathon (6 Boedromion, 490 BCE). But there were other celebrations of the dead, annual ones about which we know little except their names, traditional ones such as those that occurred on the ninth and thirtieth days after death, and personal ones that occurred at more informal times.

On the formal occasions the entire family paid honor to its ancestors, but it is clear from the scenes on vases, especially the fifth-century white-ground oil flasks (*lekythoi*) that were often left at the tombs and the fourth-century red-figure vases that marked the tombs,[6] that women by themselves often paid other and more casual visits, much as we see them doing in the modern cemeteries in Greece today. In these vase paintings, we see them bringing appropriate objects to the tomb, trays with fillets and lekythoi, special cakes, and other gifts for remembering loved ones; they would pour libations, leave gifts and bloodless offerings, and tie the fillets around the tombstone, perhaps as a gesture of remembrance and closure.

THE CEMETERY[7]

Outside the fortification wall, three roads converge at the Dipylon and Sacred Gates in northwest Athens: from the harbor at Piraeus a road (now called Gräberstrasse) joins the Sacred Way from Eleusis to follow the left bank of the Eridanos stream into the city through the Sacred Gate; east of the Eridanos, the wide road from the Academy enters the city through the Dipylon Gate. At the convergence of these three roads stretches the Kerameikos cemetery alongside and between them for some distance. Public monuments line the Academy road; here, several monumental tombs have been excavated, such as the mass tomb of the Lacedaemonian officers and Athenian polemarchs (403 BCE; Xenophon, *Hellenica* 2.4.28–33). Farther out must have been more tombs of the honored dead buried at public expense, the Demosion Sema, where Pausanias saw the stele of Pericles who gave the famous funeral oration there (Thucydides 2.34–46; Pausanias 1.29.3). The extraordinary width of the Academy road (more than 35 m in front of the Dipylon Gate) would have accommodated the funeral games that accompanied these state occasions.[8]

Most of the private cemetery plots flank Piraeus Street and the Sacred Way, filling the triangular area between them. At the convergence of the two roads was the Tritopatreion (plot 14), probably a heröon; across the Sacred Way to the south is a sanctuary to an unknown divinity (plot 20); and farther up the hill to the west is a sanctuary to Hekate (plot 32). Aside from such sacred areas, the cemetery contains hundreds, if not thousands of burials. Most of the tombs consist of unmarked sarcophagi, simple inhumations, some cremations, all stacked in several layers in the earth, grouped in plots tended by families, and marked by the tomb stelai.

Women visitors to the Kerameikos cemetery in the later Classical period would have entered it through one of the two gates, and, unless they were to pay honors to an illustrious family member buried in one of the public monuments along the Academy road, they would have turned toward the private plots along the Sacred Way and Piraeus Street.

Although in use from the twelfth century BCE to the early Roman period, the cemetery saw its principal use from the mid fifth century into the third century (early Hellenistic period). In 338 BCE, after Athens' defeat at the battle of Chaironeia, many of the cemetery's tomb markers and building blocks were hastily removed to repair the city walls. After a sumptuary law in 317/316 under Demetrios of Phaleron, tomb markers became drastically simplified; no longer the ornately sculpted stelai of the earlier period, large rectangular blocks or short columns bore only the name of the deceased (cognomen), father's name (patronymic), and the community from which they came (demotic).

In the late fifth and fourth centuries, tomb markers varied in shape, but many of all types were inscribed. Some markers took the shape in marble of the lekythoi whose oil was poured in honor of the dead and the taller loutrophoroi, which often marked the tombs of the unmarried; many of these also received relief sculpture. Most markers, however, consisted of simple, upright slabs often (though by no means always) decorated with relief sculpture. There are two major types of sculpted stelai, the tall pediment stele whose area above the relief takes the form of a temple pediment and the shorter, squarer *näískos* (little temple or shrine) stele that looks like a temple façade with flanking jambs enclosing the relief with pediment above. The deeper the relief and broader the stele, the more people it can accommodate and the later it usually is dated; in the latest naiskos stelai, the relief can be a separate slab inserted between separate jambs and crowned with a separate pediment.

The excavated area of the Kerameikos contains at least 35 identifiable ' family plots, each containing numerous burials but only a few tomb stelai; Christoph Clairmont's massive update of Conze catalogues 125 Classical stelai that can be assigned to the Kerameikos cemetery, and, of these, 54 can be attributed to the family plots they once marked. Several inscribed tomb markers identify the specific members of the family, and from these it is sometimes possible to reconstruct an extended family tree.[9] Obvious age and sex differences in the relief scenes allow for similar reconstructions of generic family groups.[10]

In many cases, the people depicted on the stelai seem to correspond to the names inscribed, and in these instances we can assume that, at least when a stele was first set up, it marked the graves of the people named on it.[11] Many other stelai, however, were reused; some were put into new bases, and others were reinscribed with new names.[12] We can imagine that modifications to a family's plot and the later burial of additional family members might have warranted such reuse; more drastically, some stelai might even have been taken from one plot to mark another, especially in the late fourth century, after the disturbances to the cemetery in 338, or perhaps when a family had died out or moved away and there was no longer any male relative to maintain the plot. It is therefore often impossible to tell whether the people named (in either the original or later inscriptions) were related to each other,[13] if the names inscribed had any relation to the people depicted in the reliefs,[14] or if the names inscribed and the people depicted were even related to the deceased buried in the plot itself.[15] Our women visitors coming to a family plot to honor their ancestral dead may have had to regard the markers with a "willing suspension of disbelief": it is possible that such a visitor, when pouring her libations and setting her offerings, had in mind deceased relatives and friends who were not the persons inscribed on the stelai or engraved in the scenes or even buried below.[16]

Though the connection between the inscribed names, the sculpted figures, and the deceased might not always have been straightforward, we may nonetheless assume that our women visitors saw some sort of generic relationship operating between names and figures on the stelai and the people whom she came to honor. Though some of the scenes on the stelai were specially commissioned, most are conventional, with several versions appearing on different stelai, and these must have been carved in a type of mass production ready to be bought, inscribed, and set up.[17] Most of these scenes depict people singly or in groups of two or three, occasionally four, rarely more. It is obvious that these people correspond to social realities and were meant to be seen as comprising ideal families, often accompanied by their servants. The inscriptions and the apparent ages of the individuals can therefore be helpful in identifying the idealized relationships among the participants in some of these scenes.[18]

Here are two examples from the Kerameikos, one straightforward, the other surprising: stele Kerameikos MG 23, I 433, depicts a standing woman clasping hands with a seated man and gives their names, Theopropis and Simonides; because she appears much younger than he, they are presumably wife and husband rather than sister and brother.[19] Stele Kerameikos P 695, I 221, depicts a woman holding an infant, as if mother and child, but the inscription tells us that the woman Amphareté is the grandmother, and all females, child, mother, and grandmother, are now deceased.[20]

I give these examples and the various factors at work in the Kerameikos of the later Classical period, because, in trying to imagine the interaction between our women visitors and the monuments, we need to keep in mind that almost every apparent "fact" about the stelai could have been a fiction. We can hypothesize that stelai were set up soon after the burial of the primary deceased whom they commemorated. At that time, the figures engraved in the reliefs probably portrayed idealized social families; inscriptions would be necessary to specify special relationships (e.g., mother and child) but not necessarily specific families (e.g., grandmother and granddaughter). Additional names could be added later, but these might not correspond to the figures sculpted in the reliefs. A family may die out or move, or a family plot might change hands, and stelai could then be appropriated to mark the tombs of other people. Such discrepancies and alterations might thus have freed our women visitors to the cemetery from the necessity of interpreting the conventional figures in the reliefs as specific individuals, allowing them therefore to be able to gaze upon them with the freedom to construct their own narratives and interpretations.

WOMEN ON THE TOMBSTONES

What is indisputable about the stelai, however, is the preponderance of women in the inscriptions and in the figured scenes. Tombstones from Athens depict and mention the cognomina of more women than men;[21] and when women and men are depicted together, it is common for the woman to be named but the man not.[22] More specifically, of the 125 catalogued stelai from the Kerameikos, inscriptions record at least 80 female cognomina and at least 66 male cognomina.[23] Of the freeborn people depicted in the reliefs (servants not being counted), there are 5 infants, 1 child, 111 males, and 131 females, with roughly twice the number of females than males in the range of young adult to adult.[24]

Depictions of women also seem more personalized. Men on the tombstones possess a number of attributes that identify them as soldiers, hunters, citizens, athletes, and devoted sons.[25] Women, too, are depicted and named in the conventional family roles of wife, mother, sister, and daughter, but they are also depicted in other roles such as priestess, dancer, midwife, and physician.[26]

The tomb markers were presumably set up to commemorate the death of a specific individual, conventionally termed the "primary deceased."[27] When the stele depicts a seated and a standing figure, Clairmont usually identifies the standing figure as the primary deceased, taking leave of the one who is remaining. This seems sensible, but other indications may elicit a different identification. Among the well-preserved Attic stelai depicting only two adult persons (Clairmont nos. 2.051–2.499) I briefly surveyed those that name just one of the figures, assuming that the named person was the primary deceased. There are 82 examples of such stelai: 61 women and 21 men are named. Of the scenes where it was clear to which of the two sculpted figures the name applied, there was a slight preference for seated figures to be named (42 seated to 34 standing) but a marked preference for figures on the left to be named (49 at left to 27 at right). In the reliefs, therefore, women on the left, especially when seated, stand a good chance of being the primary deceased; at the end of this study we shall return to this preference.

The most common composition involves two figures on stelai, one seated, the other standing, often clasping hands (*dexiôsis*: δεξίωσις).[28] Men can have masculine attributes such as staff, shield, or hunting hound (to connote citizen, warrior, or hunter), while women have a box, a wool basket (*kalathos*), or a child (fig. 6.3, 6.4).[29] When a man and woman are depicted together, they may be husband and wife or brother and sister; inscriptions sometimes state these relationships, and noticeable age differences or similarities (respectively) may imply them. In other instances, two men clasp hands, and occasionally inscriptions specify father and son or perhaps brothers.[30]

While the majority of two-figure stelai depict a man and a woman, of the ones that depict same-sex pairs, more stelai depict both women than both men.[31] Sometimes the familial relationship between these women is clear: inscriptions may specify it, or obvious age differences may imply mothers and daughters.[32] In three reliefs, the second woman assists the other who is

6.3. Stele for seated woman, in front of whom a second woman stands and holds a box. Athens, National Archaeological Museum 726; Clairmont no. 2.300. Photograph: Author.

6.4. Stele for woman who died in childbirth; woman stands and looks at seated woman; between, woman (servant?) holds infant; in back of chair, another woman. Athens, National Archaeological Museum 819; Clairmont no. 4.930. Photograph: Author.

dying; for convenience, Clairmont prefers to identify this second woman as the deceased's mother, but without an inscription that specifies her role, she equally well could be a midwife, if the woman died in childbirth, or some other professional, friend, or relative assisting.[33]

In the majority of these two-women scenes, however, the relationship between them is unclear, even if, for convenience, one may prefer to identify the women as related or as close friends.[34] As is common, almost all the scenes involving only two women have one standing and one seated, and they may or may not clasp hands.

In the following section, I concentrate on two aspects of these stelai depicting two women: whether they clasp hands or not, and whether they are named or not (assuming that naming the figures indicates they belong to the family whose plot the stele marked and that clasping hands indicates that the two figures are related). To anticipate my conclusions: when both women are named, they almost invariably clasp hands and are probably therefore close family members. But when neither woman or only one woman is named, the standing woman usually contemplates the seated woman, and they do not clasp hands; I suggest that these two women are not close family members.[35]

Of the stelai that depict the two women clasping hands, only six do not name either figure (fig. 6.5): four scenes depict one woman standing and one sitting, thereby indicating a domestic location but otherwise no specific relationship between them;[36] the fifth, however, includes a small household dog, akin to the modern Spitz, that leaps upon the figure at the right, probably to indicate the primary deceased;[37] the sixth stele includes a maid who holds a baby.[38] Of the ten stelai that depict the two women touching, five name just one of them: four depict them clasping hands,[39] and the fifth depicts an embrace (see below).[40]

When both women are named, however, they almost invariably clasp hands,[41] whether they both stand[42] or, as is otherwise the rule, one stands and one sits. Most of these scenes are simple with no object to convey the social construction of either woman;[43] occasionally, however, one of the women holds something to indicate a social role: the standing woman holds a box,[44] the sitting woman holds a *kithara* (a type of lyre),[45] a maid holds a child.[46]

The rest of the stelai, both those naming neither woman and those naming only one woman, depict no handclasping; instead, one woman stands and regards the second woman seated. For instance, a standing woman regards the seated "Arkhestrate daughter of Alexos from Sounion" fingering her veil.[47] On two stelai, the standing woman holds or offers a baby to a seated

6.5. Stele for seated woman who clasps hands with second woman who stands and looks at her; in back of chair, girl. Athens, National Archaeological Museum 870; Clairmont 3.461. Photograph: Author.

woman.[48] But most commonly (seven stelai), a young unnamed woman holds a box and regards the seated woman, who is named (the primary deceased): "Ameinokleia daughter of Andromenes from Lamptraia" with her sandal being adjusted by a maid;[49] "Pausimakhe" opening a box;[50] "Kalliarista daughter of Phileratos wife of Damokles" touching her mantle;[51] "Arkhestrate" taking a fillet from the box and regarding her daughter, who leans against her knees holding a bird;[52] "Kallistomakhe daughter of Thorykon from Trikorinthos" receiving a large bracelet; and "Glykylla" removing (or perhaps putting on) a bracelet.[53]

Even when the stele is reused, the seated figure is the one named (and thus the primary deceased even in the period of reuse); for instance, seated

"Niki]ppe daughter of Nikippos" holds some wool (a kalathos stands beneath her chair) while a young woman, against whose thigh a nude boy leans, stands and regards her.[54]

The gesture of clasping hands (dexiosis) has received much scholarly discussion.[55] It joins two people physically and in harmony; it was used in life both upon meeting and upon parting, and for closing the agreement between father and prospective groom for the daughter's hand in marriage. As a gesture in funerary art, it therefore signified that the deceased and survivor were closely joined both before and after death: "The two parties together make up a whole, the family, which the intervention of death has failed to sunder."[56]

Most of the relationships depicted on stelai showing two people were probably considered real yet conventional; having them of different sexes, naming both, and having them clasp hands was probably the surest way to imply a close family relationship (a loving husband and wife, for instance). Omitting any of these criteria throws that relationship in doubt; omitting all (having the two figures both women, naming neither woman or just one of them, and omitting the handclasp) must be seen therefore as deliberately implying that the two women were not close family members. That this relationship was depicted on so many stelai as to be conventional ought to imply that it was socially real, if not socially legitimated. I suggest, therefore, that these two women, not clasping hands, at most only one who is named, represent women who were "close friends," one woman regarding her deceased friend.

THE HOME AND TOMB

Who is this unnamed woman, the secondary deceased, if she is not a close relative? She usually stands to regard the named other woman who is most often seated—they should at least therefore be friends. Since the small range of attributes, the box, a kalathos and ball of wool, an infant or child, the small dog, and the omnipresent chair are all emblems of the home (oikos: οἶκος),[57] I take the secondary nonrelative woman to represent all members of the primary deceased's circle of intimate friends.

It is of course an ideal home, one envisioned on the stelai as an encapsulation of the one envisioned by proper society. In vase paintings, we see the same home environments where women of the household, women relatives, and women friends gathered. We see them lounging against each other, bathing, dressing one another, arranging each other's hair; producing cloth and washing clothes; playing lyres and auloi (a musical instrument like a double clarinet) for one another; and looking after their children and their women servants. Such domestic spaces were probably the realm of women once their husbands and fathers left for the agora, and it is these homosocial spaces at those times that may have been called the "gynaikonitis" (γυναικω-νῖτις) or "women's quarters."[58] I prefer to think of the gynaikonitis as the space and the women in it, a type of "woman's world."

The well-known terracotta kneeguard (*epinetron*) for working wool, the namepiece of the Eretria Painter (late fifth century), may serve to illustrate this "woman's world" (fig. 6.6). Its two main scenes depict women preparing brides, one labeled the goddess Harmonia, the other, the heroine Alkestis.[59] On the back end, the end at the thigh, there is a band decorated with palmettes. On the front, knee end, the utensil has an applied woman's head and a painted band depicting Peleus seizing Thetis in front of her father Nereus and five sisters, Altis, Melite, Eulimene, Aura, and Nao. A frieze runs along each side that hugged the thigh, and each depicts the mythological scene of women preparing a bride for marriage. On side A, we see divinities, left to right: in front of a column a seated Aphrodite selects jewelry, Eros holds a chest, Peitho and Kore flank a seated Harmonia (Aphrodite's daughter, the bride), and Hebe adjusts her hair before a seated winged male Himeros (Desire), who holds a chest of cloth and offers her a small jar, probably of perfumed oil (fig. 6.7); and on side B, we see heroines, left to right: Theo bends over two black-figure basins on stands (*lebetes gamikoi*), Kharis stands facing her and lifts her mantle, Theano arranges branches in a loutrophoros as if it were a flower vase, Asterope leans on a seated Hippolyte talking to her pet bird perched on her left hand, and inside a columned porch Alkestis (the bride) leans against a bed in front of an open door (a room is visible beyond), and on the wall hang two wreaths and a mirror (fig. 6.8).

The domestic environments on the Eretria Painter's epinetron share several interesting points with the stelai; here too we find the box and chest, jewelry, the pet, and the gesture of lifting the mantle. This gesture is akin to the formal unveiling (*anakalypsis*) that the bride does in front of her new husband.[60] But on the epinetron and on the tomb stelai, the gesture seems more casual.[61] Clairmont notes that women normally drew the cloak (*himation*) over the head to cover themselves modestly, and fingering or touching it was simply giving "the inactive hand . . . some activity," especially "in the context of the togetherness of the living with the deceased." The gesture may have indeed been absent-minded, but most stelai depict the gesture as if

6.6. Red-figure epinetron by the Eretria Painter. Athens, National Archaeological Museum 1629. Photograph from negative from the Athens, National Archaeological Museum. Courtesy Deutsches Archäologisches Institut, Athen.

6.7. Red-figure epinetron by the Eretria Painter. Athens, National Archaeological Museum 1629. Side A: preparations for the marriage of Harmonia. Drawing after Hartwig, " Ἐπίνητρον ἐξ Ἐρετρίας," pl. 10.1.

6.8. Red-figure epinetron by the Eretria Painter. Athens, National Archaeological Museum 1629. Side B: preparations for the marriage of Alkestis. Drawing after Hartwig, " Ἐπίνητρον ἐξ Ἐρετρίας," pl. 10.2.

frozen halfway between veiling and unveiling, as if ambivalent; viewers could therefore interpret it according to their own inclination: either unveiling or about to veil the face, welcoming or refusing the spectator's attention.[62]

Even more striking is the Eretria Painter's depiction of Alkestis leaning against her bed, presumably the marriage bed that she addresses in Euripides' play, *Alkestis* (177–182); since Alkestis' death heroizes her, her marriage bed is much like the couch that women in the stelai lean against or lie on having died in childbirth (see above, and n33).

Perhaps marrying, giving birth, and dying were closely linked;[63] the tomb stelai often show deceased women and their infants, and the inscriptions mention their death soon after marriage. For the daughter of Ampharete (above, and n20) and for Myrtis (above, and n32), giving birth brought on their death. In addition, on a damaged stele we read how Pamphile died early into her marriage and apparently before giving birth:

> Marriage gave her once a home in which Pamphile
> was eager to dwell most blessedly;
> she left behind her life now finished before twenty
> and the marriage home of her youth died with her.[64]

From such examples and from the large number of women named and depicted on the tomb stelai, marriage, giving birth, and death seem to have been a recurrent sequence. The cemetery may have been an extension of the gynaikonitis: both were women's spaces, with the gynaikonitis being the locus where women supported women through the dangers of marriage and childbirth, and the cemetery being the locus where women tended the tombs of those who had succumbed. Since these marriages and childbirths are subjects that focus on women's sexuality, womb, and genitals, the homosocial environments of both gynaikonitis and cemetery may also have been the loci for homoerotic feelings.

HOMOSOCIAL AND HOMOEROTIC STELAI

What might a woman think and feel when she paid honors to the dead and looked upon the women in the stelai? If we turn to the accompanying inscriptions, many seem too repetitive to be helpful, often employing a standardized vocabulary that restricts empathy: a woman's qualities are usually limited to the formulaic "virtuous and restrained (or moderate)" (*agathê kai sôphrôn:* ἀγαθὴ καὶ σώφρων), the female counterpart to the "good and upright man" (*kalos k'agathos:* καλὸς κ'ἀγαθός); her worth is conveyed by the sorrow (*penthos:* πένθος) she leaves behind and the longing/desire (*pothos:*

πόθος) her family feels at her loss. The inscriptions also sketch out conventional narratives: death cut short her marriage; now dead, she cannot enjoy the child she bore; the earth envelops her body but her memory lives on.

One remarkable stele, however, should caution us against dismissing these conventional narratives, qualities, and emotions. A painted stele once depicted two women, probably standing and facing each other and therefore not clasping hands and therefore probably not close family members; both their names, however, are inscribed, "Herophile" and "Anthemis." The accompanying elegiac couplet is remarkable for its content, sentiment, and graceful meter:

> Her companions crown this tomb of Anthemis with a wreath
> in their remembrance of her virtue and friendship.[65]

In few words this sincere memorial assures us that women, like Anthemis' companions, did tend the tombs of their friends with genuine care; the memorial also allows us to assume that Herophile was indeed one of Anthemis' companions, the secondary woman, and therefore a member of her gynaikonitis.

We therefore need to pay more attention to the reliefs and the epigrams of stelai than their conventional words and scenes might otherwise elicit:

A young woman stands holding an open box, from which the young seated Arkhestrate takes out a fillet while she looks at a small girl holding a bird:

> The earth has covered over the virtuous and restrained
> Arkhestrate most desired by her husband.[66]

Khrysanthe stands, clasping hands with a seated elderly man:

> The earth has her body within but your moderation,
> Khrysanthe, that the tomb cannot hide.[67]

Pausimakhe stands somewhat limply, holding a mirror (fig. 6.9):

> All who live are fated to die, but you Pausimakhe
> leave behind bitter sorrow for your grandparents
> and your mother Phainippe and father Pausanias;
> those standing here see this memorial of your virtue
> and moderation.[68]

As seated Melite clasps hands with her beloved Onesimos, he addresses her in the inscription and twice praises her as worthy (*khrêstê:* χρηστή)—she was probably a slave; in the last line she replies:

—Hail! tomb of Melite, a worthy woman lies here;
You constantly returned the love Onesimos had for you;
how he misses you now dead, for you were a worthy woman.
—And hail! beloved of men, do take care of my loved ones![69]

And one fragmentary stele preserves only the head of "Dionysia," a woman past her prime, and an idealizing inscription:

Neither clothing nor gold did she enjoy in life
but she loved her husband and self-restraint;
instead of your youthful beauty, Dionysia,
your husband Antiphilos adorns your tomb.[70]

The conventional persons depicted in the reliefs and the conventional narratives conveyed in the inscriptions do not have to limit the women viewers/readers of them from interpreting them as they wish. Several stelai appeal to their imagination and address them directly, inviting them to contribute to the construction of a continuing narrative. The stele of Khrysanthe, for instance, implies that the spectator can envision her "moderation"; the stele of Pausimakhe asks the spectator to imagine her "virtue and moderation"; the stele of Melite invites the spectator to wonder if her "loved ones" are indeed being taken care of; and the stele of Dionysia demands that the spectator observe if her tomb is indeed being adorned. Such appeals involve us in the process of continuing these women's lives.

PAUSIMAKHE'S MIRROR

The stelai employ several other devices that cause the spectator to identify with the women in the reliefs. The most obvious is Pausimakhe's mirror. Several stelai depict women holding mirrors. Clairmont lists twenty-four, but several are fragmentary and unclear, and three depict the woman (all facing left) not looking into the mirror she holds.[71] The other twenty-one women, however, do look into their mirror; most stand to the right, hold the mirror up, and look directly into it. One even has a dowel hole in her upraised hand; a real mirror may have been inserted there. Since an interest in depicting reflections in mirrors begins to develop contemporaneously in other fourth-century media, including South Italian vases and mural paint-

6.9. Stele for Pausimakhe. Athens, National Archaeological Museum 3964; Clairmont no. 1.283. Photograph from negative, National Archaeological Museum, Athens, © photographer H. R. Goette. Courtesy Deutsches Archäologisches Institut, Athen.

ing, it is possible that Pausimakhe's mirror had her reflection painted on it for us to gaze at.[72] Since she holds the mirror up so that we see its almost full disk, the reflection we would see, or imagine, there would have been ours as well as hers; Pausimakhe, then, is our alter ego.[73] The *memento mori* in her inscription, "All who live are fated to die," reminds us all of the passing of time and the nearness of death; the reflection, therefore, is also that of our immanent soul.[74]

A full study of ancient mirrors is beyond the scope of this paper, but a few additional comments are appropriate.[75] One of the primary purposes of mirrors is to allow us to see ourselves as we appear physically to others; thus we use them to perfect our appearance and to check our health. The image that mirrors convey, however, is an illusion that occupies no real space in this world (therefore an "outopia" [or "utopia"]).[76] This illusion would have been more obvious in antiquity, since ancient mirrors were of polished metal, usually bronze, and the reflection they gave back was dark. Within the heterotopia of the cemetery, the sculpted figure of Pausimakhe gazes at her reflection in the mirror; and as a real woman spectator envisioned that dark reflection (a stand-in for her own), the two women would have triangulated that reflection, locating it at the juncture of their two worlds.[77] As the two women, the lifeless Pausimakhe in her outopia and the living woman in the heterotopia of the cemetery, both gaze upon the mirror, like a hinge it folds the one onto the other and melds them.

ARKHESTRATE'S FRIEND

Although several stelai depict women holding mirrors precisely as Pausimakhe does, many other stelai use another device for triangulating the spectator into the scene: the secondary woman who gazes at the primary deceased, at whom all spectators of the stele also gaze. The stele of Arkhestrate, for instance (above, and nn52 and 66), depicts a young woman holding a box and gazing at Arkhestrate as she removes a fillet and, in turn, gazes at her daughter, who leans against her knees and holds a bird. Arkhestrate, the primary deceased, thus functions like Pausimakhe's mirror, to triangulate the spectator to the secondary woman and meld them. Whereas the mirror causes the deceased and the spectator to be paired, the parallel gazes of the secondary woman and of the spectator demand that they also be paired.[78] When the spectator thus assumes the role of the secondary woman, in gazing and reflecting upon the primary deceased, she is also being asked to imagine and feel the emotions that were felt by the women whom the secondary woman represents.

If our woman spectator gazes at the young woman, who in turn gazes at Arkhestrate, who in turn gazes at her daughter who gazes back, there is ample opportunity for her to imagine a narrative of love, loss, grief, and yearning, and for her to appropriate for herself, along the circle of gazes, the desire that Arkhestrate's husband felt at her passing. Our woman spectator thus builds on her perception of the relief and epigram and on her identification with the young woman holding the box to create her own metaresponse: to imagine what her own relationship to Arkhestrate would have been and to regenerate the desire that had once been felt for her.[79]

Through such devices as the mirror and the secondary woman, our woman visitor learned to identify herself as a member of the primary deceased's circle of friends and to read herself actively into the construction of a narrative that concerns her and her relationship with another woman,[80] the primary deceased. She should be able to place herself intimately in that relationship, to gaze upon the primary woman with feelings, yearnings, and regrets similar to those depicted in the relief and specified in the epigrams, even to the point of imagining the woman's life cut short, her virtue and moderation, and even the desire felt for her.[81]

GIRL-FRIENDS ON STELAI

Several stelai lead us more specifically toward this last possibility, that of homoerotic feelings being depicted in the stelai or generated by their depictions.[82] I start with three deep naiskos stelai dated to the mid fourth century; while there is nothing distinctly homoerotic about them, several aspects seem unusual: the stelai form a coherent stylistic group, only pairs of women are depicted and named on them, and no family relationship is specified (they are not mothers and daughters, sisters, or cousins). In other words, there is no mention or indication of any of the usual, socially legitimated relationships between these women.

Each of the three stelai depicts one woman standing on the left with her left hand raised in a speaking gesture, and the other woman seated on the right. One stele, provenience unknown, names its two women "Hedeia daughter of Lysikles from Athmonon" and "Phanylla daughter of Aristoleides from Athmonon"; for convenience, Clairmont identifies them as cousins, but they may simply be friends from the same community.[83] Two similar stelai, both from plot 20 in the Kerameikos, both name the women "Demetria" and "Pamphile" (fig. 6.10) and the original architrave to one of these two stelai carries additional names secondarily inscribed, "Kallistomakhe daughter of Diokles" and "Nausion daughter of Sosandros."[84] The three stelai are so similar, stylistically and compositionally, that they should all come from the same workshop, possibly destined for the same clientele or the same cemetery plot (if so, Kerameikos plot 20).

From the inscriptions, it is clear that these women, Hedeia, Phanylla, Demetria, Pamphile, Kallistomakhe, and Nausion, are not sisters. Since all their cognomina are different, they probably are not first cousins.[85] It seems unlikely that all six women would have been second cousins commemorated by stelai from a single workshop—and two of them even twice. If these six women did not belong to a nuclear family, one wonders what their relationship was. Whoever they were, they were important; perhaps they had formed some kind of an association or had been in business together, or perhaps they were just very close friends whom not even death could separate.

6.10. Cast of the stele for Demetria and Pamphile, from Kerameikos plot 20. Kerameikos inv. no. unknown; Clairmont no. 2.464. Photograph: Author.

Two stelai depict one woman embracing the other. On one (see above, and n40), a young woman embraces and touches the chin of a maiden, and the inscription above names one of them, "Mynnion daughter of Khairestratos from Hagnous." Since the gesture is directed at the maiden, she is probably Mynnion, but there is not enough of an age difference between them to identify the young woman as her mother; it is more likely that she is another relative or a slightly older close friend.

The second stele is unusual:[86] a woman embraces and touches the breast of a girl. Clairmont identifies the girl as about ten years old, and the woman as a nurse by her "garment and possibly also her physiognomy"; at the left stands a smaller girl. The top frame of the stele bears an inscription over the woman, "Soteris," and letters of a name, now illegible, over the girl. Although the gesture is unusual, a contemporary Apulian winejar depicts a similar scene with two adult women.[87] The girl may not be so young as ten, but she is certainly no older than twenty. If Soteris were a nurse, she would probably have been named as such (*titthê:* τίτθη; see above, n26); her "physiognomy" does seem crude, but that need not imply a difference in class or status. Given these peculiarities, it is possible that the stele does depict something unusual.

Even more interesting is the scene on a half-preserved, early fifth-century relief from Phalanna, Thessaly: two women stand and face each other; the woman at the left lifts up the left shoulder of her chiton and holds out a ball, probably of wool, in her right hand; the woman at the right touches the left edge of her chiton's shoulder and reaches out as if to take the ball.[88] The two gestures answer each other and seem purposeful rather than casual, as if gestures in greeting or in mutual understanding. The same gesture, also in connection with wool working, occurs in the tondo of a kylix by Douris (see Rabinowitz's essay in this volume, fig. 5.1).[89] The ball of wool that is being offered may function as a gift; and since it connotes weaving and therefore invokes that homosocial work environment, the ball of wool as a gift may have been a love gift. The gesture of lifting the shoulder of one's chiton while a ball of wool is offered may convey the women's good intentions, willingness, receptivity, or even desire.[90]

Another ball of wool occurs on Nikippe's stele from Skala Oropou mentioned above (n54), and a kalathos under her chair completes the reference to the industriousness of the deceased.[91] But Clairmont and others have also pointed out that the pose of Nikippe's right arm, raised high against the back of her chair, is reminiscent of the pose of Alkamenes' "Aphrodite of the Gardens" and this may lend some support for an erotic connotation for the ball of wool.

Finally, another early fifth-century, half-preserved relief from Pharsalus, Thessaly, shows a similar scene (fig. 6.1); it has been much discussed.[92] Two women face each other, and while the woman on the left stands, the woman on the right was probably seated; both women wear scarves to bind their hair. The woman on the left holds up a flower in her left hand and, with her right, offers a leather bag (*phormiskos:* φόρμισκος) to the woman on the right, who holds two flowers, one up in her raised right hand and another down in her lowered left hand.

The iconography here seems homoerotic in three details, the flowers, the raised and lowered hands, and the phormiskos, but most scholars seem to have shied deliberately away from such an interpretation. John Boardman (above, n92) notes vaguely that "Thessaly will present novel compositions with women, presaged in [the Pharsalus relief] with its mysterious pair," as if such mysteries are appropriate to the outskirts of civilization. Brunilde Ridgway (above, n92) assumes the relief is a tombstone and describes it as

6.11. Relief from Pharsalus, Thessaly. Louvre 701. Photograph: Author.

presenting a "moment of intimacy and companionship," but she dismisses the intimacy as something servile: "The presence of the companion [on the left] in the Pharsalus relief carries approximately the same emotional implication as the pet of other tombstones, or the small servant boy" attending athletes and youths. Since the two women seem approximately equal in stature and status, Ridgway's characterization is unfair.

Both women assume a version of the "hands up and down gesture," a gesture that is seen primarily, but not originally, in male homoerotic courting scenes.[93] The flowers may support this association. In many erotic scenes, people hold flowers, whether the scene takes place in a brothel or whether it involves men courting youths.[94] The meaning of flower holding should imply a good disposition or warm feelings; in the hands of a person offering a flower, it may also demonstrate one's good intentions or even desire,[95] and in the hands of a person being made an offer, as with youths being courted and women prostitutes being approached by men, it may signify one's willingness to accept.[96] With these possibilities in mind, Gundel Koch-Harnack found it difficult to avoid the conclusion that the two women on the Pharsalus relief are lovers: the woman on the right is older (she has a fuller bosom and heavier jaw), and "she tilts her head so as to look lovingly into the eyes of her partner."[97]

Though the contents of the leather bag are open to discussion, it is generally assumed that such bags contained either coins or knucklebones (*astragaloi*: ἀστράγαλοι). In a couple of vase paintings, people in a shop hold a phormiskos, apparently purchasing something with the coins in the bag.[98] The majority of scenes with phormiskoi, however, depict men and youths offering or showing them to women or youths; and in these cases, the phormiskoi should either contain coins for sex[99] or astragaloi as a love gift.[100]

A relief from Aigina, but undoubtedly of Attic workmanship, also features two women and a phormiskos: a seated young woman clasps hands with a standing woman, who draws her veil back with a dramatic gesture.[101] The seated woman's left hand tightly holds the phormiskos slightly above her lap and just below the handclasp. Both Athena Kalogeropoulou, who first published the stele, and Clairmont assume that the bag's contents are astragaloi. Kalogeropoulou comments (above, n100) that astragaloi are found by the hundreds in tombs, attesting their use in foretelling the future and the deceased's role in mediating between this world and the next. She also comments on the apparent similarity of the two young women's ages, which leads Clairmont to identify them as "intimate girl friends."

Since astragaloi are common as tomb offerings,[102] it is possible they are the contents of the bags on the Pharsalus and Aigina reliefs; if so, they should be gifts from one woman to the other. If the Aigina relief is a tomb stele, its composition may conform to the standards outlined above: the seated woman on the left is the primary deceased to whom the standing secondary woman on the right has given the phormiskos with its astragaloi. The Pharsalus relief reverses the conventional Attic position of the two women: the standing secondary woman on the left gives her phormiskos of astragaloi to the seated deceased woman on the right; their flowers symbolize the intimate friendship they had and their warm feelings for each other.

"SPLIT," "DOUBLE," "MULTIPLE," AND "SELF" CONSCIOUSNESS

Cemeteries are indeed heterotopias, "other" places, where we think thoughts and feel emotions that are often different from those we have in "normal" places. In cemeteries we feel the presence of the dead, and we know we shall eventually join them in that "innumerable caravan" (W. C. Bryant, "Thanatopsis"). With these feelings and knowledge, we construct a different sense of ourselves than that which we usually feel.

The Kerameikos cemetery in the Classical period was no different. It constituted a heterotopia outside the city gates, one that in the later fourth century had also lost even an internal fixity—plots had changed hands, stelai had been moved, and other people's names had been engraved over the sculpted figures.

In such situations, our woman visitor, coming to the cemetery to honor specific individuals, might realize at some level the futility of specificity; instead, she would have to rely on her thoughts and emotions induced by the conventional figures in the reliefs and the conventional sentiments in the epigrams. Both relief and epigram, however, contributed at least one agenda: to induce an identity of visitor and deceased. The sentiments in the epigrams call for the woman visitor to imagine the deceased individual's character and qualities, to feel for her the emotions that her loved ones once felt for her, and finally to remember that she will join her.

Through such a device as Pausimakhe's mirror, our woman spectator becomes one with Pausimakhe herself, and through the device of the secondary woman, our woman spectator becomes fixed in a cycle of gazes. The primary deceased on the stelai is her future self, while the secondary woman who regards her is her alter self. Her own self thus regards the deceased whom her alter self also regards. The gaze comes full circle, locking our woman visitor into a loop of gazes as tight as the two gazes into Pausimakhe's mirror.

But these gazes are not like the gaze that men turn on our woman visitor inside the city on the other side of the gates; there she is object and object alone. Instead, in this homosocial nexus of viewer and viewed, it is her own gaze that travels from her through the two women figures on the stelai and back, continuously shifting from her to secondary woman to primary deceased, from her as subject to an object that is also a subject to another object that is also a subject to another object that is again her, making all both gazer and gazed in a continuous loop or *vision en abîme*.[103] Somewhere in that cycle of women viewing should be desire, the desire that begins and ends in the homosocial worlds of gynaikonitis and cemetery where marriage, birth, and death demanded that women care for each other while living, fulfill each other's lives when surviving, and tend each other's tomb. And within that desire should be a homoerotic desire between women, a woman's desire for a woman while alive and for the other woman on the other side of the gaze when she has passed on—and since visitor and deceased are inextricable, she is finally left with a homo*io*erotic (of someone similar) desire for her own self.

NOTES

*I am grateful to Nancy Sorkin Rabinowitz for the invitation to give a paper for the panel "Retrieving Female Homoeroticism" at the annual meeting of the American Philological Association, December 29, 1996, in New York City; eventually that paper turned into this very different one. I am also grateful to Paul Rehak and Lawrence Richardson Jr. for their help, suggestions and comments, and to my many students, especially Suzanne Fisher and Christina Ponig. The translations here are the author's own.

1. Lauren Petersen, "Divided Consciousness and Female Companionship: Reconstructing Female Subjectivity on Greek Vases," *Arethusa* 30 (1997): 35–74, esp. 51.

2. Aristophanes, *Lysistrata* 387–396; Menander, *Samia* 38–46; Plato, *Phaedrus* 276B; and other sources. The Adonia: Ronda R. Simms, "Mourning and Community at the Athenian Adonia," *Classical Journal* 93.2 (December–January 1998): 121–141, esp. 132 and n49; Jane Rowlandson, *Adonis Festival: Women and Society in Greek and Roman Egypt* (Cambridge: Cambridge UP, 1998); Nicole Weill, "Adoniazusai ou les femmes sur le toit," *Bulletin de Correspondance Héllenique* 90 (1966): 664–698; and John J. Winkler, *The Constraints of Desire: The Anthropology of Sex and Gender in Ancient Greece* (New York: Routledge, 1990) 188–209 ("The Laughter of the Oppressed: Demeter and the Gardens of Adonis"). The Thesmophoria: N. J. Lowe, "Thesmophoria and Haloa: Myth, Physics and Mysteries," in *Sacred and the Feminine in Ancient Greece*, ed. S. Blundell and M. Williamson (New York: Routledge, 1998) 149–186.

3. Michel Foucault, "Of Other Spaces: Utopias and Heterotopias," in *Rethinking Architecture*, ed. N. Leach (London: Routledge, 1997) 350–356.

4. For general information about Athenian funeral rites, see Margaret Alexiou, *The Ritual Lament in Greek Tradition* (Cambridge: Cambridge UP, 1974); R. Garland, *The Greek Way of Death* (Ithaca: Cornell UP, 1985); Gail Holst-Warhaft, *Dangerous Voices: Women's Laments and Greek Literature* (London: Routledge, 1992); S. C. Humphreys, *The Family, Women and Death: Comparative Studies.* 2nd ed. (Ann Arbor: U of Michigan P, 1993) esp. 82–88, 94–118; Eva C. Keuls, *The Reign of the Phallus: Sexual Politics in Ancient Athens* (Berkeley: U. of California P, 1985) 149–152; Donna C. Kurtz and John Boardman, *Greek Burial Customs* (Ithaca: Cornell UP, 1971); Ian Morris, *Burial and Ancient Society* (New York: Cambridge UP, 1987); Thomas H. Nielsen et al., "Athenian Grave Monuments and Social Class," *Greek, Roman and Byzantine Studies* 30 (1989): 411–420; H. W. Parke, *Festivals of the Athenians* (Ithaca: Cornell UP, 1977) 53–54; and H. Alan Shapiro, "The Iconography of Mourning in Athenian Art," *American Journal of Archaeology* 95 (1991): 629–656. Solon's antisumptuary laws of 594 apparently included restrictions against ostentatious funerals; sometime later, perhaps in the early democracy before the Persian Wars, more restrictions were said to be added. The Solonian restrictions, as they have come down to us, are elaborate concerning the presence and conduct of women: women could not lacerate themselves or wail or lament anyone else than the deceased, and no women under the age of sixty could attend the funeral unless closely related to the deceased (up to first or perhaps second cousins). The early democracy further restricted funer-

ary speeches to those made only by a public magistrate; compare Pericles' funeral oration (Thucydides 2.34–46), in which he refers to the tradition of having such speeches and to the decorous silence of women. For a detailed account, see Humphreys, *Family, Women and Death* 85–89 (incorporating the ancient sources, especially Plutarch, *Solon,* and Cicero, *de Legibus* 2.64). For an interpretative account, see Nicole Loraux, *L'Invention d'Athènes: Histoire de l'oraison funèbre dans la "cité classique."* 2nd ed. (Paris: Éditions Payot & Rivages, 1993) passim, esp. 39–64. For a cautious reassessment, see Ian Morris, "Law, Culture and Funerary Art in Athens: 600–300 B.C.," *Hephaistos* 11–12 (1992–1993): 35–50.

5. The dokimasia could be conducted twice, upon being enrolled into the tribe and upon being elected to office. Men were questioned about their ancestry, about their maintenance of family cults and tombs, parents, and property, and about fulfilling their duties to the state (military service and taxes): Winkler, *Constraints of Desire* 45–70 ("Laying down the Law: The Oversight of Men's Sexual Behavior in Classical Athens") esp. 54–56.

6. See, for example, the two mid-fifth-century white-ground lekythoi by the Achilles Painter, NMA 1963 (*ARV*[2] 995.122; *Paralipomena*[2] 438; Beazley *Addenda*[2] 312; Keuls, *Reign of the Phallus* fig. 105), and Ashmolean Museum 1896.41 (*ARV*[2] 998.165; Beazley *Addenda*[2] 313; Ellen D. Reeder, ed., *Pandora: Women in Classical Greece* [Princeton: Princeton UP, 1995] 146–148); and the fourth-century Apulian hydria associated with the Ilioupersis Painter in the New York Metropolitan Museum 56.171.65 (A. D. Trendall and Alexander Cambitoglou, *The Red-Figured Vases of Apulia,* Vol. 1 [Oxford: Clarendon P, 1978] 205.114, pl. 65.2). Also see Garland, *Greek Way of Death* 104–105; and Elaine Fantham, Helene Peet Foley, Natalie Boymel Kampen, Sarah B. Pomeroy, and H. A. Shapiro, eds., *Women in the Classical World: Image and Text* (Oxford: Oxford UP, 1994) 96–97.

7. For a guidebook: Ursula Knigge, *Der Kerameikos von Athen. Führung durch Ausgrabungen und Geschichte* (Athens: Deutsches Archäologisches Institut Athen, 1988).

8. Loraux, *Invention d'Athènes* 45.

9. Alexander Conze, Adolf Michaelis, Achilleus Postolakas, Emanuel Loewy, Alfred Brüchner, Paul Heinrich, August Wolters, and Robert von Schneider, *Die asttischen Grabreliefs.* 4 vols. (Berlin: W. Spemann, 1893–1922). See, for example, Clairmont's reconstructed lineage for the family of Eubios, whose plot was on the north side of Piraeus Street in the Kerameikos (Clairmont vol. III 336), and Humphreys, *Family, Women and Death* 109, 113, 118 for other lineages.

10. R. E. Leader, "In Death Not Divided: Gender, Family, and State on Classical Athenian Stelai," *American Journal of Archaeology* 101 (1997): 683–699. For example, Clairmont no. 3.350 (vol. III 184; NMA 717) from Kerameikos plot 19 belonging to Makareus and Archebios of Lakiadai depicts (beginning with this description, I describe the stelai, proceeding from left to right as I face them) a woman ("mother") seated on a stool clasping hands with a standing young woman ("daughter"), while an elderly man ("father") between them contemplates the "daughter," probably the primary deceased for whom the stele was erected.

11. Harold R. Hastings, "On the Relation between Inscriptions and Sculptured Representations on Attic Tombstones," *Bulletin of the University of Wisconsin* 485 (1912): 1–16, esp. 8, proposes that in most cases the deceased is depicted in the reliefs. For example: Clairmont nos. 2.210 (vol. II 147–148; NMA 765), a pediment stele, possibly from Kerameikos plot 21, shows a woman "Mika" and man "Dion" standing and clasping hands; 2.214 (vol. II 152–

153; Kerameikos I 342), a painted relief stele from Kerameikos tomb 106, depicts two women "Eukoline" and "Timulla" clasping hands; and 2.383 (vol. II 441–442; NMA 920), an anthemion stele (stele with floral top) from the Kerameikos, depicts an elderly man "Piaios" seated on a throne, clasping hands with a beardless young man "Diphilos."

12. Kurtz and Boardman, *Greek Burial Customs* 136–137. For example, Clairmont no. 2.441 (vol. II 562–563; NMA 764), a deep naiskos stele, depicts a standing young woman holding an opened box and facing an older woman seated; the top frame carries a fragmentary inscription dated to the fourth century, (Ἰάλω), probably a woman's name; and the pediment carries third-century inscriptions, "Demostrate daughter of Aiscron from Halai," "Mikion son of Mantodoros from Anagyrous," and "Ameinikhe daughter of Mikon from Thria."

13. Plot 56 across the Eridanos from the Tritopatreion contained two markers, a marble lekythos and a stele. The marble lekythos, Clairmont no. 2.755 (vol. II 671–672A; Kerameikos P 1388), depicts an elderly man seated on a chair, clasping hands with a standing youth (a nude servant boy stands at right), and it carries their names, "Kleomedes" and "Amoibikhos," presumably father and son. The stele, Clairmont no. 2.710 (vol. II 652–653; NMA 884; Knigge, *Kerameikos von Athen* fig. 151b), carries in relief a loutrophoros flanked by two lekythoi and two aryballoi (globular perfume flasks); on the relief lekythos at left, a nude youth plays with a hoop, and on the loutrophoros, a youth with a traveling cap, spear, and horse clasps hands with a man leaning on a staff (a servant boy stands at right), with a man's name and demotic, "Panaitios Amaxante[us]," written above. Who is Panaitios? the youth or the man?, and is it the same youth as on the lekythos at left? And what is Panaitios's relation to Kleomedes and Amoibikhos?

14. In plot 37, a hillock between Piraeus Street and the Sacred Way, stele Kerameikos P 388 (Clairmont no. 4.420; vol. IV 95–96) carries a relief depicting a maiden (12–18 years old), two women, and a man; the original names inscribed on the architrave are of three females, Protonoe, Nikostrate, and Eukoline; there is no male name. But there are two names later inscribed in the pediment of the stele, a male name, Onesimos, and another female name, which was later erased.

15. E. A. Meyer, "Epitaphs and Citizenship in Classical Athens," *Journal of Hellenic Studies* 113 (1993): 99–121. Clairmont no. 1.081 (vol. I 235–237; Kerameikos P 1169, I 417), a pediment stele from Kerameikos plot 38a, depicts the youth "Eupheros" holding a strigil (a metal implement for scraping off sweat and grime from exercising in the gymnasium); the skeleton in the plot, however, was too short (1.35 m = 4.43 ft.) to be as old as a youth, implying a discrepancy between the stele and deceased.

16. Cf. Leader, "In Death Not Divided" 697.

17. Kurtz and Boardman, *Greek Burial Customs* 136–141.

18. Clairmont prefers to identify the figures in the stelai as members of a nuclear family. He sees "fathers," "mothers," "sons," and "daughters" and identifies them according to their gender and ages for which he devises a precise terminology: infant (1 year), baby (2–3 years old), boy and girl (4–12), youth and maiden (12–18), young man and young woman (18–25), man (bearded) and woman in their prime (25–45), elderly (45–60), and old (60+). In the descriptions of the stelai below, I include Clairmont's identifications of family members.

19. Clairmont no. 2.346 (vol. II 333–334).

20. Clairmont no. 1.660 (vol. 1 404–406); the elegiac inscription lacks a completing fourth line:

τέχνον ἐμῆς θυγατρὸς τόδ' ἔχω φίλον, ὅμπερ ὅτε αὐγάς
ὅμμασιν ἡελίο ζῶντες ἐδερκόμεθα
ἔχον ἐμοῖς γόνασιν καὶ νῦν φθιμένον φθιμένη 'χω.

I hold of my daughter her dear child, whom we saw
live in the light of the sun;
I hold it now dead on my knees, having myself perished.

Also see C. Clairmont, *Gravestone and Epigram: Greek Memorials from the Archaic and Classical Period* (Mainz: Phillip von Zabern, 1970) 91–92.

21. In life, naming a woman in public seems to have implied that she had a reputation; it is on tombstones that we usually learn their given names: David Schaps, "The Woman Least Mentioned: Etiquette and Women's Names," *Classical Quarterly* 27 (1997): 323–330, esp. 328–329. For the inscriptional preponderance of women's names, see Karen Stears, "Dead Women's Society: Constructing Female Gender in Classical Athenian Funeral Sculpture," in *Time, Tradition and Society in Greek Archaeology*, ed. Nigel Spencer (New York: Routledge, 1995) 109–131; and T. Vestergaard et al., "A Typology of Women Recorded on Gravestones from Attica (400 BC–200 AD)," *American Journal of Ancient History* 10 (1985): 178–190. Nielsen et al., "Athenian Grave Monuments" 411, reports 4,519 Athenian names between 400 BCE and 250 CE, of which 1,472 are women; we are not told if the 4,519 names include both the cognomen and patronymic or count the two as one. Since both men and women have male patronymics, we would expect three times as many male names than female if everyone's name was complete and if both cognomen and patronymic were counted separately (Humphreys, *Family, Women and Death* 111). Of 4,519 names, therefore, we should expect three-fourths to be male (3,389) and one-fourth (1,130) to be female. Since not all the names that Nielsen et al. recorded could have been complete, the correspondence between the ideal number (1,130) and the actual (1,472) is striking. Stears, "Dead Women's Society" 113–114, cites the catalogue by Conze, *Attischen Grabreliefs*, as including 176 tombstones for women alone and 168 for men alone; in Clairmont, I count 178 tombstones depicting one adult person whose sex is recognizable, 96 women and 82 men.

22. See, for example, two stelai depicting an unnamed man and a named woman: Clairmont nos. 2.211 (vol. II 149; NMA 851) "Chairestrate," and 2.344 (vol. II 329; Kerameikos I 181) "Anthis," both from the Kerameikos.

23. Eleven men and five women carry patronymics, and on one stele (Clairmont no. 1.154; vol. I 242–243; Chalkis Museum 2181), only the patronymic is partially preserved.

24. Within the age grades that Clairmont observes, the ratios change markedly (here: m = male, f = female): child: 5 m, 6 f; adolescent: 12 m, 8 f; young adult: 19 m, 33 f; adult: 41 m, 81 f; and elderly: 34 m, 3 f. Using just these data, one is tempted to suggest that males more often died in childhood and old age, while females more often died in the ages between 20 and 45.

25. Leader, "In Death Not Divided" 690, draws our attention to the conventional attributes for "the variety of roles by which the identity of male citizens was defined," military

garb, nudity, and athletic gear, and the staff that gave men the right to speak (cf. Homer, *Iliad* 1.10, 20, 230; 10.325; and 23.565; and *Odyssey* 2.35).

26. On the well-known stele of Dexileos (dated 394), the name of his sister Melitta was later inscribed and presented as a wife and daughter (Clairmont no. 2.209; vol. II 143–145; Kerameikos P 1130): "Melitta daughter of Lysanias from Thorikia, wife of Nausistrates from Sphettios" (for the change from Dexileos heröon to family tomb plot, see Wendy E. Closterman, "The Form and Function of the Dexileos Precinct," *American Journal of Archaeology* 103 [1999] 299). Mothers are often shown with their children, while a mother and daughter who are both adults can be named (e.g., Clairmont no. 2.434a; vol. II 551–552; Leipzig S39; "Myrtis daughter of Hierokleia"). Priestesses: e.g., Clairmont nos. 13 (vol. I 17–18; NMA 3287), a priestess of Cybele (she holds a tympanon [a kind of flat drum]); 1.248 (vol. I 277–278; Kerameikos I 430) from the Kerameikos depicting "Polystrate" carrying a temple key; 1.316 (vol. I 310–311; NMA 2309); 1.334 (vol. I 319–320; Kerameikos P 1131) from Kerameikos plot 31, a priestess carrying a hydria; 1.350a (vol. 329–330; Geneva, Private Collection), "Khoirine"; and 1.934 (vol. I 495–496; Piraeus Museum 3627 = ex NMA 1030) an old woman with tympanon. Clairmont no. 1.721 (vol. I 423; NMA 1896) depicts a dancer whom he terms a *hetaira* (ἑταῖρα: prostitute). Nurses are named as such (*titthê*: τίτθη) in the inscriptions that accompany Clairmont nos. 1.376 (vol. I 347; NMA 3935), "Pyraikhme worthy nurse"; 1.969 (vol. I 510–512; British Museum 1909.2–21.1), perhaps "Melitta"; 1.980 (vol. I 516; Athens Epigraphical Museum 10506), "Phanion Corinthian nurse"; and the following stelai record just the word, "titthe": 1.350 (vol. I 328–329; Athens Epigraphical Museum 8844) from Piraeus, 1.949 (vol. I 503; Agora Museum I 6508), and 2.337d (vol. II 316; NMA 2076). Clairmont no. 1.249 (I 278; NMA 978) is inscribed "paideusis worthy nurse" (*paideusis titthê khrestê*: παίδευσις τίτθη χρεστή)—paideusis, meaning "education," may have been her name or nickname or another of her duties; the adjective "worthy" indicates she was a slave (see below, n69). Clairmont no. 2.890 (vol. II 780–782; NMA 993) from Menidi names "Phanostrate midwife (or nurse) and doctor" (*maîa kai iatros*: μαῖα καὶ ἰατρός); 1.969 may title Melitta as the "nurse." Stears, "Dead Women's Society" 123–124, thinks there were "only a limited number of occupations. These were centered on the domestic and were chiefly child-raising, woolworking and interacting with family members and slaves," but she also lists tombstones that depict priestesses and a nurse, and adds a prostitute. Vestergaard et al., "A Typology of Women," mention all these and add a vendor of salt.

27. Of course, whatever actual persons were represented by the figures on the stelai are now all dead. As Clairmont says of Nikomeneia, the secondary woman (not the primary deceased) on no. 3.442 (vol. III 371–372; Kerameikos P 290, I 174) from the Kerameikos, "To be sure, Nikomeneia will have died some day."

28. There appears to be only one stele depicting two standing women, and these do not clasp hands: Clairmont no. 3.703 (vol. III 450; Kerameikos P 663), a stele from the Kerameikos, carries a loutrophoros-hydria in relief on which appear a standing maiden (to Clairmont, "close friend") with a box, and two young women facing each other and holding an infant.

29. For example: Clairmont nos. 3.427 (vol. III 347; NMA 2729), a lekythos from the Kerameikos, probably plot 20, depicts a simple scene: a seated woman clasps hands with a standing young woman, while, at right, a maiden stands frontally; 2.390 (vol. II 465–466;

NMA 820), a pediment stele, depicts a seated woman turned almost frontally and a standing young woman; 2.300 (vol. II 245–246; NMA 726), a naiskos stele, depicts a standing young woman with a box and a seated woman (to Clairmont, the latter is an "older sister or friend"); 2.871 (vol. II 752–753; present whereabouts unknown), a pediment stele from Oreoi, Euboea, depicts a standing young woman with short hair and carrying a large kalathos (to Clairmont, a "close relative"; for kalathoi, see below, n91), and a girl leaning against the knees of a seated woman; 2.652 (vol. II 647–648; Leiden I 1903/2.1), a pediment stele, carries a standing young woman (to Clairmont, a "close relative . . . just past maiden age") holding a baby (boy?) out to a seated young woman in a chair; and 4.930 (vol. IV 152–153; NMA 819), a naiskos stele from Piraeus, depicts a young woman, a younger woman holding a swaddled baby with a bonnet, a seated woman, and a maid behind the chair who touches the baby (to Clairmont, the seated woman died in childbirth, and the other figures are her maid and "very close relatives").

30. Husband and wife, e.g., from the Kerameikos, Clairmont nos. 182 (vol. I 63; NMA 242) records "Sostratos" and "Praxagora" from Aigilia, and 2.154 (vol. II 102–103; Kerameikos P 280, I 192), a loutrophoros, depicts a standing young woman clasping hands with a standing adult man ("-os from Skambonidai"). Brother and sister, e.g., Clairmont no. 3.420 (vol. III 334–336; Kerameikos I 277) records, among others, "Euphrosyne" and "Eubios" the daughter and son of "Phanippos of Potamos." Father and son, e.g., from the Kerameikos, Clairmont no. 2.418 (vol. II 513–514; Reading, PA), a lekythos from the Kerameikos, records "Sostratos son of Sonautides" and his son "Prokleides son of Sostratos," both from Aigilia. Brothers?: Clairmont no. 2.425b (vol. II 531; Athens Epigraphical Museum 8892), a stele from the Kerameikos, depicts a seated old man clasping hands with a standing old man and records "Adeistos Mi..k[."

31. From Clairmont's two-figure stelai (nos. 2.051–2.499) whose figures are recognizably men or women, I count 224 with a woman and a man, 75 with both men, and 110 with both women.

32. Clairmont no. 2.434a (vol. II 551–552; Leipzig S39) depicts seated Hierokleia clasping hands with standing Myrtis, the names engraved above their heads; Myrtis is named a second time on the frame and then described by an elegiac couplet:

Μύρτις—Ἱεροκλείας θυγατὲρ Μόσχου γυνὴ ἐνθάδε κεῖται
πλεῖστα τρόποις ἀρέσασα ἀνδρί τε τοῖς τε ἔτεκε.

Myrtis—daughter of Hierokleia and wife of Moskhos lies here;
she pleased her husband in many ways, including giving birth.

Clairmont no. 2.376d (vol. II 421–422; Leiden 1859: KAG) depicts a similar scene and names the two women as "Demostrate wife of Khorokles from Aixone" and "Lysippe daughter of Khorokles," mother and daughter or step-mother and step-daughter; Lysippe's name is a secondary inscription, and it may have been added to the stele erected first for Demostrate.

33. Clairmont no. 3.375 (vol. III 244–245; Louvre 3115), a marble lekythos said to be from Athens, depicts a woman (to Clairmont, the mother) helping another woman lie down on a couch with a maid in back; the deceased is named "Killaron daughter of Pythodoros from Agryle"; no. 4.470 (vol. IV 120; NMA 749), a pediment stele from Oropos, depicts

"Tolmides of Plataia" grieving, a woman assistant (to Clairmont, his wife) holding out both hands toward his daughter, "Plangon of Plataia daughter of Tolmides," leaning against a couch (or perhaps a birthing stool), while a maid in back helps; and no. 3.442 (vol. III 371–372; Kerameikos P 290, I 174), a pedimental stele from the Kerameikos, depicts the young woman "Nikomeneia" holding what may be a sponge in her right hand and extending her left towards a woman, "Stephane," who leans on a stool, while a maid in back helps (to Clairmont, Nikomeneia was important enough to the family of the deceased Stephane to be named, but he is unsure of their relationship, "mother and daughter" or "close relative" — or she may have been a respected midwife [see above, n26]).

34. In Clairmont, I find 46 stelai with 2 women and an additional 11 with 3 whose relationship is unclear. As is his practice, Clairmont narrates relationships for these women; if he detects an age difference, he identifies a "mother" and "daughter"; if he sees no such distinction, he often will identify the secondary woman as a "close friend or relative."

35. Close family members would obviously include members of the nuclear family (parents and children), plus grandparents and grandchildren; since women were forbidden to attend the funerals of relatives more distantly removed than first (or possibly second) cousin (see above, n4), we may consider first cousins at least also as close family members.

36. Clairmont nos. 2.291b (vol. II 233; NMA 922), a naiskos stele, depicts a seated woman clasping hands with standing younger woman (to Clairmont, the standing deceased daughter of the seated mother); 2.466 (vol. II 596; NMA 968; Athens), a naiskos plaque, depicts a woman seated on a stool leaning forward to clasp hands with a standing woman who raises her right hand in a speaking gesture (to Clairmont, this is "seated mother with her standing daughter, . . . the deceased"). Two stelai include a third woman: Clairmont nos. 3.461 (vol. III 397–398; NMA 870), and 3.466 (vol. III 407–408; Piraeus 429) are duplicates, each a separate slab for a naiskos stele, depicting a woman seated on a stool, clasping hands with a standing woman, the primary deceased, who leans toward her; a girl in a long-sleeved chiton, and therefore probably a maid, stands behind the stool (3.461 adds a speaking gesture to the standing woman and a partridge under the stool).

37. Clairmont no. 2.284 (vol. II 219; Piraeus 23), a stele, depicts a standing woman clasping hands with a standing woman, on whom a small fuzzy dog (a Spitz) jumps. To Clairmont, these are the deceased daughter and mother, although the attention the Spitz shows the "mother" might rather imply she is the primary deceased; cf. no. 2.386, which depicts a standing maiden and a seated "Habrosyne" (named and therefore the primary deceased) at whom the Spitz jumps.

38. Clairmont no. 3.842 (vol. III 472; NMA inv. no. unknown), a lekythos, depicts a maid in a long-sleeved chiton holding a baby, while a seated woman clasps hands with a standing young woman (to Clairmont, the seated "mother" and standing daughter who "died in childbirth").

39. On one stele from the Kerameikos, Clairmont no. 2.891 (vol. II 782–783; Kerameikos P 666, I 211), "Timagora daughter of Euthykleos from Xypete" lifts her veil with her left hand and clasps hands with a seated woman, while a young maid stands at left with a box (to Clairmont, Timagora is the daughter of the seated woman)—the scene is similar to ones involving youths (cf. Clairmont nos. 2.890a, 2.892, 2.892b); 2.362 (vol. II 377; Piraeus 217) carries the inscription "Nikomakhe wife of Eukleies" above a seated woman with a large tympanon who clasps hands with a standing young woman (to Clairmont, the nar-

rative is complex: Nikomakhe, dead not long after her marriage to Eukleies, as priestess of Cybele gave her mother her tympanon); 3.319a (vol. III 140; NMA 3341), a lekythos from the Kerameikos, depicts seated "Hesykhia" clasping hands with a standing young woman, while a second standing young woman gestures at right; and 3.858 (vol. III 478–479; NMA 1026), a pediment stele from Athens, depicts a seated woman clasping hands with a standing "Kotion," while a girl with a bird and a young woman stand at right (Clairmont observes that "the respective ages are hardly distinguished").

40. Clairmont no. 2.421 (vol. II 520–521; NMA 763; "near Royal Stables, 1858") presents a standing young woman embracing and touching the chin of a standing maiden, "Mynnion daughter of Khairestratos from Hagnous" (to Clairmont, Mynnion is the maiden, and the young woman is her mother, but she does not appear to be old enough).

41. Clairmont no. 3.388 (vol. III 276–278; Karlsruhe 66/64), a moderately deep naiskos stele, depicts two women standing, "Plathane" and "Khoiros," contemplating the seated "Myrrhine"; the top frame gives the names, while "Kallisto" (not depicted) was inscribed later in the pediment (to Clairmont, Plathane, Khoiros, and Myrrhine are all "close relatives/friends"). Clairmont no. 2.441 (vol. II 562–563; NMA 764), a deep naiskos stele from the Kerameikos, depicts a standing young woman holding an open box and contemplating the seated older woman (to Clairmont, the two women are relatives). On the top frame, a few letters remain of the original fourth-century inscription; third-century inscriptions in the pediment attest a reuse of the stele for "Demostrate daughter of Aiscron from Halai," "Mikion son of Mantodoros from Anagyrous," and "Ameinikhe daughter of Mikon of Thria." Regardless of the reuse, Clairmont identifies the standing and seated woman by the later names, and he makes no mention of Mikion.

42. Clairmont nos. 2.214 (vol. II 152–153; Kerameikos I 342), a painted stele with relief from the Kerameikos, depicts a standing "Eukoline" clasping hands with a standing and headless "Timylla" (to Clairmont, Eukoline is the primary deceased, daughter of Timylla); and 3.407a (vol. III 309; NMA 1019), a pediment stele from the Kerameikos, depicts a seated "Malthake" clasping hands with a standing "Nikippe," with a woman frontal ("close relative") between. On the top frame, after the name "Nikippe" is the word "khrêstê" (χρηστή), which Clairmont translates literally to describe Nikippe as "worthy," but the word is commonly used to modify a slave (see below, n69); "khrêstê" should therefore describe the frontal woman between Malthake and Nikippe.

43. Clairmont nos. 2.311d (vol. II 265; NMA 1034), a pediment stele from the Kerameikos, depicts a standing "Phileia," fingering her veil, and clasping hands with the seated "Nikeso" (to Clairmont, Phileia is the "principal deceased"); 2.347 (vol. II 336; NMA 1075), a lekythos from the Kerameikos, depicts a standing "Theopropis" clasping hands with the seated "Aristonike" (to Clairmont, the two women are probably "sisters," but there is no direct evidence for this; see nos. 2.346, 3.348, and 3.349, which mention, by cognomen only, Simonides and Theopropis; Simonides, Anthippos, and Aristonike; and Theopropis, Anthippos, and Simonides respectively). Clairmont nos. 2.377a (vol. II 423; British School of Archaeology, Athens S.87), an anthemion stele, depicts a standing young "Myttope" clasping hands with seated "Myrrhine" (to Clairmont, Myttope is the "principal deceased," and Myrrhine is her "mother"); 2.428a (vol. II 538; NMA 1032), a pediment stele, depicts a standing young "Ariste" fingering her veil and clasping hands with seated "Mika" (to Clairmont, the two women may be "mother and daughter"); 2.272 (vol. II 195–196; Piraeus 234), a fragmen-

tary stele, depicts seated "Meliboia" probably clasping hands with standing "Nikarete" (to Clairmont, Nikarete is the primary deceased, and Meliboia her "older sister or close friend"); 2.328 (vol. II 291; NMA 3923), a lekythos from Sepolia, depicts a seated "Mika" clasping hands with standing young "Philtate" (to Clairmont, Philtate is the primary deceased and Mika is her "mother"); and 2.396a (vol. II 482; NMA 1108), a lekythos from the Kerameikos, perhaps plot 55, depicts a seated "Dionysia" clasping hands with standing young "Myrte" (to Clairmont, Myrte is the primary deceased, and Dionysia is perhaps her "mother").

44. Clairmont nos. 3.423 (vol. III 341; NMA 830), a naiskos stele found between Kouvara and Keratea, depicts a standing young "Kleostrate" clasping hands with seated "Menestrate," while, between them, an unnamed young woman stands and holds a box (to Clairmont, Menestrate is the primary deceased and mother to Kleostrate, while the second woman is a "close relative, perhaps younger sister"); and 3.404 (vol. III 303–304; New York Metropolitan Museum 06.287), a moderately deep naiskos stele, said to be from Salamis, depicts a seated woman clasping hands with a standing figure, while a young woman with a box stands between and faces towards, but does not look at, the standing figure. The standing figure at right was originally conceived as a young man with a himation but was turned into a young woman wearing a sleeveless chiton. Names are on the top frame, "Lysis[t]rate" over the seated woman and, over the standing figure, "Panathenais" over an erasure (the young man's name?); the woman with the box is unnamed.

45. Clairmont no. 3.411 (vol. III 317–318; Kerameikos P 1139), a naiskos stele from the Kerameikos, Piraeus Street, depicts a seated woman "-s" holding a kithara and clasping hands with the standing "Doris," while a young woman stands mourning between them (to Clairmont, the seated woman is Doris' mother who holds Doris's kithara [see nos. 2.161 and 2.183, with youths holding lyres]); for the narrative, cf. no. 2.362 (above, n39).

46. Clairmont no. 2.894 (vol. II 788; Kerameikos P 233, I 167), a painted anthemion stele from the Kerameikos, depicts a standing young maid holding an infant, and a young standing "Medontis" fingering her veil and clasping hands with the seated "Nikandra." The composition is the same as that on no. 2.891, where the maid holds a box (see above, n39). Clairmont no. 4.910 (vol. IV 149–150; Louvre Ma 3113), a naiskos stele said to be from Athens, depicts a woman "Bako" fingering her veil and clasping hands with the seated "Aristonike"; at left, a boy looks and gestures at Bako; between the two women stands a frontal maid holding a box, and at right, a younger maid holds an infant. The top frame carries the names Bako, Socrates, and Aristonike. Clairmont identifies the boy Sokrates and states that Bako "died soon after having given birth to her second child," and he identifies Aristonike as the grandmother. Aristonike, however, is not visually much older than Bako.

47. Clairmont no. 3.471 (vol. III 413–414; Leiden 1821), a naiskos plaque from Glyphada (ancient Aixone) (to Clairmont, the standing woman is Arkhestrate's "daughter" [see more of the family on Clairmont no. 4.471, vol. IV 121–122, NMA 2574 + 2584]).

48. Clairmont no. 2.780 (vol. II 686–687; NMA 3790), a pediment stele from Psychiko, depicts a standing maiden or young woman (to Clairmont, a "close relative") holding out a child, which stretches out its left arm towards the seated "Philonoe daughter of [. . .]" and the mother of the child; a conventional elegiac couplet once gave her patronymic:

ἐνθάδε Φιλονόη κεῖται θυγατήρ [˘˘−] ο
σώφρων εὐσύνετος πᾶσαν ἔχ [οσ' ἀρετή] ν

Here lies Philonoe daughter of [. . .]o
praiseworthy for her modesty, having every virtue.

Clairmont no. 2.806 (vol. II 699–700; Chalkis 104), a shallow naiskos stele, depicts a young woman (maid or "rather close relative") holding the infant "Aristion" (recarved from a box?) in front of a seated "Paranome," who lifts her left hand (to Clairmont, another complex narrative: "When first used, the relief depicted a woman whose name was probably inscribed and who died soon after having given birth to a child. The close relative to the [left] may originally have held a box the [left] corner of which still subsists but was then given an infant to indicate the reason for the death of the seated woman").

49. Clairmont no. 3.370 (vol. III 229–230; NMA 718), a shallow naiskos stele from Piraeus, the north polyandreion (a mass tomb), names the slightly older young woman (to Clairmont, the younger woman is a "younger sister or a friend"); the box has generated some discussion (see Clairmont), although it looks conventional. The kneeling maid is unusual, but she would be the perfect parallel for what Eva Stehle and Amy Day have in mind when they discuss the chitoned kneeling figure O in the east pediment of the Temple to Zeus at Olympia and identify "her" as adjusting the sandal of figure F, "Sterope" ("Women Looking at Women: Women's Ritual and Temple Sculpture," in *Sexuality in Ancient Art*, ed. Natalie Kampen [Cambridge: Cambridge UP, 1996]: 101–116).

50. Clairmont no. 2.306 (vol. II 253–254; Marathon 3599, BE 103), a naiskos stele from Marathon (to Clairmont, the standing woman is a "close relative, perhaps younger sister" of Pausimakhe).

51. Clairmont no. 2.235b (vol. II 310–311; Rhodes), a pediment stele from Rhodes (to Clairmont, the standing woman looks like a servant maid but may instead be a clumsy Rhodian rendering of a "younger sister or relative" of Kalliarista). The epigram (two elegiac couplets and a closing pentameter) lavishly gives her generic virtues:

ὅστις ἄριστος ἔπαινος ἐν ἀνθρώποισι γυναικός
Καλλιαρίστα Φιληράτο τοῦτο ἔχουσα ἔθανεν
σωφροσύνας ἀρετᾶς τε ἀλόχωι πόσις ὄν<ε>κα τόνδε
Δαμοκλῆς στᾶσεν μνημόσυνον φιλίας
ἀνθ' ὧν οἱ δαίμων ἐσθλὸς ἔποιτο βίωι.

Whatever great praise exists for women amongst men
Kalliarista daughter of Phileratos has it, now dead,
for her moderation and virtue; for his wife, her husband
Damokles has set up this memorial because of his regard
for which her noble spirit might attend his life.

52. Clairmont no. 2.820 (NMA 722, Markopoulo), a shallow naiskos stele from Markopoulo (to Clairmont, the standing woman is a "close relative or friend" of Arkhestrate). The clumsy elegiac records her generic virtues and her husband's grief (for the translation, see below, in the text):

ἐνθάδε τὴν ἀγαθὴν καὶ σώφρονα γαῖ' ἐκάλυψεν
Ἀρχεστράτην ἀνδρὶ ποθεινοτάτην.

53. Clairmont no. 2.319a (vol. II 279; NMA 1140), a shallow naiskos stele from Piraeus (to Clairmont, the standing woman is a "close relative," and the bracelet may imply that

Kallistomakhe was not married at the time of her death); and on no. 2.223a (vol. II 165–166; British Museum 1893.6–27.1), a deep pediment stele said to be from Thebes, the seated "Glykylla" is wearing the bracelet that she had taken from the box held by the "close relative"(?) standing in front of her.

54. Clairmont no. 2.650 (vol. II 644–646; Piraeus, inv. no. unknown), a late fifth-century pediment stele from Skala Oropou with a first-century inscription. Clairmont cites Despinis for thinking that the seated woman is the primary deceased but identifies the standing woman as the mother of the boy. The boy, however, must have been included to show that his mother had died and left him bereft, which implies the standing figure is the primary deceased. Which of the two women was meant to represent the first-century "Nikippe" is an open question. Clairmont and other scholars notice the resemblance of the standing woman with boy to Alkamenes' Prokne and Itys, and the pose of the seated woman's upper body to his "Aphrodite of the Gardens" (see the Aigina stele, discussed below).

55. E. G. Pemberton, "The Dexiosis on Attic Gravestones," *Mediterranean Archaeology* 2 (1989): 45–50; and Glenys Davies, "The Significance of the Handshake Motif in Classical Funerary Art," *American Journal of Archaeology* 89 (1985): 627–640. Kurtz and Boardman, *Greek Burial Customs* 140, suggest that naming both figures clasping hands implied both were the primary deceased (e.g., Demetria and Pamphile, here Figure 6.10).

56. Clairmont, Introductory Volume 115, quotes K. Friis Johansen, *The Attic Grave-reliefs of the Classical Period* (Copenhagen: E. Munksgaard 1951) 151; compare Leader, "In Death Not Divided" 698: "Death becomes an occasion to stress the oikos as unbroken."

57. Leader, "In Death Not Divided" 688, comments on how "the medium, context, and style of stelae associate them with civic art, [but] their iconography and its prescriptive force in presenting visually ideal gender roles in domestic contexts associate them with the visual sphere of the oikos." She then sees stelai as occupying "a liminal position that complicated and confused the divisions between" "civic and domestic, public and private" "polarities."

58. See Rabinowitz's essay in this volume. S. Isager, "Gynaikonitis," *Museum Tusculanum* 32–33 (1978): 39–42. Neither archaeology nor textual studies have provided an exact location for a specific room or area for women called the "gynaikonitis."

59. NMA 1629 published in *ARV*[2] 1250.34; *Paralipomena*[2] 469; *Beazley Addenda*[2] 354; P. Hartwig, "Ἐπίνητρον ἐξ Ἐρετρίας," *Ἀρχαιολογική Ἐφημερίς* 1897: cols. 129–42, pls. 9–10; Adrienne Lezzi-Hafter, *Der Eretria-Maler: Werke und Weggefährten* (Mainz: Philipp von Zabern, 1988) vol. I cat. no. 257, pp. 253–262 and 347–348, vol. II pls. 168–169; Paolo E. Arias and Max Hirmer, *Tausend Jahre griechische Vasenkunst* (Munich: Hirmer Verlag, 1960) 95, pl. 203; John Boardman, *Athenian Red-Figure Vases: The Classical Period* (London: Thames and Hudson, 1989) fig. 235; Keuls, *Reign of the Phallus* fig. 234; and Carola Reinsberg, *Ehe, Hetärentum und Knabenliebe im antiken Griechenland* (Munich: C. H. Beck, 1989) fig. 24.

60. John H. Oakley, "Nuptial Nuances," in *Pandora: Women in Classical Greece*, ed. Ellen D. Reeder (Princeton: Princeton UP, 1995) 63–73, esp. 67, fig. 12; John H. Oakley, "The Anakalypteria," *Archäologischer Anzeiger* (1982): 113–118; and D. L. Cairns, "Veiling, Αἰδώς, and a Red-Figure Amphora by Phintias," *Journal of Hellenic Studies* 116 (1996): 152–158.

61. In the short descriptions of the stelai in this study, I have tried to convey the casualness of the gesture and its different character from the marriage gesture of "anakalypsis" by using a conventional and short phrase, "fingering the veil" or "touching the mantle."

Both gestures may indicate a woman's erotic submission, "anakalypsis" to her husband, the casual variant (Keuls, *Reign of the Phallus* 253) to someone not her husband: Amymone makes the gesture as Poseidon pursues her on a red-figure lekythos by the Phiale Painter (New York Metropolitan Museum 17.230.35; *ARV²* 1020.100; Beazley *Addenda²* 316; John H. Oakley, *The Phiale Painter* [Mainz: Philipp von Zabern, 1990] 82 no. 100, pl. 79; Keuls, *Reign of the Phallus* 240, fig. 216); among the pairs of women and men at a party, one of the women makes the gesture on a red-figure skyphos by the Brygos Painter (Louvre G156; *ARV²* 380.172; *Paralipomena²* 366; Beazley *Addenda²* 227; Keuls, *Reign of the Phallus* fig. 154); and Iphigeneia makes it, thinking Agamemnon is leading her to Achilles, on a white-ground lekythos by Douris (Palermo NI 1886; *ARV²* 446.266; *Paralipomena²* 375; Beazley *Addenda²* 241; Ellen D. Reeder, "Catalogue," in *Pandora: Women in Classical Greece* [Princeton: Princeton UP, 1995] 330–332, fig. 101, both sides).

62. Clairmont, Introductory Volume 86. Leader, "In Death Not Divided," 695, interprets the gesture "as a formal gesture of welcome."

63. Barbara McManus, "Multicentering: The Case of the Athenian Bride," *Helios* 7 (1990): 225–235, esp. 230–231. Sara I. Johnston, *Restless Dead: Encounters between the Living and the Dead in Ancient Greece* (Berkeley and Los Angeles: U of California P, 1999) 184–199.

64. Clairmont no. 2.365d (vol. II 386–387; present whereabouts unknown), a pediment stele from the Laurion area, depicts a fragmentary figure standing, probably a woman, regarding a seated woman, probably Pamphile, since most stelai that name only one woman name the seated one (Clairmont, however, thinks it possible that "Pamphile" regards her "mother"):

[οἶκον ἔδοχ' ὑ]μέναιος ἐν ὧι πότε Παμφίλη ἥδε
ζῆλον ἔχοσ' ὤικει τὸμ μακαριστότατον
ἢ πρὶν ἔτ]η τελέσαι β[ίον] εἴκοσι[ν] ὀρφανίσασα
νυμφίδιος οἶκος ἡλικίας ἔθανεν.

65. Clairmont no. 146 (vol. I 47–48; present whereabouts unknown), a stele probably from Piraeus:

Ἀνθέμιδος τόδε σῆμα κύκλωι στεφανοῦσ<ι>ν ἑταῖροι
μνημείων ἀρετῆς οὕνεκα καὶ φιλίας.

The meter demands the iota adscript not be pronounced (cf. κουριδίωι in Clairmont no. 2.850) and that only the –οῦ– in στεφανοῦσ<ι>ν be long.

66. Clairmont no. 2.820 (above, n52).

67. Clairmont no. 2.282b (vol. II 216–217; Copenhagen Ny Carlsberg 199 [IN 1595]):

σῶμα μὲν ἐντὸς γῆ κατέχει τὴν σωφροσύνην δὲ
Χρυσάνθη τὴν σήν ο<ὐ> κατέκρυψε τάφος.

68. Clairmont no. 1.283 (vol. I 293–294; NMA 3964), a pediment stele from Paiania; the inscription is elegiac, although verses three and four should be reversed if a standard elegiac is to be maintained (and the last line is an addition although it completes the dactylic verse begun by the last *written* line of the inscription):

πᾶσι θανεῖν [ε]ἵμαρτα[ι], ὅσοι ζῶσιν σὺ δὲ πένθος
οἱ | κτρὸν [ἔ]χε[ι]ν ἔλιπες Παυσιμάχη προγόνοις

μητρ[ὶ] τ[ε Φ]αινί[π]πηι καὶ πατρὶ Παυσανίαι
σῆ[ς] δ' ἀρετῆ[ς μ]νη Ι μ[ε]ῖον ὁρᾶν τό[δ]ε τοῖς παριοῦσιν
σωφροσύνη[ς] τ[ε].

69. Clairmont no. 2.406 (vol. II 489–491; Piraeus Museum 20), anthemion stele probably from Piraeus; the meter of the inscription is unusual, two lines of awkward dactylics and two lines of trochaic tetrameters:

—χαῖρε τάφος Μελίτης χρηστὴ γυνὴ ἐνθάδε κεῖται
    φιλοῦντα ἀντιφιλοῦσα τὸν ἄνδρα Ὀνήσιμον ἦσθα κρατίστη
    τοιγαροῦν ποθεῖ θανοῦσαν σε ἦσθα γὰρ χρηστὴ γυνή
—καὶ σὺ χαῖρε φίλτατ' ἀνδρῶν ἀλλὰ τοὺς ἐμοὺς φίλει.

Nielsen et al., "Athenian Grave Monuments" 419, state that the epithet "worthy" (*khrêstos*: χρηστός) and the greeting "hail!" (*khaire*: χαῖρε) are never used for citizens and only very rarely for metics; "the occurrence of either term is a strong indication that the inscription commemorates a slave," perhaps a concubine in this case, since Melite seems to refer to her children. Other tomb stelai that name slaves include Clairmont nos. 1.249 (above, n26), 3.407a (above, n42) and perhaps 2.399d (vol. III 488; NMA Theseion 151), which names the seated woman "Syra" as if from Syria (cf. no. 1.220, below, n91).

70. Clairmont no. 1.417 (vol. I 362–363; NMA 2054), a fragmentary stele from Piraeus (I have restored her husband's name for convenience):

οὐχι πέπλους οὐ χρυσὸν ἐθαύμασεν ἐμ βίωι ἥδε
ἀλλὰ πόσιν τε αὐτῆς σωφροσύ[νην τ' ἐφίλει]
ἀντὶ δὲ σῆς ἥβης Διονυσία ἡλικίας τε
τόνδε τάφον κοσμεῖ σὸς πόσις Ἀντίφ[ιλος].

71. Clairmont, vol. VI Indexes 129 (omitting no. 1.967, woman with mirror case): the woman looks into the mirror—she stands to right: nos. 1.148/2.148 (fragmentary), 1.152, 1.170, 1.283 (Pausimakhe), 1.291 (mirror doweled into the hand), 1.305 (fragmentary), 1.471 (Hellenistic girl with melon coiffure), 2.209b, 2.291a, 2.831 (mirror held up by serving maid), 4.378 (unclear; the mirror might be lowered), or she stands to left: 1.188, 1.768 (fragmentary), 3.345b (held up by serving maid), 4.190, 4.386 (unclear); woman sits to right: 2.208, 2.210; woman sits to left: 2.187; and the woman does not look into the mirror—she stands to left: 2.266a, or she sits to left: 2.255, 2.313.

72. Winfried Herrmann, "Spiegelbild im Spiegel: Zur Darstellung auf frühlukanischen Vasen," *Wissenschaftliche Zeitschrift der Universität Rostock. Gesellschafts- und sprachwissenschaftliche Reihe* 17 (1968): 667–671, discusses vase paintings that depict reflections in mirrors and attributes the interest in them to Orphism; and Hélène Cassimatis, "Le miroir dans les représentations funéraires apuliennes," *Mélanges de l'École Française de Rome, Antiquité* 110.1 (1998): 297–350, esp. 306 and n17, gives a recent bibliography even while noting that mirror reflections do not appear in Apulian funerary vases. Add: a Lucanian pelike in the Primato Group, Louvre K545 (A. D. Trendall, *The Red-figured Vases of Lucania, Campania and Sicily* [Oxford: Oxford UP, 1967] 184, no. 1119); a Lucanian hydria in Boston Res. 41.56 (Boston Museum of Fine Arts, *Vase-painting in Italy: Red-figure and Related Works in the Museum of Fine Arts* [Boston: Boston Museum of Fine Arts, 1993] 51, no. 3); a skyphos by the Palermo Painter (ca. 400) in Palermo 961 (Trendall, *Lucania* 53.275, pl. 23.2); and two Apulian bell kraters in the Boston Museum of

Fine Arts, one by the Torpoley Painter (1970.237), and the other the name piece of the Painter of Boston 00.348 (Trendall and Cambitoglou, *Apulia* I, 48.16 and 267.48 respectively; and A. D. Trendall and Alexander Cambitoglou, *Second Supplement to the Red-Figured Vases of Apulia, Part I [Chapters 1–20]* [London: Bulletin of the Institute of Classical Studies, Supplement 60, 1991] 12 and 62 respectively). Two other vases show Athena holding up a shield with Medusa's reflection on it: a pelike in a Taranto Private Collection and another vase in Boston 1970.237 (Trendall and Cambitoglou, *Apulia* I, 51.44; and Boston Museum of Fine Arts, *Vase-painting in Italy* pl. IV). If the mural prototype of the Alexander Mosaic was indeed painted by Philoxenos of Eretria (end of the fourth century), we may add the image of the trampled Persian soldier whose face we see only as reflected in his shield (Bernard Andreae, *Das Alexandermosaik* [Stuttgart: Philipp Reclam jün., 1967] 27, fig. 11). In the Hellenistic period, we see reflections used, for example, in the Campanian paintings showing Narcissus at the Spring (Brigitte Rafn, "Narkissos," in *LIMC* vol. VI.1, 703–711, nos. 1–24; VI.2, 415–416, figs. 1–17).

73. Leader, "In Death Not Divided" 693, specifies the woman viewer's double consciousness when looking at reliefs depicting women looking into mirrors: "The image on the relief—a woman looking at herself—suggests the action of the viewer in the cemetery looking at the woman on Pausimakhe's memorial."

74. Cassimatis, "Le miroir" 311–312, and n 91 on 350, where she cites a discussion of an idea first proposed by L. Dreger ("Das Bild im Spiegel. Ein Beitrag zur Geschichte der antiken Malerei" [privately printed PhD Dissertation, U of Heidelberg, 1940]: 169–170), that, in a funerary context, the mirror can be taken to reflect the soul; in support of this idea, Cassimatis cites the Lucanian nestoris (a wine-mixing bowl), Naples 82124, in the Brooklyn Group that depicts the Furies menacing Orestes with a mirror in which he sees the face of his mother Clytemnestra (Trendall, *Lucania* 113.588; D. Knoepfler, *Les imagiers de l'Oreste. Mille ans d'art antique autour d'un mythe grec* [Zurich: Akanthus, 1993] no. 78, pl. XX).

75. Maria Wyke, "Woman in the Mirror: The Rhetoric of Adornment in the Roman World," in *Women in Ancient Societies: An Illusion of the Night,* ed. Léonie J. Archer, Susan Fischler, and Maria Wyke (New York: Routledge, 1994) 134–151. Gay Robins, "Dress, Undress, and the Representation of Fertility and Potency in New Kingdom Egyptian Art," in Natalie Kampen, ed., *Sexuality in Ancient Art* (Cambridge: Cambridge UP, 1996) 27–40, esp. 32–33, writes about the mirror in pharaonic Egypt: how mirrors symbolized health and fertility and helped "the deceased to achieve rebirth into the afterlife." For mirrors as a site for erotic depictions, see Andrew Stewart, "Reflections," in Natalie Kampen, ed., *Sexuality in Ancient Art,* (Cambridge: Cambridge UP, 1996) 136–154.

76. "Between these two [utopias and heterotopias], I would then set that sort of mixed experience which partakes of the qualities of both types of location, the mirror. It is, after all, a utopia, in that it is a place without a place. In it, I see myself where I am not. . . ." (Foucault, "Of Other Spaces" 352).

77. Leslie Kurke, "Inventing the *Hetaira:* Sex, Politics, and Discursive Conflict in Archaic Greece," *Classical Antiquity* 16 (1997): 106–150, esp. 136, uses the verb "triangulate" to describe the way male viewers of a psykter by Euphronios depicting an all-female symposion (Hermitage B644; *ARV*² 16.15; *Paralipomena*² 509; Beazley *Addenda*² 153) would have been drawn to experience a homoerotic desire for "Leagros" invoked in an accompanying inscription. The verb "triangulate" is used primarily in geometry and surveying: from two

points, two lines are drawn to intersect at and locate a third point. Another, and perhaps more apposite use, is in hunting: two dogs stand staring at a prey, establishing viewpoints at whose intersection stands the object of their regard.

78. Leader's separation of stelai into an early group of stelai "commemorating men or women with representations of members of the deceased's sex alone" and a later group "commemorating both sexes" ("In Death Not Divided" 698–699) implies, correctly I think, that the secondary woman represents the primary deceased's homosocial circle of women friends and family.

79. James C. Anderson, "Aesthetic Concept of Art," in *Theories of Art Today*, ed. Noël Carroll (Madison: U of Wisconsin P 2000) 65–92, esp. 71: "Both aesthetic pleasure and aesthetic appreciation are metaresponses (pleasure) to base responses (admiration or positive judgment) to some object or event."

80. Cf. Winkler, *Constraints of Desire* 162–187 ("Double Consciousness in Sappho's Lyrics") and esp. 178–180.

81. Both Adrienne Rich, "Compulsory Heterosexuality and Lesbian Existence," *Signs* 5.4 (Summer 1980): 631–660 (revised edition in *Lesbian and Gay Studies Reader*, ed. Henry Abelove, Michèle Aina Barale, and David M. Halperin [New York: Routledge, 1993] 227–254), and Martha Vicinus, "Lesbian History: All Theory and No Facts or All Facts and No Theory?" *Radical History Review* 60 (1994): 57–75, argue that woman-woman relationships are often so intimate that they assume a homoerotic aspect.

82. Similarly, three stelai may depict pairs of soldier lovers: Clairmont no. 2.156 (vol. II 104–106; Piraeus 385), a stele, depicts the nude young man "Chairedemos" standing close to and overlapping the bearded adult "Lykeas," who is wearing a knee-length chiton; both are soldiers with shields and lances (to Clairmont, the two are brothers or close friends); no. 2.354 (vol. II 355–356; Moscow Pushkin Museum F-1601), a naiskos plaque, depicts a bearded soldier and a youthful soldier facing each other; and no. 2.910 (vol. II 795; NMA 1069), a lekythos, depicts the adult soldier "Leophoreides son of Eunomos from Melite" clasping hands with a youth in chitoniskos with incised shield crest and holding a painted lance; two squires carrying shields flank the two men. In this last scene, Clairmont identifies the youth as Leophoreides' "nephew," perhaps referring to the role that maternal uncles often played in socializing their sister's sons in adolescence; see Aristophanes, *Clouds* 124; and Jan Bremmer, "The Importance of the Maternal Uncle and Grandfather in Archaic and Classical Greece and Early Byzantium," *Zeitschrift für Papyrologie und Epigraphik* 50 (1983): 173–186. In many cultures the relationship between adolescent and maternal uncle is often homoerotic; see David F. Greenberg, *The Construction of Homosexuality* (Chicago: U of Chicago P, 1988) 26–40.

83. Clairmont no. 2.426b (vol. II 533–534; Copenhagen, Ny Carlsberg 219 [IN 514]); "Phanylla" may be a later inscription, referring either to the second woman or to the seated woman in a reuse.

84. Clairmont no. 2.426 (vol. II 532–533; NMA 2708), a deep naiskos stele, depicts standing "Pamphile" clasping hands with the seated "Demetria daughter of Nikippos"; and no. 2.464 (vol. II 593–595; Kerameikos inv. no. unknown) has "Demetria" standing and "Pamphile" sitting, both looking out to the spectator and fingering their veils. A secondary inscription (*Inscriptiones Graecae* II^2 11797) on the original architrave to 2.426 adds two names in reuse, "Kallistomakhe daughter of Diokles" and "Nausion daughter of Sosan-

dros. Clairmont cites Brückner for thinking that when Kallistomakhe and Nausion reused stele 2.426, 2.464 was commissioned to continue commemorating Demetria and Pamphile, and they date this second stele twenty years later than the first—but if Demetria and Pamphile could commission a second stele for themselves stylistically very similar to their first one, so could Kallistomakhe and Nausion have commissioned their own. Even so, Clairmont thinks that all these women belonged to a single household. On Clairmont no. 2.427 (vol. II 535–536; Kerameikos I 260), a marble lekythos from the same precinct, Pamphile is also depicted seated next to a standing "Hegetor son of Kephisodoros," and Clairmont thinks they may be brother and sister.

85. First cousins tended to have similar cognomina and to be distinguishable through their different patronymics. Clairmont no. 4.416 (vol. IV 93–94; Louvre Ma 767), a naiskos stele from Attica, depicts a standing man, named "Phanippos," clasping hands with "Mnesarete daughter of [. . .]ost[. . .]," seated on a stool; between them stands "Mnesarete daughter of Sokrates" looking at Phanippos; in back of the stool is a maid. Because the two women's cognomina are identical but their patronymics are different, it can be assumed that they are first cousins and that their mothers or fathers were siblings.

86. Clairmont no. 1.943 (vol. I 500; provenience and whereabouts unknown).

87. Red-figure Apulian vase by the Truro Painter (Taranto no. unknown; Keuls, *Reign of the Phallus* fig. 81).

88. John Boardman, *Greek Sculpture: The Classical Period* (London: Thames and Hudson, 1991) fig. 55.

89. Berlin 2289 (*ARV*[2] 435.95; *Paralipomena*[2] 375; Beazley *Addenda*[2] 238; Keuls, *Reign of the Phallus* fig. 232): one woman sits, baring her leg; a woman stands in front of her, pulling up the right shoulder of her chiton; a wool basket sits on the floor nearby. A similar scene occurs in the tondo of a kylix by the Stieglitz Painter (Florence 3918; *ARV*[2] 827.7; Beazley *Addenda*[2] 294; Keuls, *Reign of the Phallus* fig. 233); here, the standing woman holds a mirror, and on the wall hangs an alabastron. A similar woman sits baring her leg on a skyphos by the Phiale Painter (Palermo, Fondazion Mormino 788; Oakley, *Phiale Painter* 90, no. 154*bis*, pl. 132C; John Oakley, "Images in Non-wedding Scenes of Myth," in *Pandora: Women in Classical Greece*, ed. Ellen D. Reeder [Princeton: Princeton UP, 1995] 71, fig. 20); she wears a veil—perhaps the gesture is imminent (see Stears, "Dead Women's Society," 119–120).

90. McManus, "Multicentering" 231, calls the gesture of anakalypsis, which these more casual gestures resemble, "the bride's consent."

91. Kalathoi appear in several stelai, usually placed discretely under the chair on which the primary deceased sits (Clairmont nos. 120, 1.176, 1.184, 1.246, 1.691, 2.650 [the Nikippe stele; above, n54], 2.829, 2.948, 3.384b) or beside the chair (Clairmont nos. 1.894, 1.986); on two stelai, a woman holds a large kalathos in front of the seated woman (Clairmont nos. 2.335 and 2.871), but on three stelai, the kalathos plays a more prominent role, sitting on the floor in front of the seated woman who works wool above it (Clairmont nos. 247, 1.220, 1.309). Two of these last stelai deserve special comment: no. 1.220 (vol. I 268; Leiden 1821) depicts a kalathos on the floor in front of "Kypria," passing yarn and perhaps holding a distaff (Clairmont calls her "a metic rather than a slave" [but see no. 2.399d, above, n69], and takes the kalathos to connote her "active involvement in household work"); and no. 1.691 (vol. I 391 and 413; NMA 792) depicts a seated woman holding an infant; under the chair is the kalathos, an oddly shaped loutrophoros sits on the floor in front of the woman,

and on the wall above hangs a box (to Clairmont, the odd shape of the loutrophoros indicates that the artist may not have been an Athenian; in any case, the assortment of objects indicates "the realm of the gynaikonitis").

92. Louvre 701: Hägen Biesantz, *Die thessalischen Grabreliefs* (Mainz: Philipp von Zabern, 1965) 22 no. K36, pl. 17); Boardman, *Greek Sculpture* 68, fig. 54; Brunilde S. Ridgway, *The Severe Style in Greek Sculpture* (Princeton: Princeton UP, 1970) 46–47, 55, fig. 68; Gundel Koch-Harnack, *Erotische Symbole: Lotosblüte und gemeinsamer Mantel auf antiken Vasen* (Berlin: Gebrüder Mann, 1989) 180–181, fig. 48.

93. John D. Beazley, "Some Attic Vases in the Cyprus Museum," *Proceedings of the British Academy* 33 (1947): 195–244, esp. 198–223, catalogues three classes of homosexual courting scenes: a) the young beloved (*erómenos:* ἐρώμενος) stands usually nude, at the right facing left, his left hand down often holding a wreath, his right hand up often holding a spear, and the older lover (*erastés:* ἐραστής) beseeches from the left, his hands in the "up and down" position, left hand "up" towards the face of the erómenos, the right hand "down" towards his genitals; b) the presentation or acquisition of animals as love tokens; and c) embraces or actual depictions of intercrural copulation. Kenneth Dover, *Greek Homosexuality* (Cambridge, MA: Harvard UP, 1978) 94, presents these three groups more narratively; and Martin F. Kilmer, *Greek Erotica* (London: Gerald Duckworth, 1993) passim, discusses and illustrates them in detail. Beazley further describes his group a: most scenes occur in black figure, where the erastes is a bearded man and the eromenos a youth, but in early red figure, the two are younger, the erastes a youth and the eromenos a boy. Some Attic red-figure vases, however, do present bearded men with youths (cf. Dover's vases R520, R684, R934, etc.). The earliest depiction of the "hands up and down position" occurs between a man and a woman on an Orientalizing jug from Arkades in Crete, now in the Herakleion Museum (Doro Levi, "Early Hellenic Pottery of Crete," *Hesperia* 14 [1945]: 1–32, esp. 14–15, pl. 16; Reinsberg, *Ehe, Hetärentum und Knabenliebe* fig. 108; Günter Neumann, *Gesten und Gebärden* [Berlin: Walter de Gruyter, 1965] fig. 32).

94. In brothel scenes, for example, both the male customer (man or youth) and the woman prostitute can hold a flower; see the red-figure pelike in the manner of the Pig Painter (Adolphseck 41; *ARV*² 566.6; Beazley *Addenda*² 261; *Paralipomena*² 389; Keuls, *Reign of the Phallus* fig. 206; Koch-Harnack, *Erotische Symbole* fig. 63b), a kylix by Makron in Toledo (1972.55; Keuls, *Reign of the Phallus* figs. 141, 142; Reeder, *Pandora*, 183–187), and the red-figure alabastron (Berlin 2254) by the Pan Painter (Keuls, *Reign of the Phallus* figs. 141, 205, 206, and 238 respectively). In male homoerotic courting scenes, both man and youth may hold flowers (Dover, *Greek Homosexuality* 92–93); see, for instance, the red-figure kylix by Douris (Vatican 16545; *ARV*² 437.116; *Paralipomena*² 375; Beazley *Addenda*² 239; Françoise Frontisi-Ducroux, "Eros, Desire, and the Gaze," in *Sexuality in Ancient Art*, ed. Natalie Kampen [Cambridge: Cambridge UP, 1996] 81–100, fig. 34: the youths "caress their own face with a flower, emphasizing their beauty"). Koch-Harnack, *Erotische Symbole* 179, fig. 46, discusses a fragmentary kylix by Douris in Leipzig (T 550; *ARV*² 438.139; *Paralipomena*² 375) depicting two women facing each other below a phallic lotos flower (above, fig. 5.2a,b).

95. See, for instance, a red-figure alabastron by Paseas (NMA 1740; *ARV*² 163.13, 1630; *Paralipomena*² 337; Jane Sweeny, Tam Curry, and Yannis Tzedakis, *The Human Figure in Early Greek Art, Athens* [Athens: Greek Ministry of Culture, 1988] 170–171, no. 60): a woman offers a flower to another who dances with castanets (*krotala*).

96. Gundel Koch-Harnack, *Knabenliebe und Tiergeschenke* (Berlin: Gebrüder Mann Studio-Reihe, 1983) 161–172.

97. Koch-Harnack, *Erotische Symbole* 181 (my translation).

98. A red-figure lekythos in the Fogg Museum of Art (1977.216.2236, cited in Keuls, *Reign of the Phallus* 419) depicts a woman purchasing an eel and sponge; the tondo of a red-figure kylix by Phintias (Johns Hopkins U; *ARV*² 24.14; *Paralipomena*² 323; Beazley *Addenda*² 155; Keuls, *Reign of the Phallus* fig. 240) depicts a youth purchasing pottery.

99. Many vase paintings on all sorts of red-figure pots depict men or youths offering phormiskoi to women, as if negotiating for sex. See, for example, an amphora in Leningrad (B1555; Reinsberg, *Ehe, Hetärentum und Knabenliebe* fig. 71); a pelike by the Hephaistos Painter in Rhodes (12887; *ARV*² 1116.40; Beazley *Addenda*² 331; Keuls, *Reign of the Phallus* fig. 241); a column krater by the Harrow Painter in the Villa Giulia (*ARV*² 275.50; Beazley *Addenda*² 207; Reinsberg, *Ehe, Hetärentum und Knabenliebe* fig. 68); an oinochoe by the Berlin Painter in San Antonio (*Paralipomena*² 345.184*ter*; H. Alan Shapiro, *Art, Myth, and Culture: Greek Vases from Southern Collections* [New Orleans: New Orleans Museum of Art, 1981] no. 63); a lekythos by the Painter of London E342 in the University of Arkansas, Fayetteville (57–27–42; *ARV*² 669.45; Beazley *Addenda*² 278; Shapiro, *Art, Myth, and Culture* no. 65); an alabastron by the Pan Painter in Berlin (2254; *ARV*² 557.123; *Paralipomena*² 387; Beazley *Addenda*² 259; Keuls, *Reign of the Phallus* fig. 238; Reinsberg, *Ehe, Hetärentum und Knabenliebe* fig. 65); an epinetron by the Painter of Berlin 2624 (NMA 2180; *ARV*² 1225.2); a skyphos by the Amphitrite Painter in Altenburg (271; *ARV*² 83231; Beazley *Addenda*² 295; Reinsberg, *Ehe, Hetärentum und Knabenliebe* fig. 74; Keuls, *Reign of the Phallus* fig. 242); and a kylix by Makron in Toledo (1972.55; Keuls, *Reign of the Phallus* figs. 141, 142; Reeder, *Pandora* 183–187). Men also offer leather bags to youths: see the tondo of a red-figure kylix by Makron (Bochum S507; *ARV*² 472.206*bis*; Beazley *Addenda*² 246; Koch-Harnack, *Knabenliebe und Tiergeschenke* fig. 82), the tondo of a kylix by Douris (New York Metropolitan Museum 52.11.4; *ARV*² 437.114; Beazley *Addenda*² 239; Keuls, *Reign of the Phallus* fig. 266; and Koch-Harnack, *Knabenliebe und Tiergeschenke* fig. 83), another kylix by Douris, once in Dresden (Reinsberg, *Ehe, Hetärentum und Knabenliebe* fig. 103), and an amphora by the Tyskiewicz Painter (Copenhagen 3634; *ARV*² 293.51; Beazley *Addenda*² 211; Koch-Harnack, *Knabenliebe und Tiergeschenke* figs. 84 and 85). On the exterior of a kylix by the Briseis Painter, a youth holds out his leather bag, while in the tondo, a youth stands in front of a seated youth, the leather bag hanging on the wall above (Tarquinia Museum 703; *ARV*² 408.32); and a white-ground mug from Selinus perhaps by the Hegisiboulos Painter shows three youths, two of whom hold leather bags (Palermo 2139; I. Wehgartner, *Attisch weissgrundige Keramik: Maltechniken, Werkstätten, Formen, Verwendung* [Mainz: Philipp von Zabern, 1983] 99–100, pl. 33.1–2).

100. Gloria Ferrari Pinney, "Money Bags?" *American Journal of Archaeology* 90 (1986): 218. For a general discussion of astragaloi and a citation of the ancient sources, see Athena Kalogeropoulou, "Drei attische Grabreliefs," *Archaische und klassische griechische Plastik: Akten des internationalen Kolloquiums vom 22.–25. April 1985 in Athen*, II, *Klassische griechische Plastik*, ed. Helmut Kyrieleis (Mainz: Philipp von Zabern, 1986) 119–133, esp. 124–125.

101. Clairmont no. 2.196 (vol. II 130–131; Aigina 2222); and Kalogeropoulou, "Drei attische Grabreliefs" 122–126, pls. 123–124, publishes the relief and discusses its iconography. Clairmont identifies the relief as a tomb stele, while Kalogeropoulou identifies it as a dedication because of its small, square size (0.96 m), and the presence of a large tang at the bot-

tom for insertion into a base (cf. the dedicatory relief NMA 1601, square and tanged, from the sanctuary of Aphrodite at Daphni; Semni Karouzou, *National Archaeological Museum. Collection of Sculpture: A Catalogue* [Athens: General Direction of Antiquities and Restoration, 1968] 96). Though Clairmont is unsure about the identity of the primary deceased (he finally opts for the standing woman), Kalogeropoulou is sure that the seated woman is the primary deceased.

102. Kurtz and Boardman, *Greek Burial Customs* 208–209.

103. See Winkler, *Constraints of Desire* 162–187 ("Double Consciousness in Sappho's Lyrics"); and Petersen, "Divided Consciousness" 58–60.

CHAPTER SEVEN

GLIMPSES THROUGH A WINDOW

An Approach to Roman Female Homoeroticism through Art Historical and Literary Evidence

Lisa Auanger

 To have even a partial understanding of the place and meaning of homoeroticism within a Roman context, one must abandon one's modern notions. We must realize that we cannot find our twins or clones in the past: we cannot assume that for the ancient Romans the dominant form of female homoeroticism was manifested in cultural institutions such as marriage (or formal domestic partnership) or that it was necessarily acting against those gender expectations we might hold, for example, having short hair, wearing men's clothes, and speaking like a man.[1] Largely constructs of modern definition, these criteria should not form our views of ancient society and its norms, especially for women's relationships. Accepting this, we may be tempted to conclude that since no exact parallel existed, we cannot know anything. In fact, we really need to know what we are looking for.

It is quite true that there are few images of explicit sexual activity between women, especially in Roman art. In her recent study Bernadette Brooten includes only two Roman examples of female homoeroticism, only one of which is sexual (or genital): (1) an Augustan grave relief showing two freedwomen, Fonteia Eleusis and Fonteia Helena, with hands clasped in a "*dextrarum iunctio*"—one was evidently recut in the later centuries to show a man; and (2) a wall painting from Pompeii that seems to show women having oral sex.[2] Although there may be others hidden away in museum cellars, it is clear that the physicality of the sexual aspect of women's relationships is not frequently present in Roman representations. On the other hand, when we have representations (verbal and visual) that are strongly suggestive of sexual activity between women, we cannot assume that they are depicting lesbian relationships. Such a definition is limiting and as misleading as applying the term "lesbian," with the connotations of a distinct culture that this twentieth-century usage evokes, to female models posing together in pornographic magazines addressed to men.

The depiction of female homoeroticism in Roman times may be more in line with a definition of female friendship that has not been the object of extensive academic consideration.[3] Thus, we may be able to find aspects of women's relationships in our sources by refining our definition. Although no one definition can describe all the relationships between women, for this paper, the "homoerotic" consists of behaviors and words that constitute a variety of situations, such as relationships expressing deep personal attachments between women, ranging from romantic friendships that include emotional, spiritual, intellectual, and physical ties, to brief physical encounters without commitment to normative everyday interaction that includes varying degrees of physicality and closeness. The "homosocial" includes some of the same but does not necessarily include or exclude an erotic or even physical component.

In real life, then and now, the homoerotic and the homosocial are accompanied by a variety of visual and verbal signs and symbols; we find these in works of art and literature. Yet the materials come from an incomplete record and are not articulate in themselves, so they generally require interpretation or extrapolation. The aspects of women's interpersonal relationships and their vestiges appear at a variety of levels in the Roman materials. Sometimes the relationships, in a broad sense, have parallels of expression in heteroeroticism, in the interaction between people of different sex that is easily defined by marriage, social interaction, courtship, touching, or simply sharing lives. The iconography (visual language) of men's and women's relationships provides us with a core, definitive set of motifs or symbols that at the very least, helps us to identify these interactions.

Sometimes the evidence is but a glimpse through a window, and it must be read as such; we know that things are not always as they appear. Yet these glimpses of intimacy are quite real. Sometimes there is a fairly obvious reference to genital sexuality. Quite often, however, as in many cases in antiquity, the images go far beyond the realm of sexual intercourse, showing the sort of intimacy we see in the Song of Solomon, which preserves for us parts of the love songs of the desert peoples.[4] Would we see the erotic and romantic in this text if it were preserved in fragments, as 1.15: "Your eyes are like doves. . . .; 2.1: I am a rose of Sharon, a lily growing in the valley. . . . I have come to the garden, my sister, my bride; 7.2: Your navel is a rounded goblet that will never lack spiced wine. . . .; 7.8: I said, 'Let me climb up into the palm to grasp its fronds'"? In many cases, fragments are all that we have of the female homoerotic; occasionally we overlook them as a result of our modern beliefs and ignorance about the private aspects of women's lives.

Nevertheless, although historical circumstances have largely written the mutual loves of women and their normal everyday existence out of public knowledge, there is evidence for them in antiquity, and scholars have made some headway in an excavation of materials. In recent decades a corpus of pioneering and trailblazing scholarship has emerged that has illuminated ancient female homoeroticism in many ways, though from mainly modernist perspectives on the materials, with a tendency to search for verbal naming and equivalents to modern concepts. That is, people looked for lesbians and dykes named or described as such in the ancient materials and for explicit depictions of sex between women. Cantarella, Lilja, Martos Montiel, Hallett, Brooten, and others have presented superb research on the topic in various forms and have made great advances in viewing women's relationships.[5] The recent scholarship aims in general at pulling the evidence for female homoeroticism from our materials and bringing together materials concerning women whose sexualities—desires and actions—were directed at women or viewed as transgressing the societal norms. As a result, the scholarship has led to the definition of a written vocabulary of female homoeroticism, ironically often drawn from and defined through comic or polemical texts, often modeled on paradigms of coarse male eroticism. For example, words such as "tribas" (Martial 7.70; Plato, *Phaedrus* 4.16.13) and "frictrix" (Tertullian, *De resurrectione mortuorum* [On the Resurrection of the Flesh] 16.6 and *De pallio* [On the Philosopher's Cloak] 4.9) were brought to light as ancient analogs to "dyke" and other such words.[6] A sort of canon of dominant materials has emerged, a selective and fairly negative one that has its basis largely in the language of the modern world, where a language has sprung up drawn and reclaimed from those perceived as having an inferior status.[7] Although these ancient words certainly depicted real types, and the later centuries of early Christianity witnessed the oppression of women's physical relationships in certain contexts,[8] the definitions of what constituted homoerotic behavior among Roman women are too limited.

Overall, our sources for homoeroticism in the Roman world are the same as for other historical matters. Writings and visual depictions provide a wide array of evidence about its place and nature. Usually one can only glimpse women's interactions, especially the homoerotic; rarely are they central to the artifact or the text, and we see them only as we understand and know them, from our own culturally constructed sensibilities and meanings.

The Roman era, in fact, offers a wide variety of evidence that attests or shows female homoeroticism in Europe, Asia, and Africa and in different times. More than five hundred years of arts and writings show women interacting. The materials range from writings about Sappho, including quotations from her poems, to images with iconography similar to heterosexual eroticism, to subtle expressions of relationship presented in symbolic verbal and visual language.

In this paper I present a summary of several Roman materials attesting women's relationships, focusing on selected themes in which iconography and latent symbolism express intimacy that may indicate the prior existence of something greater—an informal institution that is no longer extant or never officially existed. The materials range from the second century BCE through the era marked by the spread of Christianity throughout the Mediterranean, as late as the sixth century CE, and concern both mortal and immortal. Although using such a span of places and periods has its intrinsic problems, most of the evidence considered belongs to a "cultural set," structured institutions (e.g., cults, myths) where continuity of tradition is demonstrated largely through the materials themselves, and so a reference in the sixth century may illuminate a picture of the second century.[9]

DYKES AND DEVIANTS?
OVERSTEPPING THE PRIVATE LINE

Roman legal texts are strangely quiet about the matter of women's relationships with other women. There seems to be no mention of regulation of women's relationships to women in the *Digest of Justinian,* which preserves a great deal of earlier legislation.[10] Lilja believes that the Lex Sca(n)tinia, dated between 226 and 149 BCE, must have dealt with same-sex relations between freeborn Roman citizens, mainly on the grounds of attestation in Juvenal's (fl. 100/110 CE) second *Satire* and Suetonius' *Domitian* (84), but she points out that the type of same-rex relations remains unspecified.[11] In Juvenal's *Satire* (47–49), Laronia says that there is no such thing among women (*non erit ullum exemplum in nostro tam detestabile sexu*). While Lilja regards Laronia as a hypocrite, since "everyone (not only Juvenal) knows there were lesbians," maybe Laronia was right: if she understood homosexuality to consist of penetration and domination, then this passage should signify that female homosexuality was not regularly defined through this particular lens. Instead, it appeared as a mode of sensuality and may not as such have officially existed, being more like informal close, romantic friendship among equals.

The sole reference to female homoeroticism in Sarah B. Pomeroy's valuable classic *Goddesses, Whores, Wives, and Slaves: Women in Classical Antiquity* considers Juvenal's comments (6.306–348) on the Roman women Tullia and Maura to be merely an observation that they attach a phallus to the deity at the temple of Pudicitia and take turns riding it.[12] Some use this passage to conclude that the Romans looked upon women's erotic relationships with condemnation. Although we see women engaging in sexual activity here, it is appropriate to consider the sacred context to understand the expressed distaste for what the women were doing. Romans were very serious about religion and proper public behavior for women. Some spaces, for example, consecrated to cults and divinities were generally regarded as vulnerable to pollution. In *Roman Questions* 20, Plutarch, who lived from about 50 to 120 CE, tells us that it is possible that even myrtle was not allowed in the cult of Bona Dea because it was sacred to Venus and hence represented venery. The "condemnation" for the actions of Tullia and Maura here may lie in violation of sacred space and public lewdness of women, something for which even Augustus' own daughter Julia was punished.

Norms of gender were like other rules of propriety. The Romans, especially of the upper classes, were very inflexible about acceptable behavior for women in many aspects of everyday life. These included where they would eat, speaking in public, manners in general, and the full segregation of certain sectors of their life. It is in this context that we should understand those writings (including the aforementioned) that have become part of a canon of "documents" concerning female homoeroticism, possibly condemning it.[13] These images usually involve claims of abnormal female masculinity, sometimes the inclusion of a male sex organ, acting against a husband's wishes or in a manner that would threaten his reputation, leaving a husband for a woman, and often engaging in an embarrassingly public sexual act.[14] Some Romans even made fun of a woman's sexuality—physically/mechanically defined—when it overstepped the private boundary or became "unfeminine." Such an attitude is found in a poem of Luxorius, a sixth-century North African, about a hermaphroditic "girl":[15]

> (31) Two-organed monster of the female sex, whom enforced lust turns into a man, why do you not enjoy the normal way of making love? Why does violent vain pleasure deceive you? You do not give that with which you are passive and also active. When you offer that part of you which proves you are female, then you may be a girl.[16]

By and large, these materials overlook other aspects of female friendships and interactions in the private sphere. There is no significant condemnation of love or close friendship, kissing, touching, hugging, and similar activity among women, which indicates that the Romans did not disapprove of all demonstrations of affection between women. These materials refer to fairly specific situations and are often satirical; as such, their value as historic sources is questionable.[17]

So where are we to find female homoeroticism? The real sources are those cultural objects prevalent in everyday life and often reproduced in some manner through different times and places.

A DIGRESSION:
THE VERY REAL PROBLEM OF HELLENISM

Although we have a great deal of material from the Roman period, we are faced with some serious problems in its interpretation. Often the difficult fact is that the Roman images were copied from Greek originals and were far removed from their original place of production—the context and the setting. Scenes from Greek myth and life were reproduced and quoted in the same terms as they had been created several centuries earlier. How are we to treat these? What sort of historical evidence do they offer? Did these convey their original meaning to the Romans? Was the artist's focus merely an accurate reproduction? What do these tell us about the consumer? Was accuracy such a part of the Roman aesthetic that content would be overlooked? Would offensive content be modified?

Unfortunately, these are difficult questions, and the truest answer is rarely absolute. As Touchette has pointed out, the traditional view of excerpted figures losing their original and religious meaning "oversimplifies the many levels—none of which were mutually exclusive—on which Roman perception . . . must have functioned."[18] Mediterranean culture, especially in Italy, appreciated and integrated Greek art into their ways of living from as early as the Etruscans, late in the eighth century BCE.[19] We demonstrate a similar willingness, as Touchette suggests, to see in Roman literary and artistic copying the value they found in Greek models.

We do have literary paradigms that can help us understand these problems, concerning both revivals and adaptations of Greek myths and themes, as in Ovid. Further, a great deal of the Roman "homosexual" vocabulary was derived from or directly imported from Greek words.[20] Roman discussions of Greek art and myth also sometimes illuminate. One case of continuity of Hellenic tradition particularly important for the study of female homoeroticism is that of Sappho.

Sappho's Value

Materials about Sappho and copies of her actual writings in the Roman era provide the most important basic corpus of evidence for homoeroticism, as we can define it.[21] Although there has been controversy, a tradition of special relationships with women—not necessarily exclusive of erotic activity—followed the writer from the Augustan era onwards. These Roman copies, commentaries, allusions, and other references, as preserved, allow us access to a set of positivistic facts: each can be certainly attributed to a time and place of production. The materials vary widely in date and origin, and so they provide evidence from particular communities. Although one cannot fully generalize about the nature of Roman female homoeroticism and homosexuality from any of these sources, overall, the Roman commentary provides us with evidence about how Sappho and her relationships were regarded and understood—or misunderstood—and simultaneously gives us a richly diverse vocabulary that may let us define female homoeroticism from an ancient's perspective. The materials show some variance in perception and interests between the Latin- and the Greek-speaking worlds—the Roman west and the Greek east—but the scarcity of sources, the varying contexts of the writers, and the diverse literary traditions require that we interpret these differences carefully.

Little attention appears to have been given Sappho during the Republican period. Cicero tells only of a statue of Sappho (*Second Verrine Oration* 2.4.126).[22] Yet from the time of Augustus onward, there appears to have been substantial interest in her erotic relationships. Horace envisions her as a preeminent poet and mentions her work bemoaning girls or young women (*puellis querentem de popularibus*) (*Carmina* 2.13.24).[23] Lilja finds homoerotic parallels for the lamenting, "*puellis querentem*," with Valgius' mourning of Mystes (*Carmina* 2.9). Horace also envisions Sappho as "*mascula*" (*Epistulae* 1.19.28). Given the common association of masculinity with lesbianism in modern times, it is fitting to pursue inquiry into his use. Dionysius Latinus in his commentary on Horace explained the "*mascula*": "not soft, neither broken in desires nor unchaste" (*non mollis, nec fracta voluptatibus nec impudica*).[24] Porphyrio (ca. 234 – ca. 305) later also speculated on whether the "mascula" refers to her being "maligned as a tribad" (*vel quia tribas diffamatur*). By his time, he certainly has lost the ability to differentiate between the masculine and the tribad.[25]

It is not clear what Horace means by "*mascula*," but the overall usage of the word in Latin and the concept in both Greek and Latin indicate that it does not refer solely to female homoerotic types. Nor is there any need to connect the expression with words for sexual acts that would make Sappho like a man. Horace was quite specific when this was his goal, as in *Epode* 5.41, where he specifically used masculine libido (*masculae libidinis*) to describe Folia in reference to her sex drive. Soranus, the physician of the early second

century CE who practiced in Rome, frequently described women as masculine (*androdeis*), in his *Gynecology*.[26] For him, there was a masculine type of
woman in body build (1.23), a type that may not have been menstruating regularly (1.29), or a type not able to conceive (1.34).

Horace may have intended to convey a meaning similar to "*androdeis,*" but
that is unlikely, given the varying physical descriptions. In Campbell's opinion, the "*mascula*" refers to Sappho's ability to keep pace with men, and Horace's respect for her poetry is evidenced through his metrical imitation of it.
Martianus Capella wrote (9.995): "We recognize that rhythm is masculine
and melody feminine. For melody is the subject which, lacking a particular form, is judged on its own; rhythm, however, as a result of the manly
activity involved in it, produces form, as well as various other effects, by
sounds."[27] Martianus Capella also (6.573) tells us that Pallas, since she pre-
sided over the councils of men, was "called the masculine goddess (*virago*)."
Horace's Sappho may have been perceived in this way; her intellect was key.[28]

In addition, Horace provides a reference to Sappho's erotic feelings (*Ode*
4.9.10–12): "The love still breathes, and the passions sent from the lyre
of the Aeolian girl are still living" (*spirat adhuc Amor / vivuntque commissi Calores
Aeoliae fidibus puellae*).[29] Here Sappho is presented in a list of poets, for her
inspiration. Campbell points out that there are "striking verbs at the beginning of each clause." These verbs show a sort of personification of both
Amor and the *Calores:* "Her Love/Amor still breathes and Passions live."[30]
These images are paralleled in the arts of the Roman era that have a basis
in religion and often are derived from the Hellenic. Lilja pointed out the
strength in "*calere*" as a verb, used elsewhere in Horace to contrast girls' and
boys' feelings. Interestingly, Horace then moves on to a discussion of Helen,
a discussion including "*adulteri,*" a sex crime that should be understood in
reference to Augustan moral legislation. Horace's allusion might further suggest that female homoeroticism had no place in Augustan moral legislation.

At about the same time, Ovid (who lived from 43 BCE to ca. 17 CE) wrote
an account of a romance of Sappho that is similar to the modern genre of
historical fiction, imagining the well-known letter from Sappho to Phaon
(*Heroides* 15), in which Ovid imagines Sappho writing to her male lover, who
has abandoned her.[31] In modern terms, Ovid's Sappho may have been bisexual, having at one time loved a woman, at another time, a man. Ovid's
descriptions of Sappho's relationships with women and men may provide
some information about how female homoeroticism was talked about in his
times. Sappho's focus in this letter is love, once again "*amor,*" for both women

and Phaon, though her passion for Phaon is emphasized (or perhaps even invented) in the interest of Ovid's story line.

> 15–20 Neither the maids of Pyrrha charm me now, nor they of Methymna, nor all the rest of the throng of Lesbian daughters. Naught is Anactorie to me, naught Cydro, the dazzling fair; my eyes joy not in Atthis as they once did, nor in the hundred other maids I have loved here to my reproach; unworthy one, the love that belonged to many maids you alone possess.[32]

> *nec me Pyrrhiades Methymniadesve puellae,*
> *nec me Lesbiadum cetera turba iuvant.*
> *vilis Anactorie, vilis mihi candida Cydro;*
> *non oculis grata est Atthis, ut ante, meis,*
> *atque aliae centum, quas non sine crimine amavi.*[33]

Ovid, then, saw the emotional manifestations of women's relationships in "*iuvare,*" "*grata,*" and "*amor.*" These are the same terms used to express fondness in heterosexual relationships. In addition, the gaze (*oculis*) played a significant role in Sappho's feeling for women.

It is sometimes argued that the language of such texts, mainly the reference to the beloved as "girl" or "*puella,*" is evidence of a sort of female pederasty equivalent to Greek male relationships. Ovid, however, also uses the word "*puella*" as a term of address and endearment, from Phaon to Sappho, as Sappho imagines it (line 100), and thereby suggests that the use in erotic contexts had nothing to do with age.[34] The *Tristia* provide more information about Ovid's perception of Sappho's relationships with women (365–366): "What does Sappho teach if not to love girls/girlfriends, or girls/girlfriends to love" (*Lesbia quid docuit Sappho, nisi amare, puellas?*)[35] The verbs again show a sort of equality between the sexes; the relationships are presented in the same terms: in Ovid's eyes, Sappho *loved* a woman as she *loved* a man (*amare*). The "Lesbia" seems to refer to Sappho's birthplace, but it may also indicate that the adjective was associated with female homoeroticism by this time.[36]

A variety of language was used to describe Sappho and her life in the following centuries. The younger Seneca, who lived from approximately 5 BCE to 65 CE, also mentions (in *Letters to Lucilius*) a passage by Didymus that raises the question of whether Sappho is "*publica.*"[37] Although sometimes translated "prostitute," as by J. M. Edmonds, "*publica*" has been given many meanings, but frankly, we do not always know what it means: it is a disservice to the text to try to find a single word to serve as an equivalent. Given the expectation for most mortal women to remain outside public life and to stay away from political matters, we should inspect the term further. Sometimes "*publica*" is quite literally equivalent to "public." It also then may be a term similar in import to "out of the closet."

Martial, who lived ca. 40–104 CE, does not speak of Sappho with the generally derogatory vocabulary he uses for females such as Bassa or women who have sex like men. Instead he describes Sappho as a lover or perhaps even a romantic (*Carmina fingentem Sappho laudabat amatrix*). Martial's different treatment from "tribades"—the oversexed women such as Philaenis (7.70) —suggests a duality of perspectives in Latin on ancient female homoeroticism, the common and the refined, and the public and the private. These threads are in line with general norms of appropriate behavior for women. Martial also uses "*docta*" and "*pudica*" to describe the woman, learned and chaste. He envisioned Sappho as a lover as "*pudica*" in her love for women; as such, a similarity with the "virgin goddesses" is demonstrated.

The Greek east also provides many Greek writings in which Sappho is mentioned or in which her works are quoted. These show a somewhat different treatment of the woman than do the Latin writings. The Greek focus often is on her eroticism, her friendships, and their nature, and it even compares her to Socrates. Sappho's companions are more frequently mentioned but in general without consistency. There were several ways of describing the females with whom Sappho associated herself. To some they were "*hetairai*," to others, "*philai*," and to others, "*parthenai*."[38] The erotic aspect of the feelings, the link to Eros and to Aphrodite herself, is more often brought out in the Greek texts, as is Sappho's relationship to weddings through song. This inconsistency suggests to us that male writers themselves, outsiders to the sphere of women, were not sure how to categorize them.

One of the most enlightening Greek sources is nearly contemporary with the earlier Latin writings. Longinus, of the first century CE, writes in *On the Sublime* (10)[39]: "Sappho, for instance, never fails to take the emotions incident to the passions of love (*erotikais maniais pathemata*) from the symptoms that accompany it in real life. And wherein does she show her excellence? In the skill with which she selects and combines the most striking and intense of those symptoms." Longinus then quotes the poet about stunned lovesickness, emphasizing both physical and spiritual aspects of the romantic or erotic feelings.[40] He comments:

> Is it not wonderful how she summons at the same time, soul, body, hearing, tongue, sight, colour, all as though they had wandered off apart from herself?

She feels contradictory sensations, freezes, burns, raves, reasons—for one that is at the point of death is clearly beside herself. She wants to display not a single emotion, but a whole congress of emotions. Lovers (*erontas*) all show such symptoms as these, but what gives supreme merit to her art is, as said, the skill with which she chooses the most striking and combines them into a single whole.[41]

His description would pertain to any erotic love, male or female, same sex or other. So to Longinus, Sappho is most simply a lover. Yet several of the Greek texts discuss the nature of Sappho's friendship in the Greek philosophical manner; the authors search for the right word to describe her and her relationships. Maximus of Tyre, 125–185 CE, compares Sappho's "*eros*" to that of Socrates.[42] Maximus writes: "What else could one call the love of the Lesbian woman than the Socratic art of love? For they seem to me to have practised love after their own fashion, she the love of women (*gunaikes*), he of men" (*Orations* 18.9). The beloveds are good or beautiful (*kalai*).

Philostratus, born around 170 CE, writes of a Damophyla, who like Sappho was said to have had maiden companions "*parthenous . . . omiletrias*" (*Life of Apollonius of Tyana*).[43] Lucid are the words presented in the Oxyrhynchus Papyrus of the second or third century CE, where it is written that Sappho is sometimes said to be a woman-lover, "gunaike[pas]tria."[44] Athenaeus in his *Deipnosophistae* of around 200 wrote that "free women and girls even now call their close/intimate friends *hetaerai* or companions as did Sappho" (*hai eleutherai gunaikes eti kai nun kai hai parthenoi tas sunaetheis kai philas hetairas, hos hae Sappho*) (13.571).[45] The key words there are "*sunaethe*," "*phila*," and "*hetaera*"; all are used to describe a realm of women's friendship that saw fulfillment outside the sphere of men but had similarities with Greek male friendships.

The third and fourth centuries also witness several mentions of Sappho: Himerus, Julian, Libanius, and others all speak of her loves, life, or poetry. By the *Suidas* or *Suda* lexicon of the tenth century, Sappho's companions are still referred to as "*hetairai*" or "*philai*." The author of this work reports that Sappho was slanderously declared to be bound by an impure affection (*aischras philias*), probably a result of later Christian bias, possibly a reference to changing norms of marriage and married life. The writings as a group suggest that female homoeroticism had a place in the lives of the educated, the people who are generally represented by the authors—in the writers' interests, in personal interactions, in ritual, and in theories of love—through the Roman period in different parts of the empire, from Rome to Asia Minor. Despite its ambiguity, the language of these texts is more lucid than that of the visual arts and other texts where homoeroticism seems absent—it provides us with a core group, a sort of definitive homoerotic set, to which other terms and concepts can be added. The definition of the set includes a tradition of "*amor*," "*eros*," friendship, closeness, virginal states of being, and learnedness. In addition, some of our manuscripts and papyri that preserve writings of Sappho are products of the Roman empire, providing evidence about her writings' relevance for the Romans. These documents show that certain figures, themes, and motifs were long associated with her, including Muses, Aphrodite, Erotes, and weddings. As a result, I extrapolate that these themes may have been associated with female homosociality and homo-eroticism in general and further examine pertinent materials.

VISUAL LANGUAGE AND ALLEGORY: THE OTHER MATERIALS

In the study of other media and genres, we are faced with a different type of problem. Roman pictorial arts are complex and not often explained by unequivocally associable texts. The images stand alone, and their historical significance—what they meant to the ancients—can be approached only through analysis and interpretation. One must therefore isolate a set of sig-nifiers to piece together the picture that defines intimacy between women. Physical contact—briefly, touch, gaze, physical proximity, and position— are visual signifiers of relationships between the figures represented.[46] These signifiers are all multifaceted and do not show their full meaning, but they can be read more wholly when taken in conjunction with other evidence. The position of figures and the use of iconographical elements also contribute to meaning. Symbols and types used in heteroerotic scenes appear among women, sometimes obviously, sometimes not, suggesting the presence of *eros* and affection as it was commonly represented.

Granted we do not fully know what these signifiers and images meant to the ancients, but they show up regularly in the depiction of certain myths.[47] We then can conclude that certain mythic themes, including those that writ-ers of the Roman era transmitted from Sappho, lend themselves to interpre-tation as evidence of homoeroticism. These include stories and represen-tations of all-female groups such as Muses, Graces, and Maenads, whose "sisterhood" is only as significant as the reader's level of understanding and whose relationship is sometimes even expressed as "sisterly" or "sisterlike" by the ancients. The same idea is expressed in the *Song of Solomon* 2:1: "I have come to the Garden, my sister, my bride." Arnobius of Sicca (who experi-enced a late third-century conversion to Christianity), critical of myth that includes incestuous behavior, provides evidence for the ancient view of why overt incest would not offend the pagans (5.32–45):[48]

> For not what is written and indicated on the surface of the words is what is actually meant and said; but all these things are taken in an allegorical sense and with mystical interpretations. Therefore, he who says "Jupiter lay with his mother" does not mean the incestuous and vile embraces of physical love, but instead "Jupiter" means rain, instead of "Ceres," the earth. . . . In like manner also in the other stories, one thing is said but another is meant, and the common and obvious sense contains an underlying hidden meaning and a profound truth shrouded in mystery.

So we need to examine our views of the past, such as in images of the Graces, who are often shown with such a detail as a caress of the breast or shoulder.[49] The Graces, although sisters in the tradition, make several obviously homosocial, possibly homoerotic, appearances in ancient art and literature; they are regularly represented as three nude women. For example, on an agate onyx cameo from Pompeii, they are depicted with a touch of the hand and placement of the hips that together demonstrate a very sensual interaction. On a sarcophagus they are thematically placed with *erotes* (fig. 7.1).[50] The "*germanitas Gratiarum*" is mentioned by Martianus Capella (7.733), who provides further evidence of how the Graces function through homoerotic acts (2.132) in nuptial ceremony.[51] The one kisses the bride on the forehead and between the eyebrows to breathe joy and honor into her eyes; the second embraces her face to lay grace upon her tongue; the third embraces her waist to give her gentleness of spirit. The Graces, including Capella's, also engage in all-female dance (1.33).

Despite the problem of Hellenism[52]—understanding the meaning of Greek copies—the visual representation of pagan myths sometimes may reflect contemporary reality: the gods looked and acted to some extent like the people who imagined them; that is, humans and human interaction often served as models in the production of the arts. General literary conflation of the mortal with the divine, or comparison of the mortal and the divine, is also a regular feature in Roman art and literature and sometimes demonstrates homoeroticism. Other times homoeroticism is more simply expressed in metaphorical language, usually complimentary. Luxorius, for example, wrote about a woman who appears to have been one of his contemporaries, likening her to goddesses in different aspects:

7.1. Sarcophagus showing Graces and Erotes. Hever Castle. Deutsches Archäologisches Institut, Rome, Neg. 72.601. Photograph: Singer.

Although you have a beautiful snow-white body, you desire to observe all the rules of chastity. It is wonderful how gloriously you control nature, inasmuch as you pass for a Minerva in your way of life and for a Venus in your body. You find no happiness in taking to yourself the comfort of a husband, and you often choose to shun the sight of men. Nevertheless, you have a fancy for this pleasure, hateful though it may be to you! Is it not possible for you to be the wife of somebody like yourself? (78) [53]

Rosenblum suggests in his commentary that there is no male equal to the woman in beauty, and "an obscene meaning is implied," that is, woman marrying woman, comparing the passage to Martial's (6.64.5): "your own wife might well call you a wife" (*et possit sponsum te sponsa vocare*). Objectively Luxorius' woman is in some ways like the depictions of Sappho: chaste, goddesslike, and a lover of women.

By the time of Augustus and through the years of empire, it was not uncommon for mortals to be presented in the guise of divinities and figures of myth. For this reason, the divinities and mythical figures represented with homoerotic characteristics can be read as reflectors of Roman social reality. Female homoeroticism appears both in the divine realm and in the mortal realm, which overlap in Roman art. It especially can be seen among Muses, Aphrodite, and Erotes. [54] The art is crafted to serve expressively in a variety of ways, through allegory, iconography, and visual semiotics. Roman art is particularly imbued with multiple meanings in this way and hence resembles the writings of and about Sappho.

MUSES AND MUSICIANS

The Muses, who appear in the poetry of Sappho, are often presented in Roman art together in a group.[55] The Muses are associated with different areas of creativity: Calliope, epic poetry; Euterpe, lyric poetry; Erato, romantic poetry; Polyhymnia, song and pantomime; Melpomene, tragedy; Thalia, comedy and bucolics; Clio, history; Terpsichore, dance; and Urania, science. Although some take them to be sisters, there is substantial disagreement among ancient writers about the birth and the origins of these women. When they are presented as sisters, their sisterhood should be read as only as significant as the brother-sister relationship of Jupiter and Juno, that is, not excluding an erotic dimension.[56] Some evidence suggests that these divinities (Muses) also were associated with a homosocial, and even homoerotic, tradition in antiquity. In *On Brotherly Love* (480e), Plutarch paraphrases Hesiod and reports that the Muses received their name because they were always together (*homou ousa*) in concord and sisterly affection (*philadelphian*).[57] Plutarch also provides information about the activities of the Muses (*Bravery of Women* 243), calling a gathering with the Graces a joining and consorting ("*sugkatamignos*" and "*sukugian*"). Arnobius (4.24) provides information that preserved in his day was a tradition in Myrtilus that the Muses were the "handmaids of Megaclo, daughter of Macarius."[58] Clement of Alexandria (*Protrepticus* 2.31.4) provides a connection of the Muses with Sappho's homeland, when he tells us that Myrsilus of Lesbos says that the Muses were Mysian handmaids of Megaclo, daughter of the Lesbian king Macar, and were taught by Megaclo's mother to sing and play the lyre to soothe the king's temper.

In the literary tradition, Sappho also becomes one of the Muses, a transformation that is mentioned in the Palatine Anthology and elsewhere from the first century onward.[59] Plutarch, for example, wrote (*Amatores*) that "Sappho fully deserves to be counted among the Muses. . . . Sappho utters words really mingled with fire and gives vent through her song to the heat that consumes her heart, thus healing in the words of Philoxenus, 'the pain of love with the melodies of the Muse.'" He also claims that it is proper to mention Sappho at the Muses' shrine (*Dialogue on Love* 762–763).[60] Catullus (35.16) addresses a contemporary as a "girl more learned than the Sapphic Muse" (*Sapphica puella Musa doctior*). In the Palatine Anthology is preserved part of an encomium ascribed to Antipater of Sidon (7.14): "Memory was astonished when she heard the honey-voiced Sappho, wondering whether mankind possessed a tenth Muse." Preserved from the same is a reference to Sappho, "who among the immortal Muses is celebrated as the mortal Muse" (7.14). Another, written by Tullius Laurea, freedman of Cicero, also associates the poet with the Muses (7.17).

In the visual arts, the Muses are often presented in an exclusively homosocial context, and occasionally their images gaze in a possibly erotic way at each other; the gaze is sometimes accompanied by a touch that seems homoerotic, perhaps reflective of the Sapphic strand in the literary materials. In addition to its presence in Sapphic writings, as argued in Greene's essay in this volume, ancient writers also provide other examples of a variety of erotic gazes in homoerotic contexts, especially male. For example, Philostratus describes a painting in which satyrs gaze upon the sleeping Olympus, pupil of Marsyas, a well-known homoerotic myth: "A band of satyrs gaze lovingly upon the youth, ruddy grinning creatures, one desiring to touch his breasts, another to embrace his neck, another eager to pluck a kiss" (*Imagines* 1.20). Philostratus also describes the gaze in a painting of Narcissus, who has fallen in love with his own image: "The eye, surely, is that of a man deeply in love . . . and he perhaps thinks he is loved in return, since the reflection gazes at him in just the way he looks at it" (1.23).

Extant relief sarcophagi, especially works of the second century CE, show the gaze and related physical manifestations of closeness particularly well among the Muses. Erato, with her connections to romantic, even erotic poetry, appears especially significant in these images. A drawing of a sarcophagus from Ostia, in Rome's Villa Vigna Pacca, presents the Muses in pairs or groups that are compositionally closed by their mutual gazes; one group of three, in which Erato is present, reflects visually the Muse's connections with romantic poetry in this way.[61] On the sarcophagus, Clio is represented with a diptych as an attribute and seems in fact to grasp the drapery of Erato (or perhaps Terpsichore) to get her attention, which is drawn by Urania, whose hand reaches behind the draped outstretched arm towards her abdomen. Plutarch tells us that "Erato eliminates the mad, frantic element in pleasure, which reaches a conclusion in love and trust" (*Table Talk* 9.746F).[62] Another sarcophagus, found by the Porta Latina in Rome, shows Muses, represented as musicians, although their individual identities are uncertain.[63] In the central group, the Muse who seems to be Polyhymnia, leaning on a stone wall, is staring intently at a Muse with a cithara, perhaps also Erato, who is entertaining her. Similar in iconography, and as striking, is a group in the Louvre where two Muses (possibly Urania and Melpomene) are lost in each other's eyes, lost in serenade (fig. 7.2).[64] In addition to the intent

7.2. Sarcophagus showing Muses. Paris, Louvre, MA 475.

gaze, male gender implications may be expressed through phallic symbol-ism, with the Muses connected to male sexuality.[65] Visually, this depiction of Urania may carry a latent reference to Aphrodite Urania through the ico-nography, especially her attire, thereby enhancing the implications of Eros.

Yet Muses are immortal, so what do they have to do with women? Are they to be echoed? By the Roman period, for example, Sappho had become elevated to the extent of no longer existing as a mortal, but in the minds of many, she was a Muse. Further, sometimes one can hardly determine if the images representing the Muses are really Muses or women depicted as Muses, since women other than Sappho also were associated with them. A fifth-century Sicilian inscription, for example, states: "Here lies Euterpe, the companion of the Muses. She lived chastely and piously and blamelessly for 22 years, 3 months."[66]

The musical aspect of the Muses was often emphasized in the eroticized groups, as on a sarcophagus in Vienna.[67] The first four Muses in the line are presented in pairs, closed by intent gazes. The Muse who appears to be Er-ato is shown in a stylistic manner that evokes images of Aphrodite, with her drapery clinging to her body and her pose similar to various images of the goddess. It may be no accident, then, that when mortal musicians are de-picted in art, they appear to share affinities with their immortal counterparts, the Muses. Musicians, mortal offshoots of Muses, also are depicted in ho-mosocial groups in which closeness, intimacy, and eroticism are demon-strated. Such images occur both in sculpture and in painting, suggesting that they were part of the common iconographic vocabulary of artists. Since it receives little comment in the sources, the eroticism of musicians may have been a part of Roman life that was common or at least not regarded as odd. A painting in the Metropolitan Museum shows a woman with a cithara, coupled with a woman who could be a lover, or perhaps as Ragghianti proposed, an *ancella*, a handmaid or a sister in some sense.[68] The image is somewhat evocative of both Erato and her audience, and of Sappho as performer for women. A painting in Naples, from Pompeii, shows a similar musical theme: identified as depicting a concert, the painting shows a musician and her intent female audience of three sharing a woman's space.[69] Written sources sometimes confirm the connection between musicians and homoerotic behavior. In fact, Leaena of Lucian's famous homosexual *Dialogue of the Courtesans* (5.290) is a musician.[70]

Sarcophagi and other sculpture also include the motif of female couples sharing an instrument and engaging in dance that is eroticized to varying extents. On a fragment of a sarcophagus in the Studio Canova in Rome, a pair of female musicians is depicted in an embrace, one holding the other from behind (fig. 7.3).[71] Another fragment shows a pair of female musicians strolling and sharing an instrument, one with her arm around the shoulder of another, like young lovers or close friends whose interaction includes the physical.[72] Another with more symbolic homoerotic qualities shows a couple dancing around an altar upon which a fire is burning (fig. 7.4).[73] One participant whose body is bared looks into the flame, while the other holds her face towards the sky in an image suggesting ecstasy. This last figure holds a thyrsus, which may hold phallic symbolism in its visual expression.[74] The flame serves as signifier of the heat of passion and genitalia. Eros was a keeper of a torch, and Plutarch (*Roman Questions* 1 and 2) tells us that torches are lit in marriage rites and that fire and water are both part of the ritual, fire representing the masculine element and water, the feminine. Similar, more highly eroticized, heterosexual groupings can also be found.[75]

APHRODITE

The Muses have their effects on and analogs in mortals, but what about the other goddesses, including the more common cult figures? One aspect of ancient religion that is foreign to most of us is women's relationship to the female divine. To understand the breadth of the relationship, one can look at relationships between the mortal and the divine in modern religion, where we see the projection of a physical/romantic relationship with the divine. On a popular level, talking about one's relationship to or with God is common, and sometimes, in the case of nuns, it is regarded as marriage. The marriage is only one aspect in the history of Christianity and other religions.

7.3. Sarcophagus showing musical activity. Studio Canova. Deutsches Archäologisches Institut, Rome, Neg. 31.48. Photograph: Faraglia.

7.4. End of a sarcophagus showing two musicians dancing around an altar. Pisa, Campo Santo. Deutsches Archäologisches Institut, Rome, Neg. 34.614. Photograph: Felbermeyer.

From the times of early Christianity (and perhaps even earlier), women made vows to God that were equated to relationships they would otherwise have only with men.[76] The relationships had a place in the visual arts, where occasionally there are highly eroticized images, as in Bernini's *Transverberation of Saint Theresa*, in which the angel, resembling Eros, comes to the woman, Theresa, who is depicted in an ecstatic state.[77] The eroticization of the mortal-divine relationship also appears in art connected with ancient Greco-Roman religion in situations such as the leader's interactions with eroticized Victories, whose iconography is similar to what is frequently used for Venus or Aphrodite, and in men's dreams of sexual or erotic interaction with the female divine, as presented by Artemidorus of Ephesus (*Oneirocritica* 1.80).[78] In the second century CE, some writers regarded Mary as a New Eve, evidently looking at a sort of pure eroticism in the immaculate conception.[79]

Female homoeroticism in Greco-Roman religion is especially notable in works that contain representations of Aphrodite or Venus.[80] This goddess had a very personal, one-on-one relationship with the cult members to the extent that she could physically guide them. Tibullus tells us (1.2) that she assists young women in the actual mechanics of their love relationships, from opening a bolted door to teaching how to move quietly from the bed so as not to be discovered in their affairs. The tradition of Aphrodite helping lovers was an essential part of her cult and was known throughout the world. Sappho herself addresses Aphrodite about romantic matters in a hymn (1.1) preserved by Dionysius of Halicarnassus and in fragments preserved by Strabo (1.5), Athenaeus (1.6), and Apollonius (1.7, 8, and 9). Indeed, Sappho's (5.86) writing also compares a female beloved to a goddess (as preserved in a seventh-century manuscript).[81]

The physical aspects of the perceived nature of the relationship are illuminated by the visual arts. Some representations of women with Aphrodite depict the mortals in situations with the female goddess—the woman possibly under the influence of Eros; the depictions sometimes include genital or other erotic contact. A very literal homoeroticism is occasionally demonstrated in these depictions of the quasidivine or mortal with the divine, as in depictions of Helen and Aphrodite. Perhaps this depiction is derived from a tradition that reaches back to the composition of the *Iliad*, where Aphrodite says to Helen in frustration at her resistance to go to Paris: "Damn you woman, don't provoke me—I'll get angry and let you drop! / I'll come to hate you as terribly as I now love you!" (3.314–315).[82]

There are definitely erotically charged images of the goddess with the human or semihuman female, especially mythic, just as there are with males

7.5. Helen and Aphrodite relief. Alinari 11189. Alinari /Art Resource New York.

but in terms appropriate for the females in ancient tradition. A famous scene of Helen and Aphrodite is shown in a manner that highlights the erotic interaction between the two, as on a relief in Naples (fig. 7.5).[83] Inscriptions identify the figures. The goddess is shown seated at the side of Helen, sharing her chair; Peitho is perched above; on the right are Eros and Alexandros. While the obvious interpretation is heterosexual, there is a submerged homoeroticism both in the balanced, traditional boy group[84] of Paris (Alexandros) and the adolescent Eros, and in the Helen/Aphrodite group. Aphrodite is depicted frontally with bared breast at Helen's side; her arm is around Helen, at whom she gazes. Helen's hand is placed near Aphrodite's pubic area in a gesture that simultaneously suggests that she may gain erotic power from the goddess and that she is in a mode of providing homoerotic pleasure. Suggesting a long-lived tradition in its existence as an original and a copy, Aphrodite's role here is like that of Venus in Capella's *Marriage of Philology and Mercury:* "And beautiful Venus, alone familiar with the flames of love, will caressingly console you Obstinate maiden, knowing not how to yield to a new love, Venus will prepare your heart" (9.903).[85] The erotic gesture and imagery also appear on a Neo-Attic krater in the Palazzo dei Conservatori.[86] Here Aphrodite is attired differently, with both breasts exposed, and a group of Muses or musicians takes the place of Peitho. A group of highly archaized women appear in the background, as if to give a setting (fig. 7.6). These figures may hold a reference to Sappho's time and her eroticism, since they are holding hands and approaching a flower, a lover's gift from early times.[87] A much younger Eros also is shown (fig. 7.7).[88] Aphrodite points to Eros, and the modest Helen again places her hand near Aphrodite's pubic area. The visual indications of the homoerotic seem to function as a foreshadowing of heterosexual relationship: the goddess stimulates the woman, in the visual terms of homoeroticism, to lead her into her heteroerotic context, perhaps sometimes as a rite of passage. Horace's mention of Sappho together with Helen (4.9) appears to be thematically similar and may be a reflection of this motif. It is interesting to note that Helen is also present in Sappho's ode to Anactoria (1.38), a work preserved in a second-century papyrus; this poem contains an allusion to Helen's erotic "choice" to leave for Troy, almost a metaphor for Sappho's words.[89]

The interaction of other females occasionally also is eroticized by the presence of Aphrodite. A painting preserved through an engraving and identified as the myth of Venus and Adonis shows what appears compositionally and contextually to be a couple of women. Venus, Adonis, and Eros are flanked by groups that balance the composition (fig. 7.8).[90] On the left is a group of youths, and on the right are the two women who stand together in a possible embrace. Adonis is mentioned before Aphrodite in a fragmentary sixth-century parchment with Sappho's poetry.[91] Moreover, in Ovid's *Metamorphoses* (10.560–739) within the Orpheus cycle, Venus tells Adonis the story of Atalanta, who avoided men.

Not just Aphrodite but logically her meanings (erotic feeling, erotic expression, passion, desire) are expressed through conflations of iconography that present mortals in her guise or with some of her characteristics. Pompeian painting contains several other images in which Aphrodite's implied presence suggests eroticism in groups of women, especially when considered in conjunction with other elements of the depiction. An Aphroditelike/eroticized female is one of the figures in the painting known as the Colloquio di Donne.[92] Given the norms of proper female dress, the seminudity

7.6. Archaistic women from Neo-Attic krater. Rome, Capitoline Museums, Promoteca, inv. mc 1200. Deutsches Archäologisches Institut, Rome, Neg. 28.86. Photograph: Faraglia.

7.7. Eros, from Neo-Attic krater. Rome, Capitoline Museums, Promoteca, inv. mc 1200. Deutsches Archäologisches Institut, Rome, Neg. 28.84. Photograph: Faraglia.

7.8. Engraving of Venus and Adonis. Rome, from Domus Aurea. Deutsches Archäologisches Institut, Rome, Neg. 1104. Photograph: Gauss.

of this figure suggests that she may not be physically present but is there as an allegory or personification.[93] Her gaze is directed at the other seated female. A wall painting from the Aventine, now lost, but preserved in a drawing, also shows couples of women.[94] Aphrodite seems to be uniting the pair on the left in the same way as Concordia unites married couples on sarcophagi and in other media.

The Aldobrandini Wedding

Perhaps the most striking appearance of Aphrodite in a homosocial context occurs within the so-called Aldobrandini Wedding, a painting that has not yet been exhaustively interpreted (fig. 7.9).[95] A figure, generally regarded as Aphrodite herself, interacts homoerotically with a woman, this time on a bed, within a chamber depicting something similar to the image presented by Martianus Capella. The theme is variously identified, most recently by Müller, who interprets it as a story of Hippolytus. Although I am not fully in disagreement with Müller's reading, especially in its treatment of details, this painting requires reading on a greater variety of levels and with less fixed labeling than Müller has argued. A homoerotic pre-nuptial ritual/myth may be presented at a secondary, more general level. Represented are two small

7.9. Aldobrandini Wedding. Biblioteca Apostolica Vaticana. Deutsches Archäologisches Institut, Rome, Neg. 30.174. Photograph: Felbermeyer.

7.10. Male-female chamber scene. Rome, from villa under Farnesina, National Museum of the Terme, inv. 1188. Deutsches Archäologisches Institut, Rome, Neg. 77.1295. Photograph: Rossa.

genderless figures, probably female, an older woman with a fan, two semi-draped female figures, a heavily draped female, a semidraped male, and three fully draped women, one of whom holds a lyre. The figures are situated in front of a wall that bends and seems to show delimitations of setting, possibly separating vignettes. There are three altars, a bed, and two platforms.

Following Müller, the painting can be read as three distinct segments. The first, with three women, one of whom is hooded, usually is read as a scene of ritual, perhaps the invoking of a divinity. The group is homosocial, as often is the case in prenuptial images presented in texts. The second, with four figures, may read from the semidraped female to the semidraped male, who also may work transitionally with the third segment. The Aphrodite-like figure, identifiable by her seminudity, sits on the bed; Peitho (Persuasion, daughter of Aphrodite), as Müller has argued convincingly, stands at the side. Beside Aphrodite on the bed is a figure wearing a light-colored gown and veil, the bride, reacting to the presence of Peitho and Aphrodite. The interaction between Aphrodite and the bride is of the type used with Helen: the gaze of the figures demonstrates their connection. Further, it is not unlike a male-female chamber scene. Clarke, for example, has pointed out the similarities in dress, and the women's pose with a male-female chamber scene caused "Andreae to see this picture as a young married couple on their wedding night" (fig. 7.10).[96] As for married couples, the scene implies preconjugal relations and is one of prenuptial homoeroticism. Peitho's presence here is not unexpected. In addition to being combined with Aphrodite in the visual arts, she is also recorded in literature at weddings, as Martianus Capella wrote (9.996): "Persuasion, Pleasure, and the Graces, singing to the accompaniment of a lyre and dancing hither and thither with the rhythmic beat. . . ."[97] Peitho also is mentioned in Antipater of Sidon's *Epitaph on Sappho*, in a second-century papyrus commentary on Sappho, and in a sixth-century parchment preserving fragments of Sappho.[98] These show Roman-era knowledge of Sappho's relations with the goddess.

The seminude male may be allegorical or a personification or may represent the bridegroom, as Müller suggests (he supports this interpretation by a comparison with the painting from the Casa del Citarista, which also sports a figure at the foot of the bed), but it seems more likely, in conjunction with the various associated deities and in line with earlier interpretations, that the figure may represent a personification, perhaps Hymen.[99] With the other elements here, we would expect Eros, and so Hymen is a logical replacement. He is mentioned in Dioscurides' (third century BCE) inscription in the Palatine Anthology: "Sweetest support of love for passionate youths, Sappho, with the Muses does Pieria or ivied Helicon honor you, whose breath is equal to theirs, the Muse in Aeolian Eresus; or Hymen, God of Weddings, holding his bright torch, stand with you over bridal beds. . . . " [100] Hephaestion (second century CE) too quotes Sappho associating Hymenaeus and weddings.[101]

The third scene is one of ritual: the women are presented like Muses in a homosocial environment. The goddess' place in a nuptial context then seems to be as an intercessor between the present and future. Earlier interpretations focused on water and fire in the first and third vignettes, aspects of marriage ritual.[102] These elements then also have significance in the homoerotic realm.

A different type of homoeroticism can also be seen in some aspects of Aphrodite cult. In one ritual attested by Ovid (*Fasti* 4.133–162), women bathe the statue of Aphrodite in celebration of a holiday.[103] The homosocial environment of the bath, perhaps this specific bath, with its erotic qualities may be attested by a situla from Herculaneum (fig. 7.11).[104] A woman, sometimes identified as Aphrodite, is in the bath with three attendants: in general the scene is not highly eroticized: the nude women/girls interact, evidently completely unself-consciously. Yet a certain sensuality is evident: the central figure's foot with outstretched toes, for example, brushes against the leg of the attendant. Andrew Scholtz has shown that washing the feet sometimes was a metaphor for sexual intercourse in antiquity.[105] On the other side, a figure is disrobing before the two nude attendants; she lifts her dress, exposing her legs and pubic area.

Aphrodite's homoeroticism stretches beyond the realm of the nuptial and the physical. Glimpses through the window reveal quite a variety of actions, including expression of a sincere appreciation of female beauty. In Luxorius, amidst a full description of her physical beauty, Venus expresses regret that a woman will leave her band for a wedding (91.42).[106] A cameo sports the same sort of context, an image of Aphrodite flanked by two females attempting to catch Erotes.[107] Martianus Capella also reflects a homoerotic scene with a possible allusion to an embrace of Mars and Venus (Aphrodite), as presented in the introduction of Lucretius, *De Rerum Natura* (On the Nature of Affairs): "Thus Venus spoke, and, lying backward, leaned into the embrace of Pleasure, who was standing beside her." A sarcophagus in Rome's Capitoline Museum shows a woman kneeling before Aphrodite, or an Aphroditelike figure, offering her a bowl of what appear to be apples, one of her

7.11. Situla from Herculaneum. Naples, Museo Nazionale, inv. 25289. Waldstein and Shoobridge, *Herculaneum: Past, Present, Future*, pl. 44, facing p. 170.

main attributes in Roman art, representing the apple won in the beauty con-
test against her sisters.[108] It is always possible to read too much into such
images, but the possibilities for interpretation remain endless.

We have good evidence to suspect that the scene as a whole may hold
some homoerotic significance. The erotic significance of the apple is far
ranging in Roman art. The apple was presented as a gift between lovers as
in Longus' *Daphnis and Chloe* (3.33–34) and in Philostratus' *Imagines* (1.6) Cupids are represented playing ball with apples, one kissing the apple before
tossing it, a symbol that they are beginning to fall in love.[109] Further, its usage with Eve in early Christian art reflects its erotic symbolism.

EROTES OR AMORES

Little male figures, often winged (namely, Eros or Erotes, Amores, Putti, or
Cupids), also carry their allegorical meaning in scenes showing women interacting. In ancient Rome the concept of *eros*, simply translated as "erotic
love," was broadened by definition of types, both literarily and visually, a
practice that may have had its origins in Greek art and thought. Just as the
gods and goddesses had many faces and aspects, so did Eros as an allegori-

cal god, and *eros* as a concept. Generally, the overlap is not quite comprehensible to the modern monotheistic mindset, which is also limited by the modern homo-hetero binary. Eros was presented in a variety of moods and aspects: among them, playing, sleeping, and working.[110] Philostratus' image includes different symbolic acts of the figures as represented in painting (*Imagines* 1.6). For example, in addition to tossing apples, other Cupids shoot arrows to perpetuate love.

Roman relief sarcophagi are often laden with Erotes, and later artists often understood the representation of Eros and Erotes as expressors of a backdrop of feeling for the scene. Often this was used to indicate the erotic and make further expression of it, as Mary Sheriff has shown was the case in Neoclassical images in which Jupiter disguised himself as Diana to seduce the Nymph Callisto.[111] In a work by Angelica Kauffman, for example, the figure of Eros sits at the left of the couple with his fingers to his mouth in a gesture to silence, as if indicating that something is secret—Jupiter's identity —or perhaps that something cannot be told, the women's passion.

Sheriff's work provides a paradigm for looking at the images in Roman art and understanding how we might read the art. For though the women are from no special social group, there is depiction of homoeroticism in the women's closeness. The Kauffmann images show further that in the eighteenth century, the viewer was imagining an erotic kiss between women and how it would be expressed. The situation may be similar in certain paintings and sculpture produced during the Roman period, artworks especially for private consumption. There is a variety of evidence that shows connections of women or groups of women with Eros; our understanding of these is quite limited. In the Greco-Roman images, the Eros or Erotes, as appropriate to their actual place in Roman religion, serve as more than signifiers and often function as actual characters in the images.

Sometimes the Erotes may be presented solely to express different types, as is the case with the painting from the Casa dell' Amor Punito in Pompeii.[112] This image represents two women, each with an Amor. It presents a homosocial setting, and in this way it resembles later images such as Boucher's "The Graces Chaining Cupid" of 1736–1737 or Angelica Kauffmann's "Cupid Distressed by Three Nymphs (or Virgins)" of 1777. Yet how are we to interpret this? Is literary evidence significant? On what level should we examine these—literal, allegorical, metaphorical, other?—and how should we find their meaning? Perhaps when we generalize about the iconography, we should read for meaning as an oppression of a type of Eros, a sort of moralizing allegory so common in Roman art, an oppression that has its literary parallel in Ovid's Iphis and Ianthe story.[113] Yet since the scene from the Casa dell' Amor Punito is at most homosocial, it is unclear what type of love may be punished and to what level we should read the Erotes as allegorical. Certainly, however, the women shared the Erotes, perhaps a symbol of erotic choices. There is further evidence in Bion (mid second–mid first century BCE) that would suggest that this painting falls more in the genre of the Muses with Eros (Bion, Fragments 3 and 9).[114] Fragment 9 reads: "Either the Muses are intimidated by savage Eros or they love him heartily, and they follow in his train. And so if anyone sings with a loveless soul, him they flee and refuse to teach. But if anyone sings sweetly with a mind awhirl with love, to him they hurriedly gravitate all together." Reed points out that this selection may contain a possible allusion to Sappho.

Such paintings, then, present us with an enormous interpretive problem. All in all, we may never know what they mean. Sometimes there is little more than homophobia that prevents us from making the sort of interpretation that we would make about heteroerotic images, which are so obvious to many.

Yet there are some images where there is evidence, internal and external, to support more fully a homoerotic reading, though the evidence is very fragmentary, and even somewhat circumstantial. One Pompeian painting is titled "Two Women at an Amor Market," which depicts two women deciding together what sort of Eros or Amor they want (fig. 7.12).[115] In other Pompeian frescoes, Venus shows Adonis a nest of little Cupids, a sort of heteroerotic parallel. The significance of these paintings may then indeed be illuminated through Horace's reference to Sappho's love and desires still breathing and living: the Erotes may have served to express the women's erotic choices, something they shared. Another Pompeian painting shows two nude women and an Amor; Stuveras identifies this as an inversion of the theme of Venus and the two Amores (fig. 7.13).[116] Since Roman women often were presented in the guise of Venus, one should read this painting for what is on one level a homoerotic theme: two women connected by Eros. This image is not dissimilar to heterosexual marriage scenes in which Eros appears between men and women whose hands are clasped in the "*dextrarum iunctio*." [117]

Women interacting with women and Eros also can be found in media other than painting, notably on relief mirrors, gems and finger rings, and sarcophagi. The theme of the women chasing Erotes occurs on a sardonyx cameo of the imperial period.[118] Gisela Richter identified the figures as Aphrodite with two attendants and three baby Erotes. With due respect to

7.12. Women at an Amor market. Naples, Museo Nazionale. Deutsches Archäologisches Institut, Rome, Neg. 75.1481. Photograph: Rossa.

7.13. Eros between Two Women. From Pompeii II.3.3. Deutsches Archäologisches Institut, Rome, Neg. 57.881. Photograph: Bartl.

Richter, such specific identification is not necessary or even desirable since this is Roman art (in which conflation of images served a practical propagandistic purpose), and it conceals the universality of the female homoerotic theme, its meaning for and about mortals. The eroticization of the females, resembling Aphrodite, is fact. Although an erotic energy is not shown between women on one gem, another fragmentary gem (in the Metropolitan Museum) shows a subtle eroticism. On this, the central figure's foot brushes playfully against the drapery of the figure on the left.[119]

In the cases of many of these erotically laden scenes, the setting is a sensual garden. Luxorius presents a verbal image of such a homosocial space in one of his poems. Cupid/Eros, is the only male in this depiction, as in the others; thus the poem demonstrates genuine desire (i.e., Eros/Cupid) between women. Luxorius (46) wrote:

> Garden where the wood nymphs gently flit about, where the dryads frolic in a verdant troop, where Diana cherishes the tender nymphs, where Venus hides her rosy limbs, where tired *Cupid*, now free after hanging up his quivers, restores his smooth flames,[120] where the Muses retreat; Garden whose beautiful foliage never grows thinner, whose spring balsam is always fragrant, whose delicate fountain of clear water gives rise to a spot well watered by a mossy stream; Garden where the sweet singing of birds resounds,—Whatever is carried to other cities this garden obediently supplies in this one spot.[121]

There are several scenes that show gardens or pastoral spaces similar to this in art—sometimes other males are included, and often the scenes are set in a cult space or a similar pastoral place. An Eros and a priapic figure also appear in a scene in Naples that shows women in rustic ritual celebration.[122] This image is laden with erotic symbolism, including the goat (see below) and the filling of a seated woman's vessel by a standing woman.

Another potentially homoerotic and allegorical scene can be found on a sardonyx cameo of the imperial period, which shows Erotes controlling the maneuvering of a chariot.[123] Dionysos reclines with a figure identified by Richter as a young satyr, in a male homoerotic vignette: one holds the reins and a torch "like a whip" over a pair of winged female figures identified by Richter as Psyches, who pull the vehicle. The other Eros pushes from behind, in a reference to the male homoeroticism.

A silver dish from Aquileia in the Vienna Kunsthistorisches Museum suggests homoeroticism in a utopian setting at the service of state religion.[124] The emperor (or an official) is presented in the guise of Triptolemus in a verdant garden, bringing fecundity to his world. At his side is an altar where Erotes stand. Behind him, above the altar, is a pair of goddesses, one sensually resting her arm on the shoulder of the other, who is an Aphroditelike figure. Another female pair interacts with the snaky, phallicizing heads of the creatures that draw the chariot.[125]

Homoeroticism in the expression of fecundity can also be found on a Mars and Rhea sarcophagus in Rome's Palazzo Mattei.[126] In the lower right corner, two semidraped female personifications of place, each accompanied by an Amor, recline over a goat, an animal known for erotic implications. One also holds a symbolic, full cornucopia, positioned perhaps to evoke a phallic image: the idea of being full through plenty, through the phallus and also the planting of seed. Similar conceptions of plenty and bountiful landscape in which homoeroticized personifications are present appear on other sarcophagi, most notably those showing themes of Endymion, who was loved by Luna or Diana. On the left of a frieze in the Louvre stands a pair of semidraped personifications, one with her foot on a goat; the one woman leans on the other, enhancing the sense of the eroticism.[127]

CONCLUSIONS

This essay has considered a wide variety of evidence for female homoeroticism and homosociality in artifacts, literary and visual, of the Roman period, from about 200 BCE through the sixth century CE. It suggests primarily that the lens of modern heteroerotic language—the penetration and pornographic model of sex—is misleading when applied to the ancient materials. The paucity of pornographic materials in the arts is convincing in itself. Ancient feminine sexuality had a different aspect that was not commonly the object of discussion. The evidence suggests that female homoeroticism in many of its visual manifestations—touching, gazing, appreciating beauty—was not regarded as a rarity or unusual during the period of Roman domination of the Mediterranean, among goddesses or among women. The arts, especially under Greek influence, suggest that varying degrees of physical and spiritual interaction were common among the goddesses, and women's relationships to women were not denigrated if they remained in the private realm.

The homoerotic aspects of life were so engrained, so much a part of everyday life and ritual, that they were not at all strange, which may help explain the paucity of literature on the topic. That is to say: what was significant in the relationships was not sensational. Just as different modern communities

7.14. Nereid Thiasos with Erotes. Rome, from under San Crisogono. Deutsches Archäologisches Institut, Rome, Neg. 32.347. Photograph: Sansaini.

have a variety of terms to express their lives, and the modern period shows a variety of women living together (e.g., as friends, as lovers), the ancient Romans also had a broad vocabulary to describe women's relationships with one another, a vocabulary that appears to have differed throughout the empire. The language of the visual arts merges Sappho, the Muses, Aphrodite, Erotes, weddings, and what was associated with these—symbols, gestures, gazes, and more—to present glimpses of intimacy between women. All these recur with evidence that further supports homoerotic readings in different materials, as on a sarcophagus showing a Nereid Thiasos with Erotes (fig. 7.14).[128] The Thiasos is replete with Erotes, music, seminudity, and the gaze; the "men" who are there are removed from the realistic human female realm.

The ancients living under Roman rule held a compartmentalized view of what we today regard as female homoeroticism. They saw in general both a vulgar type and a type that was so well known and accepted that it did not merit mention. Sources that focus on the sexual—especially the genital—are more critical. It appears that one type of homosocial, even homoerotic, behavior may have been expected among girls through a certain age. It is ritualized in images of weddings and may have continued in some forms throughout the life of a Roman woman. The acceptability of behaviors varied widely in correlation with public act and proper setting, and historically the different parts of the empire showed different normative behaviors for women. Many of the behaviors (e.g., loving, caressing) had parallels in language in male/female relationships. The difference is like that of the masculine and feminine expressed by St. Ambrose of Milan (*On Virginity* 15.93): "Of course, the soul has no gender in itself, but perhaps it is a feminine noun (*anima*) because when the turbulence of the body acts violently upon it, the soul softens bodily assaults by its gentle love and a certain persuasive rationality."[129]

NOTES

1. The Vestals' hair, however, was ceremonially cropped. Sir Thomas Cato Worsfold, *The History of the Vestal Virgins of Rome* (London: Rider, 1932) 23 and 53. Sources attesting the haircut include Pliny, *Natural History* 16.44.85, Dionysius 8.89, Juvenal 4.4, and Lucan 1.597. On marriage, see John Boswell, *Same-Sex Unions in Pre-Modern Europe* (New York: Villard Books, 1994).

2. Bernadette J. Brooten, *Love between Women: Early Christian Responses to Female Homoeroticism*, Chicago Series on Sexuality, History, and Society (Chicago: U of Chicago P, 1996) 59–60; n138 demonstrates the uncertainty of the identification. Further, even though oral sex between women may be depicted, it is clearly not a representation of everyday private life.

3. Recent feminist scholarship has helped to rectify this and to define women's friendships from different perspectives, e.g., Lillian Faderman, *Surpassing the Love of Men: Romantic Friendship and Love between Women from the Renaissance to the Present* (New York: William Morrow, 1981). See also Rabinowitz's introductory essay in this volume.

4. M. Jack Suggs, Katharine Doob Sakenfeld, and James R. Mueller, eds., *The Oxford Study Bible, Revised English Bible with the Apocrypha* (New York: Oxford UP, 1992). The composition is variously dated from the tenth century BCE through the fourth century CE.

5. Studies about, pertaining to, or including ancient Roman female homoeroticism include John Boswell, *Christianity, Social Tolerance, and Homosexuality: Gay People in Western Europe from the Beginning of the Christian Era to the Fourteenth Century* (Chicago: U of Chicago P, 1980); Brooten, *Love between Women*; Eva Cantarella, *Bisexuality in the Ancient World*, trans. Cormac Ó. Cuilleanáin (New Haven: Yale UP, 1992); Judith Hallett, "Female Homoeroticism and the Denial of Roman Reality in Latin Literature," in Judith P. Hallett and Marilyn B. Skinner, eds., *Roman Sexualities* (Princeton: Princeton UP, 1997) 255–273; Saara Lilja, *Homosexuality in Republican and Augustan Rome*, Commentationes Humanarum Litterarum 74 (The Finnish Society of Sciences and Letters: Ekenäs, 1983); Juan Francisco Martos Montiel, *Desde Lesbos con Amor: Homosexualidad femenina en la antigüedad*, Supplementa Mediterránea, 1 (Madrid: Ediciones Clásicas, 1996).

6. J. N. Adams, *The Latin Sexual Vocabulary* (Baltimore: Johns Hopkins UP, 1982) 97, 121–122, 190. These words seem to be fairly sexually explicit.

7. On the development of queer language, see Edmund White, "The Political Vocabulary of Homosexuality," in *The State of the Language*, Leonard Michaels and Christopher Ricks, eds. (Berkeley: U of California P, 1980): 235–246.

8. See Wilfong's essay in this volume.

9. On the conservatism of ancient religious institutions and the continuity of cult one need only to consider the images presented to the people in the coinage. See, e.g., my own doctoral dissertation, "A Catalog of Images of Women in the Official Arts of Ancient Rome" (Dissertation U of Missouri, 1997) ch. 2 (goddesses) and ch. 3 (personifications of abstractions).

10. *The Digest of Justinian*, vols. 1, 2, and 4, with Latin text edited by Theodor Mommsen,

with the aid of Paul Krueger, and an English translation edited by Alan Watson (Philadelphia: U of Pennsylvania P, 1985). I have examined parts of book 1 on justice and law, and
on human status, book 23 on betrothals and marriage, and book 48 on adulteries. If the
masculine was used as a gender inclusive term, then it is possible that adultery may have included women's homoerotic relationships. I am inclined to believe that was not the case,
since there is specification of "mulier" and "mas." See further Seneca the elder, ca. 55 BCE—
ca. 37/41 CE (*Controversiae* 1.2.23), who presents a case concerning whether the man who has
caught his wife in bed with a woman was justified in killing them as adulterous and Martial, ca. 40–104 CE (*Epigrams* 1.90), who asks if there could be adultery without a man since
Bassa was imitating a man or like a man. Martial essentially calls Bassa a "*fututor*" which
the *Oxford Latin Dictionary* defines as "a man who has sexual intercourse." I think "fucker"
is closer to the original meaning. (See also Martos Montiel, *Desde Lesbos* 106–107.)

Yet others believe that Seneca the elder and Martial provide evidence that relationships
that could be classified as sexual were considered as adulterous, regardless of gender of the
participants, as Cantarella, *Bisexuality* 167, concludes ("A married woman who has a homosexual relationship commits adultery"), based on Martial's comments.

11. Lilja, *Homosexuality* 137. See also Boswell, *Christianity* 63–70.

12. Sarah B. Pomeroy, *Goddesses, Whores, Wives, and Slaves: Women in Classical Antiquity* (New
York: Dorsett P, 1975) 209–210.

13. See, for example, Plautus' (d. ca. 184 CE) *Epidicus* (400–409) for a subtle comic representation. In short, Periphanes does not want the music girl to come in contact with his
daughter. See also John R. Clarke, *Looking at Lovemaking: Constructions of Sexuality in Roman Art,
100 B.C.–A.D. 250* (Berkeley: U of California P, 1998) 227–229 for further discussion of the
"phallic lesbian."

14. Cantarella's discussion (*Bisexuality* 164–167) provides several other examples that can
be categorized in this way. Her treatment of Petronius (first century CE), *Satyricon* 67 (165n56)
is notable, as she points out that the women in question are hardly respectable ladies.

15. Cf. Clarke's more positive interpretation of the Hermaphrodite in general. Clarke,
Looking at Lovemaking 49–55.

16. Morris Rosenblum, *Luxorius: A Latin Poet among the Vandals*, Records of Civilization
Sources and Studies (New York: Columbia UP, 1961) 130–131. The Latin reads:

In puellam hermaphroditam
Monstrum feminei bimembre sexus,
Quam coacta virum facit libido,
Quin gaudes futui furente cunno?
Cur te decepit inpotens voluptas?
Non das, quo pateris facisque, cunnum.
Illam, qua mulier probaris esse,
Partem cum dederis, puella tunc sis.

Ignorance of the sexual participant is at issue in Lucian and also may have been a concern
in Ovid's story of Iphis and Ianthe; see Haley's and Pintabone's papers in this volume.

17. E.g., they represent a single author or not what was in the laws. See also Martos
Montiel, *Desde Lesbos* 115, who comments on the deliberate misogyny and comicalness of the

texts: "Es cierto que la mayoría de estos textos son abiertamente misóginos, y que en ellos, quizás buscando un elemento de fácil comicidad, casi de caricatura, como vemos en Marcial, se exagera bastante una práctica cuyo proceso efectivo debió de ser ampliamente ignorado. Las descripciones nunca son precisas, y esa falta de claridad podría deberse, tanto o más que a una intencionalidad del autor de no herir la sensibilidad de sus lectores, a un verdadero desconcocimiento del detalle de tales prácticas. . . ."

18. Lori-Ann Touchette, *The Dancing Maenad Reliefs: Continuity and Change in Roman Copies*, Bulletin Supplement 62 (London: U of London Institute of Classical Studies, 1995) 31–35, esp. 32–33. See also Brunilde Sismondo Ridgway, *Roman Copies of Greek Sculpture: The Problem of Originals*, Jerome Lectures Fifteenth Series (Ann Arbor: U of Michigan P) 20, 24.

19. Pia Guldager Bilde, Inge Nielsen, and Marjatta Nielsen, eds., *Aspects of Hellenism in Italy: Towards a Cultural Unity?* Danish Studies in Classical Archaeology Acta Hyperborea 5 (Copenhagen: U of Copenhagen, Museum Tusculanum P, 1993).

20. Ramsay MacMullen, "Roman Attitudes to Greek Love," reprinted in Wayne R. Dynes and Stephen Donaldson, eds. *Homosexuality in the Ancient World*, Studies in Homosexuality 1 (New York: Garland, 1992) 348–358, esp. 352: "The vocabulary of homosexuality contains many Greek terms. . . . These Graecisms testify to a way of life imported as a package. . . ." See also Hallett, "Female Homoeroticism."

21. I have used David A. Campbell, ed. and trans., *Greek Lyric 1: Sappho and Alcaeus*, Loeb Classical Library 142 (Cambridge, MA: Harvard UP, 1982) for the quotation of the relevant texts in this section because the collection is unique in its comprehensiveness and notes about the preservation of the materials. The work is also widely available to readers. Likewise, the translations presented in this section are quotations from this volume. When it has been desirable to draw upon others, they are cited in the footnotes. I am not a Sappho scholar, and this section merely attempts to summarize relevant information. Other detailed studies to which I refer the reader include Ellen Greene, ed., *Reading Sappho: Contemporary Approaches* (Berkeley: U of California P, 1996) and *Re-reading Sappho: Reception and Transmission* (Berkeley: U of California P, 1996); and Jane McIntosh Snyder, *Lesbian Desire in the Lyrics of Sappho* (New York: Columbia UP, 1997).

22. There are mentions of Sappho in the works of at least ten men who wrote in Latin: Cicero, Horace, Ovid, the younger Seneca, the elder Pliny, Martial, Statius, Bassus, Aulus Gellius, and Maurus. In the interest of brevity I have not included those writers and references that focus exclusively on her writing and meter. It is nonetheless quite possible that even those that mention meter are indirect references to the erotic, since meter sometimes presented an allusion to sexual intercourse. See Adams, *Latin Sexual Vocabulary* 39, and William Harris Stahl and Richard Johnson, with L. Burge, trans., *Martianus Capella and the Seven Liberal Arts: The Marriage of Philology and Mercury*, vol. 2 (New York: Columbia UP, 1977). The wedding ritual (9.967–995, "Harmony") ends with a discussion of rhythm.

23. Horace, 65–8 BCE, was a poet who wrote in official circles during the age of Augustus. For the use of "*puella*" in erotic relationships as a term that does not express age, see pp. 219, 249n34.

24. Campbell, *Greek Lyric 1*, 18–19.

25. David A. Campbell, "Aeolium Carmen: Horace's Allusions to Sappho and Alcaeus," *EMC* 22.3 (1978): 94–97. Campbell summarized the scholiast's responses: (1) "that

she was famous [as a man could be] for her poetry" and (2) that she was homosexual, a tribad. Campbell went on to write: "I think the second explanation is wide of the mark." See also Lilja, *Homosexuality* 72.

For a discussion of the definition of "tribad" (tribas), see Hallett, "Female Homo-eroticism" 255–273, esp. 255. The author of the *Oxford Latin Dictionary* entry viewed "tribas" as "a female sexual pervert, a (masculine) lesbian," and the author of the entry in Lewis and Short the term as "a woman who practices lewdness with women."

26. Owse Temkin, trans., *Soranus' Gynecology* (Baltimore: Johns Hopkins UP, 1956) 20, 26, 32, 33, 94, 133, and 134.

27. Martianus Capella 381. Martianus Capella was a Neoplatonist who lived in Car-thage (in North Africa) in the fifth century CE. His *Marriage of Philology and Mercury* appears to have been written between 410 and 439 CE. See William Harris Stahl and Richard John-son, with L. Burge, trans., *Martianus Capella and the Seven Liberal Arts: The Quadrivium of Martianus Capella, with a Study of the Allegory and the Verbal Disciplines*, vol. 1 (New York: Columbia UP, 1971) 11–15, esp. 15. Cf. Danuta Shanzer, *A Philosophical and Literary Commentary on Martianus Capella's De Nuptiis Philologe et Mercurii Book 1*, U of California Publications in Classical Studies 32 (Berkeley: U of California P, 1986) 5–17. Shanzer is also convincingly inconclusive. The Latin (9.995) reads: *numerum autem marem esse, melos feminam noverimus. et enim melos materies est, quae sine propria figure censetur, rythmus autem opere quodam virilis actus tam formam sonis quam varios praestat effectus.*

28. Other divinities also were presented like men or masculine, as is shown in Pleasure's description of Geometry in the *Marriage of Philology and Mercury* (6.704): "Pleasure, for some time relaxed among the beautiful girls, 'For what reason has this pitiless boor with coarse limbs completed her circuit of the earth and, after traipsing over so many mountains, rivers, seas, and crossroads has come to relieve boredom? I could believe that her limbs prickle with thorns and shaggy hair. She is so covered with dust and so tough and peasant-like that one would naturally suppose her to be a man (*credatur mascula*)'."

The representation of abstract concepts as men and women was a common practice in Greco-Roman religion from the earliest times. On the personified women, see Auanger, "Catalog" 64–203.

29. The text cited is from Stephanus Borzsák, ed., *Q. Horati Flacci Opera* (Leipzig: Teub-ner, 1984) 116–117. See also Lilja, *Homosexuality* 72.

30. Or to preserve the word order, emphatically, "Breathing, her Love is; Living, her Passions are."

31. Pamela Gordon, "The Lover's Voice in *Heroides* 15: Or, Why is Sappho a Man?" in Judith Hallett and Marilyn B. Skinner, eds., *Roman Sexualities* (Princeton: Princeton UP 1997) 274–294. See esp. 288–289 for an argument about the authenticity of this letter. See also Howard Jacobson, *Ovid's Heroides* (Princeton: Princeton UP, 1974) 277–299, esp. 277–278, and Campbell, *Greek Lyric* 1 23. Campbell, in *Greek Lyric* 1, following Bowra, postulates: "Pos-sibly Phaon was another name for Adonis, and a poem of S. in which Aphrodite declared her love for him . . . was misinterpreted as expressing S.' love for a living man."

32. Grant Showerman, trans., *Ovid, Heroides and Amores*, Loeb Classical Library (Cam-bridge, MA: Harvard UP, 1914) 183.

33. Gordon, "Lover's Voice" 278. Variants of line twenty (*"quas non sine crimine amavi"*) show *"hic"* rather than *"non."* Gordon points out that either way there was shame involved

in the love, but Gordon does not consider the plethora of possible reasons, including loving too much, being hurt, or putting oneself in too lowly or vulnerable of an emotional situation.

34. See Rabinowitz's introduction in this volume and Holt N. Parker, "Sappho Schoolmistress," in Ellen Greene, ed. *Re-Reading Sappho: Reception and Transmission* (Berkeley: U of California P, 1996) 130–162, esp. 158. Parker points out (158), ". . . *puella*, of course, is used equally of girls, mature women, and goddesses, especially as objects of love, and Horace calls Sappho herself a *puella* at *Odes* 4.9.12." Cf. Martos Montiel, *Desde Lesbos* 19–20, on Maximus of Tyre.

35. Hallett, "Female Homoeroticism" 260, pointed out the appropriateness of dual interpretation of the line.

36. See below for the cult of Muses on Lesbos and their frequent association with Sappho.

37. Campbell, *Greek Lyric 1* 22–23. Campbell n1: "An allegation derived perhaps from the general opinion of the Lesbians as immoral."

38. It is misleading to translate any of these terms into English, since the corpus of evidence that is presented in this paper provides a basis for their definition and related complexities as regards women's relationships. In short, these women were Sappho's companions. Rabinowitz includes a discussion of *"hetairai"* in this volume. The later significance may have changed and even have come to influence our understanding of the earlier usages. *"Philai"* approximates "loved ones" or "dear ones," and *"parthenai"* would commonly be translated "virgins," as in the Parthenon.

39. W. Hamilton Fyfe, trans., *Aristotle,* The Poetics, *"Longinus"* On the Sublime, *Demetrius* On Style, Loeb Classical Library 199 (Cambridge, MA: Harvard UP, 1982) 154–157.

40. Campbell, *Greek Lyric 1* 78–81. Sappho is quoted: "He seems as fortunate as the gods to me, the man who sits opposite you and listens nearby to your sweet voice and lovely laughter. Truly that sets my heart trembling in my breast. For when I look at you for a moment, then it is no longer possible for me to speak; my tongue has snapped, at once a subtle fire has stolen beneath my flesh, I see nothing with my eyes, my ears hum, sweat pours from me, a trembling seizes me all over, I am greener than the grass, and it seems to me that I am a little short of dying. . . ."

41. Fyfe, *Aristotle* 157.

42. Campbell, *Greek Lyric 1* 20–21.

43. Campbell, *Greek Lyric 1* 20–21.

44. The word is not an equivalent to the modern "lesbian." Pollux (3.69–70) includes the term. See Rabinowitz's essay in this volume for problems of drawing equivalents.

45. Campbell, *Greek Lyric 1* 156–157. According to Athenaeus, Sappho wrote that Leto and Niobe were *"philai hetairai."*

46. For similar work in other periods, see College Art Association, Gay and Lesbian Caucus, *Bibliography of Gay and Lesbian Art* (New York: The Caucus, 1994).

47. Consider Ganymede and the Eagle or Leda and the swan. In both of these cases, erotic interaction is depicted.

48. Arnobius of Sicca, *The Case against the Pagans,* vol. 2, bks. 4–7, trans. George E. McCracken, Ancient Christian Writers: The Works of the Fathers in Translation, no. 8. The Catholic U of America (Cork: Mercier P, 1949) 440–451.

49. *Le collezioni del Museo Nazionale di Napoli,* under the care of Archivio fotografico Pedicini, vol. 1.2 (Rome: De Luca, c1986–) 224–225, no. 19.

50. Hever Castle sarcophagus of the late second century CE. "Charis, Charites/Gratiae," *LIMC* 3, 205, no. 26.

51. Contrast Rhetoric (5.565), who noisily kissed the forehead of Philology. The Graces also sometimes were depicted with married couples, as "Charis, Charites/Gratiae," *LIMC* 3, no. 30, pl. 160.

52. As above, p. 216.

53. Rosenblum, *Luxorius* 156–159. The Latin of the poem is as follows: *In mulierem pulcram castitati studentem / Pulcrior et nivei cum sit tibi forma coloris, / Cuncta pudicitiae iura tenere cupis. / Mirandum est quali naturam laude gubernes / Moribus ut Pallas, corpore Cypris eas. / Te neque coniugii libet excepisse levamen; / Saepius exoptas nolle videre mares. / Haec tamen est animo quamvis exosa voluptas: / Numquid non mulier conparis esse potes?*

54. It also can be seen among other goddesses, in stories of women who spurn men, women of a "tribe," and transgendered myths.

55. There are several (possibly more than ten) references and allusions to Muses in Sappho's work transmitted through the Roman era. These include Oxyrhynchus Papyrus 2294, where the Pierian Muses are present in a bridal song. The passages are quoted by several Roman era writers: Apollonius Dyscolus, Hephaestion, Maximus of Tyre, Aelius Aristides, and Himerius. See Campbell, *Greek Lyric 1,* 81, 93, 99, 101, 129, 147, 161, 183, 191, and 203.

56. See above, pp. 222–223.

57. *Moralia,* vol. 6, pp. 260–261 (480e).

58. Arnobius of Sicca, *The Case against the Pagans,* vol. 1, bks. 1–3, trans. George E. McCracken, *Ancient Christian Writers: The Works of the Fathers in Translation,* no. 7. The Catholic U of America (Westminster, MD: Newman P, 1949) 220–221, 395–396; Arnobius (3.37) comments on varying traditions about the birth, sexual status, and number of Muses.

59. Campbell, *Greek Lyric 1,* 49n1. Several of the fragments preserve a much earlier tradition; the nature of the original—true or another step in the process—is rarely, if ever, known.

60. *Moralia,* vol. 9, pp. 389–390.

61. Max Wegner, *Die Musensarkophage,* Antiken Sarkophagreliefs (Berlin: Mann, 1966) 83, no. 218, pl. 2a.

62. *Moralia,* vol. 9, pp. 286–287.

63. Wegner, *Musensarkophage* 21–22, pl. 2b, "Leningrad." The identity of the figures on this sarcophagus is unclear because the attributes are repeated: three hold citharalike instruments.

64. Wegner, *Musensarkophage* 36–37, no. 75, pls. 3 and 6. Other eroticized Muses can be found in Munich, 27–28, no. 55, pls. 24 and 25 (where proximity, gaze, and hand gestures serve as signifiers); Villa Borghese in Rome, 78, no. 205. pl. 27; London, 24, no. 43, pl. 28; Woburn Abbey 90–91, no. 231, pl. 42; Palermo, 33–34, no. 68, pl. 66; Rome, Museo Vaticano, 57–58, no. 138, pl. 68; and Tunis, 86–87, no. 225, pl. 102. These show varying levels of physical interconnectedness among the Muses. The Munich sarcophagus includes an almost comically intent Minerva.

65. On the phallic symbolism, see Adams, *Latin Sexual Vocabulary* 14ff., on sharp or pointed instruments.

66. Ross S. Kraemer, ed., *Maenads, Martyrs, Matrons, Monastics: A Sourcebook on Women's Religions in the Greco-Roman World* (Philadelphia: Fortress P, 1988) 205, no. 76.

67. Wegner, *Musensarkophage* 88–89, no. 228, pls. 9b, 11, 12.

68. Carlo Ludovico Ragghianti, *Pittori di Pompei* (Milan: Edizioni del Milione, 1963) 89, fig. 7. There is no reason why the two categories must be mutually exclusive. See Rabinowitz's essay in this volume.

69. *Napoli* 1.1, 53 and 138, no. 107. On the association of music with the erotic, see Adams, *Latin Sexual Vocabulary* 21 and 25; Lilja, *Homosexuality* 28; and Philostratus (*Imagines* 1.20). In the continued description of the painting of satyrs gazing upon Olympus, Philostratus writes, "The cleverest of them [satyrs] draws out the tongue of the second pipe [reeds already yielding music that lie beside Olympus] which is still warm and eats it, thinking he is kissing Olympus, and he says he has tasted the boy's breath." Philostratus (1.1) also tells of a painting of a spirit of Comus, revelry, where transgendered dressing is part of the scene in a heteroerotic context. The image is laden with sound.

70. See Haley's essay in this volume. Also, the father's concern in Plautus' *Epidicus* had to do with a music girl. On the lives of musicians, see Chester Starr, "An Evening with the Flute Girls," *Parole del Passato* 33 (1978): 410.

71. Friedrich Matz, *Die dionysischen Sarkophage*, vol. 4, pt. 4, Deutsches Archäologisches Institut, Antiken Sarkophagreliefs (Berlin: Gebr. Mann Verlag, 1968) 486, no. 323, pl. 126.

72. Carl Robert, *Einzelmythen*, vol. 3.2 (Rome: "L'Erma" di Bretschneider, 1969) 181–182, no. 153, pl. 47. The end of a Hercules and Hesione sarcophagus in Cologne also shows a homoerotic pair of dancers, Bacchantes, 159–161, no. 137a, pl. 42. This is a work carved in the provinces, probably of the third century.

73. Matz, *Dionysischen* 4.4, 455–456, no. 260, pl. 288. The other end shows a scene of heteroerotic dance.

74. Adams, *Latin Sexual Vocabulary* 28 and 229 (thyrsus) and 86–87 (hearth/flame). One might also consider the relevance of the flame in the homosocial context of the Vestals. On Eros, see below pp. oo. Further, in Prudentius' *Psychomachia*, the allegory "*sodomita Libido*" (l.42) is the bearer of a flame. Prudentius goes into detail describing her action against "*virgo Pudicitia*" with a very fire-laden vocabulary. Macklin Smith (*Prudentius* Psychomachia: *A Reexamination* [Princeton: Princeton UP, 1976] 286) connects the image to the *Aeneid*, where torches are "associated either with destructive burning or with the Passions of love." Fire also had a place in the wedding ceremony (Frank G. J. M. Müller, *The Aldobrandini Wedding*. Iconological Studies in Roman Art 3 [Amsterdam: J. C. Gieben, 1994] 26–27). See also Ovid's description of Sappho's passion, above.

75. Matz, *Dionysischen* 4.2, 274–275, no. 138, pl. 63; Robert, *Einzelmythen* 3.2 178–181, no. 152b, pl. 47. A fragment of a sarcophagus in Girgenti shows a fully homosocial bridal group, where a veiled woman seems affected to the point of fainting. Two musicians and a figure of Eros are also shown. The Muses were present at the wedding of Philology and Mercury (Martianus Capella 2.117–125), singing and performing with instruments in the chamber in which the bride was being prepared. There was also a great deal of music and dancing (2.133).

76. As, for example, the fourth-century St. Agnes, *Butler's Lives of the Saints*, vol. 1 (New York: Kenedy, 1956 [repr. Westminster, MD: Christian Classics, 1981]) 133–137, esp. 133: "Her riches and beauty excited the young noblemen of the first families in Rome to contend as

rivals for her hand. Agnes answered them all that she had consecrated her virginity to a heavenly husband, who could not be beheld by mortal eyes."

77. Jean-Noël Vuarnet, *Extases féminines* (Paris: Arthaud, c1980) 102. Other images in this book also show representations of relationships with the sacred or holy in erotic terms. See also Moshe Idel and Bernard McGinn, eds., *Mystical Union and Monotheistic Faith* (New York: Macmillan, 1989) esp. 59–86: McGinn, "Love, Knowledge and the *Unio mystica* in the Western Christian Tradition." The volume also includes papers on Judaism and Islam.

78. Robert J. White, trans., *The Interpretation of Dreams, Oneirocritica by Artemidorus* (Park Ridge, NJ: Noyes P, 1975) 65.

79. J. A. Ross MacKenzie, "The Patristic Witness to the Virgin Mary as the New Eve," *Marian Studies* 29 (1978): 67–78, esp. 71 (from Justin Martyr) and also 74–76 (Ephraem). According to MacKenzie (76–77), "By the fourth century the concept of Mary as the counterpart of Eve had been incorporated into the soteriology of the Greek speaking church, where it was a commonplace. In the fifth century parallels between Eve and Mary proliferated, at times to the point of preciousness."

80. Except in a direct quotation in which "Venus" is used, I shall refer to the goddess as "Aphrodite," since most of the materials are strongly under Hellenic influence.

81. See also Skinner's essay in this volume. In addition, the following explore Sappho's relationship with Aphrodite: Paul Friedrich, *The Meaning of Aphrodite* (Chicago: U of Chicago P, 1978) 104–128, esp. 123–125, and Snyder, *Lesbian Desire* 7–25: "Sappho and Aphrodite."

82. The translation is from Anne Carson, *Eros the Bittersweet: An Essay* (Princeton: Princeton UP, 1986) 4–6.

83. Bieber, *Sculpture* 153, fig. 652; Müller, fig. 15; Roger Stuveras, *Le putto dans l'art romain*, Collection Latomus 99 (Brussels: Latomus, 1969) pl. 6, fig. 14; *Napoli* 1.2, 148–149, no. 261. There is also a cast at the University of Missouri-Columbia, Pickard Hall. Similar iconography can also be found in "Helene," by Lily Kahil and Noëlle Icard, *LIMC* 4, pp. 526, 527, nos. 143, 147, esp. 147. Bieber regards the relief itself as Hellenistic but is not dissonant with later reproduction.

84. The boy group, Eros and Alexandros, is represented in the manner of homoerotic male couples in the traditional language of Greek pederasty. The balancing of pairs occurs elsewhere. One of the Hoby silver cups, probably produced in the first century CE, the so-called Priam Cup, shows women interacting in a manner that compositionally balances a male scene of definite eroticism. D. E. Strong, *Greek and Roman Gold and Silver Plate* (Ithaca: Cornell UP, 1966) 136, pl. 35b.

85. Martianus Capella 350. The translation is not verbatim. A similar concept can be seen in a certain cult of Juno. Near the end of the marriage festivities, Martianus Capella, vol. 2, p. 345 (9.888) tells us that a goddess, probably Juno Pronuba, is present, "she who delights in loosing maiden girdles and in caressing maiden hearts with fond desires" (*interulos gaudens dissoluere nexus blandificaque libens stringere corda face*). The language foreshadows the heterosexual foreplay yet to come.

86. Dagmar Grassinger, *Römische Marmorkratere*, Monumenta Artis Romanae XVIII (Mainz am Rhein: P. von Zabern, 1991) 190–192, 280, cat. no. 33, figs. 102–104; Müller, *Aldobrandini Wedding* figs. 11–13. This eroticism is not shown in all interpretations of this theme: a painting in Naples, from the Casa di Amandus shows a diminished eroticism in a Venus

who could be a Roman matron, and a Neo-Attic Crater in Cardiff does not demonstrate anything erotic.

87. On the flower as a lover's gift, see Younger's essay in this volume.

88. This interesting substitution also pertains to interpretation of the eroticism among musicians discussed in the previous section.

89. Norman Austin, *Helen of Troy and Her Shameless Phantom* (Ithaca: Cornell UP, 1994) ch. 2, "Sappho's Helen and the Problem of the Text"; Page DuBois, *Sappho Is Burning* (Chicago: U of Chicago P, 1995) esp. ch. 5, "Helen"; and Jack Lindsay, *Helen of Troy: Woman and Goddess* (Totowa, NJ: Rowman and Littlefield, 1974) esp. ch. 7, "From Gorgias to Late Antiquity." Austin, Dubois, and Lindsay overlook the homoeroticism latent in some of the materials yet make valuable contributions to the study of Helen. Austin brings out the similarities of situation between Helen and Sappho.

90. Müller, *Aldobrandini Wedding* fig. 2 (after L. Mirri and G. Carletti, *Le antiche camere delle terme di Tito* [1776] pl. 25).

91. Campbell, *Greek Lyric 1* 120–123. Further some scholars draw connections between Adonis and Phaon (23).

92. *Napoli* 1.1, 138, no. 108. The seminude figure resembles the official iconography of Aphrodite. The color scheme enhances the differences between the female figures represented and may support the divine/mortal theory.

93. It was common to represent mortal together with divine in Roman art. Notable examples include triumphal arches in which Roma and Victory appear with the emperor and troops.

94. Müller, *Aldobrandini Wedding* fig. 4. Aphrodite brings together the women more convincingly than Eros (see pp. 240–241), with her hands on the shoulder of each.

95. Müller, *Aldobrandini Wedding* 26–34 (earlier interpretations), pls. I–VI (color). The painting is now in the Vatican Museums and was for many years in the Aldobrandini Collection.

96. Clarke, *Looking at Lovemaking* 101, 103: male-female chamber scene; Rome, from villa under Farnesina, National Museum of the Terme, inv. 1188. DAI, Neg. 77.1295. Clarke himself views the Aldobrandini Wedding as "a truncated and very free interpretation of the rituals that would occur at an actual wedding."

97. Martianus Capella, vol. 2, p. 345n3. The positioning of the figures in the "Aldobrandini Wedding" is not unlike that used in a painting from Pompeii's Casa del Citarista, an image showing a couple who are identified as Mars and Venus. *Napoli* 1.1, 132–133, no. 62.

98. Campbell, *Greek Lyric 1* 26–29, 114–115, 120–123.

99. Müller, *Aldobrandini Wedding* 28–30.

100. Campbell, *Greek Lyric 1* 48–49.

101. Campbell, *Greek Lyric 1* 134–137.

102. Müller, *Aldobrandini Wedding* 26.

103. Kraemer, *Maenads* 25. The holiday is on April 1; the women also offer incense to Virile Fortuna at this time.

104. *Napoli* 1.1, 98–100 and 214–215, no. 63; Charles Waldstein and Leonard Shoobridge, *Herculaneum, Past, Present, and Future* (London: Macmillan 1908) pl. 44. Silver situla: h. 270 mm; d. 260. The situla is dated to the late second or early third century CE, which

may be too early. I am not fully convinced that the woman being bathed represents Aphrodite since the image is so unusually naturalistic.

105. Andrew Scholtz, "Perfume from Peron's: The Politics of Pedicure in Anaxandrides Fragment 41 Kassel-Austin" *Illinois Classical Studies* 21 (1996): 69–86. See also Catherine Osborne, *Eros Unveiled: Plato and the God of Love* (Oxford: Clarendon P, 1994) 93–101, Eros the Socratic Spirit, "Bare Feet."

106. *Aeneid* 11.586. For other depiction in the arts, see, for example, Gisela M. A. Richter, *Metropolitan Museum of Art, New York, Catalog of Engraved Gems, Greek, Etruscan, and Roman* (Rome 1956) 365–366, no. 371, pl. 47. MMA no. 81.6.189. A carnelian ring stone, owned by a Dionysius of Smyrna, shows two female figures performing what in other contexts is a gesture of courtship and imminent marriage. The one figure holds a (measuring) stick, and the other holds a sistrum. Richter identified these as Nemeses and pointed to the similarity of the images on coins that may show the two famous cult statues of the city. This gem is dated by Richter to the second or third century CE on the grounds of letter forms.

107. Richter, *Metropolitan Museum* 615, no. 612, pl. 57; G. M. A. Richter, *Engraved Gems of the Greeks, Etruscans, and Romans*, vol. 2 (London: Phaidon, 1971) no. 144.

108. Matz, *Dionysischen 3* 351–353, no. 200, pl. 215.

109. For further discussion of this passage and the apple as gift, see Carson, *Eros* 87–90. See also Richter, *Engraved Gems* no. 224. Accompanied by a Priapic figure carrying a basket of fruit, perhaps apples, Venus attempts to catch a winged female figure wearing a short tunic, a figure that Richter identified as Pudicitia following Chabouillet's 1858 interpretation. Later writers also quoted Sappho on apples (Campbell, *Greek Lyric 1* 130–137). According to the fourth-century writer Himerius (*Orationes* 9.16), "It was Sappho who compared the girl to an apple," and Syrianus (*On Hermogenes*) mentions Sappho and quotes, "As the sweet apple reddens on the bough-top, on the top of the topmost bough; the apple-gatherers have forgotten it—no they have not forgotten it entirely, but they could not reach it." A second-century CE papyrus on lyric poetry preserves "strike with an apple . . . and Sappho . . . and Calliope" (Campbell, *Greek Lyric 1* 202–203).

110. See also Philostratus, who writes of Cupids riding sacred birds (*Imagines* 1.9). One Cupid stretches his hand out over a promontory to the sea to indicate the future suicide of the doomed heteroerotic couple in what Philostratus describes as "the painter's symbolic suggestion of the tale" (1.12). The painter "uses the Cupids as his assistants in the device so as to connect it with something of Aphrodite" (1.16, Daedalus). In addition, Philostratus the Younger includes an image of Eros and Ganymede playing dice (8). Erotes also were represented as musicians and dancing in art, as in *LIMC 3*, "Eros/Amor, Cupido," by Nicole Blanc and Françoise Gury, nos. 449–479.

111. Mary D. Sheriff, "Reading Jupiter Otherwise," in *Myth, Sexuality and Power: Images of Jupiter in Western Art: Papers Delivered at the Georgia Museum of Art in Connection with the Exhibition, Jupiter's Loves and His Children, February 8, 1997,* ed. Frances van Kueren (Providence, RI: Center for Old World Archaeology and Art, Brown U, 1998) 89–93, figs. 5 and 6. Sheriff's unique and creative treatment of the art, especially her methods for looking at and interpreting homoeroticism in myth, makes her work of very broad significance to the person working with the ancient materials, since so little has been done in the past on any era.

112. *Napoli* 1.1 45 (color plate), 132–133, no. 71; Stuveras, *Le putto* fig. 81. The painting is from Pompeii. The theme was popular in various forms from the sixteenth century onward.

113. See Pintabone's essay in this volume.

114. J. D. Reed, ed., *Bion of Smyrna: The Fragments and* The Adonis (Cambridge: Cambridge UP, 1997) 2–3 (date); 108–109 (Fr. 3); 162 (Fr. 9). Fragment 3: "Let Eros call the Muses, let the Muses bear Eros; let the Muses give me song while I forever desire; sweet song, than which no medicine is sweeter."

115. Stuveras, *Le putto* pl. 82, fig. 176; *LIMC* 3, "Eros/Amor," 964–965, no. 54, pl. 682. On the heteroerotic Cupids, see *LIMC* 1.964, nos. 48–49.

116. Stuveras, *Le putto* 129–130, pl. 72, fig. 156. From Pompeii II.3.3.

117. See, for example, *LIMC* 3, "Eros/Amor, Cupido" 965, nos. 56–60, pl. 682. For bibliography on the *dextrarum iunctio*, see Brooten, *Love between Women* 89n136. Nancy Rabinowitz informs me that the same situation holds true in the Greek materials.

118. Richter, *Engraved Gems* 40–41, nos. 144 and 145. MMA acc. no. 29.175.2. See also, Richter, *Metropolitan Museum* no. 612. In the MMA's catalog, Richter identifies the composition as a Hellenistic type. See also the *Anakreonteia* 25.

119. On the erotics of the foot in antiquity, see above, p. 237.

120. See above p. 228.

121. Rosenblum, *Luxorius* 138–139. (46) *De laude horti Eugeti; Hortus quo faciles fluunt Napaeae, Quo ludunt Dryades virente choro, quo fovet teneras Diana Nymphas, Quo Venus roseos recondit artus, Suspensis refecit liber pharetris, Quo sese Aeonides fruunt puellas Cui numquam minus est amoena frondis, Cui semper redolent amoena verni Cui frons perspicuis tener fluentis Muscoso riguum parit meat, Quo dulcis avium canor resultat— Quidquid per varias refertur urbes, Hoc uno famulans loco resultat.*

122. *Napoli* 1.1, 226–227, no. 51. There is also a goat between the women here.

123. Richter, 43, *Engraved Gems* no. 164. As far as themes and production goes, it should be noted that Ganymede and the Eagle were popular themes on these gems, as nos. 256–259. Europa and the Bull also appear, no. 261. The Ganymede theme appears on the relief mirrors of the type that sport the Graces.

124. Strong, *Greek and Roman Silver Plate* 150, pl. 44a.

125. On snakes as phallic, see Adams, *Latin Sexual Vocabulary* 30–31. The snake was also associated with several goddesses and personifications in official cult. In Roman art, phallus-like shapes and textures are sometimes used symbolically, as in depictions of Leda and the Swan.

126. Robert, *Einzelmythen 3.2* 233–235, no. 190, pl. 61 (Rome, Palazzo Mattei). See also no. 188 for variations in composition but similar eroticizing components. On the erotic implications of the goat or ram, see Jeffrey Henderson, *The Maculate Muse: Obscene Language in Attic Comedy* (New York: Oxford UP, 1991) 127. The cornucopia placed as a phallus also can be found in an image of a male on a sarcophagus in Rome's Palazzo Doria (*Einzelmythen 3.1* 92–94, no. 77a, pl. 20).

127. Robert, *Einzelmythen 3.1* 86–89, no. 72, pl. 18. See also 92–94 and 96–98, nos. 77 and 79, pls. 20 and 22 for similar homoerotic couplings on Endymion sarcophagi. The one is laden with Cupids.

128. Andreas Rumpf, *Die Meerwesen auf den antiken Sarkophagreliefs*, Die Antiken Sarkophag-Reliefs, vol. 1 (Rome: "L'Erma di Bretschneider, 1969) 35, no. 87, pl. 26. Nereid Thiasos with Erotes, Rome, found under San Crisogno.

129. Daniel Callam, trans., *St. Ambrose, On Virginity* (Saskatoon: Peregrina, 1980) 32.

CHAPTER EIGHT

Ovid's Iphis and Ianthe

When Girls Won't Be Girls

Diane T. Pintabone

 Ovid's story of Iphis and Ianthe in the *Metamorphoses* has always raised more questions than it has answered about ancient concepts of female homoeroticism. The myth itself concerns Iphis, a girl raised as a boy, who ultimately is changed into a boy so that she can marry Ianthe. By placing the tale in the contexts of feminist theory and classical scholarship, we can at least identify the questions. By additionally looking at this story within the framework of Ovid's *Metamorphoses* as a whole, we can approach some answers. In this essay, I hope to add to the current body of scholarship a sense of Ovid's unique approach to female same-sex desire.

THE MASCULINE WOMAN

Scholarship examining the works of Roman authors suggests that those authors conceptualized as masculine a woman who sexually desired women. The insightful work of Judith P. Hallett, "Female Homoeroticism and the Denial of Roman Reality in Latin Literature," locates the story of Iphis and Ianthe within the (relatively small) body of ancient Roman sources that refer to female same-sex desire; these sources tend to, as she puts it, masculinize, hellenize, and anachronize female homoeroticism,[1] removing it from the realm of Roman contemporary reality. Hallett notes that Roman authors most often depict a *tribas* (tribad most often refers to the[2] "active" female partner in female-female sex) as masculine and aggressive and as the one who wishes to penetrate, while her lover's gender role is left ambiguous.[3] In her work *Love between Women: Early Christian Responses to Female Homoeroticism*, Bernadette Brooten finds that the precise meaning of *tribas* is difficult to define:

> Since the ancient sources do not clearly define the sexual position and sexual acts of a *tribas*, some sources designate both partners as *tribades*, whereas others call only the "active" partner a *tribas*. And while most sources seem to assume that a *tribas* has sex only with women, according to one source she just prefers

women to men. Whereas the ancient authors are rather vague about the sexual acts of a *tribas,* they vividly depict her as one who takes on a male role and male desires. (24)

The word *tribas* is a Greek word (borrowed by Romans), probably derived from a verb "to rub," itself implying an "active" sexual partner but often further suggesting penetration.[4] Some women (Iphis among them) are so masculinized in these sources, Hallett observes, that they are said to become men.[5] She cites telling words used by various authors to describe the "manly" practices of tribadic women, indicating a negative judgment. She cites, for example, Seneca the Younger (*Moral Epistles* 95.20.2) who claims that such women, their lust equal to that of men, "having devised so perverted a type of shamelessness, enter men" (*adeo perversum commentae genus impudicitiae viros ineunt*) ("Female Homoeroticism" 214–215). As Hallett's work suggests, same-sex desire among women was condemned as socially unacceptable,[6] and the females said to experience such desire were chastised primarily on the grounds that they were manly.[7]

Brooten adds to this image and finds that the masculinization of such women extends to thoughts of females genitally penetrating females; this masculinization depends on a concept of an "overly large clitoris," which provided a possibility for a sort of female erection (*Love between Women* 50). She further locates this idea of female homoeroticism within a broader spectrum of responses present in the ancient Mediterranean, finding that there is some evidence for female-female marriages associated with Canaanites and Egyptians (50, 332–336).

In a recent study of Sappho in Ovid's *Heroides* 15, a work by Ovid consisting of a fictional letter written "by Sappho" to her (male) beloved Phaon, Pamela Gordon[8] finds that Ovid has his Sappho exhibit what Ovid elsewhere associates with masculine sexual desire. The characteristics that Gordon notes in "The Lover's Voice in *Heroides* 15: Or, Why Is Sappho a Man?" can be summarized briefly: Ovid's Sappho expresses her sexual passion (rather than simply bewailing her predicament); she plays the active role (Ovid presents her gaze to readers) while her male beloved is seen as passive; she describes herself as sexually experienced; and she notes her own faithlessness to her former female lovers (280–284).

Such "masculine" women are described as seeking the active/penetrating position, which, according to Roman thought, could be taken only by men. The sources examined by Hallett, Brooten, and Gordon locate the woman who desires women in the Roman ideological construction of sexuality described by Amy Richlin[9] (and others), which holds that one partner is conceived of as sexually active/penetrating and the other as passive/penetrated. In "The Teratogenic Grid," Holt Parker further argues that in Roman thought, "'active' is *by definition* 'male' and 'passive' is *by definition* 'female'" (his emphasis; 48).[10] He finds that Romans conceived of even female-female sex in phallocentric terms, that women in tribadic sex are described as either "rubbing together their vulvas or one using a dildo on the other" (citing examples from Seneca, Martial, and Juvenal; "Grid" 59). Parker states: "The women have to perform a parody of intercourse. Even when women become active, a woman is still the passive object of fucking" ("Grid" 59). To the Roman mind, Parker notes, there are exactly four sexual categories for people: the normal/active male, the normal/passive female, the passive/abnormal male, and the active/abnormal female ("Grid" 48).

Gordon argues that Romans ascribe a "different nature" to women who desire women. She states: "In fact, the tribad's object choice seems to be viewed as a symptom of her masculine makeup, rather than the essential core of her tribadism" ("Lover's Voice" 286).[11] On the broader question of nature, Lillian Faderman, in her study of romantic friendship and love between women from the Renaissance to the twentieth century,[12] traces changes in female same-sex love both in its various manifestations and in the responses to it. In *Surpassing the Love of Men: Romantic Friendships and Love between Women from the Renaissance to the Present,* Faderman suggests that love between women occurs naturally, but that responses to it are culturally constructed. She argues: "Contemporary lesbianism . . . is a combination of natural love between women, so encouraged in the days of romantic friendships, with the twentieth-century women's freedom that feminism made possible" (414). Key to its reception (i.e., either negative or positive/dismissive), she finds, is the perception of women either as accepting their "assigned gender roles" —and as such, not threatening the patriarchic hold of men over women— or conversely, as a serious threat that could overthrow heterosexuality. Heterosexuality, she states, "has meant not only sex between men and women, but patriarchal culture, male dominance, and female subservience" (411).

The negative attitude in Roman literature toward women said to exhibit such "masculine" desire, thinking, and behavior, then, focuses on these women breaking from culturally assigned gender roles and being too manly by virtue of their sexuality. Although women were thought to be passive by nature,[13] these women, by desiring women, are seen as both male and active —and, as Hallett points out, in most instances such desire or behavior is explicitly indicted. Gender performance, then, is tied to sexual performance.

But what about Ovid? With regard to Ovid's Iphis and Ianthe, Hallett notes:

> Admittedly, Iphis' revulsion at female homoerotic passion must not be confused with a view of Ovid himself. Indeed, Ovid's narrative displays immense sympathy with Iphis' plight, a sympathy contrasting to Iphis' own self-condemnation and negative view of female homoeroticism. ("Female Homoeroticism" 217)

Yet, John Makowski in "Bisexual Orpheus: Pederasty and Parody in Ovid," a recent study of male homosexuality (in the story of Orpheus) in Ovid's *Metamorphoses*, points to this narrative as Ovid's clear condemnation of same-sex unions:

> However, it is the *Metamorphoses* which contains Ovid's most damning denunciation of homosexuality. This occurs in the story of Iphis, in its denouement a happy story of marriage, but at heart a tale of lesbian passion, confusion of gender, and trans-sexualism. (30–31)

And so, which is it? Is Ovid's Iphis cut from the same "lesbian" cloth that weaves together a negative portrait of a manly woman, aggressively seeking to penetrate the object of her (masculine) desires? As a male Roman author (writing first century BCE–first century CE), does Ovid fit neatly into the tradition that presents a woman who desires a woman as usurping male prerogatives and thus threatening the maintenance of the established (patriarchal) hierarchy? And, in what terms does Ovid frame the problem? In Ovid's *Metamorphoses* is Iphis' passion for Ianthe conceptualized as both homoerotic and "natural"? Is Ovid's portrayal an indictment or an endorsement of female homoeroticism?

Ovid, as is common in his works, has it almost all ways: he manages to present both a positive and a negative portrait of woman-for-woman[14] passion—suggesting that it is both natural and unnatural—precisely by simultaneously overturning stereotypes and reinforcing them. He provides no firm judgment of his own (i.e., as narrator), either for or against female homoeroticism. To see how Ovid achieves this, we need to look at the elements of his narrative, located as they are within the larger framework of the *Metamorphoses*, which itself is located in the broader context of Roman literature (which Hallett, Brooten, and Gordon describe). Ovid is unique in his approach to this topic, just as his *Metamorphoses* is unique: often described as an "anti-epic," the epic poem itself mixes and fractures traditional notions of genre—and here, gender—while pointing nonetheless to the traditional standards that it overturns.

OVID'S *Metamorphoses:* THE BIGGER PICTURE

Ovid's *Metamorphoses* is a poem wholly concerned with power: who has it, how it is used, and what its effects are. From the beginning, Ovid shows that there is a clear hierarchy in the universe. In Book 1, the creation of human life is described in terms of the power relationship between humans and other creatures:

> An animal more holy than these and more capacious of mind / was still lacking and one which could dominate the others: / the human is born, whether he made him from divine seed, / that maker of things, origin of a better world, / or whether the new earth did, which, recently led apart from the high / aether, retained the seeds of her kindred sky.[15] (1.76–81)

Humans are described as at least somewhat divine, having originated either "from divine seed" or from "seeds of (aether's) kindred sky." Humans are animals but "more holy" than other animals (*sanctius his animal,* 1.76). They can, among other things, "dominate" the rest of the creatures (*quod dominari in cetera posset,* 1.77). In this power relationship humans are supreme. In further describing humankind, Ovid states:

> [Earth] which, mixed with rainwater, the son of Iapetus / shaped into the likeness of the gods who control everything, / and although other animals look at the earth, / he gave to man a raised-up face and ordered him to see the sky / and to lift his upright face toward the stars. (1.82–86)

The hierarchy is developed more here: people are in this instance made from earth mixed with water "in the shape of the gods who control/govern everything" (*in effigiem moderantum cuncta deorum,* 1.84). We are explicitly told who stands at the top of this hierarchy of power: gods control everything. Humans are like gods in some ways but like animals in others. As people dominate beasts, so gods dominate people. Unlike other animals, however, a human is bidden to see the sky/heaven (*caelumque videre iussit,* 1.86). Thus even though humans are upward-looking, it is the god who bids the human to look and who resides at the farthest reach of that gaze.

Ovid succinctly describes a change at the very top of this universal hierarchy; Jove's rise to supremacy is conveyed in about one and a half lines: "After, with Saturn sent into shadowy Tartarus, the world was under Jove" (1.113–114). Once his father is put "in his place," order is achieved. With Saturn in shadowy Tartarus, the world is (literally) "under" Jupiter (*sub Iove mundus erat,* 1.114), signifying both the spatial relationship and the notion that the world was then subject to him. Within this hierarchy is patriarchy: within every category (i.e., deities, people, animals), the male ranks higher than the female.

Ovid relates stories that are generally concerned with the maintenance of this order: (perceived) challengers to authority are often summarily punished. Deities are shown to exercise awesome powers, often excessively and beyond what is just;[16] the narrator's voice calls into question and criticizes the very structure it exposes. It is in the context of such stories[17] that we find the unusual tale of Iphis and Ianthe (*Metamorphoses* 9.666–797), a story that seems to show a woman "out of order," that is, she plays the part of a man, is entitled to male prerogatives, and eventually even becomes a man.

So What's the Story?

Ovid sets the story of Iphis on Crete, telling us that this narrative is about *miracula*, "wondrous things"—a miracle concerning "Iphis, having been changed." In a nutshell,[18] the story is as follows: a poor couple is about to have a baby, and the father (Ligdus) tells his pregnant wife (Telethusa) that if it is not a boy, the child is to be killed (9.669–679). "The other lot," he says, "is more burdensome, and fortune denies them strength" (9.676–677). Telethusa cannot change Ligdus' mind, although he seems to have reached this decision reluctantly. Telethusa is told in a dream or vision by the goddess Inachus (or Isis)[19] to rear the child, regardless of its sex (9.696–701; lit. "whatever it is" [*quidquid erit*], 9.699). This Telethusa does: Iphis (a name common to males and females, we are told) is raised as a boy and, after thirteen years have passed, her father (unaware of the biological sex of his child) betroths Iphis to her lifelong friend, Ianthe (9.704–717). Although the two love each other equally, Iphis despairs of what to do, since there will be two brides at the wedding (9.718–763). Eventually, both Iphis and her mother, Telethusa, pray desperately at the altar of Isis (9.770–781). The temple quakes, and as the two leave, Iphis changes into a man (9.782–791). On the next day, Iphis and Ianthe are married, with the traditional Roman wedding deities in attendance (9.795–797).

Ovid's "Moral Character"

By examining the characters involved, looking at what they say and do, what is said and done to or about them, we can see if Ovid tries to steer us toward judgment about them. Ovid tells us that Ligdus, for example, is not of noble birth, nor is he a wealthy man, but one "whose life and trustworthiness were blameless" (9.672–673). He shows him in a somewhat sympathetic light, telling the reader, for example, that Ligdus hates to order his wife to dispose of a female child and hopes that *pietas*—"familial duty"—will forgive him (9.677–679). Ovid then describes both Ligdus and Telethusa crying over the instructions, but Ligdus nevertheless remains firm in his decision (9.680–684). Later, Ovid portrays him as the proud father of the supposed boy, piously paying his vows and naming the child after its grandfather (9.708–709). We can see the patriarchal hierarchy: the husband issues orders, the male child is valued over the female, thanks are given to gods, the father arranges the marriage; the child is even named patrilineally. In other words, all seems "in order."

Telethusa is likewise given a sympathetic portrayal: according to Roman views, a "good" wife should (among other things) obey her husband, bear children (preferably males)—and then not wish to kill them, under any circumstances—and be pious/observant of the deities. Here Telethusa is caught between the orders of her husband, her desire as a mother not to kill her child, and the instructions of her goddess. Obedient to the perceived wishes of the goddess, Telethusa constructs a fiction that she carries off for thirteen years (9.704–717). On the day before the wedding—in despair—she turns to the goddess for help (9.768–781). Telethusa prays, "having embraced the altar" (9.772):

> "Isis, who inhabits Paraetonium and the Mareotic fields and Pharos, / and [who inhabits] the Nile, divided into seven horns, / bring aid, I pray," she said, "and heal our fear! / You, goddess, you I once saw and your symbols / and I recognized all, the sound and your companions and the torches / and the noise of the sistra, and I marked your orders in my remembering mind. / The fact that this girl sees the light, that I am unpunished, behold, / is your counsel and your gift. Have pity for us two, / and help with your aid!" Tears followed the words. (9.773–781)

By including Telethusa's words to the goddess, Ovid further emphasizes the sympathetic portrait of her: she is faithful and respectful toward the goddess, grateful for past aid, hopeful of future aid, and most of all, obedient to the will of this higher power. Telethusa, in effect, very diplomatically reminds Isis that it was her appearance and her orders that have led to the current predicament. She even suggests her acknowledgement that she has been doing wrong ("that I have gone unpunished"), but that the goddess has saved her from censure. Telethusa manages to seem grateful for past help ("is your counsel and your gift"), yet her words tactfully emphasize the goddess' role in this situation (e.g., "you, goddess, you I saw").[20]

Thus Ovid provides a portrait of a caring mother, whose devotion to her revered goddess outweighs her strict obedience to her husband. By his provision of these attendant circumstances, Ovid depicts Telethusa as a "good" wife and mother, and above all, a pious follower of her goddess; she appropriately weighs the divine over the human. There seems to be no negative judgment, implicit or explicit, of Telethusa nor of her actions and motivations.

Ianthe, to whom Iphis is betrothed, is an unwitting participant in this play of fictions. Ovid describes Ianthe as "most praised among Phaestian women for her dowry of beauty" (9.716–717). This "dowry of beauty" (*formae dote*) may imply that Ianthe is economically the equal of Iphis: her looks may be the only dowry she brings to the marriage. The two girls are described as equals in other ways:

> Equal was the age, equal the beauty, and they received their first arts / from the same teachers, the rudiments of their age / From here love touched the inexperienced breast of both and gave an equal / wound to each.[21] (9.718–721)

Their love, as Ovid describes it, is mutual and develops over time. He paints a portrait of the girls which is similar to that of two elementary-school children who grew up together and grew to love one another.

Although equal in many ways, their hopes for the future are quite disparate:

> But unequal was the confidence: / Ianthe looks forward to the marriage and the time of the agreed-upon wedding / and thinks her to be a man whom she trusts would be *her* man; / Iphis loves her whom she has no hope to be able to enjoy, / and this itself increases the flames, and the virgin burns for a virgin. (9.721–725)

Clearly, Ianthe is presented as believing that Iphis is a man. For her part, then, there is no dilemma; she is simply betrothed to the boy with whom she has grown up and whom she has grown to love. She looks forward to the appointed day; later, indeed, her passion makes her impatient. Ovid then says of her: "Nor does the other virgin [Ianthe] burn more gently and she prays, Hymen,[22] that quickly you may come" (9.764–765). Again, we have the image of a blameless girl, who looks forward with some considerable passion to her impending wedding, unaware that she loves and is betrothed to a woman. Clearly, she is erotically attracted to Iphis: Ovid uses words —common in Roman elegiac poetry—that indicate the sexually charged desire of lovers.[23] She is, nevertheless, a virgin, which would be expected (according to Roman values) of a "good" girl of marriageable age. Ovid's portrait seems neither to state nor to imply any negative connotations about Ianthe.

As we turn now to Iphis, we have a more complex figure: a girl, raised as a boy, loves a woman and cannot seem to find a viable solution to the riddle of a wedding of two brides. Ovid portrays her, too, in a sympathetic light. Although Iphis is born female (*nata est . . . femina*, 9.705), she is raised as a boy (*cultus erat pueri*, 9.712) and would be found attractive whether seen as a girl or a boy (*facies, quam sive puellae / sive dares puero, fieret formosus uterque*, 9.712–713). As we saw above, love touches her as it did Ianthe; the only difference is that Iphis knows that this love is of a woman for a woman. Clearly, she is erotically attracted to Ianthe ("and the virgin burns for the virgin," *ardetque in virgine virgo*, 9.725). Ovid evokes sympathy for his character by having her be the one to raise objections to her own desires (cf. Hallett's views, above). Picking up the story's thread from the disparity of their hopes, we find that Iphis longs for Ianthe all the more since their union seems impossible (another feature common to Roman love elegy). She contemplates her situation, running through the circumstances and possibilities:

> And barely holding back her tears she said, "What outcome awaits me, / whom a heartache, known to no one, holds, a monstrous / heartache of a new love? If the gods wished to spare me, / they should have spared me; otherwise, if they wanted to destroy me, / they at least should have given a natural and customary ill." (9.726–730)

By her own account, Iphis' love (here, *novaeque / cura . . . Veneris*, 9.727–728) is monstrous/unheard of (*prodigiosa*, 9.727), and she refers to it as strange or novel (*novaeque / . . . Veneris*, 9.727). Her use of *Veneris* to name the troublesome matter may further suggest that she specifically means the sexual aspects of their love.[24] She frames the problem in terms of nature: to her, her love is unnatural and abnormal.[25] Still arguing along the lines of nature, she turns to zoological examples in an effort to show how strange her love is:

> Love does not make a cow burn for a cow, nor mares for mares: / a ram desires ewes, and his female counterpart follows the stag. / Thus, too, do birds mate, and among all animals / there is no female seized with desire for a female. / I wish I were no female![26] (9.731–735)

Iphis concludes that no examples of female-for-female desire exist. Her focus is on sexual attraction, *not* on marriage: the words used to describe Iphis' passion are *amat* (9.724), *flammas* ("flames," 9.725), *ardet* ("burns," 9.725), and *ignes* ("fires," 9.746). Her own examples, too, describe sexual attraction: "love burns" (*amor urit*, 9.731), "burns" (*urit*, 9.734), "seized with desire" (*conrepta cupidine*, 9.734)—again, all words commonly associated with the plight of the elegiac lover.

Iphis then thinks of another "prodigious" desire associated with her homeland, Crete:

> Nevertheless, that Crete / might bear all monstrosities, the daughter of Sol desired a bull / —a least a female for a male. My love is madder than that (*meus est furiosior illo*), / if truth be told. Even so, she followed / the hope of love; even so, she, through tricks and the image of a cow, / had sex with the bull, and it was he, the adulterer, who was deceived. / But even if all cleverness from the whole world should flow together here, / let Daedalus himself fly back on waxen wings, / what will he do? Will he make me into a boy from a girl / with his learned arts? Or will he change you, Ianthe? (9.735–744)

This passage perhaps suggests her own fear of being famed, like Pasiphaë (the woman who desired the bull), for a strange new love. Iphis suggests that Pasiphaë had better odds for a successful union with the bull than Iphis has with Ianthe—a curious thought, since it took quite a lot of ingenuity for Pasiphaë to play the part of a cow to seduce her beloved. Iphis, on the other hand, has already successfully played the part necessary to "obtain" Ianthe; the only problem here, then, is sexual consummation of the relationship.

Reasoning along these lines, Iphis concludes that her desire to unite *sexually* with Ianthe is impossible: to her mind, one or the other of them must be male (9.743–744). As she concludes that the desired union is hopeless, she attempts to rein in her passion:

> But no, be strong-minded, Iphis, collect yourself and strike out these fires that are foolish and ill-counseled. / See what you were born—unless you deceive yourself, too / —and seek what is right and love what a female ought to love! / It is hope that might seize love, it is hope that feeds love. / Reality takes this hope from you. (9.745–750)

Here Ovid has Iphis display strength of character by her attempt at self-control. She examines the cold, hard facts: she has been born female, and that is reality (*res*). Only in fantasy, then, can the union take place—in a fantasy wherein either she or Ianthe would become a man.

With (Ovidian) irony, Iphis lists the usual obstacles to the thwarted lover that one finds throughout Roman love elegy:

A guardian does not block you / from the dear embrace, nor does the concern of a wary husband, / nor the harshness of a father, nor does she herself deny herself to you seeking her; / and yet she is not to be obtained by you nor, even if all things should happen, / are you able to be happy, even if gods and men should work for you. (9.750–754)

Ovid has her run through the elegiac lovers' usual woes to emphasize the point that hers is an unusual problem. She cannot even say that gods or people thwart her desire to be united with Ianthe:

Now, too, no part of my prayers is unfulfilled, / and the gods, favorable to me, have given whatever they could; / and what I wish, my father wishes, and she herself wishes it, and my future father-in-law, too. / But nature, more powerful than all these, does not wish it, / nature that alone harms me. (9.755–759)

Here Iphis claims that the gods cannot help her: they have given what they can, but they cannot make her into a man—only nature could have done that, but nature does not wish it (*at non vult natura*, 9.758). With bitter irony, Iphis notes that the "hoped-for day" for which she claims she has no hope, has arrived:

"Behold, the hoped-for time has come, / the wedding day is here, and now Ianthe will become mine / —and not belong to me: in the midst of waters we will thirst. / Bridal Juno, Hymen, why do you come to these / rites, in which he who leads is absent and we both are brides?" / She broke off her speech with these words. (9.759–764)

Iphis concludes her speech to herself by stressing again the irony of traditional Roman wedding gods attending a wedding that is anything but traditional. It is a wedding, she says, where "he who leads is absent," again pointing to the male as the *active* member of a couple who—in Roman thought, practice, and language—leads a bride. The bride is *passive*; she is to be led. Iphis says, "We both are brides" (*nubimus ambae*), emphasizing (by the feminine ending of *ambae*) that two females will be at the wedding as brides. And then, with Iphis silently accompanying her mother to Isis' temple, Telethusa prays for aid.

In the end, changed into a man, Iphis pays his thanks to the gods and marries Ianthe:

They give gifts to the temples, / and they add a tablet: the tablet has a short poem: / THESE GIFTS, WHICH AS A WOMAN IPHIS HAD

PROMISED, IPHIS, A BOY, PAID. / The next light had revealed the broad earth with its rays, / when Venus and Juno and accompanying Hymen meet at the fires / and the boy Iphis gains his Ianthe. (9.791–797)

Ovid thus has the pious character of Iphis continue on, and like his father and mother above, he pays thanks due to the gods. Iphis, like each of the other characters, is portrayed consistently in a positive light, that is, in accordance with Roman standards of acceptable and proper behavior. For Iphis, this means that she is shown to be respectful of and obedient to her parents (showing a sense of "familial duty" [*pietas*]); she, like Ianthe, is a *virgo* at the time of her marriage; and both as a female and later as a male, Iphis seems to have proper respect for the Roman deities.

A Question of Sex

Iphis implies that the problem here is a question of sex: the question is, Is the problem "sex" in terms of sexual fulfillment or of biological sex? We can see that Ovid has Iphis frame the problem as one of sexual fulfillment that, to her, is impossible because of her biological sex. The two are interconnected. Ovid states that Iphis loves one "whom she has no hope to be able to enjoy" (*frui*, 9.724), which clearly indicates "to enjoy sexually." We can infer from her reasoning that, to her mind, sexual enjoyment cannot exist between two females. The problem is not marriage: Iphis can marry Ianthe and even states about the wedding, "and Ianthe will become mine—and not belong to me" (9.760–761).[27] She follows this up by stating, "In the midst of water we will thirst" (*mediis sitiemus in undis*, 9.761). Clearly, she sees this "water" as undrinkable by her (impot*ance*?). This tallies with Roman notions of "normal" sexual conduct, which—as we noted earlier (cf. Richlin's and Parker's views, above)—is set up in terms of active/penetrator (seen as male) and passive/penetrated. Iphis' logic runs along these lines, that if both partners are passive and receptive (i.e., female), how can one of them "enjoy" (*frui*) the other? In Iphis' asking if Daedalus could help them, Ovid further cues us to her thinking: Daedalus is known for *making* things—he is even said to have made the wooden cow disguise that enabled Pasiphaë to "seduce" the bull.[28] The inference is that the problem here is specifically the couple's lack of a penis. The concept of an active female (penetrating?) sexual partner, or of sex without a penis, is inconceivable to Iphis.

Iphis' speech implies much, both by what is omitted and by what is included. For example, Iphis focuses on *exempla* that are concerned with sexual desire, rather than, say, laws concerning marriage. She does not say that in all the world no female has ever *wed* a female, rather, that no female animal ever desires another female. She argues that nature alone bars her way (*at non vult natura*, 9.758). By arguing along the lines of nature, Iphis has already veered from the path of considering the rules established by civilized human society. She considers animals—clearly viewed as subhuman in this poem—as the standards against which to measure her own desires. From these examples she turns to Pasiphaë, who by most standards went outside the bounds of civilized human behavior when she had intercourse with a real bull. We must remember, too, that Pasiphaë is not said to have desired marriage; her goal was sexual intercourse.

Moreover, Ovid signifies Iphis' ability to see only active male penetrator and passive female penetrated by the way Iphis uses the example of Pasiphaë and the bull (even though *we* might think of Pasiphaë as having been very active). Iphis looks to Pasiphaë as a "hometown" example (i.e., also from Crete) of a strange, prodigious love, and she concludes that at least Pasiphaë, a female, desired a male and thus could fulfill her desires through sexual union. Iphis sees her own as a sexual and a biological problem: since the problem is not one of opportunity nor of a third party's objection to their union, Iphis can see the obstacle only as consisting of the fact that she and Ianthe both have female genitalia.

Her description of Pasiphaë with the bull intimates this in a more subtle way as well—*passa bovem est, et erat, qui deciperetur, adulter* (9.740), in Latin is something of a play on words: "She had sex with the bull, and it was he, the adulterer, who was deceived." More literally, this means, "She endured the bull," etc., using a verb (*passa est*, from *pati*) often used in the *Metamorphoses* of a woman who is raped[29] and that indicates the "normal" female position. The point is that Pasiphaë is still the passive, penetrated partner in the sexual situation, despite that she, a woman, actively pursued a male for sex and that she, a human, actively pursued an animal. It is still she who "endured" or, in the old sense of the word, "suffered" the bull (passive).

So, too, is there more to the bull's being "deceived." Elsewhere in the *Metamorphoses* (e.g., in the story of Arachne's tapestry, 6.103–128), women who are raped are said to have been "tricked" or "deceived" by the disguises of rapist gods. The words in the tapestry that are associated with deceit and trickery but that actually mean rape are *elusam* 6.103, *luserit* 6.113, *fallis* 6.117, *luserit* 6.124, and *deceperit* 6.125. The gods, we might note, often rape after appearing in the guises of animals. In effect, Ovid has Iphis say that while

Pasiphaë "endured" the bull, it was really she who raped him, by tricking him with her animal disguise. So even where the active (rapist) and passive (raped) are reversed, it is still the female who is the passive, penetrated partner in heterosexual sexual intercourse. Pasiphaë is behaviorally active but sexually passive: while her aggressive pursuit of sexual desires (rape, in particular) is more associated with male activity, her passivity in sexual intercourse corresponds to the Roman concept of the female role in sexual intercourse. The story confirms the traditional sexual roles (penetrated female, penetrator male) while pointing to its subversion of them (rapist female, raped male). Iphis' concept of sex maintains the standard hierarchic power structure even, as here, with a female rapist involved in bestiality.

Iphis fails to see an important distinction—and there are many—between herself and Pasiphaë, namely, that Pasiphaë actively pursued her forbidden love, while Iphis herself does nothing. Pasiphaë's desire went outside the category of humans; she had sex with a creature outside (and below in rank) her hierarchic group; Iphis goes outside hers only to search for examples. Pasiphaë masqueraded as a cow to have sex with the bull. Although Iphis is a pretend male, she makes no attempt to seduce or rape Ianthe by her (human male) disguise, and the motivations for the disguise were quite different from the outset. Thus the overall assessment of Iphis' actions (or lack of action) is quite different from that of Pasiphaë. Iphis maintains the standard behavior expected of women: passivity.

Ovid shows that Iphis is wrong in her thinking: she goes outside her hierarchic group to judge/validate her own behavior; she compares her passion with Pasiphaë's (which is quite different). Most importantly, however, Ovid proves she is wrong by the very outcome of the story. Iphis claims that she cannot be happy even if all things go her way and "even if gods and people work" for her (9.753–754). She claims the gods have given all that they can (*dique mihi faciles, quicquid valuere, dederunt*, 9.756). Yet clearly this is not so: shortly after Telethusa and Iphis pray at the altar of Isis, Iphis becomes a man:

> The goddess seemed to have moved—and had moved—her altars, / and the doors of the temple shook, and her horns, which imitated the moon, / shone and the resounding sistrum rattled. / Not indeed free from care, but happy nevertheless by the auspicious omen, / the mother leaves the temple. Her companion Iphis follows her as she goes, / with a longer stride than her usual one, nor did the brightness remain in her face, / and her strength was increased, and

the face itself was sharper / and her hair of shorter length, and she had more vigor than she had as a woman. For you, / recently a woman, are now a boy! (9.782–791)

We see, then, that Iphis was wrong: the gods did have this, too, within their power to give. The author even breaks into the narrative to let us know that the goddess, *in fact*, reacted to the prayer: to the statement "the goddess seemed to move," Ovid adds, "and she *had* moved."[30]

Knowing the outcome of the story, one can see that the points of argument in Iphis' speech to herself are completely off the mark. Her love has nothing to do with animals and perhaps has nothing to do with the gods either. It is, after all, Iphis who states that if the gods had wished to ruin her, they should have given a natural malady (*naturale malum*, 9.730), implying that her desire, as a female for a female, is both unnatural[31] and god-given. But Ovid tells us simply that "love touched the inexperienced breast of both, and gave an equal wound to each" (9.720–721). And so, does their love come from nature, or from the gods? Ovid leaves us hanging on this question, for the text is ambiguous. For "love touched" (*amor tetigit*, 9.720) could be "Amor touched," meaning Amor/Cupid (the god) did this. Given the context, this is an unlikely but possible meaning; elsewhere in the poem where Ovid has Amor do something, he tends to indicate the god clearly (e.g., in the story of Daphne, Amor speaks to Apollo, he shoots an arrow, etc.), thus drawing a distinction between nature and the act of the god. It is more plausible to take this, as I have, that love simply came to the two naturally, but the question, I believe, is irresoluble.

Perhaps it is with Ovidian irony that love comes naturally here (that is, without the involvement of Isis, Venus, or Amor/Cupid), and what the gods (Isis, in this case) have given is a viable solution so that love can be consummated by heterosexual sex within marriage. From the poem's outset, Ovid distinguishes between god and nature (*deus et melior . . . natura*, 1.21), and throughout the poem we are forced to ask whether parts of Ovid's landscape came about naturally or were made so by gods. For example, in the *Metamorphoses*, a tree might be a tree naturally or it might have been a person changed by a god into a tree. Gods can give things that otherwise occur naturally (the flood of Book 1, for instance, is god-given and not "natural"). Iphis is shown to be wrong in her seeing her problem as both god-given (i.e., not having come about naturally) and also irresolvable by gods: the gods have overruled or changed nature, by changing her biological sex from female to male. Moreover, she may be wrong in thinking that her love for

Ianthe is not "what is right" (*quod fas est*, 9.748); after all, the gods do not change her love, they change her sex, which facilitates the union of Iphis and Ianthe.

ACTIVE VERSUS PASSIVE:
FEMALE AGGRESSORS IN THE *Metamorphoses*

Examining this story within the context of the larger poem, we can see that Ovid elsewhere indicates a negative attitude toward many females who express sexual desire, particularly when the object of desire is taboo by Roman standards. That is not to say that there is a similar story in the *Metamorphoses* (this is, in fact, the only narrative that has a female desire a female), but there are other tales that involve similarities and verbal echoes. The story that directly precedes this is the story of the incestuous passion of Byblis for her brother Caunus (9.454–668). Ovid links these two stories in the segue from one to the next: finishing Byblis' story, he turns to the tale of Iphis:

> Fame of this new monstrosity [= Byblis' story] would perhaps have filled the hundred Cretan cities, / if Crete had not recently borne its own miraculous things, / with Iphis having been changed. (9.666–668)

The Latin word *monstrum* suggests the translation "monstrosity," in contrast to the word used of Iphis' transformation (*miracula*, "miraculous things"), since, when Ovid began the story, he indicated a negative judgment against a passion such as the one Byblis had for her brother:

> Byblis is an example that girls should love what is allowed, / Byblis, seized with desire for her Apollonian brother: / she loved not as a sister loves a brother, not as a sister ought.[32] (9.454–456)

Ovid (as narrator) does not withhold judgment: he clearly points the reader to a moral evaluation of this passion. Nevertheless, there are similarities here to the story of Iphis: Ovid at first, for example, depicts Byblis in a sympathetic light, as he did Iphis. In the beginning, Byblis herself did not recognize her passion for what it was (9.457–471). He portrays Byblis as resistant to her desire; in her waking hours she does not dwell on her "obscene hopes" (*spes obscenas*, 9.468) but nevertheless has erotic dreams about herself and her brother (9.469–471). We should note, too, that here the author (as narrator) calls these hopes "obscene"; in Iphis' case, he has the character express the negative view of her own desire. In a lengthy speech to herself (9.474–516; cf. Iphis' speech to herself), Byblis discusses her predicament and comes up with a plan. She regrets that the only thing that stands in the way of their union is that she, by lot (*sortita*, 9.493), got the same parents as he. She considers the examples of the gods:

> May the gods forbid! But surely the gods have had their sisters. / Thus Saturnus wed Ops, who was joined to him by blood, / Oceanus wed Tethys, and the ruler of Olympus wed Juno. / The gods have their own laws! Why do I try to measure human customs / against celestial, different sets of terms? (9.497–501)

Unlike Iphis, Byblis notes the difference in the hierarchic arrangement of the universe: humans cannot justify their behavior based on the standards of behavior of other hierarchic groups (i.e., gods or animals, in this poem). In particular, comparing mortal actions to those of immortals would suggest a hubristic miscalculation of the human position within the broader hierarchy of the universe. Byblis' examples build to the top of, and thus reflect, the hierarchy: at its apex is the ruler of Olympus, Jupiter, who wed his sister Juno.

After a brief attempt to shake off this love, Byblis cites an example from myth of brothers who wed their sisters:

> But the Aeolidae did not fear the bedchambers of their sisters! / Whence do I know these? Why have I furnished these examples? / Whither am I going? (9.507–509)

Perhaps comically here, Ovid has Byblis question her own knowledge of literary *exempla*/mythology. We can note, however, that while this may be a well-worn topos, Ovid's Byblis seems much better versed in literary *exempla* than Iphis is. Iphis uses exclusively "hometown" examples (Pasiphaë, Daedalus), while Byblis displays a more "worldly" knowledge than even she herself thinks possible. By contrast, this may add to the impression of Iphis' virginal innocence and inexperience when the reader gets to her story.

After another brief attempt to suppress her love, Byblis decides to take action: she composes a letter to Caunus professing her desire for him (9.530–563). Byblis rationalizes:

> Let old men know rules and talk about what is allowed, and what is permitted and what is not right / and what is right (*nefasque/fasque*), and let them preserve the considerations of laws: / Venus is fit for and fearless for our time of life! / We still do not know what is permitted, and we believe all things are permitted, / and we follow the examples of the great gods. (9.551–555)

In this passage, Byblis shows that she has broken with her own previous line of reasoning: now she states that they follow the examples of the gods, which she earlier recognized was a faulty comparison. Having stated that she knows that such a love is wrong (by human standards), she states in the letter, "We still do not know what is permitted" (*quid liceat, nescimus adhuc et cuncta licere / credimus*, 9.554–555), clearly contradicting the truth of the matter. In addition, Byblis intimates that she is aware of laws (*iura*, 9.551, *legum*, 9.552) that prohibit such a union, laws that she is willing to ignore.

Her brother, having read only part of the letter, casts it down in a fit of rage, and exclaims to the messenger who brought it:

> "O wicked promoter of forbidden lust, / flee while you can!" he said, "You, who if your fate did not draw with you / our own disgrace, would have paid me a penalty of death!" (9.577–579)

Her brother's outrage and his assessment that this is "forbidden lust" (*vetitae libidinis*, 9.577) provide an internal negative judgment of Byblis' desire. After her advances are repulsed, however, Byblis finds fault only with the methods she had used: no longer does she feel that her love is wrong, only that her technique did not produce the desired result (9.585–612). She believes she could have accomplished in person what her letter failed to do (9.605–609). She resolves to persist in her suit, and she does so until her hapless brother flees the land (9.613–634). Then, consumed by grief and madness, Byblis "openly out of her mind, confesses the forbidden hope of love"[33] (9.638–639) and deserting her homeland, follows after her brother. Ultimately, having wandered over many lands, inconsolable and "consumed by her own tears," Byblis is changed into a fountain (9.659–665).

The two stories, then, are linked together by Ovid, and they manifest similarities in the characters' speeches to themselves and in the forbidden nature of their respective passions. One main difference, however, is the negative judgment explicitly expressed against Byblis' passion, condemnation expressed by the author from the start of the story, by Byblis herself (although waveringly) and by her beloved, Caunus. Iphis differs from Byblis in that she does not act on her desires; it is only she who expresses a negative view of her passion, and she ultimately obtains her beloved.

Female aggressors of the *Metamorphoses* as a group are stunning failures in their attempts to obtain the objects of their sexual desires.[34] By looking at some of the female characters of this type, that is, those who both desire and then act on their desires, we can see how or if Iphis fits. We have already seen Byblis' failure to win over her brother with words, and she claims she should have gone in person so that she could put her arms around "his unwilling neck" or in some other way persuade him to submit to her desires. Other sexually desiring female figures from the *Metamorphoses* leap to mind;

looking briefly at each, we can see if a pattern emerges. Each character's name here is followed by a brief assessment of her "success" rate:

- Semele (has affair with Jupiter)
- Echo (is rejected by Narcissus)
- Thisbe (shares mutual love, but Pyramus kills himself before they unite)
- Clytie (is loved then rejected by Sol)
- Salmacis (is rejected by Hermaphroditus)
- Medea ("wins" Jason, but he later remarries, casting her aside)
- Aurora (is said—by Cephalus—to have raped Cephalus, but he pines for his wife until Aurora releases him)
- Scylla (is rejected by Minos)
- Byblis (is rejected by Caunus)
- Myrrha (sleeps with her father Cinyras until he discovers who she is, then she is rejected by Cinyras)
- Hylonome (shares mutual love with Cyllarus, but he is killed)
- Circe (is rejected by Glaucus; is rejected by Picus)
- (unnamed) women (are rejected by Orpheus; he is later killed by the scorned women of the Cicones)
- Alcyone (shares mutual love with Ceyx, but he dies)
- Venus (enjoys relationship with Adonis, but he is killed).

Of these, only Semele, Thisbe, Hylonome, and Alcyone are presented as having mutual loves mixed with erotic attraction; the other instances are described mainly as one-sided erotic attractions that except for the cases of Medea, Aurora, Circe, and Venus, all end in the destruction of the female aggressor herself. As for Medea, Aurora, Circe, and Venus, each enjoys a superhuman status.[35] Thus a pattern is established in which women who express sexual desire are destroyed or at least lose their human form: Semele is incinerated by Jupiter (during sex); Echo fades away until she is all echoing voice; Thisbe kills herself; Clytie becomes a flower; Salmacis is subsumed into Hermaphroditus;[36] Scylla becomes a bird, Byblis, a fountain, Myrrha, a tree; Hylonome kills herself; the women who killed Orpheus become trees; and Alcyone becomes a bird.

Ovid's pattern of destroying female aggressors is most pertinent to our Iphis: she differs greatly from these other women who express sexual desire because Iphis simply does nothing. Unlike Byblis, Iphis does not talk herself into pursuing her love, into acting on her desire. Passive, she ultimately leaves the whole matter to her mother and to the goddess Isis. By making her passive, Ovid breaks with the notion posited in Roman literature (cf. Hallett's and Brooten's analyses, above) that women erotically attracted to women are very aggressive pursuers of their desires. By not acting on her desire, Iphis maintains the passivity associated in Roman thought with women —and then she turns into a man.

BEYOND THE *Metamorphoses:* WHEN GIRLS WON'T BE GIRLS

If the ancient Roman stereotype of a woman who desires a woman, then, is one of an aggressive woman who actively pursues her "masculine lusts" (cf. the views of Hallett, Brooten, Gordon, and Parker, above), we find that Ovid's Iphis breaks with this tradition. Iphis both behaves passively and conceives of the female role in sexual activity as one of passivity. In asking if Daedalus could make her into a boy from a girl, Iphis adds, "Or will he change you, Ianthe?" (9.744). Ovid makes Iphis completely without a preference as to which of them becomes a man, only believing that one of them must to make their sexual union possible. Iphis identifies herself as female[37] (9.747–748), even though her gender has been culturally constructed as male (*cultus erat pueri*, 9.712). It seems not to matter to Iphis which of them penetrates the other (i.e., performs the male role), so long as sexual intercourse becomes possible for the two.[38]

That a woman is essentially passive and penetrable[39] is stated explicitly in another narrative of Ovid's *Metamorphoses*—and it too is a story that involves female to male sex-change. Caenis[40] (12.169–535) was the beautiful daughter of Elatus, raped by Neptune and given in return anything she wished. Caenis tells Neptune:

> This outrage calls for a great prayer: / to be able to suffer[41] nothing like this; grant to me that I not be female: / you will have given all.[42] (12.201–203)

Caenis equates rapability with being female; Neptune equates "like this" (i.e., rape) with any penetrability, particularly by weapons. Ovid writes that the god granted her wish (she became the male Caeneus) and gave her "in addition" (*dederatque super*, 12.206) that s/he be invulnerable to any weapons. This essentializing in Roman thought may be further demonstrated if we consider that this Caenis appears in the underworld of Virgil's *Aeneid*

(6.448–449): there, after her life as a woman and then as a man, Virgil places Caenis/Caeneus among the shades of famous women. It is as if she, upon death, reverted to her "true" underlying female identity.

In Ovid's story of Iphis and Ianthe, gender is framed in terms of cultural stereotypes that are first shown, then overturned, and then reaffirmed. Ovid's Iphis is raised as a male but thinks and acts, in Roman terms, like a female: although she recognizes her own biological sex (female) and her sexual desire for a woman (which is seen as essentially male in Roman thought), she remains passive (which is seen as essentially female in Roman thought) both by not acting on her desire and by expressing no preference that she be the penetrator in her relationship with Ianthe. The essentializing effect suggests that in her obedience to/acceptance of her "female nature," Iphis is rewarded by becoming a male. Unlike Ovid's sexually experienced "active" Sappho in Gordon's analysis ("The Lover's Voice"), Iphis laments her situation, has no sexual experience, and while passionate, can think of no viable outlet with Ianthe for her desires (i.e., does not conceive of two women engaging in satisfying sexual acts); Iphis remains passive.

In addition, the basis for Ligdus' initial objection to keeping a female child is both supported and overturned: he had stated that females are "more burdensome" (onerosior altera sors est, 9.676) and that "fortune denies them strength" (vires negat, 9.677), suggesting a definition of the female as different from (weaker than and more trouble than) a male. At first glance, we might say he is wrong, since for thirteen years Ligdus noticed no difference. Even so, while thought to be male, Iphis is betrothed at an age more appropriate to females,[43] suggesting that she is treated like a female even when thought to be male. Then, as Iphis changes into a man, Ovid states that, among other things, her strength increased (vires augentur, 9.788), suggesting that Ligdus' assertion (that a woman is weaker than a man) was in fact true. By showing the stereotype, seemingly overturning it, and then reinforcing it, Ovid provides a multifaceted reading.

Thus, Ovid suggests that Iphis is born female, has an attributed[44] male gender (i.e., is thought by others to be male), but self-identifies and acts according to female gender standards. Then Iphis becomes male (i.e., has sex characteristics made to match attributed gender). We might wonder, too, how Iphis earlier had passed for a male: in transforming into a man, Iphis walks differently, has a different complexion, different facial features, a different hair length, and becomes stronger and more vigorous (9.786–791).[45] In retrospect, by Roman standards she must have seemed an effeminate male, indeed, if these physical signs of masculinity previously were lacking. Yet Ovid makes no mention of anyone doubting that she was male.

Ovid may overturn expectations in yet another way. If (in real life and not simply in fictional works) female same-sex marriages were associated in Roman thought with Egypt, as Brooten argues (*Love between Women* 332–336), this could explain why Ovid has the Egyptian goddess Isis facilitate the union. A Roman audience may have expected that this was an exotic tale that could end with two female spouses. But then Ovid has Isis change Iphis, so that we have instead a heterosexual wedding sanctioned by the traditional Roman deities of marriage.

As for Ianthe, she, too, passively awaits the day of their union, and although passionate, she does not seek to unite with Iphis beyond what has been arranged for her. We are left to ponder whether in her case we can even call this homoerotic attraction, since she does not know that Iphis is female. However, the fact remains that she loves Iphis, and Iphis is female. Our interpretation depends on what we see as female homoeroticism: is it desire of a woman for one known to be a woman or for one who *is* a woman (i.e., both in self-identification and in biological sex)? Is gender or biological sex the determining factor? Or is homoeroticism based on the two partners knowing that both are the same biological sex? Ovid provides no hint as to whether Ianthe's love would have remained if Iphis had been revealed a woman. That Ianthe loves and desires a woman is nevertheless the reality in the story (cf. Iphis' distinction of *res*), despite her belief that Iphis is a man. The love they have, in fact, seems to transcend biological sex and self-identification, since there is no mention of a change in love—for either Ianthe or Iphis—once Iphis changes into a man, and her biological sex is changed to fit her outwardly male gender.

The question of nature arises again: Ovid leaves ambiguous whether love came naturally or was given by Amor, but he suggests the former. Their love seems to be natural, mutual, and equal; Iphis maintains a female self-identification even while she is believed to be male. But consider for a moment if Ovid had written a different story: that although raised as a male, the woman Iphis desires males.[46] This would suggest that heterosexual sexuality was naturally occurring and arose and remained despite culturally instilled gender roles. Because in this story Iphis was socialized as a male, we might conclude that her passion for Ianthe derives from her upbringing according to male gender roles, suggesting that her passion, then, is culturally created. Yet this is contradicted by Ovid's own story, which suggests a naturally occurring love by a (self-identified) woman for a woman. For example, Ovid shows the two girls as alike in every way, even in the way love touched them; Iphis exclaims to herself:

> See what you were born—unless you deceive yourself, too / —and seek what is right and love what a female ought to love![47] (9.747–748)

Iphis sees herself as a "natural female," that is, made female by nature, and female *in her nature*, and yet she recognizes her passion for a woman. She has no misconceptions about her biological sex nor about her female gender, only problems concerning whether her love is "what is right" (*quod fas est*, 9.748). By having Iphis remain a "female-minded" woman despite her upbringing as a male (all by Roman standards), Ovid suggests that the love occurs naturally and not as the result of a cultural construct of gender and sex roles.

OVID AND THE OLD SWITCHEROO (OR GENRE/GENDER-BUSTING)

Iphis' change into a man remains the key reason that some readers conclude that Ovid condemns female-female relationships (cf. Makowski, "Bisexual Orpheus" 30, that this tale is "Ovid's most damning denunciation of homosexuality"). Once she becomes a man, there is no female-female love. Yet while there were two women, Ovid as narrator did not denounce their passion (as he did, for example, Byblis' desire), only Iphis did. Ovid manages to allow the reader to come to his or her own conclusions without pointing explicitly in one direction or another—or by pointing in several directions. There is no definitive interpretation; any attempt at one is undermined by nagging contradictions. The reader can interpret the love of Iphis for Ianthe as socially unacceptable and improper, by Iphis' assessment of her predicament: she calls her desire both prodigious (*prodigiosa novaeque / cura tenet Veneris*, 9.727–728) and a malady (*malum*, 9.730), and she compares her situation to that of Pasiphaë, whose desire she includes among Cretan monstrosities (*monstra*; cf. *monstrum* of Byblis' desire above).

Yet, there is room to see her passion as acceptable and proper, since Iphis and Ianthe are ultimately united, while so many others in the *Metamorphoses* are punished/destroyed for improper or impious behavior. Alternatively, Ovid suggests that when they were two women, the love was impossible, since consummation of the love within marriage was impossible.[48] In addition, Iphis in a sense suffers the same fate as other female figures in the *Meta-*

morphoses who express sexual desire: just as Ovid provides us with female aggressors who are destroyed throughout the *Metamorphoses*, here he shows Iphis destroyed in the sense that she is no longer a woman. However, she is the only woman among the desiring human women in the poem to retain a human existence.[49] In fact, some might argue that she is elevated, according to her position in a patriarchal structure; Hallett, for example, states of Iphis' human identity that Iphis "even improves upon the one the gods have given her" ("Female Homoeroticism" 217).

Ovid has other mixed messages here: one main theme of the poem as a whole is the acceptance of the hierarchy set forth (in descending order: Jupiter-gods-people[male-female]-animals). In the hierarchy, obedience is key, and any perceived challenge to this hierarchy—and specifically to the authority of the gods—is severely punished. But to be obedient within this hierarchy, that is, to obey the instructions of the goddess, Telethusa must disobey the orders of her husband. Obedience to the goddess saves her female child, but nevertheless destroys that female child by making it male.

In every way, Ovid has it more than one way.[50] Even the genre is mixed: in his "anti-epic" *Metamorphoses*, this story has elements of elegy (see above), New Comedy, tragedy, and melodrama. Aside from elegy, the most obvious elements come from New Comedy, which usually has the following basic outline: boy loves girl, an obstacle thwarts their hopes for marriage, adventures ensue, the obstacle is overcome, and the two wed in the end. Ovid, known for expanding genres beyond standard expectations, presents a type of New Comedy scenario in which the very premise is overturned: girl loves girl, period. The rest of the outline is superfluous, since the obstacle and adventure are built right into the statement itself. Not only is the protagonist female, contrary to New Comedy's tradition, but in Ovid's "new twist" on this genre, he eliminates every other obstacle to heighten the sense of irony. The character of Iphis reflects the mixed genre—she is a different "type": she is of unique gender in that she is essentially female while having been raised as a male; then, after her passivity has proven her female nature, Iphis becomes a man.

The question of sex (both sexual activity and sexual identification) suggests that the core problem may be the potential threat to patriarchy (patriarchy, that is, enacted in heterosexual sex).[51] The love of Iphis and Ianthe is characterized by mutuality and equality, two ingredients normally lacking in most of the heteroerotic stories Ovid relates, and more importantly, lacking in the Roman sexual ideology, which establishes a hierarchy of sexual activity (penetrator) over passivity (penetrated). Like Faderman in *Surpassing,* some feminist theorists postulate that heterosexuality maintains patriarchal order through both gender (male/female) and sexual (active/passive) roles. Andrea Dworkin has further theorized that the act of heterosexual inter-course—under any circumstances—constitutes a claim of the man's own-ership of the woman and his assertion of his dominance and her inferiority and subordination to him.[52] Ovid's tale of Iphis and Ianthe confirms at least Iphis' belief that this is so: Iphis states, "Nevertheless, she is not to be ob-tained by you" (*nec tamen est potiunda tibi,* 9.753), and later she exclaims that at their wedding Ianthe "will be mine—and not belong to me" (9.760–761); since she cannot possess her sexually, she cannot truly "have" her. This con-cept is confirmed in the last line of the story when "the boy Iphis gained his Ianthe" (*potitur*—also "obtained"/"acquired," i.e., as a possession).

Ovid's tale of Iphis and Ianthe is a complex conundrum posing as a simple narrative. If we accept that Iphis by Roman standards is essentially female but a woman who loves a woman (i.e., essentially male, to the Ro-man mind), then there is a curious problem in having her become a man at the end. What sort of man could she be, thinking as she does like a woman (passive, not preferring to penetrate)? The outcome of the story always re-minds me of a joke, which I heard (again) recently. A man said to another man, "I'm just a lesbian trapped in a man's body." After her transformation, Iphis would seem such a one: Ovid portrays her as conforming to the stan-dards of behavior and thought more associated with women than with men and then has her change into a man. He gives us no indication of what in-ternal changes (or if a change in self-identification) may or may not have taken place after the change of sex.

Ovid's story of Iphis and Ianthe both overturns and affirms readers' ex-pectations through the possibility of various, even contradictory, interpreta-tions. Ovid makes the story open to the interpretations of others. His focus throughout the poem on the uses and abuses of power within the hierar-chy he describes calls into question every aspect of this "order." Even so, we started with two women who loved each other mutually, passionately, and equally. This, however, was impossible. The patriarchal hierarchy of Ovid's poem is restored at the end of the story, even though, to do so, Telethusa violated this order by disobeying her husband in the first place. When we finish with a heterosexual married couple, a man who "got" his girl, grate-ful humans thanking helpful gods, all again is "in order." We are left with the impression that within such a patriarchy—which by its nature insists on rank and position, obedience and subordination—mutual and erotic love between women, while not absolutely condemned, has no place.

NOTES

1. Judith Hallett, "Female Homoeroticism and the Denial of Roman Reality in Latin Literature," *Yale Journal of Criticism* 3.1 (1989): 209–227. Rpt. in Judith P. Hallett and Marilyn B. Skinner, eds., *Roman Sexualities* (Princeton: Princeton UP, 1997) 255–273. Hallett cites examples from Plautus, Phaedrus, Ovid, the elder Seneca, Seneca the Younger, Martial, Juvenal, Pliny, and Gellius.

2. I say "the" here, since the Roman concept of sexual activity (as we shall see) allows for only one partner to be conceived of as active and the other as passive.

3. Hallett does mention, however, that the elder Seneca seems to use *tribades* to refer to both the "active and passive tribadic partners" ("Female Homoeroticism" 223). Bernadette Brooten (discussed below) adds to our understanding of *tribas* in her *Love between Women: Early Christian Responses to Female Homoeroticism* (Chicago: U of Chicago P, 1996) esp. 14–26. Also, cf. conceptualized roles of "butch" and "femme."

4. As Hallett also notes ("Female Homoeroticism" 213), the "rubbing" contained within the word *tribas* (i.e., in the origin of this term's use) is, to me at least, ambiguous as to exactly what was thought of as rubbed by what. As Brooten (*Love between Women* 24) notes, ancient authors are "rather vague" on this point.

5. Hallett notes that Pliny and Gellius relate other stories of female-to-male transformations ("Female Homoeroticism" 221–222).

6. Hallett cites Phaedrus, too, who states that same-sex desire is consummated in *pravo gaudio*, "depraved enjoyment" (Phaedrus, *Fabulae* 4.16; cited by Hallett, "Female Homoeroticism" 209–210).

7. Both Hallett's and Brooten's analyses point out that the main criticism among Roman authors of women's sexual practices with women is that the tribad is like a man. See also Stephen M. Wheeler, "Changing Names: The Miracle of Iphis in Ovid *Metamorphoses* 9," *Phoenix* 51.2 (1997) 190–202. Wheeler explores the etymology of names in this tale and argues that the name "Iphis" prefigures the character's ultimate change to the male sex.

8. Pamela Gordon, "The Lover's Voice in *Heroides* 15: Or, Why Is Sappho a Man?" in Judith P. Hallett and Marilyn B. Skinner, eds., *Roman Sexualities* (Princeton: Princeton UP, 1997) 274–291.

9. For a more detailed discussion, see Amy Richlin, *The Garden of Priapus: Sexuality and Aggression in Roman Humor* (rev., Oxford: Oxford UP, 1992) esp. chs. 2–7 and Appendix 2, and Holt Parker, "The Teratogenic Grid," in Judith P. Hallett and Marilyn B. Skinner, eds., *Roman Sexualities* (Princeton: Princeton UP, 1997) 47–65.

10. Hallett, too, points out the Roman view that "normal" women were "naturally" passive ("Female Homoeroticism" 220–221).

11. Here we must note the distinction between (1) biological sex, (2) sexual identity or gender identification, and (3) sexual preference or "orientation." Gordon finds that while Romans acknowledge the tribad as female (in biological sex), they see her as masculine (in gender), and because of this "masculine makeup," the tribad has a female "object choice."

For a detailed and insightful study of various aspects of identity and the language used to discuss gender and identity, see esp. Judith Butler, *Gender Trouble: Feminism and the Subversion of Identity* (New York: Routledge, 1990; New York and London: Routledge, 1999).

12. Lillian Faderman, *Surpassing the Love of Men: Romantic Friendships and Love between Women from the Renaissance to the Present* (New York: William Morrow, 1981), deals with sources from England, France, Germany, and the United States, spanning from the sixteenth to the twentieth centuries.

13. Hallett cites the infamous saying of Seneca the Younger (*Moral Epistles* 95.20.2), that women of his day "even rival men in their lusts . . . although born to be passive" (*virorum licentiae aequaverint . . . pati natae*) ("Female Homoeroticism" 214–215).

14. The problematic use of the term "woman" may be noted here; in this context, I simply mean a person with female biological sex characteristics. Obviously, the word "woman" is not monolithic in meaning; on the broader implications (and the problems with using such categories), see the discussion by Judith Butler in *Gender Trouble* and also in her work, "Imitation and Gender Insubordination," in *Inside/Out: Lesbian Theories, Gay Theories*, ed. Diana Fuss (New York: Routledge, 1991) 13–31. Also useful for a summary of some leading arguments in queer theory (prior to 1996) is Annamarie Jagose's *Queer Theory: An Introduction* (New York: New York UP, 1996).

15. Unless otherwise noted, the translations throughout are my own and are based on W. S. Anderson's text: William S. Anderson, ed., *P. Ovidii Nasonis:* Metamorphoses (Lipsiae: Teubner, 1993). All quotations from the *Metamorphoses* are also from this edition.

16. Some examples: Diana with Actaeon, Juno with Tiresias, Bacchus with Pentheus, Apollo with Marsyas, Athena with Arachne, Latona, Apollo and Diana with Niobe, and Juno with Galanthis.

17. This is certainly not to imply that the story of Iphis (9.666–797) follows directly after these opening lines, only that the programmatic opening of Book 1 alerts us to the themes of power and order that course throughout the poem. In its immediate context, this story follows the tale of Byblis (who desired her brother Caunus [9.450–668]; see discussion below) and ends Book 9. Book 10 then begins with stories concerning Orpheus.

18. The story, only summarized here, will be looked at in greater detail below.

19. Romans associated Inachus with the Egyptian goddess Isis; here, Telethusa sees Inachus but later calls her Isis (9.773).

20. The repetition of Latin words containing "you" or "your" emphasizes this point: *te* (9.776), *te* (9.776), *tuaque* (9.776), *tua* (9.778), *tuum* (9.780).

21.

Par aetas, par forma fuit, primasque magistris
accepere artes, elementa aetatis, ab isdem;
hinc amor ambarum tetigit rude pectus et aequum
vulnus utrique dedit. (9.718–721)

I have translated *rude pectus* as "inexperienced breast," but *rude* may also be "untrained" or "unskilled."

22. Hymen/Hymenaeus is a Roman deity associated with marriage; often the name substitutes for the word "marriage."

23. *amor* (9.720), "love"; *vulnus* (9.721), "wound"; and, later, *non lenius . . . / aestuat* (9.764–5), "nor does [Ianthe] burn more gently."

24. Venus may refer to the Roman goddess of love, beauty, and sexuality, but it may be also used to refer to love or even specifically to sex.

25. She wishes *naturale malum saltem et de more dedissent* (9.730). She also uses the words *cura* (9.728), literally, "concern" or "anxiety" and *malum*, "ill" (or "evil"/"malady") here: in Roman love elegy, we often see the lover refer to love as a disease, sickness, madness, anxiety, and the like.

26.

nec vaccam vaccae, neque equas amor urit equarum;
urit oves aries, sequitur sua femina cervum;
sic et aves coeunt, interque animalia cuncta
femina femineo correpta cupidine nulla est.
vellem nulla forem! (9.731–735)

27. *et iam mea fiet Ianthe— / nec mihi continget* (9.760–761). William S. Anderson states, "Note the nice distinction in 760–61 between legally owning Ianthe and erotically possessing her." *Ovid's Metamorphoses: Books 6–10* (Norman: U of Oklahoma P, 1972) 471.

28. E.g., Apollodorus 3.15.8.

29. We often find the phrase *vim passa est*, "she experienced his force." In his study of rape in the poem, Leo Curran states: "*vim passa* and its variants verge on the formulaic in the *Metamorphoses*." "Rape and Rape Victims in the *Metamorphoses*," *Arethusa* 11 (1978): 221.

30. *moverat* is in the indicative (i.e., stated as a fact).

31. The *malum*, to Iphis, seems to be the combination of her desire for Ianthe and her own biological sex: she goes on both to list female animals who do not desire females and to wish that she herself were no female (9.731–735).

32.

Byblis in exemplo est, ut ament concessa puellae,
Byblis Apollinei correpta cupidine fratris:
non soror ut fratrem, nec qua debebat, amabat. (9.454–456)

33. *iamque palam est demens, inconcessamque fatetur / spem veneris,* 9.638–639; cf. *tamen illa secuta est / spem veneris* (9.739) of Pasiphaë.

34. In fact, given the failure rate, it is no wonder Iphis chooses Pasiphaë, one of the very few who actually has sex with the object of her desire.

35. Venus and Aurora are goddesses; both Medea and Circe are said to possess magical powers (and they both have deities for ancestors). Pasiphaë, too, we should note, suffers no demotion in form; she is, however, the daughter of the sun-god Sol/Helius. One could argue that Salmacis and Hylonome also are greater than human (Salmacis a water nymph, and Hylonome, a centaur).

36. Hermaphroditus' consciousness remains: it is he who notices that he is now "half-male" (*semimarem*), and it is he who then prays to the gods (4.380–388).

37. Again, I distinguish here between sex and gender identities. Gender studies (e.g., Butler, *Gender Trouble*) and studies of transsexualism are most helpful in this area. However,

we should note that in many accounts of transsexualism, there is a notion to the effect that "sex is between the legs, gender is between the ears," intimating the distinction of biological sex as determined by genitalia (externally recognized) and gender as self-identification (internally perceived). See, for example, Claudine Griggs, *S/he: Changing Sex and Changing Clothes* (New York: Berg, 1998). Butler, on the other hand, asserts: "Gender is a performance that *produces* the illusion of an inner sex or essence or psychic gender core" (her emphasis; "Imitation" 28).

38. She focuses primarily on herself becoming a man, but this seems due more to the circumstance that she is already the presumed male. She is, therefore, the more convenient choice.

39. Jonathan Walters argues a related point in his "Invading the Roman Body: Manliness and Impenetrability in Roman Thought," in Judith P. Hallett and Marilyn B. Skinner, eds., *Roman Sexualities* (Princeton: Princeton UP, 1997) 29–43, adding into the mix the aspect of social standing. Walters states: "The Roman sexual protocol that defined men as impenetrable penetrators can most usefully be seen in the context of a wider conceptual pattern that characterized those of high social status as being able to defend the boundaries of their bodies from invasive assaults of all kinds" (30).

40. Hallett mentions Caenis' transformation, particularly as told by Gellius and Pliny ("Female Homoeroticism" 221). Like Caenis, the daughter of Erysichthon in the *Metamorphoses* was granted a boon by Neptune after he had raped her: she gains the ability to change her form and changes temporarily into a (fisher)man to elude her would-be owner (8.843–868).

41. Here we again have *pati* used of the rape; earlier the rape itself was described: *aequorei vim passa dei est* (12.197), literally, "she experienced the force of the god of the sea."

42.

> "'Magnum,' Caenis ait 'facit haec iniuria votum,
> tale pati iam posse nihil; da, femina ne sim:
> omnia praestieris.'" (12.201–203)

43. Anderson notes: "Boys did not usually marry at thirteen in Rome or Greece, but girls could." *Ovid's Metamorphoses: Books 6–10* 469, n. ad 714.

44. "Attributed gender" refers to that which is perceived or acknowledged by others, regardless of self-identification, dress, or even screaming assertions to the contrary. See Griggs, *S/he*.

45. The text of Iphis' transformation:

> mater abit templo, sequitur comes Iphis euntem,
> quam solita est, maiore gradu; nec candor in ore
> permanet, et vires augentur, et acrior ipse est
> vultus et incomptis brevior mensura capillis,
> plusque vigoris adest, habuit quam femina. nam quae
> femina nuper eras, puer es. (9.786–791)

46. Consider, for example, the Hollywood version of this in the 1983 musical/drama *Yentl*, directed by Barbra Streisand.

47.

quid sis nata, vide, nisi te quoque decipis ipsam,
et pete, quod fas est, et ama quod femina debes. (9.747–748)

48. Hallett argues that Roman authors deny the existence of female homoeroticism in Roman reality and that mutually gratifying sex between women (i.e., without a penis) was inconceivable ("Female Homoeroticism").

49. Salmacis (*Metamorphoses* 4.271–388) may be an exception, although she is not human per se; as a naiad (water nymph), she enjoys a superhuman position, as does her male beloved. She, however, is subsumed into Hermaphroditus, causing *him* to have both male and female characteristics. It is nevertheless he who remains and sees that he is now a "half-man" (*semimarem*, 4.381), although he had entered the waters as a man (*vir*, 4.380). He prays to his divine parents (again, suggesting that it is he who remains) that the pool will have the same effect on any man who thereafter should touch its waters (4.382–388).

50. Cultural aspects are mixed as well: the story is set on Crete (= Greek), the Egyptian goddess Isis plays an integral role, Isis and Inachus are assimilated, and traditional Roman wedding deities are called upon (i.e., Juno, Hymen, and Venus).

51. As Faderman argues (*Surpassing*). See also Adrienne Rich, "Compulsory Heterosexuality and Lesbian Existence," in *Powers of Desire: The Politics of Sexuality*, ed. Ann Snitow, Christine Stansell, and Sharon Thompson (New York: Monthly Review P, 1983).

52. Andrea Dworkin, *Intercourse* (New York: Macmillan/Free P, 1987) 63–79.

CHAPTER NINE

Lucian's "Leaena and Clonarium"

Voyeurism or a Challenge to Assumptions?*

Shelley P. Haley

> The Dialogues of the Whores by Lucian is not an erotic book at all but a collection of comic anecdotes with a left-wing bias showing that whores are part of the oppressed proletariat but can get along all right if they know the ropes.
>
> Wayland Young, *Eros Denied: Sex in Western Society* (1964) 71

> The advent of lesbian chic has given heterosexuals—and probably some gay men who heretofore lived lives without any contact with lesbians—a window onto an all-girl world, but that window, like the one in a peep-show booth, has always been available in het male porn. Much to many lesbians' anger and chagrin (and a lucrative fact of life for many others), voyeuristic straight men discovered live lesbian sex acts long ago.
>
> Carol Queen and Lawrence Schimel, *Switch Hitters* (1996) 13

> It's an obvious but crucial fact that lesbians are, first and foremost, women and that straight guys—who program the radio stations, sell the records to retail, and call the major label shots—like women. Lesbians don't threaten the dudes, particularly when their commercial potential has already been proved.
>
> Barry Walters, "Rock's Queer Evolution," *The Advocate* (December 9, 1997): 31

As the movement for the civil and human rights of gays, lesbians, bisexuals, and the transgendered and transsexual communities has progressed, it has brought greater visibility to the cultural aspects of these groups. This in turn has given rise to a subfield of critical theory, known as "queer" theory. Like any theoretical critique of the dominant culture, whether it is feminist theory, Afrocentric theory, or Black feminist thought,[1] queer theory developed as an oppositional stance, in this case, to the dominant heterosexist paradigms. As a term, one of its earliest uses was in a special issue of the journal *differences* edited by Teresa de Lauretis and entitled "Queer Theory: Lesbian and Gay Sexualities."[2]

Like other types of academic theory, however, queer theory has often fallen into the pitfall of jargon, making it inaccessible and alienating to non-academics, particularly those who are queer themselves. Furthermore, there still exists some confusion as to what constitutes queer theory and whether there is any significant difference among queer theory, queer studies, or lesbian, gay, and bisexual studies. Such confusion is neither surprising nor unique, since it occurs in other interdisciplinary fields. For example, what is the connection between Women's Studies and Feminist theory? Or Black Studies and Afrocentric theory?

At the core of these theories is identity politics. Closely linked to identity politics is the theoretical stance that identities, personal as well as collective, are seen as social constructions and have no givens in nature, anatomy, or some other essence. Social construction allows us to enter the political contestation around issues like sexuality and sexual identity, which up to now have been considered to lie outside politics.

One consequence of social construction is the fluidity this introduces to categories of identity. At the same time, this very fluidity can create contradictions and challenges. Many identities have been repressed, denied visibility, stigmatized, and marginalized. Identity politics does offer opportunities for these voices to be heard, but often the trap of essentializing looms large and is hard to avoid. Identity politics can open people up to regulation, force them to invoke "community." Queer theory offers one framework to articulate discomfort with identity politics, no matter how strategic they may be. For instance, for an Asian lesbian living in the United States, the assumed but unspoken subject of "Asian American" may not feel like her because she is not an American-born, heterosexual male. Since she is dependent on a hetero-normative logic to perpetuate "community," she transgresses. I once saw on a women's restroom wall this exchange: "Sisters! Drop your white boyfriends! Have you tried an Asian Brother?" In red marker was the reply, "No, but I have tried an Asian sister—does that count?" For this Asian lesbian, the questions became, Do I want to force my inclusion? Can I critically queer this?

At the same time that queer theory offers this framework and can be strategic, it too can sometimes fall into the same regulation and coercion of community found in identity politics. A problem arises with the identity of any marginalized group when sanctioned categories are created. If a person cannot or does not want to fit into one of these categories, a challenge to her "authenticity" can occur. For example, am I, as a woman of African descent who participates in the white-dominated world of the academy as a tenured full professor of Classics, "authentically Black"? Am I as a bisexual woman "authentically queer"? One of the challenges to early queer theory was that it was often quite exclusionary, overlooking people of color and deliberately omitting bisexuals and the transgendered. There has been in recent years an attempt to correct these omissions,[3] and queer theory itself is continually undergoing transformation. Perhaps it is inevitable that queer theory has become the yardstick by which authentic queerness is judged. But what happens when a person feels that, in the words of Kate Bornstein, she "doesn't quite fit in one of the sanctioned queer worlds"?[4] In response to this, Queen and Schimel developed a "queer" queer theory that they call "pomosexuality," that is, *post modern* sexuality:

> Pomosexual references homosexuality even as it describes the community's outsiders, the *queer* queers who can't seem to stay put within a nice, simple identity.[5]

Later they state,

> Pomosexuality lives in the space in which all other non-binary forms of sexual and gender identity reside—a boundary free zone in which fences are crossed for the fun of it, or simply because some of us can't be fenced in. . . . It acknowledges the pleasure of transgression as well as the need to transgress limits that do not make room for all of us.[6]

Pomosexuality, like poststructuralist and postcolonial feminist theory, unpacks binary oppositions and problematizes the supposedly universal subject of queer discourses. It makes its central focus the instability of identity and the gap of dis-identification.

The purpose of this essay is to apply this theory of "pomosexuality" to a dialogue of Lucian that has received little critical attention, either from classicists or from queer theorists. For me, it is intriguing to apply a fluid theory of identity such as pomosexuality to an author who created a literary piece within a seemingly rigid framework of "set pieces." The dialogue in question is one of the pieces in a larger work, *The Dialogues of the Courtesans,* and it has been ignored for two possible reasons: it deals with what today would be termed transgendered lesbianism, and it is from late antiquity. Unfortunately, the application of pomosexuality may raise more questions than it answers. For example, what, if anything, does Lucian's dialogue teach us about the social constructs of gender and sexuality of his time? Raising the questions, however, opens a new path for interpreting these constructs and, particularly, those of female homoeroticism in ancient times. First, it may be useful to provide some background material, since Lucian is not a well-known author outside an elite circle of scholars.

Who Was Lucian?

Lucian (*ca.* 120 – *ca.* 180 CE) lived and published during a period that is traditionally known as the "golden age"—both materially and politically—of the Roman Empire. No major wars were fought, peace and prosperity reigned, and the upper and middle classes were comfortable. In terms of social status, there was unity in diversity. The provincials were no longer regarded as stepchildren but were the very stuff of which nobility was made. People descended from municipal aristocracies were represented in the senatorial and equestrian classes. "Private fortunes, local centers of culture, even a sense of meritocratic opportunity within the imperial bureaucracy are all hallmarks of provincial urban society of the period."[7]

Lucian himself represents the ideal of diversity that can occur in a multiculture. He was born in Syria, specifically at Samosata, Commogene. Commogene was annexed by the emperor Vespasian and incorporated into the province of Syria. Since the Romans were not interested in cultural proselytization, the principal social and cultural institutions remained Persian, Semitic, and Greek, even where the Romans made material alterations such as creating roads, bridges, and public monuments.

Lucian, although educated in forensic rhetoric and rather successful with public lecturing in Ionia, Greece, Italy, and Gaul, retained great affection for Syria and its culture. Allegedly, he always wore a Syrian caftan and spoke Greek, acquired as a second language, with a pronounced accent.[8] He apparently knew Latin as well but appears to have used it for his writings only occasionally; he preferred Greek for the most part. It is certain that Lucian gave up lecturing for a short period to take up a post in the imperial bureaucracy in Egypt, perhaps about 170 CE. He abandoned this position for unknown reasons and returned to lecturing. Shortly after the death of Marcus Aurelius in 180 CE, Lucian seems to have dropped out of the literary scene and is presumed to have died about then.

Mimesis or Imitation?

Lucian is considered part of the "second sophistic" but was not a sophist in the manner of Aristides or Polemon.[9] The Second Sophistic is the term regularly applied in modern scholarship to the period *c.* AD 60–230 when declamation became the most prestigious literary activity in the Greek world. . . . The term sophist . . . seems restricted to rhetors (public speakers . . .) who entered upon a career of public displays.[10]

Under the same entry, the *Oxford Classical Dictionary* states that declamation was not the only influence on the writers of the Second Sophistic. The exercise of *ecphrasis* or set-piece description was found in rhetorical handbooks and engendered a whole genre. Lucian is credited with not only the use of *ecphrasis* but also the development of the dialogue "into a humorous art-form: its use for lighter entertainment is already discernible in Dio but only from Lucian . . . do we have a wide range of entertaining works."[11]

Indeed, Lucian claimed as his niche the composition of dialogues, which some scholars have dubbed satirical.[12] Lucian asserts during a humorous courtroom scene that he turned from rhetoric to dialogue in his forties. In the same passage he characterizes rhetoric as tainted by prostitution, while "Dialogue who is said to be the son of Philosophy" was more appealing because of such solemn and respectable ancestry.[13]

Much of the scholarship on Lucian has focused on whether he was a traditionalist. If so, he would have been totally absorbed by *mimesis,* the imitation of conventional themes and forms, thereby producing new works with their own artistic validity. Some scholars, notably Barry Baldwin, analyze Lucian's use of Greek cultural heritage as "a set of conventions which Lucian used to relate his animadversions to contemporary issues and targets."[14] However, the French scholar Jacques Bompaire is the most cited proponent of the interpretation that Lucian's use of Greek cultural heritage is a literary end in itself.[15] Indeed, Bompaire seems nearly obsessed with *mimesis* and sees it everywhere. While both schools of thought agree that Lucian worked within a well-established framework of ideas and methods, the difference hinges on the role of *mimesis.* Lucian's use of imitation is important for our discussion, since it raises the question of how much of his own worldview, or own cultural stance, is reflected in the dialogues. Christopher Robinson, who follows Bompaire rather than Baldwin argues that

Lucian himself is a prime example of the traditionalism that permeates all literature of his period. The world around him occurs incidentally in his work, and the events of his own life equally peripherally, because he is wholly taken up with the task of making out of the imitation of traditional themes and forms works which have themselves independent artistic validity. It is the theory of *mimesis,* or imitation, which gives the clue to what Lucian's audiences looked for, and enjoyed, in his work.[16]

Following this argument, the sociological details of the dialogues were not as important to Lucian's audience as the manipulation of traditional themes and forms. In short, we can draw no firm conclusions about how Lucian himself felt about the issues or topics that were the subjects of his writings. We can make only judgments about how well he manipulated motifs and conventions. Even so, what piques the interest of the queer theorist is the possibility that female homoeroticism could constitute a traditional theme. What are some questions that this possibility raises? Is there an assumption that female homoeroticism is a traditional theme that can be reframed? Does the mere inclusion of female homoeroticism in the dialogue represent an innovation by Lucian? To what extent did this theme add to the literary success of *The Dialogues of the Courtesans*? To what extent did it simply add a sexually titillating flavor to a traditional theme? Could it be that female homoeroticism was seen as a cultural stereotype, and once certain ethnicities were mentioned, audiences expected it to be represented? In this case, omission of it might spell critical failure for the author.

Whichever interpretation one chooses, it is certainly true that imitation is the principle that underlies the educational curriculum in Rome both in the second century of the common era and earlier. The purpose of education at this time was to learn about life, but life as it was codified, analyzed, and exemplified in great works of art and literature. To write about life was to reproduce such writing as was presented in great literature. Beginning in primary education, young children were exposed to the great poets of Greek and Roman literature by memorizing pithy sayings from them. Pupils were taught to choose authors according to their appropriateness for a particular topic, to read carefully and transfer what was read to their own writings. The emphasis was always on imitating what clearly had worked in the past. There was no praise or no reward for being radically original. This doctrine of imitation did produce great works of art, most notably the *Aeneid*, and was the standard training for learned people not only of Lucian's time but also of previous generations.

However, Lucian—and many others—claimed other cultural heritages in addition to those of Greece and Rome. It was through the educational system particular to the Roman Empire that Lucian became assimilated to and intimate with the Greek and Roman cultures and their expectations. Lucian was, according to Robinson, "perhaps particularly drawn to a profession devoted to the Greek past by some personal compulsive need for thorough self-hellenization." [17] Nearly all the scholarship follows in this vein: the role and influence of convention and the extent to which Lucian was innovative within those conventions and within the paradigm of *mimesis* so prevalent during the Second Sophistic. A consequence of such a scholarly focus is that the individual vignettes and their details become irrelevant to the discussion of how closely the work reflected *mimesis,* and they can be ignored in favor of discussion of generalized cultural principles and Aristotelian categories of oratory. For instance, in his discussion of Lucian's diverse renderings of the dialogue form, Robinson states,

> The diversity to be found in Lucian's use of dialogue on a philosophical pattern is fully matched by the diversity of his dramatic dialogue, though here it is as much a diversity of matter as of manner. There is a clear difference in manner and purpose between *The Dialogues of the Courtesans,* on the one hand and dialogues such as *Timon* or *The Dead Come to Life.* In the former, types and situations are plainly drawn, for the most part, from New Comedy. Each dialogue is the transposition of a scene or scenes, with the familiar range of characters and situations: a lovers' quarrel and misunderstanding put right (*Dial.* 2 and 12); rivals in love quarrel (*Dial.* 9); the madam instructs the young courtesan (*Dial.* 6); the courtesan confessing her love for a penniless young man (*Dial.* 7).[18]

For the purpose of this essay, this statement is telling evidence of how the processes of erasure and denial occur. For it is within the borderlands of Robinson's "for the most part" that we find examples of female homoeroticism in Lucian's dialogues. Because he references and frames vignettes as coming from New Comedy and therefore focuses on dialogues that are heteroerotic (or seem to be), *Dialogue* 5, which deals explicitly with female homoeroticism, slips through the cracks. It also limits interpretation of *Dialogue* 12, which does indeed revolve around a "lovers' quarrel and misunderstanding put right," but the questions of the nature of the misunderstanding and how it is resolved are not dealt with. Consequently, an opportunity to explore female homosociality (if not homoeroticism) is again lost.

The Dialogues of the Courtesans

At this point, it might be best to take a closer look at *The Dialogues of the Courtesans.* I believe a starting point has to be the translation of the word ἑταίρα (*hetaira*). It is a word that in its masculine form means "comrade, companion, fellow, mate." In a military context, the word takes on that flavor as well: "brother-in-arms, shipmate, mess-mate." What happens when it becomes feminine? The meaning shifts to a sexual relationship; *hetaira* becomes in the Attic dialect a parallel to a legal wife. She is, according to the Greek lexicon, "a concubine, a courtesan, harlot." This lexical definition erases the specific role the *hetaira* had in Athenian society. It was the author now known as Pseudo-Demosthenes who outlined the roles available to women in his time: "We have mistresses for our enjoyment, concubines to serve our person, and wives for the bearing of legitimate children."[19]

The ancient Greeks, who seem to have had a word for everything, divided the status of "nonwives" into three categories. *Hetaira* is most often translated as "mistress" or "courtesan." A *pallakê* (παλλακή) was a woman of slave status who served as a concubine for the males of the house, whether she was bought for that reason or for some other. Finally, *pornai* (πόρναι) were women of slave or freeborn status who sold their sexual services. Leslie Kurke discussed the differences between the *hetairai* and the *pornai:*

> According to the traditional scholarly account, the opposition of the hetaira and porne is one of status. The hetaira is a "courtesan" or "mistress," often supported by one or two men alone, serving as their companion at symposia as well as servicing their sexual desires. The porne, in contrast, is the common street-walker or occupant of brothels, providing sex for payment to a large and anonymous clientele.[20]

Furthermore, James Davidson sees the difference as one of discourse. The discourse associated with *hetairai* was about gift exchange and seduction. The emphasis is the control the *hetairai* exercised over men and their desires. The discourse around *pornai* is one that objectified and commodified their bodies.[21] Neither discourse is flattering. The one regarding *hetairai* is phobic; the other around *pornai* is contemptuous.

To comprehend the sexual objectification of ancient Greek *hetairai* by their lovers and patrons, we can look to other times and other places. It can be enlightening to analyze how, in other historical periods, women who were constructed as foreign or "Other" were transformed into sexual objects by men. For instance, during the early part of the nineteenth century, in the territory colonized by the French and now known as Louisiana, there was a custom of *placage* initiated by the French colonizers from which we can draw striking parallels with the *hetairai* of ancient Greece. The system depended heavily upon the French construction of slavery and race. *Placees* were free-born or freed women of African descent, usually of the castes of quadroon and octoroon.[22] In some cases, *placees* inherited their occupation from their mothers. (It is unlikely that they would inherit their mothers' lovers, since there was a high likelihood that these men were their fathers.) Like the *hetaira*, a *placee* was more than a prostitute and less than a wife. Their patrons were almost exclusively white or Creole men who were light enough to pass for white.

Unlike the *hetaira* and the concubine, distinct physical markers divided *placees* and slave women. Enslaved women were darker skinned, while women with lighter skin color—presumably due to their mixed racial heritage—found themselves in the position of being *placees*. This is not to say white men did not take sexual advantage of slave women as well as *placees*. However, in terms of social status, the slave woman was always beneath the *placee*, just as the *pallake* was beneath the *hetaira* of ancient Greece. Indeed, both the *hetaira* and the *placee* could and did own slaves.[23] In general, *placees* and *hetairai* shared dependence on men for their social and economic status and needs.

Placees served as an important sexual outlet for wealthy (or cash poor but socially prominent) white men who often, because of the patriarchal nature of French/Creole Louisiana, were partnered in arranged marriages. Like *hetairai*, the *placee* couplings were heterosexual and monogamous in the sense that a man could apparently have a wife and a *placee* simultaneously, so long as it was only one of each. In Lucian's dialogues, most of the young men are serially monogamous. That is, they start out their "relationship" careers with a *hetaira* and then move on to a legitimate marriage and a lawful wife.

In much the same way, the Periclean citizenship law of 451 BCE was an expression of the construct of Athenian citizen identity. After the passage of this law, ethnic and national origin became a marker of *hetairai*. The law certainly did not have the same impact on non-Athenian men; in point of fact, the presumption is that the patrons and lovers of the *hetairai* were Athenian citizens.

The Dialogues of the Courtesans is a series of fifteen set rhetorical pieces in which Lucian examines a range of personal and intimate relationships involving *hetairai*. At this chronological, spatial, and cultural distance, it is sometimes difficult to know when the dialogues are tongue-in-cheek and when they are bringing a serious issue to light. *Dialogue 5* and *Dialogue 12*, each in different ways, deal with woman-to-woman relationships. *Dialogue 5* takes place between two courtesans, Clonarium and Leaena. Clonarium begins by reporting to Leaena the "strange" (καινὰ) rumors that have been circulating about her:

> . . . τὴν Λεσβίαν Μέγιλλαν τὴν πλουσίαν ἐρᾶν σου ὥσπερ ἄνδρα καὶ συνεῖναι ὑμᾶς οὐκ οἶδ' ὅ τι ποιούσας μετ' ἀλλήλων.

... that Megilla, the rich woman of Lesbos, is in love with you just like a man, that you live with each other, and do I don't know what together.

Leaena responds by blushing and admitting that the rumors are true, adding

Ἀληθῆ, ὦ Κλωνάριον αἰσχύνομαι δέ, ἀλλόκοτον γάρ τί ἐστι.

But I am ashamed, for it is *unnatural* (emphasis mine).

The dialogue proceeds with Clonarium pumping Leaena for details about her relationship with Megilla: how they met, what Megilla looks like, and what exactly they did together. In Leaena's description of Megilla, there are close correspondences to transgenderism. According to Nancy Nangeroni, transgenderism is

the practice of transgressing gender norms. A transgender person is someone whose gender display at least sometimes runs contrary to what other people in the same culture would normally expect. Transgender folk come in several flavors: FTM (female to male) are people who were born female but see themselves as partly to fully masculine; MTF (male to female) are people who were born male but see themselves as partly to fully feminine. Intersexed are those born with some combination of male and female physiology [similar to hermaphrodite], who may accept as natural their mixed gender.[24]

Clonarium, perhaps not surprisingly, given the culturally pluralistic world in which she lives, has some information about the women of Lesbos but not enough graphic details to satisfy her voyeuristic appetite. For instance, Clonarium says,

They say there are such masculine-looking women in Lesbos, and unwilling to be with men, but only with women as though they themselves were men. (γυναῖκας ἀρρενωπούς ὑπ' ἀνδρῶν μὲν οὐκ ἐθελούσας αὐτὸ πάσχειν, γυναιξὶ δὲ αὐτὰς πλησιαζούσας ὥσπερ ἄνδρας.)

Leaena responds to this probe with a noncommittal answer of "it's something like that." Leaena goes on to describe how she first met Megilla and their first sexual encounter. Leaena was to provide music at a drinking party organized by Megilla and Demonassa, her partner (as we learn later) who was from Corinth, was wealthy, and had similar "tastes."

In describing Megilla as a woman of Lesbos and Demonassa as a woman of Corinth, Lucian is very careful to provide markers to guide his audience

towards female homoeroticism. Both these ethnicities carry with them cultural stereotypes, and Lucian chose them deliberately. Such a choice also
reveals factors about Lucian's audience, namely, the audience would have
known the stereotypes about the sexual customs and attitudes of women
from Lesbos and Corinth. Corinth was seen as the center of the sex trade, and
Corinthian women were regarded as sexually adventurous, as were women
from Lesbos. Neaera, the *hetaira* of Demosthenes' speech, spent most of her
time in Corinth. Lucian alludes to this stereotyped perception of women
from Lesbos when he has Clonarium say a generic "they say that . . ." before
divulging what she knew about women from Lesbos. Lucian could assume
his audience had at least a passing familiarity with sexual relations between
women, even if it were at the level of stereotype and popular fantasy.

Megilla invited Leaena to sleep between her and Demonassa, where they
"kissed" (ἐφίλουν)[25] her "like men" (ὥσπερ οἱ ἄνδρες). Here Leaena gives
rather more details:

> . . . οὐκ αὐτὸ μόνον προσαρμόζουσαι τὰ χείλη, ἀλλ' ὑπανοίγουσαι τὸ στόμα, καὶ
> περιέβαλλον καὶ τοὺς μαστοὺς ἔθλιβον· ἡ Δημώνασσα δὲ καὶ ἔδακνε μεταξὺ
> καταφιλοῦσα· ἐγὼ δὲ οὐκ εἶχον εἰκάσαι ὅ τι τὸ πρᾶγμα εἴη.

> . . . not simply bringing their lips to mine, but opening their mouths a little, em-
> bracing me, and squeezing my breasts. Demonassa even bit me as she kissed, but
> I didn't know what to make of it.

At this point, Megilla became aroused (ὑπόθερμος . . . οὖσα) and passionately pulled off her wig to reveal "the skin of her head shaved close,
just as on the most energetic of athletes." Megilla teased Leaena about her
shocked reaction and asked whether she had ever seen such a "good-looking
young *man*" (emphasis mine). Leaena was confused and remarked that she
still didn't see a man. Megilla responded,

> Don't make a *woman* out of me; my name is *Megillus,* and I've been married to
> Demonassa here for ever so long; she's my wife.

Leaena still did not "get it" and insisted that Megilla must be anatomi-
cally male and drew a parallel to the myth of Achilles on the island of Scyros.[26] Megilla answered that she did not have "that": "I do not need it at
all. You'll find I've a much pleasanter method of my own ('Εκεῖνο μὲν . . .
οὐκ ἔχω· δέομαι δὲ οὐδὲ πάνυ αὐτοῦ· ἴδιον δέ τινα τρόπον ἡδίω παρὰ πολὺ
ὁμιλοῦντα ὄψει με)." Leaena, still working through all the possibilities, hit

upon the idea that Megilla was a hermaphrodite and made the interesting remark that many people were said to be hermaphrodites. To this Megilla responded, "No, Leaena, I'm all *man*." Leaena was clearly struggling and mentioned the myth of Teiresias,[27] who changed from a man to a woman and back to a man. She wondered if this is what happened to Megilla. Megilla answered, "No, Leaena. I was born a woman like the rest of you, but I have the mind and desires and everything else of a man." She begs Leaena to "just give me a chance, and you'll find I'm as good as any man; I have a substitute of my own." Leaena gives in: Megilla "went to work, kissing me, and panting, and apparently enjoying herself immensely."

This is not good enough for Clonarium. She wants details, and towards the end of the dialogue she says explicitly, "What did she do? HOW? That's what I'm most interested to hear." The dialogue ends with Leaena cautioning Clonarium not to inquire too closely into the details because "they're not very nice," and for that reason, Leaena refuses to divulge them.

What are scholars living in a postmodern, postcolonial, "pomosexual"[28] world to make of this dialogue? Is it about gender, sexuality, or working-class oppression (à la Wayland Young)?[29] The dialogue seems to be strong evidence for the social construction of gender and sexuality in the ancient world. Megilla represents more than simple transvestism. Her statement, "I was born a woman like the rest of you, but I have the mind and desires and everything else of a man," fits closely with Nangeroni's female-to-male "flavor" of transgenderism. Had Megilla been an historical figure, she might well have found herself represented in Leslie Feinberg's *Transgender Warriors* and would have felt at home in the modern transgender community. Indeed she and Demonassa would have found a niche in the polyamorous community ("Come along Leaena, it's high time we were in bed; you sleep here between us."); and in the butch-fem community (". . . there are women like that in Lesbos . . . unwilling to suffer 'it' from men and consort only with women as if they themselves were men").

Megilla and Demonassa's relationship resembles the butch-fem roles that were prevalent in the pre-1970s lesbian communities in parts of the United States. As Elizabeth Kennedy and Madeline Davis explain,

> In terms of image butches affected a masculine style while fems appeared characteristically feminine. Butch and fem also complemented one another in an erotic system in which the butch was expected to be the doer and giver, and the fem's receptive passion was the butch's fulfillment.[30]

True to the butch role, Megilla pursues Leaena and tempts her with a "much pleasanter method" of sex. Although Lucian left it to the audience's imagination exactly what the method was, Megilla was the "doer," the butch, and she expected Leaena to be the passive one, the fem.

One can see how modern queer communities could embrace the characters of *Dialogue* 5. However, how does the inclusion of this dialogue relate to the various interpretations of Lucian's use of Greek cultural heritage? If *mimesis* is the primary organizing principle, we can safely draw two conclusions: Lucian is using female homoeroticism as a literary end in itself, and one would expect to find such a set piece among the works of others writing in this genre. A very cursory review finds that Alciphron,[31] possibly a contemporary of Lucian who drew from the same comedic sources, included in his series of letters a set piece similar to Lucian's *The Dialogues of the Courtesans*, which he titled "Letters of the Courtesans." There is, however, no exact parallel to *Dialogue* 5. Bernadette Brooten in her discussion of this letter finds "homoerotic overtones" in Alciphron's framing of a party given by courtesans for one another.[32] She says, "Although a male writer has cast this fictitious scene of an all-female party, it can nevertheless help us to imagine the homoerotic possibilities of a homosocial environment, even when the women are connected with men."[33] During this party, women danced sensual dances for other women and expressed appreciation for the bodies of other women. However, there is no explicitly sexual activity between the women as there is between Megilla and Leaena. While I agree with Brooten that this party is certainly homosocial and that the piece may help modern audiences to imagine "homoerotic possibilities," I am not convinced that we can project that back to the ancients.

Nonetheless, a degree of voyeurism occurs throughout Lucian's *Dialogue* and Alciphron's "Letter." The fundamental question is, Does this voyeurism indicate Lucian's sympathy for women or exploitation of them? Is it genuine curiosity or a need to ridicule women that forms the basis of this voyeurism? The role of *mimesis* comes into play here as well. If Lucian is reworking literary tropes or cultural stereotypes, and if it is a given that misogyny is a recurrent motif throughout the history of Greek literature, then Lucian's voyeurism could constitute yet another form of that misogyny. If we believe Lucian is making hostile, critical remarks about contemporary issues and targets, the dialogue could represent voyeurism that is homophobic, misogynistic, or both. Even if we accept this interpretation, however, it would appear that transgendered female homoeroticism was a familiar enough cultural phenomenon or literary trope that Lucian can satirize it.

Problematic in authenticating Lucian as a pomosexual,[34] that is, a challenger to assumptions about gender and sexuality, is his lack of detail about sexual relationships between two women, which may be related to his employment of *mimesis*.[35] How much *did* Lucian know? We cannot escape the fact that this is a *man* in a male-dominated and male-oriented culture writing about women loving other women. Lucian's character Clonarium kept pressing Leaena for details. Significantly none were forthcoming, except in the area of kissing. Lucian goes into the most detail about this activity, which alludes to an interesting folk etiology. Judith Hallett discusses a fragment in Latin by the fable writer Phaedrus (*ca.* 15 BCE–50 CE) in which Prometheus creates the female tongue: "Lately [Prometheus] formed the tongue of woman from the molding of the male organ."[36] The female tongue was seen as related to the penis, and if the female tongue "penetrated" the lips (mouth or vulva) of another woman, a kiss became an act of sexual intercourse.

Although Lucian was writing over a century after Phaedrus, Phaedrus' folk etiology imbues another level of meaning to Lucian's "kissing like a man." It is possible that in the popular culture of Lucian's time, "kissing like a man" had become a euphemism or idiom for the sexual penetration of one woman by another. If that is the case, it could be that such details were so common that it was *Clonarium* with her "out-of-it" mentality who was being satirized. We certainly do not want to fall into the masculinist trap of thinking that women can receive sexual pleasure only from penetration. Brooten interprets Megilla's "much pleasanter method" as being mental and spiritual. She says, "Thus for Lucian sexual love between women does not originate from women's having male genitals. For Lucian, the mind seems to be the most powerful sex organ."[37] Following this interpretation, one could argue that Lucian is sympathetic toward women and female homoeroticism. At the same time, the inability of Lucian, of Phaedrus, and of other male writers to imagine sexual intercourse that does not involve penetration can be discerned. In their discussions, both Brooten and Hallett remark upon the limits of the ancient male imagination regarding this issue. Brooten writes,

> While ancient female homoerotic behavior probably included a full range of sexual expression, the ancient (and often modern) male imagination seems limited to postulating a physical substitute for the penis on the apparent assumption that sex occurs when a male organ penetrates a human orifice. Thus ancient male representations of female homoeroticism show an obsessive preoccupation with trying to imagine what women could ever possibly do with each other.[38]

Hallet offers this observation,

> Whereas Roman men passed beyond the passive sexual stage during which they
> could be penetrated by another male when they reached their early twenties, Ro-
> man women were to remain in the passive role throughout their adult lives. The
> easiest way to understand women's rejection of the passive sexual role was to
> imagine that they, like the men, had passed on to the next stage, which involved
> "penetrating behavior." [39]

According to these observations, Lucian was working within established
conventions in his treatment of women's sexuality. However, *Dialogue* 5 could
also be an expression of solidarity on Lucian's part. To begin to explore this
interpretation, we need to speculate on Lucian's sexuality. However, it must
be stated at the outset that identifying the sexual identity of a figure from the
past—even the recent past—is a process fraught with the traps and dangers
of anachronism, misperceptions, and misunderstandings of cultural codes.
As discussed earlier, the very category of identity is a problematic one, even
for modern critics. Who defines the identity? Who belongs? Who does not?
For ancient peoples, can we justifiably speak of a category of sexual identity?

Still, even having said that, there seems to be evidence that Lucian was,
at the very least, bisexual. According to Jones, comments made by Lucian in
The Mistaken Critic seem "to suggest that Lucian admitted to the usual taste
for boys." [40] Yet, at the same time, "a weakness for grown males, as opposed
to boys, was a standard charge preferred by Lucian against the 'Mistaken
Critic'." [41] Even with a tentative identification of Lucian as bisexual, this
would not *necessarily* make him sympathetic to women or have any bearing on
his inclusion of a female homoerotic situation in *The Dialogues of the Courtesans.*
However, Lucian's inclusion of such a vignette may indeed indicate some
sympathy on his part.

It is difficult to know how much of an impact Lucian's own bisexuality
had on his creative process. Several interpretations can arise. We could suppose that it might make him more inclined to draw a sympathetic portrayal
of a female homoerotic couple. On the other hand, we can wonder if even a
bisexual man could feel sympathy for women in general in a male-dominated
culture. Another possibility is that Lucian is poking fun at women "imitating" men and so reproducing the misogyny of Greek culture. If bisexuality
was the "sexual norm" for the men of Lucian's time and culture, however,
perhaps it is the monosexuality of Megilla that he is satirizing. She is "married" to a woman; she seeks out a woman as her *hetaira* and reveals no attraction or interest in men. Perhaps Lucian is merely portraying the diversity of

hetaira arrangements. Lucian may well have been attempting to create a dialogue between homoerotic women from a woman's perspective.

In the act of writing of female homoeroticism as a man, bisexual or not, Lucian has crossed a boundary and destabilized an identity. In short, he has created a dialogue within the parameters of pomosexuality. By so doing, he challenged his culture's assumptions about gender and sexuality.

Notes

*This essay is dedicated to all the transgender people who have been killed or who have suffered humiliation or rejection just for being who they are. It is also dedicated with deep appreciation to Leslie Feinberg, Ashley Merriman, Julie Shepherd, and Erin Lydick. Thanks for helping me break through the barrier of dualistic thinking.

1. Many Black feminists, myself included, prefer the word "thought" to theory.

2. Teresa de Lauretis, "Queer Theory: Lesbian and Gay Sexualities: An Introduction," *difference: A Journal of Feminist Cultural Studies* 3 (Summer, 1991).

3. One of the more successful has been Brett Beemyn and Mickey Eliasen, eds., *Queer Studies: A Lesbian, Gay, Bisexual and Transgender Anthology* (New York: New York UP, 1996).

4. Kate Bornstein, "Queer Theory and Shopping: Dichotomy or Symbionts," in *Pomosexuals: Challenging Assumptions about Gender and Sexuality*, ed. Carol Queen and Lawrence Schimel (San Francisco: Cleis P, 1997) 14.

5. Carol Queen and Lawrence Schimel, eds., *Pomosexuals: Challenging Assumptions about Gender and Sexuality* (San Francisco: Cleis P, 1997) 20.

6. Queen and Schimel, *Pomosexuals* 23.

7. Christopher Robinson, *Lucian and His Influence in Europe* (Chapel Hill: U of North Carolina P, 1979) 1.

8. Lucian, *The Double Indictment*.

9. Robinson, *Lucian* 4.

10. Ewen Lyall Bowie, "Second Sophistic," in the *Oxford Classical Dictionary*, 3rd ed. (Oxford: Oxford UP 1996).

11. Bowie, "Second Sophistic" 1377.

12. Robinson, *Lucian* 9.

13. Lucian, *Double Indictment* 28.

14. Barry Baldwin, *Studies in Lucian* (Toronto: Hakkert, 1973) 4.

15. Jacques Bompaire, *Lucien Ecrivain: Imitation et création* (Paris: Belles Lettres, 1958).

16. Robinson, *Lucian* 4.

17. Robinson, *Lucian* 5.

18. Robinson, *Lucian* 11.

19. Pseudo-Demosthenes 59.118–122.

20. Leslie Kurke, *Coins, Bodies, Games, and Gold* (Princeton: Princeton UP, 1999) 178.

21. James Davidson, *Courtesans and Fishcakes: The Consuming Passions of Classical Athens* (New York: HarperCollins, 1997) 109–36.

22. One of the legacies in the Americas of the Spanish and French colonizers was a complicated hierarchy of racial castes. Octoroons were highly prized because they claimed

only an eighth African ("Negro") ancestry; quadroons were next, with a quarter. Oddly, mulatto/as were the most highly prized, even though they had the most African ancestry (i.e., one of their parents, usually the mother, was African). As miscegenation continued, mulatto/as came to stand for any person of mixed (African/European) racial heritage, no matter what the percentages. As late as 1989, Louisiana still had on its books a law validating the "one-drop rule": any trace of Black African heritage made a person Black. Browsing through high school yearbooks from Louisiana schools in the 1940s and 1950s shows that beneath the pictures of students are the fractions of racial heritage.

23. Barbara Hambly, *A Free Man of Color* (New York: Bantam Books, 1997) presents a lucid picture of the world of the *placee*. A *placee* was recognized as the partner of a white man within the separate spheres in which they traveled. For example in Hambly's novel, two balls take place on the same night during Mardi Gras in the same location. White wives were in one room and *placees*—women of color—were in another. The men went back and forth between the two. They apparently believed their wives were naïve—or stupid—enough not to know of the existence of their *placees*.

24. Nancy R. Nangeroni, International Foundation for Gender Education, "Transgenderism" n.d., 27 July 2000 <http://www.altsex.org/transgender/Nangeroni.html>.

25. Philein does have as its first lexical meaning "to love," but I have chosen the secondary meaning "to kiss" for two reasons. First, it more accurately reflects what is happening in the passage, and second, "kiss" ties in more closely with my discussion below of the tongue.

26. According to an alternative tradition, Thetis knew that her son Achilles was fated to die if he went to Troy. She sent him to the court of Lycomedes on the Aegean island of Scyros. He was only nine years old when Calchas, the prophet attached to the Greek forces, announced that Troy could not be taken without the boy's aid. At Thetis' insistence, Lycomedes dressed the boy as a girl and reared him under the name Pyrrha along with his own daughters. The girls must have been in on the secret, for Lycomedes' daughter Deidameia later bore Achilles a son who was named Neoptolemus or Pyrrhus.

27. Teiresias was a Theban seer who as a young man saw two snakes copulating and killed the female. Immediately he found himself transformed into a woman. Several years later, coming upon the same snakes (or another pair), he killed the male snake and returned at once to his masculine form. Not long after, while Zeus and Hera were disputing whether man or woman takes the greater pleasure from the act of sex, it occurred to them to call in Teiresias as an impartial judge, since he was the only man on Earth who could answer the question from first-hand knowledge. The young man said that women experienced nine or ten times more satisfaction. This reply infuriated Hera, who blinded Teiresias on the spot. Zeus, on the other hand, rewarded him with the gift of prophecy and gave him long life as well.

28. For an example of the latest trend in queer Queers, see Jill Nagle, "Girl-FAG!" *Curve* (January 1999): 30–31.

29. See the epigraph at the beginning of this essay.

30. Elizabeth Lapovsky Kennedy and Madeline Davis, eds., *Boots of Leather, Slippers of Gold: The History of a Lesbian Community* (New York: Routledge, 1993) 152.

31. Very little is known of Alciphron's life. His literary relationship to Lucian is contentious, and his dates are based on common references to historical figures found in his literary "Letters" and those of Aelian.

32. Bernadette Brooten, *Love between Women: Early Christian Responses to Female Homoeroticism* (Chicago: U of Chicago P, 1996) 53.

33. Brooten, *Love between Women* 53–54.

34. One of the striking factors about Queen and Schimel's modern collection of erotic writing, *Switch Hitters*, is how authentically lesbians can write gay male erotica and vice versa. This adds a new layer to the depth of queerness and clearly led to the work of these authors around pomosexuality.

35. I do not subscribe to the notion that because Lucian was writing in the second century of the common era, he could NOT have written out of a "postmodern" sensibility. As Alice Walker has said, the idea that we moderns are more advanced in our theoretical processes than the ancients is "trash": Alice Walker, *My Life as Myself*, audiocassette, Sounds True Recordings, 1995.

36. Judith P. Hallett, "Female Homoeroticism and the Denial of Roman Reality in Latin Literature," *Yale Journal of Criticism* 3 (1989): 210. Phaedrus quoted from *Fable* 4.15.

37. Brooten, *Love between Women* 52.

38. Brooten, *Love between Women* 154.

39. Hallett, "Female Homoeroticism" 226–227n29.

40. C. P. Jones, *Culture and Society in Lucian* (Cambridge, MA: Harvard UP, 1986) 109n38, 111.

41. Jones, *Culture* 109.

CHAPTER TEN

"FRIENDSHIP AND PHYSICAL DESIRE"

The Discourse of Female Homoeroticism in Fifth-Century CE Egypt*

Terry G. Wilfong

 Taêse and Tsansnô, two women living in the White Monastery in Southern Egypt sometime in the fifth century CE, were sentenced to beatings by Shenute, their monastic superior, for engaging in homoerotic activity. Shenute ordered the punishment of these women (and provided a justification for it) in a letter to the women of his monastic community. He described Taêse and Tsansnô as "running after" other women in "friendship and physical desire." Although Shenute's letter, with its specific listing of individual women to be punished for homoerotic activity, is unique in many ways, his language and attitude are typical of contemporary Coptic monastic writing on the subject.

Shenute's letter provides an entry point into the discourse of female homoeroticism in the work of Late Antique Egyptian writers—a discourse shaped by the attitudes and concerns of the (male) heads of the monastic communities in which women lived. Other contemporaneous authors used this discourse to describe—and condemn—homoerotic activity between women. Moreover, their writings described recognizable groups of individuals within the monastic communities who engaged in homoerotic activity. This evidence from Egypt is of considerable relevance to the more general study of sexuality in antiquity. These Late Antique Egyptian sources not only provide a different set of data and a different perspective on the subject, but they also offer evidence of a sort unparalleled for much of the ancient world.

LATE ANTIQUE EGYPT
AND THE MONASTIC BACKGROUND

Life in Late Antique Egypt was the product of a variety of cultural, political, and religious influences, both internal and external.[1] By the end of the fourth century CE, the majority of Egyptians could be called Christians of some kind, although the sectarian and doctrinal divisions were such that there was no single, unitary Christianity in Egypt. Pagan cults were not yet gone from the scene, but they were entering their final phases of active worship. Greek was the language of administration in Egypt at this time and was also the language of business and culture for a significant portion of the population. The indigenous Egyptian language was known as Coptic, the final phase of ancient Egyptian, written in an alphabet based on Greek and Demotic Egyptian characters, using both Egyptian and Greek vocabulary.[2] Coptic served as a language of everyday life for much of Egypt's population and had come into its own as a vehicle for literary expression (largely through the Coptic translation of the New Testament). Many Egyptians of this period were bilingual, although the full extent of Coptic/Greek bilingualism in this period remains uncertain. The great majority of the sources relevant for the present essay were written in Coptic, which means that they were intended for an audience in Egypt, as opposed to Greek works written in Egypt that could be understood by a wider Mediterranean audience.

Evidence for the discourse of female homoeroticism in Late Antique Egypt comes largely from monastic contexts, not surprising considering the predominantly homosocial environments of the monasteries and their importance in shaping general discourse in this period. While most monasteries were self-contained and often self-sufficient units, such establishments were also part of larger regional communities. Monasteries were integral elements of local economies, and the heads of monasteries often exerted considerable influence with local authorities through their control of monastic landholdings and production. Monastic superiors were often important spiritual leaders outside the monastery, while monitoring and commenting on the activities and morals of the nearby secular population. Monasteries were also important cultural centers in Late Antique Egypt not just for their inhabitants but also for the nearby towns and villages. Production and distribution of books and the teaching of both Coptic and Greek often centered on monasteries, which resulted in a significant monastic influence on both language and literature. Through these interconnected spheres of influence, monastic leaders were in a unique position to shape discourse outside their community walls as well as within them. The monastic origin of nearly all the evidence relating to female homoeroticism does not, therefore, imply that these sources were exceptional but rather suggests that the discourse of this evidence would have been typical even outside the monasteries.

The most extensive Late Antique Egyptian evidence relating to female homoeroticism comes from two religious communities: the Pachomian

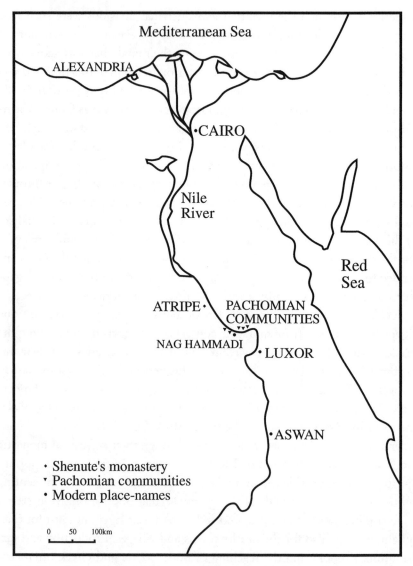

Mediterranean Sea

ALEXANDRIA

•CAIRO

Nile
River

Red
Sea

ATRIPE •

PACHOMIAN
COMMUNITIES

NAG HAMMADI

•LUXOR

•ASWAN

• Shenute's monastery
ᵛ Pachomian communities
• Modern place-names

0   50   100km

10.1. Map of Egypt showing the location of Shenutean and Pachomian monastic communities. Map by author.

monasteries and the monastery of Shenute and his successors, both in southern Egypt just above the bend of the Nile (see map, fig. 10.1). The concentration of relevant sources on these two points of origin is due to both their leaders' extraordinary literary output and their specific involvement with women's monasticism. Women are attested as monastics in Egypt as early as monasticism itself: a number of women who lived as ascetics and hermits are known from the third and fourth centuries CE.[3] Pachomius, the originator of community-based monasticism and author of the earliest known rule for monastic behavior, is credited with founding the first women's monastic community for his sister Maria near his own monastery in Tabennisi in the mid fourth century.[4] Pachomius later founded a second women's community nearby, initially supervised by a man but later placed under the direct authority of an elder woman, known as the "old woman" or the "mother." Pachomius did not write a separate rule for women but placed them under the same rule as that of the men in his own monastery.[5] In addition to devotional exercises, this rule prescribed manual work and obedience for the monastic population. Pachomius' successors Theodore and Horsiesios carried on the Pachomian tradition of supervising women's communities.

Probably the best-known women's community of this period was at the White Monastery, home of the famous author and abbot Shenute and his successor Besa, at ancient Atripe near modern Sohag.[6] A Coptic biography of Shenute claims that the women in the community totaled 1,800, compared to 2,400 men—clearly a very substantial population. Shenute's tenure as head of the White Monastery is well documented because of his extensive literary output of Coptic sermons, letters, and related compositions, organized into a series of "canons" and "discourses" that survive in varying degrees of completeness and remain only partly published.[7] Shenute's work is noted not only for its subject matter but also for its highly complex and involved style; he was one of the earliest Egyptian writers to explore the literary and stylistic possibilities of Coptic.

A substantial amount of Shenute's writing directly concerns the women under his authority and is a valuable source for women's monasticism in Late Antiquity. Shenute's successor Besa wrote a much less extensive series of letters that in their negative tone seem to be characteristic of contemporary attitudes to female monastics. In general, women's religious communities from the fifth century onward were often regarded as sources of potential trouble that required constant supervision, and Besa's letters give evidence of this attitude. The roots of these negative perceptions of women's communities, though, are already found in the Pachomian and Shenutean writings, with their emphasis on regulation and control of women's behavior.

Within Pachomian and Shenutean monasteries, men and women were kept separate from each other, in terms of both administration and physical space.[8] However, men and women were under the same rule and parallel administrative hierarchies. Ultimate authority resided at the top in the (male) heads of the monasteries: Pachomius, Shenute, and their successors. Although their authority did not go unchallenged, these leaders had a crucial advantage in that they not only made and enforced the rules but also shaped the entire discourse under which the inhabitants of the community operated. The heads of monasteries were the arbiters of daily life in the monastery and also of the spiritual life and ultimate salvation of the community members. Although the monks were exposed to other systems of thought and expression through their premonastic experiences, their readings of scripture, and their interaction with the outside world, these were interpreted by and filtered through the words of the leaders by means of their teachings. In a sense, Pachomius, Shenute, and their successors dictated the discursive universe of the members of their communities and, in doing so, shaped their possibilities for action and interaction. The leaders' control of the discourse of the lives of their communities can be seen in how they treated homoerotic relations between women.

THE TEXT

The discourse of female homoeroticism prevalent in these monastic communities can be best introduced through a composition by Shenute preserved in the Bibliothèque Nationale in Paris; it was once part of White Monastery codex BZ containing Canon 4 of the Shenutean corpus, as identified by Stephen Emmel. The beginning of the composition is missing and there are gaps throughout, but the surviving portions show it to be a letter addressed to the women's community about the monastic life, specifically, how it is to be lived and how infractions against rules are to be handled.[9] Shenute first discussed the importance of, and rationale behind, his punishments. After a gap of four missing pages, Shenute passed from the theory of punishment to some specific cases (the sections of special relevance to the following discussion are highlighted in italics):[10]

> And I know the punishment that should be given to all of you, in place of what you did among yourselves not because you are lacking in your fasting, your prayers, your meditation and your zeal, evening and morning, all day and all

10.2. Record of punishment of women for homoerotic activity: Canon 4 of Shenute from White Monastery Coptic Codex BZ, p 347 (= Bibliothèque Nationale 130.1, 140 recto). Drawing after Young, *Coptic Manuscripts*, pl. 40. Case of Taese occupies lines 12–27 of the left column.

night but instead because you are not perfect in the truth with yourselves, like me also. Because of this, may god forgive you so that he may forgive me also. However:

Thensnoe, daughter of Apa Hermêf. This one, concerning whom you sent to us before, saying, "She has committed iniquities through wicked manners," and also, "She has stolen." Thirty blows of the stick.

The sister of Apa Psyros. This one, concerning whom you sent to us before, saying, "She has stolen some things." Twenty blows of the stick.

Tsophia, sister of Hllo the younger. This one, concerning whom you sent to us, saying, "She talks back and argues hardheartedly with those who teach her and with many (others) for no reason," and also, "She has struck the face of the female Elder or hit her on the head." Twenty blows of the stick.

Tsh(e)nbiktôr, sister of John the younger. This one, concerning whom you sent to us, saying, "She is deficient in wisdom and understanding." Fifteen blows of the stick.

Taêse, the sister of Pshai the younger. This one, concerning whom you sent to us, saying, "She runs after Tsansnô in friendship and physical desire." Fifteen blows of the stick.

Takous, who is called Rebecca. This one, whose mouth has learned to speak with lies and emptiness. Twenty-five blows of the stick.

Tsophia, sister of Zacharia. Ten blows of the stick; and I know for what matter they shall be given to her.

And Tapolle, her sister. It was fitting that they (the beatings) also be given to her, but because of god and the anxiety that is upon her, we forgive her on this occasion, either because of that disturbance or because of the garment that she wove herself in covetousness—this (garment) that we cut down the middle and sent south to you. I have set her at ease only because I know that she cannot bear it, for it (the garment)[11] is thick and very wide. And if you are wise, you are able to know that width and thickness.

Tsophia, sister of Joseph. Fifteen blows of the stick; and I know for what matter they shall be given to her.

Tsansnô, sister of Apa Hllo. This one, who says, "It is others whom I teach." Forty blows of the stick, because sometimes she ran after her neighbor in friendship, and sometimes she lied about empty things that will perish, so that she forfeit her own soul. This one, of whom the whole world is not worthy, much less a plate or a bowl and cup; (yet) she lies about them.

(As for) all these (beatings), the male Elder shall administer them with his own hands on the bottoms of their feet, while they are sitting down on the ground, while the female Elder and Takhôm, with other senior women, hold them down for him, and while the other Elders who are there with them helping him hold (them) down with rods over their feet for him, until he has finished disciplining them, as we have also done to some in the past.

Shenute went on to discuss further disciplinary issues and the importance of reporting others who should be punished. The manuscript breaks off shortly thereafter.

Summary of the Text

To sum up the relevant portions of this text: A woman named Taêse was accused of running after[12] a woman named Tsansnô "in friendship and physical desire." A woman named Tsansnô (and the name is uncommon enough that it is likely to be the same person)[13] was accused of running after her neighbors (understood to be women with cells near hers in the monastery) in "friendship." She was also quoted as saying, "It is others whom I teach" and described as being proud and lying about small objects—a plate, a bowl, a cup (perhaps things that she has stolen?). Other named women in this group were charged with lying, stealing, insubordination, and even assault; two charges were not articulated, but Shenute said that he knew why the punishments were to be administered. In many cases, as the text confirms, the charges were based on information supplied by the other women in the community; Shenute stressed in many writings that community members should not cover up for the infractions of others but should instead report them.

The punishment prescribed for Taêse and Tsansnô is comparable to that set for the other women accused of lying, stealing, and so on. Tsansnô's punishment was greater than that of Taêse, but she was also accused of more. Shenute attributed to Tsansnô the unparalleled statement, "It is others whom I teach," using a special grammatical feature of Coptic (the "second tense") to focus the sentence on the "others," namely, the women Tsansnô was teaching. The quotation is followed by the charges of pride and lying, and the pride in particular emphasizes the point of the quote: that she, Tsansnô, was teaching others in the monastery. Shenute emphasized in other writings that he was to be directing the teaching and that it was unacceptable for women to teach of their own accord. The authority of teaching was to be with men, specifically with Shenute, and Tsansnô's defiance seems to have exacerbated his ire. The punishment of the women was to be administered by the male Elder, who was to beat the women on the feet with a stick, while the female Elder and a senior woman named Takhôm[14] were to hold them down, and other women to hold down their feet with more sticks. The beating of feet was a traditionally Egyptian punishment found in Pharaonic sources, intended to be a painful and long-lasting reminder to those punished.[15]

THE LANGUAGE

Although this listing of punishments for named women involved in homoerotic activity is unique in Coptic literature,[16] its language is entirely consistent with the usage in other writings of Shenute and the works of the Pachomian writers. The terminology for the "physical desire" with which Taêse ran after Tsansnô is relatively simple. The "desire" here is a very common Coptic word (*ouôsh*). The range of things that can be objects of this "desire" is wide; but the qualification of the desire as "physical, fleshly, carnal" (*-nsarkikos*) narrows the range of possibilities considerably. Although one could experience physical desire for food or drink, for example, physical desire directed at another person in Coptic is erotic, though not necessarily genital-sexual. The phrase occurs elsewhere in Shenute's writing in similar contexts and with the same meaning; Shenute also used a related and synonymous phrase *ouôsh nsarks*. In another letter of Shenute to the women in the community, he wrote "about the young women, concerning whom we have heard that they will run after each other in physical desire."[17] Shenute also accused women of showing favoritism toward other women for whom they felt physical desire in such matters as the distribution of food.[18] Although the mechanics of such physical desire (and its fulfillment) were not explicitly articulated in monastic texts such as the writings of Shenute, Coptic magical texts could be quite direct about the flesh (*sarks*) and its desires, and this term and derivatives (like *sarkikos*) appear frequently in sexual spells.[19] From both the meaning of the phrase and the context in which it appears, the "physical desire" of one woman for another represents at least homoerotic desire, if not fulfilled homoerotic activity.

Taêse also ran after Tsansnô in "friendship," and Tsansnô herself was described as running after other (unspecified) women in "friendship" as well. "Friendship" appears in other instances in Shenute's writing (accompanied by "physical desire" or not), and in roughly contemporary compositions of monastic origin, to describe the behavior of women (and men) in such a way to make it obvious that some sort of homoerotic activity or desire is involved. Such an understanding of "friendship" in a monastic milieu is clearly articulated by the monastic authorities themselves and reinforced by a close examination of the evidence for the meaning of the Coptic term for "friendship."

"Friendship" in Coptic

In Coptic, the word translated as "friendship" is the prefix of abstraction (*mnt-*) added to the noun "friend" (*shbêr*).[20] It is used, in the Coptic version of the New Testament, to translate Greek *philein*. In discussing friendship in the ancient world, scholars have tended to assume that its characteristics have remained constant and unchanging throughout history. The recent work by David Konstan[21] (among others) has gone a long way toward reassessing the meaning of "friendship" in the ancient world: how such relationships tended to be asymmetrical relations between individuals of differing status covering a wide range of situations, many of which bear little relation to modern ideas of friendship. Little attention has been paid to the dynamics and parameters of "friendship" in Coptic. In Coptic, friendship existed between individuals of the same sex, mostly men, who were not closely related. There was usually not much age difference but sometimes an inequality of status between friends, although not always a great disparity. In a secular context, friendship was seen as a virtue, and the neglect of a friendship was a matter of reproach.[22]

Shenute himself wrote of friendship outside the monastery and of friendship in a metaphorical sense without disapproval.[23] Between members of a monastic community, however, "friendship" is seen in a predominantly negative light. In part, this could be explained by seeing it as a relationship that interferes with a person's relations with god. This is certainly true in many Christian monastic traditions, although within certain parameters, friendship is sometimes considered desirable.[24] However, the terminology of friendship is most often used euphemistically in Coptic sources to describe homoerotic relations between monastics, and this is also found in eastern and western Christian monastic sources in a number of traditions, from Late Antiquity through the Middle Ages and even into the present.[25] Given the indebtedness of monasticism, ancient and modern, eastern and western, to Egyptian monastic traditions, the persistence of this terminology is not surprising. Although there are many centuries and great cultural differences separating Shenute's use of the term "friendship" and modern uses of terms like "particular friendships" to denote lesbian relations, either potential or realized,[26] there are clear connections across time. In Egyptian monastic sources in Coptic, "friendship" between monastics almost always had very specific connotations of homoerotic relations, which were vigorously condemned.

HORSIESIOS ON "FRIENDSHIP"

The most extensive statement on the subject appears in an instruction of Horsiesios, who was the head of the Pachomian monasteries in the late fourth and early fifth centuries—a contemporary and near neighbor of She-nute. The work in question is the seventh instruction in a series by Horsiesios,[27] addressed to the inhabitants of the Pachomian community: the work is entitled:

> These are the teachings that our holy father Apa Horsiesios delivered on the things about which his heart was pained, and concerning this matter, that is, friendship.

Horsiesios began by attacking friendship and anticipating possible objections to his argument, noting that he was including friendship between women. Further, he provided examples of the kind of friendship he is condemning.

> O wicked friendship, this thing that is hated by god and his angels! O vile laughter, whose sweetness is bitter! O, you are cursed, friendship, concerning which I speak and which the wrath of god will pursue! O wicked friendship! Its laughter has also destroyed many exceedingly great ones, whether priests, or superiors of men, or superiors of women, who prided themselves in their glorious monastic habit and the word of their mouth! I invoke god for you, my brother, that you remove yourself from evil friendship. But perhaps you will answer and say, "By this you are teaching me enmity." But no; rather, be at peace with your neighbor, because of god and the commandment. But, instead you anxiously glance this way and that, you watch until you have found the opportune moment, then you give him what is (hidden) under the hem of your garment, so that god himself, and his Christ Jesus, will pour out the wrath of his anger on you and on him. At (that) time, there will be no way for you to turn this way and that. Or truly, foolish one, if there was no shame in your friendship, then why are you ashamed and afraid to talk with him openly?

Horsiesios went on to condemn monks for leading others into this friendship. There are breaks in the text of uncertain length. At one point, Horsiesios furnished an extraordinary description of the behavior and appearance of these friends, describing them as if they are a recognizable and, to some extent, self-identified group within the monastery:

But listen to me! I shall create an enmity and a division between your friendship and his. Now, some from your (circle of) friendship go out with their faces shaved,[28] wearing veils around their faces and throwing on a black thing over their eyes with the excuse of illness. They tie multitudes of rings to their hand-kerchiefs and fringes come down behind them from their belt, like calves jumping around in an enclosure. They often strip naked while washing when they do not need to. Light sandals on their feet—"She went out taking pride in the desire of her soul"[29]—they clatter with their feet in the midst of the assembly. They greet their friend with high laughter, like the sound of thorn branches burning under the cauldron. They make window niches (for themselves). They take on the habits of crows and vultures out in nature for themselves, bringing away for themselves from their food dead meat and spoiled game. They fill their window niches with every transgression: the words of the prophet[30]—"Death has entered through your windows"—are fulfilled in them. Moreover, on some occasions, warning is given that the superior is coming to examine the window niches, where the abominations of Israel are located. Then they run in confusion to take them away from the window niches, burying them in the ground or casting them out right away, and then ask the men to come in so that they (the friends) might receive favor for themselves.

This passage situates the activities of the friends within the physical environment of the monastery; the references to window niches refer to the common practice of using niches below windows for storage of books and personal possessions. Horsiesios seems to be condemning the friends' accumulation of possessions, perhaps as a result of the secret exchanges of gifts described earlier. Horsiesios continued about the wickedness of friendship and how monks who do not prevent this are culpable too. He went on to outline briefly the only acceptable form of "friendship" in his eyes, which was that of a spiritual brotherhood, clearly not what is meant by "friendship" in the Shenute text involving Taêse and Tsansnô. There are gaps in the text, and the composition breaks off before its end, so we cannot be completely sure of the full range of his condemnations. It is likely that Horsiesios ended his text with a return to his argument that spiritual brotherhood was preferable to friendship as practiced by the monks he had described.

Shenute on "Friendship"

The equation between a particular kind of "friendship" and homoerotic relations in a monastic environment is clear from Horsiesios' instruction.

Such terminology is not limited to this author; Shenute in particular used the term frequently in this sense, sometimes (as in the list of punishments) without additional modifiers, sometimes qualified as "physical" or "carnal" (*mntshbêr nsarkikos*, as in the example translated below). Shenute wrote of such friendships and of the importance of reporting to him about people involved in them, a theme also found in Horsiesios' instruction:

> Woe to you who run after (your) neighbors among us with physical desires, and woe to you who are friends to (your) neighbors in blasphemy, gossip, and every wickedness. . . . Those among us, whether man or woman, who shall run after their neighbor in fleshly desire (*ouôsh nsarks*) and carnal friendship (*mntshbêr nsarkikos*), they shall be called by the prophet "the originators of uncleanness and pollution and every wicked deed," according to the way it is written: "She is the origin of sin, the daughter of Zion, because the wickedness of Israel was found in you." [31] And as for those among us, whether man or woman, who will be caught being friends to their neighbor in physical desire, they will be cursed in all their deeds that they do. (But), if they are in ignorance, they shall be free from all the curses that are written down. As for those among us, whether man or woman, who will hide (literally, cover) people who are friends to one another in physical desire, they will be cursed in all their deeds. (But), if they are in ignorance, they shall be free from all the curses that are written down. [32]

Shenute made a significant distinction in this passage between those who engage in homoerotic activity knowingly and those who do so in ignorance, the latter being excused from his disapprobation. This distinction fits well with Horsiesios' depiction of the monks involved in homoerotic relationships as being identifiable and, to some extent, forming self-conscious groups.

Not being content with relying on the force of his own threats, Shenute even set up a whole system whereby individuals could and should report their knowledge of incidents of "friendship and physical desire." He spent much effort justifying the network of spying and reporting that he had set up, in an attempt to convince the inhabitants of his community that it was their duty to god to report such goings on. Shenute specifically singled out for blame those who failed to report any of these friends. It is likely that Shenute relied on this system of internal informants for much of his data, so that Taêse and Tsansnô, and the other women cited in the list, were probably reported to Shenute by their sister monastics.

Female Homoerotic Activity
in the Writings of Shenute

The cases of Taêse and Tsansnô, and the other references to women involved in "friendship" and "physical desire," are unmistakably accusations of female homoerotic activity of some sort. It is clear that inhabitants of the White Monastery were expected to be on the lookout not only for what is explicitly described as friendship and physical desire but also for other activity that was taken as an indication of a homoerotic relationship; certainly, the discourse for discussing female homoerotic activity in Shenute's writings was not limited to the language of "physical desire" and "friendship." Both Bernadette Brooten and Michael Foat have pointed out instances of physical contact with sexual intent in Shenute's writing: the condemnation of touching or groping between monastics sleeping on the same mat or between older and younger monastics:[33]

> Cursed is a woman among us who will run after younger women, and anoint them and is filled with a passion or is [...] them in a passion of desire and slothfulness and laughter and vain error....[34]

> As for those among us (the men) or among you (the women) who will touch younger men or younger women (respectively), either while they are asleep or while they are awake, and those who will touch them that they might ascertain that they have reached adulthood, they shall be cursed, whether man or woman.[35]

However, the interpretation of these texts as references to sexual contact between adults and children is misleading; the phrase Brooten and Foat give as "young girl" (*sheere shêm*) is also used for a younger monastic, or one inferior in rank, and is unlikely to refer to actual children in this context. One also finds warnings against touching between monastics of apparently same rank, age, or status:

> Those, also, who will sleep, two on a mat, or those who will come too close so that they might touch or feel each other only in a passion of desire—they shall be cursed, whether man or woman.... Those, also, who will rise from their sleeping place, and approach the sleeping place of their neighbors so that they might, with a passion of desire, grope their neighbor while they sleep and do not know it, or, knowing (what is happening) they are patient with each other, saying [....[36]

Contrary to what Brooten suggests, these passages are not warnings against any kind of sexual contact with either males or females; the segregation by sex within the monastic community would make opposite-sex contact a much more "serious" offense, for which the same-sex sleeping quarters would not have afforded opportunity. Instead, Shenute was specifically prohibiting both male and female homoerotic activity. He repeatedly used phrases like "whether man or woman" in discussing punishable actions; this was not, however, in reference to the possibility of erotic relations with either sex but was instead making it clear that both men and women were capable of (and to be punished for) homoerotic acts.

FEMALE HOMOEROTICISM IN OTHER COPTIC SOURCES

Shenute's treatment was entirely consistent with the language found in Pachomian writings as well. Indeed, Pachomius' rules clearly indicate anxiety on the part of the monastic authorities to prevent the occasions for homoerotic activity within their domains. Pachomius, Shenute, and their successors stressed the importance of physical separation of monastics[37] to prevent physical contact between the monks, which was clearly envisioned as at least having the potential to lead to homoerotic activity. Thus, in his monastic rule, Pachomius made the following instructions:

> [94.] No one shall speak with his neighbors in the dark. [95.] You shall not sit, two together, on a mat or carpet. A man shall not grasp the hand of his friend, or any other part of him, but instead, whether sitting, or standing, or walking, you shall leave an arm's length between you and him. [96.] Nor shall anyone remove a thorn from a man's foot, except the housemaster or the second-in-command or one who is ordered. [97.] No man shall shave his head without his housemaster('s approval); nor shall a man shave another without being ordered; nor also shall a man shave another man while they are both seated.[38]

This separation was not limited to sleeping quarters but also affected the monks in the course of their work, as seen in a rule designed to keep men from touching each other found in the midst of regulations relating to agricultural work: "[109]. Two men shall not ride a bare-backed donkey or a wagon-shaft together."[39] In such cases, Pachomius did not specifically address homoerotic activity but instead sought to limit its possibility by not allowing his monks to touch at all. Although not explicitly directed to the women of his community, Pachomius' regulations applied to both the men and women.[40] These passages from Pachomius' rules, incidentally, give some clues as to the kind of homoerotic activity that the monastic authorities were trying to prevent, although much less explicitly than the writings of Shenute. Clearly, touching, manual stimulation, and the rubbing of bodies were what Pachomius had in mind; he may have known of other forms of homoerotic contact but was not willing even to give a hint of this. Shenute was slightly more specific about the kinds of touching to be condemned and informed upon than Pachomius, as seen in the passages discussed earlier, and it may be that these kinds of activities were why Taêse and Tsansnô were to be punished.

Shenute's successor at the White Monastery, Besa, addressed homoerotic relations between women in a few passages but was less explicit about the matter than Shenute, making only allusions to desires of the flesh (*sarks*) and women corrupting each other with costly gifts.[41] Other references to female homoeroticism in Coptic literature rely more on general biblical language than the specialized monastic language for such actions, perhaps because they seem to be addressed to the wider population rather than an exclusively monastic audience. An otherwise unidentified author known to scholars as pseudo-Shenute provides a very typical example, drawn from the language of the New Testament:

> Some useless women, having left behind the natural use of their husbands— these whom god granted to them that they be in a worthy marriage—they burn in their wicked desire for one another doing shamefulness. Unclean and miserable women, shamelessly they fulfill the abominable business with each other. They are repaid the wages of their error in themselves.[42]

This passage followed a condemnation of men who engage in homoerotic activity in very similar terms.

Other Coptic sources exist that suggest homoerotic activity between women to a modern reader, but it is difficult to know if this was the original intent. A good example of such ambiguity is the Coptic story of Hilaria, one of two legendary daughters of the Byzantine emperor Zeno.[43] In this account, Hilaria left Constantinople and disguised herself as a man to live as a monk in Egypt. After a period of solitary asceticism, Hilaria was accepted into a men's monastic community as a eunuch (because of her beardless state) named Hilarion. Meanwhile, emperor Zeno's other daughter became possessed by demons, and he sent her to the very monastery where Hilaria/Hilarion was living to be healed. Upon her return to Constantinople, emperor Zeno was concerned to hear that his daughter had been cured by an ascetic monk named Hilarion, who had kissed her on the mouth and slept with her. He sent for the monk and demanded an explanation, whereupon all was revealed. The vivid scene of Hilaria disguised as a man embracing and kissing her unknowing sister is highly evocative to a modern reader but may not have had the same overtones for its ancient audience: Zeno was clearly upset at the idea of his daughter having spent the night with what he thought was a *male* monk. Identifiable instances of homoerotic activity were, in general, mentioned in much different terms, as we have seen above.

THE DISCOURSE OF HOMOEROTIC ACTIVITY IN MONASTIC SETTINGS

The discourse of homoerotic activity in Late Antique Egypt was shaped by the monastic authorities opposed to it, on the grounds that it was inimical to their spiritual well-being. All the writings of Pachomius, Horsiesios, Shenute, Besa, and other monastic authorities relating to homoerotic activity explicitly described such activities as a threat to the spiritual life of the individuals who engaged in them and, ultimately, as a very real threat to their salvation. But it was also a matter of power. As Rebecca Krawiec notes, "Shenute's control of the discourse of sexuality . . . was the basis for the power structure of the monastery, a structure that existed to exercise authority as a means of guiding its members to salvation."[44] The underlying theme implicit in the monastic leaders' writings was that homoerotic activity was a threat to their authority, an infraction of discipline and order that if engaged in knowingly, amounted to disobedience and a direct challenge to the head of the monastery.

Their control of the discourse of sexuality enabled them to limit the contexts and the ways in which sexual activity could be addressed within the monastery. These limits ultimately were intended to restrict the possibilities of action on the part of the individuals under control of the monastic heads. The "friends" of Horsiesios and Shenute were not permitted the discursive space in which to advocate their "friendship." In all cases, the viewpoints presented by Pachomius, Shenute, and their successors are clearly their own; they had nothing to gain by presenting the point of view of the "friends" in their monasteries and did not do so.

We have very little evidence of the attitudes of those who were involved in homoerotic relations themselves, whether male or female. Horsiesios (admittedly a hostile source) suggested that both men and women who engaged in homoerotic activity referred to their behavior as "friendship" and formed recognizable groups of such friends, with their own set of signals and space within the monastery. Horsiesios gives a clear impression of these "friends" as a self-identified group of individuals who engage in homoerotic activity.

He does not, however, provide this information about the clothing, mannerisms, and actions of the "friends" simply to describe such groups; Horsiesios goes into detail as a warning to the other monks on how to recognize the groups of friends so as to avoid them. These friends may call themselves "friends" and refer to their "friendship," but otherwise Horsiesios does not allow them to speak. Shenute's exemption from punishment of "friends" who are not aware of what they are doing suggests that he felt that those he did punish had some sort of self-consciousness of themselves as "friends." It is tempting to read the quotation Shenute attributed to Tsansnô, "It is others whom I teach," in the context of notions of "friends" leading others into "friendship" found in Horsiesios. This statement could be not only Tsansnô's defiance of Shenute's right to be sole teacher but also a statement of her "teaching others" about friendship and physical desire. This is, however, far from certain. Apart from the reported instances of monastics calling themselves "friends," self-identification by men or women engaging in homoerotic activity is not found in these monastic writings.

Homoerotic Activity in Other Coptic Sources

Indeed, articulation of any kind of homoerotic desire in Late Antique Egypt is rare.[45] As I have discussed elsewhere, there are scenes in the Coptic stories of certain male martyrs in which a pagan governor makes veiled sexual advances on a martyr-to-be, complimenting his body and suggesting that his punishment could be lessened by acceding to the governor's otherwise unexpressed desires.[46] These scenes, however, use the discourse of homoerotic desire for rhetorical purposes; they come from writers clearly hostile to the idea who used it to reinforce the portrait of a depraved pagan governor.

Self-expression of homoerotic desire in Coptic sources is known or, perhaps more accurately, recognized only in a single magical text now in the Ashmolean Museum, perhaps from the sixth century.[47] In this document, a man named Papapolo sought to enchant a man named Phello. Papapolo wanted Phello to be given no rest and to seek after him "until he comes to me and subjects himself beneath my feet . . . until I fulfill with him my heart's desire and the longing of my soul."[48] The sexual desire of one man for another here is not expressed in exceptional terminology. Although the original editor of the text noted that the "embarrassing identity of the sex of charmer and charmed probably renders this spell unique in Coptic magical literature," in fact the language of the text is typical of Coptic spells to compel desire between men and women. Other Coptic magical texts allude to the possibility of homosexual activity but typically in the presentation of

a range of potential sexual activity. A Coptic magical text in the Oriental Institute Museum in Chicago, for example, is a spell to make a man named
Pharaouô impotent and unable to have sex with a woman named Touaein
or "any other woman, man, or beast." [49] In this case, homoerotic activity is
invoked in a range of sexual possibility, but there is no specific term (such
as "friend") used to describe individuals involved in homoerotic relations.

There was a specific term in Coptic for individuals who engaged in
homoerotic activity, but it was used only for men and is unparalleled for
women. The compound word *refnkotkmnnhoout* was used in literary texts with
reference to men involved in homoerotic acts. Broken down, the components of this compound reveal its literal meaning: *ref-* (prefix for personal
characteristics "man who regularly [does something]") *-nkotk mn-* ("sleeps
with" [in Coptic, as in English, often euphemistic for "has sex with"])
-nhoout ("males").[50] Thus a literal rendering of the term would be "man-who-
sleeps-with-males." [51] This term first appeared in the Coptic translation of
the Greek New Testament, where it is used to render Greek *arsenokoites*—a
term of some ambiguity—in a list including prostitutes, idolaters, adulterers, effeminate men, and slanderers (cf. I Cor. 6:9–10, I Tim. 1:10). Shenute
himself sometimes used this term in contexts obviously intended to evoke
the biblical lists,[52] but the majority of the contexts in which *refnkotkmnnhoout*
appears in Coptic make it clear that the term should be taken at its literal
meaning. In one case, Shenute mentioned the *refnkotkmnnhoout* in conjunction
with the Greek term *malakos*, usually translated "effeminate man" or something similar.[53] In discussing this text, Heike Behlmer has suggested that the
refnkotkmnnhoout was the "active" partner and the *malakos*, the "passive." [54]

A similar distinction between the *refnkotkmnnhoout* and another category of
individual engaging in homoerotic activity is found in the Gnostic composition *Pistis Sophia*, which uses a slightly different variation on the term (*rôme
nrefnkotkmnnhoout*; literally, "man of man-who-sleeps-with-males") in describing the punishment to be meted out to "the man-who-sleeps-with-males
and the man with whom he sleeps." [55] A fragmentary sermon or letter, once
thought to be by Shenute but now attributed to John the Archimandrite,[56]
addressed the *refnkotkmnnhoout* directly as a group: "O men-who-sleep-with-
males! You became one with the devil with wantonness that is not fitting for
you. . . ." Further, the author used an abstract formed from this compound
noun (*t-mnt-refnkotkmnnhoout*) to describe the reason that fire came down
on the men of Sodom and Gomorrah: "It burned them because of men-
sleeping-with-males" (literally, "because of the-state/condition-of-men-
who-sleep-with-males"). All the instances of these terms are applied gener-

ally and usually in a proscriptive context; they do not occur in reference to specific individuals and, perhaps significantly for the present discussion, are not applied within monastic contexts. With reference to the discourse of female homoeroticism, it is relevant to note that although theoretically a comparable compound word for "woman-who-sleeps-with-women" might be possible in Coptic, none is known to exist.

The lack of a specific term for women who engage in homoerotic activity is not surprising, given the general asymmetry of terminology for male and female homoeroticism that has been remarked on in a number of premodern cultures.[57] But there may also be a more specific reason for the absence of such a term in Coptic. The term *refnkotkmnnhoout* does not appear to exist in earlier phases of the Egyptian language and seems to have been coined by the early Coptic translators of the New Testament to render what they understood the Greek term *arsenokoites* to mean. But there was no parallel term for women in the New Testament to be translated and thus no need to be specific. The very absence of a word for women in homoerotic relations in Coptic allowed the monastic writers to shape the terminology themselves. "Friendship and physical desire," in the end, covered nearly all the activities and relationships that Shenute, Pachomius, Horsiesios, and the other monastic leaders would permit to exist within the discursive world of their communities. Our knowledge of the interactions of Taêse and Tsansnô with each other and with other women is ultimately circumscribed by the limits of Shenute's discourse. Within these limits, we can find some clues as to what the women might have been doing with each other: the passages cited above suggest strongly that the women manually stimulated each other and rubbed their bodies together. But whatever took place between Taêse, Tsansnô, and the other women at the White Monastery and the Pachomian communities can, at present, be known only through the words of the men who sought to prevent it.

CONCLUSION

The cases of Taêse and Tsansnô, however meagerly documented, have given brief glimpses into the understanding of female homoeroticism in their time, but this should not be their only significance for us. In the preface to his classic study on ascetic monasticism *Body and Society,* Peter Brown reminds his readers that the evidence he is about to discuss deals with the real lives and often the real pain of real individuals.[58] This is an essential reminder: in discussing the fragmentary, disjointed evidence enumerated above, it is easy to lose sight of the reality that the names in these texts represent actual, individual human beings. Certainly, the lives of Taêse and Tsansnô within the White Monastery cannot have been especially easy, but their stories remain largely untold. They do not reappear in any of the published works of Shenute, and we do not even know if they received the punishments Shenute directed for them; defiance of Shenute's orders for punishments was one of his recurring complaints in writing to the women of the community. So perhaps it is best to end with Tsansnô and the defiant quotation attributed to her: "It is others whom I teach." This was clearly not the first time one of the women in his community challenged Shenute's authority. But the prominence this statement was accorded suggests that Shenute saw Tsansnô's statement as a threat, however unsuccessful it may have ultimately been, to his role as arbiter of women's lives at the White Monastery. In the end, it was Shenute who had the last word on Taêse and Tsansnô.

NOTES

*This essay has been a long time in the making, and for their constructive criticism, I would like to thank the organizers and audiences of the panels and colloquia in which I have developed it. The editors of the present volume have been very generous with their time in helping me refine this essay, and I appreciate their efforts greatly. I would also like to thank Heike Behlmer, Sarah Clackson, Remko Jas, Chuck Jones, Lynn Meskell, Richard Parkinson, Jennifer Sheridan, Laurie Talalay, and especially Dominic Montserrat for specific help, suggestions, and general encouragement. I am deeply indebted to the work of Stephen Emmel and Rebecca Krawiec; I would also like to thank these scholars personally for directing me to relevant sources, patiently answering questions, and volunteering useful information. Responsibility for the use to which I have put this assistance and information, though, rests solely with me. Translations of Coptic texts quoted in this essay are my own, taking note of earlier translations when available. The survey of Heike Behlmer, "Koptische Quellen zu (männlicher) 'Homosexualität'," *Studien zur altägyptischen Kultur* 28 (2000): 27–53, came to my attention too late for inclusion. Its primary focus is on male homoerotic activity and provides a valuable complement to the present article.

1. For useful overviews of Egypt in this period, see Roger S. Bagnall, *Egypt in Late Antiquity* (Princeton: Princeton UP, 1993) and James G. Keenan, "Egypt," *Cambridge Ancient History* XIV (Cambridge: Cambridge UP, 2001) 612–637; for the religious situation in Egypt at this time, see also David Frankfurter, *Religion in Roman Egypt: Assimilation and Resistance* (Princeton: Princeton UP, 1998).

2. Coptic words and phrases cited in the present essay are conventionally transliterated using the following alphabet: a b g d e z ê th i l m n o p ks r s t u ph kh ps ô sh f h j c ti. For readers unfamiliar with the language, it may be helpful to note the frequency of consonantal clusters in Coptic and the occasional use of very long compound words.

3. Susanna Elm, *'Virgins of God': The Making of Asceticism in Late Antiquity*, Oxford Classical Monographs (Oxford: Clarendon P, 1994) 227–228, 253–282.

4. An overview of the Pachomian women's communities and their origins can be found in Elm, 'Virgins of God' 283–296.

5. Separate rules specifically for women's communities are unusual in early eastern monasticism, but note the Syriac rule published in Arthur Vööbus, *History of Asceticism in the Syrian Orient III*, Corpus Scriptorum Christianorum Orientalium, Subsida 81 (Louvain: Peeters, 1988) 181–185; thanks to Remko Jas for this reference.

6. For the essential overview and study of the women's community at the White Monastery, see Rebecca Krawiec, "Women's Life in Shenute's White Monastery: A Study in Late Antique Egyptian Monasticism," Dissertation, Yale University, 1996, also Rebecca Krawiec, "Space, Distance and Gender: Authority and the Separation of Communities in the White Monastery," *Bulletin of the American Society of Papyrologists* 35 (1998): 45–63 and Elm, 'Virgins of God' 296–310. Janet Timbie, "The State of Research on the Career of Shenoute of Atripe," in *The Roots of Egyptian Christianity*, ed. Birger A. Pearson and James E. Goehring, Studies in Antiquity and Christianity (Philadelphia: Fortress P, 1986) 258–270, provides an overview of Shenute's career and Johannes Leipoldt, *Schenute von Atripe und die Entstehung des national ägyptischen Christentums* (Leipzig: J. C. Hinrichs, 1903), remains an important study, although outdated in some respects.

7. The essential study of Shenute's writings is Stephen Emmel, "Shenute's Literary Corpus," Dissertation, Yale University, 1993, which provides a guide to the manuscripts of the known works of Shenute, reconstructs the series of "canons" and "discourses," and examines the attribution of works to Shenute. Emmel's system of identification of the compositions and manuscripts of Shenute's work is followed in the present essay.

8. For the gender-based separation at the White Monastery, see Krawiec, "Space, Distance and Gender."

9. Krawiec, "Women's Life" 51–52, places the letter in the context of Shenute's other writing to the women.

10. See fig. 10.2; the page illustrated shows the entries concerning Tshenbiktor (end), Taêse, Takous, Tsophia and Tapolle (beginning). Although long known from Leipoldt's German translation in *Schenute von Atripe* 142–143, the Coptic text was first published only in 1993 (with English translation and comments) by Dwight Wayne Young, *Coptic Manuscripts from the White Monastery: Works of Shenute*, Mitteilungen aus der Papyrussammlung der österreichischen Nationalbibliothek (Papyrus Erzherzog Rainer), n.s. 22 (Wien: Brüder Hollinek, 1993) 91–113 and plates 31–42. The present translation varies in details from Young's and incorporates the suggestions in Krawiec, "Women's Life" 160, 243–244.

11. "It" in this case is feminine and must refer back to the feminine noun for "garment," used as a metaphor for the stick in the averted beating; Young notes other metaphorical garments in Shenute's work (*Coptic Manuscripts* 113n491). Tapolle reappears in other writings of Shenute: Krawiec, "Women's Life" 246–248.

12. Literally "runs in to Tsansnô," presumably into her cell; Young translates "hastens to Tsnasno." I have adopted Rebecca Krawiec's suggestion "runs after" as being more idiomatic. The rendering of this phrase as "running up to greet a sister in desire" by Michael Foat ("I Myself Have Seen: The Representation of Humanity in the Writings of Apa Shenoute of Atripe," Dissertation [Brown University, 1996] 12) is less apt, for reasons apparent in the discussion below.

13. The name Tsansnô is also likely to indicate a local origin for the woman, since most attestations of this and related names come from the area near the White Monastery; note for example the instances of the related Sansnos in documentary texts from nearby Nag Hammadi (J. W. B. Barns, G. M. Browne, and J. C. Shelton, *Nag Hammadi Codices: Greek and Coptic Papyri from the Cartonnage of the Covers,* Nag Hammadi Studies 16 [Leiden: E. J. Brill, 1981] Coptic texts 2 and 8, Greek texts 44, 68, 69, 72, 73, 75–78).

14. For Takhôm's career, see Krawiec, "Women's Life" 244–246; much of what we know about her life relates to her involvement in (and opposition to) Shenute's punishment of the women under her charge.

15. Philip Rousseau, *Pachomius: The Making of a Community in Fourth-Century Egypt,* Transformation of the Classical Heritage 6 (Berkeley: U of California P, 1985) 95–96, notes that the only corporal punishment prescribed in the Pachomian rule is for, apparently, homoerotic activity: "He shall be beaten before the gates and he shall be given only bread and water to eat outside until he is cleansed from his filth" (from the Latin version of Pachomius' rule, translated Armand Veilleux, *Pachomian Koinonia,* Volume Two, *Pachomian Chronicles and Rules,* Cistercian Studies Series 46 [Kalamazoo MI: Cistercian Publications, 1981] 176). Shenute relied much more heavily on physical punishment for a wider range of situations than Pachomius did.

16. And unusual in other pre-modern cultures as well; see Judith C. Brown, *Immodest Acts: The Life of a Lesbian Nun in Renaissance Italy* (Oxford: Oxford UP, 1986) 6–8, for the relative scarcity of records of the punishment of women for homoerotic activity in western monastic traditions.

17. Possibly in reference to the incidents described in the list of punishments, although it is difficult to be certain. Text in E. Amélineau, *Œuvres de Schenoudi* (Paris: Ernst Leroux, 1907–1914) vol. 1, p. 17, brought to my attention by Rebecca Krawiec (thanks to Sarah Clackson for a photocopy of the relevant passage).

18. For example, in a work from Canon 2 formerly attributed to Besa: K. H. Kuhn, *Letters and Sermons of Besa,* Corpus Scriptorum Christianorum Orientalium, Scriptores Coptici, 21–22 (Louvain: Imprimerie Orientaliste L. Durbecq, 1956) 132–133 (Coptic text) and 125–126 (translation), discussed in Krawiec, "Women's Life" 138–139.

19. Krawiec ("Women's Life" 159–163) notes the use of "according to the flesh" (*kata sarks*) when describing biological family relations (as opposed to the metaphorical family relations between members of a religious community), but "physical desire" (*ouôsh nsarkikos, ouôsh nsarks*) does not appear in contexts referring to familial love.

20. See W. E. Crum, *A Coptic Dictionary* (Oxford: Clarendon P, 1939) 553. Note that *shbêr* can sometimes be translated as "companion, comrade," and *mntshbêr* can sometimes be translated as "community"; in the following examples, though, "friend, friendship" is clearly the best rendering.

21. Note especially *Friendship in the Classical World.* Key Themes in Ancient History (Cambridge: Cambridge UP, 1997) and "Philosophy, Friendship and Cultural History," in *Inventing Ancient Culture: Historicism, Periodization and the Ancient World,* ed. Mark Golden and Peter Toohey (London: Routledge, 1997) 66–78.

22. See, e.g., references to the Coptic legend of Theodosios and Dionysios in Terry Wilfong, "The Coptic Story of Theodosios and Dionysios," in *P. Michigan Koenen* (= *P.Mich. XVIII*): *Michigan Texts Published in Honor of Ludwig Koenen,* ed. Cornelia Römer and Traianos

Gagos, Studia Amstelodamensia ad Epigraphicam, Ius Antiquum et Papyrologicam Pertinentia, 36 (Amsterdam: Gieben, 1996) 351–356.

23. See, for example, Klaus Koschorke, Stefan Timm, and Frederik Wisse, "Schenute: De Certamine Contra Diabolum," Oriens Christianus 59 (1975) 60–77, text p. 65, translation p. 70, and Johannes Leipoldt and W. E. Crum, Sinuthii Archimandritae vita et opera omnia: Textus III, Corpus Scriptorum Christianorum Orientalium, Scriptores Coptici, Series II 4 (Paris: E typographeo reipublicae, 1908) 60–61, translated in Foat, "I Myself Have Seen" 108–109.

24. Note the discussion in Brian Patrick McGuire, Friendship and Community: The Monastic Experience 350–1250, Cistercian Studies Series 95 (Kalamazoo, MI: Cistercian Publications, 1988); the discussion of Egyptian sources on 13–25 of this work is, however, in marked contrast to the reading of the same sources in the present essay.

25. McGuire, Friendship and Community 418–423.

26. See, e.g., the interviews cited in Rosemary Curb and Nancy Manahan, Lesbian Nuns: Breaking Silence (Tallahassee: Naiad P, 1985) esp. xxvi–xxvii, 8–9, 133–136, 369.

27. L. Th. Lefort, Œuvres de S. Pachôme et de ses disciples, Corpus Scriptorum Christianorum Orientalium, Scriptores Coptici, 23–24 (Louvain: Imprimerie Orientaliste L. Durbecq, 1956) 75–80, of both Coptic text and French translation; English translation Armand Veilleux, Pachomian Koinonia, Volume Three, Instructions, Letters and Other Writings of Saint Pachomius and his Disciples, Cistercian Studies Series 47 (Kalamazoo MI: Cistercian Publications, 1982) 145–151. Veilleux (7–8) considers the attribution to Horsiesios dubious on the grounds that "it does not correspond much to Horsiesios' usual line of thought." However, Horsiesios did warn his monks away from "friendship" in his "Testament," which is accepted as authentic, and, in view of the similarities in language and scriptural allusion, I see no reason to doubt the attribution of the instruction on friendship to Horsiesios. Note the discussion of manuscripts in Emmel, "Shenoute's Literary Corpus" 1212 and Bentley Layton, Catalogue of Coptic Literary Manuscripts in the British Library Acquired since the Year 1906 (London: British Library, 1987) 91–92.

28. Male monks typically did not shave their beards.

29. Quoting Jer. 2:24.

30. Jeremiah, quoting Jer. 9:20.

31. Citing Micah 1:13.

32. Like the list of punishments, this is from Canon 4; Leipoldt and Crum, Sinuthii III, 154–156 and Alla I. Elanskaya, The Literary Coptic Manuscripts in the A. S. Pushkin State Fine Arts Museum in Moscow, Supplements to Vigiliae Christianae 18 (Leiden: E. J. Brill, 1994) 250–251 (text) and 293 (translation).

33. Bernadette J. Brooten, Love between Women: Early Christian Responses to Female Homoeroticism, Chicago Series on Sexuality, History and Society (Chicago: University of Chicago Press, 1996) 349–350; Foat, "I Myself Have Seen" 82–83.

34. From one of Shenute's Canons. Johannes Leipoldt and W. E. Crum, Sinuthii Archimandritae vita et opera omnia: Textus IV, Corpus Scriptorum Christianorum Orientalium, Scriptores Coptici, Series II 5 (Paris: E typographeo reipublicae, 1913) 169–170; discussion and translation in Brooten, Love between Women 349 and Foat, "I Myself Have Seen" 82–83.

35. From one of the Canons; Leipoldt and Crum, Sinuthii IV, 171, Brooten, Love between Women 349, Foat, "I Myself Have Seen" 82–83.

36. From Canon 3; Leipoldt and Crum, *Sinuthii* IV, 124, first part only in Brooten, *Love between Women* 349, both parts in Foat, "I Myself Have Seen" 82–83.

37. Note the discussion in Peter Brown, *The Body and Society: Men, Women and Sexual Renunciation in Early Christianity* (New York: Columbia UP, 1988) 246, on Horsiesios' instruction on friendship from this perspective.

38. Lefort, *Œuvres de S. Pachôme* 31, and Veilleux, *Pachomian Koinonia*, Vol. Two, 161 (English translation).

39. Lefort, *Œuvres de S. Pachôme* 32, and Veilleux, *Pachomian Koinonia*, Vol. Two, 162 (English translation).

40. Compare the case cited in a letter, attributed to sixth century writer Paul Helladicus of Elusa, of a female monastic superior who urged the women under her charge not to look needlessly at each other's faces lest they feel desire for each other. The Greek text is in Vilelmus Lundström, *Anecdota Byzantina e codicibus Upsaliensibus*, Fasc. 1 (Uppsala: Libraria Lundequistiana, 1902) 21, lines 18–24; I owe this reference to Dominic Montserrat, who also made his unpublished translation available to me.

41. Kuhn, *Besa* 33, 38–40 (Coptic text) and 31, 36–37 (translation).

42. K. H. Kuhn, *Pseudo-Shenoute on Christian Behavior*, Corpus Scriptorum Christianorum Orientalium, Scriptores Coptici, 29–30 (Louvain: Secrétariat du Corpus CSO, 1960) 23–24 (Coptic text), 22 (translation).

43. Text and translation in James Drescher, *Three Coptic Legends: Hilaria, Archellites, the Seven Sleepers* (Cairo: Imprimerie de l'Institut Français d'Archéologie Orientale, 1947) 1–13, 69–82. Note discussion in Valerie R. Hotchkiss, *Clothes Make the Man: Female Cross Dressing in Medieval Europe*, The New Middle Ages (New York: Garland, 1996) 23, 136 and Terry G. Wilfong, "Reading the Disjointed Body in Coptic: From Physical Modification to Textual Fragmentation," in *Changing Bodies, Changing Meanings: The Human Body in Antiquity*, ed. Dominic Montserrat (London: Routledge, 1998) 127–130.

44. Krawiec, "Women's Life" 35.

45. As it is in other periods of Egyptian history; see the insightful discussion in R. B. Parkinson, "'Homosexual' Desire and Middle Kingdom Literature," *Journal of Egyptian Archaeology* 81 (1995): 57–76.

46. Wilfong, "Reading the Disjointed Body in Coptic" 131–132.

47. Paul C. Smither, "A Coptic Love-Charm," *Journal of Egyptian Archaeology* 25 (1939): 173–174, recent translation and comments by David T. Frankfurter in Marvin Meyer and Richard Smith, eds., *Ancient Christian Magic: Coptic Texts of Ritual Power* (San Francisco: HarperSanFrancisco, 1994) 177–178, discussion in Dominic Montserrat, *Sex and Society in Graeco-Roman Egypt* (London: Kegan Paul, 1996) 156–157. The homoerotic magical spells for women discussed in Brooten, *Love between Women* 113–173 come from a slightly earlier period and are in Greek; to her references should be added the discussion in Montserrat, *Sex and Society* 158–160.

48. The folds in the parchment on which this spell was written make it likely that it was actually put into practice.

49. See Meyer and Smith, *Ancient Christian Magic* 178–179, but their translation of the final phrase as "any woman, whether wild or domesticated" is clearly incorrect and an artifact of the original editor's embarrassment with the subject matter (note Robert Ritner's objection on p. 369 of the same volume and the earlier discussion by the present author in

Bulletin of the American Society of Papyrologists 29 [1992]: 93–95). Clearly, the caster of the spell is jealous that the man Pharaouô was having sex with the woman Touaein, but there is no clue as to whether this person was a man or a woman.

50. Crum, *A Coptic Dictionary* 224–225; most of the examples discussed below are not cited in this entry.

51. Although such compound words with *ref-* are common in Coptic, there are no close parallels that concern sexual activity. A much more recent cross-cultural parallel to the Coptic term can be found in Peter the Great's criminal code, which uses a compound term meaning "men-lying-with-men"; see Laura Engelstein, *The Keys to Happiness: Sex and the Search for Modernity in Fin-de-Siècle Russia* (Ithaca: Cornell UP, 1992) 59—reference thanks to Dominic Montserrat.

52. E.g., K. H. Kuhn, "Two Shenoute Texts," in *Festschrift zum 100-jährigen Bestehen der Papyrussammlung der österreichischen Nationalbibliothek: Papyrus Erzherzog Rainer (P. Rainer Cent.)* (Wien: Verlag Brüder Hollinek, 1983) 187–189.

53. The text is Leipoldt and Crum, *Sinuthii* III, 97:29–98:2.

54. *Schenute von Atripe: De Iudicio,* Catalogo del Museo Egizio di Torino, Serie prima, 8 (Torino: Museo Egizio, 1996) 204–205n69.

55. Carl Schmidt, and Violet MacDermot, eds. and trans., *Pistis Sophia,* Nag Hammadi Studies 9 (Leiden: E. J. Brill, 1978) 379–380; see also 309–310, 319–320. The components of the compound terms used are age/status-neutral, so MacDermot's translation "pederast" is not particularly appropriate.

56. John Rylands Library Coptic Manuscript 71, partially published in W. E. Crum, *Catalogue of the Coptic Manuscripts in the Collection of the John Rylands Library, Manchester* (Manchester: UP, 1909) 35; for the attribution, see Emmel, "Shenoute's Literary Corpus" 1204.

57. See, for example, Valerie Traub, "The (In)significance of Lesbian Desire in Early Modern England," in *Queering the Renaissance,* ed. Jonathan Goldberg, Series Q (Durham: Duke UP, 1994) 62–83.

58. Brown, *Body and Society* xviii.

WORKS CITED

Abbott, Sydney, and Barbara Love. *Sappho Was a Right-On Woman.* Briarcliff Manor, NY: Stein and Day, 1972.

Abelove, Henry, Michèle Aina Barale, and David M. Halperin, eds. 1993. *Lesbian and Gay Studies Reader.* New York: Routledge, 1993.

ABV. See under Beazley.

Adams, James Noel. *The Latin Sexual Vocabulary.* Baltimore: Johns Hopkins UP, 1982.

Ahmed, Leila. *Women and Gender in Islam.* New Haven: Yale UP, 1992.

Alexiou, Margaret. *The Ritual Lament in Greek Tradition.* Cambridge: Cambridge UP, 1974.

Alexiou, S. "Καθαρισμός αργυρών αντικειμένων στο εργαστήριο του Μουσείου Ηρακλείου, ενεπίγραφες περόνες καὶ εγχειρίδια." *Athens Annals of Archaeology* 8 (1975): 133–139.

———. "Περὶ μινωϊκῶν δεχαμενῶν καθαρμοῦ." *Kretika Chronika* 14 (1972): 414–434.

Amélineau, E. *Œuvres de Schenoudi.* 2 vols. Paris: Ernst Leroux, 1907–1914.

Amigues, Suzanne. "Le crocus et le safran sur une fresque de Théra." *Revue Archéologique* (1988): 227–242.

Anderson, James C. "Aesthetic Concept of Art." In *Theories of Art Today.* Ed. Noël Carroll. Madison: U of Wisconsin P, 2000. 65–92.

———. *P. Ovidii Nasonis:* Metamorphoses. Lipsiae: Teubner, 1993.

Anderson, William S. *Ovid's* Metamorphoses: *Books 6–10.* Norman: U of Oklahoma P, 1972.

Andreae, Bernhard. *Das Alexandermosaik.* Werkmonographien zur bildenden Kunst 119. Stuttgart: Philipp Reclam jün., 1967.

Archer, Léonie J., Susan Fischler, and Maria Wyke, eds. *Women in Ancient Societies: An Illusion of the Night.* New York: Routledge, 1994.

Arias, Paolo E., and Max Hirmer. *Tausend Jahre griechische Vasenkunst.* Munich: Hirmer Verlag, 1960.

Armstrong, D., and A. Ratchford. "Iphigenia's Veil: Aeschylus, *Agamemnon* 228–248." *Bulletin of the Institute of Classical Studies, London* 32 (1985): 1–12.

Arnott, R. *Disease, Healing and Medicine in the Aegean Bronze Age.* Leiden: E. J. Brill, forthcoming.

Arthur, M. B. "The Dream of a World without Women: Poetics and the Circles of Order in the *Theogony* Proemium." *Arethusa* 16 (1983): 97–116.

Auanger, Lisa Ann. "A Catalog of Images of Women in the Official Arts of Ancient Rome." Dissertation U of Missouri, 1997. Ann Arbor: UMI, 1998.

Austin, Norman. *Helen of Troy and Her Shameless Phantom.* Ithaca: Cornell UP, 1994.

Babbitt, Frank Cole, trans. *Plutarch's* Moralia. Cambridge, MA: Harvard UP, 1927–1969.

Bagnall, Roger S. *Egypt in Late Antiquity.* Princeton: Princeton UP, 1993.

Baldwin, Barry. *Studies in Lucian.* Toronto: Hakkert, 1973.

Barber, Elizabeth J. W. *Prehistoric Textiles: The Development of Cloth in the Neolithic and Bronze Ages with Special Reference to the Aegean.* Princeton: Princeton UP, 1991.

———. *Women's Work: The First 20,000 Years.* London: W. W. Norton, 1994.

Barnes, Ruth, and Joanne Bubolz Eichler, eds. *Dress and Gender: Making and Meaning in Cultural Context.* Providence: Berg Publications, 1997.

Barns, J. W. B., G. M. Browne, and J. C. Shelton. *Nag Hammadi Codices: Greek and Coptic Papyri from the Cartonnage of the Covers.* Nag Hammadi Studies 16. Leiden: E. J. Brill, 1981.

Beard, Mary. "Taking an Approach II." In Rasmussen and Spivey, *Looking at Greek Vases.* 12–35.

Beazley, John D. *Attic Black-Figure Vase-Painters.* Oxford: Oxford UP, 1956.

———. *Attic Red-Figure Vase-Painters.* 3 vols. 2nd ed. Oxford: Oxford UP, 1963; New York: Hacker Art Books, 1984.

———. *Paralipomena: Additions to* Attic Black-Figure Vase-Painters *and to* Attic Red-Figure Vase-Painters. 2nd ed. Oxford: Clarendon P, 1971.

———. "Potter and Painter in Ancient Athens." *Proceedings of the British Academy* 30 (1946): 1–43.

———. "Some Attic Vases in the Cyprus Museum." *Proceedings of the British Academy* 33 (1947): 195–244.

Behlmer, Heike. "Koptische Quellen zu (männlicher) 'Homosexualität.'" *Studien zur altägyptischen Kultur* 28 (2000): 27–53.

———. *Schenute von Atripe: De Iudicio. Catalogo del Museo Egizio di Torino*, 1st ser. 8. Torino: Museo Egizio, 1996.

Bérard, Claude, and Christiane Bron. "Satyric Revels." In Bérard et al., *City of Images.* 131–150.

Bérard, Claude, Jean-Pierre Vernant, et al. *Die Bilderwelt der Griechen. Schlüssel zu einer "fremden" Kultur.* Mainz: Philipp von Zabern, 1984.

Bérard, Claude, Christiane Bron, Jean-Louis Durand, Françoise Frontisi-Ducroux, François Lissarrague, Alain Schnapp, and Jean-Pierre Vernant, eds., Deborah Lyons, trans. *A City of Images: Iconography and Society in Ancient Greece.* Princeton: Princeton UP, 1989.

———. "The Order of Women." In Bérard et al., *City of Images.* 89–108.

Bergren, A. L. T. "Language and the Female in Early Greek Thought." *Arethusa* 16 (1983): 69–95.

Bernal, Martin. *Black Athena: The Afroasiatic Roots of Classical Civilization,* Vol. I, *The Fabrication of Ancient Greece.* New Brunswick: Rutgers UP, 1987.

Bieber, Margarete. *The Sculpture of the Hellenistic Age.* New York: Columbia UP, 1955, 1961.

Biesantz, Hägen. *Die thessalischen Grabreliefs.* Mainz: Philipp von Zabern, 1965.

Bilde, Pia Guldager, Inge Nielsen, and Marjatta Nielsen, eds. *Aspects of Hellenism in Italy: Towards a Cultural Unity?* Danish Studies in Classical Archaeology Acta Hyperborea 5. Copenhagen: U of Copenhagen, Museum Tusculanum P, 1993.

Bing, Peter. *The Well-Read Muse: Present and Past in Callimachus and the Hellenistic Poets.* Hypomnemata Heft 90. Göttingen: Vandenhoeck & Ruprecht, 1988.

———, and Rip Cohen, trans. *Games of Venus: An Anthology of Greek and Roman Erotic Verse from Sappho to Ovid.* New York: Routledge, 1991.

Bloom, Allan. *The Closing of the American Mind.* New York: Simon and Schuster, 1987.

Bloom, H. *The Anxiety of Influence: A Theory of Poetry.* New York: Oxford UP, 1973.

Blundell, Susan. *Women in Ancient Greece.* Cambridge, MA: Harvard UP, 1995.

Boardman, John. *Athenian Black Figure Vases.* New York: Oxford UP, 1974.

———. *Athenian Red Figure Vases: The Archaic Period.* London: Thames and Hudson, 1975.

———. *Athenian Red Figure Vases: The Classical Period.* London: Thames and Hudson, 1989.

———. *Greek Sculpture: The Classical Period.* London: Thames and Hudson, 1991.

———, and Eugenio La Rocca. *Eros in Greece.* Milan: Arnoldo Mondadori, 1975.

Bolling, G. "POIKILOS and THRONA." *American Journal of Philology* 79 (1958): 275–282.

Bompaire, Jacques. *Lucien écrivain: Imitation et création.* Bibliothèque des Écoles Françaises d'Athènes et de Rome 190. Paris: Belles Lettres, 1958.

Bonfante, Larissa. "Nudity as a Costume in Classical Art." *American Journal of Archaeology* 93 (1989): 543–570.

Bornstein, Kate. *My Gender Workbook.* New York: Routledge, 1998.

———. "Queer Theory and Shopping: Dichotomy or Symbionts." In Queen and Schimel, *Pomosexuals.* 14.

Borzsák, Stephanus, ed. *Q. Horati Flacci Opera.* Leipzig: Teubner, 1984.

Boston Museum of Fine Arts. *Vase-painting in Italy: Red-figure and Related Works in the Museum of Fine Arts.* Boston: Museum of Fine Arts, 1993.

Boswell, John. *Christianity, Social Tolerance, and Homosexuality: Gay People in Western Europe from the Beginning of the Christian Era to the Fourteenth Century.* Chicago: U of Chicago P, 1980.

———. *Same-Sex Unions in Pre-modern Europe.* New York: Villard Books, 1994.

Bothmer, Dietrich von. *Ancient Art from New York Private Collections. Catalogue of an Exhibition Held at the Metropolitan Museum of Art. December 17, 1959–February 28, 1960.* New York: Metropolitan Museum of Art, 1961.

Boulotis, Christos. "Nochmals zum Prozessionsfresko von Knossos: Palast und Darbringung von Prestige-Objekten." In Hägg and Marinatos, *Function of Minoan Palaces.* 145–156.

Bourriau, J. A. *Pharaohs and Mortals: Egyptian Art in the Middle Kingdom.* Cambridge: Cambridge UP, 1988.

Bowie, Ewen Lyall. "Second Sophistic." In *The Oxford Classical Dictionary.* 3rd ed. Oxford: Oxford UP, 1996. 1377–1378.

Bowie, Theodore, and Cornelia V. Christenson, eds. *Studies in Erotic Art.* New York: Basic Books, 1970.

Bowman, L. "Nossis, Sappho and Hellenistic Poetry." *Ramus* 27 (1998): 39–59.

Bowra, C. M. *Greek Lyric Poetry.* 2nd rev. ed. Oxford: Clarendon P, 1961.

Bremmer, Jan. "The Importance of the Maternal Uncle and Grandfather in Archaic and Classical Greece and Early Byzantium." *Zeitschrift für Papyrologie und Epigraphik* 50 (1983): 173–186.

Brice, W. C. "A Silver Pin from Mavro Spelio with an Inscription in Linear A: Heraklion Museum 540." *Kadmos* 11 (1972): 113–124.

Bron, Christiane, and François Lissarrague. "Looking at the Vase." In Bérard et al., *City of Images.* 11–22.

Brooten, Bernadette J. *Love between Women: Early Christian Responses to Female Homo-eroticism.* Chicago Series on Sexuality, History, and Society. Chicago: U of Chicago P, 1996.

Brown, Judith C. *Immodest Acts: The Life of a Lesbian Nun in Renaissance Italy.* Oxford: Oxford UP, 1986.

Brown, Peter. *The Body and Society: Men, Women and Sexual Renunciation in Early Christianity.* New York: Columbia UP, 1988.

Brown, Shelby. "Feminist Research in Archaeology: What Does It Mean? Why Is It Taking So Long?" In Rabinowitz and Richlin, *Feminist Theory.* 238–271.

———. "'Ways of Seeing' Women in Antiquity: An Introduction to Feminism in Classical Archaeology and Ancient Art History." In Koloski-Ostrow and Lyons, *Naked Truths.* 12–42.

Buchholz, Hans-Günter. "Das Symbol des gemeinsamen Mantels." *Jahrbuch des Deutschen Archäologischen Instituts* 102 (1987): 1–55.

Buckley, T., and A. Gottlieb. *Blood Magic: The Anthropology of Menstruation.* Berkeley: U of California P, 1988.

Buffière, Félix. *Éros adolescent: la pédérastie dans la Grèce antique.* Paris: Belles Lettres, 1980.

Buitron-Oliver, Diana. *Douris: A Master-Painter of Athenian Red-Figure Vases.* Kerameus 9. Mainz: Verlag Philipp von Zabern, 1995.

Burkert, Walter. *Greek Religion.* Cambridge, MA: Harvard UP, 1985.

———. *Homo Necans: The Anthropology of Ancient Greek Sacrificial Ritual and Myth.* Berkeley: U of California P, 1983.

Burn, Lucilla. *The Meidias Painter.* Oxford: Oxford UP, 1987.

Burnett, Anne. "Desire and Memory (Sappho Frag. 94)." *Classical Philology* 74 (1979): 16–27.

———. *Three Archaic Poets: Archilochus, Alcaeus, Sappho.* Cambridge, MA: Harvard UP, 1983.

Burton, B. T. *Human Nutrition.* New York: McGraw-Hill, 1988.

Butler, Judith. "Against Proper Objects." In Weed and Schor, *Feminism Meets Queer Theory.* 1–30.

———. *Gender Trouble: Feminism and the Subversion of Identity.* New York: Routledge, 1990; New York and London: Routledge, 1999.

———. "Imitation and Gender Insubordination." In *Inside/Out: Lesbian Theories, Gay Theories.* Ed. Diana Fuss. New York: Routledge, 1991. 13–31.

Butler's Lives of the Saints. Ed., rev., and suppl. by Herbert Thurston and Donald Attwater, foreword by Basil Hume. New York: Kenedy, 1956; repr. Westminster, MD: Christian Classics, 1981.

Cairns, D. L. "Veiling, Αιδως," and a Red Figure Amphora by Phintias." *Journal of Hellenic Studies* 116 (1996): 152–158.

Calame, Claude. *Les choeurs de jeunes filles en Grèce archaïque. I: Morphologie, fonction religieuse et sociale.* Rome: Edizioni dell'Ateneo & Bizzarri, 1977.

————. *Choruses of Young Women in Ancient Greece: Their Morphology, Religious Role, and Social Functions.* Trans. Derek Collins and Jane Orion. Lanham, MD: Rowman and Littlefield, 1997.

————. *The Poetics of Eros in Ancient Greece.* Trans. Janet Lloyd. Princeton: Princeton UP, 1999.

————. "Sappho's Group: An Initiation into Womanhood." In Greene, *Reading.* 113–124.

Callam, Daniel, trans. *St. Ambrose, On Virginity.* Saskatoon: Peregrina, 1980.

Cameron, A. "Sappho's Prayer to Aphrodite." *Harvard Theological Review* 32 (1939): 1–17.

Cameron, Alan. "Love (and Marriage) between Women." *Greek, Roman, and Byzantine Studies* 39 (1998): 137–156.

Cameron, Averil, and Amélie Kuhrt, eds. *Images of Women in Antiquity.* Detroit: Wayne State UP, 1983.

Campbell, David A. "Aeolium Carmen: Horace's Allusions to Sappho and Alcaeus." *Echos du monde classique. Classical Views* 22.3 (1978): 94–97.

————, ed. and trans. *Greek Lyric 1: Sappho and Alcaeus,* Loeb Classical Library 142. Cambridge, MA: Harvard UP, 1982.

————. *Greek Lyric Poetry.* London: Macmillan, 1967.

Cantarella, Eva. *Bisexuality in the Ancient World.* Trans. Cormac Ó Cuilleanáin. New Haven: Yale UP, 1992.

Carpenter, Edward. *The Intermediate Sex: A Study of Some Transitional Types of Men and Women.* London: George Allen, 1912.

Carpenter, Thomas H., ed. *Beazley Addenda: Additional References to* Attic Black-Figure Vase-Painters, Attic Red-Figure Vase-Painters[2] *and* Paralipomena. Oxford: Oxford UP, 1989.

Carruthers, M. J. "The Re-Vision of the Muse: Adrienne Rich, Audre Lorde, Judy Grahn, Olga Broumas." *Hudson Review* 36 (1983): 293–322.

Carson, Anne. *Eros the Bittersweet: An Essay.* Princeton: Princeton UP, 1986.

Case, Sue-Ellen. "The Student and the Strap: Authority and Seduction in the Class(room)." In *Professions of Desire.* Ed. George E. Haggerty and Bonnie Zimmerman. New York: Modern Language Association of America, 1995. 39–46.

Casey, Mary, Denise Donlon, Jeannette Hope, and Sharon Wellfare, eds. *Redefining Archaeology: Feminist Perspectives. Proceedings of the 3rd Australian Women in*

Archaeology Conference. Research Papers in Archaeology and Natural History 29. Canberra: Australian National U Publications, 1998.

Cassimatis, Hélène. 1998. "Le miroir dans les représentations funéraires apuliennes." *Mélanges de l'École Française de Rome, Antiquité* 110.1 (1998): 297–350.

Castelli, Elizabeth A., David Halperin, Ann Pellegrini, Ken Stone, Deirdre Good, and Natalie Boymel Kampen. "Lesbian Historiography before the Name?" *GLQ: Journal of Lesbian and Gay Studies* 4 (1998): 557–630.

Cavalier, Odile, ed. *Silence et fureur: La Femme et le mariage en Grèce: Les Antiquités grecques du Musée Calvet.* Avignon: Fondation du Muséum Calvet, 1996.

Cavallini, E. "Noss. A.P. V 170." *Sileno* 7 (1981): 179.

Cazzaniga, I. "Critica testuale ed esegesi a Nosside A.P. VII 718." *Parola del Passato* 25 (1970): 431–445.

Chapin, Anne P. "The Sanctuary Rhyton from Kato Zakros and the Representation of Space in Aegean Art of the Bronze Age." *American Journal of Archaeology* 96 (1992): 334. Abstract.

Chauncey, George. "From Sexual Inversion to Homosexuality: Medicine and the Changing Conceptualization of Female Deviance." *Salmagundi* 58–59 (1982–1983): 114–146.

Christiansen, Jette, and Torben Melander, eds. *Proceedings of the 3rd Symposium on Ancient Greek and Related Pottery. Copenhagen, Aug. 31–Sept. 4, 1987.* Copenhagen: Nationalmuseet; Ny Carlsberg and Glyptotek Thorvaldsens Museum, 1988.

Christopher, K. *Blood Relations: Menstruation and the Origins of Culture.* New Haven: Yale UP, 1991.

Clairmont, Christoph W. *Classical Attic Tombstones.* 9 vols. Kilchberg: Akanthus, 1993.

———. *Gravestone and Epigram: Greek Memorials from the Archaic and Classical Period.* Mainz: Phillip von Zabern, 1970.

Clarke, John. *Looking at Lovemaking: Constructions of Sexuality in Roman Art 100 B.C.–A.D. 250.* Berkeley: U of California P, 1998.

Clay, J. S. *The Wrath of Athena: Gods and Men in the* Odyssey. Princeton: Princeton UP, 1983.

Cline, Eric. "Monkey Business in the Bronze Age Aegean: The Amenhotep II Faience Figurines at Mycenae and Tiryns." *Annual of the British School at Athens* 86 (1991): 29–42.

Closterman, Wendy. "The Form and Function of the Dexileos Precinct." *American Journal of Archaeology* 103 (1999): 299.

Cohen, Beth. "Divesting the Breast of Clothes in Classical Sculpture." In Koloski-Ostrow and Lyons, *Naked Truths.* 66–92.

Cole, Susan G. "The Social Function of Rituals of Maturation: The Koureion and the Arkteia." *Zeitschrift für Papyrologie und Epigraphik* 55 (1984): 233–244.

College Art Association, Gay and Lesbian Caucus. *Bibliography of Gay and Lesbian Art.* New York: The Caucus, 1994.

Le collezioni del Museo Nazionale di Napoli. Under the care of Archivio fotografico Pedicini. 2 vols. Rome: De Luca, 1986.

Compton, T. "The Barbed Rose: Sappho as Satirist." *Favonius* 1 (1987): 1–8.

Conte, G. B. *The Rhetoric of Imitation: Genre and Poetic Memory in Virgil and Other Latin Poets.* Trans. C. Segal. Ithaca and London: Cornell UP, 1986.

Conze, Alexander, Adolf Michaelis, Achilleus Postolakas, Emanuel Loewy, Alfred Brüchner, Paul Heinrich, August Wolters, and Robert von Schneider. *Die attischen Grabreliefs.* 4 vols. Berlin: W. Spemann, 1893–1922.

Cook, A. B. *Zeus.* 3 vols. Cambridge: Cambridge UP, 1914–1940.

Couëlle, Colombe. "La Loi d'Aphrodite: entre la norme et le plaisir." In Cavalier, *Silence.* 229–248.

Crum, W. E. *Catalogue of the Coptic Manuscripts in the Collection of the John Rylands Library, Manchester.* Manchester: UP, 1909.

———. *A Coptic Dictionary.* Oxford: Clarendon P, 1939.

Curb, Rosemary, and Nancy Manahan. *Lesbian Nuns: Breaking Silence.* Tallahassee: Naiad P, 1985.

Curran, Leo. "Rape and Rape Victims in the *Metamorphoses.*" *Arethusa* 11 (1978): 213–241.

D'Agata, Anna Lucia. "Late Minoan Crete and Horns of Consecration: A Symbol in Action." In Laffineur and Crowley, *EIKΩN.* 247–256.

Darcque, Pascal, and Jean-Claude Poursat, eds. *L'Iconographie minoenne: Actes de la table ronde d'Athènes (21–22 avril 1983). Bulletin de Correspondance Héllenique* Suppl. 11. Athènes: École française d'Athènes; Paris: Dépositaire, Diffusion De Boccard, 1985.

David, E. "Hair as Language." *Eranos* 90 (1992): 11–21.

Davidson, James. *Courtesans and Fishcakes: The Consuming Passions of Classical Athens,* New York: HarperCollins, 1997.

Davies, Glenys. "The Significance of the Handshake Motif in Classical Funerary Art." *American Journal of Archaeology* 89 (1985): 627–640.

Davis, Ellen. *The Vapheio Cups and Aegean Gold and Silver Ware.* New York: Garland, 1977.

———. "Youth and Age in the Thera Frescoes." *American Journal of Archaeology* 90 (1986): 399–406.

Davis, Whitney. "Winckelmann's 'Homosexual' Teleologies." In Kampen, *Sexuality in Ancient Art.* 262–276.

DeForest, Mary, ed. *Woman's Power, Man's Game: Essays on Classical Antiquity in Honor of Joy K. King.* Wauconda, IL: Bolchazy-Carducci, 1993.

Degani, E. "Nosside." *Giornale filologico ferrarese* 4 (1981): 43–52.

DeJean, Joan. "Female Voyeurism: Sappho and Lafayette." *Rivista di letterature moderne e comparate* 40 (1987): 201–215.

———. *Fictions of Sappho, 1546–1937.* Chicago: U of Chicago P, 1989.

———. "Sex and Philology: Sappho and the Rise of German Nationalism." *Representations* 27 (1989): 148–171.

de Lauretis, Teresa. "Queer Theory: Lesbian and Gay Sexualities." *differences* 3 (1991): iii–xxviii.

Demand, Nancy. *Birth, Death and Motherhood in Classical Greece.* Baltimore: Johns Hopkins UP, 1994.

De Martino, F., ed. *Rose di Pieria.* "Le Rane" Collana di Studi e Testi 9. Bari: Levante Editori, 1991.

———. "Saffo ed Esiodo, fr. 1, 21–24, Voight." *Giornale filologico ferrarese* 10 (1987): 51–55.

Dentzer, Jean-Marie. *Le Motif du banquet couché dans le proche-orient et le monde grec du VII au IV siècle avant J.-C.* Rome: École Française de Rome, 1982.

DeShazer, M. K. *Inspiring Women: Reimagining the Muse.* New York and Oxford: Pergamon P, 1986.

Detienne, M. *Les maîtres de vérité dans la Grèce archaïque.* Paris: Maspero, 1967.

———, and J.-P. Vernant. *Cunning Intelligence in Greek Culture and Society.* Trans. J. Lloyd. Atlantic Highlands, NJ: Humanities Press, 1978.

Deubner, Ludwig. *Attische Feste.* Berlin: H. Keller, 1932.

Devereux, George. "The Nature of Sappho's Seizure in Fr. 31 LP as Evidence of Her Inversion." *Classical Quarterly* (1970): 17–31.

DeVries, Keith. *Homosexuality and the Athenian Democracy.* Oxford: Oxford UP, forthcoming.

Diehl, J. F. "'Come Slowly—Eden': An Exploration of Women Poets and Their Muse." *Signs* 3 (1978): 572–587.

Dierichs, Angelika. *Erotik in der Kunst Griechenlands.* Antike Welt, Zeitschrift für Archäologie und Kulturgeschichte 19. Feldmeilen, Switz.: Raggi-Verlag, 1988.

———. *Erotik in der Kunst Griechenlands.* Mainz: Verlag Philipp von Zabern, 1993.

Diplock, A. T. *Fat-Soluble Vitamins: Their Biochemistry and Applications.* Lancaster, PA: Technomic Publishing, 1985.

Doane, Mary Ann. *The Desire to Desire: The Woman's Film of the 1940's.* Bloomington: Indiana UP, 1987.

———. "Film and the Masquerade: Theorising the Female Spectator." *Screen* 23 (1982): 74–87.

Dodds, E. R. *The Greeks and the Irrational.* Boston: Beacon Press, 1957 [1951]; Berkeley: U of California P, 1968.

Doumas, Christos. "Conventions artistiques à Théra et dans la Méditerranée orientale à l'époque préhistorique." In Darcque and Poursat, *L'Iconographie minoenne.* 29–34.

———. "Η Ξεστὴ 3 καὶ οἱ κυανοκέφαλοι στὴν τέχνη τῆς Θήρας." *ΕΙΛΑΠΙΝΗ. Τόμος τιμητικός για τον Καθηγητή Νικολάο Πλάτωνα.* Athens: Athens Archaeological Society, 1987. 151–159.

———. *The Wall-Paintings of Thera.* Athens: Thera Foundation, 1992.

Douskos, I. "The Crocuses of Santorini." In *Thera and the Aegean World: Papers Presented at the Second International Scientific Congress, Santorini, Greece, August 1978.* Ed. C. Doumas. London: Thera Foundation, 1980. vol. II.1, 141–145.

Dover, Kenneth J. *Greek Homosexuality.* Cambridge, MA: Harvard UP; New York: Vintage, 1978.

Dowden, K. *Death and the Maiden: Girls' Initiation Rites in Greek Mythology.* New York: Routledge, 1989.

Dowling, Linda. *Hellenism and Homosexuality in Victorian Oxford.* Ithaca: Cornell UP, 1994.

Dreger, L. 1940. "Das Bild im Spiegel. Ein Beitrag zur Geschichte der antiken Malerei." Heidelberg: privately printed PhD Dissertation U of Heidelberg, 1940.

Drescher, James. *Three Coptic Legends: Hilaria, Archellites, the Seven Sleepers.* Supplément aux Annales du Service des Antiquités de l'Égypte 4. Cairo: Imprimerie de l'Institut Français d'Archéologie Orientale, 1947.

duBois, Page. "Sappho and Helen." *Arethusa* 11 (1978): 89–99.

———. *Sappho Is Burning.* Chicago: U of Chicago P, 1995.

———. "The Subject in Antiquity after Foucault." In Larmour, Miller, and Platter, *Rethinking Sexuality.* 85–103.

Duggan, Lisa. "Making It Perfectly Queer." In Duggan and Hunter, *Sex Wars.* 155–172.

————, and Nan D. Hunter. *Sex Wars: Sexual Dissent and Political Culture.* New York: Routledge, 1995.

Durante, M. *Sulla pristoria della tradizione poetica greca, II: Risultanze della comparazione indoeuropea.* Rome: Edizioni dell'Ateneo, 1976.

Dworkin, Andrea. *Intercourse.* New York: Macmillan/Free P, 1987.

Dynes, Wayne R., and Stephen Donaldson, eds. *Homosexuality in the Ancient World.* Studies in Homosexuality 1. New York: Garland, 1992.

Edgeworth, R. "Saffron-Coloured Terms in Aeschylus." *Glotta* 66 (1988): 179–182.

Edwards, Mark. "Representation of Maenads on Archaic Red-Figure Vases." *Journal of Hellenic Studies* 80 (1960): 78–87.

Effinger, Maria. *Minoischer Schmuck.* BAR International Series 646. Oxford: Tempus Reparatum, 1996.

Elanskaya, Alla I. *The Literary Coptic Manuscripts in the A. S. Pushkin State Fine Arts Museum in Moscow.* Supplements to Vigiliae Christianae 18. Leiden: E. J. Brill, 1994.

Elm, Susanna. *'Virgins of God': The Making of Asceticism in Late Antiquity.* Oxford Classical Monographs. Oxford: Clarendon P, 1994.

Emmel, Stephen. "Shenoute's Literary Corpus." Dissertation Yale U, 1993. Ann Arbor: UMI, 1994.

Engelstein, Laura. *The Keys to Happiness: Sex and the Search for Modernity in Fin-de-Siècle Russia.* Ithaca: Cornell UP, 1992.

Evans, Peter, and Lyle Eveille. *Symposia and Women on Greek Vases.* London: Old Vicarage Publications, 1992.

Faderman, Lillian. *Surpassing the Love of Men: Romantic Friendships and Love between Women from the Renaissance to the Present.* New York: William Morrow, 1981.

Fairbanks, Arthur, trans. *Philostratus,* Imagines; *Callistratus,* Descriptions. Loeb Classical Library. New York: G. P. Putnam's Sons, 1931.

Fantham, Elaine, Helene Peet Foley, Natalie Boymel Kampen, Sarah B. Pomeroy, and H. Alan Shapiro, eds. *Women in the Classical World: Image and Text.* Oxford: Oxford UP, 1994.

Faraone, Christopher. "Aphrodite's ΚΕΣΤΟΣ and Apples for Atalanta: Aphrodisiacs in Early Greek Myth and Ritual." *Phoenix* 44 (1990): 219–243.

Farwell, M. R. "Toward a Definition of the Lesbian Literary Imagination." *Signs* 14 (1988): 100–118.

Feinberg, Leslie. *Transgender Warriors: Making History from Joan of Arc to RuPaul.* Boston: Beacon P, 1996.

Findlay, Heather. "Freud's 'Fetishism' and the Lesbian Dildo Debates." In *Out in Culture: Gay, Lesbian, and Queer Essays on Popular Culture*. Ed. Corey K. Creekmur and Alexander Doty. Durham: Duke UP, 1995. 328–342.

Fischer, H. G. "Another Pithemorphic Vessel of the Sixth Dynasty." *Journal of the American Research Center in Egypt* 30 (1993): 1–9.

Flacelière, Robert. *Love in Ancient Greece*. Trans. James Claugh. New York: Crown, 1962.

Foat, Michael Eugene. "I Myself Have Seen: The Representation of Humanity in the Writings of Apa Shenoute of Atripe." Dissertation Brown U, 1996.

Foucault, Michel. *The History of Sexuality: An Introduction*. Vol. 1. Trans. Robert Hurley. New York: Vintage, 1978.

——. *The History of Sexuality: The Use of Pleasure*. Vol. 2. Trans. Robert Hurley. New York: Vintage, 1985.

——. "Of Other Spaces: Utopias and Heterotopias." In *Rethinking Architecture*. Ed. N. Leach. London: Routledge, 1997. 350–356.

Fränkel, Hermann. *Early Greek Poetry and Philosophy*. Trans. Moses Hadas and James Willis. New York: Harcourt, Brace, Jovanovich, 1973.

Frankfurter, David. *Religion in Roman Egypt: Assimilation and Resistance*. Princeton: Princeton UP, 1998.

Friedman, S. S. "Creativity and the Childbirth Metaphor: Gender Difference in Literary Discourse." In *Speaking of Gender*. Ed. Elaine Showalter. New York and London: Routledge, 1989 [1987]. 73–100.

Friedrich, Paul. *The Meaning of Aphrodite*. Chicago: U of Chicago P, 1978.

Frontisi-Ducroux, Françoise. "Eros, Desire, and the Gaze." Trans. Nancy Kline. In Kampen, *Sexuality in Ancient Art*. 81–100.

——, and Jean-Pierre Vernant. *Dans l'oeil du miroir*. Paris: Odile Jacob, 1997.

Furiani, P. L. "Intimità e socialità in Nosside di Locri." In De Martino, *Rose di Pieria*. 177–195.

Fyfe, W. Hamilton, trans. *Aristotle, The Poetics, "Longinus" On the Sublime, Demetrius On Style*. Loeb Classical Library 199. Cambridge, MA: Harvard UP, 1982.

Garland, R. *The Greek Way of Death*. Ithaca: Cornell UP, 1985.

Garrison, R. H. *The Nutrition Desk Reference*. New Canaan, CT: Keats, 1985.

Gentili, Bruno. *Poetry and Its Public in Ancient Greece: From Homer to the Fifth Century*. Trans. A. Thomas Cole. Baltimore: Johns Hopkins UP, 1988.

Gesell, Geraldine. "Blood on the Horns of Consecration?" In *Proceedings of the First International Symposium: The Wall Paintings from Thera: Petros M. Nomikos Confer-*

ence Centre, Thera, Hellas: 30 August—4 September 1997. Ed. S. Sherrat. Piraeus, Greece: Petros M. Nomikos and the Thera Foundation, 2000. 947—956.

———. *Town, Palace, and House Cult in Minoan Crete.* Studies in Mediterranean Archaeology 67. Göteborg: P. Åströms Förlag, 1985.

Giacomelli [Carson], Anne. "The Justice of Aphrodite in Sappho Fr. 1." *Transactions of the American Philological Association* 110 (1980): 135—142.

Giangrande, G. "Arte Allusiva and Alexandrian Epic Poetry." *Classical Quarterly* 17 (1967): 85—97.

Gigante, M. "Nosside." *Parola del Passato* 29 (1974): 22—39.

———. "Il manifesto poetico di Nosside." *Letterature comparate, problemi e metodo: Studi in onore di Ettore Paratore.* Vol. 1. Bologna: Pàtron Editore, 1981. 243—245.

Gilbert, S. M., and S. Gubar. *The Madwoman in the Attic: The Woman Writer and the Nineteenth-Century Literary Imagination.* New Haven and London: Yale UP, 1979.

Gill, David. "Art and Vases vs. Craft and Pots." *Antiquity* 67 (1993): 452—455.

Ginouvès, René. *Balaneutikè: récherches sur le bain dans l'antiquité grecque.* Paris: Boccard, 1962.

Gladstone, Walter E. *Studies on Homer and the Homeric Age.* 3 vols. Oxford: Oxford UP, 1858.

Goff, Barbara. *Citizen Bacchae: Women's Ritual Practice in Ancient Greece.* Berkeley: U of California P, forthcoming.

Gold, Barbara. "Hroswitha Writes Herself: *Clamor Validus Gandeshemensis.*" In *Sex and Gender in Medieval and Renaissance Texts: The Latin Tradition.* Ed. Barbara K. Gold, Paul Allen Miller, and Charles Platter. Albany: State University of New York P, 1997. 41—70.

Golden, Mark. *Children and Childhood in Classical Athens.* Baltimore: Johns Hopkins UP, 1990.

———. "Thirteen Years of Homosexuality (and Other Recent Work on Sex, Gender and the Body in Ancient Greece)." *Echos du Monde Classique/Classical Views* 35 n.s. 10 (1991): 327—340.

Gomme, A. W. "The Position of Women in Athens in the Fifth and Fourth Centuries." *Classical Philology* 20 (1925): 1—25.

Gordon, Pamela. "The Lover's Voice in *Heroides* 15: Or, Why Is Sappho a Man?" In Hallett and Skinner, *Roman Sexualities.* 274—294.

Gould, Virginia Meacham. *Henriette Delille: "Servant of Slaves."* New Orleans: Sisters of the Holy Family, 1999.

Gourevitch, Danielle. "La Sexualité de l'Antiquité: essai à propos de publications récentes." *Antiquité Classique* 68 (1999): 331–334.

Gow, A. S. F., and D. L. Page, eds. *The Greek Anthology: Hellenistic Epigrams.* 2 vols. Cambridge: Cambridge UP, 1965.

Graham, Walter. *The Palaces of Crete.* Rev. ed. Princeton: Princeton UP, 1987.

Grahn, Judy. *Another Mother Tongue: Gay Words, Gay Worlds.* Boston: Beacon, 1984.

————. *The Highest Apple: Sappho and the Lesbian Poetic Tradition.* San Francisco: Spinsters, Ink, 1985.

Grassinger, Dagmar. *Römische Marmorkratere.* Monumenta Artis Romanae XVIII. Mainz am Rhein: P. von Zabern, 1991.

Greenberg, David F. *The Construction of Homosexuality.* Chicago: U of Chicago P, 1988.

Greene, Ellen, "Apostrophe and Women's Erotics in the Poetry of Sappho." *Transactions of the American Philological Association* 124 (1994): 41–56.

————, ed. *Reading Sappho: Contemporary Approaches.* Berkeley: U of California P, 1996.

————. "Re-Figuring the Feminine Voice: Catullus Translating Sappho." *Arethusa* 32 (1999): 1–18.

————, ed. *Re-Reading Sappho: Reception and Transmission.* Berkeley: U of California P, 1996.

Griggs, Claudine. *S/he: Changing Sex and Changing Clothes.* New York: Berg, 1998.

Grimal, Pierre. *L'Amour à Rome.* Paris: Hachette, 1963.

Gubar, Susan. "Sapphistries." In *The Lesbian Issue from Signs.* Ed. Estelle Freedman, Barbara C. Gelpi, Susan L. Johnson, and Kathleen M. Weston. Chicago: U of Chicago P, 1984. 91–110. Rpt. Greene, *Re-Reading.* 199–217.

Guillory, Monique. "Some Enchanted Evening on the Auction Block: the Cultural Legacy of the New Orleans Quadroon Balls." Dissertation New York U, 1999. Ann Arbor: UMI, 1999.

Gutzwiller, K. J. *Poetic Garlands: Hellenistic Epigrams in Context.* Berkeley: California UP, 1998.

Habinek, Thomas N. *The Politics of Latin Literature: Writing, Identity, and Empire in Ancient Rome.* Princeton: Princeton UP, 1998.

Hägg, Robin. "Pictorial Programmes in Minoan Palaces and Villas?" In Darcque and Poursat, *L'Iconographie minoenne.* 209–217.

————, and Nanno Marinatos, eds. *The Function of the Minoan Palaces: Proceedings of the Fourth International Symposium at the Swedish Institute in Athens, 10–16 June 1984.*

Acta Instituti Atheniensis Regni Suciae 4, 35. Stockholm: Swedish Institute in Athens, 1987.

Haigh, A. E. *The Attic Theatre.* 3rd ed. Oxford: Clarendon P, 1907.

Halbherr, Federico, E. Stefani, and L. Banti. "Haghia Triada nel periodo tardo palaziale." *Annuario della Scuola Italiana di Atene* 31 (1977 [1980]): 9–342.

Hallett, Judith. "Female Homoeroticism and the Denial of Roman Reality in Latin Literature." *Yale Journal of Criticism* 3 (1989): 209–227. Rpt. Hallett and Skinner, *Roman Sexualities.* 255–273.

———. "Sappho and Her Social Context: Sense and Sensuality." *Signs* 4 (1979): 447–464. Rpt. Greene, *Reading.* 125–142.

———, and Marilyn B. Skinner, eds. *Roman Sexualities.* Princeton: Princeton UP, 1997.

Halperin, David M. "Lesbian Historiography before the Name?" *GLQ: Journal of Lesbian and Gay Studies* 4 (1998): 557–630.

———. *One Hundred Years of Homosexuality and Other Essays on Greek Love.* New York: Routledge, 1990.

———. "Questions of Evidence: Commentary on Koehl, DeVries, and Williams." In *Queer Representations: Reading Lives, Reading Cultures.* Ed. Martin Duberman. New York: New York UP, 1997. 39–54.

———, John J. Winkler, and Froma I. Zeitlin, eds. *Before Sexuality: The Construction of Erotic Experience in the Ancient Greek World.* Princeton: Princeton UP, 1990.

Hambly, Barbara. *A Free Man of Color.* New York: Bantam Books, 1997.

Hanson, A. E. "Conception, Gestation, and the Origin of Female Nature in the Corpus Hippocraticum." *Helios* 19 (1992): 31–71.

Hanson, Victor. *Who Killed Homer?: The Demise of Classical Education and the Recovery of Greek Wisdom.* Berkeley: U of California P, 2000.

Hardy, D. A., C. G. Doumas, J. A. Sakellarakis, and P. M. Warren, eds. *Thera and the Aegean World III: Proceedings of the Third International Congress, Santorini, Greece, 3–9 September 1989.* London: Thera Foundation, 1990.

Harriott, R. *Poetry and Criticism before Plato.* London: Methuen, 1969.

Harris, R. S., and W. H. Sebrell, *The Vitamins: Chemistry, Physiology, Pathology, Methods.* New York: Academic Press, 1968.

Harrison, Evelyn B. "Greek Sculptural Coiffures and Ritual Haircuts." In *Early Greek Cult Practice: Proceedings of the Fifth International Symposium at the Swedish Institute at Athens, 26–29 June 1986.* Ed. Robin Hägg, Nanno Marinatos, and Gullug C. Nordquist. Stockholm: Swedish Institute in Athens, 1988. 247–254.

Hart, Lynda. *Between the Body and the Flesh: Performing Sadomasochism*. New York: Columbia UP, 1998.

Hartmann, Heidi. "The Unhappy Marriage of Marxism and Feminism: Towards a More Progressive Union." In *Women and Revolution: A Discussion of the Unhappy Marriage of Marxism and Feminism*. Ed. Lydia Sargent. Boston: South End P, 1981. 1–42.

Hartwig, P. " Ἐπίνητρον ἐξ Ἐρετρίας." *Ἀρχαιολογικὴ Ἐφημερίς* (1897): cols. 129–142.

Harvey, David. "Painted Ladies: Fact, Fiction and Fantasy." In Christiansen and Melander, *Proceedings*. 242–254.

Harvey, Elizabeth. "Ventriloquizing Sappho, or the Lesbian Muse." In Greene, *Re-Reading*. 79–104.

Haspels, C. H. E. "Deux fragments d'une coupe d'Euphronios." *Bulletin de correspondance hellenique* 54 (1930): 422–451.

Hastings, Harold R. "On the Relation between Inscriptions and Sculptured Representations on Attic Tombstones." *Bulletin of the University of Wisconsin* 485 (1912): 1–16.

Hawley, Richard, and Barbara Levick, eds. *Women in Antiquity: New Assessments*. London: Routledge, 1995.

Henderson, Jeffrey. "Greek Attitudes toward Sex." In *Civilization of the Ancient Mediterranean: Greece and Rome*. Vol. 2. Ed. Michael Grant. New York: Charles Scribner's and Sons, 1988. 1249–1263.

———. *The Maculate Muse: Obscene Language in Attic Comedy*. 2nd ed. New York: Oxford UP, 1991.

Herrmann, Winfried. 1968. "Spiegelbild im Spiegel: Zur Darstellung auf frühlukanischen Vasen." *Wissenschaftliche Zeitschrift der Universität Rostock. Gesellschafts- und sprachwissenschaftliche Reihe* 17 (1968): 667–671.

Herzfeld, Michael. "Silence, Submission, Subversion: Toward a Poetics of Womanhood." In *Contested Identities: Gender and Kinship in Modern Greece*. Ed. Peter Loizos and Evthymios Papataxiarchis. Princeton: Princeton UP, 1991. 79–87.

———. "Within and Without: The Category of 'Female' in the Ethnography of Modern Greece." In *Gender and Power in Rural Greece*. Ed. Jill Dubisch. Princeton: Princeton UP, 1986. 215–233.

Hinds, S. *Allusion and Intertext: Dynamics of Appropriation in Roman Poetry*. Cambridge: Cambridge UP, 1998.

Höckmann, O. "Theran Floral Style in Relation to That of Crete." In *Thera and the Aegean World 1: Papers Presented at the Second International Scientific Congress, San-*

torini, Greece, August 1978. Vol. 1. Ed. Christos Doumas. London: Thera and the Aegean World, 1978. 755–764.

Holst-Warhaft, Gail. *Dangerous Voices: Women's Laments and Greek Literature.* London: Routledge, 1992.

Hood, Sinclair. *The Arts in Prehistoric Greece.* Harmondsworth: Penguin, 1978.

———. "The Primitive Aspects of Minoan Artistic Convention." In Darcque and Poursat, *L'Iconographie minoenne.* 21–26.

Hotchkiss, Valerie R. *Clothes Make the Man: Female Cross Dressing in Medieval Europe.* The New Middle Ages. New York: Garland, 1996.

Humphreys, S. C. *The Family, Women and Death: Comparative Studies.* 2nd ed. Ann Arbor: U of Michigan P, 1993.

Hupperts, Charles. "Greek Love: Homosexuality or Paederasty? Greek Love in Black Figure Vase-painting." In Christiansen and Melander, *Proceedings.* 255–268.

Idel, Moshe, and Bernard McGinn, eds. *Mystical Union and Monotheistic Faith.* New York: MacMillan, 1989.

Immerwahr, Sara A. *Aegean Painting in the Bronze Age.* University Park: Pennsylvania State UP, 1990.

Irigaray, Luce. *This Sex Which Is Not One.* Trans. Catherine Porter, with Carolyn Burke. Ithaca: Cornell UP, 1985.

Isager, S. "Gynaikonitis." *Museum Tusculanum* 32–33 (1978): 39–42.

Jacobson, Howard. *Ovid's Heroides.* Princeton: Princeton UP, 1974.

Jagose, Annamarie. *Queer Theory: An Introduction.* New York: New York UP, 1996.

Jakobsen, Janet R. "Queer Is? Queer Does? Normativity and the Problem of Resistance." *GLQ: Journal of Lesbian and Gay Studies* 4 (1998): 511–536.

Jameson, Michael. "Private Space and the Greek City." In *The Greek City from Homer to Alexander.* Ed. Oswyn Murray and Simon Price. Oxford: Clarendon P, 1990. 171–195.

Jebb, R. C. *The Growth and Influence of Classical Greek Poetry.* Boston and New York: Houghton, Mifflin, 1893.

Jenkins, I. D. "Is There Life after Marriage? A Study of the Abduction Motif in Vase Paintings of the Athenian Wedding Ceremony." *Bulletin of the Institute of Classical Studies* 30 (1983): 137–145.

Jenkyns, Richard. "Bernal and the Nineteenth Century." In Lefkowitz and Rogers, *Black Athena Revisited.* 411–420.

———. *Three Classical Poets: Sappho, Catullus and Juvenal.* Cambridge, MA: Harvard UP, 1982.

————. *The Victorians and Ancient Greece.* Cambridge, MA: Harvard UP, 1980.

Jocelyn, H. D. "A Greek Indecency and Its Students: ΛΑΙΚΑΖΕΙΝ." *Proceedings of the Cambridge Philological Society* 206 n.s. 26 (1980): 12–66.

Johansen, K. Friis. *The Attic Grave-reliefs of the Classical Period.* Copenhagen: E. Munksgaard, 1951.

Johns, Catherine. *Sex or Symbol: Erotic Images of Greece and Rome.* Austin: U of Texas P, 1982.

Johnston, Sarah I. *Restless Dead: Encounters between the Living and the Dead in Ancient Greece.* Berkeley: U of California P, 1999.

Jones, Bernice R. "Revealing Minoan Fashion." *Archaeology* 53.3 (2000): 36–41.

Jones, C. P. *Culture and Society in Lucian.* Cambridge, MA: Harvard UP, 1986.

Kahil, Lilly. "Mythological Repertoire of Brauron." In Moon, *Art and Iconography.* 231–244.

Kaiser, Bernd. *Untersuchung zum minoischen Relief.* Bonn: Habelts Dissertationsdrücke 1976.

Kalogeropoulou, Athena. "Drei attische Grabreliefs." In *Archaische und klassische griechische Plastik: Akten des internationalen Kolloquiums vom 22–25. April 1985 in Athen, II, Klassische griechische Plastik.* Ed. Helmut Kyrieleis. Mainz: Philipp von Zabern, 1986. 119–133.

Kamboj, V. P. "A Review of Indian Medicinal Plants with Interceptive Activity." *Indian Journal of Medical Research* 87 (1988): 336–355.

Kampen, Natalie. "Epilogue: Gender and Desire." In Koloski-Ostrow and Lyons, *Naked Truths.* 267–278.

————, ed. *Sexuality in Ancient Art.* Cambridge: Cambridge UP, 1996.

Karageorghis, Vassos. "Rites de Passage at Thera: Some Oriental Comparanda." In Hardy et al., *Thera,* vol. 1. 67–71.

Karouzou, Semni. 1968. *National Archaeological Museum. Collection of Sculpture: A Catalogue.* Athens: General Direction of Antiquities and Restoration, 1968.

Katz, Marilyn Arthur. "Ideology and the 'Status of Women' in Ancient Greece." *History and Theory* 31 (1992): 70–97.

Keenan, James G. "Egypt from 425 to 600." *Cambridge Ancient History* XIV. Cambridge: Cambridge UP, 2001. 612–637.

Kenna, V. E. G. *Corpus der Minoischen und Mykenischen Siegel,* VII, *Die englischen museen.* Berlin: Gebrüder Mann Verlag, 1967.

Kennedy, Elizabeth, and Madelyn Davis. *Boots of Leather, Slippers of Gold: The History of a Lesbian Community.* New York: Routledge, 1993.

Kerber, Linda K. "Separate Spheres, Female Worlds, Woman's Place: The Rhetoric of Women's History." *Journal of American History* 75 (1988): 9–39.

Keuls, Eva C. "Attic Vase-Painting and the Home Textile Industry." In Moon, *Ancient Greek Art.* 209–230.

————. *The Reign of the Phallus: Sexual Politics in Ancient Athens.* Berkeley: U of California P, 1985.

Kilmer, Martin F. "Genital Phobia and Depilation." *Journal of Hellenic Studies* 102 (1982): 104–112.

————. *Greek Erotica on Attic Red-Figure Vases.* London: Duckworth, 1993.

King, H. "Bound to Bleed: Artemis and Greek Women." In Cameron and Kuhrt, *Images.* 109–127.

Kitto, H. D. F. *The Greeks.* Harmondsworth: Penguin, 1951.

Klaich, Dolores. *Woman + Woman: Attitudes toward Lesbianism.* New York: Simon and Schuster, 1974; Morrow, 1975.

Klein, A. *Child Life in Greek Art.* New York: Columbia UP, 1932.

Knigge, Ursula. *Der Kerameikos von Athen. Führung durch Ausgrabungen und Geschichte.* Athens: Deutsches Archäologisches Institut Athen, 1988.

Knoepfler, Denis. 1993. *Les imagiers de l'Oreste. Mille ans d'art antique autour d'un mythe grec.* Zurich: Akanthus, 1993.

Koch-Harnack, Gundel. *Erotische Symbole: Lotusblüte und gemeinsamer Mantel auf antiken Vasen.* Berlin: Gebrüder Mann Verlag, 1989.

————. *Knabenliebe und Tiergeschenke.* Berlin: Gebrüder Mann Studio-Reihe, 1983.

Koloski-Ostrow, Ann, and Claire Lyons, eds. *Naked Truths: Women, Sexuality and Gender in Classical Art and Archaeology.* New York: Routledge, 1997.

Konstan, David. *Friendship in the Classical World.* Key Themes in Ancient History. Cambridge: Cambridge UP, 1997.

————. "Philosophy, Friendship and Cultural History." In *Inventing Ancient Culture: Historicism, Periodization and the Ancient World.* Ed. Mark Golden and Peter Toohey. London: Routledge, 1997. 66–78.

Kontorli-Papadopoulou, L. *Aegean Frescoes of Religious Character.* Studies in Mediterranean Archaeology 117. Göteborg: P. Åströms Förlag, 1996.

Koschorke, Klaus, Stefan Timm, and Frederik Wisse. "Schenute: De Certamine Contra Diabolum." *Oriens Christianus* 59 (1975): 60–77.

Kozloff, A. P., and B. M. Bryan. *Egypt's Dazzling Sun: Amenhotep III and His World.* Cleveland: Cleveland Museum of Art in Cooperation with Bloomington: Indiana UP, 1992.

Kraemer, Ross S., ed. *Maenads, Martyrs, Matrons, Monastics: A Sourcebook on Women's Religions in the Greco-Roman World.* Philadelphia: Fortress P, 1988.

Krawiec, Rebecca. "Space, Distance and Gender: Authority and the Separation of Communities in the White Monastery." *Bulletin of the American Society of Papyrologists* 35 (1998): 45–63.

———. "Women's Life in Shenute's White Monastery: A Study in Late Antique Egyptian Monasticism." Dissertation Yale U, 1996. Ann Arbor: UMI, 1999, c 1997.

Kuhn, K. H. *Letters and Sermons of Besa.* Corpus Scriptorum Christianorum Orientalium, Scriptores Coptici, 21–22. Louvain: Imprimerie Orientaliste L. Durbecq, 1956.

———. *Pseudo-Shenoute on Christian Behavior.* Corpus Scriptorum Christianorum Orientalium, Scriptores Coptici, 29–30. Louvain: Secrétariat du Corpus CSO, 1960.

———. "Two Shenoute Texts." In *Festschrift zum 100-jährigen Bestehen der Papyrussammlung der österreichischen Nationalbibliothek: Papyrus Erzherzog Rainer (P. Rainer Cent.).* Vienna: Verlag Brüder Hollinek, 1983. 187–189.

Kurke, Leslie. *Coins, Bodies, Games, and Gold: The Politics of Meaning in Archaic Greece.* Princeton: Princeton UP, 1999.

———. "Inventing the *Hetaira:* Sex, Politics, and Discursive Conflict in Archaic Greece." *Classical Antiquity* 16 (1997): 106–150.

———. "The Politics of ʽαβροσύνη in Ancient Greece." *Classical Antiquity* 11 (1992): 91–170.

Kurtz, Donna Carol, and John Boardman. "Booners." In *Greek Vases in the J. Paul Getty Museum.* Vol. 3. Malibu, CA: J. Paul Getty Museum, 1986. 35–70.

———. *Greek Burial Customs.* Ithaca: Cornell UP: 1971.

Laffineur, R., and J. L. Crowley, eds. *EIKΩN: Aegean Bronze Age Iconography: Shaping a Methodology: Proceedings of the 4th International Aegean Conference, University of Tasmania, Hobart, 6–9 April 1992.* Aegaeum 8. Liège: Université de Liège, Histoire de l'art et archéologie de la Grèce antique, 1992.

Lamos, Colleen. "The Postmodern Lesbian Position: *On Our Backs.*" In *The Lesbian Postmodern.* Ed. Laura Doan. New York: Columbia UP, 1994. 85–103.

Lanata, G. "Sappho's Amatory Language." Trans. W. Robins. In Greene, *Reading.* 11–25.

Laqueur, Thomas. "Amor Veneris, vel Dulcedo Appeletur." In *Fragments for a History of the Human Body.* Part 3. Ed. Michael Feher. New York: Zone, 1989. 91–131.

Lardinois, André. "Lesbian Sappho and Sappho of Lesbos." In *From Sappho to de Sade: Moments in the History of Sexuality.* Ed. Jan Bremmer. London: Routledge, 1989. 15–35.

————. "Subject and Circumstance in Sappho's Poetry." *Transactions of the American Philological Association* 124 (1994): 57–84.

————. "Who Sang Sappho's Songs?" In Greene, *Reading.* 150–172.

Larmour, David H. J., Paul Allen Miller, and Charles Platter, eds. *Rethinking Sexuality: Foucault and Classical Antiquity.* Princeton: Princeton UP, 1998.

Lawler, Lillian Beatrice. *The Dance in Ancient Greece.* Middletown: Wesleyan UP, 1964.

————. "The Maenads: A Contribution to the Study of the Dance in Ancient Greece." *Memoirs of the American Academy in Rome* 6 (1927): 69–110.

The Lawrence Review of Natural Products. St. Louis: Facts and Comparisons, June 1996.

Layton, Bentley. *Catalogue of Coptic Literary Manuscripts in the British Library Acquired since the Year 1906.* London: British Library, 1987.

Leader, R. E. "In Death Not Divided: Gender, Family, and State on Classical Athenian Stelai." *American Journal of Archaeology* 101 (1997): 683–699.

Lee, Mireille. "Deciphering Gender in Minoan Dress." In *Reading the Body: Representations and Remains in the Archaeological Record.* Ed. Alison E. Rautman. Philadelphia: U of Pennsylvania P, 2000. 111–123.

Lefkowitz, Mary. "Ancient History, Modern Myths." In Lefkowitz and Rogers, *Black Athena Revisited.* 3–23.

————. "Critical Stereotypes and the Poetry of Sappho." *Greek, Roman, and Byzantine Studies* 14 (1973): 113–123.

————, and Guy MacLean Rogers, eds. *Black Athena Revisited.* Chapel Hill: U of North Carolina P, 1996.

Lefort, L. Th. *Œuvres de S. Pachôme et de ses disciples.* Corpus Scriptorum Christianorum Orientalium, Scriptores Coptici, 23–24. Louvain: Imprimerie Orientaliste L. Durbecq, 1956.

Leipoldt, Johannes. *Schenute von Atripe und die Entstehung des national ägyptischen Christentums.* Texte und Untersuchungen zur Geschichte der altchristlichen Literatur, 25. Leipzig: J. C. Hinrichs, 1903.

————, and W. E. Crum. *Sinuthii Archimandritae vita et opera omnia: Textus III.* Corpus Scriptorum Christianorum Orientalium, Scriptores Coptici, Series II 4. Paris: E typographeo reipublicae, 1908.

————, and W. E. Crum. *Sinuthii Archimandritae vita et opera omnia: Textus IV.* Corpus Scriptorum Christianorum Orientalium, Scriptores Coptici, Series II 5. Paris: E typographeo reipublicae, 1913.

Levi, Doro. "Early Hellenic Pottery of Crete." *Hesperia* 14 (1945): 1–32.

Lewis, W. H., and M. P. F. Elvin-Lewis. *Medical Botany*. New York: John Wiley and Sons, 1977. 325–329.

Lexicon Iconographicum Mythologiae Classicae. Zurich and Munich: Artemis Verlag, 1981–1997.

Lezzi-Hafter, Adrienne. *Der Eretria-Maler: Werke und Weggefährten*. Mainz: Philipp von Zabern, 1988.

Licht, Hans (P. Brandt). *Sexual Life in Ancient Greece*. Trans. J. H. Freese. London: Abbey Library, 1932.

Lilja, Saara. *Homosexuality in Republican and Augustan Rome*. Commentationes Humanarum Litterarum 74. Finnish Society of Sciences and Letters: Ekenäs, 1983.

Lindsay, Jack. *Helen of Troy: Woman and Goddess*. Totowa, NJ: Rowman and Littlefield, 1974.

Lipking, Lawrence. *Abandoned Women and Poetic Tradition*. Chicago: U of Chicago P, 1988.

Lissarrague, François. "Figures of Women." In *A History of Women in the West*, Vol. 1, *From Ancient Goddesses to Christian Saints*. Ed. Pauline Schmitt Pantel. Trans. Arthur Goldhammer. General eds. Georges Duby and Michelle Perrot. Cambridge, MA: Belknap P of Harvard UP, 1992. 139–229.

———. "Regards sur le mariage grec." In Cavalier, *Silence*. 415–434.

———. "The Sexual Life of Satyrs." In Halperin, Winkler, and Zeitlin, *Before Sexuality*. 53–81.

———. "Unpublished Seminar on Eros." Presented at the Centre Louis Gernet, March 22, 2000.

———. "Women, Boxes, Containers: Some Signs and Metaphors." In Reeder, *Pandora*. 91–101.

Liventhal, Viveca. "What Goes on among the Women: The Settings of Some Attic Vase Paintings of the Fifth Century B.C." *Analecta Romana Institute Danici* 14 (1985): 37–52.

Lobel, E., and D. Page, eds. *Poetarum Lesbiorum Fragmenta*. Oxford: Clarendon Press, 1963 [1955].

Loraux, Nicole. *L'Invention d'Athènes: Histoire de l'oraison funèbre dans la "cité classique."* 2nd ed. Paris: Éditions Payot & Rivages, 1993.

Lowe, N. J. 1998. "Thesmophoria and Haloa: Myth, Physics and Mysteries." In *Sacred and the Feminine in Ancient Greece*. Ed. S. Blundell and M. Williamson. New York: Routledge, 1998. 149–186.

Luck, G. "Die Dichterinnen der griechischen Anthologie." *Museum Helveticum* 11 (1954): 170–187.

Lundström, Vilelmus. *Anecdota Byzantina e codicibus Upsaliensibus,* Fasc. 1. Uppsala: Libraria Lundequistiana, 1902.

Mace, Sarah. "Amour, Encore! The Development of δηὖτε in Archaic Lyric." *Greek, Roman, and Byzantine Studies* 34 (1993): 335–364.

Mackail, J. M. *Lectures on Greek Poetry.* London: Longmans, Green, 1911.

MacKenzie, J. A. Ross. "The Patristic Witness to the Virgin Mary as the New Eve." *Marian Studies* 29 (1978): 67–78.

MacLachlan, B. C. "Love, War, and the Goddess in Fifth-Century Locri." *Ancient World* 26.2 (1995): 205–223.

MacMullen, Ramsay. "Roman Attitudes to Greek Love." Rpt. in Dynes and Donaldson, *Homosexuality.* 348–358.

Madan, C. L., B. M. Kapur, and U. S. Gupta. "Saffron." *Economic Botany* 20 (1966): 377–385.

Makowski, John F. "Bisexual Orpheus: Pederasty and Parody in Ovid." *Classical Journal* 92.1 (1996): 25–38.

Manniche, Lise. *Sexual Life in Ancient Egypt.* London and New York: Routledge and Kegan Paul, 1987.

Marcadé, Jean. *Eros Kalos: Essay on Erotic Elements in Greek Art.* Geneva: Nagel, 1962.

Marcovich, Miroslav. "Sappho Fr. 31: Anxiety Attack or Love Declaration?" *Classical Quarterly* 22 (1972): 19–32.

Marinatos, Nanno. *Art and Religion in Thera: Reconstructing a Bronze Age Society.* Athens: D. and I. Mathioulakis, 1984.

———. "The Function and Interpretation of the Theran Frescoes." In Darcque and Poursat, *L'Iconographie minoenne.* 219–230.

———. *Minoan Religion: Ritual, Image, and Symbol.* Columbia: U of South Carolina P, 1993.

———. "An Offering of Saffron to the Minoan Goddess of Nature: The Role of the Monkey and the Importance of Saffron." In *Gifts to the Gods.* Ed. T. Linders and G. C. Nordquist. Uppsala: Academia Ubsaliensis, 1987. 123–132.

———. "Role and Sex Division in Ritual Scenes of Aegean Art." *Journal of Prehistoric Religion* 1 (1987): 23–34.

———, and R. Hägg. "On the Ceremonial Function of the Minoan Polythyron." *Opuscula Atheniensia* 16 (1986): 57–73.

Marinatos, Spyridon. *Excavations at Thera.* 7 vols. Athens: Athens Archaeological Society, 1968–1976.

————, and Max Hirmer. *Crete and Mycenae.* New York: Abrams, 1960.

Marry, J. D. "Sappho and the Heroic Ideal: *erôtos aretê.*" *Arethusa* 12 (1979): 71–92.

Martos Montiel, Juan Francisco. *Desde Lesbos con Amor: Homosexualidad femenina en la antigüedad.* Supplementa Mediterránea, 1. Madrid: Ediciones Clásicas, 1996.

Matthäus, H. *Die Bronzegefässe der kretisch-mykenischen Kultur.* Prähistorische Bronzefunde II.1. Munich: C. H. Beck, 1980.

Matz, Friedrich. *Die dionysischen Sarkophage.* 4 vols. Deutsches Archäologisches Institut, Antiken Sarkophagreliefs. Berlin: Gebr. Mann Verlag, 1968.

McCracken, George E. *Arnobius of Sicca, The Case against the Pagans.* 2 vols. Ancient Christian Writers: The Works of the Fathers in Translation, 7 and 8. Catholic U of America. Westminster, MD: Newman P, 1949; Cork: Mercier P, 1949.

McEvilley, Thomas. "Sappho, Fragment 94." *Phoenix* 25 (1971): 1–11.

McGeorge, P. J. P. "Biosocial Evolution in Bronze Age Crete." In *ΕΙΛΑΠΙΝΗ. Τόμος τιμητικός για τον καθηγητή Νικολάο Πλάτωνα.* Athens: Athens Archaeological Society, 1987. 407–416.

————. "A Comparative Study of the Mean Life Expectation of the Minoans." *Acts of the 6th Cretological Congress.* Vol. A1. Herakleion, 1990. 419–428.

————. "Νέα στοιχεία για το μέσο όρο ζωής στη μινωκή Κρήτη." *Κρητική Εστία.* 4th ser. 1 (1987): 9–15.

McGuire, Brian Patrick. *Friendship and Community: The Monastic Experience 350–1250.* Cistercian Studies Series 95. Kalamazoo, MI: Cistercian Publications, 1988.

McManus, Barbara. *Classics and Feminism: Gendering the Classics.* New York: Twayne, 1997.

————. "Multicentering: The Case of the Athenian Bride." *Helios* 7 (1990): 225–235.

McNally, Sheila. "The Maenad in Early Greek Art." *Arethusa* 11 (1978): 101–135.

Medhurst, Andy, and Sally R. Munt, eds. *Lesbian and Gay Studies: A Critical Introduction.* London: Cassell, 1997.

Merck, Mandy, Naomi Segal, and Elizabeth Wright, eds. *Coming Out of Feminism?* Oxford: Blackwell, 1998.

Merkelbach, R. "Sappho und ihr Kreis." *Philologus* 101 (1957): 1–29.

Meyer, E. A. "Epitaphs and Citizenship in Classical Athens." *Journal of Hellenic Studies* 113 (1993): 99–121.

Meyer, Marvin, and Richard Smith, eds. *Ancient Christian Magic: Coptic Texts of Ritual Power.* San Francisco: HarperSanFrancisco, 1994.

Mihalopoulos, Catie. "Images of Women and Concepts of Popular Culture in

Classical Athens: 450–400 B.C." Dissertation U of Southern California, 2001.

Miller, M. C. "The Parasol: An Oriental Status-Symbol in Late Archaic and Classical Athens." *Journal of Hellenic Studies* 112 (1992): 91–105.

Mohanty, Chandra Talpade. "Under Western Eyes: Feminist Scholarship and Colonial Discourses." In *Third World Women and the Politics of Feminism.* Ed. Chandra Mohanty, Ann Russo, and Lourdes Torres. Bloomington: Indiana UP, 1991. 51–80.

Mommsen, Theodor, and Paul Krueger, eds., and Alan Watson, trans. *The* Digest *of Justinian.* Philadelphia: U of Pennsylvania P, 1985.

Montserrat, Dominic. *Sex and Society in Graeco-Roman Egypt.* London: Kegan Paul, 1996.

Moon, Warren G., ed. *Ancient Greek Art and Iconography.* Madison: U of Wisconsin P, 1983.

Morgan, Lyvia. "Island Iconography: Thera, Kea, Milos." In Hardy et al., *Thera,* vol. III. 252–266.

Morley, Neville. *Writing Ancient History.* Ithaca: Cornell UP, 1999.

Morris, Ian. "Archaeology and Gender Ideologies in Early Archaic Greece." *Transactions of the American Philological Association* 129 (1999): 305–317.

———. *Burial and Ancient Society.* New York: Cambridge UP, 1987.

———. "Law, Culture and Funerary Art in Athens: 600–300 B.C." *Hephaistos* 11–12 (1992–1993): 35–50.

Most, Glenn. "Reflecting Sappho." In Greene, *Re-Reading.* 11–35.

Mountfield, David. *Greek and Roman Erotica.* New York: Crescent Books, 1982.

Mras, Carl, ed. *Luciani Dialogi Meretricii.* Berlin: Walter De Gruyter, 1930.

Mulas, Antonia. *Eros in Antiquity.* New York: Erotic Book Society, 1978.

Müller, Frank G. J. M. *The Aldobrandini Wedding.* Iconological Studies in Roman Art 3. Amsterdam: J. C. Gieben, 1994.

Mulvey, Laura. *Visual and Other Pleasures.* Bloomington: Indiana UP, 1989.

Murray, Gilbert. "The Value of Greece to the Future of the World." In *The Legacy of Greece.* Ed. Richard W. Livingstone. Oxford: Clarendon P, 1928. 1–24.

Murray, P. "Poetic Inspiration in Early Greece." *Journal of Hellenic Studies* 101 (1981): 87–100.

Nadkarni, K. M. *Indian materia medica with Ayurvedic, Unani-Tibbi, Siddha, allopathic, homeopathic, naturopathic and home remedies, appendices and indexes.* Bombay: Popular Prakashan, 1976.

Nagle, Jill. "Girl/FAG!" *Curve* (January 1999): 30–31.

Nangeroni, Nancy R. "Transgenderism." *http://www.altsex.org/transgender/ Nangeroni.html.*

Napoli. See under *Le collezioni del Museo di Napoli.*

Neumann, Günter. *Gesten und Gebärden.* Berlin: Walter de Gruyter, 1965.

Nevett, Lisa C. *House and Society in the Ancient Greek World.* Cambridge: Cambridge UP, 1999.

Newton, Esther. "The Mythic Mannish Lesbian: Radclyffe Hall and the New Woman." *Signs* 9 (1984): 557–575.

Nielsen, Thomas H., Lars Bjertrup, Mogens Herman Hansen, Lene Rubinstein, and Torben Vestergaard. "Athenian Grave Monuments and Social Class." *Greek, Roman and Byzantine Studies* 30 (1989): 411–420.

Niemeier, Wolf-Dietrich. "Iconography and Context: The Thera Frescoes." In Laffineur and Crowley, *EIKΩN.* 97–104.

Noble, Joseph Veach. *The Techniques of Painted Attic Pottery.* Rev. ed. New York: Thames and Hudson, 1988.

Nordfeldt, AnnCharlotte. "Residential Quarters and Lustral Basins." In Hägg and Marinatos, *Function of Minoan Palaces.* 187–193.

Norton, Robert. "The Tyranny of Germany over Greece?" In Lefkowitz and Rogers, *Black Athena Revisited.* 403–410.

Nussbaum, Martha. "Platonic Love and Colorado Law: The Relevance of Ancient Greek Norms to Modern Sexual Controversies." *Virginia Law Review* 80 (1994): 1515–1651.

Oakley, John H. "The Anakalypteria." *Archäologischer Anzeiger* (1982): 113–118.

———. "Nuptial Nuances: Wedding Images in Non-Wedding Scenes of Myth." In Reeder, *Pandora.* 63–73.

———. *The Phiale Painter.* Mainz: Philipp von Zabern, 1990.

———, and Rebecca H. Sinos. *The Wedding in Ancient Athens.* Madison: U of Wisconsin P, 1993.

———, William D. E. Coulson, and Olga Palagia, eds. *Athenian Potters and Painters.* Oxford Monograph 67. Oxford: Oxford UP, 1997.

Olsen, T. "One out of Twelve: Writers Who Are Women in Our Century." *Silences.* New York: Dell, 1978 [1971]. 22–46.

Osborne, Catherine. *Eros Unveiled: Plato and the God of Love.* Oxford: Clarendon P, 1994.

Osborne, Robin. "Desiring Women on Athenian Pottery." In Kampen, *Sexuality in Ancient Art.* 65–80.

Padgett, Michael. "The Workshop of the Syleus Sequence: A Wider Circle." In Oakley, Coulson, and Palagia, *Athenian Potters*. 213–230.

Page, Denys. *Sappho and Alcaeus: An Introduction to the Study of Ancient Lesbian Poetry*. Oxford: Oxford UP, 1955.

———, ed. *Epigrammata Graeca*. Oxford: Oxford UP, 1975.

Palyvou, Clairy. "Architectural Design at Late Cycladic Akrotiri." In Hardy et al., *Thera*, vol. III. 44–56.

Pantel, Pauline Schmitt, ed. *A History of Women in the West*, Vol. 1, *From Ancient Goddesses to Christian Saints*. Trans. Arthur Goldhammer. General eds. Georges Duby and Michelle Perrot. Cambridge, MA: Belknap P of Harvard UP, 1992.

Parke, H. W. *Festivals of the Athenians*. Ithaca: Cornell UP, 1977.

Parker, Holt N. "Sappho Schoolmistress." *Transactions of the American Philological Association* 123 (1993): 309–351. Rpt. Greene, *Rereading*. 146–183.

———. "The Teratogenic Grid." In Hallett and Skinner, *Roman Sexualities*. 47–65.

Parker, Patricia. "African Vervets on Crete and Thera during MM IIIB – LM IA." *American Journal of Archaeology* 101 (1997): 348. Abstract.

Parkinson, R. B. "'Homosexual' Desire and Middle Kingdom Literature." *Journal of Egyptian Archaeology* 81 (1995): 57–76.

Pasquali, G. "Arte allusiva." *Italia che scrive* 25 (1942): 185–187.

Pastre, Geneviève. *Athènes et "le péril saphique": Homosexualité féminine en Grèce ancienne*. Paris: "Les Mots à la bouche," 1987.

Pater, Walter. *Plato and Platonism*. London: Macmillan, 1899.

———. *Walter Pater: Three Major Texts (The Renaissance, Appreciations, and Imaginary Portraits)*. Ed. William E. Buckler. New York: New York UP, 1986.

Patrick, Mary Mills. *Sappho and the Island of Lesbos*. London: Methuen, 1912.

Paul, Aaron J. "A New Vase by the Dinos Painter: Eros and an Erotic Image of Women in Greek Vase Painting." *Harvard University Art Museums* 3.2 (1994–1995): 60–67.

Pellegrini, Ann. "Lesbian Historiography before the Name?" *GLQ: Journal of Lesbian and Gay Studies* 4 (1998): 557–630.

Pemberton, E. G. "The Dexiosis on Attic Gravestones." *Mediterranean Archaeology* 2 (1989): 45–50.

Petersen, Lauren. "Divided Consciousness and Female Companionship: Reconstructing Female Subjectivity on Greek Vases." *Arethusa* 30 (1997): 35–74.

Pini, Ingo. *Corpus der Minoischen und Mykenischen Siegel*, II, *Iraklion Archäologisches Museum*, 5, *Die Siegelabdrücke von Phästos*. Berlin: Gebrüder Mann Verlag, 1970.

Pinney, Gloria Ferrari. "Fugitive Nudes: The Woman Athlete." Paper Delivered at the Annual Meeting of the American Institute of Archaeology. Abstract in *American Journal of Archaeology* 99 (1995): 303–304.

———. "Meaningful Figures." Paper Delivered at the Annual Meeting of the American Institute of Archaeology. Abstract in *American Journal of Archaeology* 100 (1996): 361.

———. "Money Bags?" *American Journal of Archaeology* 90 (1986): 218.

Platon, N. "Bathrooms and Lustral Basins in Minoan Dwellings." In *Europa: Studien zur Geschichte und Epigraphik frühen Ägäis, Festschrift für Ernst Grumach*. Ed. W. Brice et al. Berlin: de Gruyter, 1967. 236–245.

———. *Zakros: The Discovery of a Lost Palace of Ancient Crete*. New York: Scribner, 1971.

———, and I. Pini. *Corpus der Minoischen und Mykenischen Siegel*, II, *Iraklion Archäologisches Museum*, 3, A. *Die Siegel der Neupalastzeit*, B, *Undatierbare spätminoische Siegel*. Berlin: Gebrüder Mann Verlag, 1984.

———, I. Pini, and G. Salies. *Corpus der Minoischen und Mykenischen Siegel*, II, *Iraklion Archäologisches Museum*, 2, *Die Siegel der Altpalastzeit*. Berlin: Gebrüder Mann Verlag, 1977.

Pollock, Griselda. *Vision and Difference: Femininity, Feminism and Histories of Art*. New York: Routledge, 1988.

Pomeroy, Sarah B. *Families in Classical and Hellenistic Greece: Representations and Realities*. Oxford: Clarendon P, 1997.

———. *Goddesses, Whores, Wives, and Slaves: Women in Classical Antiquity*. New York: Dorsett; Boston: Beacon, 1975.

———, ed. and trans. *Xenophon*. Oeconomicus. Oxford: Clarendon P, 1994.

Potts, A. "Sign." In *Critical Terms for Art History*. Ed. R. S. Nelson and R. Schiff. Chicago: U of Chicago P, 1996. 17–29.

Prins, Yopie. "Sappho's Afterlife in Translation." In Greene, *Re-Reading*. 36–67.

———. *Victorian Sappho*. Princeton: Princeton UP, 1999.

Pucci, P. *Hesiod and the Language of Poetry*. Baltimore and London: Johns Hopkins UP, 1977.

Putnam, M. C. J. "*Throna* and Sappho 1.1." *Classical Journal* 56 (1960): 79–83.

Queen, Carol, and Lawrence Schimel, eds. *Pomosexuals: Challenging Assumptions about Gender and Sexuality*. San Francisco: Cleis P, 1997.

———. *Switch Hitters: Lesbians Write Gay Male Erotica; and Gay Men Write Lesbian Erotica*. San Francisco: Cleis P, 1996.

Rabinowitz, Nancy Sorkin. *Anxiety Veiled: Euripides and the Traffic in Women.* Ithaca: Cornell UP, 1993.

——, and Amy Richlin, eds. *Feminist Theory and the Classics.* New York: Routledge, 1993.

Ragghianti, Carlo Ludovico. *Pittori di Pompei.* Milan: Edizioni del Milione, 1963.

Rasmussen, Tom, and Nigel Spivey, eds. *Looking at Greek Vases.* Cambridge: Cambridge UP, 1991.

Rayor, Diane, ed. and trans. *Sappho's Lyre: Archaic Lyric and Women Poets of Ancient Greece.* Berkeley: U of California P, 1991.

Reed, J. D., ed. *Bion of Smyrna: The Fragments and* The Adonis. Cambridge: Cambridge UP, 1997.

Reeder, Ellen D., ed. *Pandora: Women in Classical Greece.* Baltimore, MD: Trustees of the Walters Art Gallery, in association with Princeton UP, 1995.

Rehak, Paul. "Aegean Breechcloths, Kilts, and the Keftiu Paintings." *American Journal of Archaeology* 100 (1996): 35–51.

——. "The Aegean Landscape and the Body: A New Interpretation of the Thera Frescoes." In *From the Ground up: Beyond Gender Theory in Archaeology. Proceedings of the Fifth Gender and Archaeology Conference, University of Wisconsin-Milwaukee, October 1998.* Ed. N. L. Wicker and B. Arnold. London: BAR-IS 812, 1999. 11–21.

——. "The Construction of Gender in Late Bronze Age Aegean Art—A Prolegomenon." In Casey et al., *Redefining Archaeology.* 191–198.

——. "Crocus Costumes in Aegean Art." Forthcoming.

——. "The Monkey Frieze from Xeste 3, Room 4 Reconstruction and Interpretation." In *MELETEMATA: Studies in Aegean Archaeology Presented to Malcolm H. Wiener as He Enters His 65th Year.* Ed. P. P. Betancourt, V. Karageorghis, R. Laffineur, and W.-D. Niemeier. *Aegaeum* 20. Liège: Université de Liège, Histoire de l'art et archéologie de la Grèce antique, 1999. 705–709.

——. "Seated Figures in Aegean Art and the Function of the Mycenaean Megaron." In *The Role of the Ruler in the Prehistoric Aegean: Proceedings of a Panel Discussion Presented at the Annual Meeting of the Archaeological Institute of America, New Orleans, Louisiana, 28 December 1992.* Ed. Paul Rehak. *Aegaeum* 11. Liège: Université de Liège, Histoire de l'art et archéologie de la Grèce antique, 1995. 95–117.

——, and Roman R. Snihurowych. "Is Female to Male as Nature Is to Culture? Medicine, Myth and Matriarchy in the Thera Frescoes." *American Philological Association Abstracts of Papers Presented at the One Hundred Twenty-Ninth Annual Meeting.* New York: American Philological Association, 1997. 180.

————, and John G. Younger. "Review of Aegean Prehistory VII: Neopalatial, Final Palatial, and Postpalatial Crete." *American Journal of Archaeology* 102 (1998): 91–173.

Reilly, Joan. "Many Brides: 'Mistress and Maid' on Athenian Lekythoi." *Hesperia* 58 (1989): 411–444.

Reinsberg, Carola. *Ehe, Hetärentum und Knabenliebe im antiken Griechenland.* Munich: C. H. Beck, 1989.

Renfrew, Colin. *The Archaeology of Cult: The Sanctuary at Phylakopi.* Supplementary volume (British School at Athens) 18. London: British School of Archaeology, Thames and Hudson, 1985.

Rich, Adrienne. "Compulsory Heterosexuality and Lesbian Existence." *Signs* 5 (Summer 1980): 631–660; rev. *Signs Reader: Women, Gender, and Scholarship.* Ed. Elizabeth Abel and Emily Abel. Chicago: U of Chicago P, 1983. 139–168; *Powers of Desire: The Politics of Sexuality.* Ed. Ann Snitow, Christine Stansell, and Sharon Thompson. New York: Monthly Review P, 1983. 177–205; rev. ed., *Lesbian and Gay Studies Reader.* Ed. Henry Abelove, Michèle Aina Barale, and David M. Halperin. New York: Routledge, 1993. 227–254.

————. "'It Is the Lesbian in Us' . . . " In *On Lies, Secrets, and Silence: Selected Prose 1966–1978.* New York and London: Norton, 1979. 199–202.

Richlin, Amy. "The Ethnographer's Dilemma and the Dream of a Lost Golden Age." In Rabinowitz and Richlin, *Feminist Theory.* 272–303.

————. "Foucault's *History of Sexuality:* A Useful Theory for Women?" In Larmour, Miller, and Platter, *Rethinking Sexuality.* 138–170.

————. *The Garden of Priapus: Sexuality and Aggression in Roman Humor.* Rev. ed. New York: Oxford UP, 1992. New Haven: Yale UP, 1983.

————. "Not before Homosexuality: The Materiality of the *Cinaedus* and the Roman Law against Love between Men." *Journal of the History of Sexuality* 3 (1993): 52–73.

————, ed. *Pornography and Representation in Greece and Rome.* New York: Oxford UP, 1992.

————. "Zeus and Metis: Foucault, Feminism, Classics." *Helios* 18 (1991): 160–180.

Richter, Donald. "The Position of Women in Classical Athens." *Classical Journal* 67 (1971): 1–8.

Richter, Gisela M. A. *Engraved Gems of the Greeks, Etruscans, and Romans.* 2 vols. London: Phaidon, 1971.

————. *Metropolitan Museum of Art, New York, Catalog of Engraved Gems, Greek, Etruscan, and Roman.* Rome: "L'Erma" di Bretschneider, 1956.

———, and Lindsley Hall. *Red-Figured Athenian Vases in the Metropolitan Museum of Art.* 2 vols. New Haven: Yale UP, 1936.

———, and Marjorie J. Milne. *Shapes and Names of Athenian Vases.* New York: Metropolitan Museum of Art, 1935.

Riddle, John M. *Contraception and Abortion from the Ancient World to the Renaissance.* Cambridge: Harvard UP, 1992.

———. *Eve's Herbs: A History of Contraception and Abortion in the West.* Cambridge, MA: Harvard UP, 1997.

Ridgway, Brunilde Sismondo. *Roman Copies of Greek Sculpture: The Problem of Originals.* Jerome Lectures, 15th ser. Ann Arbor: U of Michigan P, 1984.

———. *The Severe Style in Greek Sculpture.* Princeton: Princeton UP, 1970.

Riedweg, C. "Reflexe hellenistischer Dichtungstheorie im griechischen Epigramm." *Illinois Classical Studies* 19 (1994): 141–150.

Rissman, Leah. *Love as War: Homeric Allusion in the Poetry of Sappho.* Beitrage zur klassischen Wissenschaft 157. Königstein: Anton Hain 1983.

Robbins, E. "Sappho, Aphrodite, and the Muses." *Ancient World* 26.2 (1995): 225–239.

Robert, Carl. *Einzelmythen.* 3 vols. 1897–1919. Rome: "L'Erma" di Bretschneider, 1969.

Robert, Martin. "Taking an Approach I." In Rasmussen and Spivey, *Looking at Greek Vases.* 1–11.

Roberts, Sally. *The Attic Pyxis.* Chicago: Ares, 1978.

Robins, Gay. 1996. "Dress, Undress, and the Representation of Fertility and Potency in New Kingdom Egyptian Art." In Kampen, *Sexuality in Ancient Art.* 27–40.

Robinson, Christopher. *Lucian and His Influence in Europe.* Chapel Hill: U of North Carolina P, 1979.

Robinson, David. *Sappho and Her Influence.* Boston: Marshall Jones, 1924.

Rohrbach, Erika. "H.D. and Sappho: 'A Precious Inch of Palimpsest.'" In Greene, *Re-reading.* 184–198.

Rosaldo, Michelle. "The Uses and Abuses of Anthropology: Reflections on Feminism and Cross-cultural Understanding." *Signs* 5 (1980): 389–417.

———. "Woman, Culture, and Society: A Theoretical Overview." In *Woman, Culture, and Society.* Ed. Michelle Zimbalist Rosaldo and Louise Lamphere. Stanford: Stanford UP, 1974. 17–42.

Rosenblum, Morris. *Luxorius: A Latin Poet among the Vandals.* Records of Civilization Sources and Studies. New York: Columbia UP, 1961.

Rousseau, Philip. *Pachomius: The Making of a Community in Fourth-Century Egypt.* Transformation of the Classical Heritage 6. Berkeley: U of California P, 1985.

Rousselle, Aline. *Porneia: On Desire and the Body in Antiquity.* Trans. Felicia Pheasant. Oxford: Basil Blackwell, 1988.

Rowlandson, Jane. 1998. *Women and Society in Greek and Roman Egypt.* Cambridge: Cambridge UP, 1998.

Rubin, Gayle. "Thinking Sex: Notes for a Radical Theory of the Politics of Sexuality." In Vance, *Pleasure and Danger.* 267–319.

———. "The Traffic in Women: Notes on the 'Political Economy' of Sex." In *Toward an Anthropology of Women.* Ed. Rayna R. Reiter. New York: Monthly Review P, 1975. 175–210.

———, with Judith Butler. "Sexual Traffic. Interview." In Weed and Schor, *Feminism Meets Queer Theory.* 68–108.

Rumpf, Andreas. *Die Meerwesen auf den antiken Sarkophagreliefs.* Deutsches Archäologisches Institut, Die Antiken Sarkophag-Reliefs. Rome: "L'Erma di Bretschneider, 1969.

Saake, H. *Zur Kunst Sapphos: Motiv-analytische und kompositionstechnische Interpretationen.* Munich: F. Schöningh, 1971.

Sabetai, Victoria. "Aspects of Nuptial and Genre Imagery in Fifth-Century Athens: Issues of Interpretation and Methodology." In Oakley, Coulson, and Palagia, *Athenian Potters.* 319–335.

———. "The Washing Painter: A Contribution to the Wedding and Genre Iconography in the Second Half of the Fifth-Century B.C." 2 vols. Dissertation U of Cincinnati, 1993.

Säflund, G. "The Agoge of the Minoan Youth as Reflected by Palatial Iconography." In Hägg and Marinatos, *Function of Minoan Palaces.* 227–233.

Saïd, Edward. *Orientalism.* New York: Vintage, 1979.

Savoy, Eric. "You Can't Go Homo Again: Queer Theory and the Foreclosure of Gay Studies." *English Studies in Canada* 20 (1994): 129–152.

Scarborough, J. "The Pharmacology of Sacred Plants, Herbs, and Roots." In *Magika Hiera: Ancient Greek Magic and Religion.* Ed. C. Faraone and D. Obbink. Oxford: Oxford UP, 1991. 138–174.

Schadewaldt, W. *Sappho.* Potsdam: Eduard Stichnote, 1950.

Schaps, David. 1977. "The Woman Least Mentioned: Etiquette and Women's Names." *Classical Quarterly* 27 (1997): 323–330.

Scheid, J., and J. Svenbro. *The Craft of Zeus: Myths of Weaving and Fabric.* Cambridge, MA: Harvard UP, 1996.

Schmidt, Carl, and Violet MacDermot, ed. and trans. *Pistis Sophia.* Nag Hammadi Studies 9. Leiden: E. J. Brill, 1978.

Schmitt, R. *Dichtung und Dichtersprache in indogermanischer Zeit.* Wiesbaden: Otto Harrassowitz, 1967.

Scholtz, Andrew. "Perfume from Peron's: The Politics of Pedicure in Anaxandrides Fragment 41 Kassel-Austin." *Illinois Classical Studies* 21 (1996): 69–86.

Scodel, Ruth. "Δόμων ἄγαλμα: Virgin Sacrifice and Aesthetic Object." *Transactions of the American Philological Association* 126 (1996): 111–128.

Sealey, Raphael. *Women and the Law in Classical Greece.* Chapel Hill: U of North Carolina P, 1990.

Sedgwick, Eve Kosofsky. *Between Men: English Literature and Male Homosocial Desire.* New York: Columbia UP, 1985.

———. *Epistemology of the Closet.* Berkeley: U of California P, 1990.

Segal, Charles. "Eros and Incantation: Sappho and Oral Poetry." *Arethusa* 7 (1974): 139–160.

———. "The Tragedy of the *Hippolytus:* The Waters of Ocean and the Untouched Meadow." *Harvard Studies in Classical Philology* 70 (1965): 117–169.

———. "Underreading and Intertextuality: Sappho, Simaetha, and Odysseus in Theocritus' Second Idyll." *Arethusa* 17 (1984): 201–209.

Sergent, Bernard. *Homosexuality in Greek Myth.* Boston: Beacon P, 1986.

Sgourou, Marina. "Attic Lebetes Gamikoi." Dissertation, U of North Carolina at Chapel Hill, 1995.

Shanzer, Danuta. *A Philosophical and Literary Commentary on Martianus Capella's De Nuptiis Philologe et Mercurii Book 1.* U of California Publications in Classical Studies 32. Berkeley: U of California P, 1986.

Shapiro, H. Alan. *Art and Cult under the Tyrants in Athens.* Mainz: Philipp von Zabern, 1989.

———. *Art, Myth, and Culture: Greek Vases from Southern Collections.* New Orleans: New Orleans Museum of Art, 1981.

———. "Eros in Love: Pederasty and Pornography in Greece." In Richlin, *Pornography.* 53–72.

———. "The Iconography of Mourning in Athenian Art." *American Journal of Archaeology* 95 (1991): 629–656.

Shaw, Joseph. "Evidence for the Minoan Tripartite Shrine." *American Journal of Archaeology* 82 (1978): 429–448.

Showerman, Grant, trans. *Ovid, Heroides and Amores*. Loeb Classical Library. Cambridge, MA: Harvard UP, 1914.

Simms, Ronda R. "Mourning and Community at the Athenian Adonia." *Classical Journal* 93 (1998): 121–141.

Sissa, Giulia. *Greek Virginity*. Trans. Arthur Goldhammer. Revealing Antiquity 3. Cambridge, MA: Harvard UP, 1990.

Skinner, Marilyn B. "Aphrodite Garlanded: *Erôs* and Poetic Creativity in Sappho and Nossis." In De Martino, *Rose di Pieria*. 77–96.

———. "Nossis *Thêlyglôssos:* The Private Text and the Public Book." In *Women's History and Ancient History*. Ed. Sarah B. Pomeroy. Chapel Hill and London: Johns Hopkins UP, 1991. 20–47.

———. "Sapphic Nossis." *Arethusa* 22 (1989): 5–18.

———. "Woman and Language in Archaic Greece, or, Why Is Sappho a Woman?" In Rabinowitz and Richlin, *Feminist Theory*. 125–144. Rpt. Greene, *Reading*. 175–192.

Smith, Macklin. *Prudentius* Psychomachia: *A Reexamination*. Princeton: Princeton UP, 1976.

Smither, Paul C. "A Coptic Love-Charm." *Journal of Egyptian Archaeology* 25 (1939): 173–174.

Smith-Rosenberg, Carroll. "The Female World of Love and Ritual: Relations between Women in Nineteenth-Century America." *Signs* 1 (1975): 1–29.

Snell, Bruno. *The Discovery of the Mind: The Greek Origins of European Thought*. Trans. T. G. Rosenmeyer. New York and Evanston: Harper & Row, 1960.

Snitow, Ann, Christine Stansell, and Sharon Thompson, eds. *Powers of Desire: The Politics of Sexuality*. New York: Monthly Review P, 1983.

Snowden, R., and B. Christian, eds. *Patterns and Perceptions of Menstruation: A World Health Organization International Collaborative Study in Egypt, India, Indonesia, Jamaica, Mexico, Pakistan, Philippines, Republic of Korea, United Kingdom, and Yugoslavia*. New York: Published in cooperation with the World Health Organization by Croom Helm, and St. Martin's P, 1983.

Snyder, Jane McIntosh. "The Configuration of Desire in Sappho Fr. 22 L.-P." *Helios* 21 (1994): 3–8.

———. *Lesbian Desire in the Lyrics of Sappho*. New York: Columbia UP, 1997.

———. "Love in the Apple Orchard: Sacred Space in the Lyrics of Sappho." Unpublished Paper Presented at the U of North Carolina at Chapel Hill, February 6, 1998.

———. "Sappho in Attic Vase Painting." In Koloski-Ostrow and Lyons, *Naked Truths*. 108–119.

———. "The Web of Song: Weaving Imagery in Homer and the Lyric Poets." *Classical Journal* 76 (1981): 193–196.

———. *The Woman and the Lyre: Women Writers in Classical Greece and Rome.* Carbondale: Southern Illinois UP, 1989.

Sourvinou-Inwood, Christiane. "Ancient Rites and Modern Constructions: On the Brauronian Bears Again." *Bulletin of the Institute of Classical Studies, London* 37 (1990): 1–14.

———. "Male and Female, Public and Private, Ancient and Modern." In Reeder, *Pandora.* 111–120.

———. "Persephone and Aphrodite at Locri: A Model for Personality Definitions in Greek Religion." *Journal of Hellenic Studies* 98 (1978): 101–121.

———. *Reading Greek Culture: Texts and Images, Rituals and Myths.* Oxford: Oxford UP, 1991.

———. *Studies in Girls' Transitions. Aspects of the Arkteia and Age Representation in Attic Iconography.* Athens: Kardamitsa, 1988.

Specchia, O. "Recenti studi su Nosside." *Cultura e scuòla* 23 (1984): 49–54.

Stahl, William Harris, and Richard Johnson, with L. Burge, trans. *Martianus Capella and the Seven Liberal Arts: The Marriage of Philology and Mercury.* Vol. 2. New York: Columbia UP, 1977.

———. *Martianus Capella and the Seven Liberal Arts: The Quadrivium of Martianus Capella, with a Study of the Allegory and the Verbal Disciplines.* Vol. 1. New York: Columbia UP, 1971.

Stanley, K. "The Rôle of Aphrodite in Sappho Fr. 1." *Greek, Roman and Byzantine Studies* 17 (1976): 305–321.

Starr, Chester. "An Evening with the Flute Girls." *Parole del Passato* 33 (1978): 401–410.

Stears, Karen. "Dead Women's Society: Constructing Female Gender in Classical Athenian Funeral Sculpture." In *Time, Tradition and Society in Greek Archaeology.* Ed. Nigel Spencer. New York: Routledge, 1995. 109–131.

Stehle, Eva. *Performance and Gender in Ancient Greece.* Princeton: Princeton UP, 1997.

———. "Retreat from the Male: Catullus 62 and Sappho's Erotic Flowers." *Ramus* 6 (1977): 83–102.

———. "Sappho's Gaze: Fantasies of a Goddess and a Young Man." *differences* 2 (1990): 88–125.

———. "Sappho's Private World." In *Reflections of Women in Antiquity.* Ed. Helene Foley. New York: Gordon and Breach, 1981. 45–61.

———, and Amy Day. "Women Looking at Women: Women's Ritual and Temple Sculpture." In Kampen, *Sexuality in Ancient Art.* 101–116.

Steiner, D. *The Crown of Song: Metaphor in Pindar.* New York: Oxford UP, 1986.

Stewart, Andrew. *Art, Desire, and the Body in Ancient Greece.* Cambridge: Cambridge UP, 1997.

———. "Rape?" In Reeder, *Pandora.* 74–90.

———. "Reflections." In Kampen, *Sexuality in Ancient Art.* 136–154.

Stimpson, C. "Adrienne Rich and Lesbian/Feminist Poetry." *Parnassus* 12.2–13.1 (1985): 249–268.

Strasser, Thomas. "The Blue Monkeys of the Aegean and Their Implications for Bronze Age Trade." *American Journal of Archaeology* 101 (1997): 348. Abstract.

Strawczynski, Nina. "Echange sous le manteau: analyse iconographique d'un motif archaïque." Unpublished essay, 1993.

Strong, D. E. *Greek and Roman Gold and Silver Plate.* Ithaca: Cornell UP, 1966.

Stuart, James, and Nicholas Revett. *Antiquities of Athens and Other Monuments of Greece.* 2nd ed. London: Henry G. Bohn, 1858.

Stuveras, Roger. *Le putto dans l'art romain.* Collection Latomus 99. Brussels: Latomus, 1969.

Suggs, M. Jack, Katharine Doob Sakenfield, and James R. Mueller, eds. *The Oxford Study Bible, Revised English Bible with the Apocrypha.* New York: Oxford UP, 1992.

Sutton, Robert F. Jr. "The Interaction between Men and Women Portrayed on Attic Red-Figure Pottery." Dissertation U of North Carolina at Chapel Hill, 1981. Ann Arbor: UMI, 1992.

———. "Pornography and Persuasion on Attic Pottery." In Richlin, *Pornography.* 3–35.

Sweeny, Jane, Tam Curry, and Yannis Tzedakis. *The Human Figure in Early Greek Art, Athens.* Athens: Greek Ministry of Culture, 1988.

Symonds, John Addington. *Essays Speculative and Suggestive.* London: Chapman and Hall, 1890.

———. *A Problem in Greek Ethics.* London, 1901. New York: Haskell Hall House, 1971.

———. *Studies of the Greek Poets.* 2 vols. New York: Harper and Brothers, 1880.

Taylor, D. *Red Flower: Rethinking Menstruation.* Freedom, CA: Crossing P, 1988.

Televantou, Christina. "Η απόδοση της ανθρώπινης μορφής στις θηραϊκές τοιχογραφίες." *Αρχαιολογική Εφημερίς* (1988): 135–166.

———. "Η γυναικεία ενδυμασία στην προϊστορική Θήρα." *Αρχαιολογική Εφημερίς* (1982): 113–135.

———. "Κοσμήματα από την προϊστορική Θήρα." *Αρχαιολογική Εφημερίς* (1984): 14–54.

Temkin, Owse, trans. *Soranus' Gynecology.* Baltimore: Johns Hopkins UP, 1956.

Terrace, E. "'Blue Marble' Plastic Vessels and Other Figures." *Journal of the American Research Center in Egypt* 5 (1966): 59–60.

Thalmann, W. G. *Conventions of Form and Thought in Early Greek Epic Poetry.* Baltimore and London: Johns Hopkins UP, 1984.

Thomas, R. F. "Virgil's *Georgics* and the Art of Reference." *Harvard Studies in Classical Philology* 90 (1986): 171–198.

Thornton, Bruce. "Constructionism and Ancient Greek Sex." *Helios* 18 (1991): 181–193.

———. *Eros: The Myth of Ancient Greek Sexuality.* Boulder: Westview P, 1997.

Thurston, Herbert, and Donald Attwater, eds. *Lives of the Saints.* 4 vols. New York: Kenedy, 1956.

Tigerstedt, E. N. "Furor Poeticus: Poetic Inspiration in Greek Literature before Democritus and Plato." *Journal of the History of Ideas* 31 (1970): 163–178.

Timbie, Janet. "The State of Research on the Career of Shenoute of Atripe." In *The Roots of Egyptian Christianity.* Ed. Birger A. Pearson and James E. Goehring. Studies in Antiquity and Christianity. Philadelphia: Fortress P, 1986. 258–270.

Touchette, Lori-Ann. *The Dancing Maenad Reliefs: Continuity and Change in Roman Copies.* Bulletin Supplement 62. London: U of London Institute of Classical Studies, 1995.

Traub, Valerie. "The (In)significance of 'Lesbian Desire' in Early Modern England." In *Erotic Politics: Desire on the Renaissance Stage.* Ed. Susan Zimmerman. New York: Routledge, 1992. 150–169; *Queering the Renaissance.* Ed. Jonathan Goldberg, Series Q. Durham: Duke UP, 1994. 62–83.

———. "The Psychomorphology of the Clitoris." *GLQ: Journal of Lesbian and Gay Studies* 2 (1995): 81–113.

Trendall, A. D. *The Red-Figured Vases of Lucania, Campania and Sicily.* Oxford: Oxford UP, 1967.

———, and Alexander Cambitoglou. *The Red-Figured Vases of Apulia.* Oxford: Clarendon P, 1978.

———, and Alexander Cambitoglou. *Second Supplement to the Red-Figured Vases of Apulia, Part I (Chapters 1–20).* London: Bulletin of the Institute of Classical Studies, Supplement 60, 1991.

Turner, Frank M. *The Greek Heritage in Victorian Britain.* New Haven: Yale UP, 1981.

Tzachili, I. "All Important Yet Elusive: Looking for Evidence of Cloth-Making at Akrotiri." In Hardy et al., *Thera,* vol. III. 380–389.

Tzachili-Douskou, I. "Τα ποίκιλα θηραϊκάιμάτια και η τοιξογραφία του στόλου· Μια ιδιόμορφη τεξνική στα ύφαντα τῇ Θήρας." *Athens Annals of Archaeology* 14 (1981): 251–265.

Van Gennep, A. *Les rites de passage.* Paris: É. Nourry, 1909; Paris: Á. & J. Picard, 1981, 2000.

Van Keuren, Frances, ed. *Myth, Sexuality and Power: Images of Jupiter in Western Art: Papers Delivered at the Georgia Museum of Art in Connection with the Exhibition, Jupiter's Loves and His Children, February 8, 1997.* Providence, RI: Center for Old World Archaeology and Art, Brown U, 1998.

Vance, Carole S., ed. *Pleasure and Danger: Exploring Female Sexuality.* Boston: Routledge and Kegan Paul, 1984.

Veilleux, Armand. *Pachomian Koinonia,* Volume Three, *Instructions, Letters and Other Writings of Saint Pachomius and His Disciples.* Cistercian Studies Series 47. Kalamazoo, MI: Cistercian Publications, 1982.

———. *Pachomian Koinonia,* Volume Two, *Pachomian Chronicles and Rules.* Cistercian Studies Series 46. Kalamazoo, MI: Cistercian Publications, 1981.

Vermeule, Emily. "The World Turned Upside Down." In Lefkowitz and Rogers, *Black Athena Revisited.* 269–279.

Vernant, Jean-Pierre. "Preface." Bérard et al., *City of Images.* 7–8.

Versnel, H. S. "Wife and Helpmate: Women of Ancient Athens in Anthropological Perspective." In *Sexual Asymmetry: Studies in Ancient Society.* Ed. Josine Blok and Peter Mason. Amsterdam: J. C. Gieben, 1987. 59–85.

Vestergaard, T., L. Bjertrup, and M. H. Hansen. "A Typology of Women Recorded on Gravestones from Attica (400 BC–200 AD)." *American Journal of Ancient History* 10 (1985 [1993]): 178–190.

Veyne, Paul. "Homosexuality in Ancient Rome." In *Western Sexuality: Practice and Precept in Past and Present Times.* Ed. Philippe Ariès and André Béjin. Trans. Anthony Forster. Oxford: Blackwell, 1985. 26–35.

Vicinus, Martha. "Lesbian History: All Theory and No Facts or All Facts and No Theory?" *Radical History Review* 60 (1994): 57–75.

———. *Lesbian Subjects: A Feminist Studies Reader.* Bloomington: Indiana UP, 1996.

Vickers, Michael. *Artful Crafts: Ancient Greek Silverware and Pottery.* Oxford: Oxford UP, 1994.

Villaneuva-Puig, Marie-Christine. *Images de la vie quotidienne en Grèce dans l'antiquité.* Paris: Hachette, 1992.

Vööbus, Arthur. *History of Asceticism in the Syrian Orient III.* Corpus Scriptorum Christianorum Orientalium, Subsidia, 81. Louvain: E. Peeters, 1988.

Vorberg, Gaston. *Glossarium Eroticum*. Hanau: Verlag Müller und Kleipenheuer, 1965.

Vuarnet, Jean-Noël. *Extases féminines*. Paris: Arthaud, c 1980 [1991].

Waldstein, Charles, and Leonard Shoobridge. *Herculaneum, Past, Present, and Future*. London: Macmillan, 1908.

Walker, Alice. *My Life as Myself*. Audiocassette: Sounds True Recordings, 1995.

Walters, Barry. "Rock's Queer Evolution." *The Advocate* (9 December 1997): 24–31.

Walters, Jonathan. "Invading the Roman Body: Manliness and Impenetrability in Roman Thought." In Hallett and Skinner, *Roman Sexualities*. 29–43.

Warren, Peter. *Minoan Stone Vases*. Cambridge: Cambridge UP, 1969.

Wasowicz, Aleksandra. "Miroir ou quenouille? La Représentation des femmes dans la céramique attique." In *Mélanges Pierre Lévêque*. Ed. Marie Madeleine and Evelynne Gery. Vol. 82. Paris: Centre de récherches d'Histoire Ancienne, 1989. 413–438.

Waszink, J. H. *Biene und Honig als Symbol des Dichters und der Dichtung in der griechisch-römischen Antike*. Rheinisch-Westfälische Akademie der Wissenschaften Vorträge G 196. Opladen: Westdeutscher Verlag, 1974.

Webster, T. B. L. *Potter and Painter in Classical Athens*. London: Methuen, 1972.

Weed, Elizabeth, and Naomi Schor, eds. *Feminism Meets Queer Theory*. Books from *differences*. Bloomington: Indiana UP, 1997.

Wegner, Max. *Die Musensarkophage*. Deutsches Archäologisches Institut, Antiken Sarkophagreliefs. Berlin: Mann, 1966.

Wehgartner, I. *Attisch weissgrundige Keramik: Maltechniken, Werkstätten, Formen, Verwendung*. Mainz: Philipp von Zabern, 1983.

Weill, Nicole. 1966. "Adoniazusai ou les femmes sur le toit." *Bulletin de Correspondance Héllenique* 90 (1966): 664–698.

Welcker, Friedrich Gottlieb. *Sappho von einem herrschenden Vorurtheil befreyt*. Göttingen: Vandenhoek und Ruprecht, 1816.

West, M. L. "Burning Sappho." *Maia* 22 (1970): 307–330.

Wharton, Henry. *Sappho: Memoir, Text, Selected Renderings, and a Literal Translation*. London: Simpkin, Marshall, Hamilton, Kent, 1898.

Wheeler, Stephen M. "Changing Names: The Miracle of Iphis in Ovid Metamorphoses 9." *Phoenix* 51.2 (1997): 190–202.

White, Edmund. "The Political Vocabulary of Homosexuality." In *The State of the Language*. Ed. Leonard Michaels and Christopher Ricks. Berkeley: U of California P, 1980. 235–246.

White, H. "The Rose of Aphrodite." In *Essays in Hellenistic Poetry*. Ed. Heather White. Amsterdam: J. C. Gieben, 1980. 17–20.

White, Robert J., trans. *The Interpretation of Dreams, Oneirocritica by Artemidorus*. Park Ridge, NJ: Noyes P, 1975.

Wicker, Nancy L., and Bettina Arnold, eds. *From the Ground up: Beyond Gender Theory in Archaeology. Proceedings of the Fifth Gender and Archaeology Conference, University of Wisconsin-Milwaukee, October 1998*. London: BAR-IS 812, 1999.

Wilamowitz-Moellendorff, Ulrich von. *Sappho und Simonides*. Berlin: Weidmannsche Buchhandlung, 1913.

Wilfong, Terry G. "The Coptic Story of Theodosios and Dionysios." In *P. Michigan Koenen (= P.Mich. XVIII): Michigan Texts Published in Honor of Ludwig Koenen*. Ed. Cornelia Römer and Traianos Gagos. Studia Amstelodamensia ad Epigraphicam, Ius Antiquum et Papyrologicam Pertinentia, 36. Amsterdam: Gieben, 1996. 351–356.

———. "Reading the Disjointed Body in Coptic: From Physical Modification to Textual Fragmentation." In *Changing Bodies, Changing Meanings: The Human Body in Antiquity*. Ed. Dominic Montserrat. London: Routledge, 1998. 116–136.

Williams, Craig. *Roman Homosexuality: Ideologies of Masculinity in Classical Antiquity*. Oxford: Oxford UP, 1999.

Williams, Dyfri. "Women on Athenian Vases: Problems of Interpretation." In Cameron and Kuhrt, *Images*. 92–106.

Williamson, Margaret. "Sappho and the Other Woman." In Greene, *Reading*. 248–264.

———. *Sappho's Immortal Daughters*. Cambridge, MA: Harvard UP, 1995.

Wilson, L. H. *Sappho's Sweetbitter Songs: Configurations of Female and Male in Ancient Greek Lyric*. London and New York: Routledge, 1996.

Wilton, Tamsin. *Lesbian Studies: Setting an Agenda*. London: Routledge, 1995.

Winkler, John J. *The Constraints of Desire: The Anthropology of Sex and Gender in Ancient Greece*. New York: Routledge, 1990.

———. "The Ephebes Song: *Tragôidia* and *Polis*." In *Nothing to Do with Dionysos: Athenian Drama in Its Social Context*. Ed. John J. Winkler and Froma I. Zeitlin. Princeton: Princeton UP, 1990. 20–62.

Withee, Diana. "Physical Growth and Aging Characteristics Depicted in the Theran Frescoes." *American Journal of Archaeology* 96 (1992): 336. Abstract.

Worsfold, Thomas Cato. *The History of the Vestal Virgins of Rome*. London: Rider, 1932.

Wycherley, R. E. *How the Greeks Built Cities.* 2nd ed. Garden City, NY: Doubleday, 1969.

Wyke, Maria. 1994. "Woman in the Mirror: The Rhetoric of Adornment in the Roman World." In Archer et al., *Women in Ancient Societies.* 134 –151.

Young, Dwight Wayne. *Coptic Manuscripts from the White Monastery: Works of Shenute.* Mitteilungen aus der Papyrussammlung der österreichischen National-bibliothek (Papyrus Erzherzog Rainer), n.s. 22. Wien: Brüder Hollinek, 1993.

Young, Wayland. *Eros Denied: Sex in Western Society.* New York: Grove P, 1964.

Younger, John G. "Non-sphragistic Uses of Minoan-Mycenaean Sealstones and Rings." *Kadmos* 16 (1977): 141–159.

———. "Representations of Minoan-Mycenaean Jewelry." In Laffineur and Crowley, *EIKΩN.* 257–293.

Zaidman, Louise Bruit. "Pandora's Daughters and Rituals in Grecian Cities." In Pantel et al., *A History of Women in the West.* 338 –376.

Zimmerman, Bonnie, and Toni A. McNaron, eds. *The New Lesbian Studies: Into the Twenty-first Century.* New York: Feminist P, 1996.

Zweig, Bella. "The Primal Mind: Using Native American Models for the Study of Women in Ancient Greece." In Rabinowitz and Richlin, *Feminist Theory.* 145 –180.

Notes on Contributors

Lisa Auanger received her B.A. in Latin from Southwestern University and her M.A. and Ph.D. in Art History and Archaeology from the University of Missouri. Her Ph.D. dissertation was entitled "A Catalog of Women in the Official Arts of Ancient Rome." In 1997 she was awarded the Superior Graduate Achievement Award in Art History and Archaeology from the University of Missouri. She is currently an editor for the *Bibliography of the History of Art* at the Getty Research Library, Getty Research Institute.

Ellen Greene, Associate Professor of Classics at the University of Oklahoma, is the author of *The Erotics of Domination: Male Desire and the Mistress in Latin Love Poetry* (Baltimore: Johns Hopkins UP, 1998). She is the editor of *Reading Sappho: Contemporary Approaches* (Berkeley: U of California P, 1996) and *Re-Reading Sappho: Reception and Transmission* (Berkeley: U of California P, 1996). She has published articles on Catullus, Propertius, Ovid, Sappho, and Anyte and is currently working on a book-length study of gender and genre in Roman elegy.

Shelley P. Haley is Professor of Classics and Women's Studies at Hamilton College, where she is also Director of the Africana Studies Program. The Chief Faculty Consultant for the Advanced Placement Latin Program, Haley has published and lectured extensively on black feminist thought and antiquity, including writing the introduction to a new edition of Fanny Jackson Coppin's *Reminiscences of School Life and Hints on Teaching* (New York: G. K. Hall, 1995); she has appeared on the BBC series "Time Watch," discussing Cleopatra, and on "Rome: The Power and Glory" on the Learning Channel. She actively works for the eradication of all oppressions through her leadership in the National Coalition Building Institute.

Diane T. Pintabone received her B.A. in Classics from Boston College (1987), her M.A. from University of Colorado at Boulder (1990), and her Ph.D. in Classics from the University of Southern California (1998). She has taught as a part-time Lecturer at California State University in Long Beach, California, and at Scripps College of Claremont University. She is currently teaching in the Classics Department of the University of Southern California.

Nancy Sorkin Rabinowitz is Professor of Comparative Literature at Hamilton College, where she teaches courses in Greek tragedy, feminist theory, and queer theory, as well as the nineteenth-century and twentieth-century novel. Author of *Anxiety Veiled: Euripides and the Traffic in Women* (Ithaca: Cornell UP, 1993), coeditor of *Feminist Theory and the Classics* (New York: Routledge, 1993), coeditor and translator of *Women on the Edge: Four Plays by Euripides* (New York: Routledge, 1998), her current research focuses on representations of women and gender in Greece.

Paul Rehak has a B.A. from the University of Michigan and an M.A. and Ph.D. in Classical and Near Eastern Archaeology from Bryn Mawr College. He is currently an Assistant Professor of Classics at the University of Kansas. His main research interests are gender in the Prehistoric Aegean and Early Imperial Rome. He edited *The Role of the Ruler in the Prehistoric Aegean* (Austin, TX: University of Texas at Austin, Program in Aegean Scripts and Prehistory, 1995) and is the author of numerous articles on Aegean iconography and art; he is currently coeditor of book reviews for the *American Journal of Archaeology.*

Marilyn B. Skinner, Professor of Classics at the University of Arizona, is the author of *Catullus' "Passer": The Arrangement of the Book of Polymetric Poems* (New York: Arno P, 1981) and coeditor of *Roman Sexualities* (Princeton 1998). She has also written numerous articles on the ancient Greek women poets and the female poetic tradition in antiquity. Currently she is working on a book-length study of Catullan elegiac verse and an article about the Hellenistic woman poet Moero of Byzantium.

Terry Wilfong received his Ph.D. in Egyptology from the University of Chicago in 1994. He is currently Assistant Professor of Egyptology in the Department of Near Eastern Studies and Assistant Curator for Graeco-Roman Egypt in the Kelsey Museum of Archaeology at the University of Michigan. He is author of a forthcoming book on women's lives in Coptic texts from the University of Michigan Press and has published and lectured extensively on a variety of topics relating to ancient Egypt.

John G. Younger is Professor of Classical Archaeology at Duke University. He received his B.A. from Stanford University in 1967 and his Ph.D. from the University of Cincinnati in 1973. Although Younger works primarily in the traditional areas of Aegean and Greek archaeology, he also deals with gender and sexuality in his book *Music in the Aegean Bronze Age* (Studies in Mediterranean Archaeology Pocket Book 96. Jonsered: Paul Åströms Förlag, 1998) and in essays such as "Gender and Sexuality in the Parthenon Frieze," in *Naked Truths*, ed. Ann Olga Koloski-Ostrow and Claire L. Lyons (New York: Routledge, 1997) 120–153, and "Waist Compression in the Aegean Late Bronze Age," *Archaeological News* (forthcoming 2001).

Index

Abanthis, 66, 68

abortion, 41, 48, 50

Achilles on Scyros, 296, 302n26

actions, 95

active/passive roles, 14, 18, 20, 31n69, 82, 88–89, 90, 91, 256–258, 266, 267–268, 269, 298, 322

adolos (honestly), 93

Adonia, 167

Adonis, 232, 234, 240, 248n31

adornment scenes, 116, 123

adultery, 218, 268

adulthood, 48

Aegean art, depiction of relations, 34

Aeneid, 275–276

aestheticists, 107

African descent, 288, 293, 302n22

agathé (good), 181

agency, 97

ages: depiction of, 35; grades, 172, 194n18, 195n24; prepubescent, 36; puberty, 36, 125

aggression, female, 273, 279

aglaïa (splendor), 71

Aigina, 190

aischras (shameful), 221

Akrotiri, Thera, 19, 34–59

alabastron, 107, 138

Alcestis (Alkestis), 125, 179–181

Alciphron, 298

Alcman, 67, 125, 130

Aldobrandini Wedding, 234–237

Alexandros. *See* Paris

Alkaios, 142

Alkamenes, 188, 202n554

allegory, 234, 236, 238

amare, 264

Amasis painter, 128, 129, 130

Amatores, 225

Amazons, 137

Ameinokleia, 177

Amigues, Suzanne, 47

Amor, 218, 219, 222, 270, 277. *See also* Eros

Amor market, 240, 241

Amphareté, 172

amphora, 128–129, 137

anakalypsis (unveiling), 179, 181, 202n61, 207n90

anakalypteria (marriage gifts), 120

Anakreontic vases, 108

Anaktoria, 99, 100, 101, 102

Andokides, 137

androdeis (masculine), 218

Andromache, 67

andron (men's room), 115

anima (soul), 245

animals, 260, 264, 268, 270

anointing, 137, 148

anthea (flowers), 70

Anthemis, 182

Antipater of Sidon, 225–226, 236

antisumptuary, 192n4, 198n35

Aphrodite, 19, 50, 60–72, 90, 125, 126, 127, 128, 224, 228–238, 264, 272, 283n24; cult statue of, 71; Cupris as cupbearer, 65; descent of, 86–87; function in eroticizing, 232; of the gardens, 188; gaze of, 88; invocation of, 86; models for, 86; and Peitho, 236; *poikilothronos*, 67; powers of, 40, 69; roses of, 70; smile of, 87; as source of inspiration, 63, 64; as *summachos*, 69, 90; temple of, 71; Urania, 227

Aphrodite-like, 243

Apollodorus, 141, 149

apotropaic, 38

apples, 237, 239, 254n109; trees, 65

aprons (as costume), 36, 40

Apulia(n), 147; pelikê, 147

archaeology, 19, 20–21

archaism, 232–233

ardeo (burn for), 264

aretê (manly excellence), 67

Aristophanes, 42, 134, 135

Arkhestrate, 176, 177, 182, 185

Arnobius of Sicca, 222–223, 225

arsenokoites (lying with men), 322–323

Artemidorus of Ephesus, 230

Artemis, Sanctuary of at Brauron, 125; and marriage, 119; as Mistress of Animals, 45–46

artists, gender of, 109

ascetism, 323

Asian Americans, 287

astralogoi, 190

Atalanta, 232

Athena, 87

Athenaeus, 221

Athens: Benaki Museum, 123; National Archaeological Museum, 123, 124, 175, 177, 180, 184

Atripe, 307

Atthis, 66

Attica, 20

attributes, 174, 176, 178, 183, 185

audiences, 64, 153n24, 319; gender of, 109, 135, 138

authority, 320; male, 22; artistic, 61

authorship, 2; anxiety of, 61; male, 2, 22, 106

Bacchae, 128

bacchantes, 127, 128, 129, 160n82

balance, 232, 234, 252n84

Baldwin, Barry, 290

bama (step), 101, 102

banquets, 140

Barber, Elizabeth, 40

Bassa, 220

bathing, 135–138, 163n113, 237

battle, 90

beards, 108

beauty, 71, 91, 97, 99–102, 263; female, 71, 84, 237; idealization of, 84

Beazley, J. D., 107

beds, 176, 179, 181, 197–198n33

belt, 41

Bérard, Claude, 110

Berlin, Staatliche Museum, 128

Bernini, Gian Lorenzo, 230

Besa, 307, 319

betrothal (*eggyê*), 119

biases: introduction, passim; twentieth century, 211

binary oppositions, 5, 6, 9, 14, 16, 26n21

biological sex, 267, 276, 281n11

Bion, 240

bisexuality: of Lucian, 300; of Sappho, 218

blood, 41, 42

Bloom, Allan, 13

blue monkeys, 37

Boardman, John, 107, 147, 148, 188

bodies, women's, 19, 51, 71

Bompaire, Jacques, 290

Bona Dea, 215

booners, 108

Boston, Museum of Fine Arts, 144

Bothmer, Dietrich von, 107, 147

Brauron, 125, 129

Bravery of Women, 225

breasts, 36, 53, 147, 223, 232; size of, 138; touching of, 187

brides, 119, 123, 124, 125, 126, 179, 236; bathing, 135

Bronze Age, 19, 34–59

Brooten, Bernadette, 1, 18, 134, 147, 211, 213, 256–257, 277, 298, 299, 317–318

brotherhood, spiritual, 315

buildings, public, 34

Burn, Lucilla, 126

butch-femme, 16, 297; butch, 18

Byblis, 271, 272, 273

Caenis/Caeneus, 275, 276
Callo, 71
Calores, 218
cameo, 223
Campbell, 218
Cantarella, Eva, 35
carotenes, 49
Carpenter, Edward, 9, 10, 28n43, 29n45
Carson, Anne, 88–89
castes, racial, 301–302n22
categories, 22, 83, 258, 287, 288; conceptual,
    111, 112. *See also* definitions
Catullus, 225
Caunus, 272, 273
celebration, 65
cemeteries, 20, 167–173, 190
chamber scene, heteroerotic, 235
charites, 161n92. *See also* Graces
cheir epi karpou (hand on wrist gesture), 122
Chicago, Oriental Institute of, 322
childbirth, death in, 176, 181, 197n29,
    198n38, 201n48
children, 317; female, 276; prepubescent,
    44, 48; on tombstones, 176, 178, 182, 185,
    195n20, 200n48, 202n54
chiton-lifting, 188
choral groups, 126–130, 161n89
Christianity, 19, 22, 213, 221, 228, 230, 238,
    304–329
Cicero, 217
citizens, 116
citizenship, Athenian, 294
civil rights, 286
Clairmont, Christopher, 172, 173, 183, 186,
    188, 190
Clarke, John, 14, 236
classics and classical studies, 1, 5, 8, 9, 11,
    13–15, 73–74; development of, 30n63
Clement of Alexandria, 225
clitoris, 162–163n103, 257
Clonarium, 22, 286, 294–297, 299
clothing, 36, 40; for males, 36
coinage of words, 323
coins, 190
Colloquia di Donne, 232

colonialism, 5, 26n19
colonists, French, 293
community, 287
companions, 182, 220, 221
comparison: of beloved to goddess, 230; to
    male pederasty, 113; of women's relation-
    ships to heterosexuality, 113
Concordia, 234
condemnation, of women's relationships,
    278
conquest, language of, 86
conrepta (seized with), 265
consciousness (self-, multiple, divided),
    167, 190–192
conservatism, of religion, 245n9
constructionist (constructivist), 15, 18
consummation, 112, 278
continuity, 214
convention, 292
copies, 223
Coptic sources, 304–305, 307–313, 318–324
copulation, lesbian, 135
Corinth, 295, 296
corneas, 49, 50
courtship, 119, 131, 189
cousins, 207n85
creativity, 64, 72; female, 60–61
Crete, 261, 268, 271; influence, 34; women
    of, 130
crocus, 41, 42, 50; gathering, 43
Cupid. *See* Amor, Eros
cupido (desire), 265
curatorial choices, effect of, 108

Daedalus, 267
damna (subdue), 86
Damophyla, 221
Danae Painter, 117, 118
dancing, 116, 130, 141, 142, 223, 228, 229,
    251n72, 298; homosocial, 20; nude, 125,
    129
Daphnis and Chloe, 238
darkness, 318
Davis, Ellen, 48–49
Davis, Madeline, 297

dead, honors to, 168, 170

death, 65, 93

deceased: primary, 174; secondary, 178

deceit, 268

decorative, women as, 116

dedications, temple, 71

definitions, 2–4, 249n38; erotic, 3; friendship, 133; homoerotic, 3, 111–112, 146, 212; homosexual, 3, 14, 15; homosocial, 2–3, 146, 212; lesbian, 3, 4, 15, 18, 61, 75n7, 112, 133, 165n132, 211; respectable, 133; sexual, 3; tribad, 247–248n25; women, 4

Deipnosophistae, 221

DeJean, Joan, 83

de Lauretis, Teresa, 16

Demeter, 51, 140

Demetria, 186, 187

Demodokos, 62

Demonassa, 295, 296, 297

Demosion Sema, 170

Demosthenes, 115

denial, 292

depilation, 148, 164n120

De Rerum Natura, 237

desire, 113, 114, 115, 312, 316, 319, 321; depiction of, 110; feminine, 84; fulfilled, 96; homoerotic, 69, 82; masculine, 82; and music, 117; mutual, 90–91; and Nossis, 70–72; and performance, 64; physical, 310, 311; and Sappho, 20, 66, 99–101; sexual, 16, 62, 256–257, 268, 270, 271, 276; women's, 4, 16, 22, 271

despair, 94

deutê (again), 66–68, 87–88

dexiosis (clasping hands), 174, 178

dextrarum iunctio (joining right hand), 211, 240

Dialogue of the Courtesans, 22, 112, 134, 228, 286, 288, 291, 292–303

Dialogue of the Whores, 286

Dialogue on Love, 225

Diana, 242, 243; seduction of Callisto, 239

Dierichs, Angelika, 140

diet, 48, 49

Digest of Justinian, 214

dildos, 20, 140–146, 165n135, 166; arguments about, 146; function of, 145; used in homoerotic setting, 142

Diomedes, 67, 87

Dionysia, 183

Dionysius Latinus, 217

Dionysos, 127–130, 140, 242

Dioscurides, 236

Diplyon Gate, 170

disciplines, academic, 287

dish, silver, 242

disrobing, 138

divinities and mortals, 126–127

docta (learned), 220

doctors, 196n26

dogs, 176, 178, 198n37

dokimasia (scrutiny), 170, 193n6

domestic scenes, 116, 119

dominant-submissive, 130

domination, 88

Douris, 110–111, 113, 114, 138, 139, 188

Dover, Kenneth J., 14, 140

dowry, 263

dreams, 230

dresses, 45, 66

dressing, 139; women, 138

duBois, Page, 84, 98, 100

ducks, 46, 57n50

Dworkin, Andrea, 280

dykes, 213, 214

Ecclesiazousae, 135

ecphrasis (set piece), 290

education, 65, 291

effeminacy, 42, 108, 276, 322; associated with orientalism, 9–10

eggs, 113

ego, 98–99, 100, 105n32

Egypt, 1, 10, 22, 37, 46, 304–329; map of, 306

elders, 307; female, 310

elthe (come), 89

embracing, 176, 187, 223, 228, 237

Endymion, 243

energy, fusion of erotic and creative, 64

epaulia (post-wedding gift-giving), 120
epic type-scenes, 67
epigrams, 69, 182, 183, 191, 201n51; dedicatory, 64
Epiktetos, 144
epinetron, 125, 179, 180
epiphany, 65, 68
equality, 83, 89, 90; in relationships, 91, 130,
   146, 263, 279
erastes (lover), 83
erasure, 292
Eretria Painter, 125, 126, 179, 180, 181
eromenos (beloved), 83
Eros, 3, 26, 68, 117, 125, 126, 160n79, 223,
   228, 230, 231, 232, 233, 236, 242; between
   women, 241; oppressed, 239
erôs, 3, 19, 62, 64, 67, 70–71, 72, 84, 97, 101–
   102, 223, 238–239; as game, 88
Erotes, 119, 125, 126, 133, 158n66, 223, 224,
   226, 237, 238–243, 254n110
erotic power, 231
erotica, 3
eroticization, of images, 230; of women, 119
ethnicity, 296; non-Greek, 44
Eudaimonia, 126
Eunomia, 126
euphemism, 313
Euripides, 79n40, 128
Europa, 51
Euthymides, 135
Eve, 230, 238, 252n79
evidence, 18, 21; Greek vases, 107; historical,
   211–255; problems of, 2, 25n6, 18, 21
explicitness, sexual, 8, 33–34, 111, 146
exposure, genital, 237
eyes, 49, 50. *See also* corneas, gaze

Faderman, Lillian, 15, 112, 258
fas (right), 271
Fasti, 237
favoritism, 312
fecundity, 243; homoeroticism in expression of, 243
feet, 142, 237, 242, 318; arousing desire, 142;
   beating of, 310, 311

Feinberg, Leslie, 297
feminine, 112; desire, 18; use of dildo, 146
femininity, 21
feminism, 16, 18; in the academy, 15; scholarship, 13
fillet, 138
fire, 228, 237; torch, 237
flames, 242, 251n74
flammae (flames), 264
flirtation, 110
flowers, 38, 42, 44, 50, 51, 65, 70–71, 80n53,
   113, 155n39, 188–189, 190, 232. *See also*
   roses
Foat, Michael, 317
Fonteia Eleusis, 211
Fonteia Helena, 211
food, 142, 312
foreplay, 112
foreshadowing, 232
Foucault, Michel, 1, 3, 12, 14, 16, 24n3, 30n61,
   31n71, 32n87
fountain, 117; Byblis changed into, 273
frescoes, 19; Bronze Age, 34–59; function
   of, 46–47
frictrix (one who rubs), 21, 213
friends, 124, 178, 321
friendship, 15, 22, 32n79, 310, 311, 312, 313;
   carnal, 316; Horsiesios on, 314; language
   of, 313; monastic, 313, 314; neglect of, 313;
   physical, 316; and power, 320; Shenute
   on, 315
Frontisi-Ducroux, Françoise, 110, 145, 148
frui (enjoy), 267
funerals, 116–117

games, funeral, 170
gamos (wedding), 119, 120
Ganymede, 133, 255n123
garden, 242, 243
garlands, 62; of roses, 72
garments, 66
gay and lesbian studies, 1, 16–17, 287
gay men, 286
gaze, 21, 88; Aphrodite and, 112–113, 125,
   190, 191, 222; erotic, 83, 100–102, 117,

130–131, 226; on gems, 240; male erotic, 135, 167, 251n69; Sapphic, 20, 91, 95, 97

gender, 278; of creativity, 60–61; external markers, 108; norms, of, 215

Genesia, 170

genitalia, cakes in shape of, 142; models of, 140, 142; symbolism, 140

genre, 286

Geometry (personified), 248n28

gestures, 117, 120, 130, 155n37, 181, 186, 187, 188, 189; lifting mantle, 179; "up and down," 161n94, 189; on vases, 110

ghettoization, 62–63

gifts, 64, 72, 113, 114, 125, 126, 138, 188, 190, 232, 319; to dead, 170; wedding, 120

girlfriends, 186, 190

Gladstone, William, 5, 7, 27nn28,29

Glykylla, 177

Gnosticism, 322

goats, 52n3, 242, 243

goddesses, 46, 179

gods, 266; as examples, 272, 273

Gomme, A. W., 8

Gongyla, 66

Gordon, Pamela, 257, 258, 276

Graces, 64, 223, 224, 236

grata (delightful), 219

Greece, 20, 34–59, 60–81, 82–105, 106–166; as concept, invention of, 5, 6; influence on Rome, 216; modern, 6; privileging of, 26n18

Greeks, defense of, 7, 8

groom, 119, 120, 121, 236

groves, sacred, 65

gymnasium, male: comparison with, 138

gynaeceum (women's space): debated, 115–116; gynaikonitis, 10, 115–116, 179, 181

Haigh, A. E., 7

hairpins, 41

hairstyle, 36, 48; adult male, 36

Hallett, Judith P., 256, 257, 258, 259, 279, 299, 300

Haloa, 140

Halperin, David, 13, 14, 31nn69–71, 134

d'Hancarville, Baron, 106–107

hands, clasping, 174, 176, 178, 182; touching, 117

hare, 128

Harmonia, 125, 179, 180

Hasselman Painter, 141

headdress, 71

Hector, 67

Hedeia, 186

Helen, 97, 99, 100, 102, 230, 231, 236

Hellenes, 6; Hellenism, 8, 216, 223

Hera, 40, 51, 87

Herculaneum, 8

hermaphrodites, 145, 215, 297

heroic life, 98

Heroides, 82, 218

Herophile, 182

Herzfeld, Michael, 6, 26, 27nn24,26

Hesiod, 63, 68, 72; model for Nossis, 70

hetairai (elite prostitute or courtesan) 7, 10, 134, 135, 162n100, 196n26, 208n94, 209n99, 220, 292–293, 294; on vases, 116

hetairistria (women who love women), 134

heteroeroticism, 130, 212

heterosexism, 16

heterotopias, 190, 191, 205n76

hierarchy, 262, 272, 279; dissolution of, 84; universal, 260, 261

Hilaria/Hilarion, 319, 320

Hippolytus, 234

historical method, 106

historicity, 172, 173, 178–179, 290, 291

historiography, 5

holidays, celebrated by women, 116

Homer, 63; use as model, 67

Homeric Hymn to Demeter, 51

homes, 167; houses, 115–116. See also gynaeceum

homoeroticism, 2, 20, 21, 50, 62, 133, 189, 206nn81–82, 237, 313; definition of, 3, 111–112; female, 3, 130, 149, 181, 186, 289, 296, 313, 317, 318, 321; and government, 321; as literary end, 298; in Lucian, 292; male, 126 (comparison with female, 146, 189, 321); physical, 304

homo-hetero binary, 31n69, 239
homophobia, 4, 149–150, 240
homosexuality, male, 3, 14, 300; discourse
    of, 8–10; of Ovid, 259; Roman vocabu-
    lary of, 216
homosexuals, 322
homosocial, 181; defined, 2–3; environ-
    ments, 19, 35, 72, 116; scenes, 121; setting,
    124–125; sisterhood, 48; space, reading
    and, 11
Homou Ousa, 225
honey, 70
Horace, 217, 240
Horns of consecration, 38
Horsiesios, 307, 314, 316, 320, 321; attacks
    friendship, 314
humans: as animals, 260; with divinities,
    228; in images of gods, 223
humor, 290, 300
hydria, 107, 135
Hymen, 236, 237, 263, 282n22

Ianthe, 21, 240; and Iphis, 256–285
iconography, use of, 222
ideal: female beauty, 84; nonhierarchical, 84
identity, 97, 287, 301; politics, 287
ideology, 2, 5, 12
ignis (fire), 265
ignorance, 316
Iliad, 40, 230
imagery, 107; military, 101, 102
images, function of, 109
imagination: male, 299; spectrum of, 63
Imagines, 226, 238, 239
imitation, 289–292; in education, 291
immortality, 65
incest, 223, 271, 272, 273
inequality, 313
informants, 316
inscriptions, 172, 182, 183, 227
inspiration, 63; male, 72. See also Aphrodite:
    as a source of
intellect, 218
intercourse, 108
interpretation, 106

intimacy, 113
Iphis, 21, 240; and Ianthe, 256–285
irony, 270
Isis, 262, 266, 269, 277, 279
iuvare, 219

jewelry, 36–37, 40
Johns, Catherine, 8, 145
John the Archimandrite, 322
Jove, 260
judgment, 273
Julia, 215
Juno Pronuba, 252n85
Jupiter, as Diana, 239
justice, 89
Juvenal, 214

kalathoi, 177, 178, 188, 207nn89,91
Kalliarista, 177
Kallistomakhe, 177, 186
kallos (beautiful), 100; kalê, 142, 221
Kalogeropoulou, Athena, 190
kantharos, 142, 144
Katz, Marilyn, 5, 25n8
Kauffman, Angelica, 239
Kennedy, Elizabeth, 297
Kerameikos, Athens (cemetery), 20, 167,
    172, 186–187, 191
kerchief, 36
Keuls, Eva, 110, 140, 147
Khresté, 183
Kilmer, Martin, 135–138, 145
kissing, 223, 239, 250n51, 296, 297, 299
kithara, 176, 200n45
Kitto, H.D.F., 8
Kleopatra, 126
knowledge, 316; of vases, 107–108
Koch-Harnack, Gundel, 130, 189
kôma, 65
komos (revel), 140, 148
Konstan, David, 313
Kore, 125
kottabos (drinking game), 135
krater, 118, 232
Krawiec, Rebecca, 320

krokotos (yellow robe), 42
Krysanthe, 182, 183
Kurke, Leslie, 293
kylix, 107, 117, 121, 131, 135

labeling, 108
labor, 41
laikazein (to fellate or engage in promiscuous behavior), 17, 33n90
lamenting, 217
landscapes, floral, 50
Laronia, 214
Late Antiquity, 288, 304–329
laughter, 315
law, 22, 268, 273, 214, 245–246n10; citizenship, 294
Lawler, Lillian, 128
leaders, 323
Leaena, 22, 228, 286, 294–299
leaning, 243
leaving, 94
lebes gamikos, 107, 122, 123, 124, 179
legs, intertwining of, 135
lekythoi, 131, 193n6; white-ground, 170
lesbian, 4, 16, 17; continuum, 15, 17, 112, 133; imagination, 61; lesbianism, 286 (literary, 20; transgendered, 288); studies, 156n47
"lesbian in us," 60–61
lesbians, 126, 147, 213, 219
lesbiazein (to fellate or indulge in lascivious behavior), 17, 21
Lesbos, 225, 296; women of, 295, 297
letters, 308, 322
Lex Sca(n)tinia, 214
Libido, 251n74
Ligdus, 261, 262, 276
Lilja, Saara, 213, 214, 217
Locri, 69
London, British Museum, 117, 118, 141
Longinus, 220, 221
Longus, 238
Louisiana, 293
loutrophoroi, 107, 171, 179
love, 258, 271, 277

lovers, 266; absence of, 96
lubricants, 140
Lucian, 4, 22, 112, 134, 228, 286–303; biographical information, 289; as pomosexual, 299; sexuality of, 300
Lucretius, 237
Luna, 243
lust, masculine, 275
lustral basin, 37–38, 42
Luxorius, 215, 223–224, 237, 242
Lykurgus, 129
Lysias, 115

Mace, Sarah, 87
Mackail, J. M., 11
Madrid, Museo Arqueológico Nacional, 136
Maenads. *See* bacchantes
magic, 90, 312, 321; magical texts, 321, 322
Makowski, John, 259
Makron, 128
male homoeroticism, comparison with, 189
male(s): in Aegean art, 42–43; artists, 109; erotic gaze, 97; homoerotic, 83; relationships, 1
malum (malady), 278, 283nn25,31
mania (spiritual possession), 63
mantles, 130–133, 161n94
manual stimulation, 323
Marathon, 170
Marcadé, Jean, 8, 145
Maria, 307
Marinatos, Nanno, 47
marriage, 20, 119, 122, 125, 127, 178, 179, 180, 181, 182, 221, 224, 228, 234, 236, 263, 267, 277; heterosexual, 93, 117, 120; of Iphis and Ianthe, 261; readiness for, 40; same-sex, 257, 277
Marriage of Philology and Mercury, 232
Mars, 237, 243
Martial, 220, 224
Martianus Capella, 218, 223, 232, 234, 236, 237, 248n27
martyrs, 321

Mary, 230, 252n79
mascula (manly), 217–218
masculine, 256, 257
masculinism, 4
masculinity, 2, 7, 112, 115, 217, 248n28, 275, 277, 297; of women, 295
masculinization, 82
matriarchy, 13
Maura, 214, 215
Maximus of Tyre, 221
medicine, 35
Megaclo, 225
Megilla, 295–300
Meidias Painter, 126
Meleager, 70, 71
Melite, 183
memento mori, 184
memory, 86, 94, 100
men, 321; and breasts, 53; friendship, 9, 313; Greek, 8–9; love of women, 9. *See also* male(s)
Menander, 119
menstruation, 41–42, 48, 50
Metamorphoses, 21, 232, 256–285
metaphor, 224; flowers, 51
methods, 108, 112, 151n6, 222, 254n111; art historical, 110, 113, 114; historical, 13–14, 21; interpretive, 113
midwives, 196n26
military imagery, 90, 101, 102. *See also* weapons
mimesis, 289–292, 298, 299
mind as sex organ, 299
Minerva, 224
miracula (wondrous things), 261
mirror, 157n53, 182–185, 191, 240nn72,74
misogyny, 298, 300
Mississippi University, 132
models: ancients for moderns, 7; Greek, 216; Hesiodic, 68; Homeric, 67, 68, 86, 87; *Homeric Hymns*, 98; male pederasty as, 130
modesty, 112
monasteries, 22, 305, 320; control of, 308; life in, 304, 308; structure of, 320

monkeys, 37; imported from Egypt, 37
monks, 308; physical contact of, 318
monosexuality, 300
monstrum (monstrosity), 271, 278
mortals and divinities, 133, 252n76
Müller, Frank, 234, 236
Munich, Staatliche Antikensammlungen und Glyptothek, 136
Murray, Gilbert, 7
Muses, 19, 61–65, 68, 69, 161n88, 225–227, 232, 237, 240, 242, 250n55, 251n75; comparison of mortals with, 62; with Eros, 255n114; within household, 64; metonymization of, 74; names for musicians, 129; and truth, 69; twentieth-century women writers', 72
music, 117; musical instruments, 135; musical performances, 129
musicians, 118, 123, 138, 227–228, 229, 246n13, 251nn70,75
Mynnion, 187
Myrtilus, 225
Myrtis, 181
myrtle, 41, 215
mythology, 51, 256–285; explaining sexual orientation, 134

näiskos stele, 171
names, 171, 172, 173
naming, 195n21; on tombstones, 176, 196n26
Nangeroni, Nancy, 295
Naples, Museo Nazionale, 231
Narcissus, 226
nature, 268, 270, 277, 278
Nausion, 186
Neaera, 296
Necklace swinger, 39, 41, 48
nectar, 71; song as, 65–66
negative attitude to women's community, 307
neo-classicism, 239
Nereids, 244
New Comedy, 279, 292

New Testament, 322; 1 Cor 6:9–10, 322; 1
Tim 1:10, 322; language, Coptic, 322;
neologisms, Coptic, 323
New York, Metropolitan Museum of Art,
117, 118, 120, 121, 131, 139, 228
Nikippa, 178
Nikippe, 188
Nikosthenes Painter, 144
Niobid Painter, 118
Nossis, 19, 62–63, 69, 72–74; absence of
erotic epigrams, 71; Aphrodite in, 69–
70; Muses in, 69, 70; use of Sappho as
model, 69, 70
nova (strange or novel), 264
-nsarkikos (carnal), 312
nudity, 163nn107,111, 229, 315; female, 135,
137, 138; significance of, 135
nuns, 22, 228, 304
nurses, 187, 196n26
NWSA (National Women's Studies Association), 61
nympheutria (bridal attendant), 120
nymphokomos (woman who prepares the
bride), 120

Oakley, John H., 124, 125
obscene language, 142
oculis (eyes), 219
Oeconomicus, 110, 115
oikos (household), 157n58, 178, 202nn56–57
olbia (delights), 70
olisboi, 140, 145. *See also* dildos
Oltos, 135, 136
Olympia, Temple to Zeus, 201n49
Olympus, 226
On Brotherly Love, 225
Oneirocritica, 230
optimists, 13
oral sex, 211
oriental, 7; "oriental seclusion," 7, 11–12,
17, 27n30
Orpheus, 232
Ottomans, 6
ouôsh (desire), 312

outopia, 184, 205n76
Ovid, 4, 21, 82, 218–219, 232, 237, 240,
256–281; bisexuality of, 259
Oxford, 8; Ashmolean Museum, 321

Pachomian monasteries, 305, 307–308, 315
Pachomius, 307, 318–319
paederastia, 8, 9, 10, 31
pagchu (entirely), 99
Paidia, 126
Painter of Athens 1454, 124
Painter of Bologna, 121
painters, identification of, 107
painting, 71, 228, 230, 232, 234, 236, 239–
240, 241; conventions, 35; mural, 183; of
stele, 182
palaistra, 137
Palatine Anthology, 225, 237
pallake (concubine), 293, 294
Pamphile, 181, 186, 187
Panathenaic festival, 110
Pannychides, 128
Papapolo, 321
Paris (Alexandros), 230, 231
Paris, Bibliothèque Nationale: MS 130.1,
308–310; Cabinet des Médailles, 129;
Musée du Louvre, 122, 137, 143, 227, 243
Parker, Holt, 258
parthenai (maidens), 220
parthenia (maidens' songs), 130
Pasiphae, 265, 267, 268, 269
passa est (endured), 268
passivity, 300; appropriate to sex change,
275
Pater, Walter, 8, 20n46
patriarchy, 167, 261, 279, 280
Pausimakhe, 177, 182–184, 185, 191
pederasty, 113, 130, 154n32, 252n84; female,
219. *See also paederastia*
Pedieus Painter, 142, 143
Peitho, 125, 126, 231, 236
pelike, 140, 142, 147
penetration (sexual), 83, 145, 165n132, 214,
256, 258, 259, 275, 280, 299, 300

penises, 127, 267; as plants, 142; substitution, 140
Pentheus, 128, 129
pénthos (sorrow), 181
Perikeiromenê (cropped), 119
Persephone, 51
personal voice, 98–99
personifications, 126, 218, 234, 236, 243
persuasion, 88, 90, 273
Petersen, Lauren, 147, 167
Pezzino group, 138
Phaedrus, 299
Phalanna, Thessaly, 188
phallicizing, 243
phallocentricism, 3, 258
phallus, 83, 140, 142, 243; birds, 142
Phanylla, 186
Phaon, 218–219
Pharaouo, 322
Pharsalos, Thessaly, 188, 189, 190
Phello, 321
Philadelphia, 225
Philaenis, 220
philai (girlfriends), 220
philein (to love), 313
Philhellenes, 6
philia (love), 3
Philostratus, 221, 226, 238, 239
Phintias, 135, 136
phórmiskos (bag), 188, 190, 209nn99–100
physical desire, 310, 311
physicality, 211
physical proximity, 222
physiological markers, 127
pictorial program, 46
Pierian Muse, 65
pietas (piety), 262, 267
Pistis Sophia, 322
placage, 293
placees, analogous to hetairai; 293–294, 302n23
Plato, 8, 63, 134
Pleasure, 236
Plutarch, 129, 215, 225, 226, 228

poetry, 19, 20, 60, 63, 66, 70, 74, 82–105; composed by women, 61, 63, 64; healing power, 66; production, circumstances of, 64
poets: as victims, 68; women, 2, 25n7
poikilothron (elaborately carved throne), 67, 86
Polyarchos, 71
Pomeroy, Sarah, 214
pomosexuality, 288, 297, 301; Lucian as pomosexual, 299
Pompeii, 8, 223; Casa dell' Amor Punito, 239–240
porne (prostitute), 134, 162n100, 293
pornography, 3
Porphyrio, 217
position, 222
positions: antidildo, 146; prodildo, 146
possessions, 96, 315
post-modern sexuality. *See* pomosexuality
pothos (longing/desire), 66, 181–182
potnia theron (Mistress of Animals), 45, 46. *See also* Artemis
pottery. *See* vases
power, 320
prayer, 269; formula, 86
prehistory, 34–59
pre-marital homoeroticism, 125, 234
presence, 96
Priapic figures, 242
priestesses, 196n26, 198–199n39
private realm, appropriateness of, 243
proaulia (offerings before wedding), 119
prodigiosa (monstrous), 264, 278
prohibitions, 318
Prometheus, 299
proof, 133
prooimion (poetic preamble), 68
propaganda, 157n55
prostitutes, 111, 134; male, 162n101
Protrepticus, 225
Prudentius, 251n74
Pseudo-Demosthenes, 293
Pseudo-Shenute, 319

Psyches, 242
puberty, 36
public, women in, 215
publica, 220
pudica (chaste), 220
Pudicitia, Temple of, 215
puella (girl), 219
punishment, 304, 308–312, 326n15; for being
    manly, 257
pursuit, active, 269
pyxides, 107, 122, 130, 132

Queen, Carol, 286, 288
queer theory, 1, 16–17, 18, 115, 286–287, 288

racism, 27n22, 30
rape, 268, 275
reading, 119
reciprocity, 72, 90
reconciliation, 89
red, 38
Reed, J. D., 240
reflections (in mirrors, shields), 204nn72,
    74
refnkotkmnnhoout (man who sleeps with
    males), 322–323
regulations, 318
Rehak, Paul, 19
relations, 185, 228; between people on stele,
    173, 174, 176; range, 4, 115; between
    women, 2, 15, 72, 186 (condemnation
    of, 278); divine and mortal, 19, 69, 73;
    spectrum of, 115; women with Aphro-
    dite, 63; women with Muses, 63
relief sculpture, 167–210
religion, 267
religious life, 304
representations, conventions of, 110
repressive hypothesis, 121
respectability, 134, 135
reuse of tombs, 172, 199n41
revenge, 88, 89
Revett, Nicholas, 6
Rhea, 243
Rhetoric (personified), 250n51

rhyta, 55n22
Rich, Adrienne, 15, 60, 62–63, 73, 112, 133
Richlin, Amy, 13–14, 24n3, 258
Richter, Gisela, 240, 242
Ridgway, Brunilde, 188, 189
rings, 240
rites of passage, 35, 42
ritualization, 42
rituals, 19, 65, 116, 119, 120; funerary, 167,
    168, 170, 173, 191, 192n4; initiatory, 126,
    159n76; mourning, 21; before wedding,
    119, 126
Robertson, Martin, 107
Robinson, Christopher, 290, 291, 292
Robinson, David, 11
Roman Questions, 228
romantic, 112
Rome, 211–255; Biblioteca Apostolica Vati-
    cana, 235; Capitoline Museum, 233, 237;
    Domus Aurea, 234; Palazzo dei Conser-
    vatori, 232; Palazzo Mattei, 243; Studio
    Canova, 228; Villa Giulia, 141; Villa
    Vigna Pacca, 226
Rosenblum, Morris, 224
roses, 70–71, 80; of Pieria, 65
Rubin, Gayle, 16
rules, 308

sacred, concept of violation of, 215
saffron, 19, 35, 37, 38, 47–50
Samosata (Commogene, Syria), 289
Samytha, 71
Sanctuary rhyton, 38, 39
sandals, 142, 165n127; adjusted, 177
Sappho, 1–2, 10–11, 19, 20, 50, 62, 63, 64–
    74, 82–105, 125, 130, 134, 155n41, 228,
    232, 236, 237, 240, 247–248n25, 250n55,
    254n109, 257, 276; addresses Aphrodite,
    230; Alexandrian editors of, 68; as Aph-
    rodite, 90; possible depiction of, 117;
    feminist view of, 17; imitation of, 69; as
    "lesbian," 18; L-P 1 as critique, 67; as
    model for Nossis, 69; and Muses, 64;
    as Muse, 75n11, 225–226, 227; as on-
    looker, 66; poetry of, 19, 20; later recep-

tion of, 82; in Roman sources, 216–222; Roman views of, 21; as schoolmistress, 11; status of, 217; Works (fragment 1 [Hymn to Aphrodite], 84–91; fragment 16, 97–102, 142; fragments 39 and 57, 142; fragment 94, 91–96, 130; fragment 96, 130)

sarcophagi, 224, 226, 228, 229, 239, 240

Sardis, 130

Satyrs, 127, 226, 242

Schimel, Lawrence, 286, 288

Scholtz, Andrew, 237

sculpture, relief, 20, 167–210, 211, 231

seated figures, in Aegean art, 40, 43

Second Sophistic, 289–290

Segal, Charles, 89

segregation of sexes, 148, 179, 308, 318

self, 99; self-expression, 321; self-identification, 321; self-knowledge, 264

semiotics, 107

Seneca the Younger, 219, 257

sensation, 95

separation, 94; forced, 93

serenade, 226

sex, 52n3, 53n12, 322; change, 266, 269, 271, 275, 276, 280; depicted between males, 130; depicted on vases, 130; with divinities, 230; drive, 217; roles, 18; segregation, 2, 7, 11–12, 21, 115, 116; work, 134

sexual intent, 317

sexuality, 304; Aegean sources, 34; history of, 14; women's, 2, 16

sexuality, post modern. See pomosexuality

shaved head, 96

Shenute, 304, 307–320; monastery of, 305–307; writings of, 317, 319

shepherds, 68

Sheriff, Mary, 239, 254n111

shoes, 165n127

shopping, 209n98, 240

shrines, 38, 96

sight, and desire, 91

signs, 212

Simonides, 173

Sinos, Rebecca, 124, 125

sins, 310

sisterhood, 222, 223, 225, 272; sisters, 186, 320

Skala Oropou, 188

Skinner, Marilyn, 19, 73–74

skyphos, 135

slaves, 108, 183, 196n26, 199n42, 204n69, 293, 294

sleeping together, 317, 319–320

smiles, 87

Smith-Rosenberg, Carroll, 15, 112

snakes, 255n125

Snyder, Jane, 61, 95, 99

social class, 116, 133–140

social construction, 287

social criticism, of art, 107

Socrates, 8, 220, 221

Sodom and Gomorrah, 322

Sohag, 307

soldiers, 90, 206n82

Song of Solomon, 212–213, 222

sóphron (moderate), 181

Soranus, 217–218

Soteris, 187, 188

soul, gender of, 244

sources: Coptic, 305; historical, 2, 18, 213, 214, 246n17; prehistoric sexuality, 34; for Sappho, 217; space, segregation, 34, 37, 308; value of, 216, 323; value of publication of, 324

sparrows, 87

Sparta, 129

speaking, 318

spectatorship, 164n117

spells, 321, 322; sexual, 312

spiritual: brotherhood, 315; life, 320

St. Agnes, 251–252n76

St. Ambrose of Milan, 244

state religion, 242

stealing, 310, 311

stelai (grave stones), 20; dedicated, 209–210n101; inscribed, 171; painted, 182

steps, 101, 102

stereotypes, 296

stigma, 15
string skirts, 40
Stuart, James, 6
Stuveras, Roger, 240
style, 157n56; masculine/feminine, 181
subject-object, 89, 191
subjects, 167
Suda, 134, 221
Suetonius, 214
sugkatamignos (joining), 225
Suidas. See Suda
sukugian (consorting), 225
summachos (ally), 79n40; Aphrodite as, 69, 90
sumptuary law, 171
suneton (intelligible), 100
Sutton, Robert, 148
symbolism, 178, 212, 242; phallic, 227, 228, 250n65, 255nn125,126
symmetrical, 96
Symonds, John, 8, 9, 10; on women, 10
symposia, 109, 134; for women, 135, 136, 163n111
Symposion, 134

Tabennisi, 307
Table Talk, 226
Taese, 304, 309, 310, 311, 312, 316, 317, 323, 324
Takhom, 310, 311, 326
Tarquinia, 149
tattling, 316
tattoos, 57n48
teaching, 321; teacher, 196n26
Teiresias, 297, 302n27
Telethusa, 261, 262, 263, 266
tenses, past, 89
teratogenic grid, 258
terminology: female homoeroticism, 323; male sexuality, Coptic, 322; military, 90. *See also* definitions
textiles, 36
texts: comic, 213; magical, 312; polemical, 213
Thebes, 128
thelo (I wish), 95
thelxis (magic spell), 89

Theodore, 307
Theopropis, 173
theory, 1, 287; feminist, 15, 17. *See also* queer theory
Thera, 146; Museum, 147
Thesmophoria, 167
Thiasos, 244
thiasos (ritual group), 77n19, 129
throne, 86
thyrsus (Bacchic wand), 228
Tibullus, 230
tombstones, 167–210. *See also* stelai
Touaein, 322
Touchette, Lori-Ann, 216
touching, 113, 222, 231, 232, 296, 317, 318, 319; breasts, 187, 226; genital, 232
traditionality, 214; of female homoeroticism, 291
tragedy, 106
transsexuality, 261
transgenderism, 295, 297
Transgender Warriors, 297
Transverberation of Saint Theresa, 230
transvestitism, 108, 297, 319–320
tribas (one who rubs), 21, 112, 213, 217, 256–257, 258, 281nn3–4, 323
Triptolemus, 242
Troy, 101
truth, Muses and, 69
Tsansno, 304, 310, 311, 312, 316, 317, 321, 324
Tullia, 214, 215
Tullius Laurea, 226

Urania, 226, 227
urit (burns), 265
utopian setting, 24

vases, 150–151n3; black and red figure, 107; function of, 151nn8–9; Greek, 20; left at tombs, 170; meaning of, 113; painting, 106–166; South Italian, 183; value, 106–107. *See also* names of individual vase shapes
veil, 42, 176; drawn, 190
Veiled girl, 39, 42, 48
Venus. *See* Aphrodite

vessel, filling of, 242
Vestal Virgins, 245n1
Veyne, Paul, 14
Vickers, Michael, 106
Victorians, 7; classicists, 12
Victories, 230
viewers drawn into image, 184, 185; at graves, 191; Sappho as, 66. *See also* audiences
Virgil, 275–276
virginal states of being, 222
virginity, 263
virgo (virgin), 267
visuals, 95
vitamins, 48–50
Vivien, Renée, 11
vocabulary, passion, 264
voices, 94, 95; female, 83; merging of, 86, 94
volcanic destruction of Thera, 34
voyeurism, 22, 298

wall paintings, 8
Walters, Barry, 286
warfare, language of, 87
Washing Painter, 122, 123
weapons, 99, 105n38, 275
weaving, 110, 128, 133–134, 153n22, 162n99; comparison with poetry, 78–79n32; hetairai, 134
weddings, 20, 116, 120, 122, 133, 142, 179, 244, 266; fire and, 237; homosocial elements, 120; night, 122
Welcker, Friedrich, 10, 11
Wharton, Henry, 10
wheat, 140
White Monastery, 22, 304, 307, 317; Coptic Codex BZ, 308–312

whiteness, of Greek statues, 6
wigs, 296
Wilamowitz, Ulrich von, 11
Williamson, Margaret, 101
wine-jar, Apulian, 187
Winkler, Jack (John), 98
women, 307, 319; ancient, 11; as Aphrodite, 240, 242; as artists, 109; Athenian, 7; in baths, 20; clasping hands, 176; comparison with later European treatment of, 8; depicted, 38 (on tombstones, 167–210; on vases, 106–166); funerary rituals, 168; at home, 20; marginality of, 105n30; marriage with men, 319; as Muse, 227; on stele, identifying, 186; naming of, 173; as objects, 167, 191; as possession, 91, 167; seclusion of, 11–12; sharing mantle, 130–132; singing, 122; social position in Greece, 6, 7; teaching, 311, 314, 324; uneducated, 65
women's monastic communities, 304–329
women's quarters, 115–116
woolworking, 110, 111, 117, 162n99, 188, 207n89
worship of Dionysos, by women, 128
Wounded woman, 39–40, 41
wreath, exchange of, 146, 147
wrists, holding, 117, 120, 122
writers and poets: twentieth-century, 72; women, 82–105

Xenophon, 110, 115
Xeste 3, 34–59

yellow, 42, 57n36
Young, Wayland, 286

Zeus, 51, 133